2.50

D1206831

DISCARD

City Portraits

City Portraits

A GUIDE TO 60 OF

THE WORLD'S GREAT CITIES

By Mimi Sheraton

HARPER & ROW 〜 PUBLISHERS

NEW YORK
AND EVANSTON

Portions of the articles on Hong Kong, Vienna, and Istanbul appeared in *Mademoiselle;* parts of the articles on Copenhagen, Stockholm, Oslo, and Helsinki in *Town & Country*. They are hereby reprinted by permission.

G
140
S 45

For Dick and Marc

Contents

Acknowledgments : *xi*

EUROPE

SCANDINAVIA

Denmark : Copenhagen, 3
Finland : Helsinki, 15
Norway : Oslo, 24   Bergen, 27
Sweden : Stockholm, 36   Gothenburg, 41

GREAT BRITAIN AND IRELAND

England : London, 53
Scotland : Edinburgh, 76
Ireland : Dublin, 89

THE CONTINENT

Austria : Vienna, 103   Salzburg, 113
Belgium : Brussels, 126
France : Paris, 136   Nice, 150
Germany (*West*) : Berlin, 168   Hamburg, 174
                    Frankfurt, 179   Munich, 183
Greece : Athens, 202

Holland (The Netherlands) : Amsterdam, 215
Italy : Rome, 227   Florence, 236   Venice, 242
        Milan, 251   Naples, 257
Portugal : Lisbon, 280
Spain : Madrid, 289   Barcelona, 298   Seville, 304
Switzerland : Zurich, 319   Lucerne, 322   Geneva, 326
Turkey : Istanbul, 337

EASTERN EUROPE AND THE USSR

Czechoslovakia : Prague, 353
Hungary : Budapest, 361
Poland : Warsaw, 370
Union of Soviet Socialist Republics (Russia) : Moscow, 378

THE MIDDLE EAST

Iran (Persia) : Teheran, 399
Israel : Tel Aviv, 407
Jordan : Jerusalem, 415
Lebanon : Beirut, 422
Syria : Damascus, 432

ASIA

Hong Kong, 441
India : Calcutta, 452   New Delhi, 455
Indonesia : Djakarta, 466
Japan : Tokyo, 475   Kyoto, 483
Pakistan : Karachi, 495
Philippines : Manila, 501
Singapore, 509
Thailand : Bangkok, 519

AFRICA

Egypt : Cairo, 533
Kenya : Nairobi, 545

AUSTRALIA

Australia : Sydney, 553   Melbourne, 556

LATIN AMERICA

Argentina : Buenos Aires, 565
Brazil : Rio de Janeiro, 573
Peru : Lima, 581
Mexico : Mexico City, 587

Acknowledgments

Obviously, a book of this kind takes a good deal of traveling—in this case several trips over a two-year period, covering many thousands of miles, from above the Arctic Circle to below the equator; from New York to Tokyo and back again, across Europe, Asia, and the Middle East. This portion of the project was the most delightful; for a woman traveling alone it could easily have been the most trying, considering the length of time involved.

The fact that the trips were so pleasant and productive is due primarily to the efforts and cooperation of the Scandinavian Airlines System—SAS. Everyone connected with that line—executives, district managers, office and flight personnel, extended every courtesy possible, offered every type of assistance I happened to be in need of, and in general solved all problems that arose en route. The offices of SAS (and throughout Southeast Asia, the offices of Thai Airways International) were to me a home away from home. Their well-informed staffs were able to provide excellent sightseeing information and make arrangements for same, and they always seemed to have the best information on hotels, restaurants, shops, and other such necessities of a traveler's life.

I can only recommend that anyone traveling would do well to make use of the SAS service and sunlit efficiency in all of its varied forms. For this reason I have included the addresses of local SAS offices in all of the cities covered in this book. Fortunately there are flights to most of them; they can accommodate you in all of them.

I would especially like to thank SAS for allowing me to use *City Portraits* as the title for this book. It is their title for the individual on-the-spot pamphlet guides which they publish; each one a city guide of unusual thoroughness and complete reliability.

I must also thank George Jones and Hal Grove, my editors at Harper & Row, for their guidance, cooperation, and patience; Jean Atcheson for her meticulous copy editing; Elisa Olsen, Mr. Jones's secretary for her help in emergencies; and Tish Thomas, who is unquestionably the world's best literary plastic surgeon. It was her tireless cutting, pasting, and organizing that turned a chaotic manuscript into a coherent book. And I could not forget to thank Joy Berry, who bore with me on the typing.

This book would have been impossible for me to do, were it not for my mother and father, who, along with Maria Dawkins, took such wonderful care of my son while I traveled. And I doubt that I will ever be able to repay the debt of gratitude I owe to my husband, Dick Falcone, for his patience, understanding, and help during the three years it took to do this book.

"Divine Nature gave the fields, human art built the cities."

—VARRO
De Re Rustica, iii

EUROPE Scandinavia

Denmark

COPENHAGEN

Lovely old queen of the sea

ALMOST anyone who has not been to Norway, Sweden, Finland, and Denmark, can tell you quickly and unequivocally what Scandinavia is like. Such a person will undoubtedly draw an ice-blue composite of these northern lands, washed by the sea and lit by the midnight sun—a cold, clear, caraway-scented world of aquavit and good golden beer, peopled by blond, blue-eyed giants, latter-day Vikings who ski and skoal, produce modern furniture and silver, and who champion, cooperatively, the blessings of "the middle way."

Such a picture, though charming enough, is merely a half truth; a convenient wrap-up of four widely dissimilar countries—four completely different styles of embroidery worked against a common cloth of race, religion, language root, geographical proximity, and a common destiny. Viewing these countries through their capitals, the visitor soon finds for every similarity a difference, for every two blondes at least one brunette. He finds that the cities themselves differ in color, style, and tone; the people in temperament, taste, and, to some extent, appearance. There are even differences in the languages and dialects, and in the cuisines. One finds, in short, as much contrast between Copenhagen and Helsinki, Stockholm and Oslo, as between Brussels and Paris, Vienna and Munich.

Copenhagen is beyond a doubt the gayest, most colorful and continental of the Scandinavian capitals—a childhood dream of a place, set around the fairytale amusement park that is Tivoli; a city giddy with cyclists and green copper spires that twirl up to the sky and glint gold in the sunlight; where great ships sail into the streets to dock at curbside canals. It's a city alive with fountains and statues and small, perfect parks and squares, dotted with shiny white stands selling paprika-bright sausages, the Danish *pølse;* a city romantic with rococo castles and palace guardsmen and legends that go back to pre-Viking days.

This is one of Europe's oldest capitals in one of the world's oldest kingdoms. It was founded in the eleventh century by the Bishop Absalon, who established the city as a merchants' harbor and named it, therefore, *København*. A Danish guidebook tells us that though no one knows what the Danes were doing in 13,000 B.C., it has been established that by 5000 B.C. they were eating oysters. The present king, Frederik IX, is a direct descendant of the tenth century ruler, Gorm the Old, which makes this Europe's longest reigning dynasty.

Copenhagen prospered from the heavy traffic on the Øresund in the sixteenth and seventeenth centuries, and, after an economic decline in the nineteenth century, grew up as a center of heavy industry with railways, breweries, and hardware factories. It was besieged by the Swedes in 1658, bombarded by the English in 1801 and 1807, and occupied by the Germans during World War II.

By all odds, Copenhagen's greatest asset is its population: one million merry, humanistic, xenophilic Danes who always manage to look as though they were up to some special piece of mischief. In appearance they are plumper and rosier than their northern neighbors; and the Scandinavian dialect they speak is so full of throat-clutching gargles that the Danes themselves say it's a throat disease, not a language. In addition to their easygoing charm, the Danes are shrewd and articulate, and have become the supersalesmen of Scandinavia, with the typical merchants' talent for driving a hard bargain. They have the Scandinavian instinct for cooperation in large affairs, but remain personally individualistic. This results in an inordinately high number of eccentrics, and one sees more out-and-out "characters" on the streets of Copenhagen than are visible in most other cities. Their two-sided personality, the combination of pleasure and purpose, accounts, in part, for some of the widely divergent talents they have produced: The late nuclear physicist Niels Bohr and the comically confused Victor Borge, the brooding philosopher Kierkegaard, and the musical bon vivant Melchior, a writer of enchanting whimsy like Hans Christian Andersen and one of Gothic grandeur like Isak Dinesen, the Baroness Blixen, who lived in her Rungsted manor house, dining only, they say, on Limfjord oysters and French champagne.

Copenhagen is the capital of a nation of four and a half million people, a country of five hundred tight little islands of glowing prosperity and well-fed warmth, lushly green islands set adrift in the blue of sea and sky, a color scheme brightened by sudden flashes of red in the white-crossed Dannebro, the Danish flag. Of these islands the three largest are Zealand, on which Copenhagen is situated; Funen, the storybook land of Hans Christian Andersen's home town, Odense; and Jutland, the windswept farmland with fields of heather, lying between the Kattegat, the Skaggerak and the turbulent North Sea. It's a land of long coastlines and sand-dune beaches. Inland, it boasts a clipped and cultivated travel-poster landscape, with red cows tethered in green pastures; long lean pigs that look as though they were made of pink marzipan; half-timbered houses in black and white or rouge red, their thatched roofs carpeted in moss.

Once a nation of Viking warriors who ruled over all of Scandinavia and the British Isles, and were the scourge of continental Europe as far south as Florence, Denmark is now considered to be a model welfare state. The Danes are known the world over for their butter, eggs, and cheese, their ham, bacon, and beef, their silver and porcelain, furniture and textiles, and have (along with the rest of Scandinavia) just about managed to eliminate poverty. Beggars are an unknown sight on the city streets. Another of Denmark's most outstanding achievements are the Folk High Schools, adapted to farmers' seasonal time schedules, so that the far-reaching educational program excludes no one. Illiteracy is as rare as poverty.

They have made an art of their smørrebrød, the little open sandwiches that are sold in shops, cafés, restaurants, and vending machines all over the city and their food is acknowledged to be among the best in Europe. Their talent for enjoying life and having fun has made their capital the playland of all Scandinavia and many Swedes come over from Stockholm just for an evening of gaiety in Copenhagen. The Danes have even devised a plan whereby one never has to go to bed at all and have arranged for what they call "A 24-hour

Night Life" of cabarets, restaurants and night clubs, ending with a stint at the Copenhagen steam baths and breakfast. "Sleep in the next country" is their advice to tourists.

If Copenhagen is the heart of Denmark, the heart of Copenhagen is Tivoli, a truly unique amusement park, smack in the center of the capital. It was established in 1843 by a well-traveled Danish showman, George Carstensen, who had visited most of Europe's amusement parks and wanted his city to have one. In essence, Tivoli is a sort of cleaned-up and shiny Coney Island laid out in a miniature Central Park. Crystal chandeliers hang in treetops; necklaces of colored lights are strung over walks; there is a Persian palace of a cabaret, a Chinese pagoda, a pantomime theater where Pierrot woos Columbine each evening when the peacock-tail curtains have parted, a concert hall, a dozen bandstands; a slew of carnival attractions; boy-soldier parades; trapeze artists; fireworks; and an offbeat student beer hall, the Ferry Boat Inn, on the Tivoli lake. Open from May to September, by day Tivoli is a park for children and strollers who admire its gardens, listen to music, and have lunch or tea at one of the twenty-four restaurants.

The true spirit of Copenhagen can best be discovered by sampling its contrasting delights—the old with the new, the simple with the sophisticated. There are, first of all, the city's handsome squares, especially the elegant Royal Square, Kongens Nytorv, with its sidewalk cafés and statuary, the Royal Theater and the Royal Academy of Art in the seventeenth century palace of Charlottenborg. The Town Hall Square, Raadhuspladsen, is the center of the city's life with flower vendors and sausage stands in front of the towering red brick City Hall. The Breughelesque fish market is a must at least one morning, as is a quiet afternoon stroll along the harborside promenade, Langelinie, where you can view the statue of Hans Christian Andersen's mermaid, and the Gefion fountain, related to the legendary founding of Zealand.

Anyone who is castle-crazy should be happy enough here, where you can visit Amalienborg, the eighteenth century rococo home of the king and the royal family, Christiansborg Palace, seat of the parliament, the supreme court, the foreign office, and the Royal State Apartments; or Rosenborg, the palace of Denmark's seventeenth century builder king, Christian IV, a fantasy of a Dutch Renaissance castle crammed full of incredible royal treasures, including the Danish crown jewels displayed on a glass encased platform that spirals under the floor if a robbery is attempted.

Some of Copenhagen's more fascinating buildings are Grundt-vigskirken, a modern church with a façade resembling organ pipes; the seventeenth century Stock Exchange with its steeple of twisted dragons' tails; and the Round Tower, where you can climb a circular ramp to the top of the tower and have a view over all the city. Legend has it that Peter the Great drove a four-in-hand up to the very top, but had to shoot the horses when they balked at the blind turns on the descent. Another interesting tower with an exterior spiral staircase tops the baroque, eighteenth century church, Vor Frelser Kirke (Our Savior's Church).

There's a museum for almost every taste too, the most famous of which are the Carlsberg Glyptoteket with an outstanding collection of French Impressionists; the Thorvaldsen Museum with some of the best works of Denmark's leading sculptor; and the National Museum with some fascinating ethnographic and prehistoric specimens. The Museum of Applied Arts will fascinate anyone interested in handcrafts, and the Arms Museum has colorful arrays of weapons, standards, uniforms, and military paraphernalia. Outside the city itself, you'll find the Frilandsmuseet, an open-air collection of old farmhouses gathered from all over Denmark, Sweden, and the Faroe Islands, some dating back to the thirteenth century. Farther along the coast is the modern art museum, Louisiana, set on an old estate at the edge of the Øresund, with long glass corridors winding between giant trees and lush fern gardens.

The Danes have worked up a number of engaging tours to help visitors see their city. You may spend a morning in a launch touring Copenhagen's canals; visit factories and design workshops on the Industrial Tour; or take the World of Tomorrow Tour, on which you can marvel at the Danish advances in schools, old people's homes, and other social institutions, and enjoy the "junk playground," where suburban children have built a miniature shantytown with "junk" donated by the townspeople.

Perhaps the most famous sight in all of Denmark lies just an hour or two away from Copenhagen: Kronborg Castle, built in 1585 by Frederik II, and better known as Hamlet's Elsinore. It is noted especially for its handsome Knights' Hall and Maritime Museum, its stony dungeons, and the view across the Øresund to Sweden. Not far from

Kronborg is Fredensborg, the summer residence of the royal family, open to the public in July when the king is not in residence, and Frederiksborg Palace in Hillerød, a picturesque Renaissance castle with moat and gardens, an outstanding art collection, and, in the chapel, an organ with a thousand and one pipes, built in 1612.

Just half an hour from the capital, at Dyrehaven (the deer park), it is possible to sample the beauty of the Danish countryside, complete with deer roaming through forests of oaks and beeches. Here you may visit the Royal Hunting Lodge, Eremitagen, relax in a café, or simply stroll through the woods.

For contrast, in this ancient but up-to-date land, you can leave the ultramodern environs of Copenhagen's Kastrup Airport and in a few minutes travel centuries back in time to the enchanting fishing village of Dragør on the island of Amager. Ducks and geese waddle through narrow, cobblestoned alleys, houses are pleasantly lopsided, and there are many traces of the Dutch peasants who were invited to develop vegetable farms here by King Christian II in the early sixteenth century.

Anyone lucky enough to have three weeks to spend in this enchanting little country can sample all of the delights on its other main islands, Funen and Jutland. On the first one can visit the ancient town of Roskilde with the beautiful twelfth century cathedral that is the Pantheon of Danish royalty, and an hour or so away is the Ladbyskibet, a fossil of a Viking ship complete with the jewels and ornaments, chains and bones of the Viking chief who was buried in this long boat with his family and entire household. Nyborg is a small town on the Great Belt, the waterway that links the Kattegat with the Baltic, and here you can visit a handsome red castle built in 1170—the oldest brick castle in Scandinavia. The capital of Funen is Odense, mentioned above, and at the southern tip of this island are several lovely lake and forest resort towns such as Svendborg, an idyllic town that celebrated its seven hundredth birthday in 1953.

Besides its heather fields and wonderful dune beaches, Jutland is interesting because of such towns as Aalborg and Aarhus. The former is interesting for its church and cloister, its zoo and museum of history and art. Aarhus, one of the oldest towns in Denmark, has an outdoor museum called the Old Town where forty-eight antique houses have been gathered from all parts of Denmark, each arranged and furnished in the authentic style of its period, a kind of quaint toy-town Danish Williamsburg that is a delight to see.

And if you're in the mood for a real get-away-from-it-all vacation, you'd do well to spend a week or two on the Baltic island of Børnholm with its plaster white beehive houses and churches, Fanø, off Jutland, where bathers are wheeled from the beach into the sea in rolling bath houses, or Aerøskøbing, off Funen, a storybook island of thatched-roof houses, flower-trimmed windows and churchyards pretty enough for picnics.

FOR THE TRAVELER'S NOTEBOOK

Official Information

Before you go: The National Travel Association of Denmark, 588 Fifth Ave., New York 36, N.Y.

In Copenhagen: SAS Office, Air Terminal, Royal Hotel, 1 Hammerischsgade; National Travel Association of Denmark, 5 Banegaardspladsen (next to Central Station, across from Terminus Hotel); U.S. Embassy, 24 Dag Hammarskjöldsalle.

Money Matters

Currency: The krone (kr. or DKR) is the chief monetary unit. It is divided into 100 øre—kr. 6.90 equals approximately $1, U.S.

Tipping: Hotels—15 per cent added to the bill covers maids and hall porters, who are also bootblacks; øre 50 per bag for baggage porters; minimum kr. 1; øre 50 to doorman for calling cab; kr. 2 when you leave. Concierge may get kr. 7 for a special service. Restaurants (unless service charge is added to check) 12 per cent with a few øre extra for exceptional service. Washroom attendants: men tip øre 50, women øre 35; barbers 10 per cent; hairdressers, tipping optional or 10 per cent; taxi drivers 10 to 15 per cent.

Climate, Clothing, and Essentials

Summers are rarely hot and there is little snow in winter, although from November to April there is a great deal of penetrating dampness, and warm coats, woolen clothes, and sweaters are essential. It is generally pleasant from April through October when temperatures range from a mild 55 to 80 degrees F. Dress is never formal unless you are invited to an official function, and normal city dress is correct at all times. Raincoats and umbrellas come in handy, and you may need a sweater or woolen suit even in summer.

Parents traveling with children may be pleased to know there are special facilities available in Copenhagen. Student-sitters can be arranged for through your concierge, and for longer periods there is Pernille's Children's Hotel, a sort of combination nursery-kindergarten-hotel, just a short drive from Copenhagen on the Zealand coast. For complete information and prices, write to the National Travel Association of Denmark or directly to the hotel at 22 Vallerød Banevej, Rungsted Kyst, Denmark.

Hotels

Copenhagen has many fine hotels noted for comfort, cleanliness, good service, and a friendly atmosphere, but it's a good idea to have confirmed reservations on arrival, especially if you plan to go between April and October. If you arrive in Copenhagen without a reservation, apply immediately to Room Service, Kiosk P, Central Station, where a room in a hotel or private home will be booked for a kr. 2 fee.

De luxe accommodations range from kr. 50 to 70 for a single with bath; kr. 80 to 150, double. Moderate: kr. 35 to 50, single with bath; double, kr. 60 to 80; inexpensive: kr. 15 to 35, single; kr. 30 to 60, double.

DE LUXE: *SAS Royal Hotel, 1 Hammerichsgade.* Scandinavia's tallest building, this newly completed, SAS-operated hotel is a monument to pushbutton efficiency. De luxe and expensive. *Hotel d'Angleterre, 34 Kongens Nytorv,* located on the city's main square; this is *the* hotel for visiting dignitaries and those who prefer old world comfort in the traditional style. De luxe and expensive. *Palace Hotel, 57 Raadhuspladsen.* Well located on the Town Hall Square, this is popular with visiting Europeans. Expensive. *Imperial Hotel, 9 Vester Farimagsgade.* New and ultramodern, rooms are simple and a bit small for the price. Garage facilities. *Hotel Tre Falke* (Three Falcons), *7 Falkoner Alle.* Modern and almost a complete little shopping center in itself, this hotel is somewhat removed from the heart of things. *Hotel Richmond, 33 Vester Farimagsgade.* Well located, this modest hotel has a good dining room and excellent facilities; popular with Americans.

MODERATE: *Terminus Hotel, 3 Banegaardspladsen.* Though lower in price than hotels in the de luxe category, this gracious place excels in charm and service. Centrally located, moderately priced, and a great favorite with Danish travelers. *Codan, 21 Sct. Annae Plads.* Many of the small, comfortable rooms have an excellent waterfront view. Three other well-located, comfortable hotels in the moderate price category are: *Hotel Mercur, 17 Vester Farimagsgade; Hotel Astoria, 7B Vesterbrogade;* and the *Grand Hotel, 9A Vesterbrogade.*

INEXPENSIVE: *Hafnia Hotel* and the *Kong Frederick,* both in *Vester Volgrade* just off the Town Hall Square, are two of the best buys in town.

Also in this category, and reliable, is the Victorian *Kongen of Denmark, 15 Holmens Kanal.*

"Shoestring" travelers will find good accommodations at rockbottom prices at various mission hotels, such as the *Hebron, 4 Helgolandsgade,* or the *Missionshotellet, 27 Løngangsstrade,* located on the Town Hall Square, with spacious rooms and a restaurant serving bountiful, simple Danish food and beer, but no hard liquor.

RESORT HOTELS: Outside the city, but still within easy reach of Copenhagen, you will find excellent resort hotels along the lovely coast of the Øresund. The *Bellevue* in Klampenborg, *Hellebaek Bade Hotel* in Hellebaek, *Marienlyst,* and *Prins Hamlet* in the vicinity of Elsinore, are all good; and *Skovriderkroen* in Charlottenlund is an enchanting old inn with quaint rooms and good food, just thirty minutes out of Copenhagen; a perfect place for anyone traveling with children.

Food and Restaurants

Danish cuisine is simple and straightforward, based on superb products prepared with a minimum of saucing and disguising. Among these specialties to be reckoned with are the already famous open-faced sandwiches, *smørrebrød* (*smørre* is the butter, *brød* is the bread). In addition, be sure to sample the mild smoked salmon (*laks*), tiny pink shrimp (*rejes*), a redspotted plaice fish (*rødspaette*), excellent lobsters, *hakkebøf,* a hamburger with sautéed onions, boiled capon with frozen cream horse-radish, roast pork with red cabbage, slices of crisp bacon in a parsley sauce, yellow pea soup, and boiled cod (*kokt torsk*) with melted butter. *Rødgrød,* the Danish national tongue-twister-dessert, is an excellent gelatin of red currants and raspberries served with lots of *flødeskum* (whipped cream). *Kransekage* are delightful finger-shaped macaroons, and *Wienerbrød,* (the Danes call it Vienna bread; we say Danish pastry), is a favorite with morning coffee. Of course, there's the famous family of Danish cheeses, and a wide assortment of sausage (*pølse*) on sale at stands all over the city.

In Danish restaurants there are no restrictions on alcoholic beverages, which can be served throughout the day, including Sundays. *Carlsberg* and *Tuborg* are the most popular beers. With herring, and sometimes with cheese, drink *snaps,* the famous *Aalborg Akvavit.* And when you're drinking with Scandinavian friends, don't forget the traditional toast, *"Skål."*

All Copenhagen hotels have restaurants, among the best of which are those at the *Terminus,* the *Imperial,* the *Richmond* (famous for its "plaice fish in a housecoat"), the *Codan,* and the *d'Angleterre* for its *Wienerbrød,* if nothing else. The *Viking* at the *Palace* is large, dressy, and de luxe, in a typically international way.

TIVOLI RESTAURANTS: This glittering amusement park has over twenty restaurants and cafés for lunch, dinner, and light snacks. The best of the formal restaurants is *Divan 2,* a bright, summery place featuring excellent Danish food (ask for the large black menu book and stick to native specialties) and the best lobster salad in the world. Prices are moderate to expensive. Just across the way is *Belle Terrasse,* a lovely flowery old place similar in feeling to *Divan 2,* but specializing in continental food prepared with a slight Danish accent. (Expensive.) These restaurants are open only during the Tivoli season, May 1 to September 15.

There is a wide range of choice and contrast in the other city restaurants: the old-fashioned charm of *Krog's* seafood restaurant, set in the heart of the fish market, the modern, touristy, Hollywood-inspired *7 Nations,* each of its rooms done in the style of a different country, with food specialties of all, or the mellow brass-and-plush *Café P. a Porta,* a favorite with Copenhagen's artists and writers. At night there's the candlelit intimacy of the *Au Coq d'Or,* where continental dishes are prepared with a definite Danish accent, or the classically French (classically expensive) *Escoffier,* which purists claim is the best in town; while Bohemian gourmets head for way-out *Galatea*—small, dark, inexpensive, and decked out with Balinese artifacts. *Oskar Davidsen's* is the city's most famous restaurant. Open sandwiches are the specialty and the yard-long menu lists over 175 combinations.

There are several excellent neighborhood restaurants fifteen minutes away from the center of town by taxi. The largest of these, known as *Glacis* or the *Victorskaelder (Østerbrogade)* has an elegant dining room as well as a handsome, wood-paneled tavern room, excellent food, and a cold table between 11 A.M. and 2 P.M. The *Bjørnekaelderen (Frederiksbergalle)* is good too and even more of a neighborhood place. Though short on English, the help is long on good will, so you will somehow make yourself understood. *Langelinie Pavilion,* set beside the Copenhagen harbor on the esplanade-park, is a sparklingly modern luncheon or dinner place, convenient if you are sightseeing in the area, though a bit on the expensive side. There is also the good, inexpensive *Glyptoteket* across from the Carlsberg Museum, and a delightful, informal luncheon place in the Copenhagen Zoo.

Lunching or dining outside of Copenhagen can be very pleasant when you are driving around the outskirts of the city. There are lovely inns along the coast between Copenhagen and Elsinore: *Kølles Gaard* in Humlebaek, *Store Bjørn Kro* in Hornbaek, and most notably the *Søllerød Kro* at Holte, established in 1677 and one of the loveliest restaurants anywhere. More elaborate, international places include the *Bellevue-Strand Hotel* on the beach at Klampenborg, and *Kystens Perle* in Shekkersten, another example of Denmark gone Hollywood.

Entertainment, Night Life, and Special Events

Tivoli is the main nighttime attraction from May 1 to September 15 (see p. 6). The outstanding cabaret here is *Nimb,* with what seems to be continuous entertainment in three languages (Danish, French, and English). My own favorite is the student beer hall, the *Faergekroen* (Ferry Boat Inn).

Night club life in Copenhagen is on the unsophisticated side, and, with the exception of the *Ambassador,* a chic supper club with dancing in the Palace Hotel, and the *Adlon,* most of the places are typical of the large European cabarets.

Lorry's, also known as *Drachmann Kroen* and *Landsbyen,* is an enormous compound of dining rooms and cabarets, the *Atlantic Palace* is huge, with dancing and a merry-go-round bar, and the *Vingaarden* offers modern jazz. The *Valencia* has friendly girls and a floor show; the *Hvid Vinstue* on the Royal Square is a handsome old tavern-pub, and there is a whole string of rowdy sailors' bars in the harbor area called Nyhavn. Though the area is a little wild by Copenhagen standards, the activities are limited to minor brawling and major drinking. If you are interested in seeing how Danish teenagers sow wild oats, look in at *Den Røde Pimpernel* (Scarlet Pimpernel) just off Strøget; and if you would like to try your luck at the gambling table, make arrangements to go to Marienlyst (see p. 11). It is possible to maintain a twenty-four hour night life in the city, ending with a hangover cure at the Copenhagen Baths or the *Sauna* at the Royal Hotel.

The Royal Danish Ballet performs nightly at the Royal Theater from September to mid-May; and the *annual Royal Danish Ballet and Music Festival* is held during the last two weeks of the month. Opera is also performed at the Royal; the concierge can check programs and reserve tickets for you.

In summer, ballet can be seen at the Pantomime Theater in Tivoli; open-air concerts are held both in the city and on the outskirts each afternoon and evening. In winter, concerts are given in the Broadcasting House and the Odd Fellows Palace.

SPECIAL EVENTS: Danes burn candles in all their windows on *May 4* to mark the end of the German occupation of Denmark in World War II, and on *Midsummer's Eve* (June 23) the summer solstice is celebrated with bonfires along the coast and special programs at Tivoli.

On *July 4* Danish-Americans flock to Rebild Park in Jutland where Danes honor the American Independence Day with special festivities. From the middle of September to the middle of October, the Danes take part in the *Scandinavian Design Cavalcade* with special displays of furniture, silver, porcelain, glass, textiles, rugs, and handcrafts.

MEET THE DANES: Arrangements can be made for you to meet and visit the home of a Danish family whose interests match your own if you apply at the National Travel Association office when you arrive in Copenhagen.

Shopping

Almost anything you want to buy can be found along the Strøget, Copenhagen's main shopping axis running from Kongens Nytorv to the Town Hall Square, Raadhuspladsen. Here you'll find the silver shops of *Georg Jensen, Just Andersen* and *Hans Hansen,* the porcelain showrooms of *Royal Copenhagen* and *Bing & Grøndahl,* the fur shops of *A. C. Bang* and *Birger Christensen,* and the kaleidoscopic array of toys at *Thorngreen's.* Across from the fashionable *Fonnesbech* store there's the exciting little shop, *Form and Farve,* with simple home accessories and casual clothing. The newly modernized *Illums Bolighus,* a department store full of the world's best home furnishings, is itself a masterpiece of design ingenuity.

The largest department store in town is the *Magasin du Nord* on Kongens Nytorv, and here too is the *Haandarbejdets Fremme,* a handicrafts society with lovely embroidery and hand-knit sweaters. The most beautiful furniture in Denmark, designed by Hans Wegner, can be seen at *Johannes Hansen;* glassware is on view in the *Holmgaard* showroom in Nyhavn; and smart sportswear for men and women can be found at *Helga Madsen's* in Østerport.

Den Permanente, a unique cooperative selling the products of Denmark's great designers, is the best starting place for any shopping tour.

Copenhagen abounds in enticing little antique shops, most of which you will find on the streets off Strøget around the d'Angleterre, all glowing with copper and brass kettles, *aebleskiver* pans, molds, samovars, and candlesticks.

And, should you forget anything, you can probably find it on your way out of the country, at the Kastrup Airport shop. Here much of the best Danish merchandise is represented, antique samovars included, plus a well-stocked food counter and a tax-free liquor shop.

For a complete guide, get a copy of the SAS booklet, "Shopping Your Way Through Scandinavia."

Background Reading

The Icicle and the Sun, by William Sansom
Denmark Is a Lovely Land, by Hudson Strode
Scandinavia, edited by Doré Ogrizek, World in Color Series
Tourist in Denmark, published by the Danish newspaper, the *Politiken*

Finland

HELSINKI

*The white city of the north, the world's
smallest, most sophisticated capital*

PEWTER-gray and brick-red, mustard and olive, mauve and charcoal,
these are the Byzantine colors of Scandinavia's most excitingly foreign
capital, Helsinki. It is a city of dramatic sweep and proportion, with
a striking resemblance to Leningrad, the czarist St. Petersburg, especially around the Senate Square with its overpowering, high-domed
Lutheran Cathedral painted brilliant salt-white, and its heavy columned
Parliament Building done in old gold, all centered on the statue of
the benevolent czar, Alexander II. It's a vigorous, sea-girt town, opening wide and flat around its gray Baltic harbor; most beautiful in
winter, when it is iced white and striped blue as ice-breakers cut sea
lanes in the frozen waters, a graphic reminder of the Finnish flag, a
wide blue cross on a field of white.

Helsinki (*Helsingfors*) is set in a land of sixty thousand lakes and
what must surely be the world's most mystically spiritual landscape.
Here flat, silent stretches of mirror-dark lakes swallow the light of the
low-hanging sky and are dotted all over with tall-timbered forest
islands—and somehow it is the wide expanses of water that seem solid,
the islands that seem to swirl and drift. And they say that nowhere does

15

the full moon look so large, so charged with white magic, as it does here. There is an end-of-the-world stillness, a calm expectancy in this wild natural setting—the landscape Sibelius set to music in his stirring and majestic *Finlandia*.

The key to the Finnish temperament lies in the word *sisu,* denoting indomitable staying power in the face of insurmountable odds, the characteristic that accounts for the Finns' victorious survival through trials that would have permanently discouraged a less stalwart people. They are in many ways the most complex and interesting people in Europe—tough and introspective, with an essential wildness, a broad underlying humor, and an international reputation for absolute integrity; it is said that if you must have a stranger hold your purse, you'd be wise to choose a Finn. They are a unique people, in looks and personality a strange combination of the races and national influences that have touched them. They are a passionate Magyar race with a pervading sense of restraint due, no doubt, to the six hundred years they spent under Swedish rule; and with a Slavic flair for the dramatic, traceable to their one hundred years as a Russian grand duchy before they became an independent republic in 1917. In the Helsinki streets one easily spots traces of the elegant blond Swedish strain, the darker Slavic breeds, the handsome Magyar descendants with flaring cheekbones and tiger eyes.

They are ardent readers, and *The Egyptian,* by their own Mika Waltari, sold some 100,000 copies in Finland, equal in proportion to 4 million books in our own country. Stockmann's department store has the largest bookshop in Scandinavia. With their strong sense of drama, they are dedicated theatergoers, with Arthur Miller, Tennessee Williams, and Eugene O'Neill the top favorites, along with Chekhov. There are two official languages here: Swedish, which is spoken by about 10 per cent of the population (Finland is, in fact, the Swedish name for the land the Finns call *Suomi*), and Finnish, an almost surrealist tongue, Finno-Ugric in origin and related only to Estonian and Hungarian. It is a language of double and triple vowels and consonants whereby "Vol-au-vent with shrimps" on a menu translates to *Katkarapuja ja parsannuppuja voitaikinavannikkeessa.*

With its "green-gold" wealth of forests, it is the wood-pulp-paper industry that sustains Finland and, as do the other Scandinavians, the Finns excel in the applied, rather than the fine, arts. The designs they produce are among the most startlingly original and influential in the world, their designers unhampered and independently self-assured. With the heritage of Alvar Aalto and the elder Saarinen behind them, their modern architects sweep across the landscape in bold brush-strokes, with vital, naturalistic buildings that seem to cut new shapes in space. One can see examples of this work in suburban developments such as Tapiola and in the modern churches—the peaked-snow pyramid at Salla and the budget-built Otaniemi church with its abstract steeple of split rails, its glass walls opening to the somber, dense pine forests. Built more than twenty years ago, but with the same articulate feeling, is the Olympic Stadium with the Aaltonen statue of Paavo Nurmi, the "Flying Finn," just outside. And in the smaller objects (the earth-toned stoneware of the Arabia artists, the classic, versatile dinnerware of Kaj Franck, the ice-carved crystal and luminous lighting fixtures of Tapio Wirkkala, in the metal work of Sarpaneva, the handsome furniture of Ilmari Tapiovaara, and the heavy silver jewelry inspired by the ancient Kalevala legends) one sees the rugged crafted look, the sensitivity to form and texture.

Sightseeing in Helsinki is pleasantly easygoing, starting at the morning market in the harbor square, directly in front of the Presidential Palace, where fruits, vegetables, flowers, fish, buttons, baskets, shoelaces, and shawls are sold noisily and colorfully side by side. Walk past the Hall of Knights, where remnants of the Finnish-Swedish nobility hold an annual full-dress high-society ball; see the Finnish paintings in the Ateneum Gallery; attend the folk dances at Seurasaari, an open-air museum of old Finnish country houses, open from May to September; and visit the impressive Hietaniemi Cemetery, where Marshal Mannerheim is buried and where, on religious and national holidays, a candle gleams on each of the three thousand graves. In summer, ferry out to Suomenlinna and dine at Walhalla, set in the ramparts of an eighteenth century harbor fortress, or spend a weekend at the park-resort hotel Aulanko and on the way visit the birthplace of Sibelius and stop at Hattula, a thirteenth century church famous for its frescoes.

But whatever else you do or do not do in Finland—whether you swim or sail in summer, or ski on cross-country trails in winter; whether you fly to Lapland to hunt, see the midnight sun, or shoot the rapids; whether you attend the Scandinavian Design Cavalcade in September or the Sibelius Festival in June—the one thing you must try is a *sauna*. A combination steam and dry-heat bath in a resin-scented pine-paneled room, the *sauna* is to the Finn a source of psychic as well as physical renewal. You can have yours complete with birch-twig "floggings" in the handsome *saunas* of the Hotel Helsinki or Palace, or go to the *Sauna* Association where you wind up with a cooling dip in the lake.

FOR THE TRAVELER'S NOTEBOOK

Official Information

Before you go: Finnish National Travel Office, 10 East 40th St., New York 16, N.Y.

In Helsinki: SAS Office, 37 Esplanaadikatu; U.S. Embassy, 21 Ita Kaivopuisto; Finnish Tourist Association (Suomen Matkailijayhdistys) 15A Mikonkatu; Helsinki Tourist Office (Helsingin Kaypungin Matkailu-toimisto) 17 P. Esplanaadikatu.

Money Matters

Currency: The unit of currency is the Finnmark (FM), also called Mark or Markka. It is divided into 100 pennies. FM 3.19 equals about $1, U.S.

Tipping: A 15 per cent service charge is added to the bill in hotels. Tip hotel desk clerk FM 3 to 10, depending on his services and the length of your stay. Luggage porter FM .20 to .30 when you check out; hall porter FM 1 to 2. A 15 per cent charge is added to restaurant checks; extra FM 2 to 2.50 for exceptional service. Terminal porters, FM 3 to 5 per bag; same for doormen, hatcheck girls, *sauna* attendants; no tip necessary for taxi drivers, barbers, or hairdressers.

Climate, Clothing, and Essentials

The tourist season lasts from June to the beginning of September. July is the warmest month, averaging about 68 degrees F. Light clothing is suitable during the summer months but bring along your raincoat. There will be snow and freezing weather from December through April—fine for ski fans. You will naturally need warm clothing, wool stockings, and heavy shoes in winter, a light topcoat in spring and fall.

The Finns dress informally in normal city attire, and evening clothes are necessary only at first-night performances at the theater or opera.

Hotels

Room charges in Helsinki vary considerably and it is difficult to generalize or to divide the accommodations into specific categories, but both luxury and economical rooms are available. All are clean and simply furnished, generally in the modern style for which the Finns are well known. Service is generally good, and all of the hotels listed here have restaurants. It is always advisable to book your reservation in advance, particularly in summer, but if you should arrive without a reservation, go to the Hotel Booking Center in the Central Station and they will make arrangements for you. Prices for a single room range from FM 13 to 25, with a de luxe price of FM 40; doubles range from FM 20 to 45, with the top de luxe price of about FM 65.

DE LUXE: *Palace, 10 Eteläranta.* This handsome hotel designed by Alvar Aalto is one of the city's chief sights—situated in an office building and with a view over the harbor—good restaurant and superb *sauna*. De luxe and with beautiful suites. *Marski, 10 Mannerheimintie.* One of the newest and most modern hotels in Helsinki, well located with comfortable rooms and a member-only night club to which hotel guests are admitted. *Vaakuna, 2 Asema-aukio.* Occupying two floors in a centrally located office building, this modern hotel has small but pleasant rooms and good *sauna* facilities. First class and rather expensive. *Kämp, 29 Esplanaadikatu.* Old world atmosphere (but few modern comforts), overlooks an esplanade-park, and its restaurant was a favorite with Mannerheim. Turn of the century brass-and-plush decor is faded but charming. Expensive. *Seurahuone, 12 Kaivokatu.* Moderately expensive, this old-fashioned hotel is centrally located, has a restaurant and complete facilities.

MODERATE: *Helsinki, 12 Hallituskatu.* Unprepossessing outside, this well-located hotel has many redecorated rooms, offers superb service and handsome *sauna* accommodations, reasonably priced; first class and corner suites are spacious. *Olympia, 2 Läntinen Brahenkatu.* A little way out of the center, this is located close to swimming and athletic facilities in the House of Sports. New and modern, moderately priced.

INEXPENSIVE: *Marttahotelli, 24 Undenmaankatu.* Modern, comfortable, and convenient; an excellent buy in the budget class. *Torni Hotel, 26 Yrjonkatu.* Comfortable, convenient, a favorite with traveling Europeans. *Klaus Kurki, 2–4 Bulevardi;* the *Carlton, 5 Keskuskatu.* These are both quite moderately priced and comfortable. *Hospiz, 23 P. Rautatienkatu* and the *Ursula,* a little way out of the center of the city at *1 Paasivuorenkatu* are economical, clean, and comfortable, with single rooms for less than FM 15 and doubles averaging about FM 25.

Food and Restaurants

Finnish food is a combination of national influences, with such Scandinavian favorites as *gravlax* and eel, with the usual ritual concerning the delectable dill-flavored crawfish, eaten with festival zeal in the late summer and served, not with akvavit, but with vodka, and smorgasbord called here *voileipäpöytä*. In addition there are such Russian specialties as borscht and blinis, shashlik and beef Stroganoff; and strictly Finnish creations such as well-smoked reindeer tongue; an oven-roasted stew of lamb, beef, and pork, called *Karjalan paisti; kalakukko,* a meat-and-herring pie; and the dark pumpernickel baked in ring-like disks that hang on long wooden poles across the bakery ceiling. Most Finns drink beer or milk with their meals, and often a curdled milk which is said to be very good for you.

Some restaurants serve all types of wines and spirits, some only wine, some beer and some nothing (that is, nothing alcoholic). *Snaps* or akvavit is a good start for your dinner; this is usually drunk in one or two swallows, often accompanied by beer. If you like vodka, you will find it here, and Finnish liqueurs are very good. Try, for instance, *Polar* ("folk brandy"), often taken as a long drink, and *Mesimarja,* a sweet liqueur made of bramble-berries and cloud berries.

One of the most surprising things about Helsinki is the great variety of restaurants it has, and in the *Torni Hotel* alone one may dine in a Chinese, Balkan, or Spanish restaurant, each with a separate, native kitchen and suitable decor. There is good French and Italian food, with music and dancing, at the *Monte Carlo,* simple bistro fare at *Chez Marius. Fen Kuan* is an Oriental snack bar featuring sukiyaki and Indonesian *Nasi Goreng,* and *Ruokabaari* is a way-out Bohemian place with inexpensive Russian food that you serve yourself (and pay for in advance), and is only for the most intrepid.

All of the hotels have dining rooms and the best of these is at the *Palace,* especially pleasant for lunch because of the harbor view, and which features continental and local dishes. Unquestionably the best and most elegant restaurant in Helsinki is *Motti,* where anything on the huge menu is superb. Prices are moderate to high, depending upon the amount you eat and drink, and it's a good idea to have your hotel direct your cab to this place since its address, *2 Töölöntorinkatu,* is hard (if not impossible) to pronounce, and almost as hard to find. The most authentically colorful restaurant, open only for lunch, and with a huge smorgasbord, is *Kestikartano,* all done up in rough-hewn wood in the typical Finnish country style. The *Savoy* is elegant and continental, suitably expensive, with a panoramic view of the harbor and city, while the *White Lady* turns out gourmet food to the sound of piano music, and *Orpheus* is an atmospheric cellar-grill. In summer it is pleasant to ferry out to the medieval harbor fortress Suomenlinna and dine at the *Walhalla,* or the outdoor restaurant *Esplanaadikappeli* near the market square. *Perho,* a little bit out of the way, is worth the trip for its superb design. Prices are moderate as this is a practical training course for home economics students.

For light lunches and inexpensive meals, there are many cafeterias throughout the city. *Pika-Pala* serves typical Finnish dishes, and restaurants of the *HOK* and *Elanto* chains are excellent for budget travelers. The *Elite* is an artists' and writers' hangout, therefore expectedly inexpensive, and there are many espresso cafés too.

Kultakukko-Coffeehouse and the restaurant *Lunnunrata,* in the suburb Tapiola, afford a wonderful tower-top view of this modern architectural wonderland. Meals are good and prices moderate. In summer the *Café Töölönranta,* in a waterfront garden near the Olympic Stadium, serves good meals at reasonable prices.

Entertainment, Night Life and Special Events

Almost everything stops here at midnight. There are three interesting night clubs in Helsinki and many restaurants have dancing and floor shows until 1 or 2 A.M. The M-Club of the *Marski Hotel* is smart, popular, and open to hotel guests; the *Monte Carlo,* also a club but open to foreign visitors, is known for its fine dance music. In both cases your hotel porter can make necessary arrangements. One place not to be missed is *Kalastajatorppa,* also known as *Fiskatorpet* (the Fisherman's Hut), a very handsomely designed circular building, more exciting for its architecture than for its food or floor show, but well worth a visit. The *Adlon* is a smart and subdued old-world supper club with dancing, while the *Fennia* is the leading cabaret-restaurant with moderately good floor shows and food to match. The *Casino* is an expensive (about FM 45 for an evening is average) dinner-and-music place a little way out of town, with a breathtaking view of the sea. *Espilä* has the closest thing to a girlie show in Helsinki. The *Teatteri Grilli* near the National Theater stays open until 4 A.M. and has a good late à la carte menu of grills and sandwiches.

Helsinki has five theaters and an opera house. The leading stages are the Finnish National Theater and the Swedish Theater. The opera presents ballets as well as the standard operatic repertoire. These theaters are closed during the summer, but you will find excellent entertainment and folk dances at the open-air theaters at Seurasaari. Ask your hotel porter or check a daily paper to get further information on performances.

Concerts are usually given in the Concert Hall of the University Senaatintori. During the winter the Municipal Orchestra of Helsinki and the Radio Symphony Orchestra give frequent performances.

From the beginning of May to the middle of September the amusement park at Linnanmäki is open.

SPECIAL EVENTS: *Walpurgis Night* on April 30, followed by *May Day* (May 1) is the time when all the students go wild, wear white caps and celebrate with bonfires, drinking, and open house, and when everyone, it seems, carries at least one balloon.

In late September and early October, Finns take part in the *Scandinavian Design Cavalcade* with special displays of home furnishings and craftwork in shops and exhibition halls; and *Sibelius Week,* the musical event of the year, is celebrated in June, with special concerts and performances by renowned conductors and soloists from all parts of the world.

From June through August you may fly Finnair on an overnight visit to the Land of White Nights in Finnish Lapland.

Shopping

Anyone who likes modern design will have a field day in Helsinki for, beyond question, some of the world's most handsome home furnishings are designed and made by the Finns.

Ceramics and dinnerware by Arabia, crystal by Karhula-Ittala, Riihimäki, and Notsjö, furniture by Alvar Aalto, cloud-soft Metsovaara blankets and elegant modern lighting fixtures, traditional wool string *ryijy* rugs (beautiful enough to make wall hangings), and ingenious kitchen cookware, sculptured wooden laminates and subtly-colored table linens—all these and more are to be had in this city so famous for its applied arts. To see the best over-all sampling, visit *Stockmann's,* a huge department store with a superb selection. In addition, you can see the furniture of Alvar Aalto at *Artek Oy;* one-of-a-kind Arabia art ceramics at a gallery-shop on Esplanaadikatu; textiles and *ryijy* rugs at the *Finnish Design Center* and *Friends of Finnish Handicrafts;* and hand-wrought jewelry at *Kalevala Koru.* The department store, Elanto, has an especially good collection of glassware; lighting fixtures can also be seen here, as well as at *Idman Oy,* and *Pohjoismainen Sähkö. Pirtti* and *Hemflit* are noted for their table linens, textiles, and knitted skiwear. There is expertly designed sportswear at the shop of the famous Olympic runner, Paavo Nurmi.

Women interested in high fashion should not miss the casual clothes impeccably designed by Armi Ratia, and sold at three *Marimekko* shops in the city.

Background Reading

The Icicle and the Sun, by William Sansom

The Land and the People of Finland, by E. Berry

Scandinavia, edited by Doré Ogrizek, World in Color Series

Journey to Finland, by D. Ashcroft

Helsinki à la Carte, by the Western Foreign Press Club, c/o Kauppakilta, 13 Snellmanninkatu, Helsinki, Finland. This is a superb on-the-spot guidebook, also full of useful information when you're planning a trip to Helsinki.

Facts about Finland, available from the Finnish National Travel Office,

10 East 40th St., New York 16, N.Y. This contains, in addition to complete facts and figures on Finland, an excellent bibliography of works on various aspects of Finnish life and culture, all written in English.

Norway

OSLO

In the Land of the Midnight Sun

OSLO, the capital of Norway, was founded in the year 1050 by Harald the Harsh, who set the foundations of his city at the point where the Akers River meets the Oslofjord. Although nothing of his original city remains today, Oslo, more than any other Scandinavian capital, recalls the days of the Vikings and the Norse legends of Thor and Odin, Bragi and Frey. It is a narrow strip of a city backed up against the mountains and facing out to sea, and it has about it the relaxed, buoyant feeling of a frontier outpost. Its most astounding feature is its crisp, clear mountain air spiked with a salt-sea bite and vigor. And from almost any point in the city you can see, all at once, mountaintops and harbor, the Holmenkollen ski jump, and fleets of pleasure sailboats.

Skis and sails give us the clue to the Norwegian terrain and the temperament of the people. It is a land of seagoing mountaineers, a country of rugged montains cut by sea-lane fjords, great deep-sea waterways that in the past lured the mountain folk down from their difficult farmlands and tempted them to explore the open seas to find easier climates. And so, in ancient times, the Vikings sailed as far west as America, which they named Vineland, south to the Mediterranean; and east to Constantinople and the Sweet Waters of Asia,

24

where they served as the personal guards of the Byzantine emperors in the all-Scandinavian Varangian Guard. In later years, Nansen and Amundsen explored the polar waters on the *Fram,* and Heyerdahl drifted with the tides from Peru to Polynesia on his balsa raft, *Kon-Tiki.*

Norway is in every way a land of the boundless, a rugged landscape of extremes, and the temperament of the people is as extreme and rugged as the terrain, a fact that made the Norwegians formidable adversaries for their German conquerors during World War II. They are given to easy laughter and easy anger and are open and friendly, completely without guile. The Norwegians are the archetype Scandinavians, tall and lean, with an athletic gait and angularity, with water-blue eyes, and gold hair that reminds one of corn silk. Their beautiful women are as coolly tempting as vanilla ice-cream sodas. The language they speak is closer to Swedish than to Danish, but with a rolling singsong rhythm. A scotch-and-soda is called here *pjolter,* and a *Konge* (Royal) *pjolter* is a highball of cognac and champagne.

Virtually all of the three and a half million people who inhabit this land are literate, for Norway instituted free compulsory education over a hundred years ago. This well-established culture has produced such introspective intellectuals as Ibsen and Grieg, Knut Hamsun and Sigrid Undset, the sculptor Vigeland, whose writhing human forms can be seen at Frogener Park, and the madly emotional Edvard Munch, whose earliest and most shattering paintings are in Oslo's National Gallery and the Munch Museum.

Norway has had a constitutional monarchy only since 1905. The present king, Olav V, is the son of Haakon VII, the Dane who was voted king when the Norwegians chose to end their hundred-year union with Sweden. Few kings in history have been as beloved as Haakon, and his return from exile in England after World War II was a time of much celebration throughout the country. King Olav is as popular as his father was, an unusual fact in a land where the innately democratic people take their aristocracy with more than a grain of salt.

While Norwegians endure a high tax rate, they profit from a high standard of living, their greatest commercial assets being their merchant fleet, their wood-pulp products, their handcrafts, and the fishing industries. One of Norway's greatest problems is a shortage of labor to work the farms and timberlands and to man the heavy industries which have grown up as a result of cheap hydroelectric power.

While there is perhaps less to do in Oslo than one finds in the other northern capitals, there is still more than enough to occupy even the most casual visitor. One could spend a week on the Bygdøy Peninsula alone and not exhaust its wonders. For here is a folk museum of back-country houses gathered from all over Norway, high-platformed log cabins with ladder entrances and box bunk beds and grass growing out of the birch-bark roofs. There is a twelfth century staved church looking like a fantastic cuckoo clock; and a beautiful old restaurant where on summer nights you can watch folk dancing and eat cured lamb with sour cream and the soft pancake bread, *lefse*. It is on Bygdøy, too, that you can see the balsa raft *Kon Tiki,* set in its hand-somely carved exhibition hall, and the three great Viking ships—one, the funeral ship of Queen Aase—and visit the soaring A-shaped con-crete building that houses the *Fram* of Nansen and Amundsen, the ship that has sailed farther north and farther south than any other single ship in the world.

Back in the center of Oslo, you will want to wander through the massive Town Hall, then walk along the harbor wharves where the morning fish market is held. At noon Oslo citizens queue up here to buy paper cones of hot shrimp, boiled at sea, and eat them as they sit along the piers and watch great ocean liners arrive and depart. One morning, well armed with camera and film, go to the flower and fruit market set in the square, Stortorget, just opposite the seventeenth cen-tury Oslo Cathedral with its sculptured bronze doors and ceiling frescoes. Stop for a Norwegian hot dog, called *pølse,* as in Danish, but wrapped in a *lompe,* a sort of potato-flour *tortilla.* And then, per-haps, visit the Arts and Crafts Museum and see the Baldishol tapestry that dates from the twelfth century, one of the last five Norman tap-estries in the world. Rest under the yellow awnings of the gay cafés along the main shopping thoroughfare, Karl Johansgate, and wonder at the Scandinavian talent for growing window-box gardens such as those around you.

Oslo offers a wide range of outdoor activities easily accessible from the city the year round. There are hunting and fishing, hiking and swimming, skiing, skating and tobogganing, and sailing. It is also the starting point for side trips to Fredrikstad to see the PLUS community of artists and artisans, or to Bergen, the old port city that was the headquarters of the Hanseatic League in Norway, or to Jotunheim, the home of the trolls and giants of *Peer Gynt,* or to the ski resort, Lillehammer.

In late spring, you can travel by boat through the enamel-blue fjord waters, when the mountaintops are sugared with snow, the valleys frosted with apple blossoms and lilacs, a sight almost as beautiful throughout the months of summer. And at the same time of year you can take an overnight trip by air to Lapland and the midnight sun.

BERGEN

A pasture amid mountains

NORWAY'S second city is a gay and robust deep-sea port, as quaintly picturesque as a storybook village, with salt-white houses topped by red-tiled roofs, a wide blue harbor with snowy gulls and fishing trawlers, merchant ships and shipbuilders' cranes, all set off by a backdrop of forest-green hills. Its streets are bustling with flower vendors and fishmongers, bubbling with a bright café life that is undaunted by the ever-present North Sea mists which seem to dampen everything but the jovial spirits of the witty, cosmopolitan Bergeners.

Bergen has been officially a part of Norway since the city's founding in 1070, and it was the country's capital from the twelfth to the fourteenth century. But until the completion of the Oslo-Bergen Railway in 1909, the city was in closer contact by sea with Great Britain and the European continent than it was with Oslo by land. The reason lies in its topography, for Bergen is walled off by a ring of seven mountains (its name in fact is a derivation of the Norwegian word *bjorgvin,* "a pasture amid mountains") and so faced westward across the sea to become Norway's leading center of shipping, shipbuilding, and fishing, and its main point of immigration. In addition, Bergen is the prime producer of dried salt cod, the beloved *baccala* of southern Europe, and so has been linked to the Mediterranean for generations; and for two hundred years it was the headquarters of the North German Hanseatic League. All of this has given the Bergeners easygoing continental manners and a special aptitude for language, although they retain a strong sense of regionalism, and a distinctive dialect of their own.

A "second city" only in terms of its 150,000 population, Bergen has many claims to distinction, among them its world-famous navigation school, its institute for weather study and another for, of all things, leprosy research. And it has made its cultural contribution to Norway as well, with its three renowned native sons: Edvard Grieg, in whose honor the Spring Music Festival is held with many concerts at his home, Troldhaugen; the "Nordic Paganini," Ole Bull, whose statue adorns the little *plass* that bears his name; and Ludvig Holberg, the "Scandinavian Molière," though he actually worked in Denmark and both countries claim him as favorite son. Ibsen, though not born in Bergen, worked there for several years as director of Norway's first National Theater. The original building was later destroyed by fire.

Since its buildings were mainly of wood, much of Bergen has met with the same fate and only a few of the original old sections are intact. Even the houses of the Hanseatic merchants set along the wharf, Bryggen, are eighteenth century reproductions of the fourteenth and fifteenth century peaked-roof, brown-wood buildings: ascetic office and living quarters for German clerks transported to Bergen to manage the affairs of the League. Here they were locked up at night, each in a cabinet bunk-bed, so short they must have slept sitting up, and each bed with its small entrance door large enough for a maid to reach in for bed making but so small she could not wriggle through completely—or at least that was the theory. Such stern measures were designed to minimize resultant intermarriage whereby German funds would slip into Norwegian hands. A great many fascinating collections illustrating Bergen's Hanseatic days can be seen in the nearby museum in Finnegaarden.

Two of the oldest buildings in Bergen are the Mariakirken, St. Mary's Church, built in the early twelfth century and used as the official church of the Hanseatic tradesmen, and the medieval cathedral honoring Norway's patron St. Olav. Its most impressive relic is the medieval fortress Bergenhus, with its thirteenth century Haakon Hall and sixteenth century Rosenkrantz Tower. It was from this fortress that Bergen forces successfully defended the city against the naval attack of the Earl of Sandwich in 1665, and one of the British cannonballs can still be seen embedded in the fortress wall. Old Bergen houses of the nineteenth century are gathered in an outdoor museum at the edge of the city, and when it comes to indoor museums, there is one for almost every taste. The Municipal Museum has a representative collection of nineteenth and twentieth century Norwegian paintings and sculptures, as well as a smaller group of European works, and the extremely fine Museum of Arts and Crafts covers the applied arts of Norway, China, and all of Europe. There is also the Hanseatic Museum already mentioned, the Fishery Museum, and, twenty minutes out of the city, the Hordaland Agricultural Museum with interesting displays of old farming utensils, silverware, and fishing boats. The Natural History Museum, the Historical Society, and the Maritime Museum are all affiliates of Bergen's university, and so is the fascinating Aquarium at Nordnes.

More of the city's past can be sampled on a three-hour evening tour to Fana where you can visit the staved church at Fantoft, the eight-hundred-year-old Fana church, watch a program given by colorfully costumed folk dancers, and enjoy some typical country food and music. Another day you can rent a car and drive fifteen miles south to the twelfth century Lysekloster monastery, or, one morning, take a boat trip from the fish market jetty and cruise around Bergen's picturesque outlying islands. And Bergen is, of course, the jumping-off point for three of Norway's most breathtaking fjords: the Hardanger, the Nordfjord, and the Sogne, absolute musts for anyone visiting Norway from May through mid-September and most beautiful in the apple-blossom months, May and June.

FOR THE TRAVELER'S NOTEBOOK

Official Information

Before you go: Norwegian National Travel Office and Norwegian Information Service, 290 Madison Ave., New York 17, N.Y.

In Oslo: SAS Office, 6 Ruseløkkevein, or 18 Karl Johansgate; U.S. Embassy, Drammensveien; Tourist Information Office, 28 Rosenkrantzgate.

In Bergen: SAS Office, 5 Nordahl Brunsgate; Tourist Office, 1 Slotts-gaten.

Money Matters

Currency: The krone (NKr.) is divided into 100 øre and is the main unit of currency. There are about NKr. 7.12 to $1, U.S.

Tipping: Hotels add 12½ per cent to the bill, but the head porter and bellhop are tipped a few kroner each for special service; restaurants have a service charge of 10 per cent, but for good service it is customary to leave an additional 5 per cent; hatcheck girls and washroom attendants 50 øre each; baggage porters 75 øre for each bag; taxi drivers are tipped 10 per cent only if they help with baggage.

Climate, Clothing, and Essentials

Norway has more daylight in summer than any other country in the world and there is practically no darkness between the end of April and the middle of August. On Midsummer's Day, for example, Oslo has eighteen and a half hours of daylight. During the warmest months, June, July, and August, temperatures average about 70 degrees F. May is the perfect time to visit Bergen's Hardangerfjord. September and October are brisk, with glorious colors, and in winter (December to Easter) when temperatures drop to 20 degrees, snows provide a paradise for sportsmen. Norwegians rarely dress formally and the usual city attire is always correct. It is wise to pack a raincoat and solid walking shoes at any time of year.

Hotels

Hotel standards are high in Norway and the law requires any establishment calling itself a "hotel" to comply with standards imposed by the government. If you are unable to make reservations, contact the Accommodation Office (*Innkvarteringssentralen*), at the East Railroad Station (Oslo *Østbanestasjon*). Almost any accommodations will be clean, modern, and comfortable. Most hotels have rooms with or without private baths, and prices quoted are without service charge or breakfast. De luxe: single with bath, NKr. 50 to 65; double, NKr. 90 to 150. Moderate: single, NKr. 40 to 50; double, NKr. 75 to 120. Inexpensive: single, NKr. 17 to 35; double, NKr. 30 to 65.

OSLO

DE LUXE: *Grand Hotel, 31 Karl Johansgate.* This de luxe hotel, located on the city's main street, is a pleasant mixture of old and new and has two of the best restaurants in town. *Bristol Hotel, 7 Kristian IV Gate.* Beautifully old world and gracious, this handsome place is conveniently located yet is out of the hustle and bustle. *Continental Hotel, 24 Stortings-gate.* Certainly the up-and-doing, brightly modern hotel of the city, located just a stone's throw from the Town Hall. Also very comfortable are: the *K.N.A. Hotel, 68 Parkvein* (Royal Norwegian Automobile Club); the *Norum, 53 Bygdøy Alle* near Frogener Park; and the *Holmenkollen Turist-hotel,* located some twenty minutes from the center of town by electric railway, on a mountainside near the famous ski run, with a magnificent view over the Oslofjord and the city; moderately priced for this class.

MODERATE: Less expensive, less luxurious, but no less comfortable are: the *Hotel Viking, 11 Gunnerusgate,* a little away from the center of things but with a very good restaurant on the thirteenth floor; the *Astoria* at *21 Akersgate;* the *Savoy,* at *11 Universitetsgaten;* and the *Ansgar Misjons-hotel, 26 Møllergate,* near the flower market. All are conveniently located and moderately priced.

INEXPENSIVE: The *Studentbyen* (Student Town), a huge new dormitory center which offers single and double rooms as well as apartments, is converted into a hotel during the summer. The charge for a single room is about NKr. 37.50, including breakfast. The address is *85 Sognsveien.* Other inexpensive accommodations include: the *Ritz, 3 Frederik Stangs-gate,* the *Gabelshus Hotel, 16 Gabelsgate,* or the modern *Indremisjons-hotellet, 4 Staffeldtsgate,* with prices from NKr. 16 to 20 for a single room.

BERGEN

Hotel space is plentiful in Bergen, but it is essential to have advance reservations during the May Music Festival and the month of July.

DE LUXE: The *Orion* is one of Norway's best and most modern hotels. It is on the waterfront; all of its rooms have baths. A first class hotel, single rooms are about NKr. 52 per day; doubles, about NKr. 80. The newly rebuilt *Norge* is the latest addition to the luxury class. The *Bristol, 11 Torgalmenning,* is also a first class hotel, very comfortable, pleasant, and recently remodeled. Also in this class is the *Terminus,* a slightly more commercial but comfortable hotel near the railroad station.

MODERATE: The *Neptun, 8 Valckendorffsgate,* has bed-sitting rooms and a café. Other moderately priced hotels are: *Slottsgaarden, 3 Sand-brogate;* the *Rosenkrantz;* the *Hordaheimer;* and *Skandia.* All can be well recommended.

INEXPENSIVE: In the summer months, the *Alrek,* a student hotel, offers comfortable accommodations at extremely low prices.

Food and Restaurants

Seafood and fresh-water fish naturally rank very high among the most popular Norwegian dishes. You will surely enjoy the large shrimp and lobster fresh from the sparkling waters of the northern seas. Trout is generally boiled or fried in sour cream. Salmon is at its best when smoked, although some gourmets prefer it boiled and served with a rich mixture of whipped sour cream and horse-radish, or topped with creamed spinach and a poached egg.

You will probably enjoy the *fjellrype* (ptarmigan), perhaps the most popular of Norway's game birds. When the autumn hunting is good, there will be woodcock, capercailzie, or wild duck. Venison, cured lamb, *spekeskinke* (cured ham), and even goat's and sheep's ham (also cured and known as *fenalaor*) served with scrambled eggs and fresh vegetables are also highly regarded. As in the rest of Scandinavia, beer, wine, and akvavit are often taken with meals.

Although all first class hotels will serve you a continental breakfast on request (just ask for "café complet" or "the complet"), people with hearty appetites will be delighted to know that Norwegian hotels generally provide a very substantial meal (*frokost*) in the morning, as a rule from 7 to 9:30 A.M. From a huge table (the Norwegians call it a "cold table" although some warm dishes are included) you may pick and choose from a great variety of delicacies based on cereals, eggs, meat, salads, various types of fish, cheese, and bread.

OSLO

Among the city's restaurants the most startlingly beautiful is *Frogner-seteran,* a vast wooden building of heavy beams and rafters and flying dragon heads, atop a mountain overlooking the ski jump, the city, and the harbor. Game is the specialty. Dine one night at the amusing and colorful artists' restaurant, *Blom's,* and try the special Black Pot, a Norwegian boiled dinner of vegetables and mixed meats. In summer, visit *Dronningen* or *Kongen,* both set out on an arm of land in the Oslofjord harbor; and for well-prepared international cuisine any time, stop at *Jacquet's Bagatelle.* On Bygdøy you will find the well-designed *Najadan,* a new restaurant with a collection of old figureheads and other ships' appointments.

In the basement of the Tostrup Building you will find *Tostrup-kjelleren,* known for its fine seafood, while on Stortorget (flower market), near the Oslo Cathedral in a seventeenth century building, the *Stortorget Gjæstgiver* has catered to generations of Oslo citizens.

Finally, there are a number of inexpensive restaurants offering simple but substantial meals at cafeteria prices: *Viking's Kafeteriaen, Restaurant Larsen's Kafeteria,* the small *Wimpy,* and the *Snick Snack.*

BERGEN

Here you should eat fish, which is served in great and delicious variety, especially boiled cod, or boiled pale, a popular local fish. International cuisine is offered in hotels and leading restaurants. Perhaps the choicest Bergen restaurant is the old and beautifully decorated *Bellevue Inn*, perched high up on the mountainside. The *Flesland Airport* restaurant is not just a place for travelers but also a favorite among Bergeners who want good fare. This, the *Chianti* and *De Sma Hjem*, in town, are popular restaurants in the city. The *Fløyrestauranten*, on the summit of the Fløyen Mountain, is very popular. There is music and dancing from 7:30 to 12 P.M. and the view over the city is superb. The *Elsesro* at Old Bergen is open from May 15 to September 30 and also has a fine view of the sea.

Entertainment, Night Life, and Special Events

OSLO

Tourists seeking entertainment after dark will discover that Oslo has little to offer in the way of night clubs. Norwegians prefer dinner-dancing with limited floor shows added; therefore, night clubs of the international variety do not thrive in the city, with the exception of the *Bristol, George's*, and the *Telle*, which is small and exclusive. For a look at Oslo's teenagers in their own world of jazz and rock 'n' roll, visit the *Metropol*.

There are three permanent theaters in the city of Oslo, the most distinguished being the National. The classical dramas of Ibsen and Bjørnson, as well as the comedies of Holberg, are presented here along with more modern plays.

The Oslo Philharmonic Orchestra gives concerts from September to May, and its high standards are further enhanced by guest artists and conductors from other countries. There are also numerous chamber music and church concerts and solo recitals. Opera and operettas are performed in the Folketeater Building.

Details are always to be found in the newspapers, in the monthly publication "Oslo Guide," or from the hall porter at your hotel, who will also tell you about the performances offered at the summer theater at Frogner Park or folk dancing and folklore culture sessions at Folkemuseet on Bygdøy.

BERGEN

There are no night clubs but there is dancing in such leading restaurants as Bellevue, *Bristol, Fløyrestauranten*, and *Rosenkrantz*. The *Stjernesalen* restaurant has floor shows as well. The theater and concert season runs from September to the middle of June, and in recent years the Bergen Festival has become an annual event at the end of May. The program includes concerts, drama, ballet and recitals in Edvard Grieg's house, Troldhaugen.

The leading theater is the *Nationale Scene* (National Stage), Symphony concerts are given at the nearby Konsertpaleet by the Harmonien Symphony Orchestra, once conducted by Edvard Grieg. In summer there are municipal entertainments in the parks, and sometimes a military band will play at midday in the City Park.

The hills around the city rise to a height of some 2,000 feet, and ski lifts, ski and toboggan runs (some floodlit at night), as well as skating rinks, are located almost everywhere. The most important sports event of the year is the *Holmenkollen Ski Competition,* which takes place annually on the first Sunday in March.

SPECIAL EVENTS: Fireworks, and open-air dancing and special celebrations at folk museums in Oslo and Lillehammer celebrate *Midsummer's Eve.* In addition, Norway takes part in the *June Music Festival,* and in the *Scandinavian Design Cavalcade,* when from mid-September to mid-October special displays of furniture, wood carvings, textiles, knitwear, ceramics, and glass are on view in shops and designers' workrooms. From May 25 to June 11, there is a famous *International Festival of Music, Drama, and Folklore* in Bergen. Norwegians pay tribute to the United States with a *July 4* ceremony honoring Abraham Lincoln in Oslo's Frogener Park. Boat trips through the fjords can be arranged from May through August.

KNOW THE NORWEGIANS: This is a program to introduce you to people whose professions or interests are similar to your own. Visits are arranged through the travel associations in Oslo and Bergen.

Shopping

OSLO

When preparing a shopping list for Oslo, remember that this is a center for superb ski wear, most notably the heavy hand-knit sweaters, gloves, and caps at *William Schmidt's* and at *Heimen's.* Luminous enameling in dazzling shades of emerald, gold, magenta, and electric blue, all on gleaming sterling silver, is to be found at *David-Andersen's* and *Tostrup's,* where you will also see fanciful jewelry and small table accessories. Ruggedly crafted furniture and home accessories are on view at three shops: *Norway Designs, Forum,* and *Rastad & Relling,* while country handcrafts are exhibited at *Den Norske Husflidforening* (*Husfliden*) in Møllergaten.

For an over-all look at the best in Norwegian home furnishings, visit the exhibition at *Forum.* Lustrous furs—blue fox, seal, or mink—can be purchased at *Pels-Backer, Carl Lunder, Walker Borther,* and the Oslo

Bundtmakeforretning. Handsome modern glass is sold at the *Glasmagasinet, L. Kløver,* and *Joh. Jørg. Backe,* while unusual pewter and ceramics are available at *Tinnboden* or the *Galligani* shop. For wonderful antiques, try *Blømquist* or *Kaare Berntsen,* and for a wide array of ski equipment there are, among others, the shops of *Marius Eriksen, A. Gresvig, Ludvig Torgersen,* and *Sigmund Ruud,* the famous Norwegian ski jumper.

BERGEN

The skillfully hand-woven articles, ski sweaters, dolls, folk costumes, rose-painted and carved wooden bowls and boxes, and other rustic articles at *Husfliden* are excellent. *Erling Krage* has a large selection of arts and crafts, pewter, pottery, and similar articles. The jewelers of Bergen, among them *David-Andersen, Safir, Magnus Aase,* and *K. Hestenes,* carry much the same stock as do their Oslo colleagues. Pewter and cutlery may be purchased at *J. Berstad* and *Peter M. Kolderup;* glass and ceramics at *Glassmagazin Thomsen,* and a little of everything at the two department stores, *Sundt & Co.* and *Kløverhuset.*

For a complete guide, get a copy of the SAS booklet, "Shopping Your Way Through Scandinavia."

Background Reading

The Icicle and the Sun, by William Sansom
Scandinavia, edited by Doré Ogrizek, World in Color Series
Skoal, Scandinavia, by Edward Streeter
How to Feel at Home in Norway, by Philip Boardman, and *Norwegian History Simplified,* by Zinken Hopp, are two interesting books, both available from Johan Grundt Tanum, 43 Karl Johansgaten, Oslo, Norway

Sweden

STOCKHOLM

City on the water

THE most serenely beautiful of the four Scandinavian capitals, Stockholm is graceful and gracious, polished and sophisticated, as elegantly formal as a Mozart sonata. It is a city that floats on a sea of Baltic blue, with green-wooded islands and white-masted ships and brick-red towers topped with lustrous gold leaf; a place of quiet voices and handsome serious men in impeccable gray suits, and tall, pale women with hair the color of candlelight.

Dating back to the thirteenth century, Stockholm is the capital of Europe's fourth largest country, a city of eight hundred thousand in a country of seven and a half million. Sweden is a land of overwhelming prosperity that reaches north to the icy mountains of Lapland, south to a gentle countryside with a tapestry landscape of flowers and forests, sunlit streams and fairytale castles—a land of factories and folklore, a welfare state with a history of witchcraft. Once the home of Vikings and powerful warriors, of Gustavus Vasa, the king who freed Sweden from the iron grip of Denmark, and his grandson, Gustavus Adolfus, whose victories made the Baltic a Swedish sea, Sweden is now a nation of equally powerful peacemakers, the country of Nobel and Bernadotte, and the greatest hero of the peace to date, Dag Hammarskjöld.

Everywhere contradictions abound: in the country, its capital, and, most of all, in its people. The Swedes love everything modern and revere everything old. They plan and design for the future without tearing up their past behind them. They are said to be cold, stiffly formal, and reserved. They are known to be hospitable, sincere, and courteous, with the typical Scandinavian fondness for saying "Thank you" (conversations are everywhere punctuated with the hammertaps, *Tack, Tack*). They have an almost Oriental sense of etiquette that governs all phases of life right down to the fine art of skoaling, and are absolute sticklers for promptness. Being five minutes too early for an appointment is as bad as being five minutes too late, with the result that dinner guests arrive a few minutes before the appointed hour and wait outside until exactly the right second before knocking. But they also have remarkably informal, relaxed rulings on all affairs of sex, marriage, and divorce and have one of the world's most progressively enlightened attitudes toward unwed mothers, of whom they have a fair number. All this indicates, perhaps, that their "coldness" carries with it the implied heat of the banked furnace and that their "reserve" is only on the surface, which is, after all, a very good place for it to be.

Along with useful inventions such as the self-aligning ball bearing and the vacuum cleaner, dynamite and the safety match, Sweden is also responsible for some of the most enchanting handicrafts: lacy straw Christmas ornaments, painted wooden birds, delicate embroideries and hand-woven rugs and fabrics. The Swede has the detached efficiency of the German, the American love of the easy life and laborsaving gadgetry, the English flair for understated humor, and a cultural leaning toward France. It is said that a Swede speaks German in the first stage of drunkenness, English in the second, and French in the third; it is to be noted that he speaks Swedish only when sober. It is indeed a language of sobriety, the most beautiful of the Scandinavian dialects, with the gentle lilt of a lullaby but with a delicate and precise attack on syllables; a language of subtle accents well suited to the cool, intense dramas for which these people have such a strong predilection—the works of their own passionately mad Strindberg and our O'Neill, whose last plays were translated into Swedish and produced for the first time in Stockholm's Royal Dramatic Theater. Sweden seems to have a special talent for movie making, too, and has given the world the two Bergmans, Ingmar and Ingrid, Greta Garbo, Viveca Lindfors, and Anita Ekberg, while their active opera company has produced Jenny Lind, Birgit Nilsson, and Jussi Björling, whose son Rolf made a promising debut in 1961. The same "practical, realistic" Swedes who created one of the swiftest jet interceptors, the supersonic, delta-winged SAAB Dragon, have as their national hero Nils Holgersson, Selma Lagerlöf's bewitched thumbling, who traveled over Sweden on the back of a flying gander.

This same unaccountable love of whimsy explains the Swedish calendar full of festivals and holidays. On April 30, Walpurgis Night is a rite of spring dating back to the Vikings, when bonfires burn all night to chase the Witch of Winter before the dawn of spring. Whitsuntide, just seven weeks after Easter is a time of picnics and countryside excursions. The most joyous holiday of all is Midsummer's Eve, during the week of the summer solstice, when, in city parks and country gardens, crossbarred Maypoles are entwined with green garlands and wild flowers and there are folk songs and dances until sunrise. There is the crayfish festival on August 8 when everyone gathers to eat the scarlet, dill-flavored *kräftor* and wash them down with icy aquavit. In September there is an eel festival when the special treat is hay-broiled eel, eaten out of doors; and in November Martin Gooseday, a holiday akin to our Thanksgiving. There are several great society balls during the winter season and the greatest social event of the year, the Nobel Prize Dinner in the Gold Room of the Town Hall on December 10. Christmas festivities begin on December 13, Lucia Day, when in homes, hotels, and offices, young girls in white robes with wreaths of candles in their hair serve hot coffee and saffron-scented cakes to family and guests; and then of course, Christmas Eve itself, with the traditional dried cod, *lutfisk,* and the Swedish Santa Claus, *jultomte,* and the candlelit tree decked out with red apples, tiny flags, gingerbread goblins, piglets, and stars.

Stockholm is a city for walkers, and although it may be covered by bus, private car or taxi, as with most cities it is best seen on foot. Stroll through the hilly cobblestoned streets of the Old Town, Gamla Stan, with its cellar antique shops and afternoon coffee-and-cake *konditoris;* wander around the Royal Palace, the golden block of buildings designed by Nicodemus Tessin; and see the Great Cathedral, Storkyrkan, first begun in the thirteenth century. Then rest a while on the benches in the city's oldest market square, Stortorget, rimmed with gabled medieval houses. This is where Christian the Tyrant of Denmark beheaded eighty-two members of the Swedish aristocracy in the infamous bloodbath of 1520. You can continue through Gamla Stan, pass the handsome Dutch-baroque House of the Nobility where the June music festival is held, and go on to Riddarholm Church, the pantheon of Sweden and the burial place of seventeen kings, a thirteenth century building with a forbidding steeple of black iron latticework. Or walk in the opposite direction and cross the bridge where Lake Mälaren joins the salt-sea Baltic, past the sprawling opera house and the fishing boats with their nets stretched out to dry in the sun like the golden wings of giant butterflies, and on past the city's luxury hotel, the Grand where you can rest again at the quayside café. From there, you can walk to the National Museum with its outstanding collection of north European and Swedish paintings and get a good view of one of the city's landmarks, the white sailing ship now serving as a youth hostel and moored permanently in the Saltsjön.

Skansen, an outdoor museum of old farmhouses, is set in a park just fifteen minutes from the center of the city. Here peacocks and pheasants roam free and unharmed, the houses are restored and furnished. At Christmas, the old houses become shops and sell handicraft gifts, and shoppers, chilled by the star-frosted air, warm themselves with *glögg,* the clove-scented claret punch, rich with currants and almonds and ablaze with sugar. Across from Skansen is the Nordiska Museum, with its displays of old country folk art, and its especially dramatic exhibits of antique table settings. And then there is Stockholm's antique attraction, the *Vasa,* a seventeenth-century war galleon. Fitted out for its maiden voyage with armaments and furnishings of every kind, it was launched, sailed a mile out to sea, then capsized and sank. Recently it was raised and pumped out, and a new museum was built for this unique time capsule and its contents.

The Stureplan section of the city is a whirl of activity, a miniature Times Square with flashes of neon, night clubs and restaurants, shops and kiosks and Sturebadet baths, where you can be massaged and steamed while your clothes are cleaned and pressed. And, finally, anyone visiting Stockholm must certainly leave half a day for the city's famous Town Hall, a modern building with dramatic medieval overtones, built in 1920 by Ragnar Östberg.

Sweden's charms are not, of course, confined to its capital and there are dozens of fascinating things to see an hour or so out of town, in almost any direction you care to travel. You might visit one of the modern, model "satellite" towns, such as Farsta, or drive to the beautiful country castle, Drottningholm, with its little Renaissance theater that has all of its stage apparatus intact, and where, in summer, performances are given in authentic period costuming and staging. Sigtuna, the oldest town in Sweden, with the ruins of the country's first cathedral dating from 1100, can easily be reached for a day's excursion, as can the ancient university town of Uppsala where you can see the gardens of the famed botanist, Linnaeus, and visit Old Uppsala, the royal residence in pre-Christian centuries.

On the way to Uppsala you can also see the seventeenth century palace, Skokloster, while the small, picturesque Gripsholm Royal Palace in Mariefred could be visited on another day for its outstanding collection of 2,400 historical portraits.

In a more relaxed mood, you can enjoy the bathing resort, Saltsjöbaden, in Stockholm's archipelago, wander around the island of Vaxholm where a hilltop castle looks out over the idyllic old town and the sea, or fly to Visby, "city of ruins and roses," on the island of Gotland, where crumbling medieval castles and walls are blanketed with trails of wild roses. And, if you have more time in this lovely land, visit the white-sanded, wide-beached Falsterbo, or take a dreamy steamboat trip on the Göta Canal from Stockholm to Gothenburg.

Sweden is divided into three main sections and each has more than enough variety and charm to tempt and satisfy the traveler. Götaland in the south includes the province of Skane with its beautiful old chateaux and beach resorts, and Kalmar with its moated and turreted castle that was built by Gustavus Vasa. The many glassworks whose products are known all over the world are set amid the pine and birch forests, the icy lakes and quiet country roads of and villages of Smaland. Gothenburg, and the Baltic islands of Öland and Gotland are also in this section. The region richest in Swedish folklore is Svealand, especially in its province of Värmland which is Selma Lagerlöf country, and in Dalarna and Dalecarlia, where some of the most picturesque old costumes are still worn at weddings and on festival days.

Norrland, the northern section of Sweden, makes up more than half of the 173,000 square miles of this land, yet includes just 10 per cent of the population. It is in these rugged highlands that you find ski and winter sports resorts, mountain hiking trails and streams practically begging to be fished. Set along the Gulf of Bothnia, the six provinces that make up Norrland, give the offbeat traveler a chance to discover a relatively un-touristed region. And if you like you can fly from Stockholm to Norrland's most northerly province, Lapland, and see the midnight sun and the nomads who roam between the icy regions of Norway, Sweden, and Finland, unhampered by borders and passports.

GOTHENBURG

Gateway to the West

GOTHENBURG (Göteborg) has been Sweden's exit to the open sea since the tenth century, when it was the point of rendezvous for Viking fleets that gathered at the mouth of the Göta River to embark on their voyages of exploration. Sweden's "second city" is the capital of Bohuslän, a coastal province so ancient it is said to be the locale of the Anglo-Saxon Beowulf epic. It is now a summer vacationland for Swedes in search of sun and sand, and the city is surrounded by dozens of charming villages, safe harbors for trawlers that fish in the North Sea banks.

Gothenburg itself is a bustling, mist-gray port on the Kattegat, with a skyline of cranes and derricks hovering over its shipyards, a city of wharves and quays, beside which fishermen dock each morning to auction off their daily catches. It is laced with canals and stamped with the red-brick baroque of Dutch Renaissance architecture, both holdovers from the Hollanders who planned this city in the seventeenth century at the request of the founding king, Gustavus Adolfus. As if it weren't enough to be the country's number one seaport and shipbuilding center, Gothenburg has its share of heavy industry as well, for it is the home of Sweden's largest automobile firm, Volvo, the headquarters of the giant SKF ballbearing complex, and has two leading institutes of industrial design, the Konstfackskolan and the Slöjdföreningens.

Add to this that Gothenburg has an outstanding cultural life and you'll begin to see how diverse a city it really is. The main center of that culture is the municipal square, Götasplatsen, where one of Europe's most modern concert halls, a civic theater and art museum and gallery are all focused on the impressive Poseidon fountain by Carl Milles. As might be expected from people whose lives are so closely linked with the sea, the easygoing, cosmopolitan, Gothenburgers take special pride in their maritime museum with its wonderful array of ship models going back to Viking days, and exhibits dealing with all kinds of maritime memorabilia.

But commerce and culture are not the only aspects of the city that give its four hundred thousand citizens cause for pride. They seem to take an inordinate delight in their parks, great green garden patches dotted all over the city. Of these, the largest and most wildly natural is Slottskogen, with miniature forests and a natural history museum; Trädgaardsföreningen is the lush botanical garden of the city's famous horticultural society and a favorite meeting place for townspeople; and Liseberg, a garden amusement park with a concert hall, restaurants, and a riot of carnival acts, is a joy to Gothenburgers and tourists alike.

Anyone with three days to spare can take an idyllic, three-day steamboat trip from Gothenburg to Stockholm (or vice versa) along the overland waterway, the Göta Canal. Drifting through picturesque farmlands and countrysides, you pass such sights at the Bohus fortress, built in 1308 and once considered north Europe's most powerful fort; the gigantic waterfalls of the Trollhättan power dam; Sweden's largest lake, Vänern, with its imposing seventeenth century Läckö Castle; the Vasa castle, Vadstena; and the ruins of the twelfth century monastery, Alvastra. Finally—240 miles and 58 locks later—you reach the Baltic skerries and sail into Lake Mälaren and the Stockholm harbor.

FOR THE TRAVELER'S NOTEBOOK

Official Information

Before you go: Swedish National Travel Office, 630 Fifth Ave., New York 20, N.Y.

In Stockholm: SAS Office, 1 Norrmalmstorg; Stockholm Tourist Information Office, 20 Gustav Adolfus Torg; Swedish Tourist Traffic Association, 3A Klara Västra Kyrkogata; U.S. Embassy, 101 Strandvägen.

In Gothenburg: SAS Office, 7 Östra Hamngatan; Tourist Information Office, Central Station.

Money Matters

Currency: The unit of currency is the crown or krona (Sw. kr.) which is divided into 100 öre. There are approximately 5.18 Sw. kr. to $1, U.S.

Tipping: In hotels, 10 to 15 per cent is usually added to the bill; tip the baggage porter öre 75 per bag when you check out. Restaurants add 10 per cent but it is customary to leave another 5 per cent for good service; öre 35 to 50 for hatcheck girls, washroom attendants, and shoeshine boys; cab drivers 10 per cent, barbers and hairdressers 10 to 15 per cent; kr. 1 per bag for porters in terminals.

Climate, Clothing, and Essentials

Though cooler than in central Europe, summer days are full of sun, and temperatures from June through August average 70 degrees F. Summer nights are short and extremely beautiful. Medium-weight summer clothing, a light topcoat, and thin suit are advisable. Spring and autumn are delightful and similar to New York temperatures. In winter, temperatures average 27 degrees F. and there is much snow in Stockholm, less in Gothenburg. May through October is the pleasantest time to visit Sweden. Normal city attire is correct at all times; the Swedes dress conservatively, and women prefer well-made suits of gray or muted tweeds by day, dark dresses at night. A raincoat is useful in either of these cities.

Hotels

Hotels in Sweden are noted for their cleanliness and superb service, and as a rule the staff speaks English, German, and French, in addition to Swedish. De luxe accommodations range from Sw. kr. 40 to 55 for a single with bath; Sw. kr. 60 to 85, double. Moderate: Sw. kr. 30 to 40, single with bath; Sw. kr. 40 to 60, double. Inexpensive: Sw. kr. 15 to 30, single with bath; Sw. kr. 29 to 30, double. Reservations are absolutely necessary during the summer months. Rates do not include the 10 per cent or 15 per cent service charge or breakfast.

STOCKHOLM

If you arrive without a hotel reservation, contact Hotellcentralen on the lower level of the Central Railroad Station. They will find a room at your price in a hotel, boardinghouse, or private home for a 3 kronor service charge.

DE LUXE: *Grand Hotel, 8 S. Blasieholmshamnen.* Beautifully situated across the water from the Grand Palace, centrally located and a popular meeting place for everyone. *Strand Hotel, 9 Nybrokajen.* Well located, overlooking the water and near the shopping centers—a favorite with Swedish high society. *Palace Hotel, 115 St. Eriksgatan.* On the top floor of an office building, near the center of the city and overlooking a lake.

MODERATE: *Hotel Reisen, 12 Skeppsbron.* Charming, very continental little hotel, located on the water in the old town. *Hotel Stockholm, 9 Nybrokajen.* Occupying the top floor of an office building, this hotel is centrally located and has no restaurant but serves breakfast to guests. *Apollonia Hotel, 53 Nybrogatan.* Fairly new and well located, with all hotel conveniences. *Carlton Hotel, 57A Kungsgatan.* Close to the shopping center and the Concert Hall, this is another modern, well-equipped hotel. *KAK Hotellet, 6 S. Blasieholmshamnen.* A well-run hotel of the Royal Automobile Club, conveniently located with a view of the Grand Palace. Other moderately priced, comfortable hotels with convenient locations include the *Hotel Gillet, 13–15 Brunkebergstorg* and the *Hotel Grand Esplanade, 7A Strandvägen. Hotel Brommaplan,* at the airport, is a comfortable, moderately priced hotel for anyone on a one-night stopover; and the *Gyllene Ratten, 285 Vantörsvägen* in Hägersten, is a modern motel four miles southwest of Stockholm.

INEXPENSIVE: *Hotel Malmen, 49–51 Götgatan.* A modern hotel with a good restaurant, near the old part of the city. Inexpensive and extremely comfortable. *Strandvägshotellet, 7C Strandvägen.* In the same building as the *Hotel Grand Esplanade,* this inexpensive hotel has some rooms with private baths and is convenient to the shopping center. Inexpensive student hotels are opened from June through September. Most rooms have private baths with showers, restaurants, and serve wine or beer. Among the best of these are the *Hotell Jerum, 21 Studentbacken* and the *Hotell Domus, 1 Körsbärsvägen.* The *Frälsningsarméns Hotell* at *66 Drottninggatan* offers extremely inexpensive, clean accommodations, but has no restaurant and serves no liquor. It is run by the Salvation Army in the manner of the mission hotels. Other good, inexpensive hotels in Stockholm include the *Park, 10 Vasagatan* and the *Aston, 3 Mariatorget.*

RESORT HOTELS: Outside of Stockholm there are several very attractive hotels, suited to longer stays, families, or those who like the resort-hotel life added to their city sightseeing. One of the loveliest of these is the

Grand Hotel Saltsjöbaden, twenty minutes from the city center, with complete facilities for yachting, golf, tennis, and swimming, located near Sweden's only gambling casino. *Hotel Foresta,* next to the Carl Milles Park, also twenty minutes away in Lidingö, is a modern hotel-apartment house with kitchen facilities, and elegant restaurant, bar and a shopping center of its own, plus regular bus service into the city about twenty-five minutes away.

GOTHENBURG

MODERATE: *Park Avenue Hotel, 36–38 Kungsportsavenyn.* The newest and best known hotel in the city, this place offers top accommodations at moderate prices. Older but still comfortable hotels in the same class include the *Eggers, 1 Drottningtorget;* the *Grand Hotel,* and the *Palace Hotel,* both of the latter on *Södra Hamngatan.*

INEXPENSIVE: The *Hotel Ritz, 25 Burggrevegatan,* is inexpensive but comfortable and the *Kontoristföreningens Hotell, 23 Stora Nygatan* and the *Hotel Kung Karl, 23 Nils Ericsonsgatan,* are extremely inexpensive but quite livable. Two inexpensive and comfortable student hotels, open from June through September, are the *Hotell Viktor Rydberg, 48 Viktor Rydbergsgatan,* and the *Guldhedens Studiehem, 2 Dr. Bexgatan.*

Food and Restaurants

Smorgasbord is, of course, as Swedish as Sweden itself and the large tables groaning under a fantastic assortment of cold and hot delicacies will delight anyone with a real appetite. Smorgasbord can be taken as hors d'oeuvres or as a complete meal, generally luncheon, in which case it is correct to go to the table three times—once for fish and herring, again for cold meats and salads, and a third time for hot dishes and cheese. The native cuisine has only a few really exclusive specialties—the mildly cured salmon (*gravlax*), a kaleidoscopic palette of herrings, pale pink caviar (*löjröm*), lamb stewed with dill, a wonderful hash called *pytipanna, köttbullar* (meat balls), excellent game, pea soup with pork, and the famous Swedish dessert pancakes served with lingonberries.

In August and September delectable crayfish (*kräftor*) are the specialty, and all you need to enjoy them is a napkin around your neck, bread, butter, aquavit (*snaps*) or beer.

As in most large cities, it is possible to dine well in inexpensive restaurants, though top prices in de luxe Swedish restaurants are lower than in comparable restaurants in New York or Paris. In a *Mjölkbar* (coffee shop), a self-service restaurant, a meal may be had for about $2.

Liquor laws have been relaxed somewhat in Sweden, but alcoholic beverages may be served only with meals and at certain hours of the day.

Cocktail bars in the big hotels have international atmosphere, but the word "bar" by itself indicates an inexpensive self-service restaurant.

STOCKHOLM

You will have superb service and excellent food whether you dine in a place as inexpensive and Bohemian as Gamla Stan's *Cattelin,* where you can have lobster soup, a perfect roast filet of beef, and an airy lemon soufflé, with wine, for less than $10 for two; or a place as elegantly luxurious as the *Hamburger Börs,* with its *King Oscar's Room,* right out of a museum, complete with arched mirrors, gilt, and baroque angels, where a red velvet cushion is placed beneath the feet of a lady guest.

You can dine beneath the street of the Old Town, in the candlelit caves and cellars of *Den Gyldene Freden,* where you may have an elaborate meal or just cold shrimps, bread, and butter. For a splendid view go high up over the city, in the restaurant that tops the Stockholm Eiffel Tower, the *Katarina Hiss.* Drive twenty minutes out of the city to the modern *Foresta Hotel* and have a lobster soufflé as light as a cloud, or relax in the red-velvet grandeur of *Riche's,* or the adjoining *Teatergrillen* with its sophisticated café atmosphere. The most beautiful restaurant of all is the *Operakällaeren,* set behind the Opera House, across the water from the Royal Palace. The mellow little art nouveau bar, the grill room with its glass broiling wall, the main dining salon—a place of potted palms and etched crystal, plush and gilt—all are as perfect as the food, as flawless as the service.

Should you find yourself leaving Stockholm and still hungry, take heart—the restaurant at Bromma Airport ranks with the city's best and has an intriguing menu of international specialties.

There are several restaurants on the outskirts of Stockholm where you can enjoy superb food in a country inn atmosphere. The best of these are the *Stallmästaregaarden* (Stablemaster's Inn), set among lovely gardens and featuring a wonderful smorgasbord at luncheon, and, a little farther away, the *Djurgaardsbrunns Wärdshus,* a delightful inn set on an old canal and offering extremely fine food.

Back in town you can have quick light lunches at the restaurants in the *Nordiska Kompaniet* or *PUB* department stores, or in the *Solliden* restaurant in Skansen Park. There are a number of very good, very inexpensive places in Stockholm too, some serving no liquor, others serving beer or wine. Among these are the *Sturehof,* an excellent seafood restaurant; *Brända Tomten* and *Bäckahästen,* both part of a national chain noted for good food; both serve wine and are likely to be crowded at lunchtime.

The several restaurants of the *Margareta Huskaallsskola* are interesting and inexpensive too. This is a restaurant and household school and the restaurants provide practical experience for the students, and, although there are few trimmings, the food is good, simple, and an excellent buy.

GOTHENBURG

As you might expect, seafood and fish are good in this city, and are as fresh as they can possibly be. The elegant *Valand* is highly recommended, especially for its atmosphere, while *Henriksberg,* with its harbor view, is famous for its fish. *Langedrags Restaurant,* in a seaside suburb, offers a wonderful view of the approaches to the city, and in the lovely botanical park, Trädgaardsföreningen, the restaurant offers good food, music and dancing as well. Both of these last are at their best in summer, as are the cafés and restaurants in the Liseberg Amusement Park, where you dine outdoors. For a touch of old Sweden, try *Frimurarelogen* where the food is good and prices moderate. The dining rooms of the leading hotels are good too.

Entertainment, Night Life, and Special Events

STOCKHOLM

Summer outdoor concerts are usually held in one of the large parks, such as Kungsträdgaarden and Skansen. On the stage in Kungsträdgaarden you will find cabarets and plays, while at well-known Skansen there is a regular open-air theater. When near Skansen don't fail to visit the amusement park called "Gröna Lund's Tivoli."

From April to August the China Theater, a variety house, gives two nightly performances. The *Kungliga Teatern* (Royal Opera House), founded during the rococo period by King Gustav III, has an extensive repertory of opera and ballet performed by leading Swedish and international artists. The *Kungliga Dramatiska Teatern* (Royal Dramatic Theater) presents first class modern and classical dramas. The theater and opera seasons run from the end of August until the middle of the following June. In summer you will often be able to see eighteenth century plays performed at the unique and historic Drottningholm Court Theater while the *Konserthuset* (Concert Building) is the center of musical life during the winter.

Stockholm is not famous for night clubs, but most of the first class restaurants offer music and dancing. (Note: In summer the following restaurants are generally open until 3 A.M.—*Trianon, Strand, Bacchi Wapen, Ambassador,* and *Vallingehus*). Few restaurants feature floor shows, but you will find variety entertainment at *Berns* and *Hamburger Börs* (see *Restaurants*) in the center of Stockholm. Special celebrations are described on p. 38.

For one of the most interesting excursions anywhere, fly across the Arctic Circle to the land of twenty-four-hour daylight, visit a market place and a sixteenth century church in Jukkasjärvi, and other wonders of the Lapland landscape, have a midnight supper, and be back in Stockholm for breakfast the next morning. For information, ask your travel agent or SAS.

SWEDEN AT HOME: Anyone interested in meeting Swedes with interests or professions similar to his own may do so by applying to Tourist Information Center, Kungsträdgaarden Park, in Stockholm, or the Tourist Office in the Central Station in Gothenburg. Applications must be made in person when you arrive in the city.

GOTHENBURG

Gothenburg's night life is limited to those restaurants and hotels offering dancing and an occasional floor show.

The *Stora Teatern* (Great Theater) at the Kungsportsavenyn often presents operas or operettas and sometimes an international show. There are several fine cinemas in the city and you will easily find one or more international films in the original language with Swedish subtitles.

In summer, Liseberg Amusement Park is a treat for everyone, with a wide choice of entertainment and a good selection of restaurants and cafés, all in a sylvan setting which, by night, is beautifully illuminated.

Those fond of music will head for the handsome, modern Konserthuset at the Götaplats. Gothenburg's fine symphony orchestra is often visited by leading conductors and soloists from all over the world.

Shopping

STOCKHOLM

The influence of modern design is apparent almost everywhere. Along the main shopping streets of Kungsgatan, Drottninggatan, Hamngatan, Regeringsgatan, and Birger Jarlsgatan you will find famous Swedish glassware from the internationally known manufacturers: Orrefors, Kosta, and Strömbergshyttan, ceramics of the Rorstrand and Gustavsberg factories, stainless steel (Gense), silverware, pewter articles, hand-woven textiles, and beautiful Swedish handicrafts, approved by the *Svensk Hemslöjd* or *Hemslöjdsförbundet*. Be sure to visit *Konsthantverkarna,* the choice shop for handicrafts at 2 Master Samuelsgatan.

A good starting point for any shopping expedition would be a visit to *Svensk Form,* a new design center of modern Swedish home accessories, gathered here to give you an over-all sampling. Although nothing at

Svensk Form is for sale, you can get the name of shops that carry the things you like. Back in the heart of town, visit the very special, very luxurious *Svenskt Tenn*. Here you can find old and new things from Sweden and anywhere else in the world; the pewter is especially handsome and the hand-screened linens look like old botanical prints. *NK,* the huge department stores, *Nordiska Kompaniet,* and *PUB* have complete collections of almost anything you want to buy and will ship it for you.

Gourmet travelers will love the well-stocked shop of *Arvid Nordqvist,* full of a staggering array of game, sausages, fish, cheeses, and such exotic imports as corn on the cob, each ear individually wrapped in colored tissue paper. You can send home such native delicacies as preserved lingonberries or golden cloudberries or the rose-pink Swedish caviar, löjrom.

For high-fashion furs try *Ivan Petersson,* with a wide range of temptation in mink, or such confections as a fur ski "sweater" of silvery seal with knitted turtleneck and cuffs, or a coat of taffy-colored broadtail as crisply slim as silk moiré. And while in the realm of fashion, plan one day to visit Countess Marg von Schwerin's *Märthaskolan,* a fashion boutique where you can have lunch and watch a fashion show of French and Italian copies, or the originals that are the shop's specialty, all of which cost in Sweden at least a third less than they do at home.

Gamla Stan is a fine district for browsing around for antiques at reasonable prices.

GOTHENBURG

Östra Hamngatan and Kungsgatan form the main shopping center of Gothenburg. Look particularly for Swedish glassware, steel, and silverware, and for the elegant and decorative Swedish handicraft articles. Leading shops include *Ferdinand Lundquist* and *Meeth's,* the city's largest department stores. Here you can find everything from dresses to toys, tearooms, and tourist agencies. Among many excellent shops, try *Hallberg* or *Landoff* for silverware and jewelry, *Klockargaardens Hemslöjd* for linens and textiles, and *Hemslöjden L. Gillblad* for Swedish arts and crafts. *Forsaljnings Magasinet* features towels and tablecloths made of pure flax. For stainless steel and cutlery, visit *Eskilstuna-Boden,* and *Lido* in the Centrum Building.

For more complete shopping information, get a copy of the SAS booklet, "Shopping Your Way Through Scandinavia."

Background Reading

Skoal, Scandinavia, by Edward Streeter
The Icicle and the Sun, by William Sansom

Scandinavia, by Doré Ogrizek, World in Color Series
The Wonderful Adventures of Nils Holgersson, by Selma Lagerlöf
Sweden, Model for the World, by Hudson Strode
Digest of Sweden, available from the Swedish Travel Office, 630 Fifth
Ave., New York, N.Y.

For a complete list of books written in English about all phases of Swedish life and culture, write to the Swedish Institute, 42 Kungsgatan, Stockholm, Sweden.

Great Britain
and Ireland

England

LONDON

> "When a man is tired of London, he is tired of life; for there is in London all that life can afford."
>
> —DR. SAMUEL JOHNSON

When a stranger enters London, even though he has been accustomed to life in a large city, he recognizes at once that here is something superior to anything he has ever known. He feels the life surge of humanity uplifting him, as the transported mariner of the lakes perceives beneath his ship the undulating swell that has swept half way round the world. The rattle of wheels, the beat of horses' feet, and the great city's ceaseless roar are in detail not unlike what he has heard elsewhere; yet underneath it all, he feels there is a difference, and as he makes his way amid the throng along the Strand, watches the endless tide of human life ebbing and flowing across London Bridge, drifts down the crowded Thames from Hammersmith to Greenwich, or hears the ponderous peal of Big Ben, half smothered by the tumult of the streets, he realizes with a sentiment akin to awe, that he is standing in the world's metropolis.*

Although London today is far from being the "world's metropolis" it was in the Victorian age, it still *feels* as though it had that title firmly in its grasp. No city in the world quite prepares one for the overwhelming fact of London, just as no lake voyage quite prepares one

* Henry L. Stoddard, nineteenth century American traveler and lecturer.

for a trip across the ocean. "If Paris suggests intelligence, if Rome suggests the world, if New York suggests activity, the word for London is experience . . . [It] has the effect of making one feel personally historic," wrote V. S. Pritchett in his magnificent book, *London Perceived*. Technically a has-been since World War I, and now merely the sentimental focal point of the empire that dwindled to a vague commonwealth after World War II, London has had to relinquish most of its claims to supremacy. The pile of humanity, the monument to confusion that is Tokyo, outranks it as the world's largest city, over-reaching London's eight and a half million population by another million and a half, and New York is now the clearinghouse of the world. But New York is younger than London by almost two thousand years; it has never had to assume the responsibilities of a capital of empire, nor does it have a royal framework to give it continuity, form, and tradition. If London makes one feel historic, New York makes one feel current, if not downright transient. Besides, Manhattan, the nucleus of New York, is a slim strip of an island, its bigness a matter of height, so that the city seems more fragile, less bulky, and easier to see in its entirety. In London, the overpowering sense of size comes from its sprawling endlessness, the width and weight of its buildings, to say nothing of the aura of tradition that hangs over the city as thickly as the brown-gray fog that Dickens called "a London particular."

"The greatest glory that has ever come to me was to be swallowed up in London," wrote James M. Barrie after his first arrival from Edinburgh. Even visitors from such vast and active cities as New York and Toyko feel "swallowed up" by the maze of serpentine streets, the web of picturesque alleys, the caverns of soot-blackened Portland stone buildings, and the far-flung innumerable sections that are towns within towns within a city.

The actual "City" of London, the original site of the Roman settlement and now the financial center of Great Britain, is a mere one mile square. But around this is the 117-square-mile area of London County, set in Greater London, the Metropolitan Police District which covers 730 square miles in a 15-mile radius measured from Charing Cross. No wonder every account of the city begins with the apology, "No one can know London completely—not even in a lifetime."

In addition to the bewilderment caused by London's unexpected size and bustle, there is the added pressure of seeing all of the places one has heard about since childhood. For to Americans raised on English literature and English history no other foreign city feels as familiar as this one; no other city evokes quite the same rush of nostalgia. The names of London's streets, squares, parks, and sections are better known to us than those of many American cities. People who have never heard of State Street, Market Street, or Bourbon Street, surely have come across Haymarket, Bond Street, or Petticoat Lane in a story or movie. Piccadilly Circus means as much as Times Square, if not more and many an American who does not know in which city he can find the Commons, knows where to find the squares named Berkeley and Leicester, though the spelling of both might come as a surprise. Limehouse, Mayfair, Soho, Chelsea, and Westminster are probably more familiar than the five boroughs of New York (how many Midwesterners would remember Richmond?) and many a schoolboy who could not name Boston's river can tell you that London's is the Thames.

This feeling of familiarity with London is bred into our consciousness from our nursery-rhyme days:

> London Bridge is falling down . . .

> Pussy cat, pussy cat, where have you been? . . .

> Do you know the muffin man
> Who lives in Drury Lane? . . .

We even know the messages spoken by London's church bells:

> Oranges and lemons,
> Say the bells of St. Clement's . . .
> I'm sure I don't know,
> Says the great bell at Bow.

Of them all, these last are the most famously talkative—the bells of St. Mary-le-Bow. For it was their chiming that lured Dick Whittington back to become the Lord Mayor, as he was leaving the city with his cat tucked under his arm. And it is said that only those born within the sound of Bow bells are Cockneys, the true Londoners.

Literary legends and allusions—it is these that make London so exciting for Americans to visit, and one is often not quite sure which of the city's places, events, and heroes are fictional and which are fact. A perfect case in point is the following letter written by a New Yorker to John Galsworthy:

Dear Mr. Galsworthy,

Thinking you may be somewhat interested, I am writing about a happening in London, where I spent considerable time a few years ago. Late one bright afternoon I walked down the Haymarket. Just as I turned into Cockspur Street I came face to face with a man whom I instantly recognized as some one I knew, but whose name for the moment had escaped me. It was apparent he did not recall me, and passed on. Trying to recall where and when I had met this man, I suddenly realized that I did know him well. It was Soames Forsyte.

Faithfully yours,

London is full of faces and caricatures out of Dickens, Hogarth, Maugham, and Galsworthy—faces, and places too. "His route lay through Pall Mall, and at the corner, instead of going through the Green Park, the cabman turned to drive up St. James's Street." The route was that of Old Jolyon, the patriarch of the Forsyte clan, but it could just as well be part of a walking-tour guide to the city. One could easily play a game called "Fact or Fiction" when in London seeing its sights. Is 10 Downing Street any more a place of pilgrimage than 22½ B Baker Street? Which Horatio is the more popular naval hero—Hornblower or Nelson? Was the *H.M.S. Pinafore* a real ship? And how about the *H.M.S. Victory?* Scotland Yard is half fact and half fancy, but what of Saffron Hill? Separate the real people from the characters in fiction: Sam Weller, Beau Brummell, Bill Sykes, Guy Fawkes, Jack the Ripper, Nell Gwynn, Little Nell, Moll Flanders, James Bond. Were the exploits of King Arthur and his Knights of the Round Table less believable than those of Henry VIII? And did the royal events that Shakespeare drew from Holinshed's *Chronicles* occur exactly as they do on stage, or how much was fact fictionalized for the sake of dramatic impact?

From Tacitus to Ian Fleming, writers have been setting the London scene in unforgettable vignettes. The Romans who conquered the Thames-side settlement of the Britons called it Londinium, after the Celtic Llyn-dun, a hill fort on a pool. Caesar arrived in 55 B.C.; by the time a well-established market town had grown up under Claudius around 43 A.D., the Romans could write of this as "an international rather than a national settlement." The Thames was, as it always has been, the deciding factor in the city's fate, for the river made the city a valuable port a short way from the North Sea. The exploits of the Saxons, and the Angles who gave England its name, are best described through the legends of King Arthur, and almost every schoolchild knows of the bravery of Alfred the Great who fought off the invading Danes. Fewer know of Ethelred the Unready, whose laxity enabled the Danes to return and rule from 1016 to 1066, when William, the conquering Norman, won the battle of Hastings and became the last invader of English soil.

It was after this conquest that London grew to lasting importance, then that its infamous and fabled Tower was begun, and the earliest section of Westminster Hall was built by William Rufus, the second king of the Norman dynasty. Playwrights, classic and contemporary, have written of the ruling Plantagenets—Henry II and his archbishop, Thomas à Becket, Richard the Lion-Hearted, King John, who was forced to sign the Magna Carta to preserve all the ancient privileges of London, and the three Edwards who fought, and finally subdued, Scotland. And certainly the London life and mores of the time of the last Plantagenet, Richard II, had a careful and colorful chronicler in Chaucer, whose Canterbury Pilgrims left from the Old Tabard Inn, the site of which is marked in High Street, Southwark.

The affairs of the much-married Tudor King, Henry VIII, and the coterie at Hampton Court that included Cardinal Wolsey and Thomas More, have been the subjects of countless plays, paintings, and legends. King Henry, infuriated at the refusal of the pope to grant him a divorce from Catherine which would legitimatize his secret marriage to Anne Boleyn, broke with the Roman Catholic Church and had himself appointed sole head of the church and clergy of England.

It was Henry and Anne's daughter, Elizabeth, who brought Britain its first golden age. This was Merrie England, where wenches served boars' head, stuffed peacocks, and bowls of mead to guests of honor seated "above the salt." It was the England of Drake, who defeated Spain's Invincible Armada, and of Raleigh who brought Europe its first shipment of Virginia tobacco. Mary, Queen of Scots, was beheaded by order of her jealous cousin Elizabeth; the East India Company got under way to handle trade with newly won lands; and for the first time improvements were made in London's dirty, deeply rutted streets. The most glittering ornaments of this golden age were its writers: Shakespeare, who met with Ben Jonson, Beaumont, and Fletcher at the Mermaid Tavern in Cheapside; Bacon, Marlowe, Drayton, and the poet laureate of chivalry and fairyland, Edmund Spenser, who died of starvation and a broken heart.

Political life was turbulent under the Stuarts. Charles I was beheaded through the efforts of Cromwell who subsequently served as Lord Protector of England from 1653 to 1658. This was the London of John Milton and George Fox, who established the Quaker faith, but an austere, disciplinarian London found sudden and uproarious release in 1660 with the return of the Stuart king Charles II, who had a fondness for ladies and lap dogs.

It was during this time that London had its greatest chronicler, Samuel Pepys, whose diary is a uniquely complete account of London life from 1660 to 1669. It covers events both trivial ("Home, and, being washing-day, dined upon cold meat") and spectacular ("I went out to Charing Cross, to see Major-general Harrison hanged, drawn and quartered; which was done there, he looking as cheerful as any man could do in that condition").

The British have always had a talent for matter-of-factness and an ability to make the best of a bad situation. Pepys's most dramatic and valuable accounts are those of the Great Plague, which took 100,000 lives between 1664 and 1666, and the Great Fire that destroyed 13,000 homes in 1666, finally ending the plague's pollution. It was then that Sir Christopher Wren designed the churches that James Bone called "the mighty fleet of Wren, with their topgallants and mainsails of stone." The most famous of these is the enormous sky-domed cathedral of St. Paul's, while the most beguiling is the delicate spire he created for the restoration of St. Mary-le-Bow.

In the reign of the Oranges, William and Mary, designs of buildings, furniture, and clothing took on a heavy, squat Teutonic cast that was somewhat refined during the time of Queen Anne. Britain won Gibraltar, a vital link in the rapidly expanding east-west empire, and again there was a flowering of great writers: Pope, Swift, Prior, Addison, and Steele.

George Frederick Handel's *Water Music* was first played in 1717 by fifty musicians floating on a barge along the Thames from Whitehall to Chelsea, at the royal command of Anne's successor, George I. Daniel Defoe developed the English novel as a literary form with, among other works, *Moll Flanders* and *Robinson Crusoe,* and was sentenced to the stocks and Newgate Prison several times for his political views. His fiction is enriched with the most minute and factual details of the dress, manners, customs, and styles of his time, for Defoe had a bookkeeper's eyes for detail.

The London of the four Georges is fairly well known to Americans through associations with our own Revolutionary War period. The neatly proportioned motifs of neoclassic design were the trademarks of such architects as the Adam brothers and cabinetmakers like Sheraton, Hepplewhite, and Chippendale. London enjoyed another burst of literary glory with such eloquent eighteenth and nineteenth century writers as Samuel Johnson, the greatest Londoner of all time; Richardson, Fielding, Smollett, Sterne, Thomson, Young, Gray, Gay, Shelley, Keats, Byron, Scott, Wordsworth, Coleridge, and Southey.

In the reign of the crude and slightly mad George III, Napoleon was beaten by Nelson at Aboukir and Trafalgar and by Wellington at Waterloo. To Londoners of that time, such a victory more than made up for the trivial loss of thirteen troublesome colonies three thousand miles away.

Barring a few glassy modern office buildings and hotels that tower above the low and even London skyline like gleaming exclamation points, the city one sees today is essentially the London of Queen Victoria, who reigned from 1837 to 1901. Since Boadicea, the Briton who hurled her Iceni troops against the invading Romans, England has flourished under her queens.

The age of exploration begun by Elizabeth I reached its peak with Victoria. Her Diamond Jubilee in 1897 was essentially a festival of empire. Disraeli made her Empress of India and, with the financial backing of the Rothschilds, maneuvered an important interest in the Suez Canal for England. The Union Jack flew on every continent. When it was midnight in Sydney it was noon in Montreal. "The sun never sets on the British Empire," was no empty expression.

The City with its Bank of England was the financial center of the world, and the newly rebuilt Houses of Parliament had such eloquent orators as Melbourne, Peel, Disraeli, and Gladstone. The Industrial Revolution got under way, taking full advantage of the raw materials pouring in from the empire and making England a manufacturing island, dependent on her colonies for food. It created Dickens's bitterly poor slum waifs and Galsworthy's moneyed upper middle classes. This was the time of Beau Brummell's elegance and the drunken squalor of Gin Alley as drawn by Hogarth.

Gilbert and Sullivan casts sang, "Bow! Bow! ye tradesmen, bow ye masses!" shortly after Karl Marx had outlined some new plans for those masses in *Das Kapital* which he wrote in the British Museum.

And at a time when English travelers were going to the most obscure corners of the globe and London was the "world's metropolis," an etiquette book advised hostesses about dinner guests: "Distinguished foreigners, if they are clean, and can talk English well, may be very agreeable, but your guests will often suspect them, and their names must be known in England to make them desirable in any point of view."

Prince Albert sponsored the Great Exhibition of 1851 for which the Crystal Palace was built, and the whole Victorian design movement started, complete with gingerbread architecture, antimacassars, portraits painted on velvet, upholstered chairs with women to match, and seashell sculptures under glass bell jars. Dickens, Galsworthy, Matthew Arnold, Carlyle, Macaulay, and Kipling, to name only a few, provided accurate pictures of all phases of London life. Liberalism and exploration flourished on all fronts—scientific, economic, political, and intellectual. None of Victoria's subjects did more for England than Winston Churchill, a soldier in the Boer War who was to give Britain its most eloquently inspiring leadership during desperate days two generations later.

Nothing done in the time of Edward VII, or of the Georges, V and VI, did much to alter the architectural appearance of London. Hitler's V-2 raids and the postwar boom of modern building have changed things a little, but the over-all aspect is the same. The heavy somber color scheme of ocher, brick-brown, puce, and charcoal is set off here and there by a statue of white marble, a green patch of park, the lacing of a black wrought-iron gate, the glint of a polished brass doorknob or bell plate, and the intermittent flashes of brilliant scarlet of the Royal Mail trucks and letter boxes, the jackets of the palace guardsmen, and the famous London double-decker buses.

The market town founded by Caesar has become the wellspring of the world's richest language, the lingua franca of half the globe and the tongue of many of the best writers who ever lived. The city in which Shakespeare first made his mark still offers some of the best theater in the world (and occasionally some of the worst), and the variousness and eccentricities of its citizens are reflected in the tremendous range of specialty shops, specialty restaurants, and specialty neighborhoods. Santayana said, "England is the paradise of individuality, eccentricity, heresy, anomalies, hobbies and humors." London is the capital of that paradise and looks it in a most exhilarating way.

Like many great and fabled cities, London is a series of set pieces; almost everything you have heard about it is true, the good as well as the bad. It is kippers and crumpets, fish and chips, roast beef and Yorkshire pudding. It is white curtained tearooms where sandwiches are wispy with cress, and hundreds of private clubs devoted to a hundred different interests. Like a character described by Samuel Johnson in a literary review, London is "a hardened and shameless tea drinker . . . whose kettle has scarcely time to cool; who with tea amuses the evening, with tea solaces the midnight and with tea welcomes the morning." (One taste of most English coffee will explain the preference for tea.) London is the city of unarmed bobbies and the Teddy boys of Notting Hill; of Marble Arch, where soapbox orators air their grievances, and offbeat Soho cabarets where anti-Establishment satirists do the same on a more sophisticated level. While the smart Mayfair set is sipping champagne in international-style night clubs and de luxe French restaurants, vagrants are given a night's lodging in the antiseptically humiliating mission houses like those described by George Orwell from his down-and-out days. There is pomp and pageantry in the Changing of the Guard and the lord mayor's annual inauguration, the daily parade of the Horse Guards in their plumed silver helmets, and the June Trooping of the Colour to honor the Queen on her birthday.

Buffets at railroad stations like Waterloo and Victoria look like the setting for Noel Coward's *Brief Encounter,* while the drab slum areas of the city are right out of the latest new wave of angry young men movies. Street entertainers called buskers; the Cockney Pearlies in button-trimmed costumes; flower girls that seem inspired by Eliza Doolittle before she met Professor Higgins; blustering mustached Watsons; bulwarks of empire like Colonel Blimp; and the candid, patient, and strong faces that typify "this happy breed"—all surround you as you wander through the city.

There are the great pubs like the dockside Charlie Brown's, known to sailors the world over; the Prospect of Whitby, dating from the time of Pepys; the Elizabethan Anchor, the galleried stagecoach inn; the George; the Victorian Red Lion, with its glittering etched-glass paneling; and dozens of lesser known places where good talk and warm beer go hand in hand.

Harley Street with its fashionable doctors; Bond Street with everything from fascinating antique shops to smart women's specialty stores; Savile Row with its exclusive men's tailors; Liberty, famed for its printed silks and cottons; and Fortnum & Mason's with its array of twenty-four carat food delicacies show only one side of the city's face. Equally typical is the London of Petticoat Lane with its Sunday push-carts, the great markets like Leadenhall and Covent Garden that feed the city; the open antique stalls of Caledonian Market and Porto-bello Road where "beautiful junk" is the specialty; Limehouse with its Chinese residents; and Whitechapel with its Jewish tailors and kosher butchers. All of these fit together like a million mismatched pieces to make an intriguing jigsaw puzzle.

It is virtually impossible to plan an orderly tour of London; there are too many enticements to lead one away from a set itinerary. It is best to consider the various attractions by packaging them off into sections of the city.

The most logical place to begin is, perhaps, where London itself got its start—in the "City." This square mile corresponds roughly to the London of Claudius' time and is now the financial heart of the British Isles. Its streets are caverns walled in by banks and insurance firms, by Lloyds and the House of Rothschild. There is the Old Lady of Threadneedle Street, otherwise known as the Bank of England, and a block away is the Royal Exchange. This is the realm of the lord mayor who lives in the Grecian-style Mansion House. He is the supreme ruler of the City, and no troops may march through his territory without his permission. Here too is the medieval Guildhall, and the famous court, Old Bailey, close to the site of Newgate Prison. The Monument marks the spot where the Great Fire began in the royal bakery on Pudding Lane, and it is in the City that one can see Wren's masterpiece, St. Paul's. Wellington and Nelson are only two of the national heroes entombed in this overpowering baroque building with its huge nave and soaring dome.

St. Mary-le-Bow on Cheapside, and London's oldest church, the handsomely austere St. Bartholomew-the-Great built in the twelfth century, the Smithfield meat market, Fleet Street with its newspaper offices, its pubs that cater to journalists, and its Johnsonian landmarks like the house of the good doctor and one of his favorite haunts, the Cheshire Cheese, are all in this area—a weekday working neighbor-hood that is ghostly quiet on Sundays. The City stretches along the Thames from Billingsgate fish market where the fishmongers are noted for their black oilskin hats and their briny, bawdy slang, to Temple

Bar, where the lord mayor grants the queen permission to enter his realm.

East of the City stands the Norman silhouette of the Tower of London, looming ominously and romantically over the Thames, just opposite Tower Bridge. A place of dark deeds and ghostly legends, the Tower is guarded by its yeomen Beefeaters in the red uniforms and starched ruffs that date from the fifteenth century. Here the crown jewels are kept and the winding stairways and bleak stone corridors are grim reminders of the illustrious prisoners of the past. The Tower Green was the site of the scaffolding where Anne Boleyn; Queen Elizabeth's favorite, the Earl of Essex; Lady Jane Grey; and Catherine Howard were executed. Many more royal prisoners are buried in the chapel cemetery on the green. To Macaulay this was the saddest place on earth. "Death," he said, "is there associated, not, as in Westminster Abbey and St. Paul's with genius and virtue . . . but with whatever is darkest in human nature . . . with the savage triumph of implacable enemies, with the inconstancy, the ingratitude, the cowardice of friends, with all the miseries of fallen greatness and of blighted fame."

Around the Tower sprawl the foreign conglomerates of Whitechapel and Limehouse, the slum settings for *Oliver Twist* and the colorful London Docks that keep this city in touch with the world. Building cranes, gulls and freighters; sailors in the uniforms of every nation, and girls waiting to welcome them; dockside pubs and the tangy scent of oil and the salt sea, make this one of the city's most exciting locales. From Tower Bridge one can look out over Wapping and Rotherhithe, the point from which the *Mayflower* set sail for Plymouth and then on to America. Opposite the Isle of Dogs, so called because it was once the site of the royal kennels, is Greenwich, with its handsome neoclassic naval academy, its maritime museum, the *Cutty Sark,* last survivor of the famous tea clippers, now in dry dock near Greenwich Pier, and the Royal Observatory and hospital designed by Wren.

Sailing west on the river, under Tower Bridge and London Bridge, past the soaring Gothic beauty of Southwark Cathedral with its Harvard Chapel, by the round Temple Church which was built by the Knights Templar on their return from the Crusades in the Middle Ages, one comes to the Strand. This is one of London's brightest, busiest sections, with the theaters of Drury Lane, the exuberance and color of the Covent Garden produce market where porters carry stacks of bushel baskets on their heads, and where the famed opera house stands.

Also on the Strand are great hotels like the Savoy, and such traditionally British restaurants as Simpson's, and Rule's, which dates from 1798; Somerset House with its government registry offices and its famous wills like that of Shakespeare on display; and the Old Curiosity Shop, the inspiration for Dickens' famous novel. The oldest and most famous actors' club, the Garrick, is another landmark in this general neighborhood. West of the Strand is Mayfair, which derives its name from a medieval fair held here each May, and the carnival spirit still pervades the area. Piccadilly Circus, where traffic swirls around the statue of Eros and neon signs flash on and off advertising Bovril and Schweppes, is the core of Mayfair. The elegant shopping streets are in this area, and Park Lane, which was once known as Millionaires' Way, still retains something of its former grandeur. Here are Burlington House with its art exhibits and Burlington Arcade with its rows of wonderful shops; great hotels like the Ritz and the Dorchester. On Grosvenor Square the statue of Franklin Roosevelt stands close by the American Embassy. Shepherds' Market; Sotheby's auction galleries; the Albany, where Byron and Gladstone lived; Ashley House, home of the duke of Wellington; Pall Mall, where Charles II and his courtiers played a kind of croquet called *paille maille* are also part of this fashionable society section.

In sharp contrast is the Bohemian atmosphere of Soho. Here are the best foreign restaurants, the sleaziest strip shows, and the dustiest antique shops. Plaques mark the houses of such famous people as De Quincey, who lived on Greek Street, and Hazlitt and Mozart, who lived on Frith Street.

Nearby Berwick Street bristles with the activity of its open markets. Among Soho's most impressive sights are St. Patrick's Roman Catholic Church and the French Protestant Church in Soho Square, an aristocratic little plaza, rimmed with houses that date from the seventeenth century. Certainly night is Soho's most colorful time, when the smartly dressed society set of the West End mingles with the uninhibited and effusive local residents, as the former seek out the latest gambling joint, the best "unknown" restaurant and spend an evening "living dangerously" in London's most offbeat neighborhood.

Anyone who can manage to tear himself away from the miles of antique books that line the dusty shelves of the shops on Charing

Cross Road will come at last to Westminster, to foreigners perhaps the best known section of all. This is official London, royal London, and the scene of the city's most historic pageantry. This is where the royal family lives, the setting for Parliament and the magnificent Abbey. It is hard to say which of Westminster's attractions is the most famous. To some it might be Trafalgar Square with its pigeons and fountains, its demonstrations on Guy Fawkes Day, its memorial column to Lord Nelson guarded by four huge stone lions, and the National Gallery, one of the seven best art collections in the world. St. Martin-in-the-Fields is a jewel of a church standing in one corner of the square, called the "Parish Church of the Empire" since it broadcasts services to the entire commonwealth once each month.

Others might consider the neo-Gothic towers and spires of the Houses of Parliament to be Westminster's if not London's most famous landmark, especially if you take into account Big Ben, booming the hours from the tower that looks over Westminster Bridge; the striped buildings of Scotland Yard; and the County Hall across the Thames from which London itself is governed.

Still others will think first of Westminster Abbey, the soul of Great Britain and its Pantheon. The Abbey, founded by Edward the Confessor before the Norman Conquest, has been the scene of every royal coronation since 1066. Its soaring columns and arches, its magnificent iron choir screen, its Chapel of the Kings with the Coronation Chair containing the Stone of Scone taken from Scotland by Edward I, the lacy beauty of the Chapel of Henry VII, with its stone fan vaulting, carved wood pews, and heraldic flags—these are only a few of the Abbey's great attractions. Nothing in it is more impressive than its crypts—the tombs of kings, queens, statesmen, explorers, scientists, artists. The Poet's Corner has memorial busts and plaques dedicated to almost every great English writer we ever read in school and more. Here are monuments to Shakespeare and to his beloved friend "O rare Ben Jonson," to Milton, Addison, Goldsmith, Bulwer-Lytton, Macaulay, Browning and Tennyson, while not far away are the tombs of Mrs. Siddons and David Garrick—all honored together in this necropolis of genius.

Westminster Hall, opposite the Abbey, is one of the city's handsomest antiques. Originally a fine example of Norman architecture, built by William Rufus, during the reign of Richard II it received a Gothic overlay. Its great hall, rising above a huge stairway and backed by the jewel-like glitter of stained-glass windows, was the scene of marriage feasts and royal banquets, and such serious events as the trials of Thomas More and Guy Fawkes, Walter Raleigh and King Charles I. Cromwell was named lord protector here.

Eight years later, after he had been buried in Westminster, the royal Stuarts returned to the throne. Charles II had Cromwell's body exhumed, his head severed and impaled on a pinnacle of this hall where it remained for twenty-five years as a grisly reminder that anti-royalist sentiments were not to be tolerated.

Walking along Whitehall toward the palace that gives this street its name, one passes the Cenotaph honoring the dead of World War I, the Admiralty, and the Horse Guards, but not without a brief detour down a slim pocket of a street to one of the city's most famous addresses, No. 10 Downing Street, the home of the prime minister. Whitehall Palace was the royal residence of kings and queens from Henry VIII to William and Mary. All that remains of the old palace since the Great Fire swept through is the Banqueting Hall, designed by Inigo Jones, with its gorgeous ceiling paintings by Rubens. This once grand palace is more commonly known today as the United Services Museum.

Those who do not head for Parliament Square to see the Abbey and Big Ben as soon as they reach London probably go to the Mall, the wide and handsome avenue edged by St. James's and Green Park, which leads up to Buckingham Palace in a majestic sweep. At almost every hour of every day, one can see tourists and Londoners alike peering through the brass-trimmed iron gate to the columned gray stone residence of Queen Elizabeth II and her consort, Prince Philip, whether or not the royal standard flies to indicate that the queen is at home. Each morning at 11 A.M. the crowd grows until it stands six deep to watch the pageant of the Changing of the Guard, the parade of men in red jackets and bearskin busbies that has fascinated viewers for generations.

The Tate Gallery, with its modern paintings, and Victoria Station mark the edge of Westminster. Beyond lies Chelsea, the London version of Greenwich Village and Montparnasse combined. One of its best known sights is the Royal Chelsea Hospital, designed by Wren for Charles II who was urged by Nell Gwyn to build it. It was the first hospital built to care for military pensioners, a role it still fulfills, and the old soldiers in their red frock coats are among Chelsea's most colorful figures.

Whistler and Henry James lived not far away, in the section noted for its teatime buns and its eighteenth century porcelain, its artists, and its air of Bohemia. Behind Chelsea is Kensington with its beautiful homes and gardens; and not far away is the Victoria and Albert Museum, crammed full of souvenirs of that overstuffed and glorious era, but also housing impressive collections of medieval and Oriental art.

And still there is more to the city that Disraeli called "a modern Babylon." There is the elegance of Belgrave Square, where once luxurious homes have become foreign embassies and consulates; and there is Regent's Park with its aristocratic streets and houses and its famous waxworks, Madam Tussaud's. There is Bloomsbury with trim eighteenth century squares and the British Museum that contains Lord Elgin's marbles taken from the Parthenon. In Marylebone is the priceless array of paintings of the Wallace Collection. Add the Royal Festival Hall; Cleopatra's Needle; the fields of Hyde Park, where sheep are allowed to graze; the palaces of Kensington, Lambeth, St. James's, and Marlborough House; Roman walls and Roman baths and every kind of playing field imaginable. Now you will begin to see why London presents a dizzying dilemma, whether you plan to see it "all" in a week, a month, a year.

To add to this already formidable embarrassment of choice, one is constantly being lured to the rest of England. Even those who have only a week or so to spend will want to see the Thames Valley, stopping by the red brick palace of Hampton Court. Further along there is Windsor which has been a royal country castle for nine hundred years and the favorite home of the present queen. One can drive northeast to the university town of Cambridge or take the Thames route followed by the clerks in Jerome K. Jerome's zany idyll, *Three Men in a Boat*. This will bring you to Oxford and the lushly green, stone-walled Cotswolds via Hampton Court, Windsor, and Eton.

One can branch off from the river route to Bristol or Gloucester, or turn north to Tewksbury and its ancient abbey. Closer to London are dozens of historic baronial homes, now open to the public; and tours of the most breathtaking gardens can be arranged if that suits your fancy.

Just beyond the Cotswolds is the Shakespeare country in Warwick. Thatched roofs, half-timbered walls, diamond panes of leaded glass, romantic herb gardens and tapestried flower gardens make this one of England's most beautiful regions.

FOR THE TRAVELER'S NOTEBOOK

Official Information

Before you go: British Travel Association, 680 Fifth Ave., New York 19, N.Y.; 39 South La Salle St., Chicago 3, Ill.; 612 South Flower St., Los Angeles 17, Calif.

In London: SAS Office, SAS House, 52 Conduit St., W.1; Tourist Information Center, 64–65 St. James's St., Piccadilly, S.W.1. *Teletourist Service:* This is a telephone service which provides information about principal events of the day in London. Dial 100 from a pay station, and ask the operator for "9211"; or from a private phone, dial "ASK 9211."

Money Matters

Currency: The monetary unit is the pound sterling (£), divided into 20 shillings (s.), each in turn divided into 12 pence (d.). One pound sterling equals $2.80, U.S., and a shilling is 14¢.

Tipping: At hotels and restaurants tip a minimum of 10 to 15 per cent, never less than 6d.; porters, 1s. for first suitcase, 6d. each additional piece. Taxi drivers not less than 6d. on fares up to 2/6 (2s. 6d.), more for special service. Barbers and hairdressers, 20 per cent of bill; washroom attendants 2d. or 3d.

Climate, Clothing, and Essentials

Great Britain and Northern Ireland have an agreeable climate. Not only in summer but in spring and autumn as well, the weather is mild, though at times blessed with "a bit of rain." The average temperature in summer is about 60 degrees F., in winter 40 degrees F. Dial WEAther 2211 for latest weather forecasts. In spring and fall a raincoat comes in handy—a good buy in London; and a sweater and light topcoat are advisable even during summer. Normal city attire is correct and although formal dress for evening is not essential, it is worn in London more than elsewhere.

Hotels

In general, hotels provide courteous service and comfortable, if not beautiful, rooms. Hotel rates generally cover "bed and breakfast" and they are somewhat higher during the peak of the tourist season, from June to August. If you need help in finding a room, the London Hotel Information Service, 88 Brook St., will come to your rescue.

Super de luxe accommodations in London range from 140 to 200s. for a single room with bath; 190 to 240s., double. De luxe hotels charge from 100 to 160s., single; 160 to 185s., double. First class rates range from 60 to 110s., single; 115 to 145s., double. Moderate rates range from 55 to 85s., single; 80 to 105s., double. Inexpensive rooms can be had from 30 to 45s., single; 55 to 75s., double, which may or may not have private baths.

SUPER DE LUXE: *Claridge's, Brook St., W.1.* is in a class by itself, even among London's most luxurious hotels, and it is home to visiting royalty. It represents the height of formal elegance; its liveried doormen are a sight not to be missed. In fashionable Mayfair and as plush as possible. *Ritz, Piccadilly, W.1.* Elegant and old world, this hotel is done in Regency décor and overlooks Green Park. *Savoy, Strand, W.C.2.* Another of London's luxury hotels, set on the banks of the Thames, and very popular with American visitors. *Berkeley, Berkeley St., W.1.* Rooms here are attractive and comfortable; the hotel overlooks Piccadilly. *Dorchester, Park Lane, W.1.* Many rooms here have windows on Hyde Park and are charmingly decorated with beautiful old furniture.

DE LUXE: *Connaught, Carlos Place, W.1.* This hotel is one of my personal favorites, as British as high tea, kippers, and crumpets. The service is reserved and impeccable, the club-like atmosphere is classically, solidly English. *Grosvenor House, Park Lane, W.1.* Many rooms on Hyde Park; the hotel is extremely popular because of its handsome décor, its excellent service, and convenient location. *London Hilton, Park Lane.* Opened in April 1963; this hotel is modern, bustling, and has all of the usual hotel facilities. *Park Lane, Piccadilly, W.1.* Conveniently located close to the shopping and theater sections, some of the rooms here overlook Green Park. *Westbury, New Bond St., W.1.* This hotel was opened in 1955 by the American Knott chain and is crisply modern and compact, with complete facilities. *Mayfair, Berkeley St., W.1.* A pleasant old hotel that has been refurbished recently.

FIRST CLASS: *Brown's, 21–24 Dover St., W.1,* is a well-known, justly popular tradition among British hotels. Commercial, comfortable, and convenient. Prices are moderately first class. *Cumberland, Marble Arch, W.1.* Located opposite Marble Arch, this huge hotel is bustling and commercial, its service impersonal but adequate. *Hyde Park, 66 Knightsbridge, S.W.1.* Some of the rooms have balconies and a view of Hyde Park; all are comfortable and pleasant. *Mount Royal, Marble Arch, W.1.* Also overlooking Hyde Park, this hotel is comfortable, convenient, and pleasant.

MODERATE: *Rembrandt, Thurloe Place, S.W.7; Piccadilly, Piccadilly, W.1; Normandie, 163 Knightsbridge, S.W.7; Eccleston, Victoria, S.W.1; Rubens, Buckingham Palace Rd., S.W.1; Tavistock, Tavistock Square, W.C.1,* and the *Grosvenor* (not to be confused with Grosvenor House), *Buckingham Palace Rd., S.W.1,* are all very good moderate-priced hotels with restaurants and convenient locations.

INEXPENSIVE: Inexpensive hotels that are well located and comfortable are the *National, Bedford Way, W.C.1,* which caters to a cosmopolitan clientele; *Kensington Gardens, Kensington Gardens Square, W.2,* which serves breakfast only; and *Worsley House, 7–19 Clifton Gardens, W.9,* set in its own little park.

Food and Restaurants

In general, everything you've heard about English food is true and while it is perfectly possible to get wonderful meals in London, few of them feature English dishes. English breakfasts are excellent and hearty, with an enormous variety of dishes. Tea is another delight when you are served delicate little sandwiches, scones, biscuits, crumpets, and luscious tea cakes of all kinds. English seafood is unsurpassed: Dover sole, Scotch salmon, the oysters and shrimp, and the popular fish and chips. The roast beef with Yorkshire pudding, mutton chops, steak-and-kidney pie, and roasts are all excellent too. Bread is by and large bad, as are most of the vegetables.

The native cheeses such as Stilton, Cheddar, Cheshire, Gloucester, and Wensleydale are of superb quality. York ham, Dublin Bay prawns, Aylesbury duckling, Norfolk turkey, and Wiltshire pork are among the other fine products. Coffee is pretty awful except in the espresso cafés. The gin is good and dry and taken usually with tonic or vermouth. The beer is winey and heady and served warm, which is not as unpleasant as you think, once you get used to it.

The restaurants and grills of the hotels already mentioned are among the city's best and most elegant dining places, especially the *Dorchester, Savoy,* and *Connaught.* In addition, many chic private clubs serve superb continental food at expectedly high prices. These clubs welcome visitors; membership can be arranged for you by the British Travel Association or your hotel. They are almost the only decent places open on Sundays. The most popular clubs are: *Ambassadeurs,* which is in the ex-House of Rothschild; the *Empress Club,* which has music and a very plush setting but no dancing; and the *"21" Club.*

Among the typically English restaurants you will enjoy are the following: *Simpson's-in-the-Strand,* renowned for its roast beef and Yorkshire
pudding and certainly a "must" for your first visit at least. *Wheeler's,
Scott's, Wilton's, Bentley's, Overton's,* and *Cunningham's* are all famous
for seafood. *Rule's* serves excellent games and grills in its Edwardian dining room; the *Antelope Tavern,* in a picturesque cellar, is a chop house of
the old school. Luncheon at Dr. Johnson's favorite pub, *Ye Olde Cheshire
Cheese,* a Fleet Street haunt of newspapermen, is one of the city's pleasantest attractions. The steak-and-kidney pie is excellent and you can see
the good doctor's original dictionary. The *Guinea* is a noisy and colorful
pub-restaurant where you may eat and drink at the bar, or walk into the
dining room, ordering from the buffet and charcoal grill as you pass.
The *Ivy* is dignified, very British, and leisurely; food and service are tops.
Dinner one night at the *Elizabethan Room* of the *Gore Hotel* is not to
be missed. The food and décor hark back to the time of the first Elizabeth, and you can sit at the long trestle tables as the "wenches" bring
such delicacies as boar's head or stuffed peacock breasts. Fine continental
food is served elegantly at *Caprice, Le Coq d'Or, L'Écu de France,* and
Mirabelle, all chic, impeccable, and expensive; and *Prunier's* serves seafood with a French accent. *Boulestin, La Belle Meunière, Au Père de Nico,*
and *Au Popote d'Argent,* are more moderately priced and serve good food,
primarily French. The *Café Royal* is a famous Victorian and Edwardian
restaurant frequented by theatrical and literary personalities; a good place
for early pre-theater dinner, as are the *Aldwych Brasserie,* and *Berkeley
Buttery,* and the *Trocadero.* The *George and Dragon* serves wonderful
Austrian food and the Hungarian *Csarda* has good goulash and Tokay
at very modest prices. In Soho, *Leoni's Quo Vadis* features excellent Italian dishes; and the *White Tower* serves delicious Greek food at moderate
prices. *Albert's* is an excellent, moderately priced Belgian restaurant in
the same area. *Veeraswamy's* is renowned for its Indian food while
Jamshid and *Shafi India* are very good too. *Choy's* offers Chinese fare and
Ox on the Roof is an informal place for sake and sukiyaki. The *George
and Vulture,* with its pew seats that date from Dickens' time, is a handsome old chop house, and *La Belle Étoile* offers a variety of well-prepared
continental dishes at moderate prices.

Several of *Peter Evans' Eating Houses* serve steaks and simple grilled
meats. For Spanish food, try *Martinez* with its Andalusian specialties, or
Majorca, which is simple and modestly priced. For snacks or full meals,
try the Schrafft-like *Lyons Corner Houses,* all over the city, the quick
hamburger places called *Wimpy*s, the inexpensive meals at the *ABC
Cafeterias, Forte's,* and *Express Dairies,* or such places as the *Bacon
and Egg,* the *Grill and Cheese,* and *Chicken Fayre.* For afternoon tea,

try such pastry shops as *Floris Bakeries, Gunther's,* and the *Tea Center* or *Claridge's* for an elegant high tea.

Entertainment, Night Life, and Special Events

The weekly publication "What's on in London" will give you information about current attractions in theater, cinemas, night clubs, etc. With over fifty theaters, London offers great variety in entertainment. Tickets are reasonably priced and your hotel porter will be able to order them for you. Among the more famous theaters you might want to visit are the Old Vic, with its internationally famous Shakespearean company; Drury Lane, where musicals are performed in the city's oldest theater, dating from the late seventeenth century; the Mermaid, which puts on a number of experimental plays; and the Royal Court. The Palladium is a well-known music hall where international stars perform. If you missed them on their world tour, now is your chance to see the Royal Ballet (formerly Sadler's Wells), and the Sadler's Wells theater; both the Royal Ballet and a superb opera company use the Royal Opera House at Covent Garden. Ballets, concerts, and operas are given in the acoustically perfect Royal Festival Hall, and other concerts and recitals are held at the Royal Albert Hall.

There are scores of night clubs, supper clubs, dance halls, and bars, and the following is the merest sampling of what London has to offer in this department. Many of the hotels and restaurants already mentioned have music and dancing in the evening. In addition there are the private clubs already mentioned which have entertainment and late dancing as well. Other clubs in this category, more for entertainment than food, are *Churchill's* and the *Embassy.* At the *River Club* you dance on a terrace overlooking the Thames; the *Astor* is intimate and entertaining; *Pigalle* is lavish, with elaborate floor shows; *Quaglino's* offers good Italian food, and Hungarian gypsy music with a late floor show. The *Jack of Clubs* in Soho is gay, colorful, and informal; and in the same area the Naughty Mile offers strip shows and other lightly clad entertainment. By contrast, the *Colony* and the *Four Hundred* are dressy, expensive favorites of the fashionable Mayfair set.

PUBS: This uniquely British institution is something to be enjoyed by all visitors. Ideally, you should just drop in to any pub you see and become part of the activity, the talk, dart games, drinking, and general conviviality. Some of the pubs are especially interesting for their historic and literary associations and a few are listed here to start you off.

The *Cheshire Cheese,* already mentioned, is primarily historic and though officially classed as a pub, it is better left to lunchtime. The *Red Lion,* one of the city's most beautiful Victorian pubs, with its etched glass, polished wood, and red plush grandeur, is a must. The *Prospect of Whitby,* down by the wharves, harks back to the London of Samuel Pepys and is also a fascinating place. The *Cock and Lion* serves good food in an authentic atmosphere; the Stilton cheese here is especially good.

The *Falstaff* is a favorite of writers, and the *Mitre* is an authentically paneled Elizabethan tavern not to be missed. The *Grandier*, too, is interesting. Other popular and famous pubs include the Victorian *Salisbury*, the *Bull and Bush*, which was the favorite of Hogarth and Dickens, and the *George and Vulture*, which also has Dickensian associations. The *George*, the last of the galleried inns which were the first English theaters, stands near the site of Shakespeare's Globe Playhouse and Southwark Cathedral.

SPECIAL EVENTS: In mid-June the queen's official birthday is celebrated with Trooping the Colour, performed by the Household Brigade in full dress uniform. From April to November the *Shakespeare Festival* is held in Stratford-on-Avon, and November 5 is Guy Fawkes Day. London has a calendar full of shows and exhibits, commercial and artistic, and it is best to check local papers when you arrive to see which are being held during your stay.

Among the major sports events near London are the *Oxford and Cambridge Boat Race* held on the second Saturday before Easter; the *Derby* and the *Oaks* at Epsom early in June; *Royal Ascot Week* later in the month; and the *Wimbledon Tennis Championships* at the end of June and the beginning of July. The Association Football (soccer) season runs from the end of August to the beginning of May. Rugby football is played largely by amateur teams. Cricket test matches between England and the Australians or West Indians can still draw big crowds.

Shopping

One of the best guides to shopping in London (and anywhere else in England, Scotland, Wales, and Ireland) is the SAS booklet, "Shopping Your Way Through Great Britain and Ireland," which you will receive when you are planning your trip. The following is merely a sampling of some of the high spots from that booklet.

There are so many wonderful things to buy in London, it is difficult to include them all. There are two main shopping areas in the city. The West End comprises the section around Oxford Street, Regent Street, Bond Street, and Piccadilly Circus. The other area is Kensington and consists of Knightsbridge, Brompton Road, and Kensington High Street. Small and enticing antique shops can be found on the King's Road (Chelsea), Fulham Road, Kensington Church Street, in Camden Town, and in the small streets off Bond and Oxford streets, as well as in Soho. Charing Cross Road is the place to find secondhand bookshops, many with collections of fine old prints. The largest of these (and the largest in the world) is *Foyle's* with a stock of more than five million books.

London's centers of shopping interest are the *Burlington Arcade,* a long and fascinating covered street full of tempting shops, and the *Piccadilly Arcade* just opposite which offers more of the same. The *Crafts Center of Great Britain* exhibits contemporary gold and silver jewelry, ceramics, sculptures, and a few pieces of modern handmade furniture. The *Design Center* is a permanent but changing exhibition of consumer goods such as home furnishings and tableware, textiles, and cutlery, and though purchases cannot be made here, you will be told where to find anything that interests you.

Some of the great shopping delights in London are its outdoor markets —generally stalls and carts full of antiques, scraps of old jewelry and what Ludwig Bemelmans once described as "beautiful junk." On Fridays, the *Caledonian Market* is a favorite with Londoners; *Berwick Market* in Soho is held on Mondays and Thursdays. On Wednesdays and Fridays, take a trip to the Tottenham Court Road. If you're looking for silver, try the *Portobello Road Market* on a Saturday, and on a fine Sunday morning, the famed *Petticoat Lane Market* should not be missed for an amusing and interesting experience. Bone china, antique or new, from such famous manufacturers as Spode, Wedgwood, Doulton, Minton, Crown Derby, and Royal Worcester, can be found in many shops in the city. *Maple & Co.* has a great selection of antique pieces, as do *Asprey's, Gered,* and *Garrard.*

Arthur Churchill is known for his antique glass, *James Oaks* for clocks; and the underground arcade, the *Silver Vaults,* is a collection of eighteen shops featuring pieces from England's finest design periods. The *General Trading Co.* is a fascinating shop in an old coach house, full of antique porcelain, pewter, and other such things. *Christie's* and *Sotheby's* are famous auction houses where you can find the best in paintings, furniture, old jewelry, and tapestries. *Cameo Corner* near the British Museum is world famous for its collections of jewels and *objets d'art. Mappin & Webb* and *Garrard* are only two of the better known sources of silver, new as well as old, and the *Pewter Shop* in the Burlington Arcade has beautiful pieces cast from original two-hundred-year-old molds.

Men's clothing and sportswear are one of the city's best buys and among the more famous shops offering ready-to-wear (and sportswear for women as well in some cases) are *Burberrys, Aquascutum, Moss Bros., Austin Reed,* and *Simpson's. Harborow's Ltd.* and *Harvie & Hudson* are two of the best known shirtmakers. *Izod's* and *Sulka* have handsome ties and accessories, and along the famed Savile Row, such custom tailors as *Henry Poole, Anderson & Sheppard, Hawkes,* and *Huntsman & Sons* are just a few of the fine London establishments. *Hoby* is the oldest custom shoemaker in the city, while *Peal,* established in 1791, is the world's largest producer of handmade shoes. *Lilley & Skinner* and *Lobb's,* noted for shoes and riding boots, are also worth visiting. *Alfred Dunhill, James J. Fox,* and the *House of Bewlay* feature pipes and tobacco blends.

Women interested in high fashion should visit London's famous couturiers and their boutiques.

The city has very good department stores featuring a sampling of most of the things mentioned here. *Harrods, Selfridge's, Swan & Edgar,* and *Derry & Toms* are just a few of the best. *Liberty* is noted for its scarves and fabrics, and *Fortnum & Mason* for its unsurpassed and absolutely fantastic gourmet shop. *Lillywhites* is a six-story sporting goods store; *Ogden Smith's* is noted for guns.

Background Reading

Here's England, by Ruth McKenney and Richard Bransten
These Are the British, by Drew Middleton
London Perceived, by V. S. Pritchett
London, by Ivor Brown
Great Britain, edited by Doré Ogrizek
A History of the English Speaking People, by Sir Winston Churchill
In Pursuit of the English, by Doris Lessing
Shortened History of England, by G. M. Trevelyan (a Penguin Paperback)

To know London in all of its aspects, one must know the London of Samuel Pepys and Samuel Johnson, Dickens, Thackeray, and Macaulay, the Sherlock Holmes world of Arthur Conan Doyle, and the seamier side of life as reported by George Orwell in *Down and Out in Paris and London* and *Keep the Aspidistra Flying.*

One of the best on-the-spot guides I've ever come across is a pamphlet called "London," available at any of the offices of the British Travel Association. It contains everything you might want to know about the city, what to see, what to do, what to buy and where, and a city map. A complete hotel guide to Great Britain and a wealth of other material is available at these offices too; and their booklet, "Hotels and Restaurants in Britain," also provides excellent sectional road maps of England, Scotland, Wales, and Northern Ireland.

Scotland

EDINBURGH

The Athens of the north

TAKING into account its reputation as a seat of learning and its numerous colonnaded Greek Revival buildings, one can easily see how Edinburgh earned its epithet. But it would be hard to think of two cities more dissimilar in tone and aspect than the sunny, salt-white Aegean city with its easygoing open-air café life, and this stone-gray, grass-green Midlothian capital, with its brisk and bracing North Sea climate and its snug wood-paneled pubs. Scott's town of "dusky grandeur" is a seaport on the river estuary called the Firth of Forth, a handsome masculine city of five hundred thousand, packed with memories and mementos of all the Scottish heroes. Its intellectual life is almost as vibrant as it was in the great nineteenth century days of the *Edinburgh Review,* the magazine for which Sydney Smith only half-jokingly suggested the motto, "We cultivate literature on a little oatmeal." The phrase might well be applied to all of Scotland, considering that it has cultivated such literary talents as James Boswell, Robert Burns, Sir Walter Scott, Thomas Carlyle, Robert Louis Stevenson, Kenneth Grahame, and Sir James Barrie, often on a diet as limited as the one described by Smith, give or take a dish of haggis or two.

Edinburgh is neat and orderly, bisected into Old and New Towns by the wide, awning-bright thoroughfare, Princes Street, that runs a rule-straight course from west to east. The north side of the street edging the New Town is lined with shops selling books and bagpipes, tartans and tweeds, sweaters and paisleys, kilts and tam-o'-shanters, brightly painted tins of shortbread and crocks of marmalade, and over sixty versions of what we call "Scotch" and the Scots call "whisky" (without an "e"), a derivative of their own Gaelic word, *uisge-beatha*, the water of life.

The south side of Princes Street is trimmed with green garden parks that lead to the soaring Gothic spires of the Scott Monument, and the Grecian-temple-style buildings of the Royal Academy and the National Gallery. Behind these, a tree-covered hill climbs to the stony mass that is the Edinburgh Castle, looming over the city from its rocky crag. This is an age-of-chivalry storybook castle come to life, complete with ramparts and battlements, towers and turrets, moat and draw-bridges, flying pennons and tartan-clad men-at-arms, who pipe and parade a military tattoo each evening during the late summer Festival of Music and Drama.

Tumbling down from the castle heights are what Stevenson called the "high-piled tottering rookeries" of the Old Town, where top-heavy stone houses lean over the winding streets and gray courtyards. Primarily the work of builders, these rough-hewn houses are in sharp contrast to the polished Georgian and Regency elegance of the New Town, the part of Edinburgh that grew up after the mid-eighteenth century. This is a precise checkerboard of planned vistas, tree-lined crescents, and such pretty squares as St. Andrew's, the financial heart of Scotland, and Charlotte Square, with its high-domed, Greek-columned Church of St. George. Everywhere the New Town is graced with the restrained neoclassical motifs—carved plaster beading and cameos, airily draped figures, Doric capitals and pediments—that distinguish the work of the city's most famous architect, Robert Adam.

Much of Edinburgh's present-day life is played out in its pubs, just as it was in the days of Burns and Scott. The atmosphere is hospitable and inviting, and the lively, colorful talk—the burr-accented arguing, conjecturing, and challenging—reminds you that the Scots are a Celtic-Gaelic people with all of the linguistic eloquence that combination implies. You can get a good-natured argument on almost anything here (especially if you take your whisky with anything as heretical as soda or ginger ale), and this is the best place to sample the unique Scottish personality: canny, free-thinking, as bristly as their national thistle, and only slightly less skeptical than their eighteenth century philosopher, David Hume, who challenged even the concepts that water refreshes and fire warms. The Scots still take less at face value than most people do, and display the kind of contentiousness that led Benjamin Franklin to say, "Men of good sense, I have observed, seldom fall into disputation, except lawyers, university men and men of all sorts that have been bred at Edinburgh."

The Scots claim to be the tallest white men in the world, and after staring at them for a few days in their capital you'll be inclined to concede the point. Added to that, if you ever see the ease and agility with which they throw the fifty-pound lead hammer or toss the caber, the trimmed tree trunk weighing more than a hundred pounds, you'll rate them among the strongest as well. Combine this strength with their disputatious natures, and you'll understand how they came by their reputation as fighters. Scotland, remember, is the country of Highland clan feuds where the Macdonalds and the Campbells waged contests in the mountains of Argyll that made our Hatfields and McCoys look like squabbling children.

The Scots' ability as fighters was acknowledged back in ancient times, when the Romans gave up trying to conquer the land they called Caledonia, and walled it off from Britain; and later, when the English suffered defeat at the hands of the great Scottish liberators, William Wallace and Robert Bruce, at Stirling and Bannockburn in the thirteenth and fourteenth centuries. Volunteer Scottish battalions were among the fiercest fighters for the Protestant cause during Europe's Thiry Years War and in the sixteenth century formed the personal guard of the Swedish king, Eric XIV; even today the Highland regiments are the pride of the British army.

Established as a kingdom in 1034, much of Scotland's history can be gleaned from the sights within its capital. The starting point must be Edinburgh Castle, the heart of Edinburgh, the very foundation of Scotland, and the place where many of its most melodramatic moments were enacted. The oldest relic on the grounds is the eleventh century chapel built for Queen Margaret, the English princess who escaped from the Normans and fled to Scotland, bringing with her the English language and customs. She became the wife of Malcolm Canmore, and the daughter-in-law of Scotland's first king, Duncan, murdered by Macbeth in 1039.

In 1313, Scottish soldiers scaled the 270-foot crag on which the castle stands to take the English garrison by surprise and claim a victory for Robert Bruce. Still guarding the battlements is the monstrous iron cannon, Mons Meg, made in Belgium in the fifteenth century, which fired the salute announcing the engagement of Mary Stuart to the dauphin of France. In the Royal Apartments you can see the tiny bedroom in which Mary gave birth to the son who would unite Scotland and England under one crown in 1603—James VI of Scotland, James I of England—though the parliamentary union was not achieved until 104 years later. It is said the infant was lowered from the window of that bedroom in a basket so that he might be baptized a Roman Catholic when the combined Protestant agitations of John Knox and Queen Elizabeth made it necessary for such a ceremony to be held secretly.

Walking Edinburgh's Royal Mile, the antique route the Stuarts took from the castle to Holyrood Palace, one passes at least a dozen places that are reminders of Scotland's literary or political past. Among them are the house of David Hume, another in which James Boswell entertained Samuel Johnson, and the lodginghouse where Robert Burns found "a share of a deal table and a chaff of a bed" when he first came to the city in 1786. About midway on the Mile is Parliament Square with its magnificent governmental buildings such as the City Chambers, an outstanding example of the work of the Adam brothers, and the National Library with its collection of illuminated manuscripts: in one corner of the square, a little heart-shaped sign marks the site of the Old Tolbooth prison, the opening setting for Scott's *The Heart of Midlothian*.

The most impressive and important building in the square is the High Kirk of St. Giles, silvery with age, brilliant with stained glass, decked out in heraldic flags, and mellow with the scars of Scotland's many religious battles. Its oldest portion, the four octagonal pillars supporting the tower, date from 1120 and Norman times, and, in its southeast corner, the Chapel of the Most Ancient and Noble Order of the Thistle, the highest order of Scottish chivalry, stands as an exquisite example of the work of the twentieth century architect, Sir Robert Lorimer.

There are many more irresistible detours along this road before you finally come to Holyroodhouse, now the official home of the British royal family when they visit Edinburgh. It is an antique companion piece to the great castle and many stories begun at one royal residence ended at the other. But no event that took place here was more dramatic than the one marked by the little brass plaque in the audience chamber of the Catholic Queen Mary. It was here that her Italian secretary, David Rizzio, died after being stabbed fifty-six times as the result of a plot between the queen's second husband, Lord Darnley, and the nobles who were attempting to establish Protestantism in Scotland.

The beautiful lawn of this gray stone palace rolls down to Holyrood Park and on to the highest hill in Edinburgh, Arthur's Seat, its 822-feet height easier to climb than you might think because of the springy turf on the slopes. Other sights in the city include its oldest square, the Grassmarket in the shadow of the Edinburgh Castle; scores of inns, houses, birthplaces, and pubs associated with every Scottish writer you've ever heard of and a few you might have missed; the magnificent acropolis of Greek buildings and monuments on Calton Hill; and Kirk o' Field, the site of a four-room house in which Lord Darnley was killed in 1567, one of the most impenetrable mysteries in all Scottish history—there are still conjectures as to the role Queen Mary and Bothwell played in the event. Wander around the group of buildings that make up Edinburgh's university and note especially the Latin inscription over the main entrance which says that the building, which is as Athenian as anything in Athens, was the work of "Architecto Roberto Adam."

Just outside of Edinburgh one can see such natural wonders as its fantastic zoo with the world's largest captive colony of penguins, or something as dramatic as the Palace of Linlithgow, where jackdaws fly in and out of the sightless windows, unable to boast of the castle's ancient past. This was a fortified position in the days of the Romans and the manor house of Scottish royalty from David I in the twelfth century to Bonnie Prince Charlie in the eighteenth, and it was occupied by Edward I of England when he besieged the castle of Stirling. It was here in 1513 that Queen Margaret, sister of Henry VIII, received the news that her husband, James IV, had been beaten by the British at Flodden; and it was here that Mary Stuart was born.

Between Edinburgh and Linlithgow is one of the most magnificent homes in all of Britain, the eighteenth century Hopetoun House with its Adam splendors and great paintings, its fine porcelain, silver, and crystal collections. The countryside offers other delights: the picturesque thatched roof village of Swanston where Robert Louis Stevenson spent his boyhood summers; Rosslyn Chapel, an exquisitely ornate flower of the Gothic style and its fourteenth century companion castle with kitchens and dungeons carved out of the foundation rock; such historic and beautiful mansions as Lennoxlove, the residence of the duke of Hamilton, and Tantallon, a forbidding seacliff ruin that was one of the strongholds of the Douglas clan.

Edinburgh is the capital of what Sydney Smith once called "the knuckle end of England," a rocky, rugged mountain country of 30,411 square miles, reaching from the southern border country and the Cheviot Hills to the far northernmost point on the British Isles, John o' Groat's. Jutting into the misty, stormy waters of the Atlantic Ocean and the North Sea, the Scottish coast is riddled on three sides with bays and coves and rimmed by islands of starkly Gothic landscapes such as the Orkneys, the Shetlands, and the Hebrides, one of which is the Isle of Skye where the head of the MacLeod clan still lives in the ancient Dunvegan Castle. Rugged though the Scottish terrain may be, it is also studded with some of the most romantic sights and associations ever to fire the traveler's imagination. Divided roughly into Lowlands and Highlands, even the former has its share of hills, and the great mountains of the north country are cut by deep sea firths, which are to Scotland what the fjords are to Norway.

The whole countryside is a tweedy scheme of amethyst heather and green-gold thistle, slate-blue hills and emerald glens; a landscape bright with the brooks the Scots call burns, the lakes they know as lochs, little villages called burghs, grouse moors, deer forests.

The gentle green grazing hills and farm country of the Galloway Lowlands and the border country are rich in memories of Scotland's two most famous writers, Burns and Scott. The simple thatched roof cottage in which Burns was born can still be seen in Alloway, in the county of Ayrshire, and his tomb in the Dumfries churchyard is a literary shrine visited by pilgrims from all over the world. It was in the Murray Arms Inn at Gatehouse of Fleet that Burns wrote "Scots Wha Ha'e"; and the real-life Annie Laurie was born at Maxwelltown House in Dumfriesshire. In the town of Burns's birth you may cross the Auld Brig o'Doon (the bridge that spans the river Doon), or stroll along the Afton's green braes.

Sir Walter Scott, born to a wealthier and more prominent family than Burns, is remembered in the counties of Roxburghshire, Selkirkshire, and Berwickshire, border country rich in relics and ruins of the many battles fought between the English and the Scots. This is the romantic setting that inspired much of Scott's poetry. Perhaps the most famous places associated with the poet is the Gothic Melrose Abbey, now almost destroyed by time, where it is said that the heart of Robert Bruce lies buried, an abbey still viewed aright "by the pale moonlight," as are other such roseate ruins as Jedburgh, Kelso, and Dryburgh where Scott is buried. This lovely area of hills, meadows, and richly wooded valleys along the river Tweed is where Scott built his mansion, Abbotsford. There one can visit the room in which he wrote the Waverley novels and see the virtual museum of medieval armor and weapons he collected.

But though Scott and Burns loved their native Lowlands, both had their hearts in the Highlands, Scott's "Caledonia, stern and wild," and certainly it is the most picturesque and typical part of the country. This is the home of the warring clans, of tartans, kilts and bagpipes, heaths and hunting moors, salmon rivers and ancient castles. In the northern part of the land, bordering on the Great Glen, you can search for the Loch Ness monster, climb Ben Nevis, the highest peak in Britain, or visit Inverness, the capital of the Highlands. The classic road to this region starts at Stirling Castle, where the infant Mary Stuart was crowned queen and where William Wallace won his famous victory from the English in 1297. Set up on a crag as is Edinburgh Castle, the Stirling ramparts offer a view of Robert Bruce's battlefield of Bannockburn. All around the area are dotted little burghs with their irregular rows of white cottages tiled with red roofs and to the north rise the hazy blue peaks of Ben Lomond, Ben Ledi, Ben Venue, and Ben Vorlich.

Wend your way through the little fishing towns on the North Sea until you come to the "Silver City," Aberdeen, the center of the regal resort area known as Royal Deeside. This thriving seaport-university town is as famous for its fish as it is for its Angus beef; and its citizens are the canny Scotsmen who are the classic originals of all the penny-pinching Scotsmen jokes you ever heard. From Aberdeen it is only a short way to Balmoral, the Scottish home of Queen Elizabeth and her family, a handsome castle set in the valley of the river Dee. And among the other attractions of the area are the annual Highland Games at Ballater, Aboyne, and especially Braemar, where the grand finale is held before the royal family every September. This is a pageant that evokes every dream one has ever had of Scotland, with the various clansmen dressed in their traditional tartan kilts and shoulder-draped plaids, velvet jackets, and brush-trimmed tam-o'-shanters, as they compete for honors in everything from playing the bagpipes and dancing the fling to tossing the caber, pole vaulting, and throwing the hammer.

In this same vicinity you can wander through Scotland's most famous castle, Glamis, of which Shakespeare's Macbeth was the thane. It is the present home of the earl of Strathmore and was the birthplace of Princess Margaret—a castle with enough ghostly legends to satisfy even the most romantic traveler.

And though less picturesque than most of the country, Glasgow is a must for anyone interested in really understanding Scotland's past and present. This is the largest city in the country, the second largest in all the British Isles, and to its proud citizens the most important in the world. It is twice the size of the capital, and was founded by St. Mungo to whom the city's magnificent thirteenth century cathedral is dedicated.

The lawn-carpeted Kelvingrove Park offers a true view of a university older than the one in Edinburgh; and the Glasgow art gallery is one of the richest in the British Isles, with masterpieces by Rembrandt, Rubens, Whistler, Raphael, Titian, and Turner, among others.

This is the city that certainly made the most of Watt's steam engine, harnessing its power for iron works and steel mills as well as shipyards, a boisterous, muscular, smoky, industrial city and one of the friendliest in Europe. Though its main attractions are more practical than idyllic, it is from here that one can take a pleasant and very sentimental journey to the bonny, bonny banks of Loch Lomond or visit the dramatic mountains of Argyll and the town of Inveraray. Here the Campbell chieftain still lives in his ancestral home, not far from the Glen of Weeping, Glencoe, where, on a terrible February dawn in 1692, members of his clan turned upon their unsuspecting hosts, the Macdonalds, and put them to the sword.

FOR THE TRAVELER'S NOTEBOOK

Official Information

Before you go: British Travel Association: 680 Fifth Ave., New York 19, N.Y.: 39 South La Salle St., Chicago 3, Ill.; 612 South Flower St., Los Angeles 17, Calif.

In Edinburgh: The Scottish Tourist Board, 2 Rutland Place.

In Glasgow: SAS Office, 173 Bath St.; Tourist Information Bureau, St. Enoch Square.

Money Matters

Currency: For currency and tipping see London.

Climate, Clothing, and Essentials

The climate is moderate, all year round, average temperatures: spring, 53 degrees F.; summer, 65 degrees F.; autumn, 54 degrees F.; and winter, 43 degrees F. Spring and autumn are Scotland's loveliest seasons, but summer is also nice. Remember to take your raincoat no matter when you go. Dress as you would in any large city. Formal evening clothes are seldom necessary, but if you should need them, you can hire them easily and inexpensively.

Hotels

Glasgow and Edinburgh have hotels to suit everyone's taste and pocket. Although hundreds of rooms are available, you are strongly advised—especially in the months of July, August or September—to make reservations beforehand. If you prefer to stay in the countryside, Scotland has many fine luxurious hotels such as the *Gleneagles Hotel* midway between Stirling and Perth, or the *Turnberry Hotel* on the southwest coast. Both offer wonderful comfort and recreational facilities. They aren't exactly inexpensive, but you will get good value for your money. For a complete list of hotels throughout Scotland, with a description of prices and facilities, see "Hotels and Restaurants in Britain," obtainable from any of the British Travel Association offices mentioned at the beginning of this chapter.

Hotel rates in first class establishments range from 50 to 95s. for a single room with bath; 90 to 175s., double. Moderate: 30 to 50s., single; 50–100s., double. Inexpensive: 25 to 35s., single; 50 to 70s., double.

EDINBURGH

DE LUXE: The *Caledonian* and the *North British*, both on *Princes Street,* offer the city's most comfortable and attractive accommodations. Both have been recently modernized, have full hotel facilities, and good locations. The *Caledonian,* opposite Edinburgh Castle, has a view of the gardens and features dinner dancing in one of its three restaurants, the *Pompadour.* The *North British* has a handsome new grill with dancing nightly and the service is extremely efficient. The *George, George Street,* also in the upper price category, is close to the shopping and sightseeing areas, and the *Roxburghe, Charlotte Square,* looking out on a pretty garden square, is gracious and very old world. Its rates are a little lower than the first three.

MODERATE: In the less expensive category you'll find the *Learmonth, Learmonth Terrace;* and the *Royal Circus, Royal Circus,* and the *Royal Stuart, Abercromby Place,* are well located. All are members of the Tourist Association of Scotland and so maintain reliable uniform standards.

GLASGOW

Hotels here are adequate and comfortable, though their appearances are generally a little forbidding. Service is good, though without frills. You will probably be most comfortable at the *Central Hotel, Central Station;* the *North British Hotel* at *Queen Street Station;* at the *St. Enoch Hotel, Enoch Square.* All are conveniently located and have good restaurants, and are in the first class price category, while the *Belhaven* at *Belhaven Terrace* and the *Grosvenor* at *Grosvenor Terrace* are good bets in the moderate price class.

Food and Restaurants

Contrary to popular belief, the Scots do not live on oatmeal and haggis, though certainly you should try both while there. The latter is a sort of pudding of oatmeal, meat, and spices steamed in the lining of a sheep's stomach, and served with mashed turnips; you will be surprised at how good this can be. As for the rest of the fare, you should try the herrings, fresh or kippered (they're wonderful grilled, and served with a mustard sauce); the incomparable smoked salmon; the finnan haddie and, in fact, all of the fish, which comes to you fresh from the sea, the rivers, and the lochs. Other fine products are the Angus beef, the assorted pancakes, scones, oatcakes, and shortbreads; and the blood-and-oatmeal puddings. Scotch broth is rich, hearty, and delicious; the game, especially grouse and partridge, is superb. The vegetable cookery leaves a lot to be desired, but the honey, marmalades, and pastries more than make up for that. "High tea" is a favorite Scottish meal, taken between 5 and 7 P.M. It features a substantial dish of meat or fish, usually followed by an inviting array of freshly baked scones, biscuits, cakes, and preserves. As you might guess, Scotch (called whisky here) is the leading alcoholic drink, though beer is also popular and good.

EDINBURGH

In addition to the restaurants of the leading hotels, you find excellent food at a number of other city restaurants. The *Cramond Inn,* a little way out of the city, is one of the most charming of these. Built in 1670, it is in a pleasant, cottagey half-timbered building with fumed oak furnishings and excellent food, most notably the shellfish specialties. Within the city itself, you will enjoy the handsome, spacious *Café Royal*, where the game is excellent; the *Handsel*, where smorgasbord and Swedish food are featured; *L'Apéritif* with very good grills, roasts, and continental dishes; and the *Doric Tavern*, a small place with a fine international menu. The *Beehive Inn*, the *Albyn Rooms*, and the *Epicure* also have loyal followings, and in the more modest price levels, you will like *MacVitties*, and the *White Cockade*. Cadbury's *Chocolate House*, with a number of hot and cold chocolate drinks, desserts, and snacks of the tearoom variety is a good place for a light lunch or tea.

GLASGOW

Two restaurants on the outskirts of Glasgow bear mentioning here as both have large menus and excellent food, carefully served in pleasant surroundings. The first of these is the *Buchanan Arms* in Drymen where the curries and Virginia ham are delectable. The second is the *Boulevard Hotel* in Clydebank; reservations are necessary for both places. The *101* is one of the most popular restaurants within the city itself. It is large, conveniently located, and has a good international kitchen. *Malmaison*, which adjoins the *Central Hotel; Rogano's*, where seafood (especially bouillabaisse) is very well done; *Guy's*, with its continental atmosphere and *Ferrari's* are other places that are justly popular. Scottish food with décor to match is featured at the *Royal Restaurant*.

Entertainment, Night Life, and Special Events

Glasgow and Edinburgh have several large theaters with all types of entertainment from classical drama to variety shows; and during the summer there are afternoon and evening concerts in the parks.

There are no night clubs in Scotland, but a number of the hotels and restaurants mentioned above offer dinner and dancing. Evening dress is usually not necessary.

SPECIAL EVENTS: From April until October there are performances of concerts nearly every day. Late August sees the opening of the *Edinburgh International Festival of Music, Drama and Art*. For three weeks, world-famous orchestras, opera, theater, and ballet companies and internationally known artists perform nightly. A unique feature of the festival is the Military Tattoo held each night on the Castle Esplanade; and one of the many pleasures of Edinburgh is to sit in the Princes Street Gardens listening to a military band with the old castle as a backdrop. For information and programs of the festival, write to the Festival Office, Synod Hall, Castle Terrace, Edinburgh, or the Festival Society, 11 Cambridge

Street, Edinburgh. It is wise to buy tickets and make room reservations by the preceding April.

Highland Games are held in many different places during the months of July, August, and September. If possible, include one of these spectacular shows in your program. You will not regret it. In recent years the annual *Pitlochry Festival of Drama, Art and Music* has become very popular with Scotland's visitors. The small town is situated forty-two miles northwest of Perth. The historically interesting St. Andrews, which is an excursion from Edinburgh, is the Mecca of golfers; and this particular sport is more popular in Scotland than in almost any other part of the world.

Shopping

Among the best buys in Scotland are the wonderful woolens, especially the tweeds and tartans, the sweaters, silver, sporting goods, antiques, and such local novelties as bagpipes, Portobello pottery, and Scotch whisky.

EDINBURGH

The main shopping districts are along Princes and George streets. Highland handicrafts are featured at *Highland Home Industries, Ltd.*, a nonprofit cooperative, and you will find interesting handicrafts and jewelry at the *Scottish Crafts Center* too. There are exquisite cashmere, Shetland, and intarsia sweaters at *R. W. Forsyth, Jenners,* the two leading department stores, and *Romanes & Paterson,* all on Princes Street; fine antiques and silver can be found at *George Cockburn,* old jewelry at *Hamilton & Inches,* and Portobello pottery at *John Henry's. J. & R. Glen* and *R. G. Lawrie* are the places for bagpipes. Lawrie's will fit you out in complete Highland dress if you wish. *Lillywhites, John Dickson & Son,* and *Thornton's* specialize in sporting goods, and for tweeds and tartans try *William Anderson, Binn's, Darling & Co.,* and the *Tartan Gift Shop.* Some of these have ready-made clothes as well as yard goods. *Roderick Tweedie* is known for a wonderful selection of sweaters.

GLASGOW

If you have Scottish ancestry and would like it traced, the Scots Ancestry Research Society can do it for you. The best and most interesting shops in the city are along Buchanan Street and in the nearby Argyle Arcade. There's a branch of *R. W. Forsyth* here, and among the other department stores you should visit are *Copland & Lye, Daly's, MacDonald's, Pettigrew & Stephens,* and *Rowan's,* noted especially for its fine clothing. The *Iona Shop, R. G. Lawrie, Robin Hood Gift House, Wiley &*

Lochhead are noted for typical Scottish souvenirs, and *Alex Martin Ltd.* has a wide range of sporting goods. For a complete shopping guide to Scotland, get a copy of the SAS booklet, "Shopping Your Way Through Great Britain and Ireland."

Background Reading

The Scot in History, by Wallace Notestein

Edinburgh, by Eric Linklater

The Edinburgh Caper, by St. Clair McKelway. (A story of the most outlandish intrigue, with modern Edinburgh as its setting.)

Great North Road: A Journey in History, by Frank Morley. (The saga of the road north from London to Edinburgh and its importance to British life and history.)

In Search of Scotland, by H. V. Morton

Republic of Ireland

DUBLIN

*The fair city of Molly Malone
and Molly Bloom*

DUBLIN is as hard to pin down as the Irish—a briny, alive, alive-o sea-port with a long and epic history, a Blarney-blessed charm, and a touch of magic in the air. It's a soft pencil sketch of a city where fantasy and fact are as inextricably intertwined as the town and its Liffey River, the *dubh-linn,* or dark pool, that was James Joyce's Anna Livia Plurabelle.

To the traveler who is tired of touristic set-pieces, the Irish capital will seem a stimulating "natural." It is handsome and unself-conscious; anyone is welcome anywhere as long as he is not a bore, and the friendly, considerate service is more a matter of genuine concern and innate hospitality than a result of hotel- and restaurant-school training. Dubliners have a talent for enjoying life. Certainly their city, with its convivial pubs and superb theaters; its magnificent horses and historic sights; its pot-still whisky and Guinness stout; its beef, bread, bacon, and plump Galway oysters, trout and salmon; and its shops full of ice crystal and snowy lace, wool tweeds and old books, high fashions and antiques, offers the visitor more than enough to keep him happy. If no red carpet is unrolled for him, neither are prices stretched to fit his more affluent standard of living; one takes this highly individualistic city as he finds it or not at all.

Known to Ptolemy as a port settlement in the second century A.D. and founded, officially, by the Danes in the ninth, Dublin is essentially a product of the eighteenth century, a city of neoclassic domes and columns and Georgian squares that glow with the rose-amber tapestry of brickwork; graceful bridges arch over the river inlets, and there are dozens of statues, each with a gossipy history. It has spawned and spurned an inordinately large number of inordinately eloquent poets and patriots, all of whom were distinguished by the unique Gaelic flair for syntax and what Sean O'Faolain described as "a Celtic-Danish-Norwegian-Norman-Tudor-Cromwellian-English-Jewish-Irish genius."

With its open watery setting and its far off view toward the blue-shadowed Wicklow Hills, this city of 500,000 has about it a sense of distance and detachment, as though it were an island adrift in the gray expanse of the Irish Sea. Blue mists and clouds of Irish rain roll in and veil it in a soft, dreamy haze, turning the parks a bright shamrock green and the colleens' complexions a dewy petal pink. And the evanescent light that licks across the sky like quicksilver changes the Dublin mood from hour to hour, keeping temperaments a little off balance and nerves a little on edge, in a pleasantly exhilarating way.

It is perhaps the city's mercurial spirit that gives the most ordinary events a way-out quality. It is the sort of a place where, as John Pentland Mahaffy put it, "the inevitable never happens, the unexpected always." Certainly he should have known, for he was one of the most colorful characters ever to decorate this city of eccentrics. No one understood the effects of the Dublin atmosphere better than John M. Woolsey, the judge who ruled that *Ulysses* could be admitted into the United States, when he justified Joyce's work by explaining, "In respect of the recurrent emergence of the theme of sex in the minds of his characters, it must always be remembered that his locale was Celtic and his season Spring." Probably it was more a matter of place than season, for Dublin, at any time of the year, has inspired some of the wildest literary rambles ever to be chronicled. This is true whether you consider Oliver St. John Gogarty's walk down Sackville Street, or the bizarre existence of J. D. Donleavy's *Ginger Man;* the twenty-four-hour odyssey of Stephen Dedalus and the garrulous Leopold, who made June 16 a commemorative Bloomsday to Joycean aficionados everywhere, or Brendan Behan's whisky-and-porter-scented tour, with the narrator bursting into song all along the way and ducking in and out of pubs as he took his readers around his "island."

Any of these memoirs is good company on a walking tour of the city. Each brings a special perspective to Dublin's long vistas, and all take you, sooner or later, past its most famous and hallowed sights. Its most familiar setting is its broad harbor, with gulls and trawlers, and kegs of porter being loaded onto freighters by black-capped stevedores, and the green-domed, white-columned landmark of the Customs House that was built in 1791 after plans by James Gandon. The city's other treasures of Greek Revival architecture are the wedding cake that is the Four Courts, and the sickle-shaped, statue-topped, windowless Bank of Ireland, which was the parliament building when Dublin was a fashionable and patrician town of the landed gentry. Students of Ireland's revolution will probably go first to the General Post Office, the headquarters of the ill-fated Easter Uprising of 1916, that was led by the soldier-scholar-poet, Padraig Pearse. Outside this granite building stands the statue of the dying hero Cuchulainn, the Hound of Ulster, who fought off the forces of Queen Maeve near Dublin, just about the time Christ was born—a symbolic monument to the many who have died for Irish freedom during the nineteen centuries between that time and the present.

From the Post Office one can walk the length of the city's main thoroughfare, formerly Sackville Street, and now named O'Connell, after the leader who fought relentlessly and successfully for Catholic religious freedom in Ireland. "The only way to deal with such a man as O'Connell," said the Rev. Sydney Smith, "is to hang him up and erect a statue to him under the gallows." This traffic-filled street, with its crowds, cars, and double-decker buses, its shops and office buildings, is lined with pedestaled statues of Ireland's heroes. From the top of the fluted pillar honoring Lord Nelson, one can watch the busy life of the broad avenue, only one of many created by the eighteenth century Commissioners for Wide and Convenient Streets. From this height one can see the whole length of the thoroughfare: south to the busy, triple-arched bridge, the O'Connell, wider than it is long; north to the mound of the Rotunda, the meeting place for I.R.A. leaders, and on to Parnell Square, named for the brooding and eloquent debater who fought for Irish Home Rule, and ended as an outcast among his own countrymen because of an affair he had with the wife of an army captain.

Parnell's fate was anything but unique in Erin's history, for the Irish have turned against their own time after time, and it is not for nothing that exile and homecoming are two of the most recurrent themes in Irish literature, along with dirges of poverty and death and songs of freedom. Read down the partial list: Yeats, Joyce, St. John Gogarty, O'Casey, O'Faolain, O'Connor, Swift, Congreve, Goldsmith, Sheridan, Wilde, Shaw, Behan, and George Moore whose *Hail and*

Farewell might well be the motto of the lot. All have loved and hated Ireland; all have gone away and returned, physically or spiritually; all have written about it; all have done everything but ignore it.

The streets that web back from Parnell Square and the thriving O'Connell Street made up the infamous north Dublin slums, for a long time the most bitter and tragic slums in all Europe. Here the great Georgian houses were warrens for the poor for almost a century. Around Mountjoy Square the cracked fanlights and glassless windows stared blindly at barefoot and starving children, black-shawled, hollow-eyed women, and tattered, defeated men. This area was home to Brendan Behan whose play *The Hostage* was set in a house on Nelson Street, and it was the birthplace of Sean O'Casey who described the house as "smirched with age-long marks of ague, fevers, cancer and consumption," with windows "lacquered by a year's tired dust from the troubled street below." Most of these slums have been torn down and their inhabitants relocated in new housing developments in the south Dublin sections of Crumlin and Kimmage.

One can still get an idea of just how elegant these houses were in their heyday by crossing south of the Liffey to the old city and its neatly landscaped greens. Walk over the O'Connell Bridge or the high-arched little iron footbridge, the Ha'penny, so called because of an old toll charge, and then on to College Green. The most noteworthy sight on the green is the sixteenth century Trinity College, founded by Elizabeth I and rebuilt in the eighteenth century in the Georgian style. Inside the railings of the college are statues of two of its illustrious graduates, Edmund Burke and Oliver Goldsmith, and close by is the Trinity library with its magnificent collection of old books and manuscripts. The prize treasure in the library is the eighth century *Book of Kells,* the world's most beautiful illuminated manuscript, and each day a page is turned to allow even exposure to the light. Across the green stands Leinster House, the seat of the *Dail Eireann,* the Irish Parliament, and behind this are the National Museum, with its folk exhibits and antiquities that range from the Stone Age to medieval times, the National Library, the largest in all Ireland, and the Art Gallery, with its rooms full of European and Irish paintings of the past.

The eastern edge of this quadrangle faces one of Dublin's handsomest greens, Merrion Square. Rose-red brick houses trimmed with white columns and pediment-capped doorways, leaded glass fanlights and wrought-iron balconies and lanterns are almost exactly as they were when Daniel O'Connell and Oscar Wilde lived here. Merrion Square is bounded by some of Dublin's smartest shops, and in one of its most classically beautiful houses Sybil Connolly designs her artful, feminine tweeds which have become a fashion trademark the world over.

Merrion Street leads one easily to St. Stephen's Green, one of the most impeccably landscaped garden parks in Europe. One of its more notorious residents was Francis Higgins, a shoeshine boy who worked his way to the top, becoming a lawyer, the owner of the *Freeman's Journal,* and a millionaire. He was called "The Sham Squire" because of the way he dressed, and it is said that he was "daily to be seen in St. Stephen's Green wearing a three-cornered hat fringed with swan's down, a canary coloured vest, a bright green coat and gold tassels on his Hessian boots."

Grafton Street, Dublin's answer to Fifth Avenue and the Rue de la Paix, takes one from St. Stephen's Green back to College Green. Turn westward along Dame Street, where the Olympia Theater stands opposite the grim gray eminence of Dublin Castle, built between 1208 and 1220, on the site of what, four centuries earlier, had been a Danish fortress. This was the official residence of the English viceroys, whose elaborate state apartments are now open to view, and hundreds of Irish resistance fighters were imprisoned within the castle's stony dungeons.

Near the castle is the heavy, square stone City Hall designed by Thomas Cooley, and Christ Church, which was built by the Danish king Sitric of the Silken Beard in 1038, with a nave that is a masterpiece of the Gothic style. About three blocks away is the city's most important church, St. Patrick's Cathedral, named after the English saint who brought Christianity to Druid Ireland in the fifth century, and incidentally cleared the land of snakes, as legend has it. Established in 1190, the cathedral has been partially destroyed, rebuilt, and added to through the centuries; the south aisle of the nave is a tribute to its best known dean, Jonathan Swift, who preached from its pulpit and is buried on its grounds. Over the door of the robing room one can read his own bitter epitaph, "He lies where savage indignation can no longer rend his heart." Behind the cathedral are clustered open markets with a flea-market assortment of household objects and exotic furnishings dating from Dublin's golden prime, junk antiques and used clothing, old clocks and coat racks, and here and there a Waterford decanter.

Walking the south quays of the river, still westward, you will come to an odd sort of landmark for a city—odd, that is, for any city but Dublin—the Guinness brewery. Barrels of malty dark stout are shipped from the brewery's own quay to ports on every continent, and one may tour inside to watch the brewing, and sample the end product. The high quality of Irish stout, porter, and whisky is said to be due to the purity of the Liffey water, and all of the distilleries and breweries are along its banks.

Perhaps the stout will give you the stamina you need to continue back north of the river and on to Phoenix Park with its 1,760 acres, one of the largest urban parks in Europe. Enter the grounds through the Chapelizod Gate, named after Iseult of Ireland who tarried nearby with her Tristan. Along the green slopes of the park are numerous playing fields; a zoo; a race course; a hospital; the United States Embassy, and the *Aras an Uachtaráin,* the official home of Sean Lemass, Ireland's *taoiseach,* or prime minister. Once a staunch and oft-imprisoned guerrilla fighter of the I.R.A., Lemass was Eamon de Valera's protégé and successor, and is now the leader of the *Fianna Fail* (Heroes of Destiny) Party. He has, almost singlehandedly, drawn aside the green curtain of the *Sinn Fein,* the "Ourselves Alone" movement that isolated Ireland for decades. In the past five years he has succeeded in luring French, German, Japanese, Dutch and South African industrialists to open plants in Cork, Shannon, Killarney, Limerick, and Dublin, convincing them of the profits to be realized from Ireland's enormous untapped labor force and granting them a number of financial inducements as well. For the first time since the ruinous potato famines of 1846 and 1847 Ireland's statistics are rising instead of dropping.

Once one of Europe's most densely inhabited countries, Ireland's 1845 population of nine million has melted away to a mere three million or slightly less. In addition to the millions who died as the result of starvation and warfare, other millions more scattered across the seas. At the same time the Irish marriage and birth rates are among the lowest in the world; almost 70 per cent of all Irish males between twenty and thirty-nine are bachelors, and with thousands of women emigrating each year, the men are in an overwhelming majority. The situation is anything but encouraging to the girls who do remain, a fact made lyrically clear by Siobhan McKenna's exquisite recording of Brian Merriman's poem, "The Midnight Court." But now the average marriage age is dropping, and the tide of emigration has been turned back steadily; the average number of emigrants has been cut from 43,000 a year to 14,000 in 1963. There are jobs at home now, and with the severe censorship on films, books, and public entertainments slackening a bit, it's not quite so dull to stay there.

All the walking and talking that is bound to go on during one of these literary strolls through the city is certain to make you thirsty. Since your guide, whether he is Joyce, O'Casey, Donleavy, Gogarty, Behan, or O'Faolain, is certain to stop by a pub for refreshment, you might as well do the same. For it is here that you will see the true Irish spirit and sample the softly poetic brogue at its best. Talking is an art here partly because of the drink that sets the mind free, partly because of the Gaelic heritage of language. If their city is difficult to capture on paper, their personality is impossible; it is a trap few writers care to fall into and one even the Irish themselves respect. A perfect case in point is Ike Dignam, a character in Sean O'Faolain's story, *Persecution Mania,* who tries to act Irish not knowing quite what that might be, with the following result:

He has a notion that the Irish have a gift for fantasy, so he is constantly talking fey. He also has a notion that the Irish have a magnificent gift for malice, mixed up with another idea of the Irish as great realists, so that he loves to abuse everybody for not having more common sense. But as he also believes that the Irish are the most kind and charitable people in the world, he ends up every tirade with Ah, sure, God help us, maybe the poor fellow has a good heart.*

The rest of Ireland differs from Dublin more than most countries do from their capitals, for the 32,585 square miles of it are, for the most part, untouched by modern innovations, other than good roads and a handful of cities. Almost no spot within the twenty-six counties is more than seventy miles from the sea, and the warm vapors caused by the Gulf Stream meet with the colder air of the Irish Sea to keep the land mild and blanketed with dewy mists, preserving the emerald greenness that has become the Irish national color.

Ireland's counties, lakes, and rivers have been celebrated in poems

* From *The Finest Stories of Sean O'Faolain,* Copyright 1949, by Sean O'Faolain, reprinted by permission of Atlantic-Little, Brown and Company, publishers.

and songs for centuries: Connemara, Killarney, Galway, Shannon. Its sights include Druid megaliths, stone-circled, carved Celtic crosses, ruined abbeys like Muckross, fairy forts, rock castles, ancient dolmens and barrows, coppery peat bogs, purple heather fields, and always the low roof of sky and the gray-blue lakes. The carts of the gypsy tinkers pass you on the road; from the starkly peaceful Aran Islands fishermen sail in their ancient currachs; and in the west counties, the Gaelic storytellers, the *shanachies,* still weave their tales of magic and mystery. It is not hard to imagine this as the land of white-robed Druids who worked spells with wisps of straw, or of the High Kings of Tara and the nobles whose jewel-colored robes and mantles gelamed with roughly cut gems of quartz and jasper, emeralds and Kerry diamonds.

Close to Dublin are the velvety golf greens and racing courses of Wicklow, and the ancient wonders of Howth Castle, where the Boswell manuscripts were discovered. There is the twelfth century castle of Swords; the Boyne and Blackwater valleys that take one back to the great days of Tara; Slane, where St. Patrick lit the fire "that would burn and consume Tara" and its pagan rites. There is Kells where the famed Book of Kells was written; and St. Kevin where the fires of learning were banked throughout the Dark Ages.

Travel to Cork to kiss the lipstick-stained Blarney Stone; to Wexford with its Danish and Norman ruins, to Waterford, famed for its crystal; or to the monastic ruins of Clonmacnois. Drive round the Ring of Kerry, the scenic route through the Killarney country, or to western Galway and on to the Aran Islands, the setting for Synge's *Riders to the Sea.* Visit what the Irish of Eire consider another part of their world—Belfast and northern Ireland, with the six Ulster counties which chose the Protestant English way of life and have never since been recognized by the Dublin government. Or visit Donegal, the *Ultima Thule* that represented the unconquered, unknown world to the ancient Romans, with its seaside resorts, it thirteenth century Sligo Abbey, and its memories of Yeats.

FOR THE TRAVELER'S NOTEBOOK

Official Information

Before you go: Irish Tourist Office: 33 East 50th St., New York 17, N.Y.; 135 South La Salle St., Chicago 3, Ill.

In Dublin: Aer Lingus, 40 Upper O'Connell St.; Irish Information Office, 14 O'Connell St.; U.S. Embassy, 15 Merrion Square.

Money Matters

Currency: Pounds (£)—and all currency here—are Irish, not English, but the dollar equivalent for each denomination is the same (i.e., a shilling equals 14¢, etc.), and English currency is acceptable anywhere.

Tipping: Tipping follows European standards, with a 10 to 15 per cent service charge added to hotel bills; 15 per cent in restaurants; cab drivers 15 per cent; doormen and bellboys get 1s.; hatcheck and washroom attendants 6d.

Climate, Clothing, and Essentials

Dublin has a mild, moderate climate with winter temperatures ranging from 40 degrees F. to 50 degrees F., and rarely over 70 degrees F. in summer. There is a good deal of rain and fog, and light raincoats and warm jackets are advisable the year round. Formal dress is needed only for top social events and conservative city attire will do for most occasions.

Hotels

For a complete list of accommodations throughout Ireland, see "Ireland, Hotels and Guest Houses," available at the Irish tourist offices mentioned above. Hotels in Dublin are fairly good. Private baths are not too plentiful, but rooms are comfortable and the service is adequate. Reservations are essential especially during the summer, Easter, Christmas, and at the time of the Horse Show in August.

You can expect to pay from 50 to 75s. for a single room with private bath in the top-price hotels; 110 to 150s. for doubles. Moderate hotels charge 30 to 50s. for single rooms without baths; 60 to 100s., double. In less expensive hotels, single rooms without baths range from 20 to 30s., single; 40 to 60s., double.

DE LUXE: The *Dublin Intercontinental,* opened in 1963, is the city's newest, most modern, and largest hotel, located close to the Botanical Gardens and the United States Embassy. De luxe and with all facilities. The *Shelbourne, St. Stephen's Green,* is one of the city's top hotels and a favorite with those who like a traditional old world atmosphere, while the *Greshan, Upper O'Connell St.,* has a somewhat more modern aspect, an up-and-doing air about it, and a very handsome grill room. The *Russell, St. Stephen's Green,* in the top price category, has a superb restaurant and an altogether continental charm. The *Royal Hibernian, 48 Dawson Street,* has a more private atmosphere and is housed in an impressive Georgian building.

MODERATE: *Jury's, College Green;* the *Central, Exchequer St.;* the *Four Courts, 9 Inns Quay;* the *Clarence, 6–8 Wellington Quay;* the *Wicklow, Wicklow St.,* and *Moira's, Trinity St.,* are good bets in the inexpensive category.

Food and Restaurants

Dublin's restaurants are relatively inexpensive and the products you can sample here are among the world's best. Irish bacon, ham, fish, seafood (especially Galway oysters and Dublin Bay prawns), and game are excellent, as are the soda breads. Try all varieties of the breads including those made with treacle and currants. The beef and lamb are of high quality and the grills are always well prepared. *Champ,* a mashed-potato dish, is made with many additions such as peas, chives, parsley, or cabbage and onions, when it is called *Colcannon champ.* Irish whisky and Guinness stout are the most typical and the best local alcoholic beverages, and this, of course, is the place to have Irish coffee with dessert.

In addition to the fine grill at the *Dolphin Hotel* and the restaurants of the *Russell, Shelbourne,* and *Gresham* hotels, Dublin's most famous dining places include *Bailey's,* a popular meeting place for writers and artists, where the seafood specialties are excellent; *Jammet's,* with its tiled bar and French food; and the *Red Bank Restaurant,* where the Dublin Bay prawns are nothing short of sensational, and the oyster bar serves forth some of the best of the Galway product. For light lunches, visit the *Buttery* of the *Royal Hibernian Hotel.* Bars, or more exactly pubs, are a favorite Irish, as well as English, institution. The leading hotels and restaurants have their own, of course, but in addition you should see the favorite meeting places of newspapermen, such as the *Pearl* or *Palace* bars on Fleet Street, or *Mooney's, O'Meara's* and *David Byrne's.*

Entertainment, Night Life, and Special Events

Dublin's night life is on the quiet side, and the only establishment that might loosely be termed a cabaret is the *Metropole Restaurant's Georgian Room* where there is dancing and a floor show. There is also dancing at several of the hotels. On the other hand, there is a wealth of theater here, most notably the performances of the Abbey Players in the Queens Theater. The Edwards-MacLiammoir Company and the Longford Players perform at the Gate Theater, and the Globe and Pike both feature experimental drama. Opera and ballet companies perform at the Gaiety, and modern dramas by visiting companies are staged at the Olympia.

SPECIAL EVENTS: In September the *Dublin Theater Festival* is celebrated with performances by Irish and foreign actors in a program of dramas, classic and modern. The *August Horse Show* is a leading sporting and social event highlighted by the international jumping competition for the Aga Khan Cup. Industrial, agricultural, and trade exhibits take place in the May *Dublin Spring Show*. *An Tóstal*, a Gaelic term for "pageant," is a nationwide festival run from May to September. It fosters all of the Irish arts and cultures in a program of dance, handicrafts, music, theater, history, archaeology, and sports.

MEET THE IRISH: If you are interested in meeting Irish people with occupation and interests similar to your own, you can arrange this at the Irish Tourist Information Office when you arrive in Dublin.

Shopping

Some of the best buys in Ireland are the rugged woolens, especially the tweeds and richly colored blankets, the crisply embroidered linens and the lustrous Waterford crystal. Carrickmacross or Limerick lace, antiques, old silver, riding boots and sporting goods, whisky, and Belleek china are among the other things to consider. The main shopping areas of Dublin are Grafton Street, O'Connell Street, Wicklow Street, and Henry Street. *Arnott & Co., Brown Thomas,* and *Switzer* are the leading department stores; *Whyte & Sons* is the largest shop specializing in crystal and porcelain; and for antiques visit *Hopkins & Hopkins, W. Weldon, West & Sons,* and *Louis Wine.* Knitwear and Aran Island sweaters are to be found at the *Donegal Shop,* and *Irish Cottage Industries,* while lace and linen are featured at *Walpole's.* Men's shoes and boots are custom-made at *T. Barry's* or *Michael Edge's,* and the most famous shop for tweeds is *Kevin & Howlin.* Irish couturiers are world famous. There are a number of fine shops for ready-made or custom clothing for men. For a good representative collection of Irish products and handicrafts, visit the *Permanent Exhibition of Irish Manufacturers,* on St. Stephen's Green.

For a complete shopping guide, get a copy of the SAS booklet, "Shopping Your Way Through Great Britain and Ireland."

Background Reading

Dubliners, by James Joyce
Brendan Behan's Island, by Brendan Behan
James Reynolds' Ireland, by James Reynolds
Tell Dublin I Miss Her, by Dominic Behan
Story of Dublin, by D. A. Chart
Joyce's Dublin, by Patricia Hutchins
The Book of Dublin, by Eric Whelpton

For a look at some of Dublin's wildly Bohemian aspects, read J. P. Donleavy's *The Ginger Man* and for more local color, the works of Sean O'Casey.

The

Continent

Austria

VIENNA

"The conversation between mankind, art and nature—a Europe in miniature"

GOETHE's description of Vienna is as valid today as it ever was. Despite the glassy inroads of modern architecture and the quick-paced busyness of a brand-new prosperity, this is still the most romantically European city in the world. Other continental capitals reflect the personalities of their own countries. A visitor to London, Paris, Madrid, or Rome sees things essentially English, French, Spanish, or Italian. But Vienna recalls that great golden bubble of a world that was Europe at its baroque best. And if the city is not quite the gay and carefree *Alt Wien* it was in its Hapsburg heyday (two wars, a Nazi *Anschluss,* bitter poverty, and a paralyzing four-power occupation were bound to leave scars), even a short stay here should be enough to prove that the Viennese pulse still beats in three-quarter time and the last waltz has not yet been played.

The Austrian capital of 1.7 million is virtually a monument to the good life and includes everything we think of as European—the *gemütlich* as well as the grand. It is the city of beer and *wurstel,* coffee and cake, candlelight and wine; of grand balls in the gold and white wedding cake of an opera house and community sings in summer beer gardens; a place of *Ach, du lieber Augustin* and *Eine Kleine Nachtmusik.* Within and around the city one can see imperial palaces set in royal parks and narrow streets that wind into cobblestoned mar-

103

ket squares. The double eagle emblem of the Austro-Hungarian empire shows up everywhere as does the red and white color scheme of the Austrian flag. Florist shop windows are brilliant the year round with arrangements of red roses and white lilacs, red carnations and white lilies of the valley, white acacia and primroses, red tulips, and anemones. You can shop for impeccable custom-made boots and haberdashery, browse through the silken splendor of *haute couture* boutiques, or choose, instead, a wardrobe of Tyrolean *lederhosen* and hats, Loden cloaks, or peasant dirndls cozily trimmed with yards of rickrack braid.

Eating is one of the favorite pastimes of the *Urwiener,* the citizen of Vienna, and he indulges in it at places posh or plebeian: street corner *wurstel* stands, simple brewery *Bräuhaus* restaurants, and in an enormous Rathauskeller where five hundred people dine at once and a schnitzel the size of a platter costs no more than a dollar. Or he might go instead to one of the city's traditionally elegant dining rooms, like Sacher's, where the same Herr Ober has served the same cut of *Beinfleisch* (boiled beef) to the same customers at lunchtime for twenty years.

After the opera, there are plush and gilt supper clubs that remind you of every wine, women, and song operetta you ever saw; and at any time of day you can read newspapers in a coffeehouse as you try one of a dozen versions of the world's best *mokka* coffee. That same coffee, black or adrift with *Schlagobers,* the whipped cream that is a Viennese trademark, can be had along with meltingly rich chocolate and cream pastries in hundreds of *Konditoreien,* of which the best known is Demel's, a landmark with a faded *fin de siècle* charm that has made it a tourists' favorite. And though you're in the heart of a modern metropolis, you can enjoy the folksy country charm of small taverns where waitresses in black bombazine serve you in quaint rooms with low-beamed ceilings and half-timbered walls.

Die gute Wiener Küche—the good Viennese cooking—is only one of the city's claims to fame. It is as well known for its scientists as it is for its strudel. The Viennese doctor, bearded and mystically intuitive in the fictional image, was for a long time considered the ultimate medical authority. As for the Viennese psychoanalyst, suffice it to say that this was the home of Sigmund Freud and earlier of Mesmer, who, in about 1775, staged the first demonstrations of the hypnotic technique later called mesmerism. A bronze statue of the analyst's black leather couch would not be out of place in the Stadtpark.

Vienna is distinguished, too, for its art collections and the taste with which they are displayed; its bootmakers; its social progress, as evidenced by some of the world's earliest low-cost housing for workers; and its horsemanship, as exhibited in the Spanish Riding School. Here, in an eighteenth century arena that looks more like a grand ballroom, with white and gold columns and balustrades and crystal chandeliers, riders in chocolate and cream liveries and black bicorn hats, put the white Lippizzaner horses through a precision ballet of caprioles, *levades,* and *courbettes.* Only in Vienna can one see this style of *haute école* riding that dates from 1580, one of the most graceful remnants of the city's baroque past.

Vienna is known as "the musicians' holy city" and was home at one time or another to Mozart, Gluck, Haydn, Beethoven; Schubert; von Suppé; Brahms, Mahler; Schönberg; Oskar Straus; Johann Strauss (both father and son); and Richard Strauss. The city reveals the range of its tastes through the music it listens to, from operas as esoteric as *Palestrina* to operettas as popularly sentimental as *The Merry Widow.* The fact that the bombed-out opera house was restored to its gold-leaf splendor before the Viennese had coal or coffee is convincing proof of their devotion to music. They listen to their boys' choir in the Burgkapelle, the chapel of the Hofburg palace, to Styrian brass bands in the parks, to symphony orchestras in the courtyard of the Town Hall, and to musical comedies in the Volksoper. If they cannot spend an evening at the royal theater of the Hapsburg summer palace, Schönbrunn, listening to chamber music, they might go to a wine cellar where the hockish white wine is accompanied by zither music or *Schrammel* singers who perform with two fiddles, a guitar, and an accordion. There are gypsy violinists in Hungarian and Serbian restaurants, string quartets in dining salons, and always, somewhere, a blonde contralto warbling of *Wien, Stadt meiner Träume*—"Vienna, city of my dreams."

As long as it is music the Viennese are happy; and, from the sound of things, the waltz makes them happiest of all. Its lilting rhythm is everywhere. It drifts out of car radios and record shops, tearooms and restaurants, dance orchestras in smart cabarets, and gazebo bandstands in the public gardens; and it tinkles from souvenir music boxes in all the tourist shops. Jazz, cool and hot, may be filtering into Vienna's musical life, but the city is still very much the home of the waltz king and the Blue Danube, the river whose waters look unexpectedly brown, unless you happen to be in love, in which case, it is said, they live up to the song's title.

Such legends suit the temperament of the Viennese, who even now have a weakness for operatic romances; for tales of star-crossed lovers like their own crown prince, Rudolph, and his mistress, Maria Vetsera, who in 1889, carried out their suicide pact in the hunting lodge at Mayerling; and for such dashing heroes as *Der Rosenkavalier,* whose exploits Richard Strauss set in the eighteenth century Vienna of Maria Theresa. There is more than a hint of romance about the courtly, courteous Viennese men who pride themselves on their *fesch,* the trim, dashing, gallant style that harks back to their imperial past. Women are fashionably dressed, completely feminine, and just a little *dramatisch.* Black velvet is the favorite for winter soirees, bibs or ropes of pearls are more often seen than chokers, and nothing smacks of *Mittel-Europa* quite so much as their hats: deep beehives and stovepipes of furry felts that clamp down over their ears and show only the tiniest wisps and curls of fine blonde hair.

Devout Roman Catholics whose standard greeting is *"Grüss Gott,"* the Austrians are a racial blend of Celts, Illyrians, Romans, Magyars, Avars, Slavs, Huns, and other tribes that have coveted this East-West junction throughout its history. And though the expected archetypes are fair, one sees almost as many brunettes as blondes; and nowhere else does one notice so many people with eyes as pale-green as Chinese jade. In love with all Austria, but proudest of their own city, the Viennese speak their special German dialect, *Wienerische,* that distinguishes them from their countrymen.

If the traditional gaiety of Vienna seems tinged with sadness, it is not hard to understand why. For this city was the capital of an empire that vanished, one that was at the peak of its power in the fifteenth and sixteenth centuries under the Spanish-Austrian Hapsburg Holy Roman emperors, Charles V and Philip II. Before the Thirty Years' War divided that realm, it was the largest empire the modern world had ever known, reaching across most of continental Europe and the Atlantic Ocean to outposts in the New World. And though the nineteenth century empire of Metternich and Franz Josef I was only a fraction of that size, it was then at its most glittering and memorable.

The era of the dual Austro-Hungarian monarchy, with its waltzes by Strauss and Lehár, its imperial balls and dashing hussars, was in fact a swan song that ended in Sarajevo on June 28, 1914, when Archduke Franz Ferinand was assassinated. At the end of World War I, the empire that had covered much of Central Europe, Yugoslavia and the Trentino in Italy, and had included fifty-one million subjects, dwindled to a republic of seven million, a truncated, landlocked island, deprived of its Adriatic seaports, its monarchy, and all of its former glories.

No wonder, then, that nostalgia is so much a part of this city. There are intimations of it in the magnificently furnished, deserted palaces, in the hushed stillness of royal gardens, in antique-shop windows, with their exquisitely wrought silver, their chunks of gleaming baroque curlicues, their delicate figurines and old gold jewelry sparkling with rose diamonds. But the relics of past grandeur are most striking of all in the Arsenal Museum, with case after case full of splendidly colorful regimental uniforms.

Much of Vienna's personality dates from the seventeenth and eighteenth centuries; more specifically, from 1683, when Prince Eugene of Savoy and the Polish armies of John Sobieski defeated the Turks who were at the city gates for the second and last time. As all things do in Vienna, the siege resulted in coffee and cake. When the sultan's soldiers fled, they left behind sacks of coffee beans. Viennese scouts, having observed the habits of their adversaries, took the beans, roasted and ground them, and brewed Europe's first cup of coffee. And the bakers who had helped defend their city baked a victory cake inspired by the sultan's turban, creating the raised and fluted *Kugelhopf,* now a Viennese classic.

Vienna's wealth of baroque architecture dates from the same period. The massive, florid ornamentation drifted over from Italy and burst upon Vienna in the wave of prosperity and joy that followed the Turkish defeat. Austrian spirits exploded in an architectural celebration of exuberant, grandiose swirls and curls. Ceilings and walls were adorned with angels and cherubs, saints and suns, fruits and flowers, waves and garlands. Buildings were palatial and grand, formally landscaped in sweeping parks and plazas. Mansard roofs, dormer windows in cartouche frames, colonnades and fairytale cupolas were standard on country mansions, town houses, palaces and public buildings, theaters and churches. Interiors shone with gold leaf, twenty-two carat and as thick as honey, set off by clouds and curves as creamy-white as the confectioners' whipped cream. Everywhere there was a feeling of elation and motion. Statues were never sculptured in repose. Great stone horses leaped over the soaring waters of fountains, their manes unfurled like silken scrolls. The mounts of heroes in equestrian statues were posed reared back on their hind legs. Buildings were supported by muscular male sculptures, their togas whipped out by an imaginary wind; and Herculean figures carved in stone seemed about to jump off their pedestals. All of the decorative intricacies of this style carried over into music, pastries, coiffures, jewelry, clothing, and manners.

The city abounds in examples of this baroque style. There are fourteen hundred rooms full of it at Schönbrunn alone. This yellow-gold miniature Versailles, begun in 1695 after plans by Fischer von Erlach, was completed in the eighteenth century during the reign of Maria Theresa. It is surrounded by a formal park with lagoons and fountains, terraced gardens and statuary, a zoo that was once the royal menagerie, and the enormous marble summerhouse, the Gloriette. The state apartments and the royal carriage museum give one a glimpse of the grandeur of the Hapsburg times. No other palace in Europe is so exactly what it was when it was a royal residence, none is more packed with memories.

Schönbrunn takes one back to Maria Theresa and her daughter Marie Antoinette; to Napoleon, his Austrian empress, Marie Louise, and their son, the little King of Rome, who died at twenty-one in the same bedroom his father had used as conqueror of Austria. There are reminders, too, of Maximilian, the dupe of Napoleon III, who was executed in Mexico, and of his Carlotta who went mad at his death. And Schönbrunn's magnificent galleries, with their crystal chandeliers, their murals and *parquet de Versailles* flooring, saw the elegance and diplomacy of the Congress of Vienna and the glittering court of Franz Josef.

Belvedere Palace, built for the triumphant Prince Eugene of Savoy, not only contains museums of modern paintings and medieval Austrian art, but is itself virtually one huge museum of the baroque style. Its graceful Marble Hall was the setting for the signing of the Austrian State Treaty in 1955, and from its terrace one can see the rooftops and chimneys of Vienna, and the spire of St. Stephen's silhouetted against the green hills of the Vienna Woods, the beloved Wienerwald.

The Hofburg, the third of the great Hapsburg palaces, is in the heart of the city, set at the edge of the Heldenplatz, the Heroes' Square. With its towering black iron gates topped by double eagles, its statues and arches and tunneled passages, its endless rooms and wings, this huge complex was a royal residence for five hundred years. Here one may see the state apartments of Franz Josef and the Empress Elizabeth and the Schatzkammer, with the crown jewels and royal souvenirs such as the prayer book of Charlemagne, whose empire extended to the eastern borders of Austria. The Hofburg encompasses several museums: the Spanish Riding School in one wing, in another the National Library, quite possibly the most extravagantly baroque building in the world. Its grand hall is a riot of columns, niches, balustrades, figures, moldings, and *tromple l'oeil* versions of the same.

The Karlskirche is another of Von Erlach's works, a great domed and columned church built in the eighteenth century to celebrate Vienna's triumph over an epidemic of plague, the same event that inspired the rococo mass of figures and saints that make up the plague column, the Pestsäule, on the Graben. Anyone who can take still more baroque should see St. Peter's Church with its copper-green dome, and the Law Courts, another masterpiece by Von Erlach.

Physically, Vienna is laid out in concentric circles, ringing out from the Innere Stadt, the central core of the old town that fans out from the Danube Canal. This section is a crowded maze of winding streets, lined with dark-gray houses antiquely mellow, and opening suddenly into baroque squares centered on fountains and edged with gabled guild houses and town mansions. Churches, houses, shops and statues are so crammed together it is almost impossible to photograph one without edging into the other, taking into account the traffic, the people, and the shallow perspective of the narrow streets. This is the tourist and business section of Vienna, the locale of its hotels, restaurants, coffeehouses and night clubs. It webs out from St. Stephen's Cathedral, a twelfth century Gothic prize, with jewel-like stained-glass windows, slim, soaring arches, and a needle-point steeple.

The Innere Stadt includes remnants of walls that enclosed the Roman settlement, Vindobona, where Marcus Aurelius died in 180 A.D.; the old ghetto around the Judengasse; the lovely fourteenth century church of Maria am Gestede; the Albertina Museum, with its wonderful collection of graphic arts; and the Kapuzinergruft, with the crypts of Hapsburg royalty. Music lovers will want to visit the house in which Mozart wrote *The Marriage of Figaro,* another in which Beethoven composed *Fidelio,* and the homes of Haydn and Schubert. Walkers will delight in antique squares like the Am Hof, once the scene of medieval jousting tournaments; the Franziskanerplatz, with its Gothic-Renaissance Franciscan monastery; the picturesque meat market, the Fleischmarkt; a dozen or so artistically historic churches; galleries and museums; wine taverns and beer cellars.

Inevitably, these crowded, curving streets open onto the airy, spacious, tree-lined boulevards that bend around the old town to form the Ringstrasse, called more intimately by the Viennese "the Ring." This mile-wide belt of parks, promenades, and public buildings, was created in the nineteenth century on the ramparts of the ancient city fortifications. It is along this Ring that one can see the neo-Gothic City Hall, the Rathaus, the university, the overpowering Burgtheater, the Greek Revival Parliament House, the State Opera House, the Museum of the City of Vienna that covers three thousand years of its history, and the new wing of the Hofburg, bordering the Heldenplatz. Opposite is the Maria Theresien Platz, with the Museum of Natural History and the breathtaking Kunsthistorisches Museum. This is one of the world's richest fine-art collections, where pearl-gray walls are hung with a staggering array of paintings. The north Europeans are especially well represented, and anyone with a fondness for Dürer, Breughel, Holbein, or Rembrandt may decide to cancel all other plans for Vienna and just stay inside this museum—which has, by the way, the best lighting and hanging arrangements I have ever seen. There are parks, churches, and, believe it or not, still more museums along the Ring, the regal Schwarzenburg Palace in its own park, the Stock Exchange buildings, and the modern skyscraper, the Ringturm, with a towertop view of the city, the Danube, and the surrounding countryside.

The Ring ends at yet another, wider circle, the Gürtel, marking the outer defensive walls that withheld the Turkish armies. Beyond the Gürtel are some of the earliest low-income housing developments, built for workers in the 1920's, and beyond these are the royal summer palaces and picturesque little towns.

The most obvious seasons in which to visit Vienna are unquestionably spring and summer, the time of trade fairs and flower fairs, music festivals and outdoor concerts. One may spend balmy evenings in the beer gardens, swim or sail in the Danube, or take boat trips to the antique towns of the Wachau Valley. On May Day children ride in open fiacres from their first communion at St. Stephen's Cathedral to the Coney Island amusement park, the Prater. This marks its opening for the season and the giant Ferris wheel, made ominously famous by the movie *The Third Man,* begins to turn once more. Summer is the time for picnics on the hillsides of the Vienna Woods, and if you climb to the top of the Kahlenberg you can see over the capital, across the Danube, and on to the borders of Czechoslovakia and Hungarian Bratislava, once part of the Hapsburg realm.

But perhaps the most delightful and typically Viennese thing to do on a spring evening is to visit a suburban *Heuriger,* a tavern with a green branch over its door to mark the arrival of the new wine, the product of the previous autumn harvest. Whether you go out on a tram, carrying your own sausage-cheese-bread supper in a basket, or hire a private car to take you to a tavern where you may order a complete dinner, you will find yourself amongst lyrically gay, hospitable people. Sievering, Grinzing, and Cobenzl are only three of the many towns noted for their pretty inns and their clear golden wine.

As charming as Vienna is in summer, its most glamorous and genuine season is winter, when its night life is aglitter, its opera in full swing, its Fasching carnival is held, and big tile stoves warm the little taverns. Vienna in December is a Christmas-card city come to life. The air is frosty and clear as glass, the night sky iced with stars, and giant Christmas trees sparkle outside the opera house. The main shopping streets, the Kärntnerstrasse, the Graben, and the Kohlmarkt, are strung with necklaces of lights and shop windows are all packed with gifts: furs, leather, copper cookware, lacy lingerie, rose-embroidered evening skirts and rose-sprigged porcelain coffee cups, antique figurines and chunks of brass, sheer crystal goblets the color of champagne, petitpoint evening bags and garlands of sausages, wheels of cheese, rare wines and exotic coffees, and lollipops that look like Christmas angels.

Christmas music is played in the churches and the two most important characters in town are Nikolo and Krampus, good and evil spirits, who visit all children on December 7 for an accounting of the year's behavior. Bad deeds are confessed to Krampus while Nikolo tallies the good, and gifts or punishments are doled out accordingly on Christmas Day. Krampus, with a devil's face and crimson suit, seems a more popular figure than the white-bearded, white-robed Nikolo, and one sees the cheery demon made into cookies and cakes and figures formed of black prunes in pastry-shop windows all over the city. Usually these spirits visit the children in the masked, costumed person of a father or relative, but in recent years Vienna papers have carried small advertisements announcing that if one calls the number listed a Krampus and Nikolo will be dispatched in haste, wherever needed.

And certainly one of Vienna's December attractions is the Wiener Christkindlmarkt, an outdoor Christmas market held each year in the little square in front of the Mariatheresienplatz. Its rows of open stalls are full of every kind of gift, toy, and Christmas decoration you've ever dreamed of: sweaters, mounds of nut-studded nougat and candy apples, gadgets for cutting carrot curls, books, and records. And at *wurstel* stands, crowds stand in the icy-clear air eating thin Debrizener sausages, bright with paprika, or hot chunks of Klobasse, rich with garlic and pepper.

But whether you see Vienna in its flowery summer season, or in its gay and sparkling fall and winter, a visit to the towns around it are a "must." Few large cities of the world lie so close to such quaint and peaceful environs. There are spas like Baden; vineyard towns like Krems and Gumpoldskirchen; all of the *Heuriger* suburbs already mentioned; and such historic, antique sites as Carnuntum, with its Roman ruins, Melk and Seitenstetten, with their Gothic abbeys, Dürnstein, with a crumbled riverside castle that was the prison of Richard the Lionhearted, and to my mind the handsomest town of all, Klosterneuberg, with narrow cobblestoned streets, low stone houses, and a twelfth century Augustine abbey. Semmering, with its mountaintop hotel, is a wooded resort as popular in summer as it is in winter when it is crowded with ski enthusiasts. The railroad here, cut through a mountainside, is one of Europe's engineering triumphs, the accomplishment of an Italian engineer, Ghega, in the nineteenth century at the cost of nearly one thousand lives.

If one has time to travel farther, he may have an idyllic and inexpensive vacation in the green-wooded, castle-topped hills of Styria, or wander around the gentle, ancient countryside of Carinthia, one of the oldest and most picturesque sections of Austria. And for an even more offbeat tour, there is the relatively unspoiled pocket-sized province of Burgenland, with its meadows, fields, and lakes, its grazing lands and old-fashioned wells, its enormous and well-stocked Lake Neusiedl, and quaint village houses topped with storks' nests. Eisenstadt, the capital, includes the tomb of Papa Haydn and the ancestral palace of his patron, Prince Esterházy, and the area contains almost as many fabled castles as it does beaches and spas.

SALZBURG

The heart of the heart of Europe

IF Vienna is essentially a European city, Salzburg is almost purely Austrian and, like a child that resembles both its parents, it reminds one alternately of Italy and Bavaria, for reasons a map should make obvious. Walled off from harsh winds by the snow-peaked Alps, and set in a green and leafy landscape reminiscent of southern Europe, Salzburg, with its ornate church spires and domes, its fountains and palaces, looks baroquely Italianate. But from its beer gardens and pastry shops, its *lederhosen* and dirndls, its polished brass and wrought-iron scrollwork, one can easily guess that Munich is not far off, though the Austrian brand of *Gemütlichkeit* is considerably more delicate than the German.

One can see the whole city and the architectural influences that have been at work in it from the old stone ramparts of the Kapuzinerberg. From that gentle height you can look across the Salzach River to the old town, to the silhouettes of steeples and domes, and the looming shadow of the twelfth century fortress, the Festung Hohensalzburg, a medieval Germanic landmark that was the castle of the bishop-princes who ruled the city and had it designed to their taste.

Few cities in Europe are more what you would expect them to be than this one, a jeweled music box of a town that tinkles out a Mozart sonata, a zither melody, or a Glockenspiel carillon. It is as famous for its fine-misted rain, the *Schnürlregen,* as it is for its soufléed dumpling dessert, the airy *Salzburgernockerl;* as popular for its brine and mud health-baths as it is for its art and music.

It is this last, of course, that is Salzburg's real claim to fame, for it is first and foremost the city of Mozart, and if his home town ignored him while he was alive it has more than made up for the neglect since his death. There is Mozartiana everywhere. The plaque on No. 9 Getreidegasse marks the house of his birth—now a museum containing, among other memorabilia, his clavichord. On the *platz* that bears his name stands a statue of the composer, and a tablet marks the house (No. 8) in which his widow, Constanze, lived from 1820 to 1842. There is another Mozart house on the Marktplatz, and the Mozarteum is a music and drama school with a library of books by and about the composer and his work. In the garden is the *Zauberflöthauschen,* the little hut where *The Magic Flute* was written and which was moved from its original site near the sixteenth century Kapuzinerkirche in 1950. The tombs of the Mozart family lie in the graveyard of the late Gothic Sebastianskirche, not far from those of Weber and Paracelsus.

But most of all, Mozart is remembered by his music: his chorales and masses are sung in the cathedral and in the Romanesque Benedictine Abbey of St. Peter's, a church which is considered to be the cradle of Christianity in the Danube-Alpine area and includes a number of early Christian catacombs. His chamber music is played at candlelight concerts in the elegant state apartments of the Archbishops' Palace, the Residenz, and his symphonies are performed in the modern Festival Theater. Mozart operas are given frequently and are even enacted by the highly skilled puppeteers in the Marionette Theater. And with its world-famous Summer Music Festival, its January Mozart Festival, and its Salzburg Musical Spring, the whole city is virtually a concert stage the whole year round.

Salzburg was founded by the Romans and it began to acquire its baroque beauty in the seventeenth century, under the aegis of the

Medici archbishop, Wolf Dietrich, and those who succeeded him: Marcus Sitticus, Johann Ernst Graf Thun, and Paris-Lodron, all of whom commissioned leading Italian and Austrian architects to design the palaces, churches, and statues that gave Salzburg its unity and elegance. This was no town of self-expressive burghers' houses but the creation of an autocratic elite. The two most famous architects who worked in the city were Fischer von Erlach and Santino Solari. The latter is responsible for the fortifying ramparts that lead to the Hohensalzburg and the simply etched Cathedral on the Domplatz that is the backdrop for the annual festival performances of Hofmannsthal's play, *Jedermann* (Everyman). and just as the Austrian Mozart is credited with having written the best "Italian" opera, *Don Giovanni,* so the Austrian architect, Fischer von Erlach, designed baroque buildings that were the apogee of the Italian idiom. His masterpiece is the Kollegienkirche, Salzburg's largest and finest church, built between 1694 and 1707, a massive, dark-magenta building with a lofty dome, diadem-like turrets and statues by Mandl, one of the best sculptors of the time.

Von Erlach's earliest work in the city was the Dreifaltigkeitskirche, with its concave façade and dome frescoes by Rottmayr. Among his other creations are the west door that was incorporated into the Festival Theater built in 1956, the Markuskirche, and, of all things, a horse trough, the Pferdeschwemme, on the Siegmundsplatz, which was designed as an ornamental screen to hide a nearby quarry that a beauty-conscious archbishop regarded as an eyesore.

Salzburg is studded with other such jewels of the baroque era: the Residenz Palace of the bishop-princes, and, on the same handsome square, the Glockenspiel, with its thirty-five bells that were sent from Antwerp; the Michaelskirche, Salzburg's oldest parish church, and the great circular fountain with its scalloped shells spouting horses, the largest baroque fountain north of the Alps. Not far away is the colorful Alter Markt, with its Renaissance ironwork, and the quay-side Town Hall, the Rathaus. No single building in the city embodies more of Salzburg's architectural history than the Franziskanerkirche, a church founded in the eighth century and added to through the ages. It is a blend of Romanesque and late Gothic, Renaissance and baroque, and its high altar is another triumph of Von Erlach. No building in Salzburg has more romantic associations than the Mirabelle Palace, the *schloss* built by the prince archbishop Wolf Dietrich for his mistress, Salome Alt, and which is famous for its carved marble Angel Staircase and its opulent splendor.

Certainly no one should miss one of Salzburg's most popular tourist meccas, the Hellbrun, an early baroque country mansion built for Marcus Sitticus by Solari in the early seventeenth century. The interior of the palace with its ceremonial hall and ceiling frescoes is almost as breathtaking as its fairytale garden, where trick fountains spout into the air and a mechanical theater is operated by water. The grounds include an alpine zoo and the Monatsschlössl, a museum of Salzburg history and folklore.

Salzburg's population has tripled from 40,000 to 120,000 in the past twenty-five years, so it should be no surprise to learn that it has expanded accordingly. Happily, though, the modern section of the city lies around its edges, and the up-to-date hotels that accommodate 1.5 million visitors each year in no way interfere with its more antique charms. Open-air markets such as the weekly Grünmarkt and Schrannenmarkt are held as they have been for generations, and local folk music and dances are performed regularly in several restaurant-*kellers* and concert halls around town. In summer, beer gardens and open cafés are lively with young voices and zither music, and in winter the town takes on the aspect of a ski resort. Floodlights whitewash the city's monuments and churches during all the festival nights and on special holidays during the year.

Salzburg is the gateway to the lakes and ski slopes and the *bad* spas that make up the Salzkammergut. Bad Ischl is still ripe with memories of Emperor Franz Josef, who spent his summers there, and the White Horse Inn of operatic fame still stands on the banks of the Wolfgangsee. The Grossglockner Highway is a scenic route through the Alps past Austria's highest mountain peak, and Bad Gastein is as popular in summer when its mountain streams and green forests are at their best as it is in winter when its slopes are a paradise for skiers.

FOR THE TRAVELER'S NOTEBOOK

Official Information

Before you go: Austrian State Tourist Department, 11 East 52nd St., New York, N.Y.; Suite 523–525, Terminal Sales Bldg., Portland, Ore.; Frank P. Anderwald, 77 West Washington St., Chicago, Ill.; 448 South Hill St., Los Angeles, Cal.

In Vienna: SAS Office, 3 Kärntnerring; Tourist Office of the City of Vienna (*Fremdenverkehrsstelle der Stadt Wien*), 6–8 Stadiongasse; U.S. Embassy, 2 Friederich-Schmidt Platz.

In Salzburg: Tourist Information Office (*Stadtverkehrsbüro*), 9 Marktplatz; U.S. Consulate, 2 Munzstrasse.

Money Matters

Currency: The monetary unit is the Austrian schilling (S) divided into 100 groschen (Gr.). One schilling equals 4¢, U.S.; S25 equals about $1, U.S.

Tipping: Service charge of 10 to 15 per cent usually added on hotel and restaurant bills, but give waiter approximately 5 per cent more, at least S1 or S2; taxi drivers, hairdressers, barbers, 10 to 15 per cent; station porters, S2 to S4 per bag, S5 for larger ones; hatcheck and washroom attendants, S1 to S2; chambermaid and hall porter S3 per day each, at the end of your stay.

Climate, Clothing, and Essentials

Vienna has a temperate climate the year round, much the same as that of New York. In midwinter you will find snow, but not to the same extent as in the ski resorts. Summer days are hot, but pleasantly so. In spring and fall, take a light coat for the evening and a raincoat. Salzburg is famous for the *Schnürlregen* (intermittent misty rain). A cocktail dress or dark suit will see you through every occasion, unless you are invited to a formal ball or plan to attend opening performances at the opera or the major theaters.

Hotels

Many of Vienna's hotels have been rebuilt or modernized since the war and offer all modern conveniences, in addition to their traditional charm. If you arrive in Vienna or Salzburg without reservations, the tourist offices in the waiting room on the Westbahnhof railroad station, will be able to help you; if you would like to live with a private family, the City Tourist Office will help you. You can get a complete guide to hotels throughout Austria from the Tourist Offices listed earlier.

De luxe hotels charge from S180 to 350, single; S300 to 650, double. The range is wide because many of the rooms do not have baths, even in the luxury hotels, so be sure you specify when making your reservation. First class hotels charge from S150 to 260, single; S280 to 400, double. Moderately priced hotel rates range from S90 to 155, single; S115 to 300, double. The inexpensive hotels, as listed below, charge about S75 to 90, single; from S120, double, generally with breakfasts included. The pensions listed range from $100 to 250, single; $200 to 350, double.

VIENNA

DE LUXE: The recently opened (1963) *Vienna Intercontinental* is a five-hundred room monument to modern design, located opposite the Vienna Stadtpark, and includes everything. *Imperial, 16 Kärntnerring.* Formerly the residence of visiting royalty and a Vienna landmark for over a century, this hotel, with its plush and gilt, has its intimations of grandeur, and excellent restaurants, a café, and a romantic little bar. *Sacher, 4 Philharmonikstrasse.* Another great name among the world's hotels, this one is famous for the mellow chocolate *torte* that was invented here by the original owner-chef, Sacher, as well as for its old-world charm and elegance. The red-carpeted halls are hung with handsome old paintings and, although some of the rooms have been redecorated and modernized, others still contain floral wallpaper, painted furniture, and starched lace curtains. *Ambassador, 5 Neuer Markt.* Modernized, but with traditional appeal, this hotel has played host to a number of celebrities. *Bristol, 1 Kärntnerring.* A delightfully comfortable, plushy hotel just across from the Opera House. The *Parkhotel Schönbrunn, 10–14 Heitzinger Haupstrasse,* is a little way out of the center of things (fifteen minutes by taxi). It is quiet, elegant, and very popular with American visitors. Prices are somewhat lower than other hotels in the de luxe category. *Europa, 3 Neuer Markt,* is modern, efficient, provides TV in all rooms on request, and is extremely pleasant. *Prinz Eugen, 15 Wiedner Gürtel,* near the South Railroad Station, is sparkling and modern, and a number of its rooms have balconies. *Dom Royal, 3 Singerstrasse,* is spacious, modern, and offers such comforts as TV, terraces, and an excellent location. *Clima, 21a Theresianumgasse.* Brand-new, this hotel offers compact and pleasant rooms at modest prices, about fifteen minutes away from the main shopping center. *AEZ Zentrum, 2a Landstrasse Hauptstrasse,* on two floors of a department store, has modern rooms, a motel atmosphere, and a rooftop garage.

MODERATE: *Kaiserin Elisabeth, 3 Weihburggasse,* is close to St. Stephen's Cathedral and is comfortable and moderately priced. Other well-located hotels to consider are the *Regina* and the restful little *Kaiserhof,* which was redecorated in 1960. *Erzherzog Rainer, 27 Wiedner Hauptstrasse,* is noted for its Weinrestaurant Altwein, its good service, and pleasant rooms. *Astoria, 32 Kärntnerstrasse,* and the *Kummer, 71a Mariahilferstrasse,* are conveniently located and attractive with comfortable rooms and hospitable service.

INEXPENSIVE: *Hotel Austria, 3 Wolfengasse,* is a wonderful buy, close to St. Stephen's and the old meat market (Fleischmarkt), with very good service and comfortable rooms. *Hotel Central, 8a Taborstrasse* (same ownership as the *Austria*), is close by and almost as desirable in the budget class. Within the "Ring," the *Wandl, 9 Petersplatz,* is good, if not the least expensive of the budget hotels, while the *Graben, 3 Dorotheergasse,* close by, is set on a picturesque little street and has very nice rooms. There are a number of inexpensive hotels near the West Railroad Station (Westbahnhof). The best of these are: the *Mariahilf, 121a Mariahilferstrasse;* the *Wimberger, 34 Neubaugürtel;* and the *Fuchs, 138 Mariahilferstrasse.*

PENSIONS: Among the city's best pensions are the *Arenberg, 2 Stubenring;* the *Atlanta 33 Währingerstrasse;* the *Elite, 32 Wipplingerstrasse;* the *Opernring, 11 Opernring;* and the *Schneider, 1 Lehargasse.*

SALZBURG

Hotel rates here are a little lower generally than those in Vienna, although at the height of the music festival they often become slightly higher.

DE LUXE: The most luxurious hotel in the city, and certainly in a class by itself, is the *Gastschloss Mönchstein, 26 Mönchsberg,* a small plush castle turned into a hotel. It contains, in all, eleven suites and charges top prices during its season—from mid-April to mid-October. *Goldener Hirsch, 37 Getreidegasse,* is set in a house eight centuries old, and has been an inn for over half of that time. It combines old-world charm with modern comfort and its country inn atmosphere is inviting and delightful. *Österreichischer Hof, 5–7 Schwarzstrasse,* is enormous and grandiose, and overlooks the river bank. *Parkhotel Mirabelle, 4 Auerspergstrasse,* offers push-button modern surroundings, radio and TV in the room if you want them, a swimming pool, and terrace. *Bristol, 2 Marktplatz,* on the market place, has been renovated and is pleasantly comfortable, with good personal service.

FIRST CLASS: *Europa, 31 Rainerstrasse,* is a modern hotel offering compact rooms and a rooftop café with a view of the Alps. *Parkhotel Kaiserhof, 31 Morzgerstrasse,* is a very good buy, with restful luxury accommodations at moderate prices in a converted castle, twenty minutes out of the city. *Schlosshotel Kavalierhaus* is located in a park outside of Salzburg and has a golf course, tennis courts, and a swimming pool. The *Winkler, 7 Franz Josefstrasse,* is modern and pleasant and the *Maria-Theresien-Schlössl, 87 Morzgerstrasse,* is old world, small, private, and full of atmosphere.

MODERATE: The *Pitter, 6–8 Rainerstrasse,* with its beer cellar and café entertainment is one of the city's best buys, and the *Stein,* also in this price category, is another you will probably enjoy. The *Judenbergalm* has a most restful setting in the mountains, about twenty-five minutes from the heart of town.

INEXPENSIVE: The *Mozart, 27 Franz Josefstrasse;* the *Hotel Gablebräu, 9 Linzergasse;* and the *Kasererbräu, 33 Kaigasse,* are all well located and comfortable in the moderate to inexpensive price category.

Food and Restaurants

Austrian food is rich, fattening, and absolutely gorgeous. Meal hours follow our own, but in addition there is a traditional midmorning snack, known as *Gabelfrühstück,* and midnight snacks as well, perhaps sausage on roll, hot potato salad, and beer. *Jause,* or afternoon coffee, gives the Viennese a chance to drink what must be the world's best coffee with clouds of *Schlagobers* (whipped cream) piled on, to go along with such pastry specialties as the famed chocolate *Sacher Torte, Indianer Krapfen* (chocolate puffs filled with whipped cream) or strudels. Other wonderful desserts include *Palatschinken,* a version of *crêpes,* and *Kaiserschmarren,* strips of pancakes sprinkled with sugar.

By all means pay a visit to *Demel's,* with its *fin de siècle* elegance and its tantalizing buffet, or the more modern but excellent *Lehmann's* and *Gerstner.*

Austrian dishes that have won world renown include schnitzel—either the familiarly breaded *Wiener* or the lighter *Natur; Weiner Backhuhn,* the crispest oven-fried chicken in the world; Hungarian-inspired goulash, and chicken *paprikash;* and *Nockerl,* tiny snowflakes of dough, sautéed in butter. Boiled beef with horse-radish sauce (*Tafelspitz*) and grilled goose liver (in winter) are not to be missed.

With your meal you may take a light Austrian beer; *Gösserbräu, Schwechater Bräu,* or *Liesinger Bier.* The local wines are good. Take a *Grinzinger, Nussberger,* or *Gumpoldskirchner* with your veal or chicken, or, if you prefer a red wine, *Burgenländer* or *Vöslauer.* Try the Austrian *G'spritzler*—a wine served with soda, and very refreshing.

VIENNA

The hotels here have truly fine restaurants and anyone who does not have one luncheon of *Tafelspitz* and a slice of the rich chocolate *Sacher Torte* with whipped cream at the Sacher Hotel, hasn't really been to Vienna. For elegant, excellent, and expensive dinners or after-theater suppers, Vienna has such beautiful, plushy restaurants as the *Drei Husaren,* with its candlelight, violins, and delectable hors d'oeuvres. Across the street, the more intimate *Stadtkrug,* a wine-and-roses setting of small, intimate rooms, has exquisite food, especially the wonderful *roulade* of rabbit with a red wine sauce and light dumplings. *Am Franziskanerplatz,* a Viennese landmark in a building six hundred years old, is widely recommended but somewhat overrated. *Kerzenstüberl,* with its imperial upstairs dining rom or its romantic little downstairs *boîte,* has superb service and food to match. Also popular with tourists and Vienna's fashionable set are the *Rôtisserie Coq d'Or* with its broiling wall and American style barbecue; *St. Stephan's Restaurant,* a new setting for authentic Viennese dishes at fairly high prices; and *Zur Linde,* which has both a formal upstairs dining room and a more charming downstairs cellar, especially good for a late supper.

The *Balkan Grill,* with a small orchestra, roving violinists, and balalaika music (not all at once, fortunately), serves marvelous Serbian and Croatian food; and the broiled goose liver here is a rare treat indeed. The *Rathauskeller* is an enormous town restaurant in the City Hall and is noisy, gay, and very good, especially for luncheon. The *Weisser Rachfangkehrer* is typically Viennese and beer tavern-y and its century-old wine bar is handsome; it also has good, moderately priced food. The *Leisingerkeller* is charming and the food delicious. *Hauswirth* is an authentic, moderately priced restaurant, popular with Austrian families; it has an outdoor garden in summer. *Zum Weissen Schwann* is a two-hundred-year-old restaurant famous for its game, especially the venison. *Pataky's* is a traditional place for good Hungarian food, and *Csardasfurstin* for the most spectacular gypsy violinists. A special word must be said about *Griechenbeisl* and *Marhold.* Both of these are in the old meat market (Fleischmarkt) just across the way from each other, and I would strongly urge you to have luncheon at each. They are the epitome of all we think of as *gemütlich.* Other inexpensive but good restaurants in the city include the *Bräuerei Ottakring* and other such *Bieerstübe* as the *Alter Hofkeller,* the *Augustinerkeller, Löwenbräukeller,* and the huge *Opernkeller,* in itself a sight not to be missed. The chain of restaurants known as *W.O.K.* serves no alcohol, but the food is good and incredibly cheap.

There are delightful old restaurants outside the city, many with outdoor dining facilities and music, all with authentic *Alt Wien* atmosphere and excellent food. The *Kaffee-Restaurant Cobenzl* and the similar *Kahlenberg* afford a breathtaking hillside view of the city and its famed Danube. And among the most colorful and delightful wine restaurants (*Heuriger*) are *Eckel* and *Martinkovich* in Sievering, *Das Alte Haus, Musil, Setzger's,* and the *Huhnerstall* in Grinzing.

SALZBURG

Many of the hotels here serve good food, especially the *Goldener*

Hirsch and the *Österreichischer Hof. Zum Eulenspiegel,* a colorful old inn, is large, gay, and very full of atmosphere, although moderately priced, while the *Winkler* is a chic, expensive restaurant with a lovely view. *Powandra,* with its famous *Schmankerltorte* dessert, is a "must," and somewhere in this town be sure to try the native specialty, *Salzburger Nockerl.* Among the best brewery restaurants are the *Augustiner Bräu Stübl,* to which you bring your own food, the *Stieglkeller,* with its folk music and dancing exhibitions, and the *Stiftskeller St. Peter,* one of the city's most traditional and famous places. The *Café Glockenspiel* is nice for light lunches, and the *Grossgasthof Sternbräu,* in a pleasant garden, serves the wares of its own sausage shop. *Festungsrestaurant,* on an open terrace overlooking the city, has folk evenings too, while *Weisses Kreuz* is noted for Balkan dishes. For inexpensive food, try the dining room in the railroad station or the Town Hall restaurant, *Ratsherrnkeller.*

Entertainment, Night Life, and Special Events

VIENNA

First and foremost is the Vienna Opera (Staatsoper). The season begins in September and continues till the end of June. Ballet and operetta—a peculiarly Austrian form, owing so much to Franz von Suppé, Johann Strauss, Edmund Eysler, and Franz Lehár—is given at the Volksoper and here the season continues till mid-July. Concerts are given by the Vienna Philharmonic, one of the most important orchestras in the world, with a tradition over a hundred years old, and the Vienna Symphony Orchestra, which has in recent years become recognized for its mastery in modern music; and there are many excellent solo recitals and chamber music evenings. The Vienna Boys' Choir (*Wiener Sängerknaben*) is one of the city's most famous choral groups and the *Deutschmeister Kapelle* is a 250-year-old brass band known the world over. If you fancy amusement in the open air, visit the Prater and take a turn on the giant Ferris wheel, almost a sinister symbol since Orson Welles's appearance in *The Third Man.* If you are in a more romantic mood, go out to the village of Grinzing, about halfway to the Leopoldsberg or Kahlenberg, and sip new wine in one of the many *Heuriger* or wine gardens. The symbol here is a green wreath posted at the door, unmistakable as you walk past the little low houses on the main street.

If you want dancing, continue to the *Cobenzl-Bar* at Cobenzl. Returning to the city, three of the best places are the *Eden-Bar,* the *Splendid Bar,* and the *Monseigneur Bar,* noted for its gypsy music. After a show, you may wish to take a glass of wine in the *Urbanikeller,* a wine cellar deep underground with old vaults, antique furniture, and zither music; but be sure to go down to the second basement. Or you may try the *Alter Hofkeller* in the Hofburg. (For late suppers see "Restaurants.") If your taste runs to night clubs with floor shows, visit the *Moulin Rouge, Casanova,* or *Lido* in *Maxim,* each with their share of strip teasers and/or magicians and acrobats. The *Marietta Bar* is a cabaret with sophisticated entertainment.

SPECIAL EVENTS: *May 1* is Labor Day and marks the opening of Vienna's Prater Amusement Park when brightly decorated carriages drive children down the Praterhauptallee after their first communion at St. Stephen's Cathedral. The *June Festival* of Vienna brings special programs in theaters and concert halls, and all summer there are special musical events here as well as in Salzburg.

The *Vienna Trade Fairs* are held in March and September and the *Vintage Festivals* in the wine taverns (*Heuriger*) are held in October. The opera season starts in September and the winter carnival, *Fasching,* a time of gala social events and formal balls, lasts from December until Lent.

Skiing is the national sport. If you are visiting Austria in winter or early spring, you may wish to spend a few days in one of the major resorts of the Tyrol or Vorarlberg, but for the Viennese, Semmering, only two hours from the city by train or car, is the main ski terrain.

SALZBURG

One of the pleasantest nighttime attractions in Salzburg is the wonderful *Café Bazar,* an old chess haunt, where you may read a newspaper and have a glass of wine. *Tomaselli's* is another landmark that is open late, and the bars of the larger hotels are generally popular and crowded, especially the one in the *Goldener Hirsch.* You can dance at several of the restaurants and hotels, and there is gambling at the local casino. The *Café Winkler* is a good after-dinner dance spot and the *Casino Alm im Tal* is a combination bowling alley, folksy night club, and daytime sports palace. Native Folklore Evenings take place several times a week in the Wappensaal of the old fortress, and in the *Stieglkeller* and the *Kongree Haus.*

SPECIAL EVENTS: The city's musical activities are not confined to festival time, and you can probably find a concert or opera any night of the week. There's a special *Mozart Festival* in January and a spring music program as well. The Landestheater has a daily program of music, drama, and small-scale revues while plays are also given at the Seminary of Dramatic Art. Check local papers, the Tourist Office, or your hotel for current programs.

Shopping

Petit-point embroidery on evening bags, handbag accessories, leather goods, jewelry (especially the old rose-diamond pieces) porcelain, crystal, men's sportswear, sweaters such as the cashmeres of Bernhard Altmann, silk blouses and lingerie, scarves, Loden coats and capes, dirndl skirts, *lederhosen,* wooden carvings, costume jewelry, enamelware, costume dolls, and the epitome of what one means when he refers to "European antiques" are to be found here. Gunsmithing and handmade riding boots are two traditional Austrian specialties.

VIENNA

The most fashionable streets are the Kärntnerstrasse, the Graben, the Rotenturmstrasse, and Kohlmarkt. Among the city's leading high-fashion boutiques are *Adlmüller, Franhammer, Elegance, Stone & Blyth,* and *Gertrud Höchsmann. Lanz* is noted for its Tyrolean dirndls, its charmingly smocked children's clothes, and its beautifully trimmed Loden capes. *Knize, Koschier, Prix on the Graben, Stros, Humhal,* and *Otto H. Schick* have handsome men's wear, especially sweaters and sports jackets. *Loden Plankl* has everything made of Loden cloth for men, women, and children. All of the streets mentioned are crammed with fine leather stores as well as enticing antique shops and you will find the leading jewelers in the city here too. The two best department stores are *Gerngross* and *Hermansky;* and the *Dorotheum* is an astounding auction palace, established three hundred years ago by the Empress Maria Theresa. *Springer's* is known for firearms; and the *Lobmeyr* showroom offers sheer, golden luster crystal. For a good selection of Austrian china, try *Ernst Wahliss, Rasper und Sohne,* or *Albin Debke.* By all means visit the beautiful shop of the *Österreichische Werkstätten* on the Kärntnerstrasse. This shop exhibits and sells a complete array of modern handicrafts and home furnishings.

SALZBURG

The main shopping areas are around Residenzplatz, Getreidegasse, and Schwartzstrasse. The *Salzburger Heimatwerk* has a complete assortment of handicrafts, ceramics, and dirndls. *Lanz* has its best shop here with the same array (only larger) of the merchandise it sells in Vienna. *Thalhammer's* is noted for its clothing, as is *Resmann: Jahn-Markl* features *lederhosen* and peasant costumes.

Chartered planes are also available. Steamship and motorboats can take you to points along the Danube or around some of the country's many lakes.

Background Reading

Blue Skies, Brown Studies, by William Sansom, which anyone going to
Austria will enjoy: "Vienna," "Out of Vienna," and "Salzburg—the
Vanishing Hotel"

Austria, by Sacheverell Sitwell

The Man without Qualities, by Robert Musil

Fielding Castle, by Edith de Born

The Hapsburg Monarchy, by Arthur J. May

Belgium

BRUSSELS

". . . A sound of revelry by night . . ."

IF one had to choose a single adjective with which to describe Brussels and all Belgium, the best choice would be "opulent," for everything about this tiny country and its sparkling capital suggests an air of luxury and splendor. Its gold-washed landscape of low blue skies, gentle green hills, and medieval towns is as neatly proportioned as the vistas seen through the arched windows of a Van Eyck painting; it is a country of forest woodlands, and white sand beaches, town-square flower markets, and treasures of Gothic architecture and Flemish art. Its restaurants serve Europe's richest butter-egg-cream cuisine and it is known for some of the world's most frankly extravagant wares: exquisitely cut diamonds from Antwerp, Bruges lace and Malines tapestries, handmade guns from Liége and the gossamer crystal of Val St. Lambert, fine linens, and impeccable leather goods; even its leading produce exports—black grapes and white endive—are intended only for markets catering to the carriage trade.

With more than 9 million people packed into 11,775 square miles, Belgium is Europe's most densely populated country and one of its richest. It is traditionally a land of merchants and plays host to numerous international trade fairs. The role of capital of the Common Market is an easy one for Brussels to assume, as it has been a central European clearinghouse since the time of the Romans. Set like a small but perfect jewel between Holland, France, Germany, and Luxembourg, with a forty-mile seacoast on the Straits of Dover, this has been Europe's battlefield as well as its market place. A list of Belgian cities recalls some of history's most decisive battles, from Waterloo to Ypres and the poppy-red fields of Flanders, to Bastogne in the Ardennes, the scene of the Battle of the Bulge, where the Mardasson Memorial marks the place from which General McAuliffe answered "Nuts" to the Nazi request for surrender.

Basically a nation of prosperous, family-proud, carnival-loving, bourgeois shopkeepers, the Belgians know the value of concerted effort and organization. Even the most typical works of such Flemish masters as Memling, Dirk Bouts, Van der Goes, Van der Weyden, Gerard David, the Van Eycks, and Peter Christus, depict the Belgian love of rich detailing, calm symmetry, and warm-hearted family life. The passionate exuberance of a Rubens and the maverick surrealism of a Bosch or Ensor are the exceptions to the Belgian rule of temperance. It is, perhaps, no accident that the concept of the "Average Man" was developed in the nineteenth century by a Belgian statistician, Adolphe Quételet, who thereby performed a great service for the market researchers and copywriters of the future.

When it comes to their national freedom the Belgians are as stubbornly hardheaded as they are in affairs of commerce, a fact that was as obvious to Caesar, who considered the Belgae the bravest of the Gauls, as it was to Hitler, who complained about their refusal to submit to discipline. This same response might have been made by all of the intervening conquerors, including Merovingian Franks and Burgundian dukes, the Hapsburgs both Spanish and Austrian, the French under Louis XI and XIV as well as Napoleon. In 1815, Belgium was united with Holland, and the histories of both countries ran parallel to each other, though Belgium retained Spain's Catholicism while the Netherlands followed Calvinist doctrines. The marriage of the two countries lasted only fifteen years, after which the Belgians became an independent constitutional monarchy under King Leopold I, uncle of Queen Victoria.

In effect, there are two Belgiums and two required national languages. The southern half of the country, hinged to France, is made up of Celtic, French-speaking Walloons, who tend to look like the pertly dark original Belgae. The Frankish Flemings who live in the northern, Breughelesque Flanders, speak Dutch-Flemish, and generally have the round faces and deep golden hair of Memling's Madonnas. The half smiling rivalry between the two groups is about equal to that of our own North and South. With the language difference, most of Belgium's cities are known by two names, one French, the other Flemish: Malines is also Mechelen, Mons is Bergen, Ghent is Gent-Gand, Bruges is Brugge, Antwerp is Antwerpen-Anvers.

But whether the capital is called Brussels, Bruxelles, or by its original eighth century name, *Bruoc-scella* (the marshy dwelling), it is here that the cultural, linguistic, and temperamental strains meet, here that the Dutch talent for order and purpose meets the French love of the gay life, and the very French disregard for traffic regulations and tax laws. This city of one million is a late-night, neon-bright metropolis, with lively cafés and elegant restaurants, concert halls and music halls, ballet theaters and operas, and shops that are busy until ten at night. Everywhere there are garden patches of flower markets, historic buildings golden with age, splashing fountains and statues of all sorts including the seventeenth century *Manneken-Pis,* the little bronze boy who has a wardrobe of costumes for holidays, and who performs one of nature's most basic functions, to the delight of Kodak-carrying tourists.

Brussels is the heart of Belgium's lushest province, Brabant, and the heart of Brussels is its Grand' Place, possibly the most beautiful square in Europe. Here where the Spanish Duke of Alva had the sixteenth century insurrectionist counts Egmont and Horne beheaded, colorful fruit, flower, and vegetable stalls are framed by gold-trimmed burghers' houses and guildhalls, and fringed with the Gothic belfry, spires and arches of the fifteenth century Hôtel de Ville. Across the way, the restored thirteenth century Maison du Roi, now the Royal Arts Museum, with its intricate stonework, its wrought-iron roof railing and carved balustrades, is as crisply delicate as a piece of starched Belgian lace. Though gay and colorful by day, the square is most romantic at night, when it is bathed in the glow of its floodlights.

A few blocks away is the Gothic Cathedral of Ste. Gudule, with its twin towers of suede-gray stone, fine tapestries, and stained-glass windows, while the handsome fifteenth to sixteenth century Nortre Dame du Sablon stands near the place of the same name, where forty-eight statues honor Belgium's traditional crafts.

The largest building in the city—and it is larger than St. Peter's in Rome—is the Palais de Justice, built in the nineteenth century by

Poelaert. It would be interesting to know what inspired this mass of architecture—a Graeco-Roman-Washington D.C. phantasmagoria. Its dome rises 339 feet into the air and the observation deck affords a view over the city and its more esthetically restrained wonders.

Among these wonders are the pretty church of Ste. Catherine and the shops of the Boulevard Anspach, the twelfth century Eglise de la Chapelle with the tomb of Breughel, the flea market near the South Station, the Botanical Gardens, and the Atomium lookout that marks the site of the 1958 World's Fair. The downtown entertainment section clusters around the Place de Brouckère where you can visit the complex of buildings from which Common Market affairs are administered, or see one of Europe's oldest stock exchanges, the Bourse.

One of Brussels' most sentimental and historic sections is around the Place Royale, the site of a castle from which the dukes of Brabant controlled the flow of trade moving from Cologne to Bruges, and the scene of the abdication of Charles V as the Holy Roman emperor. Close by is the Royal Palace, where King Baudouin and Queen Fabiola were married and where the king now has his offices.

Perhaps it is best to save Brussels' greatest treasures for the last, for once you start through the city's museums, you may never get to see anything else. There is the Beaux Arts with its collection of Dutch and Flemish paintings and sculptures, the Maison du Roi with souvenirs of the city's past, one museum devoted to modern art and another to Erasmus, the Porte de Hal with collections of weapons and armor, the Folklore Museum, the Camille Lemonnier with a wealth of illuminated manuscripts and the Wiertz collection of fine paintings. There are at least half-a-dozen more with displays of Congo artifacts, musical instruments, archeological specimens, and Oriental art.

One should certainly come out of the museums long enough to visit the Brabant countryside and sample the pastoral delights of Le Bois de la Cambre or the attractive artists' town, Uccle, with its Wolvendael Park. Laeken, with its Chinese and Japanese pagodas, its royal tombs in the Church of Notre Dame and the residence of the king and queen, is another excursion worth making, as is a visit to the battleground of Waterloo, a short distance from the capital. On the way you may stop in the thickly wooded Forest of Soignes.

Anyone with a taste for art and architecture will want several days to explore the "art towns" of Ghent and Bruges. The first, dubbed "the Florence of the North," is a living museum of Gothic beauty, and the Van Eyck triptych in the overpowering Cathedral of St. Bavon is more than enough reason to make the pilgrimage. Better known perhaps as the "Ghent Altarpiece," it is a gilded, polychromed scene of exquisite detail and polished splendor—the central panel shows the Adoration of the Lamb set in a typical Belgian landscape, and the side panels the figures of Adam and Eve, which had to be "clothed" during the reign of Joseph II.

Bruges, once Europe's leading textile center, abounds with memories and early paintings of Jan van Eyck, Christus and Memling. Its thirteenth century market place with its lofty tower atop the Market House; the Church of Notre Dame, which houses Michelangelo's white marble "Madonna and Child"; and the picturesque quays with baroque gabled houses are so charming that one might almost forget to see the Memling paintings in St. John's Hospital or the other works of the Bruges School in the City Museum.

Antwerp, Belgium's second largest city, is as important for its present as it is for its past. It is one of Europe's largest seaports and its Beurs Voor Diamant is the world's largest diamond trading center. This is one of Belgium's oldest cities: its first church, St. Amand, was built in 660 A.D., and the present cathedral, begun in 1352, took almost 270 years to complete. It is a masterpiece of stained-glass windows and soaring spires and houses an important group of paintings by Rubens, who was born in this city. Its forty-seven-bell carillon is a companion piece to forty-two other bells, the largest of which, the Carolus, was baptized by Charles V in 1507. The City Hall is a Renaissance classic, standing guard in the town square, and the churches of St. James, St. Augustine, St. Paul, and St. Charles-Borromée are virtually museums dedicated to Rubens, whose works appear in all of them. In addition, there is the actual Museum of Fine Arts, where almost all the great Flemish painters are represented, including an unusually complete collection of the modernist James Ensor. The house of the master printer Christophe Plantin is a mecca for booklovers, as is Rubens' house for art lovers. And certainly anyone visiting this city should stroll around its harbor where the tenth century ruins of the harbor fortress, the Steen, stands as a reminder of Crusader days.

Fortunately Belgium is compact enough so that all of its charms are within easy reach of the capital. The whole country is dotted with towns and villages that are medieval set-pieces. Malines, on the river Dyle, was a great center of Flemish tapestry weaving and the art still survives there; Tournai is a city of goldsmiths, with a Grand' Place all its own and Belgium's oldest belfry, built in the twelfth century; Ypres, with its thirteenth century Cloth Hall and cathedral, was an important weaving town, where now a memorial gate honors the unknown British soldiers of World War I who died in its defense; Mons is the seventh century city of bells with a huge belfry and magnificent carillon; and Liége, the most important city in the Walloony, is equally well known as a religious and educational center and was the seat of the mighty bishop-princes.

But if you think all Belgium is a museum requiring the most serious guidebook-in-hand attention, you'll be pleased to know it is almost as full of idyllic resorts. The beaches in the towns around Ostende are as relaxing as they are beguiling with their local folklore festivals, and Malmédy in the Ardennes is as popular with hunters as it is with those who want to join in its Mardi Gras. Spa is the thermal resort that gave all other thermal resorts their name; and the copper-trimmed town of Dinant is only one of the charms of the château country in the Meuse Valley, fitting competition for France's Loire. Anyone looking for the ultimate in carnivals should plan to spend the pre-Lenten Sunday, Monday, and Tuesday in the town of Binche, where the wild festivities are said to be based on Peruvian celebrations seen by the Spaniards and adopted to celebrate their conquest of that country. Everyone throws oranges and water-filled sheep bladders at everyone else and the very Incan-looking costume worn by the hero, Gille, is a puff of feathers and a towering hat. The general hilarity should help you understand why Binche gave its name to the kind of all-out spree we call a binge.

FOR THE TRAVELER'S NOTEBOOK

Official Information

Before you go: Belgian Tourist Bureau, 720 Fifth Ave., New York, N.Y. (The main office is in New York, but there are offices in Atlanta, Beverly Hills, Boston, Chicago, Cleveland, Dallas, Denver, Detroit, Houston, Kansas City, Los Angeles, Miami, Philadelphia, Pittsburgh, San Francisco, Seattle, St. Louis, and Washington, D.C.)

In Brussels: SAS Office, Shell Building, 54 Rue Ravenstein; Tourist Information Office, Place de Brouckère; U.S. Embassy, 27 Boulevard du Régent.

Money Matters

Currency: The main monetary unit is the Belgian franc (B.frs.), divided into 100 centimes. 50 francs equal $1, U.S.

Tipping: If not added onto your bill, 15 per cent in restaurants and hotels; 12 per cent in cafés; 15 to 20 per cent for taxis; theaters and cinemas about 5 francs per person; 10 francs per bag for porters. Hairdressers and barbers are tipped 10 per cent of bill.

Climate, Clothing, and Essentials

You will find the climate temperate in Brussels. The average temperature in summer is 65 degrees F. and in winter about 40 degrees F. Snow is rarely seen, except perhaps in the Ardennes; the spring and summer months are lovely. Your raincoat will always come in handy, but make it a warm one in late fall and winter. Dress is conventional but not formal. Laundry and dry cleaning facilities are available throughout the city. Service is good and delivery quick.

Hotels

Hotels throughout Belgium are excellent with high standards of comfort, service, and cleanliness always maintained. There is no shortage of accommodations, but reservations are essential in July and August when the International Trade Fairs take place. De luxe rates for a single room with bath range from 350 to 750 francs, 500 to 1,200 francs, double; moderate rates range from 250 to 400 francs, single, 350 to 500, double; inexpensive hotels charge from 175 to 250 francs, single, 250 to 400 francs, double. There is much overlapping of rates within categories so be sure you understand the charge for any room you take.

DE LUXE: In the de luxe category the *Amigo, Rue de l'Amigo,* is the most modern hotel, just behind the city's famous Grand Place. All rooms have bath and air conditioning and some have radio and television as well. The *Palace Hotel, 13 Place Rogier,* belongs to a chain of luxury hotels and is justly famous. Recently redecorated. *The Westbury, 6 Rue Cardinal Mercier,* is opposite the air terminal, and a new Hilton is under construction.

MODERATE: *Albert I, 10 Place Rogier;* the *Cosmopolite, 5–6 Place Rogier;* the *Splendid, 14 Rue des Croisades;* the *Grand, 37 Blvd. Auspach;* the *Central,* opposite the Bourse, are all first class with moderate first class rates.

INEXPENSIVE: The *Sabot d'Or, 5 Blvd. d'Anvers* and the *Mondial, 23 Avenue des Boulevards,* are inexpensive but adequate hotels. There are also a number of residential hotels and pensions around the city.

Food and Restaurants

Belgian food is justly famous. It is strongly influenced by French cuisine; the specialties are rich and opulent; and there are a number of regional dishes worth scouting for as you travel around the country. Beef, chicken, and all fish and seafood (especially *crevettes*) are of the highest quality; the butter, cream, and cheese are rich and luscious; and such specialties as endive (*witloof*), and Malines asparagus are served everywhere and should be tried. Pastries are unsurpassed anywhere.

Some of the specialties to try while in Belgium include: *waterzooi,* a soup-stew made either with chicken or fish; *carbonades flamandes,* a Flemish-style braised beef in beer; *fricadelles Bruxelloises,* braised steak and endive; eel served either fried, in aspic, or in a green sauce; trout *meunière;* goose with garlic and vegetables; and *boudin,* black or white— a sort of blood sausage that is fried and served with applesauce or grapes. Rabbit with prunes (*lapin aux pruneaux*), and *hochepot,* a Flemish stew, are excellent too. *Ardennes* ham is a real delicacy; mussels are wonderful except in May and June. Steaks such as *chateaubriand* and *tournedos* are excellent too. Try Brussels waffles, Liége rice tarts and cheese tarts. All of the delectable biscuits, macaroons, and cookies are truly mouth-watering. Though all of the country's wine is imported, Belgian beer is wonderful, and there are a number of varieties to try. *Lambic* is a wheat-and-barley-based brew, and *Kriek-Lambic* is the same thing with cherry flavoring.

Le Savoy and *Le Carlton* are two leading restaurants with high standards of food and service. *La Couronne,* facing the Grand' Place, is one of the most lushly elegant restaurants and the food and service are absolutely impeccable. *Le Cygne, Au Grand Chateau,* and *Marius en Provence* are first-rate; if you feel like getting away from downtown crowds, try *Villa Lorraine* at the border of the Bois de la Cambre. *Au Filet de Boeuf* is small and wood paneled and the chicken *waterzooi* is excellent. For seafood try *L'Huîtrière* or *Aux Armes de Bruxelles. Les Six-Jeunes-Hommes* occupies an attractive sixteenth century house, which gives it an interesting atmosphere. *The Rôtisserie Ardennaise* is reasonably priced and very good, and both *Asti* and *Peppino's* specialize in Italian food. *Comme Chez Soi* is friendly and relaxed, and *Ravenstein's* has an interesting medieval setting. If you are hunting for the unusual, eat at *l'Epaule de Mouton,* one of the best restaurants. It's very small—

only nine tables—so make a reservation well in advance. There are also a number of popular tearooms around the area of the Porte Louise.

Night Life, Entertainment, and Special Events

The theater season runs from the end of September to the first of July, though the Théâtre Royal de la Monnaie sometimes offers operettas during the summer. This is Brussels' opera and ballet theater, located at the Place de la Monnaie, opposite the Central Post Office. Popular plays are also presented at the Théâtre Royal du Parc, and the Théâtre des Galeries at the Galeries St. Hubert. Concerts are presented in the Palais des Beaux-Arts and at the Conservatoire Royal de la Musique during the regular theatrical season. For light entertainment try the Cirque Royal, a traditional music hall. The latter two are closed during the summer.

Brussels has several gay night clubs. Most famous is the *Boeuf sur le Toit*. The floor show is lavish and the prices high, but it is worth seeing. The *Crazy Horse Saloon* and *Parisiana* both have floor shows. The *Nouvelle Equipe* has no floor show, but excellent music. It is operated as a club but your passport will open the door. *Memling* is an intimate, smoky, night spot, as is the *Scotch Club*.

SPECIAL EVENTS: The Belgians preserve their old traditions and visitors almost always have a chance to see a holiday procession or national festival, with participants wearing authentic costumes. The *Manneken-Pis* will be dressed in one of his many different costumes on April 6 and 30, September 3, 4 and 5, October 27, and November 20. On or around July 17, the animated *Brussels Kermesse* begins. Since 1311 it has been traditional to plant the so-called *Meiboom* (Maytree) on August 9, while the *Duivelskeruis* begins on August 22. There are a number of folklore events in the smaller villages and towns and you can get a list of these from the Belgian Tourist Offices listed above.

Shopping

The shopping districts of Brussels are on and near the Boulevard Adolphe Max, Boulevard Anspach, Rue Neuve, the Place de Brouckère, and the Place de la Bourse. Belgium is famous for its delicately beautiful lace from Brussels, Bruges, and Malines; its Dinant copperware; Val St.-Lambert crystal; and diamonds cut in Antwerp. Tapestry, porcelain, and chocolates are excellent and comparatively inexpensive here; there are handsome antiques to be had but these are rarely "finds." *Maria Loix* is one of the best shops for lacework, including blouses, while *Delplace* has a world-wide coterie of clients who buy linens from this shop. *Tissages Réunis de Courtrai* has a wide array of fine linens as well.

De Backer Van Camp and *Ritzen* have excellent collections of porcelain and crystal, and Val St.-Lambert has its own shop on the Place Ste. Catherine. The Flea Market or the *Foire des Antiquaires* are fun on Sunday morning. For chocolates try the *Godiva* or *Corne* shops, *Godelaine* or *Neuhaus*. The leading department stores are *Bon Marché, L'Innovation, Galeries Anspach,* and *Magasins de la Bourse.*

Background Reading

Belgium and Luxembourg, by Tudor Edwards
Small Boat through Belgium, by Roger Pilkington
Flemish Painting, published by Skira
Belgium, edited by Jan-Albert Goris

France

PARIS

To have once been Lutèce and to have become Paris . . .
To have been mud and to have become spirit!
—VICTOR HUGO

PARIS sets a standard against which all other cities are measured.
Any city that has beauty, charm, gaiety, and sophistication is dubbed
a Paris of a place. Copenhagen is the Paris of the north, Buenos
Aires, the Paris of South America; Saigon is the Paris of the Orient,
Beirut, the Paris of the Middle East; Penang is the Paris of Malaysia,
and there are more. But only Paris is Paris, the city which, as Casanova said, in spite of its imperfections, is the only true town in the
world, a sentiment shared by all of the Paris-philes from the Roman
Emperor Julian to A. J. Liebling.

The capital of France, with a population of four million, Paris is
the most popular city on earth. And in the museum dedicated to its
history, the Carnavalet that was the home of Madame de Sévigné,
there are over four hundred thousand books with Paris as their subject. Its monuments, buildings, streets, parks, shops, activities, and
diversions are so familiar that even those who come to Paris for the
first time recognize its sights without benefit of guidebooks, just as
Mark Twain did when he arrived there in 1897:

136

In a little while we were speeding through the streets of Paris, and delightfully, recognizing certain names and places with which books had long ago made us familiar. It was like meeting an old friend when we read "Rue de Rivoli" on the street corner; we knew the genuine vast palace of the Louvre as well as we knew its picture; when we passed by the column of July we needed no one to tell us what it was, or to remind us that on its site once stood the grim Bastille, that grave of human hopes and happiness, that dismal prison-house within whose dungeons so many young faces put on the wrinkles of age, so many proud spirits grew humble, so many brave hearts broke.

We secured rooms at the hotel, or rather, we had three beds put into one room, so that we might be together, and then we went out to a restaurant, just after lamp-lighting, and ate a comfortable, satisfactory, lingering dinner. It was a pleasure to eat where everything was so tidy, the food so well cooked, the waiters so polite, and the coming and departing company so moustached, so frisky, so affable, so fearfully and wonderfully French-y! All the surroundings were gay and enlivening. Two hundred people sat at little tables on the sidewalk, sipping wine and coffee; the streets were thronged with light vehicles and with joyous pleasure-seekers; there was music in the air, life and action, all about us, and a conflagration of gaslight everywhere.

Paris has the world's number one travel-poster landmark, the 1,000-foot-high, steel-ribbed Eiffel Tower, topped by its waving red, white, and blue *tricolor*. No streets anywhere are more familiar looking than the Rue de la Paix with its shops and cafés, the Palace de l'Opéra with its sprawling heap of an opera house, and the Champs-Élysées, that great avenue with eight traffic lanes and two broad island promenades banked with horse chestnut trees, leading from Napoleon's Palace de la Concorde to the whirlpool of traffic that eddies around the Arc de Triomphe. Begun as a triumphal arch for Napoleon and his armies in 1806, this granite gateway with its eternal flame honoring France's Unknown Soldier, may well be the world's number two landmark, and from its top (as from atop the Eiffel Tower) one can gaze over this vast, mellow tapestry of a city. As you look out over its skyline of charcoal chimneypots and slate-gray rooftops, the mauve and pewter patina of its antique stone walls, the leafy green parks and the broad, straight *grand' boulevards,* down along the Seine where the Ile de la Cité with its prow of willows seems to drift like a huge ocean liner, you can begin to understand how its diffused silken light inspired impressionists like Renoir,

Monet, Sisley, and Manet, and most of all on a dewy summer morning, the *pointilliste* technique of Seurat. As Paris' sights need no guides so her beauty needs no poets, though she has had them by the thousands.

The Louvre, the vast complex of royal palaces built between the sixteenth and nineteenth centuries, is the best known museum anywhere. It contains the world's most famous painting, the Mona Lisa, purchased by François I from Leonardo da Vinci when the Italian painter lived in France, and two of the world's most popular sculptures, the Venus de Milo and the headless toga-clad figure of the Winged Victory of Samothrace, along with thousands of other art treasures, famous and obscure. Notre Dame, with its stained-glass rose windows, its gargoyles, and the flying buttresses that arch over the green trees on the Ile de la Cité, is probably known to more people than Rome's St. Peter's, as is the ghostly cloud of the Sacré-Coeur, the fantastic church that looms over the city from the top of the *butte* of Montmartre. Paris even boasts the world's most famous restaurant, Maxim's, and the hotel on the fashionable Place Vendôme, begun by César Ritz, is the original of Ritz hotels everywhere. No street of iniquity has a reputation more widespread than the Rue Pigalle, no girlie show is better known than that of the Folies-Bergère, no section of any city is so synonymous with bohemia as the Latin Quarter. This is the student section of Paris that centers around the Place St. Michel and the Sorbonne, the university begun by Louis IX—St. Louis—in the thirteenth century. Here, in the Middle Ages, lectures were given in classical Latin, hence the quarter's name.

Women who come to Paris from any corner of the world (and others who will only dream of seeing it), know the names of its *couturiers,* of Chanel, Dior, and Balenciaga, the labels of its great perfumes, and the hallmarks of its jewelers. No bargain junk fair has the status of the Flea Market, Le Marché aux Puces, that is open on Friday, Saturday, and Sunday, and no produce market draws tourists as does Les Halles. It is doubtful that anyone visiting Paris needs a guidebook to tell him that, from two to five in the morning, this market with its garden pyramids of fruits and vegetables, its fish stalls, and its butchershops where hang sides of meat looking just like those painted by Soutine, is one of the liveliest places in the city. And it is hard to imagine anyone not knowing about the late-night onion soup with its thick topping of toasted gruyère cheese that is Les Halles' specialty.

Throughout its history Paris has been a haven for lovers, of fact or fiction. There are the anonymous lovers of whom Edith Piaf sang, *Les Amants de Paris,* who stroll beside the Seine, who hold hands in the Métro, who dream in the gardens of the Tuileries and Luxembourg as they watch youngsters sail boats across the tiny lakes, who kiss good-night endlessly on its lamp-lit street corners and in its darkened doorways. Paris was the setting for the love affairs of Rodolpho and Mimi, of Héloïse and Abélard, of George Sand and Chopin, of Voltaire and his Emilie. And it is the only city that takes in its stride the institution known as *cinq à sept,* the evening hours from five to seven, when husbands meet with their mistresses and wives with their lovers, a system probably not necessary when the Parisian *ménage à trois* was more commonplace than it is today. Small wonder that a city so full of romance, of feminine beauty and guile has been called by Van Dyke "a woman's town, with flowers in her hair."

Paris has had one long love affair with its river, the Seine, more famous than the Thames or the Tiber, the Hudson or the Mississippi. "The Seine has gone a-wooing, and it's Paris that she loves . . ." says the words of an old popular song, and it's a sentiment that is returned. The charms of this river have been eulogized by almost every poet, novelist, essayist, painter, and lyricist who ever lived in the city. It is a country river, gentle and easy-going, a river edged with willow trees that turn its waters a delicate yellow-green in spring, deep emerald in summer, golden-topaz in fall, and etch it with reflections of wispy bare branches in winter, like the lines in a steel engraving. When Julius Caesar took this city from the Parisii tribe in 54 B.C., it was called by its Celtic name, *Lutetia,* "a dwelling in the midst of waters," for it comprised only what is now the Ile de la Cité. The city's motto even today is *Fluctuar nec mergitur*—it floats and does not founder, and as Blake Ehrlich reminds us in his beautiful book, the city's full name is Paris-sur-Seine, Paris on the Seine.

The history and destiny of Paris is as intimately entwined with its river as is the city itself. The Seine supplies Paris with its main avenues of commerce, much of its livelihood, and some of its most picturesque vignettes: the bookstalls along the quays, the lower-level walks where the city steps down to the riverbanks, the fishermen who use the longest poles imaginable to catch what surely must be imaginary fish, barges where the captains' families hang laundry out to dry, the *bateaux-mouches* excursion boats, and the thirty-two bridges that tie the city together. The most elaborate is the Pont Alexandre III, built at the turn of the century, all decked out with wildly baroque lanterns and gilded statuary. The Pont-Neuf is the most monumental and historic, built on the site of other "New Bridges" destroyed through Paris' turbulent history. Completed in the seventeenth century reign of Henri IV, it became one of the leading centers of Parisian life and remained so for two hundred years. It was said that you could not cross this bridge without seeing a monk, a harlot, and a white horse.

The Seine is, as Blake Ehrlich describes it, "one long, lovely park curving through the center of Paris." It seems more a unifying seam than a divider between the Rive Gauche—the Left Bank of Bohemia, inexpensive *bistros,* the student and artist quarters, and the tiny, smoky nighttime *boîtes*—and the Rive Droite—the Right Bank, with its expensive residential sections, its grand hotels, fashionable streets and shops, elegant promenades, smart cafés, and restaurants.

But Paris, they say, is not what it used to be, though "they" apparently have been saying that almost since the city began, some two thousand years ago. The pages of its history are brightly illuminated with countless golden ages, yet everyone who knew the city in his youth comes back to it in his middle age to bemoan the changes that have taken place, certain it is the city that is different and not himself. But in fact, if one were to flip back through these same pages and read what has been written about the city in every century he would realize that the miracle of Paris is that it has changed so little. To the outside world it still represents exactly what it always has—a symbol of light and enlightenment, of charm, beauty, gaiety and freedom, a city that is still a mecca for the young, and an unparalleled catalyst between the creative artist and his talent. Even the briefest look at Paris' history shows us the timelessness of its appeal and the many old accounts still act as modern guides.

Those who knew Paris just after World War II and go back today say it is not what it was when it was bright with the first flushes of liberation, when its intellectual life bristled with such writers as Camus, and the existentialists, Sartre and De Beauvoir, whose admiring coteries gathered to watch their idols talk and write at the Café

Deux Magots. But those who were young in the poor but protean Parisian atmosphere of the thirties as described by Henry Miller and George Orwell, would have found the forties tame—shy of spirit and short on talent, and they might remind you that in spite of the Depression, their city was alluring enough to seduce George Gershwin and thousands of other Americans in Paris. The thirties, in turn, would have seemed like dull days to those who were caught up in the Paris of the twenties, when it was the haven of the lost generation and the home of writers such as Gertrude Stein and her companion Alice B. Toklas, of Hemingway, Thornton Wilder, Fitzgerald, James Joyce, and the other literary lights that focused on Sylvia Beach's bookshop, "Shakespeare & Co." And in the twenties, the cafés of Montparnasse— the Dôme, the Rotunda, and the Coupole—had their heyday as the favored haunts of such artists as Picasso, Braque, Vlaminck, Picabia, Dérain, Matisse, Rouault, De Segonzac—the modern painters who now enjoy the stature of old masters. But Paris, they say, is not what it was in the twenties; and yet Elliot Paul's description of the section of the city he knew and loved is a valid guide today if anyone were willing to get up early enough to check it out:

At dawn, the sun rising behind the cathedral, Notre Dame de Paris, sent its first feeble rays directly down the rue de la Huchette to be reflected from the windows of the place St. Michel. A few yards away, running almost parallel to the little street, the southern branch of the Seine skirted the Ile de la Cité, and on its yellow-brown waters, in which clouds were mirrored upside down, laden barges drifted, from the north of France and Belgium, bound for Rouen and Le Havre. The Latin quarter and the Cluny lay eastward; across the river stood the grim Conciergerie, the bleak and vast Hôtel Dieu, or city hospital, and the Palais de Justice.

In the place St. Michel with its dripping fountain and stone dolphins, the café de la Gare was the first to open, to take care of early customers who arrived by underground railroad from Versailles and the workers of the neighborhood who snatched their coffee and *croissants* at the corner before descending into the Métro, near the entrance of which stood a dingy international newsstand, with a profusion of provincial and local French papers on sale as well as Paris journals.*

Yet even in the roaring twenties, there would have been those who mourned for Paris in its pre-World War I days, when the Utrillo-

* From *The Last Time I Saw Paris,* by Elliot Paul, Copyright 1942, Random House, Inc. Reprinted by permission.

esque section, Montmartre, was the city's art center, and the *salons* were just beginning to show the works of cubists and surrealists. And though Colette set her romantic story of Chéri and Léa in the Paris of 1910, one cannot help but think that the author herself might have missed the earlier Paris of the *fin de siècle,* which she knew when her husband, M. Willy, first brought her to this city, locked her in a room, and forced her to write the stories he passed off as his own. For in spite of such personal tragedy, it was a gay and gorgeous Paris to see. France had recently acquired a new African empire, the Baron Haussmann had just finished his *grand' boulevards* after gouging out some of the city's most antique quarters, and the Eiffel Tower had only recently been built for the Great Exhibition of 1889. The British Prince of Wales, the future Edward VII, officially opened the tower by making the first ascent to the top in the elevator that may well have swayed and creaked then as it does now. This was the lyrical *Gaieté Parisienne* of the can-can, of cafés and music halls like the Moulin Rouge, Bal Tabarin, and Maxim's, of stars like May Belfort and Bruant, names remembered now mostly because they were the subjects of posters by Toulouse-Lautrec. The great writers of the day were Emile Zola, Pierre Loti, and Anatole France, and the younger talents were Paul Valéry, André Gide, and Marcel Proust, who had not published anything yet but who was a well-known figure often seen in the *salons* Colette frequented.

This turn-of-the-century Paris also captivated such American writers as Richard Harding Davis, who observed:

Paris is the only city in the world which the visitor from the outside world positively refuses to take seriously. He may come to Paris to study art, or to investigate the intricacies of French law, or the historical changes in the city; or, if it be a woman, she may come to choose a trousseau; but no matter how serious his purposes may be, there is always one part of each day when the visitor rests from his labours and smiles indulgently and does as the Parisians do. Americans go to London for social triumph or to float railroad shares, to Rome for art's sake, and to Berlin to study music and to economize; but they go to Paris to enjoy themselves.

Apparently the rest of the world has changed even more than Paris has, for it is doubtful that any Americans today go to London, Rome, or Berlin for the reasons outlined by Davis, though thousands still go to Paris every year primarily "to enjoy themselves."

And if any of today's young artists who have come to the Latin Quarter from homes all over the world think their dreams, hopes, ambitions, joys, conversations, and opinions are strictly modern, utterly *avant-garde,* and all their own, they should read *Trilby,* George du Maurier's novel of Parisian Bohemian life under the Third Republic. Doubtless they would be surprised, if not downright discouraged, to learn how closely their lives and thoughts and diversions parallel those of Du Maurier's three budding English artists, the Laird, Little Billee, and Taffy.

And you hobnobbed with models, male and female, students of law and medicine, painters and sculptors, workmen and *blanchisseuses* and *grisettes,* and found them very good company, and most improving of your French . . . And then they would, arm-in-arm, descend the Rue de Seine and cross a bridge to the Cité, and have a look in at the Morgue. Then back again to the quays on the *rive gauche* by the Pont-Neuf, to wend their way westward; now on one side to look at the print and picture shops and the *magasins* of bric-à-brac, and happily sometimes buy thereof, now on the other to finger and cheapen the second-hand books for sale on the parapet, and even pick up one or two utterly unwanted bargains, never to be read or opened again.

When they reached the Pont des Arts they would cross it, stopping in the middle to look up the river towards the old Cité and Notre Dame, eastward, and dream unutterable things, and try to utter them. Then, turning westward, they would gaze at the glowing sky and all it glowed upon—the corner of the Tuileries and the Louvre, the many bridges, the Chamber of Deputies. . . .

. . . Then, still arm-in-arm and chatting gaily, across the courtyard of the Louvre, through gilded gates well guarded by reckless imperial Zouaves, up the arcaded Rue de Rivoli as far as the Rue Castiglione, where they would stare with greedy eyes at the window of the great corner pastry-cook, and marvel at the beautiful assortment of bonbons, *pralines, dragées, marrons glacés*—saccharine, crystalline substances of all kinds and colours, as charming to look at as an illumination; precious stones, delicately-frosted sweets, pearls and diamonds so arranged as to melt in the mouth; especially, at this particular time of the year, the monstrous Easter-eggs, of enchanting hue, enshrined like costly jewels in caskets of satin and gold; and the Laird, who was well read in his English classics and liked to show it, would opine that "they managed these things better in France."

Then across the street by a great gate into the Allée des Feuillants, and up to the Place de la Concorde—to gaze, but quite without base envy, at the smart people coming back from the Bois de Boulogne. For even in Paris "carriage people" have a way of looking bored, or taking their pleasure sadly, of having nothing to say to each other, as though the vibration of so many wheels all rolling home the same way every afternoon had hypnotised them into silence, idiocy, and melancholia.

And then a stroll on the crowded, well-lighted boulevards, and a bock at the café there, at a little three-legged marble table right out on the genial asphalt side pavement, still talking nineteen to the dozen.

Then home by dark, old silent streets and some deserted bridge to their beloved Latin Quarter, the Morgue gleaming cold and still and fatal in the pale lamplight, and Notre Dame pricking up its watchful twin towers, which have looked down for so many centuries on so many happy, sanguine, expansive youths walking arm-in-arm by twos and threes, and for ever talking, talking, talking— . . .

Or again, if it rained, and Paris through the studio window loomed lead-coloured, with its shiny slate roofs under skies that were ashen and sober, and the wild west wind made woeful music among the chimney-pots, and little gay waves ran up the river the wrong way. . . .

. . . Little Billee, taking with him three francs (or even four), would dive into back streets and buy a yard or so of crusty new bread, well burned on the flat side, a fillet of beef, a litre of wine, potatoes and onions, butter, a little cylindrical cheese called "bonbon de Neufchâtel," tenderly curly lettuce, with chervil, parsley, spring onions, and other fine herbs, and a pod of garlic, which would be rubbed on a crust of bread to flavour things with . . .

And after dinner, what coffee, roasted and ground on the spot, what pipes and cigarettes of *caporal,* by the light of the three shaded lamps, while the rain beat against the big north window, and the wind went howling round the quaint old mediaeval tower at the corner of the Rue Vieille des Trois Mauvais Ladres (the old street of the three bad lepers), and the damp logs hissed and crackled in the stove!

What jolly talk into the small hours! Thackeray and Dickens again, and Tennyson and Byron (who was "not deed yet" in those days); and Titian and Velasquez, and young Millais and Holman Hunt (just out); and Monsieur Ingres and Monsieur Delacroix, and Balzac and Stendhal and George Sand; and the good Dumas! and Edgar Allan Poe; and the glory that was Greece and the grandeur that was Rome . . .

Details change, of course—prices rise, restaurants acquire new owners, students dance the Twist instead of the can-can, automobiles replace carriages, and café gossip centers around new writers and artists, though the gossip itself remains pretty much the same. But, surprisingly enough, anyone who has ever written a loving account of his life in this city has touched upon the play of light in its parks and on the gray stone walls of its buildings; it delicate beauty in sun or rain; the historic sights; its food and cafés; and that very special spirit that has inspired the young of so many generations to go "talking, talking, talking . . ." and thinking that they have found out things that nobody else ever found out before. . . .

When, after all, was Paris "what it was"? Was it perhaps at its best as the triumphant city of Napoleon, or was it most exciting and inspiring in the eighteenth century when the cry of "liberty, equality, fraternity" was the death knell of the monarchy? And this spirited Paris of Voltaire and Rousseau was the city such American emissaries as Benjamin Franklin and Thomas Jefferson grew to love.

Or was it at its true golden age in the seventeenth century, with such kings as Henri IV, who built the elegant, formal Place Royale, now the Place des Vosges, Louis XIII and his aides Richelieu and Mazarin, and the *grand siècle* of Louis XIV, the Sun King, and his glittering court at Versailles. The Place Royale was the center of Parisian intellectual life in that century, and the setting of its most influential salons, where writers like Racine, La Rochefoucauld, and La Bruyère were lionized, and which Molière ridiculed so brilliantly in his play *Les Précieuses Ridicules*.

The sixteenth century was the time of the French renaissance, when Paris was the home of Rabelais, and the Louvre was rebuilt by François I, a project carried on by his son, Henri II.

To be sure, not all of Paris' history is sweetness and light. Its contentious, demonstrative, volatile citizenry has revolted and barricaded the streets many times, most notably in 1789, 1830, 1848, and 1871, when the Communists burned the palace of the Tuileries. The recent rash of *plastique* bombings over the fate of Algeria hints that this spirit is still alive. Paris was defended against Attila the Hun by St. Geneviève in 451, and during the eighth and ninth centuries was devastated five times by the Normans, who sailed up the Seine and sacked it, while France's capital was at Aix-la-Chapelle where Charlemagne had moved it. After Agincourt the English took Paris and all of France and held it for a century until Joan of Arc turned the tide that made France free.

Not even Robespierre would long for Paris during the Reign of

Terror that followed the Revolution of 1789, for though he was the inspiration for its bloody activities, the hysterical mobs he led finally turned on him and sent him to the guillotine. And when the Germans laid siege to Paris during the Franco-Prussian War the starved citizenry was reduced to eating the animals in the zoos.

But in spite of the several dark ages it has lived through, one gets the feeling that someone has always been mourning for a lost Paris. Perhaps if Julian had returned to the city as it was in the twelfth and thirteenth centuries, when it was the center of European thought and learning, or to the fifth century Paris of the Frankish king, Clovis, he would have been in a fit of despair over the changes time had wrought in his "dear Lutetia."

Undoubtedly a good many of those four hundred thousand books about Paris in the Carnavalet Museum try to explain the Parisians. They can be the most courteous and delightful people in the world, or the most maddening; people who paint "Americans Go Home" on the walls along the Seine one year, and the next year turn their city upside down to welcome a young American President and his French-speaking wife. They have been loved and hated with equal fervor by almost every foreigner who has lived in their city: loved because "the Parisians mind their own business and don't care how you live your life," hated because "the Parisians ignore you and don't care what happens to you"—attributes that are probably opposite sides of the same coin. Most of the world's artists, writers, and Bohemians-at-large have felt it worthwhile suffering from the second side of the Parisian personality to be blessed with the freedom made possible by the first.

In wandering around the sections that make up most of the world's large cities, one is struck by the sharp contrasts between them. In Paris, one is struck by the harmony. Whether you are lunching in Montmartre's little tree-filled square, the Place du Tertre, or listening to the songs of its *chansonniers* in a smoky *boîte,* or watching a flamenco dancer in one of the pocket-sized night clubs near the Odéon; whether you are shopping for fine leather goods, perfumes, or clothing in the luxury shops of the Faubourg St. Honoré, or digging through dusty antique shops around the Rue du Bac; whether you are strolling around the quiet seventeenth century quays and streets of the Ile St. Louis, where rents are the highest in the city, or picking your way through the dark winding streets and lopsided houses that tumble down from the *butte* of Montmartre to the Marais and Les Halles—you will find each area stamped with a tone and style that is strictly Parisian.

And throughout these sections are the wonderful sights of the city, sprinkled liberally like flecks of truffles in a Strasbourg *pâté*. For every famous *place*, church, museum, and monument in this city, there are two less well known but no less interesting. In addition to such great squares as the Place de la Concorde, with its obelisk and fountains, its view of the symmetrical arcaded buildings of the Rue de Rivoli and that Greek temple of a church, the Madeleine, there is the exquisite Place des Vosges in the Marais, an antique backwater that is a catchall of French history, a section with almost one hundred fine mansions dating from the seventeenth century. The Palais Royal was built by Cardinal Richelieu when he was at the peak of his power. Here, seventeenth century arcaded buildings center on their own little park, a quiet leafy island in the middle of Paris' noise and activity. Louis XIV lived here for a while before he was king as did many other crowned heads of France and Europe. Alexandre Dumas and Colette were among its other renowned residents and anyone who has read Colette's charming essay, "Paris from My Window" will be prepared for the appeal of this place. The Comédie Française is on this square, the theater Colette loved to visit, and so is the handsome Grand Véfour, a restaurant decorated with Empire paneling and wall paintings, whose proprietor, M. Oliver, used to carry Colette down for dinner when arthritis made it impossible for her to walk.

In addition to Notre Dame, the Madeleine, and the Sacré-Coeur, no one should miss the Sainte-Chapelle, a fragile jewel box of a church built by Louis IX to house a fragment of the Crown of Thorns. Its second-floor chapel is one of the most dazzling sights in all of Europe, with stained-glass windows of the smallest bits and pieces sparkling with color and brilliance so that the effect is somewhat like being inside a kaleidoscope. St. Germain-des-Prés is the oldest church in Paris, a Romanesque building with parts that date back to the eleventh century, and it was here that Charlemagne, when he was eight years old, held his candle in the procession and marveled at the ritual. St. Sévérin is a huge Gothic church that seems to crowd out the narrow university streets near the Sorbonne, and St. Julien-Le-Pauvre, not far away, is an almost pathetic, strangely moving church, used for Catholic services according to the Byzantine rite. And anyone interested in French history should travel just a little away from the center of the city, to St. Denis, with its royal crypts, and try to imagine what a ghoulish nightmare it must have been after the Revolution when crazed mobs burst in and dumped all of the corpses of their kings into lime pits, including their favorites Henri of Navarre and the Sun King.

It is doubtful that anyone going to Paris will miss seeing the room after room full of treasure in the Louvre, but the Paris museum story cannot be told in that single chapter, lengthy though it may be. There is its wonderful Museum of Modern Art, and, practically across the street in the Palais de Chaillot, the anthropological Museum of Man, and the folk art museum. There is a lovely collection of clear, sunny impressionist paintings in the Jeu de Paume, and changing exhibitions at the Orangerie, and at least two dozen other museums devoted to various art periods, coins, and instruments of war, the history of Paris, antique jewelry, ceramics, natural history, and Chinese vases. The homes of Balzac, Delacroix, and Victor Hugo have been turned into museums and at the Musée Rodin you can see the thirty-two statues of Balzac which the sculptor created before he produced one that satisfied him.

One of the most unique museums of Paris is the Cluny. The building, erected in 1490, was the palace of the abbots of Cluny. Its crenelated walls, octagonal tower, graceful openwork balcony, and windows decorated with stone shells (the symbol of the pilgrims) make an appropriate setting for a magnificent collection of medieval art and tapestries that are world-famous.

Cemeteries do not usually find a place on a tourist's itinerary, but in Paris that, too, is an exception. Even the city's burial places seem to have a special charm and dreamy quality, and on their worn gravestones are the names of many greats of French history and art. In the cemetery that hugs the side of Montmartre are the graves of Berlioz, Nijinsky, the Lady of the Camellias, Henry Murger, Gautier, and Heine; and behind the high stone walls of the cemetery of Montparnasse is the grave of Baudelaire and at least a dozen other artists and writers. Héloïse and Abélard, Sarah Bernhardt, Oscar Wilde, Balzac, Delacrois, La Fontaine, Molière, Alfred de Musset, Rossini, Chopin, and Sydney Smith lie in Père Lachaise. The tomb of Lafayette is in the cemetery of Pipcus, and, as everyone must know, the grotesque, grandiose red porphry tomb of Napoleon stands in the rotunda of the domed Hôtel des Invalides, while in the Panthéon are the tombs of such famous Frenchmen as Victor Hugo, Rousseau, Braille, Voltaire, and Zola.

Ruins of the Roman arena, ancient catacombs that were burial crypts, a tour of the sewers, or a session of classes at the world's most respected cooking school, Le Cordon Bleu—all of these are among the varied sights and activities in this city. And besides Paris' own beauties and wonders there is the countryside of the Ile de France, one of the loveliest provinces within the 213,000 square miles of this country—with forests, châteaux, rivers, and royal palaces that have inspired painters from Corot to Renoir.

The magnificent palaces and gardens of Fontainebleau and Versailles, the charming Petit Trianon where Marie Antoinette and her court friends played at being shepherdesses, Josephine's home, Malmaison, still blooming with the rose gardens she loved, Rambouillet, the château of Catherine de Médicis—all are easy to reach and see in a day's excursion from Paris. There are many interesting things to see also in the suburbs around the city. At Chantilly you may visit the royal château where the chef Vatel killed himself because the fish failed to arrive for a dinner he planned to serve Louis XIV. Now the Musée Condé, the prize treasure here is the richly illuminated calendar manuscript, the fifteenth century "Hours" of the Duc de Berri. Beauvais is worthwhile for its soaring, unfinished sixteenth century Gothic cathedral. From Paris, too, you can visit the World War I battlefields—Marne, Meaux, and Château-Thierry—en route to Reims, the capital of the champagne country, which has one of France's most inspiring Gothic cathedrals, and, on the way back, stop at Guermantes, of which Proust wrote with such detail and tenderness.

The twelfth century cathedral of Chartres has what many experts consider the finest stained-glass windows in the world, and this city is the gateway to all of the gracious châteaux in the Loire Valley. Among the handsomest of these are Amboise, where Da Vinci is buried in a small stone chapel, Blois, Chenonceaux, Chinon, Chaumont, and Chambord, each with its own romantic legends and souvenirs, each with a brief chapter of its own to add to the history of France.

But no matter which of France's beautiful provinces you visit, you will probably find that its capital is its heart and soul, and in this case some forty-six million Frenchmen will agree with you. The longer you know Paris the more you will understand Victor Hugo's tribute to it:

Cities are bibles of stone. This city possesses no single dome, roof, or pavement which does not convey some message of alliance and of union, and which does not offer some lesson, example, or advice. Let the people of all the world come to this prodigious alphabet of monuments, of tombs, and of trophies to learn peace and to unlearn the meaning of hatred. Let them be confident. For Paris has proven itself. To have once been Lutèce and to have become Paris—what could be a more magnificent symbol! To have been mud and to have become spirit!

NICE

The queen of the côte d'azur

JUST as Paris is a yardstick against which all other cities are measured, so France's Côte d'Azur sets a standard for seaside resorts. Almost every country that has a strip of sand and surf beaches of which it is particularly proud calls this its "riviera." But this flowery pocket of Provence, the azure coast that winds west along the Mediterranean littoral from Menton to St. Raphäel, is *the* Riviera, the world's most luxurious, most famous international seaside playground. It is a setting straight out of a Dufy water color, complete with cobalt-blue sea and sky, glossy green date palms and airy umbrella pines, houses done up in sugar white or the strawberry pink that is a Provençal favorite, flashes of vermilion and lipstick-red in awnings, flowers, and brick garden paths. Gaily colored yachting flags and white or sun-red sails cut across the sapphire sea and the narrow sand and pebble beaches are strewn with sun-tanned, bikini-clad bodies. Vacationers in pastel sports clothes come and go along the promenades like restless butterflies, and, when the sun goes down, the whole midnight-blue strip glitters with the activities of its cabarets and casinos.

The Riviera owes its greatest treasure—its climate—to the Alpes Maritimes, the mountains that tower behind it, walling out the cold winds that sweep down across Europe from Lapland, walling in the balmy breezes that drift up from Africa. The result is this semitropical garden with a year-round calendar of flowers that includes bougainvillaea, hibiscus, violets, wild anemones, asphodels, eucalyptus, red-flowering cacti, tuberoses, the roses of Grasse, rose-laurel, and the hybrid blue roses of Antibes. Cannes holds a festival to celebrate its feathery green mimosa trees with their downy, yellow puff-ball flowers, and Nice is noted for the clove-scented carnations that grow in the fields around it. The warm air is perfumed with rosemary, lavender, and thyme, and the mountain slopes are terraced with orange, mandarin, lemon, and olive groves. In late January and February, the almond, apricot, plum, and peach orchards are fairylands of blossoms.

No wonder Nice has made so much of its candied fruits and flower petals; no wonder that the little hill town of Grasse with its Fragonard museum has become the world's leading producer of floral perfume oils. One of the most picturesque sights in the area is this lovely town in spring and summer, when the daily carloads of blossoms arrive at the distilleries to be processed.

Many great artists have been drawn to this gentle, easy climate and have been inspired by it, leaving samples of their work in the dozens of museums dotted through these towns. Renoir lived in Cagnes, where the museum that was a medieval castle-fortress houses a collection of his works, along with others by Chagall, Kisling, and Carzou. Bonnard had a house in Le Cannet, and Braque another in St. Paul. Matisse, who spent the last years of his life in Nice, designed the simple, sunny Dominican chapel in Vence, where stained-glass windows paint the plaster-white walls with splashes of blue and yellow reflections all day long. Young artists from Paris still spend summers in this leafy, quiet town with its sleepy little square.

Picasso, who lives near Cannes, worked in Antibes, where many of his paintings hang in the fourteenth century Grimaldi Castle, and the brilliantly colored pottery he designed has put the kilns of Vallauris back in business in a big way. Léger worked at Biot and there is an entire museum dedicated to his works here. Chagall spent a great deal of time all along the Riviera and like other artists who worked here, dipped his brush into the Provençal palette of blue-green-vermilion-pink-orange-yellow for paintings of the Côte d'Azur landscape.

One of the most delightful ways to see works of many of these painters is to take an afternoon drive to St. Paul, the medieval walled town up in the Alpes Maritimes, not far from Vence. Here narrow stepped streets wind between whitewashed houses with black shuttered windows. Here you may lunch on richly delectable Provençal specialties at one of the most beautiful restaurants in France, the Colombe d'Or, where white doves strut on a garden terrace that is covered with powdered terracotta. But in addition to its food, this restaurant is famous for its art collection. Most of the great modern painters who worked in this area when they were young and struggling were friends of the proprietor, and he fed them in exchange for paintings, since they lacked the more usual, more elusive currency. The ceramic mural by Léger against the garden wall is one of the outstanding treasures in the group.

The durable, inspired poet-playwright-painter, Jean Cocteau, did the mystical surrealist frescoes in the Fishermen's Chapel of Villefranche-sur-Mer, and also designed the marriage chapel in the Town Hall of the hotly tropical Menton, the last outpost of France before one steps over into Italy. Not far away is St. Jean-Cap Ferrat, where Somerset Maugham lives, and where the local museum shows works of Fragonard, Boucher, and Sisley along with its collection of Beauvais Gobelins, and Aubusson tapestries, Chinese scrolls and Korean screens, Sèvres porcelain, and Italian Renaissance paintings.

Twenty-six harbor resort towns are strung out along the seventy miles of this Riviera coastline. Each has its own personality and attractions, its own loyal coterie of vacationers. Of these, the most slickly fashionable, slickly expensive, is Cannes, the haven of the international jet-set. Some of the world's most lavish yachts drop anchor in Cannes' semicircle of a harbor. Its main promenade, La Croisette, is lined with smart shops and hotels and decked out with flags of all nations, to welcome visitors who come to see the city's annual regatta, its mimosa fair, its Palm Beach Casino, and, in spring, its film festival, perhaps the most influential anywhere. The pretty garden sea towns of Juan-les-Pins and Cap d'Antibes hark back to their Great Gatsby heydays, and the beach at "Juan" is the best along the Riviera, a seashore resort that is surprisingly short on good beaches.

But the largest city, the capital, and the undisputed queen of the Côte d'Azur, is Nice, with a population of three hundred thousand—the sixth largest city in France, and after Paris, the most popular. It is a graceful, gracious, *grande dame* of a pleasure city, that reached its golden age at the turn of the century when it was the favorite resort of royalty: the Windsors, the Romanovs, and the Hapsburgs, Brazilian princes, Indian maharajahs, and the sheikhs of Araby. The sprawling hillside villas half hidden by palm fronds and flowering vines, and the huge white wedding-cake hotels—the Ruhl and the Negresco—take one back to the days of glass conservatories and potted ferns, rose silk lampshades, and the kind of *fin de siécle* world Cecil Beaton recreated for the film *Gigi*—all eloquent reminders of Nice's romantic, regal past.

Because Nice is known as a resort, few visitors take it seriously as a city. Just as few venture far beyond the *Promenade des Anglais,* the wide, palm-lined avenue that curves around the bright blue Bay of Angels, to find the real city that lies behind the façade of gleaming white hotels, so hardly any vacationers will forego the pleasures of the cabanas, cabarets, and casinos to delve into the city's past. Yet that past is long and colorful and is the key to the tone, quality, and character of the city itself.

For though Nice reached the peak of its splendor just about a century ago, it is actually two thousand years old, founded by the Phocian Greeks. They named it *Nike,* after their goddess of victory, and the name stuck, though Nice has since changed hands many times. The Romans succeeded the Greeks in 154 B.C. and built themselves an administrative and military center at Cimiez, remains of which can still be seen today. With the fall of the Roman empire, Nice attached itself to the French *comté de Provence;* in 1388 it chose to join the Ligurian duchy of Savoy, and was not reunited with France until 1860. But the indelible Italo-Gallic stamp was on this city, which is, in fact, one big, richly flavored Italian stew, served forth with all the refinements that might be imparted to it by a French chef. This is as true of the city's architecture as it is of its cuisine; both clearly show their

Genoese origins. Almost every dish that is a Niçoise specialty has a slightly heavier, more exuberant original in Genoa: the *ratatouille* that is an Italianate Provençal stew of eggplants, zucchini, green peppers, tomatoes, onions, garlic, and olive oil; the local pizza, called *pissaladière,* with a purée of onions and strips of anchovies and black olives on a slab of a bread base; the vermicelli-fish soup *bourride;* the ravioli and the versions of the dried stockfish that is an Italian favorite; and the vegetable soup *pistou* is enriched with the classic *pesto* sauce of garlic, olive oil, cheese, and basil, just as is the standard Genoese minestrone.

In the same way, the buildings that rim Nice's Place Masséna reflect the Italian style, great massive dark-red façades with spinach-green shutters and street arcades that provide cool and shady respites from the hot summer sun. Named after Napoleon's marshal who was born in Nice, this nineteenth century square with its lovely Albert I garden is the heart of the city's modern town, with the casino and fountain the only really contemporary things about it. The Quai des Etats-Unis, which preceded the Promenade des Anglais as the city's fashionable esplanade, stretches in front of the modern town and the labyrinth of the Vieille Ville, the old town, where the overtones of Italy are strongest. It is here that you find the beautiful flower market, a veritable garden of stalls, the colorful fruit and vegetable markets, and close to the old port where Garibaldi was born, the fish market. Here the cruise ships line up at the docks, alongside the smaller excursion boats that sail regularly to Corsica, itself a French-Italian *pastiche.*

The old town is full of seventeenth century buildings done in the grand Genoese style, most notable among them the Palais Lascaris, the St. Réparate Cathedral, and the Church of Jésu, perhaps the loveliest of all with its baroque trimmings. Roman ruins and languid palms trim the Château, the hill where Nice was founded. In the suburb of Cimiez, on the edge of the city, are reminders of some of the famous foreign visitors who have come to Nice and been enchanted by it: the Romans, who left remnants of their baths and arenas; Queen Victoria, whose statue stands in front of the Hotel Regina where she stayed in the winters from 1895 to 1899; and the czars, whose villa is still guarded by the gilded double-eagle gates.

If anyone doubts that Nice remembers its Italian heritage, he will be convinced to the contrary when he finds out that here "*si*" is heard for "yes" instead of "*oui,*" and when he discovers the Niçoise love for music that shows itself in the streets named after Meyerbeer, Paganini, Mozart, Rossini, Verdi, and Berlioz.

Three *corniches* lead east from Nice to Monaco, through the Alpine foothills. The highest of these, the Grande Corniche, is a breath-taking cliffside road that winds and bends past belvederes that look over slopes covered with silvery-green olive trees, out across the opalescent sea toward Africa. The lowest, the Baisse Corniche, is a seaside road that passes through the pretty towns of St. Jean-Cap Ferrat, Ville-franche-sur-Mer, Beaulieu, and Cap d'Ail, the best choice, perhaps, for those who want to see the museums and stop for lunch along the way. But to many travelers the middle road, the Moyenne Corniche, is the best of all to take. It offers a panoramic view of the sea and countryside only slightly less dazzling than that of the Grande Cor-niche and leads you through the enchanting white Arabic town of Eze, perched over the Mediterranean amid flower gardens and cypress and olive groves, a dream of a forgotten town, hazy with a shimmering sea-blue softness that hangs in the quiet air.

Ultimately, all of the *corniches* end at Monaco, the fairytale prin-cipality ruled over by Prince Rainier Grimaldi and his movie-star princess, the former Grace Kelly, a pocket-sized country as sparklingly clean and as full of flowers as it would be in a story book. Here palms and pines and flower beds edge the streets and villas, and rows of pawn shops line the avenues that back up to the world's most famous palace of fortune, the casino at Monte Carlo.

FOR THE TRAVELER'S NOTEBOOK

Official Information

Before you go: French Government Tourist Office: 610 Fifth Ave., New York N.Y.; 18 South Michigan Ave., Chicago, Ill.; 1001 Du Pont Plaza Center, Miami, Fla.; 323 Geary St., San Francisco, Cal.; 9418 Wilshire Blvd., Beverly Hills, Cal.

In Paris: SAS Offices: 30 Blvd. des Capucines, Paris IX, and 142 Ave. des Champs-Elysées; Tourist Information Office, 127 Ave. des Champs-Elysées; Paris Welcome Information Office, 7 Rue Balzac, and at all rail-road stations; U.S. Embassy, 2 Ave. Gabriel.

In Nice: SAS Offices: 3 Ave. Gustave V, and Airport Nice-Côte d'Azur; Tourist Information Office, Hall de l'Agence Havas, 13 Pl. Masséna; U.S. Consulate, 3 Rue Docteur Barély.

Money Matters

Currency: The unit of currency is the franc (F.), divided into 100 centimes (cts). Five francs equal $1, U.S.

Tipping: Tipping is widespread and is the custom even when service charges have been added. 12 to 15 per cent is added in hotels and restaurants. Give bellhops F 1 per bag or F 2.50 when leaving. In tourist hotels a tip is expected for each service rendered. Doormen get F 1 for calling a cab; chambermaids F 3 per week or one per day; concierge F 5 when you leave. Waiters a few francs extra, wine steward (*sommelier*) F 2 or 3; porters 50 cts. per bag, cloakroom and washroom attendants, theater and movie ushers 50 cts. Barbers, hairdressers, cab drivers, 15 to 20 per cent of the bill.

Climate, Clothing, and Essentials

The climate of Paris is temperate and follows approximately that of New York, although it is less extreme and generally a little rainier in fall and early spring. Winter (December to March) temperatures average about 43 degrees F. and there is snow as well as rain. Summer (June to September) averages 80 degrees, and it can get quite hot in July and August. Spring is the loveliest season of all in Paris though the tourist season continues through to the end of September. October, though sometimes rainy, is generally mild and lovely. Winter is the most elegant season, when the opera and theaters are in full swing and the glassed-in cafés are noisy and typically Parisian. Nice and the Riviera enjoy a milder, sunnier climate and winter temperatures rarely drop below 50 degrees. It is generally too cold to swim in November, December, and part of January, but the Nice season gets under way in February and lasts all through summer. Normal city attire is correct in Paris, with emphasis on dark colors and "little black dresses" for evenings.

Generally a dark suit is all that a man will need for evening, but some restaurants require dinner jackets on certain evenings, so check when you make reservations at such place as Maxim's, which has this regulation on Friday nights. A raincoat or waterproof topcoat is suggested for all seasons except during June, July, and August. In Nice, resort wear is correct, and this is one of the few places in Europe where slacks or shorts are acceptable for women.

Hotels

No country offers a wider range of hotel accommodations than France, and though you have heard it is the most expensive country in the world, you can still get a delightfully comfortable room with bath for about $7.50 a day, breakfast included, right in the heart of Paris. Rates go even lower than this in rock-bottom budget establishments, out of season, or outside Paris. There is an enormous range of prices within hotel categories, and rates vary, depending on the floor, the view, a private bath, and similar considerations. It is perfectly possible to get a less expensive room in a luxury hotel than in a first class establishment. To add to the confusion, the government has worked out an intricate system of hotel classification, whereby categories are designated by stars—1, 2, 3, 4—then subdivided into A, B, and C groupings. It's all pretty impossible and, for the sake of sanity, we have grouped hotels roughly as follows:

PARIS

DE LUXE: In the great and famous posh hotels, strictly for the well-to-do, rates average $30 a day, double, and can easily go much higher, only occasionally a little lower. Singles here might be available at $12 per day but $18 would be more likely.

All of the luxury hotels are on the Right Bank, and all have rooms varying from a single without bath on up to elaborate suites. All offer plush surroundings, excellent service, and have popular meeting-place bars and restaurants. They are bustling, "international" in tone, and inclined to favor "name" guests.

Hotel Ritz, 14 Place Vendôme. The Ritz to end all Ritzes, on the chic Place Vendôme—elegant and fashionable. Rooms are spacious and almost indecently comfortable. *George V, 31 Ave. George V.* A byword with well-to-do Americans; there is so much English spoken that it is hard to believe you ever left home. *Crillon, 10 Place de la Concorde.* Overlooking the Place de la Concorde and the Seine, this pleasantly old-world, luxurious hotel has an easy charm. *Plaza-Athénée, 25 Ave. Montaigne.* This hotel is to wealthy Europeans and South Americans what the George V is to the same class of American tourists. *Meurice, 228 Rue de Rivoli.* Quieter and more private than the others in this class, and a little less expensive too. *Prince de Galles.* Set right up against the George V, this de luxe hotel is smaller, friendly, and pleasant. *Raphäel, 17 Ave. Kléber.* Pleasantly old-fashioned and comfortable rooms make this private little hotel restful and luxurious. *Bristol, 112 Rue de Faubourg St. Honoré.* This hotel is as fashionable as the street it is on, and its rooms are handsomely furnished.

FIRST CLASS: A comfortable double here would range from $12 to $18 a day, though some of the best rooms and suites would be as high as in the luxury hotels; the minimum accommodations would, however, be moderately priced. Singles average $11 per day. These hotels are all centrally located and just this side of luxurious. Service is excellent, and the furnishings are for the most part pleasant and traditional.

At the upper end of the price range in this category are: the *Royal Monceau, 35 Ave. Hoche,* which is quiet and reserved; the *Ambassador, 16 Blvd. Haussmann,* busy and efficient, and a good stopping place for those traveling on business; the *Scribe, 1 Rue Scribe,* popular with American fashion buyers; the *Lotti, 7 Rue de Castiglione,* near the Madeleine, quite luxurious and known for its excellent service. The *Grand Hotel, 12 Blvd. des Capucines,* is enormous; the *Claridge, 74 Ave. des Champs-Elysées,* is pleasant and comfortable; and the *California, 16 Rue de Berri,* is popular with journalists. Two other hotels in this range are the *Westminster, 13 Rue de la Paix,* and the *De Paris, 8 Blvd. de la Madeleine.* The *Pont Royal, 7 Rue Montalembert,* (Left Bank) is very accommodating and its rooms are comfortable, if you get one that is not next to the neighboring church carillon. The *Montalembert,* next door, is an equally good choice.

Still first class but a little less expensive than those above are: the *St. James et d'Albany, 211 Rue de Rivoli,* a favorite with many well-traveled Europeans because of its excellent personal service and handy location; the *Lutetia, 43 Blvd. Raspail,* on the Left Bank, a favorite with traveling Frenchmen; and the *Du Louvre, Place du Théâtre-Français;* the *Normandy, 7 Rue de l'Echelle;* the *Castiglione, 40 Rue du Faubourg St. Honoré;* and the *Palais d'Orsay, 9 Quai Anatole France,* overlooking the river.

MODERATE: You would have to plan on spending somewhere between $8 and $10 a day, double, here, while a single room might average $7. *France et Choiseul, 239–241 Rue St. Honoré,* is near the Madeleine, and the *Vendôme, 1 Place Vendôme,* has a pretty garden and a quiet setting with excellent service. *Edward VII, 39 Ave. de l'Opéra,* is pleasant and friendly. The *Atala, 10 Rue Chateaubriand,* on the Right Bank, with unpretentious but good-sized rooms, is another good choice in this category; and the beautifully polished little *Bisson, 37 Quai des Grands-Augustines,* on the Left Bank at the edge of the Seine, has a very loyal international clientele and understandably so.

INEXPENSIVE: For a comfortable double room the average price would be $8 or $9, while singles range from $4 to $6.50. *Hotel du Quai Voltaire, 19 Quai Voltaire,* on the Seine and across from the Louvre, has been recently modernized but still retains the traditional charm that made it popular with Wagner, and Baudelaire, who wrote *Les Fleurs du Mal* while staying here. Service is good and friendly; many rooms overlook the Seine and most of them have modern baths, but not toilets. The *Claude*

Bernard, 43 Rue des Ecoles, is an excellent hotel in this category, very well run, popular with Americans and close to the Panthéon and the Sorbonne. The *Angleterre, 44 Rue Jacob,* in the heart of the St. Germain district, has a quiet garden setting, and the *Trianon Palace, 1 bis Rue Vaugirard,* close to the Sorbonne, is a bright and clean hotel, popular with students. Smaller and very charming hotels with rates ranging from moderate to middle first class are the *Bellman, 37 Rue François-1er*, and the *Montaigne, 6 Avenue Montaigne.*

NICE

Prices here are a little lower than in Paris for similar categories; and they vary with the season.

DE LUXE: The *Negresco, 37 Promenade des Anglais,* and the *Ruhl, 1 Promenade des Anglais,* are the two top luxury hotels in the city, the first being even more so than the second, and much larger. Both face the beach.

FIRST CLASS: The *Plaza, 12 Ave. de Verdun,* recently modernized, has spacious rooms and excellent service; and on the top floor is a smart bar with a beautiful view. The *Royal, 21–23 Promenade des Anglais,* and the *Atlantic, 12 Blvd. Victor-Hugo,* are comfortable and pleasant. They are also slightly less expensive than the hotels mentioned above.

MODERATE: The *Luxembourg, 7–9 Promenade des Anglais;* the *Continental, 12 Rue Rossini,* and the *Angleterre, 6 Ave. Gustave V,* are well furnished, and have pleasant locations although they are not on the beach front. The *Adriatic, 81 Rue de France,* has a sunbathing terrace; the *Scribe, 20 Ave. Georges Clemenceau,* has a separate lounge for each floor; the *West-End, 31 Promenade des Anglais,* is close to the beach and the casino. The *Westminster, 27 Promenade des Anglais,* is an older hotel with good-sized rooms, and the *Beau Rivage, 107 Quai des Etats-Unis,* is also recommended. All of these mentioned are excellent, inexpensive to moderate hotels without restaurants but more than adequate rooms and facilities.

Food and Restaurants

The excellence of French cooking is demonstrated by the fact that it has become known and imitated around the world, and indeed is synonymous with international cuisine. This is due both to the quality of meats, vegetables, fruits, and fish, and the loving care with which these ingredients are prepared. Try the oysters, both Belons and Claires, the *rouget,* which is best grilled and the wonderful small lobsters, *langoustines.*

In France the day begins with *petit déjeuner:* coffee with *croissants,* flaky, crescent-shaped rolls still warm from the bakery, or you may have fresh rolls with butter and jam or marmalade. While you are in Paris, try some of the excellent dishes such as *escargots de Bourgogne* (snails), *boeuf Bourguignon* (beef braised in wine), *coq au vin* (chicken in red wine), *grenouilles provençales* (frog legs sautéed with garlic), *jambon persillé de Dijon* (ham with parsley garnish), or some of the dishes which had their origin in Paris—for example, *boeuf miroton* (with an onion sauce), *moules marinières* (mussels in a white court-bouillon) and *entre-côte marchand de vin* (sirloin steak). A broiled *entrecôte* (steak) with a stack of *pommes frites* (French fried potatoes) is the favorite meal of Parisians. Of course you will try the rich onion soup thickly glazed with cheese. In spring the *framboises* (raspberries) and *fraises des bois* (wild woodland strawberries) are the most heavenly desserts in the world, especially when dressed with thick cream (*crème fraîche*). In addition to France's more famous cheeses, be sure to try *Fontainebleau,* a fresh cream cheese that is rarely exported and which is served as a dessert. Other superb French dishes to look for are the *quenelles de brochet à la Nantua* (tiny pike dumplings with a lobster sauce), *Gigot aux soissons* (leg of lamb roasted to pink tenderness and served with white haricot beans), *loup au fenouil* (grilled sea bass on a bed of flaming fennel branches); *pigeon au petit pois* (braised squab with tiny green peas); *pommes Dauphinoises* (sliced potatoes cooked in cream); and the famous *canard à la presse* (pressed duckling). There is a wide array of wonderful *pâtés,* the sublime truffles (*truffes*), best when they are encased in pastry and baked in ashes. Pastries are superb and you don't have to know the names to choose them, since in the cafés and *patisseries* you make your own selection from the counter and a waitress brings it to your table. Coffee, especially the *filtre,* is excellent, and for breakfast it is served half-and-half with steaming milk.

Around Nice you'll find the food specialties of Provence, with much of it scented with garlic, rich in tomatoes and olive oil, roughly a cross between French and Italian fare. The famous fish soup, bouillabaisse, and the regional *pistou* and *bourride,* the pizza-like *pissaladière* that is sold everywhere, *salade Niçoise,* and the vegetable stew, *ratatouille,* are not to be missed.

In your choice of wine, be guided by the *sommelier,* or wine waiter; the general rule is to begin with lighter wines, the white or red wines of Bordeaux, for example, and progress to heavier, stronger wines, such as the reds of Burgundy. The distinctiveness of French wines varies with each vineyard and season, and it is a good idea to try local wines on their home ground as you travel around the country. Though you'll want to try the vintage wines, you should also sample the open carafes of *vin ordinaire* which usually are a fraction of the price of the bottle wines. It is also a good idea to substitute some of France's excellent apértifs (Dubonnet, Lillet, vermouth, either plain or with *cassis,* or liquorice-flavored Pernod) for your usual pre-dinner cocktail. While a meal in the more expensive restaurants may cost F. 50 to 70, there are many modest restaurants where you can get a good meal for F. 15 to 25, particularly in the Latin Quarter. *Restaurants de tourisme* display a special shield and all restaurants post their menus and prices outside.

PARIS

Any one book attempting to guide your selection of restaurants in Paris begins with an apology and this one is no exception. Paris is so full of wonderful eating places and almost everyone has his own favorites, and one gets the feeling that unless you have told all, you have told nothing. The selection here represents the merest sampling of what Paris has to offer in many different kinds of restaurants and I would strongly recommend that anyone interested should read the descriptions of Parisian restaurants in that chapter of Waverly Root's book, *Food of France.* He is especially good on *bistros* and the restaurants that specialize in the regional food of the country.

GREAT AND FAMOUS—AND EXPENSIVE: All of these restaurants are beautiful, with excellent service and very good food. Whether or not you should make it a point to visit one, or all, depends on your interest in food and your desire to see, at least once, the famous places you have read about. All feature the classic *haute cuisine. Maxim's,* probably *the* single most famous restaurant in the world, still has its gay nineties elegance and its loyal coterie. It is very plush, the service is excellent, and anyone who hasn't been there ought to decide about the food for himself. *Le Grand Véfour,* unquestionably the handsomest of the Big Four, is in the Palais Royal and done in perfect Napoleonic décor. *Lapérouse.* Beautifully plush and private, with many small rooms and much old world elegance, this place on the Left Bank serves food that might at worst be described as uneven, at best, excellent. *Tour d'Argent.* Although the clientele here is largely tourist, the famous pressed duck is still the best in the city. The service and professional operation of this place is a delight to behold.

EXPENSIVE AND CLASSIC: The *Berkeley,* in the hotel of the same name, is to many minds the best of the *haute cuisine* establishments, while *Taillevent, Lucas Carton,* and *Lasserre* are three other very elegant, posh dining places noted for their classic cuisine. *Drouant* is famous for the superb treatment of its seafood dishes, while *Escargot* in Les Halles, in a nineteenth century building full of atmosphere, serves truly excellent food. *Le Petit Bedon* is a very chic, tiny, bright place with an open kitchen and superb game dishes. *Chez Pauline* is a small but expensive *bistro* featuring Lyonnais and Beaujolais specialties. *Chez l'Ami Louis* is a phenomenon, a small, simple, and almost discouraging-looking *bistro near* Les Halles, but it is full of surprises—first with the most beautifully refined and elegant food I've eaten anywhere, prepared by the bearded chef-impresario, Antoine Magnin. The final surprise is the check, which is staggering but worth it. *Allard, Boule d'Or, Cochon d'Or, A la Grille, Chez Moi,* and *Chez Benoit* are other interesting, expensive, and excellent *bistros.*

MODERATE: You can get delectable crackling suckling pig at *Cochon de Lait,* near the Odéon; wonderful *coq au vin* at *Bouteille d'Or* on the banks of the Seine; excellent food in the *Montmartre* restaurant, *La Mère Catherine;* and incomparable *bistro* atmosphere at *Au Grand Comptoir* with its hearty, superb bourgeois cooking. Try the hot Limoges sausage and the *steak à l'échalote. Auberge de la Truite* resembles a Norman country inn and features the food of the province. The *Rotisseries de la Reine Pédauque* is wood-paneled, large, popular, and its table d'hote meals are among the best buys in the city. *Laborderie* is known for its Basque dishes. For specialties of the Savoy region try *Quasimodo* or *Au Savoyard; La Bourgogne* serves beautiful Burgundian food. *Le Rallye, La Pergola,* and *Aux Quatre Marches,* good businessmen's lunch places, have hearty modest-priced food.

SPECIAL RESTAURANTS: *Brasserie Lipp* on the Boulevard St. Germain is one of the many Alsatian brewery restaurants in the city, featuring *choucroute garnie* (sauerkraut with sausage and ham) and excellent draught beer. *Androuet* is a cheese shop downstairs; and the restaurant upstairs serves you anything you want as long as it is made of cheese. *Pré Catalan* and *d'Armenonville* are lovely outdoor restaurants in the Bois de Boulogne with classic food, high prices, and dancing on summer nights; and *Auberge du Vert Galant* has a lovely terrace for summer dining right near Notre Dame. Paris has a number of wonderful seafood restaurants and you will find *aficionados* who claim *Porquerolles'* bouillabaisse is the best; others will do battle for the honor of *La Mediterraneé;* and still others prefer the blue-and-white tiled charm of *Relais Bisson.*

Paris has its share of budget restaurants too, mostly on the Left Bank. One of the best of these is *Restaurant Sts. Pères* on the Boulevard St. Germain, a thoroughly delightful place. *Pré au Clerc* is even less expensive and very good, and the *Beaux-Arts,* a noisy, bustling student restaurant, serves good French food without frills at very low prices—even lower if you choose to dine without a napkin. Other bargains include *Chez Drouet,* and *Au Provençal,* featuring the rich tomato-garlic-eggplant food of that region, and the *Relais de la Butte. La Puce,* near the Panthéon, serves wonderful *pistou* and *brochettes,* and offers jazz and guitar music in the late evening. The restaurant *Champollion,* on the tiny Rue Champollion in the area of Boulevard St. Michel, serves excellent Russian food at incredibly low prices and is always crowded with the Sorbonne students who favor this place. Try *Le Hoggar* and *Marrakech* for Algerian *cous-cous.*

For late-night eating there are the wonderful *bistros* of Les Halles, most especially *Au Pied de Cochon,* and for light lunches and snacks there is the *Pam-Pam,* and cafeterias such as *Poulet* near the Champs-Elysées and *Latin Cluny* on Boulevard St. Germain.

The prettiest and best restaurant just outside Paris is *Le Coq Hardi*—a pleasant, flowery country inn, perfect for a long, leisurely luncheon. It is in Bougival, about thirty minutes out of Paris.

Sidewalk cafés are a special Paris institution and they exist in all parts of the city. Each has its own coterie; all will serve you a glass of wine or a cup of coffee and let you sit there all day, and most are open for a *croissant*-and-*café-au-lait* breakfast. Cafés should be listed under "Entertainment," as well as under "Restaurants" since sitting there, watching Paris go by, is one of the pleasantest diversions, day or night. The *Café de la Paix,* in view of the Opéra on the Right Bank, is one of the most popular, and if you sit there long enough it is said you will see almost everyone you know. *Fouquet's* and *Weber's* are on the Champs-Elysées, and along the Left Bank Boulevard St. Germain, *Aux Deux Magots, Café Flore,* and *Brasserie Lipp* cater to the existentialist-artist-writer trade, as do the *Montparnasse,* the *Select,* the *Dôme, La Coupole,* or *La Closier des Lilas.*

For tearoom snacks and lunches there are places like *Marquise de Sévigné, Boissier,* and a number of *patisseries,* a personal favorite being *Caretti's* on the Place du Trocadéro.

NICE

There are wonderful restaurants in Nice and in the cities close by along the Riviera. Perhaps the most famous, and certainly the best and most delightful, is *La Bonne Auberge,* near Antibes, one of the great eating places in all of France and worth an excursion in its own right. In Juan-les-Pins, the *Poularde* is good and so is the seafood at *Brossin.*

In Nice itself, the *Raynaud* is elegant, expensive, and popular; *Poularde Chez Lucullus* is one of the city's best and is more moderately priced. *Petit Brouant* is modest in price and features good Niçoise food in a garden setting. For typical Mediterranean food in charming authentic surroundings, try *Les Pêcheurs, Le Lou Paisan, Ane Rouge* or *Coco Beach, Au Manoir Normand* is formal, handsome, and elegant with very good food and moderately high prices, and among the very native, well-priced and charming restaurants to try are *La Pergola,* somewhat like a snack bar but with excellent Niçoise dishes; *La Bourride,* famous for the fish soup of the same name; *La Trappa,* which is inexpensive, small, and very authentic; and *Da Bouttau,* a downstairs kitchen restaurant—informal, colorful, and touristy, and right for anyone interested in local color. The special chicken and fish soup there are wonderful. The *Cave Niçoise* on the Rue Masséna, with its sawdust-covered floor and rock-bottom prices, is almost unknown to tourists. It is informal and features extremely good family cooking.

Entertainment, Night Life, and Special Events

PARIS

Paris packs more *divertissements* into a few square miles than almost any other city on earth. The Opéra is world famous. The Opéra Comique presents a large repertory of the lighter French and Italian operas such as *La Bohème* and *The Barber of Seville.* The Comédie Française plays at the *Salle Richelieu,* the *Théâtre de France* at the Odéon, and the *Théâtre National Populaire* (TNP) at the Palais de Chaillot. During the winter and spring seasons there are daily concerts by international artists, ensembles and orchestras and in summer various concert series at the Palais de Chaillot, and at the Abbaye de Royaumont, and Sceaux near Paris. Operettas are given at the Châtelet. There are a number of variety music halls of which the most famous is the *Folies Bergère*—a sort of super, lightly clad version of the kind of stage show usually performed at Radio City Music Hall. The *Casino de Paris* does the same thing on a slightly less spectacular level. Paris also has a bevy of full-fledged night clubs—all quite expensive, and many featuring the most sophisticated, refined and subtle strip teasers in the world. The *Lido,* an enormous club, is luxurious, spectacular and touristy. *La Nouvelle Eve* is more sophisticated, smaller, and smarter. The *Bal du Moulin Rouge* is the place to go to see the classic can-can, while the *Crazy Horse Saloon* has what many connoisseurs consider the absolute "end" in girlie shows, with extremely seductive strippers and a wildly colorful atmosphere. For traditional Parisian atmosphere, *chanteuses* and all, there is the famed *Patachou,* the *Lapin Agile,* and *El Djazir* for Algerian food and belly dancers. On the intimate, small, and smoky side there are the excellent *Guitar* and *La Catalan*—tiny Left Bank spots featuring wonderful flamenco dancing in very close quarters—both are superb.

Those of the smart and very dressy set who like to dance to old favorites and *rumba* bands frequent *L'Eléphant Blanc, Monseigneur, Dinarzade,* with Russian food and gypsy violins, *Jimmy's Club, Keur Samba,* with African dancing, *Le Drap d'Or,* with lots of French period atmosphere, *Shéhérézade* and *Novy,* featuring more shashlik and Russian music, and *Maxim's Midnight Room.* Café sitting is as popular by night as it is by day, a visit to Les Halles after midnight is one of the city's most fascinating diversions—and don't forget the traditional onion soup in one of the market *bistros.* You should also take at least one after-dark walk along the famed Place Pigalle—a uniquely Parisian outdoor show that is fascinating and somewhat incredible. For a complete list of current attractions, get a copy of *Une Semaine à Paris.*

SPECIAL EVENTS: *Shrove Tuesday* is celebrated with fancy dress balls and confetti; *May 8* marks the end of World War II in Europe and is also *Joan of Arc's Day,* with processions before her statue in the Place des Pyramides. At the *Kermesse aux Etoiles* in mid-June the stars of stage and screen run a charity sale for veterans of the Leclerc Division which liberated Paris in 1944. *Bastille Day* celebrations on July 14 take place in every restaurant and every street in Paris, with flags, bunting, gaily colored lights, spectacular fireworks, music, and dancing all night long in the streets. Military parades are held on *May 8, July 14,* and *November 11.* The *Exhibition of Housekeeping Arts* is held in February, and the *International Aeronautical Exhibition* at Le Bourget Airport every other June.

NICE and along the RIVIERA

The *Palm Beach Casino* in Cannes ranks at the top. Besides gambling, it offers music, floor shows, and dancing under the stars. There is open-air dancing also at the *Whisky à Gogo.* A refreshing evening entertainment is the boat trip with music and dancing, and you will also enjoy strolling along the Croisette, sitting among the flower beds which border this sparkling promenade, or listening to the music from the bandstand.

The most famous night clubs in Nice are *Maxim's* and the *Folies.* At Monte Carlo you will no doubt want to visit the famous *Casino,* and later, in summer, to dance at the *Sea Club.* Concerts are often given in Cannes and Nice, usually in the casinos. Nice has a fine opera house which gives performances during the winter with internationally known artists. Theater groups frequently visit Riviera towns; there is the annual *International Film Festival* at Cannes each May, the *Music Festival* at Menton, and the outdoor cinema at Monte Carlo each summer. The biggest event of the year is the *Pre-Lenten Carnival,* beginning on the second Thursday before Ash Wednesday. This is the biggest and most colorful carnival in Europe: the days are filled with fun, flowers, parades, floats; and the nights with masked balls and revelry.

Shopping

PARIS

For a completely detailed shopping guide to Paris, be sure to get the

SAS booklet, "Shopping Your Way Through Southern Europe," when you have booked your trip. The top shopping area extends from the grand boulevards with department stores such as *Aux Trois Quartiers, Au Printemps, Galeries Lafayette,* and *Samaritaine de Luxe,* to the streets leading off the Place de l'Opéra, the Place de la Madeleine, the Place Vendôme and especially the Rue du Faubourg St. Honoré. Here you will find the best known jewelers, perfume shops, dress and accessory shops. The collections of the great *couturiers* are shown by invitation only and, unless you are a buyer, it is practically impossible to get in when the new spring or fall collections are being presented; at other times, arrangements must be made in advance and there is only limited seating at any one showing. Many famous houses also have boutiques where ready-to-wear dresses and fashion accessories are offered at prices that are modest in comparison with those of the major collections.

If you are hunting for antiques or bric-à-brac, or are plain curious, you will be intrigued by the *Flea Market* (*Marché aux Puces*) at the Porte de Clignancourt, a vast miscellany of shops and goods, but be prepared to haggle. Paris has other fascinating outdoor markets as well. The *Flower and Bird Market* on the Left Bank; the *Dog Market,* at the Rue Brancion, which has showings on Sunday afternoons; and the many neighborhood food markets that are open at various days of the week.

Perfume, gloves, silk scarves, and other accessories are good buys in Paris. You may also be attracted by crystal ware, ceramics, hand-sewn lingerie, leather goods, and other finely crafted articles. Antique hunters will love the streets around the Pont Royal on the Left Bank and the shops off the Boulevard St. Germain and Rue Bonaparte.

There are the city's great art galleries such as *Charpentier, Bernheim Jeune et Cie,* and *Louis Cave;* and fascinating bookshops and stalls along the Seine. *Brentano's* and the *Librairie Anglaise* near the Opéra are excellent too. For china from Limoges there is *Rouard* and the *Société des Produits Européens;* and *Sylvestre,* on the Left Bank, has tiles, ovenware, and tableware. *Baccarat, Daum* and *Lalique* feature their superb crystal, and *Fauchon* is one of the world's most fascinating gourmet-delicatessen food shops.

For the beautiful silks and wools for which the French are famous, try *Aux Gobelins, Corot,* or *Rodin,* as well as the department stores already mentioned. In addition to the boutiques of the *couturiers,* chic ready-to-wear (*prêt-à-porter*) for women can be found at *Henri à la Pensée, Martine,* and *Weil,* while elegant scarves and accessories are available at *Hermès, Léda, Du Muth,* and *Innovation,* with a good selection of leather coats and luggage. For gifts, try *Obéron, Maison Royale, Société des*

Produits Européens, and *Sagil. Grand Maison de Blanc* has excellent linens and gloves, and *Christofle* is known the world over for its silver.

NICE

The main shopping districts are Avenue de la Victoire, Avenue de Verdun, Rue Paradis, Rue de la Liberté, and Rue de France. The leading department stores are *Galeries Lafayette* and *Riviera. Maison de Blanc* has a large selection of plain or embroidered linens and for perfume, try *Rhul.* Pottery can be found in workshops all over the Riviera, especially at Vallauris, the town made famous by the artist, Picasso. Cannes, Nice, and Monte Carlo are good shopping centers with an infinite variety of shops, representing all the well-known fashion houses and jewelers of Paris.

Background Reading

So much has been written about Paris that it is difficult to make a choice of suggestions. But a few books which stick in my mind as being outstanding for the impressions they give of the city and the country are as follows:
Paris on the Seine, by Blake Ehrlich
The Last Time I Saw Paris, by Elliot Paul
Down and Out in Paris and London, by George Orwell. (The seamy side, but nonetheless fascinating.)
France, A Portrait in Color, edited by Doré Ogrizek
A Moveable Feast, by Ernest Hemingway
The Story of Paris by Thomas Okey in J. M. Dent's series, *Medieval Towns.*
For a glimpse of Paris' artistic life in the twenties, few books could rival *The Autobiography of Alice B. Toklas,* by Gertrude Stein, or *Shakespeare & Company,* by Sylvia Beach
An essential book for anyone interested in traveling around Paris and France is the *Guide Michelin,* an almost infallible and absolutely reliable guide to hotels and restaurants throughout the city and country.

West Germany

BERLIN

Checkpoint Charlie and die Mauer

ANYONE who gets a special thrill out of being at the Place Where Things Are Really Happening would do well to head straight for Berlin—right now the most sensitive city on the face of the earth. For if Germany is the powder keg that could explode into World War III, Berlin is the fuse that could ignite it. This artificial half-city, kept alive by transfusions from the West, is a rich and glittering showcase—an island of capitalist opulence and gaiety, 110 miles inside the gray sea of Communist austerity that is the Russian-dominated D.D.R., the German Democratic Republic. Always considered the nerve center and conscience of its country, Berlin's dilemma today pinpoints that of all Germany, for as the city is divided into east and west sectors, so is the entire country. And just as the 2.2 million people of West Berlin refuse to accept as permanent the wall that cuts them off from 1.1 million friends and relatives, so the 57 million people of the Federal Republic of Germany refuse to acknowledge that they arc permanently partitioned off from 18 million countrymen in East Germany.

Everything Berlin needs for survival is sent in from the West by trucks, trains, and planes, through the Communist-guarded traffic lanes. More subtle (but no less vital) transfusions of morale come from the strategic visits of British, French, American, and Bonn officials and celebrities—reminders to Berlin that it has not been, and will not be, abandoned. Outwardly the Berliners go about everyday affairs with the traditional German zeal and dedication to purpose. Their attitude toward their present predicament is best typified by that of the city's mayor, Willy Brandt, who has a kind of smiling but stalwart, nerveless determination to restore Berlin to what he considers its rightful role—the united capital of a united Germany.

It is easy to see how Berlin got used to being Germany's leading city for it has played the role since 1701 when it was the capital of Prussia under Frederick I and later under Frederick II, the Great. Since the fifteenth century, it had been the residence of the powerful electors of Brandenburg. (It was for one of these princes that Bach wrote the six concerti bearing that family name.) The most famous of the Brandenburg rulers, the "Great Elector" Friederich Wilhelm, gave refuge to twenty thousand French Huguenots, who founded the city's craft traditions and established Berlin as an industrial center. And as far back as the thirteenth century, fishing and trade were pursued with great success along the banks of Berlin's river, the Spree. The capital of the Prussian Hohenzollerns became the capital of the kaisers in 1871, when the Iron Chancellor, the Junker, Otto von Bismarck, unified the German empire and crowned Wilhelm its first king. It was Bismarck who helped defeat Napoleon III, Bismarck who instigated the successful fight against Austria and later was accused of provoking the Franco-Prussian War, when Alsace was annexed from France. He made Germany the most powerful country on the Continent, a position it held until World War I. It was during Bismarck's reign—and reign he did—that the image of the German superman really took hold and as it was also the time of Wagner and Nietzsche he had considerable help in selling the image. It was Bismarck, too, who created the blood-and-iron nightmare of expansion that ended with Hitler and the German defeat in World War II—a piece of history too recent to need recounting here.

There is nothing in Berlin's past that is as exciting as its present; no relic of its seven hundred years of history that is as poignantly dramatic as the three-year-old brick wall that cuts the city in half. To understand what the Wall—*die Mauer*—really means to Berliners, try to imagine what it would be like to live in New York, Chicago, or Los Angeles and awake one morning to find a fortified wall running the length of Forty-second Street, State Street, or Wilshire Boulevard. If you worked on one side of the wall and lived on the other, you could not go to your job. A son who spent the night with friends on Fifty-third Street could not get back to his family who lived on Thirty-eighth, and if you were engaged to marry someone who lived on the East Side while you were on the West, you could see each other only if one were willing to risk his life crossing over. Money deposited in banks, shoes left to be repaired, a favorite church or market—all might be suddenly walled out of your life overnight. The large-scale political, economic, and philosophic implications of the wall are fairly obvious and serious enough; the really demoralizing effect comes in the more personal aspects of daily living.

The Wall has become Berlin's leading sight since it was put up one August night in 1961. In other cities a visitor will dash off to a favorite restaurant, a famous museum, a well known shop, or an historic *place* or *piazza*. In Berlin, almost every visitor drops his bags at his hotel and makes straight for the Brandenburger Tor, the triumphal arch built in 1791 that is the city's landmark, and from here peer across into the other world of East Berlin. And later perhaps, he will cross over at Checkpoint Charlie and wander through the eastern sector, taking in its historic Opera House on Unter den Linden, the Berliner Ensemble, the spiritual home of Berthold Brecht, the Marx-Engels Platz, once the site of the royal German castle, the overpowering Russian war memorial in Treptower Park, the relics of the bunker where Hitler spent his final hours. The showcase street, Stalin Allee, is again called by its original name, Frankfurter Allee and is the pride of the Communist regime, and the main route of official tourist buses from the western sector. But just behind this thin façade of over-scaled modern apartment houses, shops, and cafés are empty lots and piles of rubble from the bombed-out buildings that have not yet been replaced. On East Berlin's Museum Island, visit the Pergamom Museum with its incredible Middle Eastern antiquities and the grounds of the city's Humboldt University, once the most highly respected in the country. But most interesting of all will be the drabness and desolation of the streets, the shops, the restaurants, and the people, as compared to the gay and glittering delights of the western sector.

Most of these delights are strung out along the main street, the Kurfürstendamm, better known to Berliners as the Ku-damm. It is along this avenue that all of the brightest treasures of the booming capitalist economy are set out like prize pieces in a jewelry-shop window. Handsome hotels offer lush comforts and impeccable service to their international clientele. Restaurants serve a world-wide array of rich and well-prepared dishes, and one de luxe establishment lists specialties from China, Japan, Korea, India, the Middle East, and Russia on its silk scroll menu. And at any one of the four thousand corner pubs—the *Eckkneipen* that are everywhere—you can try one of a dozen kind of frankfurters, washed down with a *Molle,* the Berlin pint stein of beer.

Shops along the Ku-damm display a dazzling assortment of cameras, old Meissen and Dresden porcelains, wonderful toys, antique pewter and copper, chic wool and leather-trimmed clothing for women as well as men, carved cuckoo clocks, ornate steins and hand-crafted souvenirs from the Black Forest, dirndls, *lederhosen,* and Loden cloth coats from Bavaria. At night the avenue is a blaze of lights and activity as dozens of intimate, pocket-sized bars open for business. And on the streets behind the Kurfürstendamm—on the Haseneide, the Kantstrasse and the Nürnbergerstrasse—enormous clubs are packed with patrons who come to watch the wildly spectacular floor shows. One of these clubs, the Resi, seats eight hundred people and each table is equipped with a telephone, so that if you see someone in the room you'd like to know, you merely call and invite him, or her, over for a drink. And the St. Pauli am Zoo presents a do-it-yourself strip show where patrons remove the clothing of entertainers with the aid of fishing poles. Evidently this city, always famous for gaiety and sophistication, has no intention of changing its way of life merely because it is in the most precarious position in its history.

Nor has Berlin shown signs of forfeiting its long-held reputation as Germany's leading intellectual center. This was, after all, the place where Berthold Brecht and Kurt Weill enjoyed their first triumphs and the place where the dada and surrealist art movements got under way. Berlin's Sturm Gallery held an historic exhibition of modern German and European paintings in 1913 and a year later gave Marc Chagall his first one-man show. In 1918 Hülsenbeck published his review, *Der Dada*, and the painter George Grosz did some of his greatest and most successful work.

Berlin's universities still draw students from all over the world, especially those interested in the technological sciences, politics, and art. Theaters rebuilt after World War II bombings are among the liveliest in Europe, and the *Festwochen*, the September music and ballet festival, is one of the Continent's outstanding artistic events. Berlin's symphony orchestra, under Herbert von Karajan, is perhaps the finest in the world, and dozens of other orchestras, chamber music groups, and opera companies perform throughout the city and over its radio all day long.

Aside from the interest generated by its unique political and geographical position, Berlin has many "sights" in the usual touristic sense of the word, and though most of them suffered varying degrees of damage during World War II, they have almost all been restored, some completely, others only partially. Perhaps the city's favorite park, the Tiergarten, best symbolizes Berlin's miraculous resurrection. Once a thickly wooded urban forest of 630 acres, all the trees were cut down for fuel in the bitter cold winter of 1945–1946. But now new trees and lawns are growing again and there is an especially beautiful English Garden, with hundreds of trees and shrubs donated by the British royal family—a garden dedicated by Anthony Eden and therefore called by Berliners, the Garden of Eden.

Those given to panoramic views have two choices in Berlin. There is a two-hundred-foot-high lookout platform atop the Siegessäule, the victory column built in 1873 after the Franco-Prussian War, or a five-hundred-foot-high view from the top of the modern Funkturm, the Eiffel-like radio tower on the city's fair and exhibition grounds. A ghostly reminder of Germany's National Socialist past is the ashen ruin of the Reichstag, the parliament building burned by Hitler in 1933 and only now being restored, while a hopeful forecast of the future is the reproduction of the American Liberty Bell that rings from the tower of the Schöneberg Town Hall. The bell was a gift from the United States honoring the bravery of Berliners during the Russian blockade of 1948–1949. The people of the city returned the compliment by erecting the Luftbrückendenkmal, a soaring shaft of concrete at Tempelhof Airport which commemorates the airmen who lost their lives flying supplies into the city during those trying sixteen months—

often at the rate of a thousand planes a day.

Among the city's oldest treasures are St. Mary's Church on Neuer Markt, built in the early fifteenth century, and the elegant seventeenth century palace of Charlottenburg with its magnificent baroque statue of the Great Elector. Many of the state apartments have been restored, the palace museum contains a fine collection of old musical instruments, and on the garden grounds are a number of royal family tombs. In the Grünewald, a favorite woodland resort for Berliners, the Renaissance hunting lodge, the Jagdschloss, has a fine painting collection. At night it is illuminated with wax tapers to make a romantic backdrop for the concerts given in its gardens. European paintings, covering the centuries from the thirteenth to the nineteenth, are shown in the Dahlem Museum, along with sculptures and crafts dating from Gothic times to the eighteenth century, while the Museum für Völkerkunde displays primitive tribal artifacts from Asia, Africa, and South America.

The people of Berlin are as proud of their modern sights as they are of their antique relics and with small wonder. They have one of Europe's most striking modern buildings, the double clam shell that is their Kongresshalle, and a bright balconied apartment-house block designed by Le Corbusier. And the Hansa Viertel, the restored modern housing development on the site of the old Hansa residential section, was designed by architects and town planners from all over the world.

You may visit dozens of other *Schlösser,* museums, sports palaces, and parks; you may stand on the corner of the Potsdamerplatz where the British, Russian, and American sectors meet; or visit that sad and sober reminder of the results of war—the ruin of the Gedächtniskirche that will not be restored even when the new Memorial Church is completed.

HAMBURG

The free and Hanseatic city

HAMBURG has never been "in" as a tourist stop, and probably never will be. A seaport and a center of commerce and heavy industry, it lacks the more obvious attractions of other German towns. It boasts neither the legendary Lorelei lure of the Rhineland, nor the Bavarian bonhomie of Munich. It has neither the front page of glamour of Berlin nor the sepia-etched charm of the quaint towns along the Romantic Road. While it is only a short bus ride from the Baltic beach towns of the Ostsee, Hamburg itself is an inland river port on the Elbe, and there is nothing of the resort about it. Though the history of the city goes back to the ninth century and Charlemagne who founded it, it has few authentic landmarks of that past. Its buildings are restorations of antique originals that were either burned by the Great Fire of 1842 or leveled by Allied bombs in World War II. To the tourist, then, this is a busy industrial complex with no cabana beaches and no genuine old ruins, no storybook lore and no picturesque local folkways, unless you place the uniquely lurid attractions of the nighttime Reeperbahn in that last category.

But to a traveler really fascinated by great cities, to anyone who will take the time to discover the romance and excitement of a place as vital as this one, Hamburg offers a rich reward. It invites you to live its life rather than merely scan its sights.

With its population of 1,800,000, this is the largest city in West Germany proper, and has been the country's leading seaport since the days of sailing ships and the Hanseatic League, the rich and powerful organization of Baltic towns that banded together for purposes of trade. The League got its start in the thirteenth century by gaining control of the Baltic herring supply, a vital industry in a Christian Europe that ate fish on Friday. In the fourteenth and fifteenth centuries it controlled the shipping and trade of northern Europe and had set up headquarter outposts in Bergen, Stockholm, and London; and its ships carried goods to and from eastern Europe via the Vistula, and Italy by way of the Atlantic. The League was powerful enough to force Denmark to grant access to the Baltic through Schleswig-Holstein, the area that has been a bone of contention between the two countries ever since.

Today Hamburg is soundly, solidly middle-class, a robust money-making center of trade and finance, the home of cigar-smoking, coin-clinking burghers, with a taste for culture, a talent for comfortable living, and a free-wheeling laissez faire philosophy that governs more than their business lives. "Free" is the most recurrent word in Hamburg's title through the ages. It was chartered as a free city by Barbarossa in 1189 and in 1510 Maximilian declared it a free imperial town. It was incorporated into Napoleon's empire in 1810, but after his defeat it was again designated "free." When Hamburg joined Bismarck's unified Germany it did so as a "free and Hanseatic city," a title it shared with the other great Hansa towns, Lübeck and Bremen. Hamburg takes its title seriously. In the seventeenth century it stayed out of the Catholic-Protestant Thirty Years' War that ravaged Germany and most of Europe. And in 1945 Hamburg made its own early peace with the Allies while Hitler was still screaming for the last drop of German blood.

Now a free city-state within the German Federal Republic, Hamburg is Germany's most independent and open-minded city. Each month sixteen hundred ships drop anchor in this harbor, unloading the cargoes and ideas of a thousand far-off ports. Hamburg has, throughout its history, been in closer touch with the lands it faced across the sea than with the Germany backed up behind it, so that its style has always been more international than Teutonic.

The city is made up of a combination of ingredients as diverse and unlikely as those in its two most famous dishes—the soup that contains eel, ham, pears, prunes, apricots, peas, and wine; and its *Labskaus,* a sailors' stew of meat, herring, pickles, and potatoes. The ingredients in the larger *Labskaus* that is Hamburg are as surprisingly complementary as those in its local menu specialties, and create a flavor just as rich, mellow, and subtly enticing. Some of the features of the city are as predictable as eel in eel soup; others are as unexpected as meat and herring in the same stewpot.

Since this is a seaport, one might expect to find a skyline of cranes gangling over the oil-slick waters of the Hamburg harbor. Edged by some thirty miles of docks, this section is a favorite with natives as well as visitors who take the launch tour or stroll along the piers. Either way it is a fascinating hubbub of activity, with red-and-black Alster steamers traveling from other German ports, tooting tugs and ocean liners wailing a soulful farewell, stevedores loading ships, dozens of bars and wurst stands, and over all the briny scent of the sea. But just as one might be surprised to find ham and apricots in eel soup, or pickles in a stew, so he might be unprepared for the sparkling clean garden of a town that is also Hamburg. Flowers, trees and grass-green promenades border on the twin artificial lakes, the Inner and Outer Alster, and the city is so laced with canals that it recalls Amsterdam, unless you are familiar with Copenhagen, in which case you'll note an even stronger resemblance. There are reminders of the Danish capital too in the green-gold copper steeples, in the towered Rathaus, the Town Hall that is one of Hamburg's "must" sights, and in the solid, prosperous demeanor of the city and its people.

In a thriving commercial city such as this, you would expect the smart shops you find along the lakefront Jungfernstieg, the Grindel skyscrapers, and the heavy traffic around Sprinkenhof and Chilehaus, a symbol of Hamburg's overseas connections. You would expect, too, the sixteenth century Stock Exchange on the Johannisstrasse, one of the few buildings to survive the nineteenth century fire, and the crowds in the midtown restaurants at noon. But in a city as frankly commercial as this the magnificent gardens of the Municipal Park, the lakeside esplanades, and the Planten un Blomen are less taken for granted. Hard-headed merchants and bankers who are regulars at the *Austernstuben,* where the celebrated local oysters are served with Cheshire cheese and a glass of red wine, are regulars also at Hagenbeck's, the world's most beautiful zoological garden, where thousands of animals roam in natural surroundings. Two of its leading attractions are the Tiger Jungle and the compound of prehistoric monsters sculptured in stone. This zoo, designed by Carl Hagenbeck in the mid-nineteenth century, was the inspirational forerunner of such naturalistic zoos as those in the Bronx and San Diego, and still manages to outdo its imitators.

The smoky haze that descends over Hamburg from time to time is to be expected in a city of heavy industry only sixty miles from the misty North Sea, but again there is the element of surprise when one realizes that the city is so clean and widely handsome. Hamburg has made the most of its two disasters, building sewers and orderly boulevards to replace dark, winding streets destroyed by the Great Fire, and replacing dank St. Pauli slums with model garden apartments after World War II. Glimpses of old Hamburg survive around the Fleete, the canal maze lined with gabled guild houses and cellar shops, in the eloquently baroque church of St. Michael, in St. Peter's, which was restored in the nineteenth century, and St. Catherine's, with its gold-capped steeple.

In addition to the shops, banks, factories, shipyards, office buildings, parks, waterways, and scenic suburban roads such as the Elbe Chaussee, the Hamburg *Labskaus* is generously seasoned with culture. Its Deutsches Schauspielhaus is one of the most vital and influential theaters in Germany, and the concerts in its Musikhalle are as good as they should be in the city that was the birthplace of Brahms and Mendelssohn. The Kunsthalle contains paintings that represent every major European art movement from the sixteenth century through the twentieth. It has outstanding collections of German, French, Italian, Spanish, Dutch, and Flemish works, a dazzling array of impressionist canvases, and exciting paintings by such Munich "Blue Rider" abstractionists as Kandinsky, Klee, and Franz Marc. The Völkerkunde Museum has more than 50,000 exhibits covering ethnic art and artifacts from primitive European and East Asian civilizations. The Museum of Local History tells Hamburg's story through maps, prints, and assorted memorabilia, and the Arts and Crafts Museum is a tribute to the guilds that operated in Hamburg for ten centuries, and gave the city its reputation for craftsmanship.

Hamburg plays every bit as hard as it works, as one night on the town will prove. The whole city seems to be washed in the neon haze of ultraviolet and acetylene-blue, especially in the waterfront suburb of St. Pauli. Here you will find what must be Hamburg's most famous street, the Reeperbahn, a wide and windy avenue lined with every kind of nighttime distraction known to man. Champagne clubs, sailors' dives, dance halls, music halls, cabarets, and cocktail lounges are all here to chose from. Floor shows range from plush Folies-type revues to sleazy strip shows where the girls exhibit the same kind of gum-chewing disinterest that characterized much of our own burlesque. Some shows are built around girls who perform with animals while others rely on that good old Hamburg specialty, *Damenringkampf im Schlamm*—women wrestling half-nude in slimy mud a foot deep—a spectacle every bit as revolting as its name. Jazz, hot or cool, is featured in smaller clubs along the Grosse Freiheit, the little street leading off the Reeperbahn, and if you feel like some good, clean Bavarian fun, you can find it at the big beer hall, Zillertal. In all, the Reeperbahn is a living monument to Gomorrah, a three-dimensional pornographic set-piece that gets beerier and beerier as dawn approaches and the last overblown drunks weave homeward. "Hamburg is a sailors'. town," guidebooks always say by way of explaining its night life, but even for a harbor city its after-dark hospitality seems a trifle exaggerated.

For a combined seaside vacation and a look at some of north Germany's medieval past, one could do no better than to travel to Schleswig-Holstein and the Baltic beach towns, the Ostseebäder, stopping for a while in Lübeck. This city was the "Queen of the Hansa," a strategic port at the junction of the Trave River and the Baltic. Much of its atmosphere stems from the medieval brick buildings along the docks and the forbidding Holstentor, the antique defense gate of the city. Black glazed tiles lend a feeling of power to the Gothic City Hall and the twelfth century Romanesque cathedral is noted for its soaring spires. Thomas Mann aficionados will come to this town that was his birthplace and visit Buddenbrooks House, the setting for his novel, while collectors of restaurants will not want to miss one of Germany's most historic—the Schiffergesellschaft. Once the guild house of the city's shipowners, it became a restaurant in 1863 and is famous for its vaulted ceiling and the ship models suspended from the rafters, as well as for its hearty Holstein fare: schnitzel, stuffed pork chops, and Holstein-bier, which natives drink with the juniper-flavored brandy, *Korn*.

Bremen, the third city in the Hansa triumvirate, also has handsome and fascinating relics of its medieval past: its guild houses and Town Hall, its cathedral and arcaded streets, and its landmark, the monument to the knight Roland that has loomed over the market place since the early fifteenth century. And for anyone who loves the detachment of island resorts, there is the charming North Sea Heligoland, famed for its sailors, its duned beaches, and its lobsters.

FRANKFURT AM MAIN

Germany, U.S.A.

FRANKFURT is probably the most American-looking city in Europe, a medium-sized metropolis of 672,000 people that recalls Milwaukee, Cleveland, or, even more exactly, New York's Germantown, Yorkville. It is a thriving, commercial city, a center of trade and banking, with its mind strictly on business. Looking at the modern office buildings (tall, but not quite skyscrapers), the well-dressed people, the clean streets, the automobiles, the busy shops and international restaurants, and the overwhelming number of excellent hotels, no one would guess that this city was a pile of rubble at the end of World War II.

The whole place has an air of prosperity and purpose; everyone seems to be dashing about on some vital mission. Even the stout-hatted *Hausfraus* who meet for a morning or afternoon *Kaffeeklatsch* in one of the *Konditoreien* seem merely to be pausing in a somewhat breathless shopping routine. String ensembles that play in restaurants and cafés do so, more and more, over the wheeling-and-dealing conversations of German salesmen who can pitch in any language prospective buyers happen to speak.

Frankfurt is Germany's market place, its airport is the busiest in the country, and it plays host to more Americans than any other city in the land. To tourists it is a gateway rather than a goal. It is the funnel through which they enter Siegfried's Rhine castle country or the *Baden* spas, the Grimms' fairytale land of the Black Forest, or the beer-and-*wurst, lederhosen* charm of Bavaria, the Student Prince *Schloss* of Old Heidelberg, or Mainz, the capital of the Palatinate with a thousand-year-old Romanesque cathedral and museums and monuments dedicated to its famous son, Gutenberg, who invented his movable type press and printed his first book here.

To businessmen, Frankfurt is the goal, most especially in spring and autumn when its enormous trade fairs are under way. And it is from this city, also, that they fan out to the manufacturing centers of Düsseldorf (the birthplace of Heinrich Heine), and Cologne (known for its Gothic-spired cathedral and its great artistic tradition). Those involved in matters of government head for Bonn, the birthplace of Beethoven and the capital of the ninety-six thousand square miles that comprise the Federal Republic of Germany, the western half of prewar Deutschland.

All of this coming and going is old hat to Frankfurt, for it has played a similar role since 794, when Charlemagne took up residence at what was then called *Franconoford,* the ford of the Franks. It was a free imperial city for five hundred years; twenty-three Holy Roman emperors were crowned in its cathedral. Even its trade fairs are historic: The one in spring originated in 1240, while the autumn event is a relative parvenu, a Frankfurt tradition only since 1330. And the October Book Fair is a reminder that this city was the center of the European book trade from the time Gutenberg opened his print shop there in 1454 until the end of the eighteenth century.

The city's complete name, Frankfurt am Main, is the clue to its success, for its position on the navigable Main River made it a vital link between the provinces of Hesse, Thuringia, Franconia, Swabia, and the Rhineland, as well as all of western Europe. Thus it provides a natural showcase for Germany's varied products: toys and tools; handicrafts and machinery; wine and beer; optical goods and precision instruments; automobiles and textiles; porcelain and plastics; and just about anything else that anyone wants to buy.

Frankfurt's two best known native sons typify the tone and range of interests in the city: the poet Goethe, who was born in 1749 in the little wrought-iron-trimmed house on the Grosser Hirschgraben that is now a museum. The banker Nathan Rothschild was born in the Frankfurt ghetto in 1777 and died in the same city fifty-nine years later, after founding the world's most fantastic international banking firm.

The combination of culture and commerce, of good living and good business is the way of life in Frankfurt. Being a Germany city it has its fabled zoo and its Palmengarten, one of the world's largest botanical displays; it has its Nizza garden promenade along the Main, its dozens of museums devoted to classic and modern art, stamps and coins, sculptures and handicrafts, natural history and astronomy. The Germans have a passion for collecting and observing, and the people of Frankfurt are no exception.

Sipping rich *mokka* coffee or a stein of beer at a café, you can watch the swirl of traffic that revolves around the main square, the Hauptwache, a modern spectacle in sharp contrast to the nearby St. Catherine's Church where Goethe was confirmed. The central telecommunication skyscraper of the postal department offsets the gateway to the Palace of Thurn and Taxis, the family that started Europe's first great international communications system, and ironically, you can see the administration building of the former I. G. Farben Industries, which escaped Allied bombs while most of antique Frankfurt did not. The Bourse hints at the city's still active role in world financing, while the Eschenheimer Tower is a mute souvenir of the medieval fortifications erected in 1426 to protect the city.

But by far the most romantic and historic section of Frankfurt is the Römer, once a Roman hill that predated Charlemagne. This Gothic square takes one back to the city's free imperial days. It was here that fountains flowed with wine, whole oxen were grilled on spits, and brilliant pageantry celebrated the coronation of the emperors which took place in the cathedral that still stands. Destroyed during the war but now completely restored, the Römer is etched with wrought-iron floral finials and curved railings, the gables of the medieval City Hall have been rebuilt, and the fourteenth century Cloth Guild Hall is almost completely repaired. Close to the Römer and in the inner Old Town are St. Paul's Church, where the first German National Assembly convened in 1848, and St. Nikolai's Church, dating from the thirteenth century and once the councillors' chapel.

For contrast again, see the modern square where the new opera house stands, the university, and the fair grounds with sixteen exhibition halls and ten foreign pavilions. And if the somewhat maddening whirl of Frankfurt proves too much for your nerves as well it might, you can recover quickly and delightfully at what is probably the most famous, and certainly the most handsome, spa in Europe. Baden-Baden, just two hours from Frankfurt by train, is a gracious reminder of its *fin de siècle* heyday, when it was the favorite watering place of Europe's crowned heads. It offers at least a dozen different kinds of thermal baths—steam, water, mud, inhalation, and almost anything else you can think of. At night you can try your luck at its magnificent gold baroque casino and during the day you can wander through its lovely parks, its Lichtenthaler Allee that was the favored promenade when Queen Victoria came to this town, and visit some of the pretty neighboring villages in this Black Forest setting. Baden-Baden's baths have been celebrated for their curative powers since Roman times and the new and larger bathhouse being built is ample evidence that its popularity is as great today as it ever was. Although they are primarily intended for rheumatic and arthritic cures, Baden-Baden's waters and treatments can be taken for reducing as well, and then you can go right out into one of the town's exquisite little pastry shops, such as the König, and put back any weight you might have taken off.

MUNICH

Summer surprised us coming over the Starnbergersee
With a shower of rain; we stopped in the colonnade,
And went on in sunlight into the Hofgarten,
And drank coffee, and talked for an hour.

"The Waste Land," *Collected Poems 1909–1962,*
by T. S. Eliot

T. S. Eliot is only one of the many poets and writers who have enjoyed Munich's charms. The city has won the praises of Heinrich Heine and Gottfried Keller, of Goethe and Thomas Mann, who opened his story, *Gladius Dei* with the exultant "Munich shone in all its greatness!" But no one was more inspired by it than Thomas Wolfe, who, in *The Web and the Rock* wrote, "How can one speak of Munich but to say it is a kind of German heaven. Some people sleep and dream they are in Paradise, but all over Germany people sometimes dream they have gone to Munich in Bavaria . . . And really, in an astonishing way, the city is a great Germanic dream translated into life."

The Bavarian capital is to Germany what Naples is to Italy and Seville is to Spain: the poetic southern city that gives the outside world its travel-poster image of the entire country. With their costumes, music, dances, and festivals, their food and natural settings, these places inspire the guidebook clichés that usually (and incorrectly) spill over to the country as a whole. The natives of all of these cities are more romantic, volatile, and exuberant than their countrymen to the north, and, with their broad humor, colorful idioms, and gently slurred lyrical dialects, they are generally taken for the national archetypes. (Northerners in these countries are only too eager to point out the fallacy of such imagery.)

To anyone who has never been to Germany, and to many who have, it is the land of beer and *wurst* set to the tune of the "Beer Barrel Polka" or the "ump-pah-pah" of a big brass band. In the popular image, it is peopled by stein-swinging, folk-singing burghers and *Hausfraus,* who wear *lederhosen* and aproned skirts, and speak a singsong Bayrische—an image most nearly summed up by Bavaria and its leading city, Munich.

Almost everything one thinks of in connection with Germany reaches its peak here. It is the world capital of *Gemütlichkeit*—that untranslatable word implying the spirit of warmth, friendliness, and easy good living that glows throughout Bavaria. It has been a beer-making center since the thirteenth century and boasts one-third of the world's breweries; its *Bierkellers* (a Munich invention) are numbered in the thousands, including the one in which Hitler attempted his unsuccessful *Putsch* in 1923, after which he went to jail and wrote *Mein Kampf.* Visit the Mathaser, the traditional Löwenbräukeller or the famed Hofbräuhaus on the Platzl, and you'll see thousands of people holding steins of *helles* or *dunkels* (light or dark) beer, joining in what must be the world's largest community sing.

In addition, Munich butchers know 115 different ways to make a sausage, and there's an intricate ritual about which is correct for which time of day, the local specialty being the 11 A.M. *Weisswurst.* Six meals a day are standard in this city, where the food is the best and richest in Germany. And if you visit Dahlmyer's, a Cartier's of a food shop full of cold meats, cheeses, cavair, sturgeon, salads, six kinds of mustard, and at least a dozen types of pickles, you'll remember perhaps, that delicatessen in a German word, a German idea, and practically a German obssession.

Munich is a city of promenade gardens and park cafés, statues and squares and sun-splashed fountains, innumerable restaurants, *Brotzeit* snack parlors and pastry *Konditoreien,* concert halls and a dozen theaters devoted to drama, modern and light, classical and experimental, a puppet playhouse, cabarets, and the bohemian *boîtes* of the Schwabing artist quarter. And everywhere, you see the bright blue-

and-white color scheme that flashes through the city like a banner: on tablecloths, traffic signs, and trams, in the cloud-dappled sky and on many of the striped awnings shading the fruit and vegetable stalls of the morning Viktualienmarkt.

As though life weren't gay enough in Munich, special fairs dot the civic calendar like currants in a stollen. There are flowers and food-decked observances for religious holidays such as Whitsuntide, Easter, and Christmas. There are summer music and drama festivals and trade fairs of gourmet delicacies and applied arts, folk crafts and industrial design. Three times a year a flea market rag fair, the Auer Dalt, is held as a kind of free-for-all for lovers of bargain antiques whose chances of turning up an unknown Dürer grow considerably smaller every year. Munich's pre-Lenten *Fasching* is an anything-goes winter carnival during which the city is one big masquerade ball for weeks on end, winding up on Shrove Tuesday when market women with candy-box bows in their hair dance in the open square of the Viktualienmarkt.

But to see just how gay Munich can get when it really bares its soul, one should be there during the *Oktoberfest,* the beer festival that runs from late September to early October—a tradition since 1810, when it began as a celebration of a royal wedding. Accurately described as "the greatest public merrymaking in Europe," this bottom-pinching, back-slapping paroxysm of revelry is as rowdy, raw, and raucous an event as you're likely to find anywhere. Seventy thousand people are served at once in the huge tent beer halls erected by the city's leading breweries on the Wisen fairgrounds. The air rings with sounds of screaming, laughing women, clanging Ferris wheels, carrousel calliopes, midway pitchmen, and blaring brass bands. The crisp fall nights are spiced with the scent of sizzling barbecued chickens and beer. There are parades and pageants, folk dancing, and natives in the Tyrolean costumes of Upper Bavaria. As the official guidebook says, "For sixteen days Munich lives in a whirl of hilarity"—a whirl that results in what may well be the biggest municipal *Katzenjammer* in the world.

Munich's gaiety, though traditional, is today something of a miracle, for at the end of World War II three-quarters of the city lay in ruins and one-third of its citizens were homeless. But, as in the rest of Germany, brightly balconied apartment houses rose on the ashes of bombed-out buildings, parks and squares were replanted, the

Müncheners indulged in one of their pet pastimes, street repairing, and brand-new industries cropped up on the edge of town. Today this "village of one million inhabitants" is more prosperous, brighter, and busier than it ever was, the second largest city in West Germany and one of the most beautiful. Its main square, officially Karlsplatz but more familiarly Stachus, is said to be Germany's most hectic intersection. At the height of the season, traffic signals controlled through television screens in police headquarters are supplemented by twenty patrolmen. There are underground pedestrian passageways and it is estimated that each day a quarter of a million people, twenty thousand cyclists, and three thousand pairs of tramcars cross the square. Guarded by arched gates that are remnants of Munich's medieval fortifications, both the neon-trimmed Stachus and the somewhat more gentle, tree-lined Sendlinger-Tor Platz represent Munich at its busiest and most modern.

The oldest and most picturesque part of the city is the Marienplatz, where markets were held in the Middle Ages. This square is rimmed with arcaded steets and red-roofed buildings that center around the Mariensäule, the flower-banked pedestal statue of St. Mary, the Bavarian patroness. On one side stands the nineteenth century pseudo-Gothic New Town Hall, with a tower Glockenspiel that draws tourists and Müncheners alike at 11 A.M. Mechanical knights and squires joust on horseback, red-coated coopers dance, and a rooster flaps his wings and crows as the hour strikes. In a corner of the square, the city's twin trademark, the green bulb-hatted red-brick towers of the Frauenkirche Cathedral look over the step-gabled houses, while opposite is the slate-gray Gothic spire of St. Peter's, the twelfth century basilica that was Munich's first parish church, and the Alte Peter of the popular Bavarian song. The Tal, the street leading off the square, ends at the best-preserved of the antique city gates, the Isartor, with its watchtowers and crenelated walls overlooking the Isar River just as they did when it was built in 1314.

It is to this river that Munich owes its historic role as a market town, though its name was derived from the *München*—the monks—of the Tegernsee Monastery that existed here in medieval times. Duke Henry the Lion founded the city in 1158 and established a market place and a mint, and built a bridge across the river in order to levy tolls, for it was an exact midway point on the east-west, north-south salt and grain trade routes. It later became the residence of the Bavarian kings, a fact that explains the great number of palace-museums and royal garden parks that grace the city today. Munich's reputation as a center of art, music, and learning began in the nineteenth century during the reigns of Ludwig I and Maximilian II. They started its art collections, supported it musical and theatrical activities and founded the university bearing both their names—the Ludwig-Maximilian University—close to the triumphal arch, the Siegestor, and Munich's Montmartre, Schwabing.

Other reminders of these rulers and their contributions to Munich's cultural life are everywhere in the city, most especially in the Odeonsplatz. Here an equestrian statue of Ludwig I, flanked by pages bearing his twin mottoes, "Perseverance" and "Justice," stands in front of the Residenz—the royal palace, now a museum of state apartments, crown jewels, and treasures displayed in the Schatzkammer. The square is flanked by the baroque green-doomed and towered Theatinerkirche; the Feldherrnhalle, modeled after the Loggia dei Lanzi in Florence's Piazza Signoria; and one of Munich's sunniest delights, the tree-shaded cafés and flowered walks of the royal garden turned public park, the Hofgarten.

Behind the Odeonsplatz are the theaters that began under royal patronage and still survive: the Residenz Theater and the Cuvilliés Theater—a red, white, and gold baroque masterpiece, where the renditions of Mozart operas set a high standard, just as those of Richard Strauss do when performed by the Bavarian State Opera in the Prinzregenten Theater.

Memories of Maximilian are strung out along the street that bears his name, past the highly respected National and Schauspielhaus theaters, past the Denkmal, the memorial statue honoring this king, and across the Isar to the Maximilianeum. Once a school for pages and young men headed for top government posts, this great golden building, in its wooded park, is now the seat of the Bavarian Diet and as such is, perhaps, the most fitting tribute to one of the state's greatest rulers.

Munich owes its reputation as an art center primarily to Ludwig I, who established the Alte Pinakothek. This museum now ranks as one of the seven great galleries of the world, along with the Louvre in Paris, the Uffizi in Florence, the London National Gallery, Madrid's Prado, the Kunsthistoriches Museum in Vienna and Berlin's Kaiser Fredrich. Its rooms are packed with works by Dürer and Altdörfer,

El Greco and Titian, Rembrandt and Michael Pacher, Da Vinci, Rubens, Raphael, Grünewald, Breughel, and all of the great European painters of the fourteenth to eighteenth centuries. Art of the nineteenth century, formerly part of Ludwig's Neue Pinakothek, is exhibited in the Haus der Kunst along with twentieth century and contemporary works.

Further evidence of Ludwig's interest in art is apparent in the classic square he had designed, the Königsplatz, with its Greek-inspired Propyläen and the antiquities museum, the Glyptothek. To understand the continuity of Munich's importance in the art world, cross this square to the Roman villa that houses the Municipal Gallery. Here you will see an excellent array of modern works—most especially those of Kandinsky, who came to Munich from Russia. Here he studied, taught, worked, and established two of the most significant movements in the modern art world: Die Brücke in 1900, with another Russian émigré, Jawlensky, and Der Blaue Reiter school with Paul Klee and Franz Marc in 1910. This last, named after a painting by Kandinsky, was one of the first and most influential abstract art movements in Europe, and painters such as Picasso, Dérain, Braque, Rouault, and Vlaminck joined in their exhibitions.

If you think you've heard about all of Munich's great museums and churches, you are in for a surprise, for if ever a city suffered an embarrassment of artistic riches, this one does. More museums? Try the National with its magnificent samples of Bavarian handicrafts produced between the Middle Ages and the nineteenth century: wood carvings, tapestries, peasant beds and chests, chairs and tables, suits of armor, models of old towns, porcelains, and the splendid Krippenschau collection of Christmas nativity scenes. The Munich State Museum does for the city what the National does for Bavaria, and gives a fascinating glimpse into the lives of eighteenth and nineteenth century Müncheners. Art is not the only thing that finds it way into museums here, as you will discover when you see the Deutsches Museum, sitting on a little island in the middle of the Isar. It is the largest museum of science and technology in Europe, if not in the world. A complete tour of its rooms measures some eight and a half miles and it includes a planetarium and every kind of chemical and physical exhibit one can imagine. Then there is a museum of primitive folk arts, and another, a private collection of the Schack family, in a gallery just off Prinzregentenstrasse, and exhibitions of graphics, and a theater museum near the Hofgarten.

Even the Botanical Gardens and the Hellabrunn Zoo must be ranked as museums in this city, so astonishing and complete are their collections. The first contains samples of flowers and shrubs from every continent: orchids, cactuses, rockeries where immigrant plants from the Himalyas have found a home, flaming groves of rhododendrons, tropical hothouses, and the queen of plants, the Victoria Regia. The king of beasts, the lion, is only one of eleven thousand animals that live in natural surroundings in the zoo. It includes all kinds of snakes and seals, antelopes and elephants, exotic birds and fish, with quarters arranged to simulate their native geographical conditions. And to prove just how zealous the Germans are when they begin to experiment, the zoo even includes aurochs, a species that became extinct three centuries ago, but which zoologists and geneticists have been able to breed back.

Munich numbers several churches among its artistic treasures. Besides those already mentioned, there is the Michaelskirche, an old church of the Augustines, with a great rotunda of a barrel-vaulted ceiling and a white and gold Renaissance interior that looks like a gigantic and elegant wedding cake. The modern church of St. Matthew's, looking like a ship lying at anchor, is in sharp contrast to the baroque Dreifaltigkeitskirche, while the church in Berg am Laim and the Asamkirche are outstanding examples of rococo, and the Ludwigskirche is a delicate masterpiece of neoclassic restraint.

If one should happen to forget that Munich is a German city, there are more than enough parks to remind you of the fact. In addition to the sprawling exhibition park with its Hall of Fame and the Statue of Bavaria, whose head you can climb into for a panoramic view of the city, Munich's great arboreal pride is the English Garden. It is a wooded countryside in the heart of the city, with horse-drawn carriages, a Chinese pagoda tower that is an open-air restaurant, a pretty rowboat lake, the Kleinhosseloher See, and a Greek temple-like lookout, the Monopteros.

Schloss Nymphenburg, an hour out of town, is a park, a museum, and a palace all rolled into one. It is a graceful eighteenth century château that was the summer residence of the Bavarian electors and kings, bordered by the Botanical Gardens and watered by artificial lakes and streams. Inside the palace one can see royal apartments and a treasury full of jewels, an outstanding collection of the lifelike Nymphenburg porcelain figurines, a roomful of paintings of great Munich beauties done for Ludwig I, and the Marstallmuseum, a collection of painted and gilded fairy coaches dating from the time of Ludwig II. Secluded in one corner of the royal park is the little rococo gem of a palace, the precisely elegant Amalienburg. On festive occasions women in towering powdered wigs and Marie-Antoinette-style ball gowns and men in courtly knee breeches and silk coats complete the eighteenth century atmosphere of the palace and park, moving to the tune of Mozart's *Eine Kleine Nachtmusik*.

As if Munich's charms weren't more than enough to draw tourists and vacationers, it is set in the midst of Germany's gorgeous Bavarian countryside. The entire plateau of Upper Bavaria is strewn with little churches with twinkling onion-shaped towers (the influence of eastern Europe has always been strong here and still is with immigrants pouring in from Communist countries) and castles rich with baroque and rococo curves. The great castles of the mad Ludwig II—the Neuschwanstein, the Linderhof, and the Herrenchiemsee—are not far from the Bavarian Alps, the great towering peaks that delight hikers and mountaineers in summer and skiers in winter. Heading south from the city you will come to the sailboat-bright Starnbergersee, the country's leading winter mountain resort, Garmisch-Partenkirchen, from which you can go by railway, cable car, or elevator to the summit of the Zugspitze, a peak 9,722 feet high, and then on to Oberammergau, the scene of the famous Passion Play. South, too, are the green-wooded forest, the Grünewald, and budget resort lakes like the Tegernsee and the Schliersee, with their Tyrolean mountain villages. The road heading southeast takes you to the Austrian border spa, Bad Reichenhall, or further, to Berchtesgaden, the magnificently landscaped mountain area where Hitler had his "eagle's nest" retreat.

FOR THE TRAVELER'S NOTEBOOK

Official Information

Before you go: German Tourist Information Office, 500 Fifth Ave., New York, N.Y.; 11 South La Salle St., Chicago 3, Ill.; 323 Geary St., San Francisco, Cal.

Berlin: SAS Office, 10 Joachimstalerstr.; Municipal Information Office

(*Verkehrsamt*), 728 Fasanenstr. Charlottenburg 2; U.S. Consulate, 170 Clay Allee, Dahlem.

Hamburg: SAS Office, 38 Ballindamm; Municipal Information Office, Bieber Haus, next to Main Railroad Station; U.S. Consulate, 27 Alsterufer.

Frankfurt: SAS Office, 2 Am Hauptbahnhof; Municipal Information Office, in Hauptbahnhof, Main Railroad Station; U.S. Consulate, 21 Siesmayerstr.

Munich: SAS Office, 8 Maximilianstr.; Municipal Information Office, 1 Rosental; U.S. Consulate General, 527 Königinstr.

Money Matters

Currency: The monetary unit is the German mark (DM), which is divided into 100 pfennig. $1, U.S. equals DM 3.95.

Tipping: A service charge of 15 per cent is added to your hotel check; it is customary to leave a mark or so behind when you pay your bill; 50 pfennig per suitcase in general; 10 per cent service charge in restaurants, but a small extra tip is customary.

Climate, Clothing, and Essentials

The climate is temperate all year round, spring, summer, and fall being most agreeable for travel. A light topcoat or raincoat is advisable. From November to March you will need a warm coat; January and February are the coldest months. Normal city attire is correct in all the cities.

Hotels

There are comfortable and clean hotels throughout Germany in every price category. Private baths are available with all rooms in the de luxe hotels, but in less expensive establishments only a portion of the rooms have this feature, and generally they are a little more expensive. Since there are so many trade fairs, music festivals, and other such events in many German cities throughout the year, it is always best to have reservations confirmed before you arrive.

Hotel rates range from about DM 21 to 55 for single room and bath in a de luxe hotel; DM 40 to 98, double. First class hotels charge from DM 16 to 38 for single rooms; DM 24 to 65, double. Moderately priced hotel rates range from DM 12 to 21, single; DM 20 to 35, double; and inexpensive rooms can be had from DM 9 to 12, single; DM 16 to 28, double.

Rates in Hamburg and Munich are in a slightly higher price range. De luxe hotel rates in both cities charge from DM 28 to 55 for a single room and bath; DM 45 to 98, double. First class hotels charge from DM 20 to 38, single; DM 32 to 65, double. Moderate and inexpensive rates are about the same as those in the other two cities. Any of the German

Tourist Information offices at the above addresses can send you the complete "Hotel Guide to West Germany."

BERLIN

DE LUXE: *Berlin-Hilton, Budapester Strasse.* This huge 350-room hotel is the city's largest and newest hotel, done in the standard Hilton format. Conveniently located and at the top of the de luxe price level. *Bristol Kempinski, 27 Kurfürstendamm,* is a popular international hotel. Modernized recently, it is in the heart of the shopping and amusement area. *Hotel Berlin, 63–69 Kurfürstendamm.* Prices here hover between de luxe and upper first class rates but the service, rooms, and location put it in the top class from the standpoint of comfort. *Hotel am Zoo, 25 Kurfürstendamm.* Rates range from de luxe to moderate here, depending on whether or not you take a room with a private bath.

First class: Parkhotel Zellermayer, 15 Meinekestrasse, the *Plaza, 63 Knesebeckstrasse,* and the *Windsor, 8–9 Knesebeckstrasse,* are only a few years old and offer modern appointments and good service; all three are located just a few minutes away from the city's main street, the Kurfürstendamm. *Hotel Savoy, 9–10 Fasanenstrasse,* is well known for its exceptionally good service and ultramodern appointments, and its dining room is justly popular. *Steinplatz, 197 Uhlandstrasse.* This charming and quiet little hotel has excellent food, an intimate bar, and a pleasant oldworld grace about it. It faces a pretty little square.

MODERATE: *Hotel Lichtburg, 10 Paderborner Strasse,* comfortable and modern, is located in a quiet residential area and the service puts it in the first class category, though its rates are moderate. *Roxy, 34 Kurfürstendamm.* A good restaurant and handy location make this a popular hotel, with very modest rates. It is small and private and the rooms are pleasant. *Stephanie, 38 Bleibtreustrasse,* and the *Tusculum, 68 Kurfürstendamm,* offer similar conveniences and are in the same top service–moderate price group.

INEXPENSIVE: Inexpensive hotels in Berlin include the *Hotel Pension Regina, 37 Kurfürstendamm, Hotel Frühling am Zoo, 17 Kurfürstendamm,* and the *Metro, 59–60 Kurfürstendamm.*

HAMBURG

If you arrive in Hamburg without a reservation, the Hotel Accommodation Bureau in the Railroad Station (Hauptbahnhof) will gladly help you.

DE LUXE: Hamburg's two most famous and luxurious hotels are the *Atlantic, 73 An de Alster,* and the *Vier Jahreszeiten, 9–14 Neuer Jungferstieg,* overlooking the Inner and Outer Alster lakes. Many rooms in both hotels have balconies and lake views, the restaurants are elegant, the rooms comfortable and attractive, and the service unsurpassed.

FIRST CLASS: *Alsterhof, 12 Esplanade,* close to both the lake and shopping center, is comfortable and efficient. *Reichshof, 34–36 Kirchenalle.* Many rooms here have showers and the location, close to the Central Station, is a handy one. *Continental, 37 Kirchenallee,* and the *Europaïscher Hof, 45 Kirchenallee,* are two other equally good and convenient hotels in this category. *Berlin, 1–9 Borgelderstrasse,* Hamburg's newest hotel, offers large, pleasant rooms, good food, and is close to the city's business center.

MODERATE: *Stuttgarter Hof, 10 Bremer Reihe,* and the *Linden, 53 Kirchenallee,* are small, moderate to inexpensive hotels without private baths or restaurants, but the service is adequate.

FRANKFURT

DE LUXE: *Frankfurt Intercontinental,* opened in 1963, is the city's largest and ultramodern hotel. It offers every convenience you can think of. *Frankfurter Hof, 33 Kaiserplatz,* luxurious and newly redecorated, has the popular Lippizzaner Bar and two good restaurants. Some of its rooms have balconies. *Hessischer Hof, 40 Friedrich Ebert Anlage,* offers superb service and good location and is convenient to the site of the trade fair. *Savigny, 14 Savignystrasse.* This modern and luxurious hotel is pleasantly small and private and its décor is cheerful. Centrally located with attractive dining room and bar. *Monopol-Metropol, 11 Mannheimerstrasse.* Rooms here are comfortable and large, and though the hotel is opposite the station, it is quiet. *Parkhotel, 36–38 Wiesenhüttenstrasse,* and the remodeled *Fürstenhof Carlton, 18 Am Hauptbahnhof,* are two other good choices in the luxury class. The *Schlosshotel Kronberg, 25 Hainstrasse, Kronberg,* a former royal palace, is twelve miles from the city in a lovely park setting. Rooms are small but plush, and there is a nine-hole golf course on the grounds.

FIRST CLASS: *Continental, 56 Baselerstrasse,* is small, comfortable, with good personal service, and is close to the station and the city center. *Hotel Basler Hof, 25 Wiesenhüttenplatz.* Rooms here are quiet and adequate and about half of them have private baths.

MODERATE: *Hamburger Hof, 10–12 Poststrasse,* and the *Union Hotel, 52 Münchenerstrasse,* are small, pleasant hotels with good service and moderate rates.

MUNICH

DE LUXE: Two Munich hotels are in the absolute top of the luxury class establishments in the city: the *Vier Jahreszeiten, 17 Maximilian-*

strasse, known for its most famous restaurant, the Waltherspiel, its excellent service, and luxurious rooms. *Bayerischer Hof, 4–6 Promenadeplatz,* with its terrace and swimming pool that are glass-enclosed for winter, has been recently modernized and has spacious, pleasant rooms and good food. The *Grand Hotel Continental, 1 Max-Josefstrasse,* with its roof-garden restaurant and convenient but quiet location, and the *Königshof, 25 Karlsplatz,* with its elegantly furnished, spacious rooms, are also excellent luxury hotels popular with international travelers.

FIRST CLASS: *Deutscher Kaiser, 2 Arnulfstrasse,* a skyscraper hotel with all modern facilities; the *Regina-Palast, 5 Maximiliansplatz,* and the *Platzhotel, 8–9 Münzstrasse,* right next to the Hofbräuhaus, are all comfortable, pleasant hotels in the upper first class price bracket.

MODERATE: The *Bundensbahn Hotel, Am Hauptbahnhof,* near the railroad station and with an attractive dining room; the refurbished *Schottenhamel, 3 Prielmayerstrasse,* and the *Eden-Hotel Wolff, 4–8 Arnulfstrasse,* are all well-equipped, pleasant, and most adequate, as is the new *Mark, 15 Senefelderstrasse,* with its colorful Bavarian restaurant.

INEXPENSIVE: Hotels in this category well worth considering are: the *Stachus, 7 Bayerstrasse,* one of the city's best buys—half of its rooms have showers; the *Hotel Torbrau, 37 Tal;* and the *Esplanade, 27 Bayerstrasse.*

Food and Restaurants

All of the large German cities have fine restaurants featuring the food of virtually every country on earth, but the native specialties will be more interesting to any bona fide traveler. There are *Schnell Imbiss* (quick snack) stands everywhere, and the range of restaurants includes the highest type, the *Gastätten;* the *Bierstuben* or *Hofbräus,* where simple short-order dishes and a few cooked specialties are served primarily as an adjunct to beer; and *Weinstuben,* with food meant primarily to go with wine.

The bread is without doubt the best in the world, and so are the sausages, primarily a Munich specialty. There is one for every time of day. No real Münschener would be caught eating at 11 A.M. steamed veal *Weisswurst* at four in the afternoon when the soft, spreadable, spicy *Mettwurst* is considered mandatory. Other varieties are *Schweinswurstl,* fried pork sausages, plain *Wurstl,* always served in pairs, coarsely ground *Bratwurst,* a grilled pork-and-veal sausage, fried *Cervalat* or *Jägerwurst,* and over a hundred others.

Special dishes to try are the Westphalian ham and pumpernickel, all of the pork, the cheese, and dairy products. Famous German dishes always on the menu are the oxtail soup (*Ochsenschwanzsuppe*), pea soup, turtle soup, fruit soups, and consommé with liver dumplings.

A colossal array of herring and herring salads, *Sauerbraten* (marinated pot roast), Austrian-inspired goulash and schnitzel, roast duckling, and goose are ubiquitous. Berlin is known for its two pastry specialties, the towering almond-flavored cake, *Baumkuchen* and *Berliner Pfannkuchen,* the original jelly doughnut and its *Königsberger Klops,* meatballs with a piquant caper, lemon, and anchovy sauce; and its own version of yellow-pea and bacon soup. Hamburg is noted for its eel soup and its sailor's hash, *Labskus; its Bohnen-und-Bitten,* a stew of beans, pears, and bacon; and its pea soup with pig's knuckles and snout (*Erbensupper mit Snuten und Poten).* The oysters are a local fetish and understandably so. Frankfurt (in addition to the frankfurter) is noted for its *Kassler Rippchen,* smoked pork loin served with sauerkraut, and the hard cider, *Apfelwein,* that is available throughout the country. A huge assortment of dumplings (*Knödel*) typify Munich's cuisine and in addition to *wursts,* you should try *Leberkäs,* a steamed *pâté* meat loaf of liver and spices that is served hot; and the roast suckling pig, *Spanferkel.* Pastry in this city is unquestionably the world's most exquisite.

Everywhere and with everything, you will find cucumber salads, good mustard, sauerkraut flavored with caraway or juniper, cabbage, red and white, sweet and sour, or simmered in wine, and some of the best potato concoctions imaginable. Beer is wonderful whether you order light (*helles*) or dark (*dunkels*) and *Weissbier,* taken with a dash of currant juice, is a northern favorite. Wines are light and pleasant and you may order them by the glass—*ein Schoppen.*

The Rhine wines such as *Niersteiner, Rüdesheimer* and *Assmannshause-ner* are excellent, as are the Moselles—*Zeller Schwarze Katz, Doktorwein, Bernkastell,* and the red *Ahr-Burgunder* are very good with some of the rich beef *roulades* and *Sauerbraten. Trochenbeeren* is a velvety-sweet raisin wine that is pleasant for dessert. *Schnaps,* the German whisky, is fiery and exhilarating and is very good with herring.

BERLIN

The *Berliner Kindl* and the *Schultheiss* are owned by breweries; the food is good, the portions large, the beer excellent, and prices moderate. The *Aben* is known for its game and roast goose and other seasonal specialties, and the dining room is rich in atmosphere. Expensive. *Kottler's* serves Bavarian food in a suitable setting to the music of a zither. The *Ritz* is a super-production, where the menu is printed on silk scrolls and offers a choice of Oriental, Russian, Arabic, or German dishes. It is a tourist high spot and therefore expensive, but if you go for this sort of showmanship, you may enjoy it. *Maison de France* serves French food and has dancing, while *Schlichter* is popular with artists and theater people and has just about the best German food in the city. *Hardtke* is also old, charming, good, and not expensive.

HAMBURG

One of the city's pleasantest restaurants, the *Alster Pavilion,* overlooks the Inner Alster lake and is known for its international food, its sidewalk café, and its pastry. The *Rosenhof,* also in a lovely setting, has a terrace and a good menu, while the *Fischereihaften* and *Sellmer's* near Hamburg's famed waterfront, have wonderful seafood. The *Vegetarische Gaststätte* serves interesting vegetarian dishes, and *Michelsen* has an enticing delicatessen display, while its upstairs dining room features Hamburg dishes. The large handsome *Ratsweinkeller* features a Hamburg buffet, eel soup on Fridays, and Javanese *rijstefel. Peter Lembke* serves superb local specialties. The old and very beautiful *Weinrestaurant Ehmke* has been popular for its seafood for over a century, and *Insel* is a hangout for artists and theater people. *Zum Hanseaten,* done up in décor of the Hanseatic era, has a quiet and pleasant atmosphere and good food, and the *Z.O.B. Terminal Snack Bar* is inexpensive and good for light lunches.

FRANKFURT

Be sure to pay a visit to one of the *Apfelwein* inns in this city: *Blauer Engel, Gemaltes Haus,* or *Schneider-Dauth. Grauer Bock,* which also serves *Apfelwein,* has good food, community singing, and provides an evening's entertainment along with the excellent *Rippchen. Malepartus* has a prize-winning native kitchen, and *Kaiserkeller* is famous throughout Germany for international as well as local food and for its pleasant café, which is open in summer. The *Savarin* and the *Brückenkeller* are good, very charming, and full of atmosphere; the *Neuhof Restaurant* serves well-prepared German dishes, while *Mutter Krauss,* a well-known inn, serves excellent game and seafood. The last two are outside the city. *Kranzler's* one of the most famous café-patisseries in the world, serves regular meals along with its rich pastries, hot chocolates, and whipped cream (*Schlagobers*); among the city's other excellent cafés are *Rumpelmayer's* and *Hauptwache.*

MUNICH

Humplmayer and the *Walterspiel,* of the *Hotel Vier Jahreszeiten,* are far and away the city's most luxurious and best restaurants, and each has its *aficionados.* No one who can afford it should miss either. Other de luxe restaurants in the city include the typically Bavarian *Schwarzwälder, Boettner's,* noted for seafood, *Holzmueller,* which has dancing, antique furnishings, and German as well as continental food, and the exclusive

Ewige Lampe. Franziskaner-Fuchsenstuben is a traditional beer restaurant that is large and attractive and has outdoor dining in summer. *Spatenhaus* is typically Bavarian and very handsomely done in a slightly more elegant vein than usual. The *Kaiserschmarren* (pancake strips served with powdered sugar) are especially light and delicate here. The *Peterhof Gaststätte* is noted for its mixed grill (the Glockenspiel here is as delightful as the morning *Weisswurst*), and the enormous *Ratskeller* in the Town Hall is colorful and modestly priced. Unquestionably Munich's most interesting restaurants are its *Hofbräus* and *Bierstuben.* No one should miss the colorful and excellent *Nürnberger Bratwurstglöckl,* with its Bavarian bric-a-brac and glass-enclosed kitchen; *Donisl,* with late-night entertainment and excellent soup with liver dumplings; *Platzl,* which is a world unto itself with large portions, moderate prices, and much gaiety; the *Hofbräuhaus,* the most famous beer hall in Germany and absolutely enormous and fascinating; and *Zum Spöckmeier. Mathaser* is the world's largest beer hall, owned by the Löwenbräu brewery, and *Den Rauche Onkel* is an incredible maze of snack bars, delicatessens, counters, and dining rooms, plus a take-out service as well—a sight not to be missed. Two wonderful *Konditoreien* for pastry are *Kreutzkamm* and the *Feldherrenhall Café.* Anyone interested in food should see *Dallmeyer's,* perhaps *the* most glorious delicatessen on the face of the earth.

Entertainment, Night Life, and Special Events

BERLIN

The cultural life of Berlin centers in its theaters and concert halls. The Schiller Theater, rebuilt after the war, is West Berlin's most modern playhouse, and is provided with the latest technical devices and top actors, directors, and producers. Here the classics of Goethe, Schiller, Shakespeare, and Molière alternate with outstanding modern dramas. More esoteric plays are staged at the Schlosspark Theater. Other leading stages include the Theater am Kurfürstendamm, the Renaissance Theater, the Komödie, the Tribüne, and the Hebbel Theater. Opera and ballet flourish in the Städtische Opera, and connoisseurs of music from all over the world treasure the recordings of the Berliner Philharmoniker. The late Wilhelm Furtwängler made this orchestra world famous and his succesor, Herbert von Karajan, has carried on in the noble tradition. The Radio Symphony Orchestra is also highly thought of. Principal concerts are given at the Hochschule für Musik. During the summer, one of the chief attractions is an evening in the open-air theater Waldbühne, near the Olympic Stadium. It offers a varied repertory including film shows. Also in summer there are the distinguished *Serenade-Abende* (chamber concerts) at the Grünewald hunting lodge, and in the Tegel and Charlottenburg palaces.

Berlin night life caters to almost every taste. Most visitors will enjoy the enormous variety hall–restaurant, *Ballhaus Resi* with a fine water show, dancing, and table-telephones with which you can summon any girl in the place who strikes your fancy, a feature of many German night spots. The *Badewanne* is a subterranean dance hall–jazz club favored by the city's younger set; and the *Goldenes Hufeisen* is one of the world's wildest night clubs, where you may ride a horse around the dance floor. The city is crammed with bars, mostly around the Kurfürstendamm and Budapesterstrasse. Among the most popular are the *Old-Fashioned Bar, Bojar,* the *Ciro* and *Remdi's St. Pauli am Zoo,* where guests use fishing rods to remove part of the female dancer's clothing.

There is dancing at many of the restaurants and hotels; and the *Wannsee-Terrassen,* half an hour out of the city, has fine food, dancing, and a floor show. *Haus Garow am See* is a lakeside garden restaurant with dancing, and a typical Berlin-style cabaret entertainment. It is a favorite of the local families.

The *International Film Festival* in June is one of the world's most important; in September the *Berliner Festwochen* (Berlin Festival Weeks) take place as a prelude to the winter season; and outstanding German and international ensembles and artists contribute to gala performances of drama, opera, ballet, and symphony concerts. At the same time the *German Industries Exhibition* is held.

HAMBURG

This is a sailor's town and its night life is suitably raucous and rough, though you can find clubs on the usual international level. Strip tease reaches its blatant peak in Hamburg, and the St. Pauli section, better known as the Reeperbahn, is washed in the rosy glow of its twinkling red lights twenty-four hours a day. Parts of this can get pretty rough; and if you have a chip on your shoulder this is the place to get it knocked off. *Glockenkate* and the *Washington-Bar* are the sort of places you would expect to find here, while the *Zillertal* is a huge Bavarian-style restaurant in the same area with good, clean community singing, German style. The *Bikini,* the *Jungmühle,* and the *Hippodrome,* all adjoining, are monuments to Sodom, with wild and sexy floor shows unsurpassed anywhere in the world. There are other night clubs around the central stations; and the *Münchener Hofbräuhaus* is a Bavarian-style beer hall that is popular and inexpensive. Elegant shows are given at *Tarantella* (Spanish-style). The *Vaterland,* the *Hansa,* and the *Kleine Komödie* are variety houses that are best enjoyed if you understand German.

If you can tear yourself away from the nightclub circuit, you might like to know Hamburg is famous for its fine theaters. The Staatsoper (state opera) is among the most modern in the world. If you understand German, you will long remember a performance at the Deutsches Schauspielhaus, and there are many other theaters in the city. The Operettenhaus is of particular interest to foreign visitors, with its repertory of musical comedy and operettas. Symphony concerts are held at the Musikhalle, where leading soloists from the whole world also give recitals.

FRANKFURT

There is plenty of entertainment in this city with about eighty cinemas and four famous theaters: the Städtische Bühnen, Intimes Theater im Zoo, Theater am Rossmarkt, and Die Schmiere, a sort of literary cabaret. In summer there are open air entertainments in the Carmelite Monastery in the Münzgasse. The museum symphony orchestra plays in the *Grosses Haus,* and chamber music concerts are held in the Volksbildingsheim. Orchestral concerts may also be heard in the Congress Hall or in the broadcasting studios of Radio Frankfurt (Dornbusch). If you have any taste for night life left after Hamburg and Berlin, there is more to be had here, and you can get the complete list from the booklet "This Week in Frankfurt," your hotel porter, or the Frankfurt Tourist Office. There is dancing in many hotels and restaurants and the cafés already mentioned are crowded and gay at night. Some of the most popular night clubs are the sophisticated *Hüttenbar* and the *Lippizzaner Bar* in the *Hotel Frankfurter Hof;* the *Café Regina,* and *Tropicana* are good for dancing; and the *Rheinland,* the *Parisianabar,* and the *Tabu* have floor shows, all with performers on the lightly clad side.

MUNICH

Munich Monthly, a publication on sale at newsstands, lists all the city's current attractions. If you like operettas, spend an evening at the Theater am Gartnerplatz. Here the Bayerisches Staatstheater presents the great Viennese classics. In addition to the bigger theaters like the Kammerspiele, there are smaller ones which are less expensive and which usually have very good performances. They include the Kleine Komödie, Theater unter den Arkaden, and Kleine Freiheit. Leading symphony concerts are given in the Herkulessaal of the Residenz or the Kongress-saal of the Deutsches Museum, and there are one or more concerts every evening during the winter season. Cabaret theaters are found all around the city and include the Annast-Kabarett, Die Zwiebel, and the Stachelschwein. There are also a lot of night clubs with dancing and floor shows. Schwabing, the Bohemian "Monmartre of Munich," has many night clubs and bars of all kinds including the *Käfig Gisela, Siegesgarten,* where you can have good and very low-priced food, and *Badewanne* at *Feilitzstrasse.*

Most of the Schwabing places are inexpensive. The night clubs in the city include *PI, Studio 15, Atelier,* and *Beidel Heinz,* which are rather exclusive and expensive.

All of the Christian holidays are celebrated in Germany and in most cities the pre-Lenten Carnival, *Fasching,* is an anything-goes revelry, found at its most exuberant in Munich.

The outstanding events are the *Bavarian State Opera Festival* in July and August and the gay *Oktoberfest,* held during the last week of September and the first week of October, beginning with an international costume parade that takes place on the first Sunday.

If you happen to be in Munich in May, July, or October, ask your hotel porter if the *Auer Dult* is on. It is a market place with traditions reaching far back in the history of the city, and it could perhaps best be compared with the Flea Market in Paris.

Shopping

Cameras, leather goods, woolen fabrics (especially coats made of Loden cloth) optical instruments, clocks, china, glassware, toys, cutlery, antiques, regional costumes, and wood carvings are the country's best buy.

BERLIN

You will find most of Berlin's elegant shops along the Kurfürstendamm, Tauentzienstrasse, Schlosstrasse, and Potsdamerstrasse. Women will be particularly tempted by the high fashions here: *Horn's* has an absolutely magnetic effect, and for jersey dresses it is perhaps matched only by *Leibling.* For an over-all glimpse of what Berlin has to offer, visit the department store *KaDeWe,* while *Eickelberg* is famous for its selections of toys, Maerklin electric trains and Stieff animals. The *Rosenthal* shop sells its world-famous porcelain, and *Henckel's* has a huge array of superb Solingen cutlery. It will be hard to walk twenty feet without seeing a camera shop, and for antiques, just walk along the Eisenacherstrasse, Keithstrasse or Fasanenstrasse and you will be overwhelmed.

HAMBURG

The main shopping district in the center of the city includes Mönckebergstrasse, Jungfernstieg, Grosse Bleichen, and neighboring streets. Department stores such as the air-conditioned *Karstadt* are to be found on Mönckebergstrasse. Marvelous toys are available at *Kinderparadies*—literally "Children's Paradise"—on Neuer Wall. There is one floor for trains alone.

FRANKFURT

The principal shopping districts lie between the Main Railroad Station and the Konstablerwache, along Kaiserstrasse and the Goethestrasse. Here you will find branches of many of the stores mentioned under Berlin and Hamburg. *Lorey's* has porcelain figurines and beer steins, among other things; and *Uhren Posner* and *Meister Bergmann* have a huge roundup of cuckoo clocks between them. *Haus der Kinder* and *Spielzeug Onkel* have wonderful toys, while *Ernst Nobel* and *Weber* have regional outfits such as *lederhosen*, Tyrolean hats, dirndls and such *gemütlich* wear.

MUNICH

The main shopping area here is along the Kaufingerstrasse, Neuhaserstrasse, the Lauflingerstrasse, and around the Stachus. There are specialty shops in the Hofgarten area and antiques along Maximilianstrasse and Barerstrasse. One of the city's outstanding souvenirs is a beer stein purchased directly from the *Münchener Hofbräuhaus*. *Loden Frey* sells all sorts of coats and capes made of the famous gray-green cloth; and the *Staatliche Porzellan Manufaktur*, along with the largest *Rosenthal* shop in Germany, sell china, figurines, and dinnerware. The *Deutsche Werkstätten* has local handicrafts. *Spelwaren Obletter* is an enticing toy store and *Ober Pollinger Kaufhaus* is a department store with a wide selection of just about everything.

Background Reading

Toward Understanding Germany, by Robert H. Lowie
Germany: Countryside, Cities, Villages, and People by Rudolf Hagelstange
The Linden Trees, by Carlo Levi
Unknown Germany, by Bernard Newman
The Train Was on Time, by Heinrich Böll
The Revolt of Gunner Asch, by Hans Helmut Kirst
Buddenbrooks, by Thomas Mann

Greece (Kingdom of Hellas)

ATHENS

Pindar's numinous city,
the jeweled crown of Greece

THERE are a number of reasons why tourists are flocking to Greece by the ever-increasing thousands. Some go to wander around the sun-gold, thyme-scented ruins, others to get lost on a whitewashed, wind-milled Aegean island. Some hope to follow the paths of Olympian gods, others to sail the indigo sea on a Homeric odyssey of their own. Many go to Greece because it is still one of Europe's biggest bargains; others go because it is chic to have been. Painters and writers hope that perhaps "the mother of arts and eloquence" will lend them inspiration, and some, like Isaac Hill Bromley, are "weary of the common-place" and look for the same kind of exotic diversions he sought— honey from Hymettus and stores of Attic salt. Romantics might want to visit the haunts of the poet-hero, Byron, or of such latter-day literary oracles as Henry Miller and the brothers Durrell. Any man who has seen the movie *Never On Sunday* will want to tour the Piraeus *tavernas* in search of Melina Mercouri or a reasonable facsimile.

Whatever the reasons behind the trip, chances are everyone who goes to Greece enters by way of its capital, and that can be more than a little disheartening at first glance, no matter what one's vision of the country happens to be. The situation that is Athens' dilemma—and its pride—was never summed up better than by a recent *New Yorker* cartoon. It depicted three American tourists—two women and a man— standing midst the roofless columns of the Parthenon, all looking disheveled and breathless from their climb up the slopes of the Acropolis. One of the women, indicating the view, says, in the best traditions of Polyanna, "It's worth the climb! You can see the Athens Hilton just as clear!"

That, in short, is Athens for you—a city where no one can decide whether to concentrate on the present or delve into the past, where the Hilton boasts of its view of the Acropolis and the guides on the ancient hilltop return the compliment. As a result, none of the travel-poster images of Greece apply to its capital, save the one of the Parthenon, the great golden fragment of a temple that stands over the city exactly as you expect it to. For the rest, Athens is as jumbled, hectic, and dazzling a city of one and a half million as you are likely to find anywhere—a pell-mell combination of elegance and garishness, wealth and poverty, beauty and excrescence.

The cement warrens with their paint peeling, the noisy markets and the narrow cobblestoned streets of the Plaka district at the foot of the Acropolis, are rimmed by the arc of modern Athens, a section of broad boulevards and public gardens, terraced apartment houses and vine-covered villas, the sumptuous Royal Palace and formal government buildings, and bright avenues lined with luxury hotels, restaurants, and shops. The whole town is a hubbub of activity from early morning to late at night and almost on to dawn again. No one ever seems to sleep; and everywhere there is the clamor of street drills and riveters, blaring radios and honking horns.

The city's varied life revolves around three of its squares: Constitution, Omonia, and Monasteraki, a triangle of contrasts that tells almost all there is to know about Athens. Constitution Square is the elegant center of the city and the hub of its tourist activities and plushier accommodations, all centered around a patch of park with orange trees, pines, and palmettos. It is here that you find the airline offices, smart cafés, and supper clubs, the Parliament Building, and the Grand Bretagne, the doyenne of Athens hotels, with a bustling lobby that is the meeting place for affluent visitors and local high society, business executives and governmental hierarchy. Here you see the fashionable people of the city: the slender women with black hair smoothed back in the latest coiffures, wearing dresses they bought at the Rome or Paris showings; the men in suits of English or Italian cut, who meet buyers and sellers from abroad to discuss the city's booming real-estate values and possible inducements for investment capital that will give Athens the "instant progress" it so desperately wants.

Behind this square are the magnificent National Gardens with a modern exhibition hall, the nineteenth century stadium constructed for the first international Olympic Games on the site of an ancient arena dating back to 330 B.C., and the Royal Palace. This handsome modern mansion is built of the same Pentelic marble Phidias used for the Parthenon, and is guarded by the operatic, mustachioed Evzones, dressed in short white skirts, high socks and turned-up shoes, embroidered vests, loose cotton blouses, and tasseled caps.

But walk the hypotenuse of this triangle, the wide thoroughfare that is Stadiou Street, and you come to Omonia Square, the 42nd Street workaday heart of Athens, a swirling conglomeration of crowds and traffic jams, lively cafés, quick-paced restaurants, department and dry-goods stores. This is the up-and-doing core of the city, where the biggest rage is the rotisserie-broiled chicken prepared in a shop run by a man from Brooklyn and his partner from the Bronx. Here the crowds are less chic than those in Constitution Square. The women are heavier and dress in sturdy, practical outfits of brown, maroon, gray, or black; most of the men wear trousers mismatched to jackets that once belonged to suits. And at night, the streets webbing out from Omonia Square are alive with cheap night clubs whose Arabic-looking touts buttonhole male tourists-at-large, offering to guide them to their various clubs and introduce them to the accommodating hostesses.

It is only a ten-minute walk from this brassy, twentieth century bustle to Monasteraki Square, the center of old Plaka. But in those ten minutes you enter another world, for this was the Athens of Turkish times, the village ruled from Constantinople by the Ottoman sultans who held Greece for almost four centuries. The stamp of the East has never quite been erased from this area; and the winding alleys are virtual bazaars, with tiny antique shops selling blue opaline glass, Turkish coffeepots, and pierced metal lanterns, brass-and-glass nargilehs, and bone or amber worry beads. On the smoky, noisy street named for Hephaestus, the Vulcan of Greek mythology, one hears the hammertap of coppersmiths who forge trays and cauldrons, scales and crosses, bells and chalices, and brass door knockers shaped like hands. The whole area is a maze of bicycles and motorcycles bobbing over the cobblestones. Pushcarts display sweet lemons and enormous oranges, tomatoes and eggplants, peppers and squash, figs and grapes, all carefully trimmed and arranged. There are the cries of street vendors, and the half-sad, half-gay twang of *bouzouki* music clatters out of little *tavernas,* where customers go to the kitchen and select the food themselves. Men sit at curbside tables sipping Turkish coffee from tiny white cups or drinking the milky, licorice-flavored *ouzo,* the Greek version of Turkish raki and Arabic arrack. Along the streets of Plaka you will see people wearing the standard, shabby black of the Mediterranean poor, though you might also get an occasional glimpse of a woman in an embroidered white peasant dress, carrying a bundle on her head.

Differences are not the only things one notices wandering around Athens; there are obvious consistencies as well—black curly hair and Byzantine eyes as darkly sad as those in ikon paintings; the fact that all family names seem to end in *s* just as in antique times; and everywhere the innate friendliness and hospitality of people to whom the word *xenos* means both stranger and guest. No matter where you are in Athens, you hear the constant din of voices—shouting, arguing, debating—for the Greeks have always been known as the world's greatest talkers. Even the New Testament observes that the Athenians "spent their time in nothing else, but either to tell or to hear some new thing"—an observation that would be just as valid today. The present citizens discuss as wide a range of subjects as did the Deipnosophists, whose banquet conversations, chronicled by Athenaeus, covered topics as diverse as harp players and bean soup, cockles and jesters, Plato and the Pleiades, the profligacy of Lydians and the misconduct of fishmongers, cheesecakes and Cleopatra. And though the modern, spoken, demotic Greek tongue would be unintelligible to the table-talking ancients, now, as then, the recurrent conversational themes are democracy, politics, philosophy—words as well as concepts that are part of the contribution of Greece to Western civilization.

From Plaka it is just a few minutes to the ruins of ancient Greece, most of which cluster in the southwest corner of the city, on top and around the base of the Acropolis. The hill is a complex of roofless, columned temples, so golden and mellow they seem to be carved out of nougat. Broken pediments, caryatids, and fluted columns are silhouetted against the ink-blue sky by day, and take on a silvery-satin patina when washed by the white light of the moon. From the terrace of this classic heap, you can see across Athens' rooftops to the opposite hill of Lycabettus, and the smaller hill of Pnyx, once a platform for orators. Nearby is Areopagos, the seat of the highest tribunals, from which St. Paul the Apostle warned the Athenians to mend their pagan ways. And though he was declared a "babbler" by the Epicurean and Stoic philosophers, he did leave converts behind him, among them "Dionysius the Areopagite and a woman named Damaris."

The crowning glory of the Acropolis is the Parthenon, the temple of the virgin goddess, Athena, whose jurisdiction over the realms of art, wisdom, industry, and prudent warfare made her the fitting symbol for the city of Pericles. Her temple is the most exquisitely proportioned and sophisticated building the world has ever known, for its architect, Phidias, compensated for the imperfections of the human eye, and designed a rectangular building of forty-six unevenly spaced columns that lean slightly inward to achieve a building that looks sharply upright.

The Turks used the Parthenon as a mosque and later as a munitions dump, which was shelled by the Venetian navy in 1687 and practically destroyed, along with most of the other beauties of Athens. Among these are the Erechtheion with its porch supported by gracefully draped caryatid maidens, the unfinished Propylaeum, that was to be the processional gateway to the Acropolis, and the Temple of Nike, the goddess of victory, whose wings were clipped so she could not fly from Athens.

It was the Venetian bombardment plus centuries of vandalism by Persians, Romans, Franks, Ottomans, and the Greeks themselves that reduced the Acropolis to the rubble it was when the British envoy, Lord Elgin, visited Athens in 1800. The place was a crumble of columns and fragmented ruins where, he reported, classic sculptures were being ground down into mortar, or chipped away by souvenir-seeking tourists. He got permission from the Turks to take away any pieces of stone that bore inscriptions or figures and, at tremendous cost, shipped off boatloads of statues, friezes, moldings, pediment decorations, and one of the caryatids of the Erechtheion, later replaced by a reproduction. Known as the Elgin Marbles, these pieces are displayed in the British Museum, and though Elgin has been criticized for his vandalism by everyone from Byron to modern nationalistic Greeks, had he not removed them from their original site they almost certainly would be lost to us today.

Many of the treasures that did remain on the Acropolis had to be dug up and pieced together—a job that took place mostly during the last seventy-five years. The impressive results are housed in the Acropolis Museum, just behind the Parthenon.

The slopes that descend from the Acropolis are carved with other remnants of Pericles' time. On the northwest side of the hill is the Theseum, or Temple of Hephaestus, a Doric treasure that stands by the ancient market place and civic center, the Agora, which was to Athens what the Forum was to Rome—a meeting place for orators and shoppers, and a stage for poets and politicians. It was here that the Athenians listened to the philosophies of Plato and later, Aristotle, and it was here that Socrates "ran around barefoot asking everyone to define his terms"—a description that appears in Will Cuppy's satirical history, *1066 and All That*. At one side of the Agora is the Stoa of Attalus, a two-storied, oblong building with open, colonnaded galleries—a typical promenade and shopping center; in ancient times, philosophers did much of their teaching at this and other stoas. A short way from the Agora is the Kerameikos, the cemetery of classic Athens, and in the opposite direction lie the Roman Agora, the library built by Hadrian, and the octagonal Tower of the Winds with its old Greek clock.

At the very base of the Acropolis stands the Sanctuary of Aesculapius, where the sick and crippled were brought in the hope of being cured by sacred snakes released only at night. Nearby is the Theater of Dionysius, where the tragedies of Aeschylus, Sophocles, and Euripides, and the comedies of Aristophanes were first performed. The Odeon of Herodes Atticus is the antique setting for the late summer music and drama festival held in the city.

Other sights include Hadrian's Arch, the Lysicrates Monument, and the Olympeion, the Temple of Zeus, begun in the sixth century B.C. and completed by Hadrian—all reminders of conquerors who turned the glories of Greece into the grandeurs of Rome. For a concentrated look at Athenian treasures, there are the museums. The most important of these is the National Archeological Museum, which houses masterpieces of sculpture, jewelry, and household objects dating back to the Minoan civilization that came to Athens from Crete three thousand years before Christ, and was supplanted by the Mycenaean and, later, the Hellenic cultures. There are magnificent ikons, mosaics, and other relics of Greece's early Christian history in the Byzantine Museum, and the exhibitions in the Benaki Museum close the gap between Byzantine times and the present, with Coptic paintings and fabrics, Islamic art, and regional folk costumes from all parts of the country.

The excursion sights around Athens again reflect the past and present. There is the busy harbor city, Piraeus, with its wharves and tugs and dockside *tavernas,* and the picturesque suburb of Kefissia, a market town full of enticing shops, coolly situated on the side of Pendeli Mountain, the marble quarry of ancient and modern Greece. And certainly everyone going to the Greek capital will circle through the classic towns and historic settings that inspired Byron. There is Sounion, where the "marbled steep" of the Poseidon temple hangs over the waters of the Saronic Gulf, a sight most breathtaking in the pink-gold haze of sunset. On the Sacred Way to Delphi and the shrine to its oracle cut into the slopes of Mount Parnassus, you pass the lake and battleground in the setting Byron described so well: "The mountains look on Marathon and Marathon looks on the sea." Driving the 110 miles that separate Athens from the ancient spa, Epidaurus, where a drama festival is held in the two-thousand-year-old open-air theater, you pass through Mycenae and Old Corinth with its temple, market place, and theater, and the spring that is said to have bubbled forth when Pegasus struck the hilltop with his hoof as he flew over the town.

Very close to Athens is Tatoi, the summer residence of the royal family amid the fir-forest hills of Mount Parnes. And should you be interested in seeing the center of Alexander's Macedonia, take a longer trip to Thessaloniki, better known to us as Salonika. Situated close to the Turkish border, this two-thousand-year-old city has been a mercantile center and Greece's link to Asia Minor throughout history.

And from Thessaloniki, men may visit the twenty monasteries and churches full of Byzantine art atop Mount Athos, where the traditions of the Middle Ages have survived since the fall of Byzantium; a starkly dramatic repository of magnificent art, overlooking rocky cliffs and the waters of the Aegean.

The isles of Greece, gilded by their eternal summers, are as idyllic today as they were in Byron's time. They shine like a handful of jewels scattered through the waters of the Aegean and Ionic seas, from the tip of Piraeus south toward the coast of Africa, east from the edge of Turkey, west to the borders of Albania. Each has its fabled ruins and remnants of antique civilizations, its resort diversions and beautiful scenery, and almost all have played a part in the mythological legends of the country.

The most important island is Crete, the birthplace of Zeus and the home of the great Minoan culture that was to spark the creative fire of Western civilization. Mountain goats, the *kri-kri,* graze on the sides of snow-clad Mount Ida, and the plains are lush with orange trees and date and banana palms. The island's most famous museum in Herakleion is a must for anyone interested in antiquities, as is the Palace of Knossos with its paprika-colored columns, its drainage system, and brilliant frescoes.

The two most interesting islands of the Cyclades are Mykonos, with its primitive windmills and handsome old vase collections, and Delos, the deserted granite island that was the birthplace of Apollo, a place now left to frogs and lizards, and a few families who guard the museum, while the temple of Artemis is watched over by the stone lions that bay to the sun-washed sky.

Rhodes is the most important island of the Dodecanese group, the Island of Roses and Sunshine, that was believed to be the daughter of Venus and the bride of the sun, with a hundred-foot-high bronze statue—the Colossus of Rhodes—that was one of the Seven Wonders of the ancient world. This Turkish-Greek island was a medieval walled fortress, the stronghold of the Knights of St. John, and it contains remnants of all of the cultures that have invaded it: Greek and Roman, Persian and Saracen, Venetian and Genoese. In the last war it was held by the Germans, who executed most of the population of one of the world's oldest Jewish communities.

You may cruise around little vacation islands near Athens such as Aegina, with its pistachio groves and Doric temple, or Hydra, one of the most beautiful spots in the Saronic Gulf and a hideaway for artists and writers, where the houses are painted white each year and look as though they were cut from blocks of *feta* cheese. Or you can curve around the Pelopennesus to Corfu, the Greek Kerkyra, and the Homeric Scheria, where the Phaeacians entertained Odysseus. This island seems to float like a graceful seahorse in the clear Ionian waters, a garden spot of lemon groves, almond trees, and grape vineyards, with Venetian overtones and more than its share of legends.

FOR THE TRAVELER'S NOTEBOOK

Official Information

Before you go: Greek State Tourist Service, 69 East 79th St., New York, N.Y.

Athens: SAS Office, 16 Venizelos Ave. (corner Amerikas St.); Greek Tourist Information Office, 8 Venizelos Ave.; U.S. Embassy, Mavili Square.

Money Matters

Currency: The monetary unit in Greece is the drachma (dr.), divided into 100 leptas; 30 dr. equal $1, U.S.

Tipping: A service charge is added to your bill at restaurants and hotels. Where tip is not included, 10 to 15 per cent is in order. Leave about drs. 2 for busboys. Drs. 10 is ample for your luggage; cab drivers get 5 to 10 per cent. Cloakroom attendants and ushers get about drs. 2.

Climate, Clothing and Essentials

Spring and autumn are ideal for visiting Greece, the climate being mild and temperate. The summer months are hot, with temperatures well in the 90's, but nights are reasonably cool, and even in the winter months the average temperature is seldom below 50 degrees F. A woolen cardigan and a topcoat may come in handy between November and March.

It is best to bring with you all film you may use during your stay as it may be expensive in Greece because of high import duties.

Hotels

There are many good hotels in Athens in all price ranges and there are government gradings of AA, A, B, C, and D, though for the sake of simplicity we have divided them into de luxe, first, second, and third class categories. Private baths are always available in the first two groups, often in the second class hotels, rarely in the third. Reservations are a must in Athens from March through Sept. For a complete listing of hotels throughout Athens and Greece, write to the Greek Tourist Office, 8 Venizelos Ave. De luxe rates range from 175 to 210 drs. for a single room with bath; 250 to 320, double. First class rates range from 100 to 180 drs., single; 150 to 260 drs., double. Second class hotels charge from 85 to 125 drs. for a single room (those without baths are the less expensive). Double rates in this class range from 125 to 190 drs. Third class hotels charge from 65 to 90 drs., single; 100 to 125, double.

DE LUXE: The new *Athens Hilton* near Constitution Square, is far and away the most modern hotel in the city. It is all air-conditioned, all of the rooms have balconies, and all afford a view of the Acropolis or Mount Pentelicon. The rates are de luxe and then some. *Grand Bretagne, 1 Venizelos Ave.,* the *grande dame* of Athens hotels, has complete facilities, a restaurant, and air conditioning is available on request. Rooms in the newer wing are more up-to-date and most of the rooms overlook Syntagma Square. The *King George, 3 King George St.,* is a somewhat smaller but charming de luxe hotel, and its upper floors are the more desirable. The *Athénée Palace, 1 Kolokotroni Square;* the *Acropole Palace, 28 Oktovriou, 51;* and the comparatively new *King's Palace, 4 Venizelos Ave.,* are well-located, comfortable, pleasant hotels with restaurants, private baths, and air conditioning.

FIRST CLASS: The *Aliki (Alice), 36 Kapodistriou,* near Omonia Square, has a restaurant, private baths for all rooms, and is only a few years old. The *National, 57 Venizelos Ave.,* is small and private and well located. Its restaurant, the *Pantheon,* is reputedly good. Rooms are large and service is first rate. The *Alexiou, 16 Venizelos Ave.; Aux Ambassadeurs, 67 Socrates St.;* and the three-year-old *Amalia, Amalia and Xenofondos,* are all excellent hotels in this category.

MODERATE: Many of the following hotels have private baths and showers, balcony rooms, rarely air conditioning. The *El Greco, Lycourgou-Athinas St.,* is modern and conveniently located in the area of Omonia Square; the *Plaka, 7 Kapnikazeas,* within walking distance of the Acropolis and many of the antique sights, is clean, modern, and comfortable.

INEXPENSIVE: *Estia Emboron, 47 Sofokleous,* is a wonderful, inexpensive little hotel if you don't mind staying in the colorful native area not usually frequented by tourists. It is clean, comfortable, without frills, and can be safely recommended. *Cairo City, 40 Marni St.,* offers clean accommodations and friendly service and has a few rooms with showers.

Visitors staying less than three nights at an inexpensive hotel will be charged an additional 10 per cent, but this does not apply at the de luxe hotels. In addition to the service charge of 15 per cent included in the prices quoted, expect to pay a small municipal tax. Air conditioning may be extra. In hotels with central air conditioning the charge is 10 drs. to 15 per room in winter, and 20 to 30 drs. in summer. In hotels without central air conditioning, air-conditioned rooms are sometimes available. These will be charged at the rate of 35 drs. for single rooms, 55 drs. for double.

Food and Restaurants

Greek food, while not as varied as the cuisine of most other European countries, offers a number of interesting specialties. Owing to the climate, food is usually served tepid by our standards, so if you want it really hot order it that way and you *might* get it. The Middle Eastern appetizers, *mezedakia,* are served here to, and include a number of salads, fish, olives, cheese, and sliced sausage that go well with the white, licorice-flavored *apéritif, ouzo.* Excellent soups to try are the fish stews, the lentil, the egg-lemon (*avgolemono*), and the cold yogurt soup. *Taramasalata* is a wonderful fish-roe appetizer. Being so close to the sea, a great variety of excellent fish and seafood is available, including squid (*kalamarakia*), lobster, crab, clams, and shrimp, generally served grilled, or baked.

Greek cooks are also noted for their imaginative preparation of lamb dishes. Try *entrather* (lamb stewed with artichokes); *souvlakia* (grilled on a spit); *dolmadakia* (stuffed with vine leaves); or *moussaka* (layers of eggplant, minced lamb, cheese, and a thyme-scented tomato sauce).

Olives and *feta* cheese are delicious, especially with Greek bread, *pitta. Tyropitta,* a favorite cheesecake, is rich and appetizing; other pastries follow the Middle East *baklava* honey-nut pattern. Both French and American coffee are available, although the local brew is the refreshing Turkish version. Greek fruits, especially the enormous succulent oranges and sweet lemons, are among the world's best. Greek wines are good too; try *Mavrodaphni, Samos, retsina,* which is astringently flavored with pine resin, and the special national wine, *Kokinelli.*

Continental food is served in the well-appointed hotel dining rooms and more popular tourist restaurants. It can be relatively high in price, but the native food served at the friendly little *tavernas,* where you go into the kitchen and make your own selection, can be had for $1 to $2 for a complete meal. *Zonar's,* with its sidewalk café, its main floor pastry shop, and its upstairs dining room and *Floca* are famous but too tourist-y; and the *Pantheon* of the National Hotel, with its huge menu, is a relative newcomer rapidly gaining in popularity. *Psaropoula* is favored by Greeks for its fine fish specialties. *Costis* is an old favorite that has remained so since 1840; its prices are slightly below those of the other restaurants in its class. *Averof* is a simply decorated, moderately priced restaurant that can be recommended for its food, and the *Dionysos* offers fine native food and a view of the Acroplis.

Anyone in search of authentic Greek food, local color, and the very "native" prices of the *tavernas* should not miss the excellent little *Corfu* and *Vassillis. Xynos,* another *taverna,* is to many minds the best in the city; and one of the most colorful in the old Plaka district is the *Saitis,* with its birdcages, hanging onions, and wall cartoons. *Avra,* in the Piraeus section of Tourkolimano, is an excellent seaside restaurant where you choose your own fish from huge refrigerator baskets; and you can have a ten-course meal in which each course is a different fish or seafood specialty. Restaurant *Kalamis* serves authentic Greek food inexpensively in a garden setting. Other simple but typical places to try are *Tsita* and *Gerofinikas* and the *Asterias* on the beach of the same name.

Entertainment, Night Life, and Special Events

Athens is a very cosmopolitan and active city at night. The open-air performances at the Odeon of Herodes Atticus, under the Acropolis, are major attractions during the summer months, and the State Symphony Orchestra plays here every Monday night between June and October. From April through October the city's famous monuments are illuminated at night, and each has a periodic transcribed narrative describing its history and significance. Drama, operas, ballets, and concerts are performed in the ancient theater at the foot of the Acropolis from July to mid-September.

After the theater you might like to visit one of the many night clubs with floor shows, such as the *Asteria,* the *Athenea Romantica* (winter); the *Acropole,* the *Coronet,* or the *Roxy.* Many of the night clubs maintain branches at the summer beaches of Kalamaki and Kastella.

There is dancing at the new Hilton and a few night clubs around Constitution Square, but the latter are out-and-out clip joints and it is best to avoid them.

For authentic Greek atmosphere, and to see the Athenians enjoy themselves in their leisure hours, visit one of the many *tavernas,* such as *Epta Adelphia* (Seven Brothers), *Kynos, Palaia Athina,* and *Vlahos* at Plaka, the old district of Athens under the slope of the Acropolis; the *Sarandidis,* or perhaps *Mostrous Spilia.* Your hotel porter will be able to tell you how to get there. There are also plenty of *tavernas* at Piraeus. In some you may hear the popular *bouzouki,* a strange mixture of Oriental and Greek music. One fine evening you should go to the fishing harbor of Piraeus (Tourkolimano, where the yachting club is situated) and eat seafood in one of the open-air restaurants.

SPECIAL EVENTS: The annual Athens Festival (ancient drama, music, and dance) is held here from mid-July to mid-September. Among the outstanding features are the "Sound and Light" performances presented at the Pnyx. *Kifissia's Fair,* held in the latter part of August, is a colorful sight; and October 3 is the date of the procession of *St. Dionysius,* which always draws interested spectators.

Outside Athens, mention should be made of the folklore performances given by the Dora Stratos ballet at the ancient theater of Piraeus. At Epidaurus there is a festival of ancient drama and Attic comedy from June to July; and October 3 is the date of the colorful procession of *St. Dionysus.*

The Wine Festival in Daphni, near Athens, takes place in September and October. A small fee admits you to the Greek wine exhibition where all wine is free.

Easter is the most important religious event in Greece, and impressive ceremonies of the Greek Orthodox Church are held during Holy Week. A very picturesque procession takes place on Good Friday, as *Epitafios* (Christ's body) is taken around the churches at night, accompanied by crowds holding candles. On Easter Sunday the people eat roast lamb cooked out of doors on spits, and hard-boiled eggs dyed red. Important military parades take place on the two national holidays, *March 25* and *October 28* (in Thessaloniki), and they are attended by the royal family.

Shopping

You will like browsing around in the shops on Constitution Square, Stadium Street, Ermou Street, Pandrossou Street, Argentine Republic Street, and Philhellinon Street. Antiques are sold at the shops of *Martinos, Zarakovitis, Adam,* and *Vitalis,* all on Pandrossou Street. The *Queen's Fund, Knossos, Diacosmitiki, Ergochiro, Nikoloudi,* and *Ergani Athina,* around Constitution Square, and the *Royal Fund* exhibition, sell popular art goods. The picturesque costume of the Royal Guard is frequently used for small dolls, very popular as souvenirs.

During the summer, shops are open from 8 A.M. until 1:30 P.M. and from 5 P.M. until 8 P.M., except for Saturday afternoon. The winter hours are 8:30 A.M. to 1:30 P.M. and 4 to 7:30 P.M., except Saturday afternoon.

You will no doubt want to buy the colorful embroideries, hand-woven silk, linen, and cotton fabrics from Crete, Soufli, and Kastoria; earthenware and black pottery from Rhodes; all kinds of handmade silverware and carved handwork; and some of the local sweet wine or some of the Greek liquors and brandy.

Background Reading

The Companion Guide to the Greek Islands, by Ernle Bradford
Splendour of Greece, by Robert Payne
Prospero's Cell and *Reflections on a Marine Venus,* by Lawrence Durrell
My Family and Other Animals, by Gerald Durrell
The Colossus of Maroussi, by Henry Miller
Hellenism, by Arnold Toynbee
The Last of the Wine and *The King Must Die,* by Mary Renault
The Grecian Calendar, by Christopher Rand
The Odyssey and *The Iliad,* by Homer
The Odyssey, a Modern Sequel and *Zorba the Greek,* by *Nikos Kazantzakis*

Holland (The Netherlands)

AMSTERDAM

The Prinsengracht, the Keizersgracht,
and the Heerengracht

HOLLAND is probably the first foreign country to appeal to us as children. This is the storybook land of the Zuider Zee, with a landscape of windmills and tulips, ships and sails, where apple-cheeked dairy maids wear starched lace caps and flaxen-haired boys play in baggy pantaloons and wooden shoes, a world as sparkling clean as the blue-and-white tile of Delft. Here canals freeze over in winter to the delight of the latter-day Hans Brinkers whose silver skates twinkle across the cold gray ice. This is a place where small boys become heroes by holding their fingers in leaky dykes, thereby saving their homeland from the sea.

Amazingly enough, most of the vision is true, though the work of the windmills has been taken over by hydraulic pumps that keep the sea in its place, and those that remain are restaurants, museums, or merely the subjects of countless tourist photographs; and the charming country people of Marken put on their folk costumes just before the tourist boat from Amsterdam is due to dock. Beneath the picturesque façade beats a stoutly practical heart, and nothing is more typical of Dutch determination than the country itself; 50 per cent of the thirteen thousand squares miles of Holland are nether-lands, wrested from the sea, a project that began in the ninth century when Charlemagne ruled the land and which continues to the present. When the Dutch need more land, they dam off a section of the sea and pump it dry.

The sea has not been the only adversary to challenge the persistence of the Dutch, for they have had to hold out against other waves of invaders throughout their history, including the ancient Romans and the Franks, the Burgundian dukes and Spanish Hapsburgs, the English, the armies of Napoleon, and, more than once, the Germans.

In the sixteenth century, when much of western Europe was in the grip of Catholic Spain, it was Holland and the low countries that first turned to Calvinist doctrines and rose against the infamous Duke of Alva, the governor appointed by Philip II. The Dutch were victorious under their leader, William the Silent of Orange, who stood off Spanish might saying, "I will maintain," a phrase that is still the Benelux motto. It was this particular phase of Dutch history that prompted Havelock Ellis to say, "Holland is one of the traditional lands of freedom; it was the home of independent intellect, of free religion, of autonomous morals, when every other country of Europe was closed to these manifestations of the spirit." It was this same tradition of freedom that dealt so harshly with the German occupiers of Holland, this same manifestation of spirit that sparked one of the most effective anti-Nazi undergrounds and accounted for the heroic efforts of Amsterdam citizens on behalf of such Jews as Anne Frank, whose hiding place is one of the city's sadder sights.

A nation of eleven million people, the practical, pragmatic Hollanders are talkative and gregarious, comfortable and solid, and stern Protestant disciplinarians; this is a nation of Dutch uncles, where even the Catholic half of the population is Calvinist in spirit. They produce richly mellow chocolate and cheery red-waxed cheese, the sheer crystal of Leerdam and the blue-and-white pottery of Delft, and some of the world's best beer, gin, ham, and beef. They are expert diamond cutters and incomparable flower growers. Tulips were brought to the country from Asia Minor in the sixteenth century and became the leading Dutch export, along with other bulbs such as hyacinths and daffodils, dahlias and paper-white narcissi. Josh Billings once said that if a Dutchman found himself in the Garden of Eden, he would proceed to plant it.

The Dutch are also known for the electronic products made at the

Philips factories in Eindhoven, the "City of Lights," for the ships they build, their precision machinery, and their herring, though considering how much of it they eat themselves, day and night, at the countless corner stands all over Amsterdam, it's a wonder there's any left to export. The language they speak is a German derivative with many unique twists, especially in the vowel groups such as *eeuw, oei* and the double *a*. The written Dutch has Flemish roots and is far more formal in tone, with expressions the Dutch call *stadhuiswoorden* (city hall words) or what we would call "five dollar words."

In a way, Holland owes its seventeenth century golden age to Spain, for it was the southern country that forced the Dutch to exercise their ingenuity and then gave them the wherewithal to do so. For when Spanish ports were closed to Dutch merchant ships Holland had to seek new markets, and when Jews fleeing the Inquisition and Protestant bankers banished from Flanders all settled in Amsterdam, they brought with them the capital needed to finance the task. The Dutch jurist, Grotius, pronounced the seas free, and the ships of Holland set sail across them, discovering new routes and new worlds and taking over the outposts of other European countries, especially those of Portugal. Schouten rounded the cape he named Horn after his home town, Hoorn; Mercator drew a new map projection; and Barents discovered Spitzbergen. The Dutch florin became Europe's hardest currency, backed by the wealth of spices, calico, silks, porcelain, coffee, tea, and diamonds that came to Amsterdam from the Indies, East and West, from their Brazilian settlements around Recife, and from the Cape Town possessions in South Africa. The Dutch Boers were driven north by the British on an epic trek to the Transvaal, where in 1866 they discovered the mines that made Amsterdam the diamond-cutting center of the world.

Holland's seventeenth century achievements were as important culturally as they were commercially. Spinoza, the son of exiled Portuguese Jews, wrote his *Ethics;* Van Leeuwenhoek ground the first microscope lenses; and Van Drebbel advanced practical theories of submarine navigation. But though they had success in all fields, the one area in which the Dutch have always excelled is painting. The roster of their famous artists stretches through every major art movement the Western world has known, from the seventeenth century masters such as Rembrandt, Hals, Vermeer, Jan Steen, Van Ruisdael, and De Hooch, through such early modernists as Van Gogh and the

De Stijl group led by Mondrian, to the virtual father of the abstract expressionist movement, Willem de Kooning.

There are close to three hundred art museums in Holland, an area equal in size to the combined states of Massachusetts and Connecticut. Holland can even boast one of the greatest and most maddening art forgers ever to bedevil collectors and curators—Van Meegeren, whose fake Vermeers deluded Goering and the Rotterdam museum, among others, and whose counterfeits earned him an estimated $1.5 million before he was discovered at the close of World War II.

Amsterdam dates back to the year 1200, when a few fishermen built huts near the banks of the Amstel River, and in 1275 constructed a dam, to give the city its early name, *Amstelredamme*. Now a city of almost a million inhabitants, it is essentially a product of Holland's golden age, its most characteristic houses built with the merchant and banking products of the Indies trade. The city streets circle out from the original nucleus, the Dam, like rings of age in a tree trunk, a watery-misty city, sliced into ninety islands by fifty miles of canals— the *grachten*—and all spliced together by five hundred bridges. Swimming is a required course in school here, where two hundred people and fifty automobiles are fished out of the canals every year, and a regular service is maintained to retrieve bicycles that go overboard.

The most beautiful canals—the Prinsengracht, the Keizersgracht, and especially the Heerengracht—are lined with shade trees and rows of solid, red-brick houses, their step-gabled, squat practicality belying their inner splendors: exuberant baroque interiors plastered with fruits and cherubs, ribbons and flutings, niches and trellised ceilings, and all the other rococo trappings of the Dutch Renaissance style. Although this sunny, leafy section is lovely on a summer day when glass-roofed excursion boats glide by, it is perhaps more impressive on a winter's afternoon, when skaters skim over the frozen canals and church bells ring out through the frosted air.

The church bells, the barrel organs with gleaming baroque Delft façades, the network of bicycles, the ever-present flower markets, flower stalls, and flower boats, the streets that end in quays, the quays that step down to the water—these are Amsterdam's trademarks. It is a wonderful city for walkers, and you should start in the oldest section, the Dam. Here you can see Queen Juliana's Royal Palace, built in 1674 as the Town Hall, the fifteenth century "new" Kerk, Holland's coronation cathedral as well as its pantheon, and nearby, the

Beurs, only sixty years old but reminding us that it was the Dutch who began the whole system of stock exchange financing when the Amsterdam bank was a clearinghouse for world traders. In this section you may stroll along Warmoesstraat, the city's oldest thoroughfare, past dozens of early houses, quaintly lopsided like those you see along the Voorburgwal, cross antique wooden drawbridges, see the Mint Tower, a landmark dating from 1606, pass the spot from which Henry Hudson's *Half Moon* set sail, and wander around the seventeenth century buildings of Amsterdam University. Close to the magnificently colorful pageant presented by the Rokin and Singel flower markets, lies Begijnhof, a three-hundred-year-old almshouse. This is a garden paradise for the aged, who live in ivy-covered, tile-roofed, brick houses, frosted with white gables and fronted by flower patches, all centering on a pretty grass-green park.

Along with the rest of Holland, Amsterdam combines the picturesque and the practical, the modern and antique, theory and practice. It is a city with strict Sunday blue laws, but it has a red-light district called the Aquarium, along the Zeedijk. This is a strip of houses with window showcases displaying girls—the merchandise that is for sale. Amsterdam is a port city, and the swarms of sailors out window-shopping here are reminders of that fact.

The city's modern life, its neon-lit night-time squares, its theaters and concert halls, its department stores and shops, its cafés and restaurants, center around such areas as the Thorbeckplein and the Rembrandtplein, the Leidseplein, and the streets leading off the old Damrak, where some of the large department stores and leading tourist hotels are found. Its diversions are many; its restaurants feature such worlds-apart specialties as thick pea soup with pork and Indonesian *rijstafel*. Shops offer everything from the most sophisticated merchandise, such as diamonds, to cozier souvenirs like miniature Delft windmills and wooden-shoe paperweights. The antique stores of Nieuwe Spiegelstraat spill forth irresistible treasures of mellow pewter and heavy Dutch silver, dark old gold or pale platinum jewelry pavéd with rose diamonds, shelves full of flowery porcelain, and crystal as meticulously cut as gems. And if diamonds are what really interest you, you can watch them being cut in a workshop on Zwanenburgerstraat, where you can buy yours fresh from the cutting table.

But none of Amsterdam's varied treasures—not her diamonds nor her silver, her magnificent Concertgebouw Orchestra nor her flower markets—nothing compares with the wealth of her museums. The most famous perhaps is the Rijksmuseum, with an unsurpassed collection of Rembrandt, including his "Night Watch" and "The Anatomy Lesson." Other artists represented include Vermeer, Hals, Van der Velde, Steen, and Rubens, who worked across the Flemish border in Antwerp. There are more Rembrandt memorabilia in the house on Jodenbreestraat where he lived from 1639 to 1660 and where his drawings and etchings are now exhibited, and in the Six Collection, in the home of Rembrandt's greatest patron, Jan Six. For contrast in time, see the modern sun-drenched canvases of Van Gogh at the Municipal Museum (the Stedelijk); for contrast in space, see the Indonesian and Balinesian artifacts, puppets, ceremonial headdresses, carvings, and water colors at the Tropenmuseum. Waag, an old city gate from medieval times, houses the Historical Museum where Rembrandt once painted, and the Jewish Historical Museum, with documents and diaries of Dutch Jewry from the Inquisition to the Nazis.

Although Amsterdam is officially the capital of Holland, and the country's leading commercial center, it is neither the seat of the government nor its largest port. The Hague claims the first honor, Rotterdam the second; both cities are worth visiting. Often called "Europe's largest village," The Hague is a gracious old city and the part-time residence of Queen Juliana and the royal family. It has its great parliament buildings and chambers, its imposing thirteenth century Knights' Hall (the Ridderzaal), the Peace Palace sponsored by Andrew Carnegie and finished in 1913, and, being a Dutch city, its own wonderful museums. Close to The Hague is one of Holland's leading seaside resorts. Scheveningen, with sunny sand beaches and a full complement of holiday attractions, and nearby Leiden, the birthplace of Rembrandt and Steen, is a storehouse of historic architecture dating from the tenth century to the sixteenth.

Rotterdam by contrast, is a rugged, commercial sea town, a rich old port city strategically situated at the estuary of the Rhine and Meuse rivers, an inland harbor with over 150 deep-water shipping channels. Surrounded by a ring of fishing- and church-steeple towns, Rotterdam itself is primarily modern in aspect, since it has been the most thoroughly destroyed city during each of the wars Holland has fought, and World War II was no exception.

The flat saucer that is Holland is dotted all over with fairytale villages and graceful old towns, too numerous to be completely catalogued. Fortunately, travel is easy here, whether you drive or bicycle over the flat roads or float along the four-thousand-mile web of canals in the easygoing excursion boats or private launches. Close to Amsterdam are the folk-costumed fishing village of Marken; Broek, a tile-bright place with streets that are washed every morning; and Monnikendam, a Renaissance town with a sixteenth century Tower Clock that has a cast of moving figures that parade every hour. Edam and Alkmaar have their colorful cheese markets, and Aalsmeer, in the heart of the flower-market section, is best early in the morning when its flower auction runs by automation. Haarlem not only rates a visit because it is the birthplace of Franz Hals and has a museum full of his works, but because it is in the center of the bulb-growing farmlands, and in spring the tulip and hyacinth fields are carpeted with blossoms.

Visit Delft because it was the birthplace of Vermeer and De Hooch and there are works and souvenirs of both in the Tetar van Elven Collection, or because of the blue-and-white ceramics that have been an art here since the seventeenth century and are displayed in the Van Meerten Museum. Or visit Delft simply because it is one of Holland's loveliest old cities, with a thirteenth century church that is the burial place of the royal family, and the Prinsenhof, the residence of William the Silent, who was assassinated there in 1584 after winning freedom for his country.

Arnhem's Open Air Museum is a historical collection of Holland's rural life through the centuries, complete with windmills, moss-covered, thatched-roof cottages, and people in their original native costumes. Again by way of contrast, the nearby Kröller-Müller Museum at Otterloo has an enticing display of modern art, with two hundred works by Van Gogh and scores of paintings by the most famous Cubists and Impressionists. Utrecht is a bell-ringing Gothic town with one of Europe's oldest universities; Hoorn is a dreamy, bygone-era town—a seventeenth century set-piece of gabled houses built for Indies merchants; Giethoorn, in the northeastern part of the country, has no streets at all and even the local harvest is brought in by boat; Groningen is a colorful university town with the fifteenth century Church of St. Martin, the patron saint of tourists, so perhaps a fitting place to visit. Bunschoten and Spakenburg are even more authentic costume villages than Marken; and all of the villages of the Zuider Zee (now the Ijselmeer) ringing outwards from the capital, are as typically Dutch as you remember them to be from travel posters, cocoa boxes, and the airbrush perfection of storybook illustrations.

FOR THE TRAVELER'S NOTEBOOK

Official Information

Before you go: The Netherlands National Tourist Office, 1 East 53rd St., New York 17, N.Y.

In Amsterdam: SAS Office, 95 Leidsestraat; Tourist Information Office (V.V.V.), 5 Rokin; U.S. Embassy, 102 Lange Voorhout, The Hague.

Currency: The monetary unit is the Dutch guilder (*guldens* in the plural) or florin (Dfl.), divided into 100 cents. 3.80 Dfl. equals $1, U.S.

Tipping: If a service charge is not included in your hotel or restaurant bill, tip 15 per cent; taxi drivers 15 to 20 per cent; hairdressers about 20 per cent; hotel porter, valet, maid, etc., a few guilders at the end of your stay.

Climate, Clothing, and Essentials

The climate in Amsterdam is temperate the year round with an average temperature in spring and summer from 60 degrees F. to 80 degrees F., and in winter and autumn from 25 degrees F. to 60 degrees F. Spring (mid-March through May) is perhaps the ideal time to visit Holland; the days are warm and sunny, and the fields of flowers surround you with a sea of color and fragrance.

You will need a heavy coat in winter as it is damp as well as cold, and we recommend a topcoat for summer and a raincoat at all seasons.

Hotels

Whether you choose de luxe or modest accommodations, you will always find the room spotlessly clean. Reservations are advisable for spring and summer (especially during tulip time) and it is a good idea to bring your own soap as few hotels supply any. If you arrive without reservations, an official of the V.V.V. Information Office at the Central Station or at 5 Rokin will help you find accommodations. A complete list of government-graded hotels through Amsterdam and Holland is available from the Netherlands National Tourist Office.

De Luxe hotel rates range from Dfl. 25 to 40 for single rooms with bath; Dfl. 45 to 60 for doubles. Moderate rates range from Dfl. 15 to 22, single; 30 to 40 Dfl., double. Inexpensive hotels charge from Dfl. 7 to 12, 28 single; Dfl. 14 to 28, double. Rates here vary depending on whether or not you have a private bath.

DE LUXE: The *Amstel, 1 Prof. Tulpplein,* is *the* hotel in the city for visiting dignitaries and celebrities. It is plush in every way, and is located a little way out of the center of things, adding to its quiet charm. The *Amsterdam Hilton, Apollolaan,* is brand-new and sparklingly modern, but is in a quiet location 15 minutes from the city center. *Doelen, 24 Nieuwe Doelenstraat,* is centrally located, luxurious, efficient; has large comfortable rooms. *Grand Hotel Krasnapolsky, Dam,* is very conveniently located, facing Dam Square. It affords a variety of accommodations and service; best rooms are in the new wing.

MODERATE: *Centraal Hotel, 7 Staadhouderskade,* is deluxe in service and accommodations but moderate in price, and is just a few minutes from the downtown area. *The American, 97 Leidsekade; Schiller, 26 Rembrandtplein;* and the *Park, 1–11 Hobbemastraat,* are a few of the other moderately priced, comfortable, and convenient hotels in the inexpensive to moderate price range.

INEXPENSIVE: *The Casa Academica, James Wattstraat,* is a summer student hotel with very moderate rates. There are two motels near Amsterdam: *Motel Amsterdam, 535 Sloterweg* on the southern edge of the city, and *Euremotel,* a new and modern hostelry on the road to Utrecht. The *Van Gelder, 34 Damrak,* and *De Moor, 1015–1017 Prinsengracht,* are clean, well-maintained hotels charging very low rates but offering no private baths.

Food and Restaurants

Be sure to sample the wonderfully rich and delectable Dutch specialties during your visit. Amsterdam herring is famous the world over, and between May and September, the peak of its season, it can be had at street-corner stands that sell it in much the same way we do hot dogs. *Erwtensoep* is a thick pea soup with sausages and pig's knuckles, asparagus soup (*aspergesoep*). *Hutspot* is the national beef stew. Red cabbage with spiced beef (*rodekool met rolpens*), pork chops stuffed with apples (*heete bliksem*), stuffed breast of veal (*gevulde kalfsborst*), and kale with sausage (*boerekool met worst*), are only a few of the delicious features of the Dutch menus. Dutch cheese—Gouda, Edam, Leiden, and others—are superb and are popular with bread and butter for breakfast. Beef and vegetables are of high quality and the pork is, to many minds, the world's best. Cakes and cookies made of gingerbread, marzipan tarts, and *petits fours* are excellent as the Dutch bread. The butter is of the same high quality as the cheeses. Dutch chocolate is smooth and richly flavored, the coffee is wonderful, and as for the beer, anyone who has ever tasted either Amstel or Heineken brews can tell you just how marvelous they are. The Bols gin is about the best anywhere.

Since Indonesia was a Dutch colony for so many years, Amsterdam has several restaurants serving wonderful *rijstafels*—the traditional Indonesian meal, consisting of many different foods served with rice. For a description of many of these specialties, see Djakarta, "Food and Restaurants," page 473.

Dikker en Thijs, one of the city's most famous and expensive restaurants, features both French and Dutch dishes in elegant surroundings, while *Vijf Vlieghen* (Five Flies), dating back to 1627, has a wonderfully authentic seventeenth century atmosphere that is understandably popular with tourists. The Havengebouw or Harbor Building has restaurants offering excellent food at moderate and high prices, both with views of the city. *'T Oude Binnenhofje* (The Old Courtyard) offers entertainment and serves continental and Dutch food at moderately high prices. The *Fromagerie Crignon* specializes in cheese dishes and does so at low prices, while the *Lido,* a night club-restaurant on a canal, has a menu mélange of French, Dutch, and Indonesian specialties and is expensive. *Fong Lie* is noted for its Chinese food.

Among the economical restaurants are the *Chalet Petit Suisse* with Swiss and Italian food, *Brouerswapen, De Bock, Den Groene Lantern,* and *Dorrius,* featuring simple Dutch cuisine at moderate prices. *De Boerdery* is a small, wonderfully picturesque little restaurant with a wood-paneled bar. They serve rotisserie grills and continental food along with a few Dutch specialties; expensive. *Bali* is famous for its Indonesian *grote rijstafel,* while *Kong Hing* serves the same meal less elaborately and less expensively. The *Apollo Paviljoen,* on a canal, has excellent fish and seafood. For inexpensive meals, snacks, and light lunches, try one of the cafeterias of the *De Bock, Broodjke. Kootje,Offeck Ruteck* chains.

Entertainment, Night Life, and Special Events

Amsterdam is a gay city with a night life that continues far into the dawn. The areas around the Rembrandtplein, the Leidseplein, and in the Leidsetraat glow with an array of night clubs, bars, cabarets to suit almost any preference. The neighborhood around Thorbeckeplein caters to sailors and includes a number of honky-tonks mixed in with strip joints: and anyone looking for female companionship can window-shop for it along the Oudezyds Voorburgwal and the Oudezijds Achterburgwal, starting at the Zeedijk.

The *Lido-Bar* is charming and elegant; the *Extase* has floor shows of the usual continental variety, as do *Caramella* and the *Blue Note.* Most of these close at 2 A.M., but don't think you have to go to bed if you don't want to. The *44 Club Femina* is loud and raucous and very gay, while the *Casino* has a late show and a private-club atmosphere to which your passport assures entry. The *Wiener Café* is—you guessed it—Viennese. *La Tropicana* is small and intimate and has a wonderful band; not expensive. The *Bamboo Bar* is popular with students, has good music, and is very inexpensive and gay.

The *Concertgebouw Orchestra* plays a series of concerts during the winter months. The *Stadssechouwburg Theater* presents opera, ballet, and dramas. Operettas and revues are given at the *Carré-Theater* and at the *Nieuwe de la Mar Theater.*

SPECIAL EVENTS: On May 5 (*National Liberation Day*), the streets of Amsterdam are decorated and illuminated, amusement fairs are held, and various other local festivities take place. The great event of the year is the flower season in springtime. The *Cheese Market* at Alkmaar is held each Friday in summer. The *Holland Festival* from June 15 to July 15 centers on Amsterdam, The Hague, and Scheveningen, and includes music, drama, concerts, operas, and ballet in each of the cities. The V.V.V. offices can make arrangements for you to attend any of these festivals.

GET IN TOUCH WITH THE DUTCH: If you are interested in meeting Dutch people with occupations and interests similar to your own, make your request to the V.V.V. when you arrive in Amsterdam.

Shopping

Holland's best and most beautiful buys include the lovely blue-and-white Delft porcelain, handsome pewter in modern or traditional designs, leatherwork, and if you're out for unset diamonds this is the place to stock up. There are wonderful antiques, delicious chocolates, the coffee-flavored hard candies, *hopjes,* and bargains in gin (*jenever*) and liqueurs. You can also send home flower bulbs, most especially Darwin tulips; and don't overlook the wonderful Philips recordings. The main shopping streets in Amsterdam are the Kalverstraat and Leidsestraat. Service is friendly and good and most attendants speak English. Largest department stores are the *Bijenkorf* (Bee Hive, and that's what it is) at Damrak and *Vroom & Dreesman* at Rokin. Shops are open from 9 A.M to 5:30 P.M. including Saturdays. You may buy diamonds or watch them being cut at *A. van Moppes & Zoom,* or *Asscher's. Focke & Meltzer* feature fine crystal and china, and the *"De Porceleyne Fles"* showroom displays and sells the fine ware of the same name. *Premsela & Hamburger* are known for their antique silver and jewelry; *Begeer van Kempen en Vos* is the court jeweler, noted for antique and modern silver; while *Bonebakker* is the Cartier of Amsterdam. Anyone interested in antiques will have a field day along the Nieuwe Spiegelstraat, though it's doubtful you'll find a sleeper here as most of the dealers know exactly what they have when they have it.

Background Reading

The Netherlands by Sacheverell Sitwell
Holland, Wonderful Out of the Water, by Eduard van Wijk
The Black Tulip, by Alexandre Dumas
A History of Dutch Life and Art, by Jan Timmers
Amsterdam, by E. van Moerkerken

Italy

ROME

S.P.Q.R. and La Dolce Vita

ALTHOUGH the recent crop of "new wave" films from Italy might lead you to believe otherwise, Rome has been the city of *la dolce vita* since the days of the Twelve Caesars. For centuries it has doubled as a Christian mecca and a place of pagan excess, where inhabitants pursue "the sweet life" whether they are ruled by a king, a Caesar, an emperor, a pope, a duce, or a president. The modern debauches of the Via Veneto smart set are innocent amusements compared to the spectacular orgies of their ancient Roman ancestors, or to the diversions of Renaissance popes such as Alexander VI, the Borgia who lived in sybaritic splendor in the apartments that can still be seen in the Vatican Palace—the living quarters in which he raised his two infamous offspring, Cesare and Lucrezia. In the early eighteenth century, Casanova—no prude or ascetic himself—noted on a visit to Rome that "the Romans think only of eating, drinking and enjoying themselves," and he said that he was disgusted by their "vile debauches" and "Bacchic fury." In the nineteenth century Stendhal, in his *Roman Journal,* observed, "The great and deep passions inhabit Rome." The statement is just as true today. And though the reports out of Cine-città are highly exaggerated as far as the majority of

227

Romans are concerned, these boisterous, volatile, warmhearted people still have a passion (to say nothing of a talent) for enjoying life to the fullest.

It is not hard to understand the reason, for Rome is unquestionably the world's most sensual city. There is a feeling of warmth and languor about it, derived partly from the warm sun, the ripeness of age, its mellow old buildings painted apricot, peach, and gold, its blue *duomo* of a sky, its pines and fountains, and its casual, colorful street life, that makes the city look as though it's always on a holiday. Men stand on street corners carrying on perpetual flirtations with girls passing by, and on hot summer afternoons the whole city dozes in the torpor brought on by too much *pasta* and too much wine. The very air seems charged with memories of all the romances and adventures that have taken place here since the city was founded, according to legend, by Romulus and Remus in 754 B.C. But most of all, perhaps, it is the presence of the ruins that makes the Romans so intent upon enjoying life, for they are constantly reminded of civilizations that have come and gone, and their philosophy is a combination of *Sic transit gloria mundi* and "Gather ye rosebuds while ye may."

As visitors soon find out, it is a philosophy that is catching. The average tourist goes to Rome determined to "do" the city properly— determined to see all of the sights his guidebook considers "musts." *He* will not "waste time" napping in the afternoon. Even though he knows that the museums, shops, and churches close for three siesta hours, he plans to hire a taxi and drive out along the Appian Way in the broiling sun, or to take a walking tour of the city to see some of its famous squares and streets. He sits down to lunch planning to order a chicken sandwich and some iced tea and becomes seduced by the menu, and by the Romans around him who seem to be enjoying what looks like the world's most wonderful food. Before long he has had an enormous meal of spaghetti, meat, a salad, some cheese, and for dessert he follows the example of the Italians at nearby tables, and cuts a big golden peach into what's left of his red wine. Sleep is the only activity possible after that, and he awakens at four thirsty and in need of refreshment. That means a café, some *espresso,* a chilled bitter vermouth, or tart sherbet frozen into a hollowed-out lemon shell. He might decide to see an outdoor opera in the Baths of Caracalla, where the ghostly silhouettes of arches and old walls provide the backdrops, and later he can have supper, and sit at still another café. Or, if there is a full moon the romantic atmosphere works its magic, he will take an open *fiacre* and ride through the quiet streets to see the Colosseum at its most poetic— when its ancient crumbling stones are silver-leafed with moonlight. Suddenly he finds that his determination and his planned itinerary have floated away into the warm, heady air. Next day he may start all over, certain he will get in his full quota of sightseeing, but the old spirit is gone and chances are he will succumb to the first café he passes, and play the favorite Roman game of Girl Watching. It is virtually impossible not to live as the Romans do, when in Rome, unless, of course, you are one of the weary, dazed hordes who are mercilessly prodded through "planned itineraries" by dedicated tour leaders, in which case you wind up knowing everything and nothing about this Italian capital.

For centuries everyone who has visited Rome has been over-powered and dazzled by it. It is a world in itself—Mother of the Arts, Museum of the Ages, the Holy City, the Eternal City. "It would be easier to write ten lectures upon Rome than one," said Henry L. Stoddard in the nineteenth century. "The supreme difficulty is: first, to choose what is essential to even an approximately thorough delineation of the Eternal City, and then to treat of it in words which shall not be so brief as to suggest a catalogue of names. Ancient, mediaeval, papal, ecclesiastical, artistic, and modern Rome are the fewest divisions possible for any genuine study of the subject, and these can be divided almost indefinitely."

And after seeing this city and its sights, Mark Twain's exhaustion and sense of defeat seem apparent in this summation from *Innocents Abroad:*

Day after day and night after night we have wandered among the crumbling wonders of Rome; day after day and night after night we have fed upon the dust and decay of five-and-twenty centuries—have brooded over them by day and dreamt of them by night till sometimes we seemed mouldering away ourselves, and growing defaced and cornerless, and liable at any moment to fall prey to some antiquary and be patched in the legs, and "restored" with an unseemly nose, and labelled wrong and dated wrong, and set up in the Vatican for poets to drivel about and vandals to scribble their names on for ever and for ever more . . . I have felt all the time like a boy in a candy-shop—there was everything to choose from and no choice. I have drifted along hopelessly without knowing where to commence. I will not commence at all. Our passports are in order. We will go to Naples.

His sentiments are undoubtedly those of almost anyone visiting this city for the first time. Nor does the problem of choice become easier on succeeding visits, for then you must choose between those things you haven't seen before and those you saw, liked, and want to see again. Before you start, you should perhaps toss a coin into the Trevi fountain so you will be sure of returning.

Rome is a huge, historical layer cake, where the centuries have piled on top of each other, and where almost every monument has been something else durings its lifetime. Modern sidewalks bear the seal of the imperial days: S.P.Q.R.—*Senatus Populusque Romanus* —of the Senate and People of Rome. The Stock Exchange stands on the site of one of Hadrian's temples. The city's oldest building, the domed Pantheon that seems to be the favored haunt of Rome's stray cats, was begun by Marcus Agrippa in 27 B.C. to celebrate his victory over Antony and Cleopatra, and was rebuilt by Hadrian as a pagan temple. Caracalla restored it to its original design, and in 609 it was consecrated as a Christian church and now contains the tombs of the Italian kings. The forbidding red-brick round tower fortress, the Castel Sant' Angelo that looms over the Tiber, was built by Hadrian as his mausoleum and subsequently was a place of refuge for the popes, a prison, and the setting Puccini used for the opera based on the story of Floria Tosca and her lover, Cavaradossi. The austere Renaissance palace that stands on the Piazza Venezia was built for a pope and was used as an embassy by the Venetian republic and later by the Austro-Hungarian empire. It was from a small balcony of this palace that Mussolini addressed the crowds, and in front of the square is the wild white heap of columns, steps, and statuary that is the Victor-Emmanuel Monument, called by the Romans "the wedding cake" for reasons that are all too obvious, once you have seen it. And on the Via Labicana, the Church of San Clemente includes four layers of Roman architectural history. Its lowest part dates back to pagan Rome, next comes the remains of a fourth century basilica, while the Upper Church, built in 1108, is a fine example of the primitive Christian style. This is decorated with twelfth century mosaics and fifteenth century frescoes, and a stairway leads down through the centuries to the remains of the first temple built to honor the sun god, Mithras.

Before long your head begins to swim, and all of Rome's ruins and monuments, its churches, its eras and civilizations, and its overlapping legends seem to be part of the identical moment in time. You might begin to wonder if Julius Caesar worshiped at the huge altar in St. Peter's. You might have nightmares in which toga-clad Romans dance in the sixteenth century Quirinale Palace where the Italian president now lives, or see the Vatican's Swiss Guards in the red, yellow, and blue uniforms designed by Michelangelo, shopping in the arched brick honeycomb that was Trajan's Market, or see medieval popes enjoying the marbled luxury of Diocletian's Baths, or perhaps imagine yourself at a Fellini movie called *The Rape of the Sabine Women,* starring Sophia Loren and Marcello Mastroianni.

And always there is the problem of choice. No matter where you are in Rome, you feel you should be someplace else. If you are at one of the fashionable cafés like Doney's that line the Via Veneto, you might think you would be happier at another that edges the cobblestoned Piazza del Popolo, with its twin baroque churches and obelisk sprawling below the Pincio terrace; or perhaps it should be the dimly lit, red-plush lined Café Greco, that was frequented by Keats and Shelley, among others. If you are dining at Palazzi, the restaurant on the Monte Mario that was the palace Mussolini built for his mistress, you might suddenly decide it would have been more fun to have dinner at one of the simple little *trattorie* that abound in the city's old, exciting slum area, the shadowy Trastevere. If you feel like a trip out of the city one day, you must choose between the wine-producing hill towns of the Castelli Romani; or go instead to Rome's ancient harbor beach resort, the Ostia Lido; or to Tivoli where you can visit Hadrian's Villa and the beautiful palace, fountains, and gardens of the Renaissance Villa d'Este; or perhaps you will choose to drive out along the chariot-rutted stones of the Appian Way, through remnants of arches and past fragments of aqueducts.

When you are picking your way through the garden of bleached stone ruins that is the Roman Forum, where lizards sun themselves and fluted columns lie on the ground like so many felled tree trunks, you might suddenly think the time would be better spent seeing the wonders of St. Peter's: its familiar square with the two soaring fountains, one of the eleven obelisks brought back to Rome from Egypt, and the great circling colonnade of the 284 columns designed by Bernini, a sight most impressive when the pope emerges from the balcony of his apartments to issue his *Urbi et Orbi* blessing to "the city and the world." Once inside that enormous cathedral you are again dazzled by its apses and arches, its throngs of people and its innumerable chapels, its paintings and statues. "If the foreigner who enters St. Peter's attempts to see everything, he will develop a furious headache," cautioned Stendhal. The same might be said of the entire city. Should you spend an afternoon in the cool, dark depths of the Catacombs where early Christians lived in hiding, or should you, instead, climb the heights of the Campodoglio and see the museum of antique sculptures and the beautiful square designed by Michelangelo on what was the Capitoline, one of the seven hills that surrounded ancient Rome? You can look over the length of the Forum from this point, or from another of the hills, the Palatine, the place where the original city was founded. Should you spend the morning in the Borghese Gardens with its fine museum, its magnificent umbrella pines, and formal flower beds, or should you shop in the elegant boutiques, jewelry shops, and gift shops that line the Via Condotti, the Via Sistina and the hectic Corso, once the setting for horse races? Should you go bargain hunting in one of the city's outdoor push-cart markets, or delve into the enticements of the bookshops and antique shops along the Via Babuino and eventually wend your way into one of Rome's most enchanting little dead-end streets, the quiet Via Margutta, where painters and sculptors have their studios and where the only noise is the sound of chisels chipping away at stone.

The Colosseum is the one sight that never disappoints anyone, for though its outside view is familiar, it is far more awesome on the inside, a vast oval stone melon, eaten away by time. Its façade is stripped of its original travertine and pockmarks indicate where bronze studs were removed, by Goths, Vandals, and by the Romans themselves. (Many historians have observed that no one ever did as much to destroy Rome as did the Romans.) The Colosseum was the great theater of its day, where thousands upon thousands were "butchered to make a Roman holiday." When it was dedicated by Titus in 80 A.D., it was inaugurated by a celebration lasting one hundred days. During that period, three thousand gladiators and more than five thousand lions, tigers, and other wild animals were sacrificed to honor the event.

If the Colosseum is the least disappointing sight in Rome, the most disappointing may well be the Sistine Chapel, though few people ever admit it. Because it is known as the room where the College of Cardinals meets in secret to select a new pope, and because it is adorned with Michelangelo's wall and ceiling frescoes of the "Creation of Adam," the "Last Judgment" and other such Old Testament allegories, one expects a somewhat hushed and spiritual setting. After walking through the endless lengths of the Vatican Libraries, where room after frescoed room is filled with cases of jeweled orbs and scepters, gilded manuscripts, ruby-covered Bibles, and other such gifts that the various popes have received from the crowned heads of the world, after you pass miles of paintings and statuary, you finally reach the chapel. What you see is a small room absolutely jammed with people: Germans in leather walking shorts; Californians in Hawaiian sport shirts; priests and nuns from the four corners of the world; monks in chocolate-brown robes; children who are crying because of the heat and confusion; and over all, the babbling of half-a-dozen guides, each speaking to his own group in a different language. The paintings seem faded and not nearly as beautiful as they do in close-ups you have seen in art books, and in fact, though the work is staggering because of the time and effort it took to complete it, Michelangelo was a much better sculptor than a painter, and the hundreds of figures in this room are not very well drawn. If you have the energy left after this (remember Stendhal's warning about headaches), you can continued to the Borgia apartments and the rooms decorated by Raphael.

This city that Byron called "the Niobe of nations . . . the city of my soul" contains much, much more, of course. Among its most beautiful churches are San Giovanni in Laterno, built by Borromini in the seventeenth century on the spot where an earlier basilica stood in Constantine's time. Nearby is the Palazzo Laternese, now an antiquities museum, though it was once the home of the popes, before they were exiled to Avignon in 1309 where they stayed for seventy years before returning the Holy See to Rome. At the church of San Pietro in Vincoli (St. Peter in Chains) you can see one of Michelangelo's most powerfully moving works, the lifelike statue of the prophet Moses; and the huge basilica of Santa Maria Maggiore, dating from 352 A.D., has been altered and added onto so many times in its history that it includes a sampling of almost every architectural style that ever held sway in Rome. St. Paul's Outside-the-Walls (outside the walls that bounded ancient Rome) is an exact nineteenth century copy of the original church built here by Theodosius and which was destroyed by fire. It is here that the apostle is buried. Because of its graceful columns, the mosaics on its pediments, its alabaster windows, and gold and white ceiling, many think this was the loveliest church in this city of churches. Not far away is the pyramid the Romans carried back with them from Egypt, and behind that is the peaceful, tree-shaded Protestant cemetery where Keats and Shelley are buried.

The Piazza Navona with its Bernini fountains; the Piazza di Spagna, where the grand stairway is lined with flower vendors, students, lovers, and tired tourists; the hectic Piazza Barberini with its Triton fountain; and the Piazza dell' Esedra with its Naiad fountains are just a few of the handsome squares in Rome. The Porta Pia, the city gate built after Michelangelo's design in 1561, was the place where Garibaldi's Thousand entered the city in 1870 to win the final battle in their fight for Italian unification.

It was that unification, the *Risorgimento,* that made Rome the capital of Italy, and it was the only choice that would have worked. After Roman times when the peninsula was united under the empire, it had become a collection of separate states, each with its own loyalties, interests, problems, languages, and customs. Even today there is much rivalry between north, south, east, and west: between the Tuscans and the Piedmontese; the Lombardians and the Ligurians; the people of the Veneto and those of the Campagna. Only Rome, the city that belongs to the world, could hold it together, partially because it was the spiritual capital of all the people on the peninsula, partly because of what it had symbolized in its ancient days. Now, with its 2 million people, Rome governs a country of 55 million which, since the end of World War II, has become one of the most prosperous in Europe. But even when they are poor (and poverty is still widespread in the country) the Italians have a talent for enjoying life unequaled by any other people in the world. Though they have been pioneers in the "art" of war, they have, since late Roman days, been the world's worst soldiers; just what you might expect of people who love comfort, good food, wine, and who hate regimentation so much they do not have speed limits on their roads or traffic lights in most of their cities.

Yet despite this lack of discipline they are among the world's best engineers and architects, mathematicians and scientists, and if they made an "art" of war, so have they made an "art" of everything else. As craftsmen they have perhaps only one fault, from an esthetic point of view: they often show a bent for conspicuous craftsmanship. They will inlay a piece of wood with the most intricate veneers, design the most complicated jewelry, build the most fantastic structures of reinforced concrete with great buildings that have pleated cantilevers and walls that looked ruffled—all to prove they can do it.

Confirmed Catholics, the Italians have a realistic approach to their religion; for the most part they have a warm affection for their saints and take a tongue-in-cheek attitude toward their clergy. Women and children go to church on Sunday; the men stand in the streets talking, watching, waiting. The Italians put their money in *Il Banco delle Santo Spirito* (the Bank of the Holy Ghost) and use an olive oil called *Pace, O Mio Dio* (Peace, Oh My God), a bit of good-natured sacrilege one would never see in such stern Catholic countries as Spain or Ireland. Being staunch family people, the Italians have made a family of their saints and gods. The pope is the number one *Papa* (the name he is called in Italian), the Madonna is the Mother of all time, and on her knee she holds the Bambino who is both her son and her God. Anyone who has ever known an Italian family at all well will recognize that such symbolism is more than a matter of coincidence.

Since Etruscan times, Italy has been a country of artistic as well as scenic wonders and anyone who wants to know it all should include, if he can, not only such much-visited, much-publicized sights as its large cities, the fishing and resort towns along the Adriatic and the Mediterranean, the art towns of Tuscany and the Etruscan relics at such towns as Viterbo, Orvieto, and Tarquinia. Italy is also the Trulli country in Calabria, where people live in black-roofed white huts that are shaped like beehives. It is unimaginable hamlets like Ariano Irpino, a town between Foggia and Naples that is built on a slope so steep the land cannot retain water for its farms. Italy also has eerie mountain towns like Radicofani, in the same region, where a crumbling medieval fortress castle hints at a more glorious past. And if you spend the night and order some meat for your dinner in the one old hotel there, the waiter will take a piece of beef from a bureau drawer in the warm dining room, cut off a slice and cook it for you.

But with the Italians, as with tourists, all roads in Italy lead to Rome, and this description of it written by Frederic Harrison in the nineteenth century is even truer today:

Rome, as a city, is a visible embodiment, type, or summary of human history, and, in these days of special interests or tastes, the traveller at Rome too often forgets this world-wide range and complexity. To the scholar, the vast world of Christian Rome is usually as utter a blank as to the Catholic pilgrim is the story of Republic and Empire. To the artist, both are ancient tales of little meaning, though the words are strong. He who loves "curios" is blind too often to the sunsets on the Campagna. And he who copies inscriptions is deaf to the music of the people in the Piazza Navona, or the evening Angelus rung out from a hundred steeples. All nations, all professions, all creeds jostle each other in Rome, as they did in the age of Horace and Juvenal.

FLORENCE

> " 'Tis the Past
> Contending with the Present; and in turn
> Each has the mastery."

FLORENCE, a city of four hundred thousand and the capital of the ancient province of Tuscany, is Italy's richest art treasury and, at first glance, her most discouraging city. Because it is called the City of Flowers, visitors might well expect it to be all decked out with gardens and window boxes, leafy parks and promenades. And since it is also known as the Cradle of the Renaissance, and the Tuscan Athens, they might also expect to find it a graceful set-piece that will be a joy to walkers and photographers, a mellow fragment of the past where one can quietly contemplate the majesty of Brunelleschi's dome, the elegance of Giotto's tower, or the beauty of Michelangelo's statue of David.

After three days, this same visitor, exhausted, frustrated, sadder, and wiser, begins to wonder why this city ever held so much appeal for English romantic poets and E. M. Forster heroines. He may even begin to suspect that he has made a terrible mistake, and that the city the Italians call Firenze is not really Florence at all. For though in May the gardens and fields around the city are actually carpeted with red poppies, blue irises, white lilies, violets, columbine, and buttercups, and look just as they do in Botticelli's painting, "Primavera," for the most part the city presents an aspect that is gray and stony, treeless and grassless. If one visits this city in summer, as most tourists do, he must be prepared for sweltering heat, dust, and grime, from which there is little respite, as Florence cannot offer beaches or lakes within its immediate surroundings, and certainly no one would ever think of taking a dip in the sluggish, mud-yellow Arno that flows through the city. Fiesole, the ancient Etruscan-Roman hill town that was the forerunner of Florence, does have a few breezy spots, but even this charming village that Browning called "yonder sober pleasance," is scorching by day. And though Florence does have a lovely glowing russet autumn, especially in late September and October, its winters are, in the understated phrasing of Baedeker, "disproportionately cold."

As for confirmed walkers and photographers, they may well find the city a nightmare. It would be hard to find a place more crowded, more choked with traffic, and more clamoring with traffic noises. Its narrow streets were designed long before the advent of the automobile, and since they are lined with valuable buildings that are documents of the past, nothing can be torn down to widen them. The sidewalks are merely slim strips that tilt toward the roadways, and unless you walk in single file you stand a good chance of being nudged by a passing fender. In addition, the high rows of buildings enclosing the streets act as traps for the noise and you are likely to be kept awake by roaring Vespa motor scooters far into the night and early in the morning. Even the cafés in the main square have all the charm of a parking lot.

Travelers who have come to marvel at the city's architectural wonders (which *are* considerable), will find the enormous cathedral, Brunelleschi's Duomo, with its façade of green, white, and gray inlaid marble patterning, almost always half-covered with scaffolding. Florence's grime makes its necessary for the building to be cleaned often and it is so large that by the time the last side is finished, the first is dirty again. Giotto's pink, white, and green marble bell tower, the Campanile, which Longfellow called "the lily of Florence blossoming in stone," is also grayed and perpetually in need of cleaning, and the handsomest and oldest building in this Piazza del Duomo, the black and white marble striped octagonal Baptistry, looks as though it had been stained with nicotine. (Its magnificent sculpted bronze doors are, however, always kept cleanly polished.)

If visitors to this city are disappointed, the fault lies in their expectations, not in Florence itself. Unlike Venice, which is a Byzantine-Renaissance fossil that exists only as a curio to delight tourists, Florence exists for trade and commerce, just as it always has. It was a thriving community when the Romans took it from the Etruscans, the center of European cloth trade during medieval times, and it still produces the craft articles for which it has always been famous: leather work, jewelry, fine embroideries, stone sculptures that now are used as garden ornaments, elaborately swirled and curlicued wrought iron, and beautiful "paintings" done in inlaid marble, the art of *pietra dura intarsia,* the same method used for the marble inlays of the Duomo and the Campanile. Florence is today the largest producer of Italy's luxury export products, the center of its *haute couture* industry, and the place where American buying offices have their Italian branches. Tourists do more shopping here than anywhere else in Italy and many come simply for that reason.

Known for their wit and cynicism, the Florentines are also famous for their business acumen and frugality. In the *Paradiso,* Dante wrote of "One who is now a Florentine, and changeth coin and wares"; and in the *Inferno* he said of himself, "All wiles and covert ways I knew"—about as an accurate a description of most Florentines as one can find. Even Michelangelo put his money into real estate, and as for wiliness, few have ever outdone Machiavelli. And, in the city of Cellini, it might also be expected that the Florentines show evidence of their intricate minds in their crafts: in the elaborate patterning of their silver, in the tooling of their leather, and in their exquisite laces.

The inevitable outcome of this mixture of antiquity and industry is the jumble that is Florence, and, to anyone willing to thread his way through it, one of the most handsome and exciting cities in Italy, if not in all the world. Unlike the flashy show-off, Venice, who displays her treasures openly for all to see at once, the Florentines (very much like the Japanese) keep their beauties behind high walls. The great paintings and sculptures, the dark-red Renaissance rooms, the colonnaded loggias and courtyard gardens are all there, just as you have been led to expect, but you must search them out and then gain entry to them. If Florence is rocky, it is, in fact, a rock garden, where bright blossoms are tucked between slabs of gray stone.

One of Florence's most handsome sights is the Piazza della Signoria, the medieval square that dates from Dante's time. It is the city's only set-piece, a huge cobblestoned expanse watched over by the gold brick tower of the Palazzo Vecchio that is the city's landmark, the Bargello sculpture gallery, that was first a guild hall and later the residence of the Ghibelline conqueror, and edged by the Loggia dei Lanzi, an arcaded pavilion full of wonderful sculptures, including Giambologna's "Rape of the Sabine Women," and Cellini's "Perseus." Here you may sit for hours at one of the café tables and dream your way back to the days of the Signorii, the ducal rulers of Tuscany, who held their *arrangi* here, mass meetings intended to stir up the emotions of the Florentines for purposes of war or politics. In front of the Palazzo Vecchio is a copy of Michelangelo's "David" (you can see the original in the Accademia), and at one side is the Uffizi Gallery, one of the world's greatest museums, which includes not only the works of the Italian masters, but of the Spaniards, Germans, and north Europeans as well.

Across the Arno, the massive Pitti Palace is the city's second richest museum, though the interior of the building itself, with its *trompe l'oeil* marbleized walls and columns, is probably the outstanding example of the Italian urge to exhibit "conspicuous craftsmanship." The Church of San Marco practically glows with the exquisite paintings of Fra Angelico, while the Bibliotheca Laurentiana, the Gothic church of Santa Trinitá with Ghirlandaio's frescoes and Luca della Robbia's tomb of Federighi, the church of Santa Maria Novella, and at least half-a-dozen more, are all filled with the works of the great Florentines.

It was because of these "great Florentines" that the city became known as the Tuscan Athens. Few cities since that ancient Greek metropolis have ever produced so much talent. Among its famous native sons (or sons of other Tuscan towns who came to Florence to live) the city can count Boccaccio, Petrarch, Machiavelli, Galileo, Savonarola, Amerigo Vespucci, whose cousin Simonetta was a famous beauty of her day, Bartolommeo, Andrea del Sarto, Cellini, Donatello, Ghiberti, Leonardo da Vinci, and Michelangelo.

Few cities offer as dramatic a contrast as those two Renaissance republics, Venice and Florence; and their heroes are as opposite in personality as their architecture. Where the famous men of Venice were passionate and full of bravado, those of Florence tended toward asceticism and cool reason. Even Boccaccio and Botticelli turned from their earlier voluptuous styles to more austere works in their later years, the latter having been irrevocably influenced by the fire-and-brimstone sermons of the monk Savonarola. More than one historian has referred to the "dark and bloody Florentines." Even their ducal families like the Strozzis and the Medicis, who practically financed the Renaissance singlehanded, had their crueler sides and Mark Twain detested the Florentines for honoring these "historic cut-throats." When he visited the Church of Santa Croce, where he saw the tombs of Michelangelo, Raphael, Machiavelli, and Dante's cenotaph, he rejoiced over the fact that the Florentines had never been able to get Dante's body back from Ravenna, the city to which he fled in exile. "We were glad to know his body was not in it," he wrote. "Medicis are good enough for Florence. Let her plant Medicis and build grand monuments over them to testify how gratefully she was wont to lick the hand that scourged her."

The "grand monuments" that are the Medici tombs in the Medici-Riccardi Palace are among the city's most awesome sights, as are the rooms of the palace, many of which have secret wall panels behind which vials of poison were concealed in case the castle was besieged and the Medicis taken prisoner. And at least one room here has a secret door, a wall panel that shuts behind you and becomes invisible as you enter, so that you have to feel your way around the room until you press the panel that moves—another example of the wiliness of the Florentines and of their passion for intrigue.

Although walking is far from delightful in this traffic-jammed city, there are a few places where this pastime is possible: along the streets of the Arno and across its oldest bridge, the Ponte Vecchio, where enticing jewelry shops are piled on top of each other, two stories high; through the little back alleys of the city on both sides of the river, where tiny cave-like crafts shops are wedged in between modern boutiques and food shops; along the fashionable Via Tornabuoni and under the arcade of the Straw Market, the Porcellino, one of the only places in the city where you can bargain. The Boboli Gardens behind the Pitti Palace are lovely in spring and fall, though in summer the grass is usually burned dry as straw, and from the lookout on San Miniato you see the classic view of Florence, with the tower of the Palazzo Vecchio and the rose-red dome of the Duomo outlined against the low cloud-dappled sky and the rolling gold-green hills of the Appenines.

Tuscany, the oldest province in Italy, which took its name from the Etruscans who settled it, is one of Italy's richest sections, not only in art, but in scenery and agriculture. Along the slopes of the Appenines are the vineyards that produce the Chianti wine, the orchards that produce Italy's finest olive oil, the marble quarries of Carrara, and grazing land for the sheep that have made this province famous for its wool since medieval times. From Florence, the capital of the province, one can visit many of its most antique towns: Fiesole, only twenty minutes away; Montecatini, with its spas and woodlands; Pisa on the sea coast, with its all-too-well-known Leaning Tower, its classic white Cathedral and Baptistry; and Lucca, noted for its olive oil, its eleventh-century churches, and the tree-lined walks that date from the sixteenth century and have earned the city its title as the City of Shady Walls. And Tuscany offers terrains as contrasting as the seaside fishing towns around Leghorn and the mountaintop medieval city of Siena, one of the most impressive of all Italian towns and the rival of Florence since the Middle Ages. It is everything Florence is not: a medieval stage set with a curving center called the Campo. Here every August the Palio is held, the racing and riding tournament in which all contestants wear their traditional guild or family costumes that date back to the Renaissance.

VENICE

The widowed bride of the Adriatic,
enthroned on her hundred isles

WRITERS who travel to Italy seem to agree perfectly on one point: Venice is impossible. It is purely a dream fantasy, a pseudo-Arabian Nights city spread out over 118 islands, and stapled together by 400 arched stone bridges; a glittering Byzantine mosaic that has cracked apart at the seams, its colorful glass tiles afloat on the silken blue of the Adriatic. "The Island of Hallucination," Sean O'Faolain called it in his book, *Summer in Italy;* "Neverness is the word for Venice," he concluded.

Mary McCarthy opened her book *Venice Observed* by explaining, "The rationalist mind has always had its doubts about Venice. The watery city receives a dry inspection, as though it were a myth for the credulous—poets and honeymooners."

Mark Twain, whose *Innocents Abroad* should be required reading for anyone going to Italy, reported on his arrival in Venice:

What a funny old city this Queen of the Adriatic is! Narrow streets, vast, gloomy marble palaces, black with the corroding damps of centuries, and all partly submerged; no dry land visible anywhere, and no sidewalks worth mentioning; if you want to go to church, to the theater, or to the restaurant, you must call a gondola . . .

In a few minutes we swept gracefully out into the Grand Canal, and under the mellow moonlight the Venice of poetry and romance stood revealed. Right from the water's edge rose long lines of stately palaces of marble; gondolas were gliding swiftly hither and thither and disappearing suddenly through unsuspected gates and alleys; ponderous stone bridges threw their shadows athwart the glittering waves. There was life and motion everywhere, and yet everywhere there was a hush, a stealthy sort of stillness, that was suggestive of secret enterprises of bravoes and of lovers; and clad half in moonbeams and half in mysterious shadows, the grim old mansions of the Republic seemed to have an expression about them of having an eye out for just such enterprises as these at the same moment. Music came floating over the waters—Venice was complete . . .

In the glare of day, there is little poetry about Venice, but under the charitable moon her stained palaces are white again, their battered sculptures are hidden in shadows, and the old city seems crowned once more with the grandeur that was hers five hundred years ago. It is easy, then, in fancy, to people these silent canals with plumed gallants and fair ladies—with Shylocks in gaberdine and sandals, venturing loans upon the rich argosies of Venetian commerce—with Othellos and Desdemonas, with Iagos and Roderigos—with noble fleets and victorious legions returning from the wars . . .

And Charles Dickens, reminiscing about his visit to this city, wrote, "I have many and many a time thought of this strange Dream upon the water: half wondering if it lie there, yet, and if its name be Venice."

If Venice is a dream, it is at least a dream come true. Few cities are so exactly what we expect them to be. It lives up to the advance billing it received from Shakespeare, Byron, Browning, Ruskin, Henry James, Howells, Twain, Dickens, Stendhal, Hemingway, Mary McCarthy, and the Baron Corvo, whose impossible fantasy of a novel, *The Desire and Pursuit of the Whole,* is so perfectly suited to this impossible fantasy of a city. Venice has been painted in minute and glowing detail by three Bellinis, two Venezianos, and two Canalettos; by Titian, Tintoretto, and Tiepolo; by Carpaccio, Lotto, and Veronese; Guardi, Turner, Longhi, and Giorgione. If there is a surprise left, it is that the city looks just the way you knew it would.

Nowhere is this more true than in the Piazza San Marco, the city's center and the focal point of its activity, the square Napoleon called "the most beautiful drawing-room in Europe." This great roofless "room" is walled in on three sides by triple storied Renaissance palaces that now house offices, shops, restaurants, and cafés. Their white stone colonnaded fronts are streaked black with age, burnt-orange awnings shield the upper windows from the sun, and ivory canvas curtains hang between the columns of the street arcades, to keep the shops and promenades cool and shady. That great heap of a cathedral, San Marco, sprawls along the eastern edge of the square. With its satiny green domes, its horseshoe arches, and gleaming gold mosaic façade, it is an Oriental wonder, the like of which has never been seen anywhere—not even in the Orient.

The center of this square teems with human activity. Tourists and Venetians alike sit at the café tables, eating *granite* and *gelati,* sipping *espresso* or the syrupy sweet iced drinks like *tamarindo* or almond milk *orzata* which the Italians like so much. Some mill about, dazed by the activity or marveling at the architectural splendors of the setting; others buy bags of feed for the pigeons and then have themselves photographed with pigeons in their hands, on their shoulders, and even in their hair. In the afternoon, along the shaded side of the piazza, five-piece orchestras play Viennese waltzes at some of the cafés, while at others guests are entertained by singing guitarists, Neapolitan style. Several nights a week military bands or full orchestras hold concerts from the stand set up facing the cathedral, and, at any time of day, the enclosed square throbs with the constant rippling hum of human voices, a sound very much like the dovecot cooing of the pigeons who make their home here.

If anything makes the Piazza San Marco less impressive than it was, it is the people who gather there. Modern clothes hardly do for it what the antique costumes did. The fifteenth century marchers in the papal processions painted by Gentile Bellini wore long, elegantly simple robes that matched the dull reds, golds, and olive greens of the church mosaics. And when Canaletto painted the Venice of Casanova, the piazza had all the dash and drama of a grand ball-room. The eighteenth century Venetians gathered there wore powdered wigs, tricorn hats, flowing capes; the men in silk knee breeches and waistcoats, and ruffled lace cuffs; the women in low-cut, tightly laced bodices and hooped skirts—costumes that seem more suited to masked balls than to a stroll in a public square.

Anyone who goes in for panoramic views has a good choice within this piazza. He may go to the top of the square rose-brick bell tower, the Campanile, that rises 325 feet into the air, and look over San Marco, the domes of its cathedral, and across the labyrinth of watery roadways that web out behind it. He can see a slightly different view from the lower vantage point atop the fifteenth century Clock Tower that rises over an arched gateway. Here two giant bronze Moors strike their hammer against the anvil bell every hour, sending the flocks of pigeons skyward, like flurries of paper picked up and whirled around by the wind. Or he may view the square itself from the balcony above the portico of the Cathedral of San Marco, where he can also get a closer look at its four famed gilded bronze horses. Originally Greek, these horses adorned the triumphal arch of Nero in Rome, and later that of Trajan. Constantine took them to his new eastern capital, Constantinople, as ornaments for the imperial hippodrome, and when the Doge Enrico Dandolo defeated the Turks in that city in 1204, he carried the horses back to Venice as the spoils of war. But their journeys were not quite over, for when Napoleon conquered the Venetian Republic in 1797, he took the horses to Paris where they stayed until 1815 when the Congress of Vienna returned them to Venice.

And from both the Clock Tower and the balcony of San Marco you can look across the small, precise square, the Piazzetta, set between the Cathedral and the Grand Canal. Here two pedestaled figures mark the city's main boat landing, just as they did when this was the scene of the triumphant returns of the Venetian fleets, back from their conquests in the east. On top of one pedestal is the statue of the Winged Lion of St. Mark, now Venice's trademark. On the other is its former patron, St. Theodore, seated on a crocodile, a fitting symbol for a city that is itself afloat on tree-trunk pilings and scraps of islands.

Along one side of the Piazzetta is the Old Library, with its archives and paintings. Opposite stands the Palace of the Doges, the Palazzo Ducale, built between the fourteenth and fifteenth centuries. It is a pink and white marble confection, frosted with lacy arches and balustrades in the flamboyant Moorish-Gothic style, and the place where much of Venice's history was made. Death sentences used to be pronounced in front of the palace's main doorway, and in its simple gray-stone courtyard colossal statues of Mars and Neptune mark the Scala dei Giganti—the Giants' Staircase. New doges were given their hats of office on the top landing of this stairway, and it was here that the Doge Marino Faliero was beheaded in the fourteenth century: "The gory head rolls down the Giants' Steps," wrote Byron of the event. Close to this staircase, the open mouth of the marble lion's head—la Bocca di Leone—was the place where anonymous denunciations were dropped during the Inquisition. The accused were tried by the Council of Ten, and, if found guilty, were taken across the Bridge of Sighs that links the palace to the Leads, the prison of watery, dank dungeons where Casanova was one of the more fortunate inmates. He escaped; others spent their whole lives there, remembered only by the water rats and the jailers who slipped meager rations through the iron gratings of the damp torture cells.

In the twelfth century a very special annual ceremony was begun in Venice, which continued until the city's conquest by Napoleon in 1797. Each year on Ascension Day the Venetian doge, dressed in silk brocade, would descend from the balcony of the ducal palace, walk along the Piazzetta and between the pedestaled statues, and there board a barge that was trimmed with canopies of gold and velvet, its deck inlaid with ebony and mother of pearl. Then, to the sound of martial music, that splendid vessel, gleaming in the sunlight, swept toward the open sea, propelled by eighty gilded oars. Amid the roar of cannon and the cheers of Venetians, the doge would cast a golden wedding band into the blue Adriatic waters, saying, "We wed thee, O Sea, with this ring, emblem of our rightful and perpetual domination." Though the Venetian bride has indeed been widowed, Venice is still, in a sense, wedded to the sea. Everything good or bad in its past or present can be attributed to its watery foundation.

The city was founded between the fifth and seventh centuries by Roman tribes who fled before the armies of Attila and sought refuge on the islands of this lagoon. Gradually they built a flourishing state and, during the Crusades, Venice was virtually a swinging door between the east and west. The Adriatic city grew rich as the port of entry and exit for European armies who fought in the east.

In 1204, the Doge Dandolo, already blind and aged, led the

Fourth Crusade and defeated the Turkish sultan. He sacked Constantinople, carrying back to Venice many of the jewels, icons, and artistic treasures that now adorn the walls and chapels of San Marco. The Venetian Republic was launched on its golden age. For over two hundred years it "held the gorgeous East in fee, and was the safeguard of the West. . . ." In the thirteenth century Marco Polo, nephew of a Venetian merchant, journeyed to the court of Kublai Khan and when he returned, years later, his relatives claimed not to recognize him until they saw the jewels he had sewn into the seams of his clothing. In true Venetian fashion, they then claimed him as their own.

At the peak of its power in the fifteenth century, Venice controlled shipping in the Adriatic, the Aegean, and much of the Mediterranean. Her fleet handled all of Turkey's shipping, controlled the spice, slave, silk, and sugar trade of Europe, and ruled over Genoa, the Dalmatian coast, Corfu, Crete, and Cyprus. And the people who declared themselves "Lords of Gold and Christendom" set about gilding their churches and their saints.

Venice's death knell was sounded in 1497, when it was announced in the Piazza San Marco that the Portuguese Vasco da Gama had sailed around the Cape of Good Hope to India. From that time on, commercial power drifted toward Iberia, and, Venice in a weakened position, could not successfully fight off the revolts of her possessions and the avenging armies of Bejazet. Still, Venice's golden age cast a long reflection and the republic retained its title *serenissima,* the most serene, until its final death blow came from Napoleon.

Though politically and commercially on the wane, Venice was at the peak of its artistic splendor in the fifteenth and sixteenth centuries and experienced a second revival in the eighteenth. Even then Venetian spies were dreaded in the capitals of Europe and the city's reputation for intrigue and cloak-and-dagger diplomacy were referred to frequently by Casanova in his *Memoirs.*

A flashy city with flashy heroes (Casanova, Dandolo, Marco Polo), theatrical Venice was also the home of the dramatist Goldoni, of Mozart's librettist, Lorenzo da Ponte, and of Harlequin and Pantaloon, whose lecherous, roguish doings, so typically Venetian, were exhibited in performances at the Teatro la Fenice, still the city's leading theater today.

Venice derived its exotic style from its contact with the Levant.

Although there are still many of the white-skinned redheads such as Titian loved to paint, the more typical Venetians are tall, dark, slim, with the long heads and dark Byzantine eyes seen in most of the icons in San Marco. The soft, sensual, Venetian dialect with its many *a* and *z* sounds shows strong Arabic influences, and the gondoliers' warning cry, *"a' oeil,"* that echoes plaintively under the bridges and through the narrow back-alley canals, sounds more Levantine than Italian. This is the only city in Italy where a street goes by the Moorish-Spanish name *calle,* instead of *via,* and on the island of Torcello there is a well-known tourist restaurant that calls itself a *locanda,* an almost direct steal from the Turkish word *lokantasi* that has the same meaning. *Polenta* (cornmeal) is more favored here than *pasta,* and it is probable that the *risotto* so popular throughout northern Italy entered through Venice, an only slightly altered version of the Turkish rice dish, pilaff, prepared in much the same way. It is from the East that the Venetians got their almost barbaric love of splendor and surface ornamentation and their taste for Assyrian winged lions.

Venice owes its present aspect to the sea, just as it does its history and its style. It is the sea that gives it the hushed stillness Mark Twain noticed, partly because it absorbs the harshness of sounds, but mostly because it has made it impossible for Venice to accommodate automobiles. All cars and motorcycles are stored in the huge circular garage in the Piazzale Roma, and visitors proceed by gondola or in the motor launches called *vaporetti.* The water also gives the city its luminous quality; its buildings, painted in tones of orange-turmeric, paprika-red, apricot, and lemon, flash "like wine, like flame, across the still lagoon." And in the rooms of its houses light bouncing off the water flits across the high ceilings, so that even the interiors have a limpid bubbling look. And because of the space limitations imposed on the city by the sea, it has changed less in appearance than almost any other place in Italy. There is little room for new buildings and only occasionally is some old house gutted out and replaced with a newer model. The only modern buildings are the garage and railroad station, and the pavilions of the foreign nations who take part in the Bienale, the biannual art exhibition held in the park of San Marco.

Most of all, the water provides Venice with its pageantry. Although the symbolic marriage of Venice and the sea is no longer celebrated, this city still has several regattas during the year and there is something of the pageant about every funeral, when the black-and-gold gondola hearses sail in a dark procession to the city's cemetery island, San Michele; or when the long, red fire boats, their brass horns screaming, cut across the water to answer an alarm. And if it were not for its watery location Venice would probably have been deserted long ago. Now it exists only for the tourists who come out of curiosity to see this unique island city. The 192,000 Venetians who live there earn a livelihood in the restaurants or hotels, as guides or gondoliers, or by making and selling the glass, lace, and leather that are favorite tourist souvenirs.

Since all Venice is a museum it needs few museums as such. For the most part, it displays its paintings in the churches and palaces where they originally hung. Almost any imposing building you wander into has its share of frescoes and cloudy ceiling murals, statues and gold-framed paintings. And though anyone who comes to this city will be intrigued by its narrow back streets where postage-stamp gardens grow between lopsided houses, and where every lane seems to lead into a blind alley, the classic way to see the city is, in the phrase of Shakespeare's Rosalind, "to swim in a gondola." The most impressive tour winds through the mile-and-a-half-long inverted *S* of the Grand Canal. It starts close to the railroad station and the public garage and lazes between palaces and churches, marble stoops that step into the water, striped wooden poles that are gondola moorings, and busy quays called *fondamenti*. Almost every building has a legend—poetic, tragic, or artistic—and if one lacks an interesting history, your gondolier will be happy to invent a story for your benefit.

Richard Wagner died in 1883 in the Lombard Renaissance Palazzo Vendramin, and close by is the stately mansion that belonged to Desdemona. Within another of these palaces the old Doge Foscari died of a broken heart at the ill-treatment he received from his countrymen. Byron lived in one; Robert Browning died in the Palazzo Rezzonico, where a memorial tablet bears the quotation, "Open my heart and you will see, Graved inside of it, 'Italy'." George Sand came to one of these houses with Alfred de Musset and betrayed him there with the Venetian Doctor Pagello; still another was the home of Titian. The thirteenth century Fondaco dei Turchi, the seventeenth century Ca'Pesaro, and the exquisite fifteenth century Ca

D'Oro, with pale golden walls that look like faded watered silk, the Palazzo Grimani, of which even Ruskin approved, the late Renaissance mansion belonging to Peggy Guggenheim, and another once owned by Barbara Hutton, and the fifteenth century Gothic Palazzio Giustiniani where Howells wrote *Venetian Life* and Wagner composed the second act of *Tristan*—all are strung out along this liquid highway.

The high-arched Rialto bridge with its two-tiered silver shops is in the heart of workaday Venice, close to the site of the old ghetto, the busy fish and fruit markets, and the quiet, anonymous little *trattorie* so popular with those who search for the "off-beat." Here you may buy a red-ribboned straw hat such as the gondoliers wear or sip coffee at a quayside café and watch the produce being unloaded for nearby markets.

At the Palazzo Grassi, the canal turns into the elegant, expensive Venice, with de luxe hotels like the Grand, the Gritti, Harry's Bar, and other such costly tourist haunts. You sail under the new wooden bridge that leads to the Accademia, with its fine art exhibits, and all at once you come to the wide bay formed by the Grand Canal and the Canale della Giudecca. The domed island churches of Santa Maria della Salute and San Giorgio Maggiore seem to float in the expanse of blue, as though they had been clipped off from some mainland and left to drift with the tides.

There are wonderful Venetian paintings in the Guildhall of San Rocco, the Church of the Frari, and the Palazzo Labia, as well as in the Palace of the Doges and the Cathedral of San Marco. When you are dazzled by the luminous golden works of the Venetian school, take a boat for the Adriatic resort, the Lido, where bright-blue cabanas fringe the beach and vendors come by selling pale-green grapes as cool as white wine, and stay until evening when the casino opens.

Another day take a boat to the island of Murano, where you may watch the glass blowers performing Venice's most classic craft, or go to the quiet grassy beaches of Torcello, or to Burano, where the faded painted houses will remind you of a box of broken, smudged, mismatched pastel chalks.

MILAN

Italy's second city and its capitale morale

To the bustling, prosperous *Milanesi* the rest of Italy is hopelessly awash in a sea of *dolce far niente*. With the exception of their own province, Lombardy, that contributes one-fourth of the nation's total annual income, and the neighboring, highly industrial Piedmont, all Italy is a vast cultural and commercial wasteland, living in its past and frittering away its present (and Milan's profits) on *il vino, le donne, e la canzone*—wine, women, and song. And though it ranks second after Rome in size with a population of 1.5 million, it is Italy's first city in matters of commerce and finance. Milan is head-quarters for the main offices of the country's leading banks and for its stock exchange, the center of the textile, printing, publishing, chemical, and metallurgy industries, and a clearinghouse for the agri-cultural wealth of the fertile Po Valley. Rome may be the nominal capital, but Milan has regarded itself as the *capitale morale* (the moral or virtual capital) since Italian unification in 1870.

With its gleaming white skyscrapers and nervous traffic jams, its pellmell pace and all-work attitude, and its plastic and chrome-plated stand-up coffee bars, this is the least typical of Italian cities, and has about it the brashness of Chicago combined with the boom-town urgency of Houston. Similarly, the average *Milanese* is the least typical of all Italians, both in appearance and temperament. He is likely to have light-brown hair and blue eyes instead of the dark eyes and olive coloring of his countrymen to the south, and he is more inclined to be concerned with affairs of finance than with affairs of the heart. Men idling on a Rome street corner will probably be ogling the girls who pass by; men in Milan are more probably standing around ogling a stockbroker's quotation board, trying to ascertain the latest price of the Montecatini or Fiat shares.

Square-set and solidly stocky, the Milan big-time operators are just as solidly middle class, strong family men, with flashy *nouveau-riche* tastes, who place a high value on bigness, newness, and speed. They love to race their slickly fast Italian sports cars and they go into fits of horn blowing when they stand bumper to bumper in traffic tie-ups along their narrow, curving streets. Many would gladly sacrifice their few remaining old buildings and squares for wider streets and more parking lots. Besides, they take greater pride in such twentieth century monuments as the buildings of Pirelli (tires), Locatelli (cheese), and Montecatini (chemicals and a little of everything else), than they do in the fourteenth century Duomo, the thirteenth century church of San Satiro or the twelfth century Basilica of San Ambrogio.

Milan is, after all, Italy's modern design and industrial art center, just as it was when Bramante and Da Vinci worked there in the fifteenth and sixteenth centuries. It is the home of the great architectural magazines, *Domus* and *l'architettura* and of the world-renowned designer-architect Gio Ponti, as well as of Fornasetti, a ceramic artist who has a genius for combining antique decorations with simple modern forms. And every three years this city is host to the Triannale, an international exhibition of applied arts in which almost every major country of the world participates. No wonder the *Milanesi* take their modern seriously and leave their antiquities to the tourists.

The stylish high-priced galleries along the Via Brera and the Via Manzoni sell more paintings as good investments than as good art, and boastful Milanese husbands go to La Scala performances less to hear opera than to show off their expensively dressed wives, who wear the *haute couture* fashions of Florence and Rome with little of the chic so common in the other two cities. Every Milan businessman who can afford to, sends his wife and children away for the summer to a villa he has built for them in Cortina d'Ampezzo or around the Italian lakes, and then commutes at week ends in the best traditions of his American counterpart. Not that the comparison would offend him—quite the contrary. Almost anything American is regarded as desirable here, and to say that Milan reminds you of New York is to pay it the ultimate compliment. The *Milanesi* have even created a new kind of restaurant that is fast becoming a rage and is spreading to other large Italian cities. Called the *tavola calda* (warm table), it is an overdone, jazzy, burlesque version of the American counter-luncheonette, Italian style. Perhaps an Italian Automat is just around the corner.

More than anything else, the *Milanesi* like to make money, and not too surprisingly, they hate to pay taxes. To avoid the irksome corollary, local tycoons at regular intervals pack unreported *lire* into large suitcases and drive over the border to make deposits in Swiss banks, thereby saving themselves quite a lot of money and causing quite a lot of consternation to their internal revenue bureau.

Half of the citizens of Milan claim they are the only true Italians; the other half claim they are not Italians at all. The Romans agree completely with the latter viewpoint, and consider them, *Tedeschi*—Germans—an opinion they base not only on the diligence, appearance, and lack of emotional display on the part of the Lombardians, but on past history. Time and again the northern province has been invaded, sacked, razed, ruled, and settled by Germanic tribes, beginning with Attila and the Huns, who drove the Romans out in 452 A.D., and ending when the Austrian Hapsburgs left in 1859.

Because of its position between the Po Valley and the Olona River, the Romans who took the city from the Celts in 222 B.C. named it *Mediolanum*—in the middle of the rivers—and it became the most important settlement in northern Italy, second in size (even then) only to Rome. But it rose to the peak of its power and glory in medieval and Renaissance times under its *Seignori*, leaders of bands of mercenary soldiers, who appointed themselves dukes, and established hereditary rule for their descendants. The first of these were the Torriana, and then, in 1277, the powerful Visconti, who started the building of the Duomo and made Milan Europe's leading producer of silk and armor. And it was a Visconti who, in 1396, founded the Certosina de Pavia, a Lombard Renaissance monastery

that is one of the most memorable sights to be seen a few miles outside Milan.

From 1450 to 1535, the Sforzas, along with their successor, Lodo-
vico il Moro, were the rulers of Lombardy, Piedmont, and most of
Tuscany. Their starkly grand red-brick crenelated castle-fortress,
with its defensive moat and towers, is now a museum and one of
Milan's most rewarding sights. It was these rulers who brought Milan
to the height of its Renaissance splendor, making it a center of art,
learning, and intellectual vigor. They were patrons of the architect
Bramante and of Leonardo da Vinci, who worked in Milan from
1485 to 1500 and again from 1506 to 1516. It was here that he
painted his masterpiece, "The Last Supper," the fast-fading fresco
that can still be seen in the church of Santa Maria delle Grazie,
which also has examples of Bramante's work in its choir and dome,
though it was badly hit during a World War II bombing.

In addition to Germanic invaders, Milan has lived under the rule
of Charlemagne, who ousted the Longobards, of Charles V, who
gave the province to his son Philip II, and of Napoleon from 1796
to 1814, after which the Congress of Vienna handed it back to the
Austrians. In 1805, Napoleon was crowned emperor in the city's
cathedral with the Iron Crown of Monza, the jewel-studded iron
band, said to have been hammered out of a nail of the True Cross,
which had been used for Charlemagne, Barbarossa, and Charles V.
It can be seen now in Monza, not far from Milan, a town visited
primarily because of its automobile speedway, the Autodromo, and
the Mirabello race track in its park.

Now Milan has a new wave of invaders—trainloads of laborers
from Italy's impoverished south who pour into this city every day,
looking for work in the wealthy factories of the industrial north.
They arrive as bewildered as our own Puerto Ricans in any of our
large cities, often speaking a southern dialect that no one in Milan
can understand, dressed in clothes too thin for the colder climate,
and carrying their few possessions rolled up in a bed sheet. They are
met at the station by welcoming committees of the local Communist
party who tell them how to find living quarters, how to find jobs,
how to get their relatives up from the south, and how to vote. Milan
needs these workers desperately and has built apartments on the
outskirts of the city to house them. With lines full of laundry drying
between the balconies of the buildings, and with the music of *mando-*

linos and guitars and the general uproar of life as it is lived in the south, this area looks like a miniature Naples, a sight the *Milanesi* prefer to ignore if they possibly can.

While Milan's attraction might seem pallid compared to the more richly antique cities of Italy, it is impossible to get an accurate picture of Italy today without seeing this Lombardian capital. With all of the history behind it, there are of course several fascinating genuinely "old" things to see. The most obvious is the enormous sand castle of a cathedral, the Duomo, that stands on the city's main piazza. Begun in the fourteenth century, it was finally completed in the nineteenth by order of Napoleon. It is a golden mass of spires, Gothic arches, pinnacles, 2,245 statues, and walls full of lacy stone tracery carving, and is the largest church in Italy after St. Peter's in Rome. Its stained-glass windows are magnificent, and shed a jeweled, spiritual light over the immense nave and aisles. Built in the shape of a Latin cross, the Duomo holds up to forty thousand people, and hundreds of long white candles light its many chapels. An elevator takes you to the top of the Duomo, where you can walk amongst its pinnacles with their flamboyant carvings and look across the silhouette of skyscrapers to the snow-capped Alps that rise behind them, or peer through the quatrefoil balustrades to the vast piazza below, with its pecking pigeons and scurrying people.

Besides the Duomo, the Sforza castle and its museums, and "The Last Supper," Milan's greatest treasure is the Palazzo di Brera, one of the finest art collections in Europe. It includes frescoes of the fourteenth and fifteenth centuries, outstanding examples of the Venetian and Lombard schools, works by Bellini, Mantegna, Tintoretto, Titian, Rembrandt, El Greco, Rubens, Raphael's "Marriage of the Virgin" and Della Francesca's "Sacra Conversazione."

The only remains of Milan's Roman days are the sixteen white marble columns remaining from the Baths of Mediolanum, and close by is one of the oldest churches in the city, San Lorenzo, with mosaics that date back to the fourth century. La Scala, Milan's world-famous opera house, is worth a visit even if it is the off-season for performances. The theater itself, with gold and white horseshoe balconies and red velvet trimmings, is one of the most beautiful in the world; and just next door the opera museum is full of memorabilia of all the great composers, conductors, and singers who have worked here.

One of the most rewarding museums in this city is the Poldi-

Pezzoli, a private collection of tapestries, armor, porcelain, paintings, and furniture that was left to the city by its owner in the nineteenth century. But of all Milan's sights the most impressive and charming is the Basilica of San Ambrogio, founded in 386 A.D. by the Bishop Ambrose, a descendant of an old Roman family. He composed the chants which even today are called "Ambrosian" and in his church mass was celebrated by a priest who faced the congregation, giving the name to what is now known as "the Ambrosian rite." Although none of the original building remains (the over-all appearance of the church is a result of its twelfth century restoration), parts of its two towers date back to the eighth and ninth centuries.

The Pinacoteca Ambrosiana has paintings and drawings by Da Vinci, Botticelli, Breughel, and Raphael, among others, and not far away is the medieval square, the Piazza dei Mercanti, a mercantile center for centuries, where you can see the Milan "skyscrapers" of the Middle Ages.

It would be a mistake to spend all of one's time among relics of the past, in a city that lives so very much in the present. Probably, if you had only a few hours to spend here, the best place to glimpse Milan's modern life all at once would be the Galleria Vittorio Emmanuele II, named after the king who freed Milan from Austria and made it part of Italy in 1859.

The Galleria is Milan's main forum, a great, noisy, hectic, glass-covered arcade that is a complex of bookstores, gift and clothing stores, travel agencies, banks, restaurants as elegant and French as Savini's, or as quick and clamoring as the Biffi cafeteria. Ten years ago the Galleria was crowded with black market money-changers, now extinct thanks to Italy's very stable *lira*. But it is still the place for the *Milanesi* to gather—to have a cup of *espresso* or a glass of vermouth, to meet friends, and most of all to talk business.

NAPLES

"The sun is warm, the sky is clear,
   The waves are dancing fast and bright,
   Blue isles and snowy mountains wear
   The purple noon's transparent might . . ."
                              —SHELLEY

I DOUBT that anyone has ever been lukewarm about Naples. You either love it or hate it on sight; no amount of time there ever seems to alter that first impression. If you fall into the first category, not even its tenements, dirt, pickpockets, and noise will discourage you. If you fall into the second class, not even its incomparable blue bay, its music and gaiety, its warmheartedness and humor, or its operatic street life will beguile you.

Shelley wrote odes to this "Elysian city," as did Byron and Browning. Goethe was enchanted by it and said, "One who has seen Naples can never be sad. . . . I pardon all who have lost their minds in Naples." Casanova considered it Italy's gayest city and, for him, the luckiest; Virgil chose to have his tomb on "Naples' sunny slopes;" Horace thought its bay unsurpassed by any other in the world.

"The environs of Naples form a Paradise, but the city itself is, to put it mildly, a Purgatory," advised a travel guidebook of 1898. And a 1903 Baedeker cautiously allowed for all tastes in a summation of Naples that is still applicable:

Naples is one of the noisiest cities in Europe. The clatter of wheels at all hours of the day and night, the cracking of whips and the shrill cries of hawkers, added to the ceaseless importunities of drivers, guides, street vendors, beggars, etc., are very distracting. Some travellers, especially if there be ladies in the party, will find the constant use of cabs the only sure method of escaping annoyance. But those who adapt themselves to the manners of the place will find an abundant source of interest in the life and bustle of the streets.

Whether you like Naples or not, you will certainly recognize it as the Italian archetype. Gastronomically it is the home of the pizza, the stronghold of the tomato-garlic-basil-olive oil school of cookery, and its air and water are said to make its *pasta* the finest in Italy. Naples gave the world Sophia Loren and Enrico Caruso; *O Sole Mio* and *Funiculi-Funicula,* and the *bel canto* style of singing; Pagliacio and Pulcinello, the sixteenth century marionette who was the fore-runner of Punch. It is these two characters—Pagliacio and Pulcinello —who afford us perhaps the best insight into the Neapolitan per-sonality: the first a clown who sings though his heart is breaking, the second a roguish prankster and scoundrel who is a charmer nonetheless. ". . . They began by stealing my money, in the end they stole my heart," wrote Aubrey Menen of the Neapolitans in an article for *Holiday* magazine. Troupes of sad-eyed clowns who per-form in the streets and at *festas* are still favorites in this *opera buffo* of a city, known equally well for its gaiety and its misery.

For a breathtaking view of what may well be the world's greatest scenic cliché, go to one of the belvederes that dot the slopes of the Vomero peak. There before you lies Naples, with its terraced houses burnished pink, white, and pale gold, curving in a crescent around the sapphire and turquoise waters of the Mediterranean bay, an opalescent conch shell curled beside the sea. Backed by the silvery silhouette of Vesuvius, roofed by the wide blue sky, and framed by umbrella pines, hot-orange calla lilies and glowing purple bougain-villaea, the setting will remind you of every *pizzeria* mural you've ever seen.

And if you were called upon to design a stage set for an Italian musical comedy, you could do no better than to draw on Naples for your inspiration. Its narrow streets step up behind the harbor and wind between tall apartment buildings, their walls all chipped, their paint peeling away in crumbling sheets. The fronts of these buildings are strung with clotheslines stretched between the balconies, the laundry flapping in the breeze as colorful as confetti. Barefoot street urchins in torn undershirts and short pants look around for still smokable cigarette butts, offer to be your guide, to sell you "feelthy" pictures, or simply ask for money outright. Great fat Mamas, their long black hair pulled back tightly into enormous buns, sit on stools in the doorways, braiding their daughters' hair, kneading dough, or gossiping. If you walk through these streets in the early morning and look into these open doorways you will often see four or five children piled up asleep on one bed, and at any hour the warm air, trapped in the narrow street corridors, is heavy with the smells of frying garlic, hot olive oil, the cool scent of the fresh basil that grows in big pots on every window sill, and the combined odors of poverty, dust, and humanity. Corner fruit stands are decked with garlands of oranges and lemons, sweet doughy pastries fry in open vats of sizzling oil, and everywhere there are the shouts and screams that cut through the air day and night: a husband screaming at his wife, a mother threatening her children, a child yelling to his friends, and through it all the sound of music, as much a part of Naples as the shouting. At one time it might be a lone hurdy-gurdy, another time a guitar or *mandolino,* a concertina or an accordion, as strolling musicians walk about the streets singing and playing just as they do in the crowded, lively tourist restaurants that stretch around the harbor of Santa Lucia.

With a population of 1,200,000, Naples is the capital of Campania and Italy's third largest city. If you ever see it during the Piedigrotta, the annual music festival that takes place in early September, you will think that every one of its inhabitants is in the streets. The highlight of the event which honors the city's patron, San Gennaro, is the night of music, when an outdoor competition is held to decide which of the new popular songs is the best, and which of the new Neapolitan tenors will be the favorite in the year ahead. As always, the Neapolitans set their sorrows as well as their joys to music. They sing of a Mama they miss and of the food she fed them, of the sun, the sea, and the sky of their beloved city, of unrequited love, and most of all, of farewell. *Addio bella Napoli*—"Farewell, beautiful Naples"—may be the title of a song that is a century old, but it would probably do for half the numbers that will be sung at next year's Piedigrotta. As with Dublin, Naples has been a place of good-byes, a city that has been misgoverned and exploited by foreign rulers for so many centuries that it finally was exhausted. Emigration was the only answer for its young people, as much in Naples as in the Irish capital. Most of the Italian immigrants in our own country are of Neapolitan extraction, a fact that explains why Naples looks so familiar to anyone who knows the Little Italies that flourish in our own large cities. Now for the first time in generations there is hope in Naples, for large northern industrialists are opening southern plants to take advantage of cheaper labor and cheaper real estate. After years of considering the southerners indolent, the new plant managers are surprised to find them as intelligent and as industrious as their northern *paisani*.

Many other street *festas* are held during the year in this city, all with colored lights strung across the streets in blazing, flowery arches, all with their noise, their food, their games, and their music. They illustrate another aspect of the Neapolitan's character, his love of spectacle and finery, his passion for cutting a *bella figura,* that extends even to the elaborately carved and painted horse-drawn hearses. Being theatrical, the Neapolitans wring as much drama as possible out of every phase of their simple lives. A traffic accident, bargaining for a pair of blue cotton espadrilles, a son that is hurt, an argument with a neighbor—all are opportunities for histrionics and bravado that no self-respecting Neapolitan would pass up. In addition they have an almost pagan sense of superstition. Figures of saints in the churches are covered with the flat silver medallions shaped like eyes, legs, fingers, a baby in the womb, stomachs, hearts, ears, a child, a grandmother: *ex votos* that the Neapolitans give to their saints as offerings to heal whatever part of the body is bothering them, or whoever in the family may be ill. And twice a year, in May and during Piedigrotta, they cram themselves into their Duomo, the cathedral that is an eighteenth century restoration of a thirteenth century original, to see if the dried blood of their patron saint will liquify in its glass vial. If it does, the year ahead will be good; if it does not, hard times are in the offing. Perhaps they believe in miracles because only a miracle can change the course of their lives. Present-day Neapolitans are not far removed from their seventeenth century ancestors who created the fairy tales of *Il Pentamerone,* the Italian Arabian Nights, which provided the brothers Grimm with the inspirations for Rapunzel and for Cinderella whom the Neapolitan story-tellers first called *Cenerentola.*

Naples is an old city. It dates back some two thousand years to the Greeks who founded their Neapolis, or new city, beside the town the ancients already had named Parthenope, in honor of one of the Sirens who lived on the isle of Capri, and who, it is said, was washed ashore near Naples where she was buried. In Roman times the city and its surroundings were the leading resorts of wealthy and influential Romans and it was held in turn by Goths and Lombards, Hohenstaufens and Spaniards, Angevins and Austrians, Bourbons and Bonapartes. Though the city lacks architectural distinction, it is rich in sights. Anyone who would rather see these guidebook landmarks and forsake the city's streets is welcome to his choice, but, excepting the National Museum with its treasured antiquities of Pompeii and Herculaneum, he would be making a terrible mistake.

No sight in the city—not the forbidding Castello dell' Ovo built in the twelfth century and now a police garrison, not the seventeenth century red-and-black Royal Palace or the Aquarium in the park of the Villa Nazionale, not the cathedral or the colonnaded church of San Francesco di Paolo can compare with the city itself. The Friday morning fish market beyond the Renaissance gateway, the Porta Capuana, the lunchtime activity at the harbor seafood restaurants like Zi'Teresa and La Bersagliera, the swirl of humanity along the fashionable Via Roma, Via Merghellina, and the Riviera di Chiara where the evening *passagiata* takes place, the yelling, bargaining, gesticulating crowds at any of the open markets—these are Naples' real wonders and its main delights. You may view the city from the peaks of the Pizzofalcone, from the Castle Sant' Elmo, or from the garden terraces of the Capodimonte Museum (the eighteenth century rococo building that houses a fine collection of porcelains), or hear an opera at San Carlo, where the audience is the most critical in Italy and where even the great Caruso was booed off the stage for hitting a note improperly. But whatever you do, be sure to hire a carriage drawn by a horse dressed in a hat, ribbons, bows, and bells, and ride at twilight past the modern, de luxe residential sections growing up along the slopes of the Vomero. Have dinner and see the city's lights twinkle on from the balcony of one of the restaurants that tops this peak. Or sit in the beehive of humanity that is the glass arcaded Galleria, ten times noisier, ten times more entertaining than Milan's, and notice how restless the Neapolitans are compared to the *Milanesi;* how they flit about from table to table, from one conversation to another, talking back and forth in the lilting, lyrical drawl. "All Naples is drunk with joy," said Stendhal. "As for the Neapolitan, he is half-crazed by impetuousness . . . the slave of the sensation of the moment."

The lovely cliffside seashore towns and islands around Naples have been luring visitors away from the city itself since Roman times. Horace, Hadrian, Cicero, Virgil, Caesar, Pliny, Caligula, Nero, Augustus, and Tiberius had vacation villas in this section of Campania. The wealthy families of Rome so crowded to this place that the long Appian Way approaching it was, in the season, thronged with chariots and gilded litters, and every inch of land was taken for their estates. In fact, so gorgeous were the seaside villas that Baiæ's beach was called the Golden Shore. Earthquakes, erosion, and the destructions wrought by Goths and Saracens have almost completely effaced all proof of this little town's past luxuries. Only a few fragments of marble and mosaic floors can be seen there today.

Pozzuoli, now a quiet fishing town, was the point at which St. Paul first set foot on the shores of Italy. When he landed he found there a thriving community, with a Colosseum of its own that seated thirty thousand people, second in size only to the arena in Rome. He found about him dozens of warehouses, stately ships unloading oil from Athens, corn from Egypt, grain from Sicily and African lions destined for Italian amphitheaters. Before him, on the slopes around the city, marble villas, temples, baths, and gardens rose tier on tier, just as the pale pastel houses do now. Silvery-green olive trees, terraced vineyards, and groves of flowering orange trees covered the hillsides that hung over the sea, creating the same leaf-green, glass-blue shimmer you can still see when driving through the towns that stretch between Naples and the golden, roofless Greek temples that stand on the grassy beach at Paestum.

Anyone who has ever seen them pictured on a travel poster knows exactly what to expect from such graceful and historic towns as Positano, Ravello, Amalfi, and Sorrento, and few have ever been disappointed. Floating in the Bay of Naples, like two ghostly galleons, are the resort islands of Ischia and Capri. The first, a larger, pine-covered, mountain island with hidden cove beaches is currently "in." But Capri is still the charmer if you see it off-season when the mobs of tourists have gone home. Then it has all the flowery, swashbuckling color that it had when it inspired the Nepenthe of Norman Douglas' *South Wind,* and you can easily see why it was favored by Augustus and Tiberius, and why the mythological Sirens chose it for their home.

Certainly no one who visits this enchanting section of Italy will want to miss Herculaneum and Pompeii. Both cities were partially destroyed by earthquakes in 63 A.D. and then completely buried beneath the eruptions of Vesuvius sixteen years later. Both were sealed off to become virtual time capsules, giving us an amazingly complete and fascinating glimpse of ancient Roman life. Of the two, Herculaneum is the smaller and better preserved, as it was covered by a layer of molten lava that hardened into airtight rock, while Pompeii was buried beneath a layer of porous ash. Still, it is Pompeii that is the more famous, and more often visited, and perhaps many of those who see it today will share the feelings of Mark Twain who visited the city in 1897 and reported on it as follows, in *Innocents Abroad:*

The Buried City of Pompeii

They pronounce it Pom-*pay*-e. I always had an idea that you went down into Pompeii with torches, by the way of damp, dark stairways, just as you do in silver mines, and traversed gloomy tunnels with lava overhead and something on either hand like dilapidated prisons gouged out of the solid earth, that faintly resembled houses. But you do nothing of the kind. Fully one-half of the buried city, perhaps, is completely exhumed and thrown open freely to the light of day; and there stand the long rows of solidly-built brick houses (roofless) just as they stood eighteen hundred years ago, hot with the flaming sun; and there lie their floors, clean swept, and not a bright fragment tarnished or wanting of the laboured mosaics that pictured them with the beasts, and birds, and flowers which we copy in perishable carpets today; and there are the Venuses, and Bacchuses, and Adonises, making love and getting drunk in many-hued frescoes on the walls of saloon and bed-chamber; and there are the narrow streets and narrower sidewalks, paved with flags of good hard lava, the one deeply rutted with the chariot-wheels, and the other with the passing feet of the Pompeians of by-gone centuries; and there are the bakeshops, the temples, the halls of justice, the baths, the theatres—all clean-scraped and neat, and suggesting nothing of the nature of a silver mine away down in the bowels of the earth. The broken pillars lying about, the doorless doorways and the crumpled tops of the wilderness of walls, were wonderfully suggestive of the "burnt district" in one of our cities, and if there had been any charred timbers, shattered windows, heaps of debris, and general blackness and smokiness about the place, the resemblance would have been perfect. But no—the sun shines as brightly down on old Pompeii to-day as it did when Christ was born in Bethlehem, and its streets are cleaner a hundred times than ever Pompeian saw them in her prime . . .

No—Pompeii is no longer a buried city. It is a city of hundreds and hundreds of roofless houses, and a tangled maze of streets where one could easily get lost, without a guide, and have to sleep in some ghostly palace that had known no living tenant since that awful November night of eighteen centuries ago.

FOR THE TRAVELER'S NOTEBOOK

Official Information

Before you go: Italian State Tourist Office (E.N.I.T.): 626 Fifth Ave., New York, N.Y.; 333 North Michigan Ave., Chicago, Ill.; 338 International Trade Mart, Camp St., New Orleans, La.; St. Francis Hotel, Union Square, San Francisco, Cal.

In Rome: SAS Office, 88 Via L. Bissolati; Tourist Information Office, 11 Via Parigi; U.S. Embassy, 119/A Via Veneto.

In Milan: SAS Office, 7 Via Albricci; Tourist Information Office, 4 Via Dogana or 3 Via Caserotte; U.S. Consulate, 32 Piazza Repubblica.

In Florence: SAS Office, 8 Lungarno Acciaioli; Tourist Information Office, 1 Via Tornabuoni; U.S. Consulate, 38 Lungarno Vespucci.

In Venice: SAS Office, Impremar, 4707 Campo San Provolo; Tourist Information Office, 1253 San Marco Ascensione.

In Naples: SAS Office, 1 Via Marittima; Tourist Information Office, 10/A Via Partenope; U.S. Consulate, Piazza Torreta.

Money Matters

Currency: The monetary unit is the lira (l.). There are approximately 625 lire to $1, U.S.

Tipping: Hotel bills include a service charge of 10 to 25 per cent. Tip bellboys 100 to 200 l. per bag; chambermaids 100 to 200 l. (approximately .25, U.S.) per day. Restaurants add 10 per cent, but it is customary to leave a slight additional tip, usually 50 to 100 l. per person. Taxi drivers

10 per cent of fare, slightly more for shorter trips; airport and terminal porters 60 l. for first piece, 40 for each additional piece; theater ushers 20 to 50 l.; washroom attendants 10 to 20 l.

Climate, Clothing, and Essentials

From north to south, Italy's climate varies to the same degree as that from New England to South Carolina. In Rome, Florence, Venice, Milan, and Naples, seasons parallel those of the northeastern United States. Winter clothes are needed from December to March and lightweight summer clothing from May to September. Shorts and slacks are worn by women only at resorts. Bathing resorts are always close at hand, so be sure to take a bathing suit during the summer months. Spring comes a little earlier in Naples, and you can usually swim at nearby resorts throughout October. Sleeveless or low-cut dresses are not allowed in the churches and women should also have a scarf for their heads. A raincoat will come in handy.

Hotels

The Italian State Tourist Office publishes a two-volume guide to hotels throughout Italy and will send you a copy on request. Rates tend to be higher during the summer tourist season (June to September) and every hotel has rooms at different prices, so be explicit when you make reservations. Many hotels will quote prices for full pension (all meals) or at least demi-pension (two meals), especially during the height of the tourist season and at less expensive and resort hotels. If you wish, you can generally get the rooms without meals, so be sure you and the hotel understand each other in advance. For the most part, second and third class hotels and pensions should be reserved on the recommendation of a travel agency or a friend who speaks from experience.

De luxe hotels in Italy charge from 3,000 to 4,600 l., single, with bath; 5,000 to 8,400 l., double. First class rates range from 2,000 to 3,400 l., single; 3,600 to 6,200, double. Second class, 1,500 to 2,500 l., single; 3,000 to 4,200, double. Third class, 1,200 to 1,800 l., single, 2,100 to 3,100, double. First class pensions charge from 1,800 to 2,600 l., single; 3,000 to 4,200, double. Service and tax must be added to these basic rates.

ROME

DE LUXE: *Hassler Villa Medici* is perhaps the most elegant and select, centrally located at the top of the Spanish Steps. The *Excelsior Hotel, 25 Via Veneto,* is the impressive temporary home of stage and screen stars and is popular among Americans. The *Grand Hotel, 3 Via della Terme,* is luxurious and perhaps the most distinguished in the city. The *Palazzo e*

Ambasciatori, 70 Via Vittorio Veneto, is expensive and quietly luxurious. The *Cavalieri Hilton* is Rome's newest and most spectacular hotel, complete with resort facilities. It is out of the general hubbub on the Monte Mario.

FIRST CLASS: The *Flora* is a top first class hotel, popular among the younger set and adjacent to the Borghese Gardens. The *Quirinale, 7 Via Nazionale,* was completely modernized in 1951. In the summer, meals are served in the delightful garden. The *Eden, 49 Via Ludovisi,* has been recently modernized and you will like its charming roof bar. Some other good first class hotels are the *Mediterraneo, 17 Via Cavour,* and the *Atlantico, 23 Via Cavour,* both under the same management, with large rooms, luxurious baths, and air conditioning. *Bernini-Bristol, 23 Piazza Barberini; Continentale, 5 Via Cavour; De la Ville, 69 Via Sistina;* the *Victoria, 41 Via Campania;* the *Majestic, 50 Via Vittorio Veneto;* and the *Regina Carlton, 72 Via Veneto,* are also in this class. The *Massimo d'Azeglio, 18 Via Cavour,* is a remodeled, comfortable hotel with an atmosphere suggesting northern Italy. The *Caesar Augustus, 200 Corso Francia,* is a new hotel about twenty minutes from the heart of the city, and limousine service back and forth is provided. The *Residence Palace, 69 Via Archimede,* is a new hotel in a residential district with all facilities, a roof garden, and some apartments.

SECOND CLASS: The *Parioli, 54 Viale Buozzi,* is a modern second class hotel about ten minutes by bus from the center of Rome. Two good second class hotels are the *Imperiale, 24 Via Veneto,* and the centrally located *Nord Nuova Roma, 3 Via G. Amendola.* The *Dinesen, 18 Via de Porta Pinciana,* overlooks the Borghese Gardens and is very popular with budget-minded Scandinavians. The *Inghleterra, 14 Via Bocca di Leone,* is an excellent hotel (if you get a quiet back room) frequented by journalists and located off Via Condotti. The *Tiziano, 110 Corso Vittorio Emmanuele,* a converted palace near St. Peter's, is comfortable and charming. The *Fiamma, 61 Via Gaeta,* near the Baths of Diocletian, is modern and cheerful. The *Alexandra,* situated right at the foot of the Via Veneto, is a fairly good large hotel in this class. The *Internazionale, 79 Via Sistina,* is equally well located and is one of the best buys in the city.

INEXPENSIVE: For very inexpensive accommodations, try the *YMCA, 23 Piazza Indipendenza,* which accommodates women as well as men. Among good pensions are the first class *Tea, 149 Via Sardegna;* the *Terminue, 47 Piazza della Repubblica;* the *Villa Gaia, 15-B Via A. Bosion.*

MILAN

DE LUXE: *Principe e Savoia, 17 Piazzale della Repubblica,* has been recently remodeled and is unusually comfortable. *Grande Albergo e di Milano, 29 Via Manzoni,* is one of the country's best hotels and popular with Europeans. The *Palace, 20 Pizzale della Repubblica,* is a phantasmagoria of marbled modern with all push-button conveniences. *Cavalieri, 1 Piazza Missori,* has comfortable, spacious rooms and is well located. *Continentale Grand Hotel, 7 Via Manzoni,* is close to La Scala, and many rooms offer a view of the hotel garden.

FIRST CLASS: The *Francia Europa, 19 Corso Vittorio Emmanuele,* near the cathedral, has air conditioning and comfortable rooms. *Touring e Grand Turismo, 2 Via Ugo Tarchetti,* is justly popular, located in the center of the city's activities. *Manin, 7 Via Manin;* the *Marino alla Scala, 5 Piazza della Scala;* and the *Regina e Metropole, 16 Via Santa Margherita,* are all good.

SECOND CLASS: The *Commercio, 5 Piazza Fontana,* and the *Manzoni, 20 Via Santo Spirito,* have private baths with showers available and are located right in the center of the city. The *Nord, 13 Piazza della Repubblica,* near the railroad station, is comfortable also. The *American Hotel, 2 Via Finocchiaro Aprile,* offers stall showers in all of its rooms and is a very good choice in this price range.

FLORENCE

DE LUXE: The *Excelsior Italia, 3 Piazza Ognissanti,* overlooking the Arno, is the city's top luxury hotel, with large rooms and good service. The *Grand* is on the same square and offers the same sort of luxury accommodations. The *Savoy, 7 Piazza della Repubblica,* close to the Duomo, and the *Park Palace, 5 Piazzale Galileo,* are also luxurious, as is the delightful *Villa Medici, 42 Via del Prato.*

FIRST CLASS: *Baglioni e Palace, 6 Unità Italiana,* has a popular roofgarden restaurant in summer, some rooms with balconies, and very good service. *Astoria, 9 Via del Giglio,* has a dining room noted for its Florentine food and is near the railroad station. *Roma, 8 Piazza Santa Novella,* recently renovated, is near the station; the *Anglo Americano e Regina, 9 Via Garibaldi,* and the *Lucchesi e Plaza, 38 Lungarno della Zecca,* both have some rooms with balconies, good locations, and service.

SECOND CLASS: *Berchielli, 14 Lungarno Acciaioli,* is one of the best buys, a stone's throw from the Ponte Vecchio. Service is good, the staff pleasant. Nearby is the *Continental, 2 Lungarno Acciaioli,* offering similar accommodations. The *Croce di Malta, 7 Via della Scala,* is a wonderful hotel, comfortable, and with good staff. *Helvetia e Bristol, 2 Via de' Pescioni;* the *Mediterraneo, 44 Lungarno del Tempio;* the *Della Signoria, 1 Via delle Terme;* the *Stella d'Italia e San Marco, 8 Via Calzaioli,* are all extremely good buys.

VENICE

DE LUXE: *Royal Danieli, Riva degli Schiavoni,* one of the city's most beautiful hotels, occupies an old palace and many of its rooms and its rooftop restaurant overlook the Grand Canal. There is a modern wing as well. *Gritti Palace, 2476 San Marco,* on the Grand Canal, is small and plush, with handsome rooms. *Bauer Grünwald, 1440 Camp San Moise,* also on the Grand Canal, is plush and huge, extremely well managed. *Grand Hotel, 2321 Via XXII Marzo,* is a fourteenth century palace on the Grand Canal, a national monument. The hallways are virtually museums of Venetian art and furniture. *Europa e Britannia, 2159 San Marco,* has some rooms with balconies overlooking the Canal.

FIRST CLASS: Among the most comfortable are the *Luna, 1243 San Marco,* just off the Grand Canal and next to Piazza San Marco, with a popular restaurant; the *Londres Beau Rivage, 4071 Riva degli Schiavoni,* near the *Danieli;* the new and modern *Cipriani, 10 Giudecca,* with a lovely lagoon view from its terrace restaurant; *Monaco e Gran Canale, 1325 San Marco,* well located; the *Park, 243 Fondamenta Condulmer,* close to the public gardens, the station, and the terminal, where most rooms have baths and air conditioning; and the *Gabrielli-Sandwirth, 4110 Riva degli Schiavoni,* in a handsome thirteenth century Venetian building with small but attractive rooms, many with a view.

SECOND CLASS: These hotels are acceptable; many have some private baths, and all listed have good service and authentically Italian atmosphere. The *Principe, 142 Lista di Spagna,* near the railroad station, is attractive, with canal view; the *Albergo Concordia, 367 San Marco,* is a real find; the *Hotel Diana, 449 San Marco,* and the *Montecarlo, 464 San Marco,* are also good, and in the same area. The *Metropole, 4149 Riva degli Schiavoni,* is a fine choice, very conveniently located. The *Hotel Marconi e Milano, 729 San Paolo,* and the *Rialto, 5147 San Marco,* are both in a colorful, bustling section of the city, with prices that range from second to third class level.

INEXPENSIVE: One of the best known second class pensions is *Stella Alpina, 99/D Calle Priula.* In the San Marco area the *Pensione Atlantico, 403 San Marco,* is clean and comfortable. The *Pensione Wildner, 4161 Riva degli Schiavoni,* and *Pensione Conte, 2185 Riva degli Schiavoni,* are extremely moderate and comfortable.

ON THE LIDO: If you prefer to stay at the Lido, Venice's beach resort, the top hotels are the very posh *Excelsior,* with its private beach and cabanas, and the first class *Grand Hotel des Bains.* There are also a number of second and third class hotels here.

NAPLES

It is better to save money elsewhere and get the best room you can possibly afford in Naples, as the lesser hotels here are likely to be discouraging.

DE LUXE: The *Excelsior, 48 Via Partenope,* is the city's traditional de luxe hotel, overlooking the bay and with air conditioning. *Vesuvio, 45 Via Partenope,* is a little smaller but has its own night club and pleasant rooms. *Royal, 38 Via Partenope,* is new and modern, with a breathtaking bay view from its balconied rooms and superb service.

FIRST CLASS: *Ambassadors, 70 Via Medina; Londres, 64 Piazza Municipio,* on the colorful piazza; the *Continental, 44 Via Partenope,* on the waterfront; the *Majestic, 68 Largo Vasto a Chiaia,* in a quiet residential section near the shopping area; *Parker's, 135 Corso Vittorio Emmanuele; Santa Lucia, 46 Via Partenope; Turistico, 5 Via G. Marconi;* and *Mediterraneo, Via Nuova Ponte di Tappia.* Air conditioning is available in most of them, many have bay views, all have restaurants and complete hotel facilities.

SECOND CLASS: The *Britannique, 133 Corso Vittorio Emmanuele,* has a good central location and half its rooms have baths; the *Metropole, 13 Via Partenope,* is smaller and closer to the luxury hotels.

Food and Restaurants

There are a number of fine regional specialties and wines which will be covered in connection with their home cities. Moderate and inexpensive restaurants generally have a budget-price table d'hôte menu (*prezzo fiso*) that is usually very economical. In general a *ristorante* is a more elegant restaurant with a large menu, while a *trattoria* denotes a less formal, family-style restaurant. However, the classifications have become confused through the years. An *hostaria,* originally meant to be a wine restaurant, now serves both elegant and simple fare, depending on the *hostaria* in question. A *rosticceria* is usually inexpensive, featuring grilled meats and spaghetti dishes, while a *tavola calda* is a lunch counter, sometimes with tables in the back. There are many snack bars such as the *Motta* and *Alemagna* chains, where you can pick a variety of sandwiches, pizzas, and pastry and eat them standing up, or sitting down.

Licorice-flavored *Strega* and the orange-like brandy *Aurum* are two favorite liqueurs, while *Campari* and *Carpano,* bitter vermouths, are favored as apéritifs. Products to try everywhere include the world's best fruits, clams (*vongole*), delectable in spaghetti sauce, *triglie,* a sweet, tender native fish, superb veal and baby lamb, white truffles, the fine cheese and bread, and the succulent tomatoes, peppers, and crisp salad greens. The *pasta* here will be a revelation; try it the way the Italians prefer it—*al dente,* to the teeth—meaning firm enough to chew. All the ice cream versions—*cassata, gelati, spumone,* and the sherbet-like *granite* —are cool and refreshing, and the *espresso* coffee is dark, strong, and delicious. Pastries are a bit heavy and overly rich.

ROME

Carciofi alla Giudia (artichokes Jewish style) are sautéed whole in oil and are not to be missed in late fall, winter, and early spring. In spring try the *piselli con prosciutto,* new peas with ham and butter. *Fettuccine Alfredo,* egg noodles with butter and cheese sauce, are a Roman specialty, as are the light dumplings (*gnocchi*). Two special spaghetti dishes are featured here too—*all' Matriciana,* with a sauce of cracklings, tomatoes, and onions, and *alla carbonara,* with a sauce of eggs, bacon, and grated cheese. *Cannelloni,* the rich and delectable meat-filled *crèpes* baked with cream sauce, are another noted delicacy. Spring baby lamb (*abbacchio*) and suckling pig (*porchetta*) are beautifully done here too. *Saltimbocca alla Romana* (a slice of veal rolled with *prosciutto* ham) is deservedly popular. *Spiedini alla Romana* is a mouth-watering luncheon entrée made with *mozzarella* cheese between slices of bread, deep fried and dressed with a caper-anchovy sauce. The local wines here are products of the Castelli Romani, the most famous of which are Frascati (white) and *Est! Est! Est!* of Montefiascone.

While most visitors to Rome will want to try one or two elegant places for gala dinners, it would be a mistake to miss some of the more typically Roman, very colorful little restaurants and *trattorie* around the city. Of the elegant and expensive dining places, none is more beautiful than the *Hostaria dell' Orso,* a restaurant in a fourteenth century building which was an inn frequented by Dante. *Palazzi,* in the villa once inhabited by Mussolini's mistress, a little way out of town on the Monte Mario, is another de luxe restaurant with continental food and breathtaking view. *Ulpia* has a spectacular setting amid the ruins of a Roman basilica, next to Trajan's Market; the food is very Roman and moderately expensive.

Popular with the international set is *Passetto's,* with sidewalk dining in summer and a beautiful display of hors d'oeuvres. Food here is more continental than Italian. *Capriccio* is another over-rated favorite of cosmopolitan travelers with an atmosphere similar to New York's small East Side restaurants, and the menu might easily be found there as well. *Fagiano* is a Rome classic, much appreciated for its pheasant and game dishes in the fall, and with a colorful location opening onto the Piazza Colonna. *La Fontanella* serves fine Florentine food on a pretty piazza. *Casina Valadier,* in the Borghese Gardens; *Apuleius,* in an old villa on the

Aventine Hill; and the *Belvedere della Rosa,* a pretty, touristy spot on the Appian Way, are all popular, expensive, and international in tone. The three *Alfredo's* must be mentioned separately. The one you've heard about is undoubtedly *Alfredo all'Augusteo,* where *fettuccine* was served by the first Alfredo with gold fork and spoon. There is so much ceremonious mixing that the *fettuccine* is generally cold by the time you get it. *Alfredo alla Scrofo* was originally owned by the same Alfredo and still serves the famed noodles. *Alfredo in Trastevere* is to my mind the most interesting of the three and has nothing to do with the other two; the food is more typically Roman, the setting more colorful, the prices more moderate. Also expensive but smaller is the elegant little *Ranieri,* with wonderful food. *Corsetti* is renowned for seafood; *Da Bolognese,* opening on the Piazza del Popolo, features specialties of Bologna. *Tre Scalini* is a highly touted tourist restaurant with a few overly merchandised menu items but with a fantastic view of the Bernini fountains in Piazza Navona. *Galeassi* is an old-time, justly famous Trastevere restaurant with excellent authentic Italian fare.

Da Canepa serves excellent food, moderately priced; the "library" of *Taverna la Biblioteca* has wine-bottle volumes; and *Da Meo Patacca* is another stage-set vestige of old Rome with wine-cellar atmosphere and outdoor dining. *Piperno* is justly famous for Italian Jewish food. Trastevere is the setting for *La Cisterna,* a picturesque standby with good food, strolling musicians, low prices. *La Taverna Margutta,* Via Margutta, a haunt of artists, is inexpensive and pleasant for lunch. *Trattoria ai Fori* is inexpensive and a personal favorite, close to the Forum. *Romolo a Porta Settimana* and *Trattoria Romulo e Remos* are two interesting, low-priced Trastevere restaurants. For late night snacks try *Pizzeria San Ignazio* and *Al Re degli Amici.* The most famous cafés line the Via Veneto: *Doney's* and the *Café de Paris.* The more Bohemian spots that rim the Piazza del Popolo are intriguing as is the famed *Café Greco* on Via Condotti, which was frequented by Shelley, Keats, and other literary lights.

MILAN

Risotto, savory saffron-scented rice, is a leading specialty, as are braised veal knuckle (*osso bucco*), the cornmeal (*polenta*), and wonderful mixed meats steamed in broth (*bollito misto*), *minestrone,* and *costoletta Milanese,* Milan's version of the *Wiener Schnitzel. Zuppa pavese,* a meat broth with poached egg, *cassoeula,* a stew of beans, vegetables, pork, and sausage, *ravioli* and *agnoli,* meat-filled dumplings, and *polenta e uccelli,* tiny birds and cornmeal, are other features to look for. *Panettone,* rich Christmas coffee cake, is a Milanese invention; such cheese as Mascherpone, Gorgonzola, Bel Paese and Taleggio are natives. The best local wines include red and white Valtellina, red Sassella, Grunello, Inferno, and those from Pavia, red and white Freccia and Chiaretto, Verdicchio, and Barbera.

Giannino's is the city's leading restaurant, large and fashionable, with garden atmosphere, bustling glass-enclosed kitchen, and delectable, expensive food. Still more expensive and chic is small *Barca d'Oro; Savini,* in the Galleria, is plush, continental, and frequented by the smart set—try salad of raw white truffles and chanterelles. *Biffi Scala* caters to an international and theatrical crowd. *Aldo* features superb seafood and Neapolitan fare—notice the wild chandelier. *Biffi* and *Taverna dell Giarrettiera,* in the Galleria, are good for light lunches, as is the garish but amusing *tavola calda* chain of *Gonzales. Ristorante Boeucc* has been a restaurant for seven centuries; it is popular with businessmen, as is *Crispi's,* one of Milan's best. For quick snacks visit the huge *Motta* café in front of *La Rinascente.*

FLORENCE

Two great Florentine specialties are *bistecca di manzo, ai ferri,* beefsteak grilled on a grate, and *pollo alla diavolo,* deviled chicken. *Tortino con carciofi,* the local artichoke omelette, and the fish soup, *triglie* Livornaise style, are wonderful. Bean salads are popular here and *lasagne* with meat sauce is rich and hearty. There is a local version of *minestrone* and the mixed fry here has sweetbreads, livers, artichokes, and zucchini. Rabbit in a sweet-sour sauce (*agro-dolce*) and game in fall should be tried. Since this is the heart of the Chianti region, you can find excellent examples of both the red and white wines by that name. That bottled by Ruffino seems to me consistently the best.

Buca Lapi, a little cave with travel-postered ceilings, caters to Americans, especially buyers. It features a guitar player in the evening; the food is good, if uneven. *Baldini* is another top restaurant, and *Sabatini* has been an attraction for many generations. *Doney's* operates a small popular tearoom and an elegant dinner spot next to it, and *Harry's Bar* is intimate and serves good *tortellini. Oliviero's* has an in-town restaurant the year round. In summer the view from *The Open Gate* on the Piazzale Michelangelo is fantastic, and there is dancing in the adjoining night club. There are two *trattorie* of more than passing interest: *Camillo,* across the Arno, unpretentious, with delightful food; and *Sostanza,* noisy and crowded but good and inexpensive. *Leland's* is a popular English-style tearoom. If you are in the mood for a thirty-minute drive, a really fantastic restaurant, almost unknown to tourists, is *Villa Borromeo* in San Casciano, a fifteenth century feudal villa in the hills of the Chianti district. All of the food is excellent, the game sensational, and prices are more moderate than you might expect.

VENICE

All seafood is delectable here, with giant prawns (*scampi*), served grilled in garlic butter, *granceole* (crabs), lobsters, squid, and sturgeon from the Adige River. Try also *bacala*, dried salt cod with an aromatic sauce. The local fish soup, *brodetto*, is a Friday specialty. *Fegato Veneziana*, calves liver, and *polenta e osei*, tiny birds cooked in cornmeal, are local features. The *prosciutto* of San Danieli is Italy's best. There are many rice dishes, among them *risi e bisi*, with peas, and *risotto di scampi*, with shrimp. *Torta de Mandorle* is a rich almond *torte*. Watermelons here are exceptional. Bardolino and Valpolicella are superb red wines, and the Soave from Verona is possibly the best white wine in Italy.

Beyond doubt one of the best and most romantic restaurants in the city is *La Taverna Fenice*, with open-air garden in summer and perfect food. *La Colomba* features fish dishes. *Harry's Bar*, a bit of Madison Avenue transported, is smoky and crowded. The same management runs the charming and good *Locanda Cipriani*, a rustic outdoor restaurant on Torcello, and will arrange transportation. *Quadri* is popular, chic, and continental. *Peoceto Risorto* is also good, set in a small seventeenth century house. The restaurant in Venice most interesting to the gourmet is *Al Graspo de Ua*, with an incredible *antipasto* and exquisitely prepared seafood.

NAPLES

Pizza is the most famous specialty, made in an eight-inch version and eaten with knife and fork; *calzone*, a fried, stuffed turnover, is another version. Naples specializes in dishes made with *mozzarella* (the cheese used in pizza), such as the open fried sandwich, *mozzarella in carozza*. The seafood and fish are sensational here whether you have them in Italian bouillabaisse (*zuppa de pesce*) or on spaghetti. *Braciole* is a rolled slice of beef simmered in tomato sauce. Among the special macaroni dishes is *maccheroni ai quattro formaggi*, with a sauce of four cheeses. The favorite macaroni here are the short, wide *rigatoni* and *ziti*, and stuffed baked wide noodles, *lasagna*. *Peperoni ripieni*, peppers stuffed with olives, croutons, and capers, are a delightful appetizer. This is the place to sample grilled fish such as *triglie*, sea bass, or Neapolitan *fritto misto*, mixed fish fry. The wines of Campania include the whites and reds of Capri, Ischia, and Ravello, the sparkling *Lacrima Cristi* (tears of Christ), Falerno, and the red Gragnano and Aglianico.

All of the major hotels have dining rooms, but tourists and Neapolitans seem to enjoy most the four that rim the little harbor of Santa Lucia. Of these the two most popular are *Zi' Teresa* and *La Bersagliera*, the second slightly more expensive, both similar and good. *Transatlantico* and *Da*

Ciro face these on the other side of the harbor, smaller, less crowded, less amusing. Two restaurants on top of the mountain, the Vomero, about twenty-five minutes by cab, with view of the bay and Vesuvius, are *Le Arcate* and *D'Angelo*. *Le Arcate* is a bit more fashionable and has dancing, while *D'Angelo* features macaroni *ai quattro formaggi,* appetizer pizzas, and a wonderful baked sole entrée, *sole oltremare. Ciro a Margellina* (also called *O Nase è Cane*) is a very simple typical Neapolitan restaurant with great seafood moderately priced, while *Dante e Beatrice* is a small *trattoria* where *pizza rustica,* a cold appetizer pie of meat and cheese, is a great specialty. *Ristorante Pizzeria Port' Alba* is said to be the oldest pizza house in Naples. Its pies are superb and inexpensive.

Entertainment, Night Life, and Special Events

There are dozens of special events in various parts of the country. The Italian State Tourist Offices will send you the complete and staggering list.

ROME

When in Rome do as the Romans do—go to the opera. The season begins in mid-December at the Teatro dell' Opera and ends in May. From the end of June through August you may see open-air opera performances in the Baths of Caracalla, an ancient ruin. The concert season starts in November and continues through May. Particularly noteworthy are the symphonic concerts with the orchestra and choir of the Academy of St. Cecilia. During summer, concerts are held in the ruins of the Basilica of Maxentius, part of the Forum. Rome boasts excellent theaters, presenting the best of classical and modern drama, or if you understand Italian you may find one of the numerous variety shows to your liking. These and revues are given in summer at the Casina delle Rose in the lovely Borghese Park.

One of the best of Rome's many night clubs is the sophisticated, chic, and dressy *La Cabala.* During winter, the *Palazzi* and the *Belvedere della Rose,* a little way out of the city center, are popular for dancing. The *Open Gate Club* is for members of Rome's high society though visitors from abroad can get temporary memberships. *Bricktop's,* run by the Parisian celebrity of the twenties, is an interesting *cave* and celebrity hangout with piano music and singer. The *Jicky Club* and the *Kit Kat* have dancing and hostesses, and at *Ulpia* you may dance amid ancient ruins. *El Rancho Grande* is a Latin-style night club, and the *Villa dei Cesari* on the Appian Way will take you back to ancient Rome, except for prices which are very much up to date. Don't forget the simple joy of watching *la dolce vita* glide by you as you sit in a café along the Via Veneto. It is Rome's number one nighttime attraction.

The biggest celebration is *Holy Week*, when the pope imparts his blessing, *Urbi et Orbi* (to the city and the world), from his balcony overlooking St. Peter's Square. There is an international horse show in April or May in the Borghese Gardens. During the last two weeks of July there is a carnival celebration in Trastevere, the *Festa di Noi-altri*, in honor of the Madonna del Carmine.

MILAN

There is probably no need to remind you of La Scala, Italy's most famous opera house. You'll certainly want to attend some of the operas, ballets, or concerts. The Piccola Scala is a new little theater for concerts and operas. Drama and revue theaters include the Teatro Lirico and Teatro Nuovo; the Manzoni and Sant' Erasmo for modern plays. Comedies are given at the Piccolo Teatro.

The leading night clubs are the *Astoria,* with dancing and fairly good food; the *Caprice,* with an entertaining floor show; the *Porta d'Oro;* the *Piccolo Bar,* popular, smoky, expensive; and the *Rendezvous,* in a pretty garden with outdoor dancing and dining. *Le Roi* is fashionable and has good floor shows. *Le Maschere* is a small music hall with strip teasers, and the *Embassy, Maxim's,* and the *Sans Souci* are noted for their shows and smart clientele.

The biggest special event is the *International Samples Fair* in April. The *International Triennale of Art and Design* is held every third June.

FLORENCE

Concerts are held at the Sala Bianca and the Conservatorio di Musica, and opera and ballet are plentiful during the season (January to March). The month of May is a time of music festivals and handicraft exhibitions, with concerts and operas given in several places, the loveliest of which is the Boboli Gardens. There is dancing at the *Jolly Club* and the *River Club* the year round. In summer one of the pleasantest places is the night club of the *Open Gate* restaurant on the Piazzale Michelangelo, overlooking the city. The famous medieval tournament and horse race, the *Palio,* is held in nearby Siena in early July and mid-August.

VENICE

It is hard to imagine anyone wanting to do more than sit in the glorious Piazza San Marco in the evening and listen to the concerts given there, but if you prefer to do other things, you can. You could take a moonlight cruise in a gondola or dance at the very chic little *Martini's,* next door to the Fenice Theater. The music is good and the dance floor roofless, lovely on a starry night. There is dancing on the *Danieli* roof and at the open-air *Parco delle Rose* or the *Blue Moon* on the Lido. Here, too, you will find the lively gambling casino, with floor show and dancing. Operas and some classical dramas are presented at the Fenice Theater from December to March and occasionally at other times of year. The *International Biennale,* an exhibition of modern painting and sculpture, is held every other summer. In late August or early September the *International Movie Festival* takes place. On the third Sunday in July there is a wonderful gondola festival and spectacle, and in September a canal regatta.

NAPLES

During the summer, open-air concerts are given at the Mostra d'Oltremare and operas presented on the grounds of the former palace, La Floridiana. From November to April, classic opera is presented at San Carlo, the Neapolitan answer to Milan's La Scala. The September *Piedigrotta* celebration in honor of the city's patron saint, San Gennaro, is a gala street festival and musical competition, one of Italy's most spectacular events.

Shopping

Anyone who wonders what to buy in Italy, will find the answer a simple one—everything. The superb craftsmanship and design genius of the Italians is obvious in every kind of merchandise, and the problem is more a matter of what *not* to buy. Magnificent art books, prints and paintings, handsome clothing for men and women, custom- or ready-made; fine leather goods such as handbags, luggage, shoes, and gloves; beautiful accessories such as scarves, cut velvet handbags, lingerie, shirts, ties, and lush felt Borsalino hats are to be had everywhere, as are the beautiful Italian fabrics like Como silk and the frosty Venetian lace. Jewelry ranges from the cameos and mosaic pieces of Naples to the exquisite brushed-gold modern pieces made in Milan and Rome, as well as the ornate and antique-looking Florentine silver. Wonderful things for your home can be had as well, including the fine porcelain made by Ginori and Fornasetti, Gambone or Morelli; the colorful swirled glass made by Venini in Murano; heavy and elegant sterling silver holloware; and expert reproductions of antique furniture. Italy is full of genuine antiques of every kind imaginable, and anything from a pill box to a dining table is available in inlaid colored marble, the technique of *pietra intarsia,* a Florentine art from the time of the Renaissance. If you plan to travel around the country, it is best to buy the products where they are made. Bargaining is widespread in all but the most exclusive shops, but it is less prevalent in Milan than in the other cities.

ROME

Here you will find a sampling of products made in all of the provinces of Italy. The main shopping streets are the Via Condotti with the best jewelers, fashion boutiques, and shops selling ceramics, and there is more of the same around the Piazza di Spagna. Via del Tritone, Via Barberini, Via Francesco Crispi, Via Due Macelli, and Via del Corso are the other big shopping thoroughfares. The Via del Babuino, leading off the Piazza di Spagna, is lined with enticing antique shops, modern art galleries, and bookshops, one of the best of which is the *Lion Bookshop*. *La Rinascente, CIM,* and *UPIM* are the large department stores, though their interest for tourists will be somewhat limited. For ceramics try *Ginori* and *Ars Labor Amor,* and for glass, *Venini*. For gloves, *Manco, Barra,* and *Perroni* among others. *Antinori, Gucci,* and *Siro's* sell excellent leather goods. There is a world of *haute couture* for men as well as women. *Brioni, Battistoni, Enrico, Gucci, Cifonelli, Arbiter, Byron, Fabrizi,* and *Radiconcini* all cater to men, some with custom tailorings, others with boutique accessories and hats. In women's fashions the great names are too well known to need listing here. *Laura Aponte* is famous for fashionable sweaters, *Emilio* for sportswear, *Fantasia* for good ready-made clothes, *Mingolini Guggenheim* for original dresses and accessories, *Galassi* for fine blouses, *Bellini, Rossati,* and *Cesari* for linens and laces. There are fine sportswear shops for women along the Via del Corso, and one of the most tempting fashion and gift shops in the city is *Myricae*. *Ferragamo's* large branch has high-fashion shoes and handbags.

MILAN

The main shopping streets are Via Manzoni, Via Montenapoleone, Corso Vittorio Emmanuele, Piazza Duomo, Corso Matteotti, Piazza San Babila, and Corso Buenos Aires. The main and best branch of the department store *La Rinascente* is in Milan. *Pozzi Società Ceramica Italiana* and *Ginori* have a good selection of ceramics and porcelains; for fabrics try *Marco Tessuti* and *Galtrucco*. *Calderoni, Faraone, Grassi* and the *Società Veneziana Arte Orafa* are fine jewelry shops, and for a variety of leather goods there are *Albanese, Gucci, Valextra,* and *Pirovano,* to name only a few. *Broggi* is noted for silver tableware. You'll find the famous Galleria lined with excellent shops selling all kinds of gifts and souvenirs, including toys and fine art books.

FLORENCE

This is the leading shopping city in Italy and the place to find fine leather and silver work, wonderful jewelry and articles made of straw, and dozens of other beautiful things. The main shopping district is the series of connected streets along the Arno, designated as "Lungarno"—Via Calimala, Via Calzaiuoli, Via Vigna Nova, Por Santa Maria, the Ponte Vecchio, Via Guicciardini, and Via Tornabuoni. One of the most colorful shopping places is the outdoor Straw Market, the *Porcellino,* where you can find everything from raffia billfolds to embroidered evening skirts, and where you are really expected to bargain. For fancier straw articles, visit the shops of *Emilio Paoli* and *Giovannozzi Nozzoli. Bellini* and *Ricami di Firenze* have silk lingerie and blouses, *Ferragamo* and *Rinaldi* feature high-fashion shoes for women, while *Manco, David, Gucci,* and *Silvio Luti* are only a few of the shops selling impeccable leather work. The Ponte Vecchio is lined with jewelry shops; bargain here. *Dinolevi* sells beautiful antique furniture and reproductions, and garden sculpture. There's a wonderful shop next to the Berchielli Hotel with a fine selection of inlaid marble.

VENICE

The main shopping areas are along and around the Piazza San Marco, Ponte Rialto, Calle Frezzeria, and Calle Accademia. Cut velvet and leather handbags made by *Roberta Camerino (Roberta of Venice),* objects made of glass (both new and antique), and Venetian laces are the best buys. Glass tableware, chandeliers, etc., are featured at *Venini, Angelo Nason,* and *Pauly.* Several glassmakers have shops on the island of Murano, where you may go to see glass being blown. For lace, see *Broccho, Jesurum, Maria Mazzaron,* and *Olga Asta,* all with pieces for wedding veils, handkerchiefs, and tablecloths. You will find fine leather at *Luigi Vogini,* amusing felt toys at *Navarra,* art prints everywhere.

NAPLES

If you are going to Capri or Ischia, you will find the sportswear for men and women irresistible. Take very little with you, as the beautiful shirts and slacks (especially on Capri) cost a third of what they would in the United States. They can be made up quickly, and there is also a wide selection of things ready made. Though Naples has far less to offer in shopping than other Italian cities, there is a branch of *Ginori* and of *La Rinascente. Donadio* sells the coral jewelry, cameos, and tortoiseshell articles that are a Neapolitan specialty. *Bernasconi* is a gift shop with a fairly good selection. Via Roma is the main shopping street.

Background Reading

No country is more aware of its own attractions than Italy, and the government tourist offices publish some of the very best guide material available.

Summer in Italy, and *Autumn in Italy*, by Sean O'Faolain
Italian Bouquet, by Samuel Chamberlain (food, hotel, sightseeing guide)
An American in Italy, by Herbert Kubly
Italian Holiday, by Ludwig Bemelmans
Pageant of Italy, by James Reynolds
Beyond the Alps, by Robert M. Coates (Italy's hill towns)
Italy, edited by Doré Ogrizek

ROME

Rome to Ourselves, by Aubrey Menen
A Time in Rome, by Elizabeth Bowen
A Roman Journal, by Stendhal
Hadrian's Memoirs, by Marguerite Yourcenar

MILAN

The House in Milan, by Giovanni Testori
The Constant Image, by Marcia Davenport (A love story, set in modern Milan.)

FLORENCE

The Stones of Florence, by Mary McCarthy
The Merchant of Prato, by Iris Origo (Renaissance life)
Naked Streets, by Vasco Pratolini

VENICE

The Treasures of Venice, by Muraro and Grabar
Venice Observed, by Mary McCarthy
The Desire and Pursuit of the Whole, by Baron Corvo

NAPLES

San Felice, by Vincent Sheehan
The Gallery, by John Horne Burns
The Last Days of Pompeii, by Edward Bulwer-Lytton
The Mortal Wound, by Raffaele La Capria

Norman Douglas, one of the greatest literary boosters Italy has ever had, wrote a number of entertaining and informative books on various sections of the country: *South Wind*, a wild fictional story set on an island just like Capri; *Siren Land, Old Calabria*, and *Twilight in Italy*.

For a true picture of modern Italy, one could do no better than to read the stories and novels of the country's own writers such as Soldati, Guareschi, Moravia, Pavese, Silone, Vittorini, and De Lampedusa, to name only a few.

Portugal

LISBON

Europe's window on the Atlantic

FROM the air, Lisbon looks like a confectioner's window, a wedding-cake city of sugar-frosted spires and towers done up in rose-red and green, mauve and white, a miniature candy-coated town set between green hills and the bright blue Atlantic, casting a water-color reflection into the Tagus River. It is a gentle, sunny city with a Gulf Stream climate, soft and balmy as Southern California's. And though it is in every sense a modern forward-looking city, its profusion of flowers, its cool wooded belevedere lookouts, its fanciful buildings, sidewalk cafés, and colorful fiestas and *romerias,* make Lisbon as romantic and mellow as the wines of Oporto and Madeira, a city of 900,000, or one-tenth of Portugal's total population. It is also Europe's final jumping off point for the New World, a fact that made it a place of intrigue and an escape hatch during two world wars.

Built on seven hills, Lisbon lives on two levels, a steep and hilly arrangement that would discourage walkers, were it not for the street elevators that lift one from the New World to the old. The modern section, the Baixa or lower town, is a dock-market area, and the older quarter, the Bairro Alto, is the higher section, spared by the earthquake of 1775. Most of the lower town was destroyed at that time and was later rebuilt under the exacting direction of the Marquis of Pombal who created an orderly, symmetrical area of tree-lined boulevards, public buildings, and formal squares.

The most picturesque section of the city, Alfama, winds between the upper and lower towns. Here narrow cobblestoned streets twist under Moorish arches and between walls that gleam with bright Azulejo tiling. Laundry dries on clotheslines stretched between flowered balconies, there is the twittering of caged songbirds; and at night gaslights flicker from wrought-iron street lanterns.

Lisbon's over-all stamp comes from its architectural style—a Moorish-Gothic blend called Manueline, after King Manuel I, who ushered in Portugal's golden age in the thirteenth century. It is a combination of medieval towers and Gothic arches, relieved by Moorish carvings and ornamentation, with purely Portuguese accents in the nautical motifs, so that arabesques adorning a Gothic wall are done in a series of intertwined ropes, anchors, waves, and sea-weed, a fitting touch for people who inherited the Phoenician pre-dilection for the sea. The most outstanding example of this style is the Tower of Belem, the city's trademark fortress, built by Prince Henry the Navigator in 1514, to commemorate Vasco da Gama's voyage to India. The fortress is trimmed with swirls of carved white stone, frothy as whipped cream, with delicate fluted domes and sugary statues, spires and pierced quatrefoil balconies. Jeronimo's monastery nearby, where da Gama is buried, is another fine example of this style, with a delicate cloister courtyard rimmed by a double tiered Gothic arched colonnade. Below this, at the harbor's edge, is the modern, stylized monument marking the spot from which da Gama set sail.

The Castle of St. George crowns the Alfama district and stands on the site of former Roman, Gothic, and Arabic fortresses, rem-nants of which can be seen within the palace walls. With its ten forbidding towers and beautiful inner gardens where white peacocks strut around the floral beds, the castle which was the home of Portuguese kings, provides a colorful view over the city and its river, and from here one can easily walk to the Lisbon Cathedral, dating from the twelfth century, and including Gothic, Moorish, and Renais-sance design elements.

Much of the city's present-day life revolves around the old Bairro Alto and its main square, the Rossio, the city center since the time of the Phoenicians and now a place of cafés and shops, night clubs and movie theaters. Here a central fountain is banded with a circle of serpentine patterned pavement, such as one finds on the beachside avenues of Rio de Janeiro. It is this wavy pattern that gives the Rossio its nickname, Rolling Motion Square. In the dark little restaurants off this square, one can hear the traditional *fados* sung, soulful laments on the sadness of life, touched by a nostalgia for lost glories —minor-key Arab-inspired melodies which suggest the strong strain of sadness beneath the more obvious fiesta-loving gayety of the Portuguese.

It is in this section that one can visit the Carmo Church and its Archeològical Museum, a treasury of fourteenth century architecture, and the Church of St. Roque, where the chapel dedicated to John the Baptist shimmers with inlays of pure silver and sea-blue lapislazuli. The Coach Museum displays a glittering array of royal carriages, some of which are the miniatures used by the little princes and princesses, and in the Museum of Ancient Art, you may see a handsome collection of paintings by Portuguese old masters, many of which were taken from Lisbon churches. The Museum of Folk Art has an enchanting and colorful assortment of pottery, laces, embroideries, textiles, carvings, and other native crafts, and the recurrent floral themes emphasize the Portuguese passion for flowers.

This love of flowers is further evidenced in the capital—virtually a bouquet of garden parks. The most spectacular is the Edward VII with its Estufa Fria, a lush greenhouse bursting with tropical flowers and trees, all very close to one of Europe's most luxuriously modern hotels, the Ritz. The gay market of Riberia Nova with its fishermen dressed in Scots-like tartans, and the fashionable Avenida da Liberdade, the local Fifth Avenue, are two more of the contrasting delights to be sampled in Lisbon.

The blend of old and new throughout the city is obvious too in its riverfront quarter, the Praça do Comercio, or the Black Horses Square. Redesigned after the earthquake, it is still ringed by medieval arcaded buildings and dotted with delicately carved statues and relics; one of Europe's most imposing squares, and a good starting point for walking tours.

All of its antique sights remind one that this city is the capital of what was one of the world's great empires, and it was from this port that such explorers as da Gama and Dias, the Corte Real brothers,

Cabral and Labrador set sail. By the first quarter of the sixteenth century, all of the Indian Ocean and the China Sea, the African coasts and the South American "Rivers of Silver" were chartered waters to the Portuguese.

In appearance and disposition, the Portuguese reflect the many racial strains from which they are descended: the Lusitanians and Phoenicians, Carthaginians and Visigoths, Moors and Spaniards. They are dark-eyed and olive-skinned intrepid lovers of the sea, and their nautical proficiency is obvious even in such long-established Portuguese settlements as Cape Cod's Provincetown. Though the language they speak is essentially Latin in root, it has an abundant sprinkling of very un-Latin "j's," "z's," and the almost unpronounceable vowel combination "oão," strong linguistic influences from the Galicians who lived in the northwest corner of Spain.

Strips of golden beaches and seaside castles reach north and south of Lisbon in an irresistible stretch known as the *Costa do Sol,* the sunny coast. The country seems half-museum, half-resort, with its ocean front array of Roman arches and gold-leafed Arab domes, Gothic spires and baroque cathedrals, Romanesque cloisters, and Manuelino turrets. There is Estoril, a riviera resort, full of hotels and flowery villas, beachside cabañas and royal pretenders—the ex-crown heads of Europe who live here in idyllic exile. Close by is the touristy, but still pretty, sailing and fishing harbor, Cascais, with its gay and noisy *lota,* the morning fish auction, its Moorish streets and native markets, and Praia do Guicho, a white sanded beach town backed by forests of pines and acacia. Sintra, Byron's "glorious Eden," is a fantasy town of Moorish and Manueline architecture, sprouting swirled belfries and towers that look like clowns' hats, midst a garden of magnolias and camelias, mimosa and cork trees. Some of the best samples of both architectural periods can be seen in the medieval Palacio do Sintra, while the Pena Palace, over-looking the town, is a nineteenth century nightmare built for a German prince—a wildly romantic jumble of battlements, turrets, and towers that is a mismatched collection of pseudo-Moorish, pseudo-Gothic, and pseudo-Victorian—a Disneyland of Portuguese architecture that affords one of Europe's most breathtaking panoramic views. As though the palace itself weren't mad enough, the ride to it via a winding cliffside mountain road, where big tourist buses and tiny European autos squeeze past each other on hairpin turns, rivals a Coney Island roller coaster for thrills, if that prospect interests you.

Close to Lisbon, too, are the fishing villages of Sesimbra and Setubal, the center of the country's sardine industry, where fishing boats have prows that curve like the long boats of the Phoenicians, and the assortment of ruins includes the Roman, the Romanesque, and the Renaissance. There is the quiet holy village of Fatima, with its shrine second only to Lourdes as a place of Catholic pilgrimage, and nearby, Batalha, with a flamboyantly medieval fourteenth century monastery, founded by King John I and his English queen, Philippa, the parents of Portugal's navigator prince, Henry.

FOR THE TRAVELER'S NOTEBOOK

Official Information

Before you go: Portuguese Government Tourist Information Bureau, 447 Madison Ave., New York 17, N.Y.

Lisbon: SAS Office, 236-A Avenida da Liberdade; Tourist Information Office, Palácio Foz, Praça dos Restauradores; U.S. Embassy, 39 Avenida Duque de Loulé.

Money Matters

Currency: The monetary unit is the escudo ($), divided into 100 centavos. 28.93 escudos equals $1, U.S. The $ sign is properly placed as in 28$93.

Tipping: Hotels and restaurants add a service charge of 10 to 15 per cent. Small additional tips can be given for exceptional service. Porters get about 3 escudos per bag, chambermaids 10 to 20 escudos per week, cab drivers 12 to 15 per cent of the fare; cloakroom attendants, ushers, barbers get 2 escudos, hairdressers 5 to 10 escudos.

Climate, Clothing, and Essentials

The Portuguese climate is moderate and very pleasant. In winter (December to March) the temperature seldom falls below 45 degrees F. and in summer (June to September) the average is about 70 degrees F. Spring and autumn evenings tend to be chilly; in these periods, and during the winter months, it is wise to have woolen things. A raincoat and an umbrella are indispensable during the winter months. One dresses conservatively in Portugal, although it is correct to wear sports clothes (not slacks!).

Hotels

Hotel accommodations and rates are established by the government, and a list of Portuguese hotels is available from the Tourist Information Office in Lisbon. Reservations are necessary throughout most of the year and often well in advance. Be sure to establish whether you are getting full room and board, room and breakfast, or room only, when you make your reservation.

De luxe hotels charge from 300 to 750 escudos, single; 500 to 830 escudos, double. First class hotels charge from 100 to 185 escudos, single; 175 to 340 escudos, double. Second class hotel rates range from 90 to 140 escudos, single; 125 to 210 escudos, double. Pension rates are 45 to 100 escudos, single; 80 to 150 escudos, double.

LISBON

DE LUXE: *Hotel Ritz, Rua Rodrigo da Fonseca,* is a large modern hotel with complete facilities, including balconies and air conditioning. *Hotel Embaixador, Avenida Duque de Loulé,* is comfortable and conveniently located.

FIRST CLASS: Well-located and comfortable hotels include the *Avenida Palace, 123 Rua 1º de Dezembro;* the recently remodeled *Hotel Tivoli, 179 Avenida da Liberdade;* and the *Hotel Eduardo VII, 3–5 Avenida Fontes Pereira de Melo,* which is first class but a little less expensive than the others. Other good choices would be, *Hotel Fenix, Praça Marques de Pombal; Hotel Mundial, 4, Rue Dom Duarte; Hotel Florida, Rue Duque de Palmela;* and the *Hotel Imperio, Rue Rodrigues Sampaio.*

MODERATE: Inexpensive but comfortable hotels include the *Hotel Atenas, 98 Rua Luciano Cordeiro,* and the *Hotel do Reno, 195–197 Avenida Duque d'Avila.* If you intend to stay for a week or longer, it is a good idea to choose a hotel-pension such as the *Avenida Parque, 6 Avenida Sidonio Pais,* or the *Residencia Inglesa, 32 Rua das Janelas Verdes.* For a single room with private bath the full pension rate is about 95 escudos.

ESTORIL

DE LUXE: The favorite seaside resort of Portugal, about 15 miles from Lisbon, where the de luxe hotel *Estoril-Palácio* and the new *Hotel Cibra* are wonderful places to stay. Expect to pay 160 to 280 escudos for a single room with private bath.

MODERATE: At more modest hotels, such as the *Atlantico* and the *Monte Estoril Hotel,* and the *Grand Hotel* corresponding charges are 90 to 100 escudos.

Food and Restaurants

Eating out in Lisbon is a great pleasure. Choose from refined French cuisine, the abundant Spanish kitchen, or from a wealth of special Portuguese dishes; and remember that seafood is especially fine here. *Bacalhau* (dried cod) is served with rice and pepper, or with eggs, potatoes, onions, and garlic—ask for *Bacalhau à Braz.* If you happen to be in Lisbon on a Wednesday, visit *Porto de Abrigo.* On that day they serve their specialty, *Bacalhau à Porto de Abrigo.* Portuguese lobster is excellent. A very nice version is *Langosta suada à moda de Peniche* (cooked with olives and served in a wine sauce). You will also like shrimp soup, or delicious *Caldeirada à pescador,* the Portuguese version of bouillabaisse, a thick, spicy, fish soup, and a meal in itself. Naturally, Portuguese sardines, exported all over the world, are popular in their homeland, served most often as an hors d'oeuvre.

There are not many places where you'll get finer beef than in Portugal. Try the *Bife na frigideira,* a delicious steak served on an earthenware plate. *Iscas com elas* is liver, cut in thin slices, served with French-fried potatoes. Although the world-famous port wine and Madeira are among Portugal's most renowned exports, there are many other fine table wines here. The best come from Estremadura, Ribatejo and Bairrada—fine red and white wines, still as well as sparkling. Port comes from the Douro valley; to sample the very best, visit the old wine cellars at the *Solar do Velho Porto* in Lisbon.

Continental food and some Portuguese dishes are served in the dining rooms of the leading hotels, and the same combination appears on the menu of *Tavares,* perhaps the best known and most elegant of Lisbon's restaurants. The *Aquário* is a large restaurant with piano music, dancing, and excellent seafood dishes; *Ramalhete* is a small, attractive restaurant in a remodeled private house with an open-air terrace and lovely view. The *Negresco* features dancing and continental fare and is expensive. The *Gondola* is noted for its Italian cooking; *Macau* for Chinese fare; the *Sol-Mar* has an interesting marine décor and good seafood; and the *Cortador* (Butcher Shop) has some of the best beef in the city, which you select from the glass-fronted refrigerator. *A Quinta* is inexpensive and rife with local color aimed at tourists, and *Pique-Nique* and *Mariscós* offer light lunches and snacks inexpensively. Excellent pastry is served at tearooms such as *Caravela, Ferrari,* and the *Imperio.*

For really native color and much of the lamenting *fado* music, visit the charming little *A Tipóia, Adega Machado, Folklore, Parreirinha de Alfama, A Toaca, A Severa, O Faia,* and *Mesquita.* These are the most interesting restaurants in the city if you want your food and entertainment authentically local rather than "internation." All are located in the old city, Bairro Alto.

A Barraca Muchaxo in nearby Praia do Guincho is a lovely beach-side seafood restaurant you ought to try for luncheon. In Sintra, don't miss the *Hotel Palácio de Seteais* which is a converted eighteenth century palace now a hotel and restaurant.

Night Life, Entertainment, and Special Events

Listening to the soulful and beautiful *fado* singing during dinner or drinks is one of Lisbon's pleasantest nighttime activities and can be done at all of the *fado* restaurants listed above. Hotels have dancing, as do the restaurant-cabarets such as the *Negresco* and the *Tágide*—a combination music hall and night club. The *Monte Claros* is a night club with a lovely mountainside location, while the *Hotel Embaixador* has rooftop dancing.

Lisbon has many picturesque bars, among them the *Carioca*, the *Rex Lord*, and the *Iberia*, noted for the high quality of its port. Other evening entertainment includes the permanent circus, *Coliseu dos Recreios*; and many movie theaters show international films. Performances of opera and ballet are given in the National Theater during the winter and spring seasons.

In Estoril, a short distance from Lisbon, the *Wonder Bar* is full of atmosphere and it is pleasant to stop for a drink. The night life at the *Casino Estoril* is both chic and gay. At Monte Estoril try the *Chaupana* or the *Rondo*. At Cascais, another nearby town, be sure not to miss the *Palm Beach* and *Canoa*.

A month-long music festival begins in May; an International Trade Fair runs for two weeks in June; and special carnivals and bullfights are held from June to September. There is always some kind of carnival, fair or fiesta (*Romeria*) going on in some town or city, so check when you know the dates of your visit.

Bullfighting is Portugal's leading sports attraction and the season begins at Easter and continues through September. Unlike the fights in Spain, bulls are not killed in the Portuguese version of the sport. Lisbon's leading arena is the Praça de Touros, and there are other rings at Alges, five miles from the city, and Vila Franca, nineteen miles from Lisbon. Remember that it is best to ask for seats on the shady side of the arena.

Shopping

The Portuguese do amazing things with cork and the objects they make are among the best buys in the country. Gold and silver jewelry are outstanding, and so are ceramics in traditionally colorful patterns. Port wine can be had at bargain prices, and cotton and lace textiles, woolen rugs and blankets, and embroidery are other things worth considering here. The Rua Garrett (the Chiado), the Rua do Ouro, Rua August, and Rua da Prata are the main shopping streets. All kinds of cork products are available at *Casa das Corticas*. If you are interested in handicrafts from the Azores and Madeira, you will find good selections at *Casa Regional* and *Regional Madeira*. *Fabrica de Loucas* and *De Sacavem* are the largest pottery manufacturers, and you will also find attractive glazed tiles at *Fabrica Sant'Anna* and *Viuva Lamego;* fine porcelain can be seen at *Fabrica de Porcelena da Vista Alegre*. *Caniche* and *Fantasia* have lovely gifts, while *Casa da Ilha Verde, The Madeira House,* and *Madeira Superbia* have fine linens, blouses, and embroidered organdies. For silver filigree, try *Joalharia Correia, Joalharia Mergulhao,* and *Sarmento,* while attractive jewelry and silver can also be found at *Leitão* and *Irmao, Ourivesaria Pimenta,* and *Claudine Oliveira,* who specializes in unusual modern silver jewelry. *Casa Simoes, J. Nunes da Silva,* and *Solar do Velho Porto* are all reliable wine shops, and *Blandy Brothers* is the best source of Madeira. *Casa Africana, Grandela,* and *Armazens do Chiado* are the leading department stores.

For a complete shopping guide, get a copy of the SAS booklet, "Shopping Your Way Through Southern Europe."

Background Reading

Portugal, by Roy Campbell
Portugal and Madeira, by Sacheverell Sitwell
Pleasure by the Busload, by Emily Kimbrough
Blue Moon in Portugal, by William and Elizabeth Younger
The Caravels of Christ, by Gilbert Renault
Cousin Bazilio, by José Maria Eça de Queiroz

Spain

MADRID

Under blue Velazquez skies

To understand Madrid, one must comprehend, at least in part, the land of startling contrasts and dramatic extremes that is Spain. With its 31 million people scattered over 194,000 square miles, this is the least densely populated country in Europe, one of the driest, and, after Switzerland, the most mountainous. The greatest portion of the land is its central plateau, a vast, arid, and harshly beautiful series of barren steppes, cut by river valleys and rising two thousand feet into the air; here you have the choice of baking in summer or freezing in winter. With the exception of the western edge of Spain bordering on Portugal, this adobe-colored *meseta* is ringed by snow-capped sierras that slope down to Atlantic and Mediterranean beaches, some rugged, others serene.

In the northern provinces—Galicia, Asturias, and the Basque country—the climate and terrain are reminiscent of France. The beaches on the Bay of Biscay—Santander and San Sebastian—resemble Biarritz, and the cool slopes of the Cantabrian and Pyrenees mountains are forested with pines and oaks, beeches and birches, apple orchards, and carpets of fern. But in the south, Andalusia and the Levantine coast along the Mediterranean are brushed by the hot

289

winds of Africa from Valencia to Málaga, and back to the fertile foothills of the Sierra Morena. This area is a tropical garden of date palms and olive woods; orange and lemon groves; rice swamps; banana, cotton, and sugar plantations.

In addition to differences in climate and landscape, the various regions within Spain are cut off from each other by temperament and tastes, customs and culture, dialect and dress, folklore and food, and, often throughout their long history, by conflicting loyalties and interests. Cool, green, Gothic Burgos prides itself on its thirteenth century cathedral, with its soaring marble spires, chiseled tracery, and delicate pointed arches, its rose windows of stained glass, and most of all, the treasure chest of El Cid, the epic Spanish knight who fought so bravely against the Moors, and who is Burgos' most celebrated native son. But warm, florid, Moorish Granada's prize is the Alhambra, the Mudejar castle-fortress that is a wonder of pink sandstone carved with lacy arabesques, horseshoe arches, and tiled courtyards. And dreamy Granada seems to miss the Moors almost as much as the Moors miss Granada and carefully preserves its souvenirs of Boabdil, the last Moorish king to be driven from Spain.

The Basques, who are descendants of the aboriginal tribes on the Iberian Peninsula, speak an ancient language no one else can even begin to understand, while, not far away, the Catalonian dialect is a French derivative. The Galicians are known for their wit and wiliness, the Asturian coal miners for their rebelliousness, the people of Barcelona for their independence and commercial acumen, the Andalusians for their poetry and their passion. Toledo looms from its rocky crag looking as austerely medieval as El Greco painted it; Valencia sings and dances at its flowery fiestas. The list of Spain's contradictions is endless, even to its heroes. In contrast to Torquemada, the infamous grand inquisitor, and the cruel Philip II are such Spanish saints as Teresa of Avila, St. Isidore, whose School of Seville spread the mathematical teachings of the Alexandrians, and St. Ignatius, who founded the Jesuit order.

Stitched to Europe by the narrow band of the Pyrenees but reaching out toward Africa at Tangiers, Spain since the eighth century has felt the pull of both continents, culturally, linguistically, philosophically. Nor is that the end of the Spanish dilemma. According to Byron, "Cervantes smiled Spain's chivalry away." Anyone who knows the Spaniards now, three centuries after Cervantes died, realizes that they have still to choose between the romantic idealism of Don Quixote, and the pragmatic, down-to-earth realism of his all-too-human companion, Sancho Panza. There is contrast, too, in the racial strains within this country: Iberians and Celts; Phoenicians and Greeks; Romans, Goths, and Moors; the Flemish, the French, and the Austrians; all have left their traces. In almost any large Spanish city one sees Velazquez' blue-eyed, long-chinned blondes, Murillo's dark-eyed, round-faced, negroid gypsies, and elegant, white-skinned brunettes straight out of Goya's paintings.

Amidst all this contrast and diversity stands Madrid, set in the dead center of the Iberian Peninsula, a midway point, temperamentally as well as geographically, between the country's regional extremes. This has been the secret of its success since Philip III made it the Spanish capital in 1606, precisely because he realized the value of its location. In addition, Madrid is a formal, reserved, sedate Castilian city, and it is Castile that holds Spain together, that gives it its form and its sense of history. Castilian pride is the unifying thread that runs through this varied national tapestry.

Spain's golden age, from the fifteenth to the seventeenth centuries, was essentially a Castilian age, when the court life moved from Andalusia to this central plateau province. By the sixteenth century, the Spanish-Austrian Hapsburgs ruled the largest empire in modern history, the empire that was the legacy of Don Carlos, Charles V. "Let others wage war. You lucky Austria, marry," said Charles, when he inherited Castile from Isabella, his maternal grandmother; Aragon and its holdings in Italy from his maternal grandfather, Ferdinand; the Low Countries and part of France from his paternal grandmother, Mary of Burgundy; Austria and the Hapsburg lands from his paternal grandfather, Maximilian. By the time his son Philip II built that sinister tombstone of a monastery, El Escorial, Spanish explorers had added the jewels of the Philippines, the Spice Islands, and much of the new world to the Spanish crown of empire.

And though by the seventeenth century, when Philip IV was on the throne, the English defeat of the Spanish Armada and the revolt of Flanders in the Thirty Years' War had broken Spain's grip on Europe, it was then that the country reached the peak of its artistic creativity, with the work of many of its greatest painters, and writers such as Calderón, Cervantes, and Lope de Vega. Throughout the eighteenth century, Spain had more than enough gold from her colonies to finance the buildings of great capitals like Lima, Buenos Aires, and Mexico City. The wide avenues, the fountains and flower-filled squares, the elegant parks and the huge, formal neoclassic public buildings that give Madrid its over-all character today, were products of that prosperous eighteenth century. When Napoleon named his brother king of Spain in the early nineteenth century and saw the magnificent royal palace from which Joseph was to rule, he is reported to have said, as he stood on the sweeping black-and-white-marble grand staircase, "At last I have this Spain so long desired. My brother, you will be better lodged here than I am in the Tuileries."

Perched atop the tableland of New Castile and walled off from European rains by mountains, Madrid has more sunny days than almost any other city in Europe. It is roofed by the deep blue cloudless sky that Velazquez loved to paint, and is cut by the trickling stream that is the Manzanares River. The air is dry and balmy, and, as an old Spanish proverb has it, "so fine it can kill a man but not blow out a candle." Summer and winters are extreme. The loveliest seasons are autumn, when pine-scented breezes blow in from the Guadarrama Mountains, and spring, when, it is said, "one can smell tuberoses along the Calle de Alcalá."

This street is the main thoroughfare of the city, linking it both in time and space. It starts at the Royal Palace, which was designed by an Italian architect, Sachetti, for a Spanish Hapsburg king, and was lived in by the French Bonaparte conqueror. The Calle de Alcalá leads to the Plaza Mayor, Madrid's most antique quarter, and by far its most interesting. Here, sixteenth and seventeenth century arcaded streets frame the square where in the time of Philip III fifty thousand spectators could watch the bullfights held there. And around this Renaissance square, nine arched gateways lead to ancient, twisting streets, lined with gray stone buildings and shops with weathered wood fronts. Here are Madrid's oldest restaurants, little caves with noisy bars downstairs, and simple white dining rooms upstairs; none of these is more famous than El Botín, known since 1725 for its roast suckling pig and lamb. Anyone who dines there after midnight (not an unusual hour in this city of late dining) will see the piglets for the following day pyramided on tables, with lettuce leaves in their mouths, looking as cleanly pink as marzipan in a candy-shop window. In this area, too, is the old Plaza de la Villa, with the Ayuntamiento or Town Hall, built in the seventeenth century, and the Casa de Cisneros, an outstanding work of the sixteenth century architect De la Mora.

Back on the Alcalá, one soon comes to the Puerta del Sol, the city's most important square since the eighteenth century when it was the eastern gateway to the city, the place where the sun first rose each morning over Madrid—hence its name. Its clock tower, the Gobernación, added in the nineteenth century, is Madrid's Big Ben with resonant bells that ring over the entire city. Further along are the sparkling jets of water that rise from the circular Cibeles fountains, Madrid's tribute to the goddess of fertility, and one of the city's best known picture postcard sights; and this same wide avenue runs through the enormous triple-arched gateway, the Puerta de Alcalá, built in honor of Charles III in 1778.

North of the Calle de Alcalá lies much of modern Madrid. Its most fashionable boulevard, lined with smart cafés, expensive shops, and hotels, is the Avenida José Antonio, also called the Gran Via, which leads to the Plaza de España. In this contemporary square, white skyscraper hotels overlook the grassy plaza and its statues of Spain's beloved Don Quixote on his noble Rocinante, and Sancho Panza on a tired donkey.

Most of eighteenth century Madrid is south of its main avenue. In the lushly green Retiro Park, marble statues are shaded by leafy trees and children play, watched over by uniformed nurses or doting grandmothers. Close by, Madrid's Ritz is one of the most gracious hotels to bear that name, and it is in this section, too, that you can visit Spain's outstanding treasure, the Prado Museum.

The art treasures in this museum are among the most breathtaking in the world. Only after spending weeks, perhaps months, in its galleries can one even begin to grasp the richness of its collection. Not only all of the best works of the best Spanish masters are represented, but the Prado boasts a magnificent group of Flemish and Italian paintings as well, works which the Spanish crown acquired when these countries were under Spanish rule and at the height of their artistic genius. Bosch, Titian, Rubens, Van Dyck, Fra Angelico, Raphael, Dürer, Veronese, Velazquez, Ribera, Goya, Murillo, Zurburán, El Greco, and hundreds more are represented here.

Devoted museum goers will also want to list as "musts" Madrid's Museo de Ejercito, with its arms collections, the Naval Museum, and the decorative arts collection with folk crafts from all over Spain. The Lazaro Galdiano Museum has more fine paintings from various parts of Europe, and Lope de Vega's house gives one a fascinating glimpse of life in sixteenth century Madrid. His furnishings have been preserved and the rooms completely restored, and even the garden of this dramatist who was a Don Juan prototype has been planted with the flowers he loved. Madrid's museums also include one with a collection of bullfight memorabilia and another which houses over 100,000 wine bottles. There are, in fact, more than twenty-five museums to choose from in this city of two million.

Because of Madrid's eighteenth century patterning and because it includes a little bit of everything one finds in Spain and is, therefore, a blend and a synthesis, the tourist who sees it on the run is likely to find it too colorless and "un-Spanish." Like a beautiful woman who is proud, reserved, and diffident, Madrid is hard to get to know. Only those who can take the time to chip away at the surface reserve will find the city to be as full of contrasts and history as the rest of Spain, as Spanish as Castile.

To get to know Madrid through its people, one will have to skip some of its museums, therefore, and see its present-day life. Take the time to relax at a café along the Gran Via or on the Calle de Alcalá, sip a glass of iced nut milk, the *horchata* that is this city's specialty, and watch the regal bearing and elegant dress of the *madrileños* as they take their evening *paseo*. And, listening to the subtle, precise accents of the Castilian Spanish they speak at tables around you, you might agree with Casanova, who wrote, "Spanish is undoubtedly one of the finest, most energetic, and most majestic languages in the world. When it is pronounced *ore rotundo,* it is susceptible of the most poetic harmony."

Shop one Sunday morning at the rag fair of a flea market that is El Rastro, where the fine antique shops are supplemented on this one day by curbside vendors selling everything from pins to plumbing tools, old clothes and kitchen gadgets, secondhand matadors' costumes, buttons, brass doorknobs, and paintings. This is the one shopping section of Madrid where bargaining is expected, and it is fascinating to see how it is managed without any sacrifice of Castilian pride or form.

A visitor to Madrid should, if possible, attend one of the summer *verbenas,* the neighborhood street fairs with side shows, doughnut sellers, wine and candy stalls. Or go, at least one night, to the little cabaret-bars near the Plaza Mayor where some of Spain's best known flamenco dancers perform and where the local delicacy is crisply fried bits of squid washed down with a *chato,* a short tumbler of clear white wine, or a glass of good cold Spanish beer.

Probably nowhere else in Madrid can you see so many elegantly dressed *madrileños* at one time as at the Sunday bullfights, in one of Spain's most important arenas, with a seating capacity of thirty thousand. Those who can afford to, sit in the *sombra*—the shade, those who want less expensive seats sit in the *sol,* the broiling Madrid sun. So much has been written about this spectacle, its history, and its meaning in Spanish life that it seems unnecessary to repeat any of it here. Anyone who missed the full background of this ancient rite can get more than enough information in the works of Hemingway, Pritchett, Brenan, Olagüe, and John Marks, whose *To the Bullfight* is a classic guide.

With a population that has doubled in a generation, Madrid is mushrooming out to modern suburbs, as is almost every other major city of the world, and there is little about this one to distinguish it in that respect.

But no matter how much Madrid grows, its Puerto del Sol will always be Spain's "Kilómetre O"—the central point to which all Spanish roads eventually lead, and from which distances in this vast land are measured.

Madrid itself is surrounded by a ring of fascinating towns and sights. Of these, Toledo is the number-one excursion point. It lies forty-two miles south of Madrid, past mountain villages that seem to have grown out of the ocher soil on which they stand. Toledo appears suddenly on the landscape, edged by the dark green Tagus River that flows all the way to Lisbon, and set atop a craggy peak over the Castilian plateau. The city winds up in rows of houses, palaces, convents, old Moorish walls, and towers, to its summit, surmounted by the enormous orange-colored citadel of the Alcázar. In spite of the over-eager guides and souvenir vendors who swarm around you as you enter the ancient gate, the Puerta del Sol, it is still regarded as the city most characteristic of Spain's medieval glory.

Founded by the Phoenicians, Toledo was the pride of Spain, as famous in the world as Constantinople, and known for its steel and damascene work. It was the favorite city of the exiled Jew, the stronghold of the Goth, the metropolis of the Moor, and the capital of Christian Spain, and bears the seals of its past grandeurs in walls, museums, churches, palaces, and houses. Narrow streets are lined with gray tone medieval buildings, their windows barred with black wrought iron. Heavy oaken doors are studded with hammered iron nailheads, and, in the churches, dark wood panels are rich with strapwork and linen-fold carvings. This was the adopted home of El Greco, the great painter from Crete who settled here in the six-teenth century, and for art lovers the main places of pilgrimage here are his home and the museum named after him. His works can also be seen in the Museum of San Vicente, in the Church of Santo Domingo, in the beautifully restored Hospital of Tavera, and in the city's cathedral, a Gothic masterpiece built between the thirteenth and nineteenth centuries.

Considering its size, Toledo is as rich in artistic and architectural wonders as Florence and Siena. The tenth century mosque of Cristo de la Luz, the twelfth century synagogue of Santa Maria la Blanca, the Transito synagogue, built in the fourteenth century, the convent of San Juan de los Reyes, the exquisite Renaissance hospital of Santa Cruz, and the Moorish castle-fortress, the Alcázar, are worthy of time on any traveler's itinerary, no matter how crowded it may be.

Just thirty miles from Madrid is another stupendous sight: El Escorial, the monastery built by Philip II in honor of the martyred saint, Lorenzo, who was roasted to death on a gridiron. The Spanish monarch gained an important victory over the French on the saint's birthday, and to commemorate the event he had the Escorial built in the shape of an enormous gridiron, only one of the ominous and melancholy notes about the place. It sits in a dramatic setting in the rocky foothills of the Guadarramas, wild-looking mountains that provide a suitably stark backdrop for the monastery that was a despot's frightful fancy petrified in gray slate and granite.

Some of the arcaded galleries are 700 feet long, and the building includes 16 granite courtyards, 80 granite staircases, 1,200 doors, 11,000 windows, and 50 miles of rooms and corridors to walk around in. Later kings added tapestries and works of art to brighten the surroundings, but Philip's apartment is by far the most fascinating sight of all. Here are the things he lived with—the low bench on which he rested his gouty leg, the wooden chair from which he ruled two worlds, the private altar on which he proclaimed to God after one of his purges, "Father, I have no enemies; I have killed them all." The portrait of Philip II painted by Titian hangs in the Escorial; it is indeed the face of a man who is said to have laughed outright only once in his life and that was when he heard of the Massacre of St. Bartholomew. Below the royal living quarters are the tombs of Philip's parents and of all the Spanish kings who followed him.

Another royal country palace worth seeing is in Aranjuez, a Castilian town famed for its thick white asparagus and its strawberries. Essentially eighteenth century in character, this palace with its Chinese room, its gardens, and royal barges that floated down the Tagus, was the favorite summer residence of Philip V. Not far away is the small, exquisite château built by a later king, the Casita del Labrador, the Farmer's Cottage, modeled after Marie Antoinette's Trianon.

Segovia is virtually a museum of Spanish architectural history and was a prosperous textile center in the sixteenth century and a favorite of Spanish kings. Its Roman aqueduct with 118 arches spans 795 yards. Its Alcázar is one of the most fantastic in all Spain, with slim turrets and delicately crenelated walls, and was one of the castles of Ferdinand and Isabella. And Segovia's cathedral, done in the late Gothic style, is elegant and severe.

There are scenes of breathtaking natural beauty close to Madrid in the Sierra de Guadarrama and the Sierra de Gredos, and no place close to the capital is more impressive than Avila, the city that looks very much the same as it did when St. Teresa first saw it in the sixteenth century. Avila rises out of the distance, surrounded by the towers and ramparts of its eleventh century defensive walls—a sight most dramatic at night when these antique stones glow under floodlights.

BARCELONA

The sardana and the big sell

BARCELONA is Spain's most European city, an up-and-doing Mediterranean seaport dedicated to commerce, shipping, and industry, to art, music, and good living. With a population close to two million, it is the country's second largest city, and, by all odds, its noisiest, liveliest, most industrious, and most prosperous. It is the capital of Catalonia, the province once held by the Visigoths, who called it Gotholonia. Traditionally, this has been an area of political and artistic ferment, famous for its independent style and its rebellious spirits. These traits were as obvious in the seventeenth century, when Catalonia revolted against Spain during the Thirty Years' War, as they were in the twentieth century, when it was a die-hard Loyalist stronghold in the civil war, a piece of tragic history immortalized in George Orwell's *Homage to Catalonia*. Only the Asturians can match the Catalonians for pure contentiousness, and even today Barcelona's politicians and intellectuals are under closer and more careful censorship than those in other Spanish provinces. Pocketed off by mountains into the northeastern corner of the country, this coastal province reaches up toward the Pyrenees and France. Its geographical position is symbolic. The tempo, tone, and tastes of Catalonia and its capital have always been more continental than Iberian.

To realize just how much Barcelona differs from the rest of Spain one should first see more typical cities: the flowery, romantic Seville and the proud, elegantly formal, Castilian Madrid. It is then that you will be most aware of those elements that account for Barcelona's contrasts: the wide, flower-decked, Parisian-style boulevards with sidewalk cafés and colorful kiosks, the fashionable people and their quick pace and sense of purpose, the crowded bars and international restaurants, and the Catalan dialect, closer to Provençal French than to Spanish. This handsome market-place metropolis with its pink and dove-gray buildings is set between the towering peaks of Mount Tibidabo and Montjuich, and is more reminiscent of the cities it faces across the Mediterranean than it is of those that lie behind its rim of mountains. It looks more like Marseilles than Seville and feels more like Milan than Madrid. In fact, this city is to Spain exactly what Milan is to Italy: the rich, northern industrial and financial center that regards the rest of its country as a place of indolent no-accounts, a point of view as incorrect in Spain as it has proven to be in Italy.

Barcelona is the home of stoutly square and vigorous big-time wheeler-dealers: men who move quickly and carry brief cases; merchants, manufacturers bankers who know how to make money and how to hold on to it. They pride themselves on the character trait they call *seny,* an innate sense of proportion about life, a sixth sense they claim to have inherited from Greek and Roman ancestors. Their passion for trade may well be a heritage from the Phoenicians, who founded the city some two hundred years before the birth of Christ. And Barcelona owes its name to those enterprising Phoenician descendants, the Carthaginians, who named it after Barca, one of their generals, when Hannibal drove his armies, elephants and all, through Catalonia on his way to Italy. The large number of golden-redheads is traceable to the Visigoths, as is one of the city's favorite celebrations, Midsummer's Eve, when bonfires and night-long revelries welcome the summer solstice—a most un-Mediterranean festival, but one still celebrated in northern lands.

Above all, Barcelona is the city of a progressive middle class that grew up here after the industrial revolution in the nineteenth century. Their taste is showy, individual, self-expressive, and, very often, way out. They love bigness and exaggeration; understated elegance is an esthetic concept the Catalans would never grasp. And whatever activity they are involved in, whether it is business or pleasure, they approach with diligence and zeal. They put as much energy into planning a new textile mill as they do into dancing the *sardana* in the streets on Sunday, as much enthusiasm into buying and selling as into enjoying the carnival attractions of the amusement park on Mount Tibidabo, which is just in the shadow of the garish modern church recently completed there. For people who give themselves to work the way the people of Barcelona do, it is amazing to note how wholeheartedly they welcome the fiestas and fairs that crop up all year round, none gayer than the Lady of Ransom fête held each September when amateur musicians and composers vie for prizes and recognition.

As one might expect with people who work and play as diligently as the Barcelonians, they are hearty eaters and drinkers. They like their sparkling red-wine *sangrías* brightened by orange and lemon slices and prefer their magnificent shellfish and rice dishes, their fish soups and blood sausages, their intricate pastries and candies, in portions that are best described as overwhelming.

Pleasure and purpose are the dual themes everywhere in Barcelona. The people are proud of their "firsts." This was the first city in Spain to have gaslights and a railway, the first anywhere to underwrite its shipping. But they are just as proud of the artists either born in Barcelona or who spent formative years there: Picasso, Miró, Dali, and Picabia, to name the painters; Balenciaga, whose career as a fashion designer was launched here; Antonio Gaudí, the architectural genius of the art *nouveau* movement. Gaudí's wildly modern naturalistic forms were architectural fantasies half a century ahead of Frank Lloyd Wright. He loved underwater motifs and undulating forms. His building façades imitated ocean waves, his decorative patterns included starfish and sea anemones, stalagmites and stalactites. Much of his work can still be seen around this city where he worked, most especially in the unfinished Church of the Sagrada Familia, in the apartment houses he designed that stand along the Calle Carolinas and in the Paseo de Gracia, and in the tiled and glittering Disneyland architecture he built in the Parque Güell.

To get the real sense of this city, one should spend some time wandering around its harbor district, a bustling, salt-sharp complex of activity and history. This harbor saw the Phoenician long boats; it saw, too, the returning ships of Columbus, with their New World loot of gold and Indians, and the towering pedestal monument to the Italian seaman is a reminder of that first momentous voyage. Now the harbor is a setting for fishing trawlers with nets strung up on masts to dry, freighters from every country in the world, motor boats called *golondrinas* (swallows) or *gaviotas* (seagulls) which can be hired for sightseeing excursions, a maritime museum, and the stock exchange, the Lonja, that dates from 1382, though the building was reconstructed in the nineteenth century.

There are two ways to appreciate the excitement of this harbor. One is to explore it inch by inch on foot, not forgetting to stop and see the replica of Columbus' caravel, the *Santa Maria,* or to thread your way through the picturesque sailors' quarter, Barceloneta, with its noisy bars and small, excellent seafood restaurants. On the Calle de Moncada, close by, are the antique mansions of a bygone aristocracy, with Gothic, Renaissance, and baroque styles intermingled. One of these houses contains the new Picasso Museum, and the artisans' quarter, not far away, is a section of tiny, dimly lit workrooms, enticing shop windows full of handicrafts, and an atmosphere that harks back to the Arab bazaars. In addition to walking around it, one should see this harbor in all of its panoramic splendor from the top of Montjuich, with the town spread out behind it against the backdrop of green mountains. From this vantage point one realizes how crowded the city is, how much it is wedged against its harbor, and how little room it has to grow.

Next to the harbor, Barcelona's most evocative section is the Ramblas, a series of wide streets built in the ancient ramparts of the city. Buildings here are secondary; the magic of the Ramblas lies in the people. These streets are the meeting place, promenade, park, market place, and soul of the city. They zigzag along, crowded from early morning until well after midnight with window shoppers, café-terraces, bullfight fans who gather beneath the Arco del Teatro, football fans at the Caneletas fountains, flower sellers and bird dealers hawking their wares, kiosks where newspapers, magazines, and books are displayed, cinemas and soda fountains, jewelers, and photographers, and every kind of tradesman and pleasure seeker one could dream of.

Branching off the Ramblas are innumerable tiny side streets, none more fascinating than the Arco del Teatro which leads to the Barrio Chino, Barcelona's erstwhile red-light district, and still ominous enough for policemen to patrol in pairs. As is usual in such areas, the Barrio Chino has more than its share of very good, inexpensive, *bistro*-like restaurants, fried fish shops, and bars with flamenco music that spills out onto the street, and an alluring, if seamy, night life. The Ramblas lead, inevitably, to the Paralelo, a combination Broadway-Montmartre, and expectedly the center of nightclub and cabaret activities.

The Via Layetana, running from the harbor almost parallel to the Ramblas, leads to the Gothic quarter, called the Barrio Gotico and dating from the fourteenth to the sixteenth centuries. Its high spot is the tremendous and handsome cathedral, built between 1298 and 1450 and famed for the purity of its styling. Two huge bell towers accent the soaring lines, and the wide nave has a choir with unusually fine medieval and Renaissance carvings. The silver throne of St. Martin and the *Pietá* done by Bartolomé Bermejo are two of its most valuable treasures. The heart of the Gothic quarter is the Plaza del Rey, one of Europe's most austerely impressive squares. It is edged by the city's historical museum, St. Agatha's Chapel with its five tiered round arches, and the imposing Palacio Real Mayor, the great royal palace, once the residence of the kings of Aragon, a kingdom so powerful it was said that even the fish in the sea wore its red and yellow colors.

The Ensanche, or "widening," is the modern residential district that was first laid out in Barcelona's era of rebirth, the nineteenth century. The chief street here is the Diagonal, and from the top of this one can view the tree-lined streets and orderly avenues of the whole section.

Barcelona's mountain peaks, Mount Tibidabo and Montjuich, offer sights to lure the tourist too. Mount Tibidabo, with its Coney Island amusement park, its incredibly flashy neon-lit church, and its lookout points over the city, makes a visit essential to anyone who cares to know Barcelona in all of its facets. Montjuich boasts a "must" in any traveler's itinerary: the Pueblo Español, the Spanish Village built for the World Exhibition of 1929. It is made up of reproductions of houses typical of the various regions of Spain, and its workshops are a souvenir hunter's delight, as all of the handicrafts produced there are for sale. Also on Montjuich is the Palacio Nacional, with a a staggering array of Romanesque and Catalonian art. The park on the hillside includes the Archeological Museum, with relics from pre-historic, Greek, and Roman times.

Traveling inland from Barcelona, one can visit the fabled monastery, Montserrat, the most important in the country since the twelfth century. It is a craggy, rocky vision of turrets and forbidding walls rising above the flat, arid plains around it. Said to be the inspirational setting for Wagner's *Parsifal,* the monastery is a treasury of medieval art. Other monasteries of interest, not too far from Barcelona, are Santas Creus, with its fine cloisters, and Poblet, the twelfth century pantheon of the kings of Aragon. Both of these Cistercian mona-steries are near Tarragona, in the town of Reus.

Barcelona is also the jumping-off point for the charming resort beach towns of the rugged coast—the Costa Brava that is Spain's Riviera. Rocky sandy beaches wind north up the coast to France and offer all of the seaside delights tourists seek out. From Barcelona's harbor you can take a boat for Majorca, perhaps the most famous of the idyllic Balearic Islands. Once an inexpensive hideaway for those who longed for the simple life, Majorca's highly publicized splendors are almost extinct. Hotel developments have cropped up everywhere and prices are rising right along with the island's skyline. Minorca, on the other hand, though less exotic, is now perhaps a better choice— a quieter, dreamier, almost forgotten island, for those who like to discover places for themselves. Both the English and French took turns occupying Minorca in the eighteenth century; both have left indelible traces. Evidence of the English can be found in the strain of blue-eyed blondes, in children's games, in bow windows, and in recurrent English words sprinkled through the Spanish spoken here.

SEVILLE

The home of Don Juan, Carmen, and
Figaro—the most Spanish city in Spain

ANYONE who visits Spain and sees only such northern cities as
Madrid, Toledo, Barcelona, San Sebastian, and Burgos, might well
decide that, once again, the travel posters have gone too far. No more
than a third of what they say about Spain is true. Certainly there are
bullfights straight out of Hemingway, where aficionados shout *"Olé"*
just as they should. Here and there are some wrought-iron railings
and lanterns, and nightclub floor shows include a flamenco dancer or
two, complete with guitar and castanets. One can eat paella and drink
sherry from Jerez almost anywhere in Spain, and most souvenir shops
offer lace fans and mantillas, wineskins and dolls in traditional
costumes. But Spain, one would have to conclude, is not nearly as
romantic and picturesque as copywriters, novelists, and librettists
would have us believe.

But let that disillusioned traveler go to Andalusia, the Southern
section of Spain that hangs like a shimmering Oriental pearl between
the Sierra Morena and the Mediterranean Sea, and he will realize

at once that the guidebook clichés and travel-poster images, the novels and opera stage sets, are based on solid realities. For Andalusia includes everything we think of as "typically Spanish."

Nowhere is this more obvious than in Seville, Andalusia's leading city and its spiritual heart. It was an important city in Roman times, and the birthplace of the emperor Trajan. Seville was prized by the Visigoths and the Vandals, after whom the entire province was named Vandalusia, and it was the pride of the Moors who held it from 712 to 1248, when Ferdinand III captured Córdoba and Moslem rule ended in Andalusia. But Seville had another era of glory, for it became the seat of the Spanish kings, and it was to this city that Columbus came seeking the financial backing for his voyage from Ferdinand and Isabella. The Gold Tower that stands on the banks of the Guadalquivir held the treasures of the New World brought back by Columbus and the conquistadors who followed him, among them Pizarro and Cortés. It is the city where the best fighting bulls are bred and the home of the cold vegetable soup, *gazpacho*.

Banded by the silvery waters of the Guadalquivir River, this city of four hundred thousand rises like a mirage from the green plateau around it. The glistening white Arabic skyline is reminiscent of Damascus, with domes, minarets, and rooftop gardens. It is fringed with orange groves and feathery palm fronds, vineyards and the terraced olive trees that produce the rich golden Spanish oil. The most spectacular landmark in the skyline is the rose-pink Giralda, the 300-foot-high square tower built by the Moors in the twelfth century as a minaret, and now the bell tower of the city's cathedral. It was originally topped by four enormous globes of solid gold that glittered in the sunlight and dazzled travelers up to twenty-five miles away. Partially destroyed by an earthquake in 1395, the Giralda was later restored and given its Renaissance belfry and its weathervane— a bronze female figure of Faith, a Faith never steadfast, but one blown about by every wind. One suspects that like most *sevillanos* the architect was a practical joker.

Seville's fifteenth century cathedral is the largest Gothic building in the world. It is filled with works of art by great Spanish and Flemish painters and is adorned with treasures from all of Spain's possessions: gold from Peru, silver from Mexico, and rare woods from the West Indies carved into tables and paneling. Five hundred masses are said each day in the cathedral's eighty chapels and the huge rectangular floor plan includes five enormous naves. Looking down from its belfry, one can see the neatly patterned irrigation channels in its courtyards, an invention of the Moors that enabled them to grow the palms and orange trees they brought with them from their native land.

And it is in Seville that one can see the Alcázar, the magnificent palace built by Peter the Cruel in the Spanish-Moorish style called Mudejar. Here, scalloped pointed arches and rose-gold walls covered with intricate carvings give the palace the delicate look of antique lace. The courtyard with its columns, the gardens and patios trimmed with box hedges, orange trees, palms, and brilliant *azulejo* tiles, and the great halls make it easy to see why the Spanish kings chose to live there long after the Moors had departed.

Velazquez, who became the court painter of the Spanish Hapsburgs, was born in Seville; Zurburán was trained there; and Murillo, another native son, immortalized the beggars, urchins, and humble women of the city. Dark, sad, and proud faces straight out of Murillo's canvases can still be seen in the city's gypsy quarter, Traina, the section that is famous for its potters, its bullfighters, its dancers, singers, and guitarists.

Seville's oldest section, Santa Cruz, is a Spanish set-piece, almost too good to be true. Here, fountain waters splash against blue-and-yellow Moorish tiles in cool, palm-shaded courtyards. Wrought-iron balconies cast lacy shadows on whitewashed walls, and the air is heady with the sweet perfume of jasmine and orange blossoms. As in all of Seville, there are flowers everywhere. Hot orange geraniums spill out of window boxes, red roses and pink carnations are sold on street corners, mauve wisteria and deep purple bougainvillaea climb garden walls like floral arabesques on a Spanish shawl. If you can bear to, just once, walk the narrow, yellow cobblestoned streets and twisting alleys in the blazing heat of afternoon, when they are deserted and heavy with the stillness of siesta. Then the whole town sleeps with louvered shutters shut against the sun, and stays that way until early evening, when the air is as fresh as spring water and the city comes to life.

Between five and six, the entire population of Seville seems to pour into the streets. Beautifully dressed women, in groups or with duennas, go out for a *paseo;* men watch them and play the Moorish-Spanish game of flirtation, their messages conveyed only by their eyes. Others sit at cafés drinking tiny glasses of sherry and nibbling the *tapas,* the snacks of fried fish always served with drinks. To the *sevillanos,* as to the Neapolitans and the Athenians, home is the place to eat and sleep. The street is the place to live.

There are many ways in which the *sevillanos* remind one of the Neapolitans, many ways in which they differ. The archetypes of both cities have dark, sad eyes, olive skins, and are smaller and rounder than their countrymen to the north. Both are poor, gay, musical, livened by wit and a broad punchinello humor. They speak in colorful idioms and chip the sharpness off the precisely pure northern dialects. As in Naples, the people of Seville are volatile, excitable, casual, and here, too, Roman paganism seems to blend easily with Christian Catholicism. But the Spaniards have too much pride to pick your pocket, though they are crafty enough when making deals, and the people of Andalusia have more style and elegance than those of Campagna. And they are even more theatrical, more darkened by a sense of tragedy and irony. No wonder so many operas have been based on the half-factual, half-fictional characters of Seville: Carmen, Don Juan, Figaro.

The quickest and most impressive way to understand the *sevillanos* is to see them during their two great spring celebrations, the Holy Week that precedes Easter, and the Feria, the fair that follows it. It is then that they exhibit their love of spectacle, their fanatical religious fervor that is tinged with pagan passion; their love of music, dancing, and fancy dress; their gaiety, color, and styles. Holy Week begins on Palm Sunday; and throughout the week the town is filled with religious processions in which the *sevillanos* carry flower-banked platforms holding statues of the patron saints. The figures are dressed in robes of silk and velvet, richly embroidered with jewels and silver threads, and wear lustrous halo-crowns of brilliant gold, as they are carried from their own churches into the cathedral for blessings, and back again. Marchers wear a wild array of costumes. Women in elegant mantillas held high by tortoise-shell combs walk in formal, dark evening dress; some men wear the costumes of Roman centurions while others are dressed as bullfighters; and many penitents are eerily clad in peaked white hoods and robes. At night the processions are lit by tall white tapers. On Good Friday proceedings reach fever pitch. Then the women, austerely dressed in black, walk barefoot through the streets, commemorating Christ's walk to Calvary. Feet bleed from the roughness of the cobblestones, heads bleed under crowns of real thorns, and people prostrate themselves in front of the Virgin Mary, who is carried through Seville's streets just as the figure of Venus was, some two thousand years ago. And at intervals throughout the week one hears the story of Christ's agonies sung in the mournful, minor-key *saetas,* a form of *hondo* or "deep singing" that is half Levantine, half gypsy in origin.

Feria, the fair that starts just after Easter Sunday, is another matter entirely. Gaiety, not tragedy, is the keynote here. It is a time of dancing in the streets and sparkling fiesta revelries. The best bull-fights are staged, dark-eyed girls in brightly colored dresses tuck red roses in their black hair, and ruffled skirts twirl to the provocative, sensual *sevillana,* the dance by which the world knows Andalusia. Men in satiny, fitted jackets and skin-tight trousers wear wide-crowned Córdoba hats at an angle only they can affect, and the whole city is a Spanish operetta, in which everyone plays an equal and important part. Wealthy families join in the festivities from their *casetas,* the temporary little one- or two-room houses they build near the city's park. Fine furniture, pictures, and accessories are moved into these rooms, which are open in front; the people of Seville have a passion for finery, whether in dress or in room décor.

All of the dancing, eating, and revelry is set against the constant backdrop of liquid, lyrical guitar playing and clacking castanets that produces the flamenco music for which Spain is so famous. Commonly attributed to the Moors, flamenco music is actually an indigenous product, a folk music influenced by the people who came to Spain from diverse parts of the world. One of the most influential of these groups came to Andalusia from Flanders accompanying the Flemish prince, Philip the Handsome, when he was to marry Doña Juana, the daughter of Ferdinand and Isabella. All of those in his party were called by the *sevillanos* "Flamencos," their word for Flemish. The term included the gypsies in the royal entourage, who were especially skillful at this form of sad, mystical, and melodious singing, and whose flair for the dramatic enabled them to create imaginative tales of love, life, and death, still the main themes of flamenco songs.

Seville is filled with wonderful sights. To sense the continuity of the city, one should see its modern suburbs with their lawns, mansions, and palm-lined avenues and then for contrast walk through busy narrow streets, such as the one called Sierpes, with its mosaic of cafés,

shops, noisy bars, and crowds. Anyone interested in the early development of America should visit the Casa Lonja, and the Columbine
Library, started by Christopher Columbus' son, Ferdinand. Both
contain fascinating books, documents, and memorabilia relating to the
earliest days of the New World.

Although Seville is Andalusia's largest city, it is not the only one
of interest and importance. No one should miss the living museum
that is Córdoba, the city that was the Athens of the Moorish-Spanish
world and the birthplace, in Roman times, of Seneca. Here the light
of learning shone brightly when the rest of Europe was deep in the
Dark Ages. In the tenth century, Córdoba had nearly a million inhabitants and within its walls were 600 mosques, 50 hospitals, 900
baths, 800 schools, and a library of 600,000 volumes, although, four
centuries later, the royal library of France consisted of only 900.
One could walk miles at night in Córdoba illumined all the way by
street lamps, 700 years before the first street lamp was lit in London;
and here the Moors wrote scientific treatises and encyclopedias on
geography, geometry, history, and astronomy when many Christian
princes could scarcely print their names.

There is more to Andalusia of course: the lovely coastal cities of
Cartagena, Almería, Málaga, Algeciras, and Cádiz, the city just
beyond the Pillars of Hercules that was a Phoenician trading center
and which now has a museum full of fine Zurburáns. From Gibraltar,
one can easily cross to Africa and the mélange of humanity that is
Tangiers, one of the most exquisitely exotic cities in the world. There
are the vineyards and wine cellars of Jerez, the Renaissance towns of
Baeza and Ubeda, and the quiet, Moorish squares and castles of
Ecija and Carmona. One can still visit La Rábida near Huelva, the
monastery in which Columbus stayed before he sailed to America,
and Ronda, with Spain's oldest bull ring and the cliffside palace of
a Moorish king.

But of all the sights one must see in Andalusia, none is sadder or
more beautiful than Granada, the home of the Spanish poet-dramatist
García Lorca and a city rich in Spanish history. Here one can stay in
the government hotel in the Alhambra, the most celebrated of Moorish
palaces, and for days live in Spain's past. Rising over the city like
Athens' Parthenon on the Acropolis, the Alhambra is a rose-gold
vision in sandstone, with pierced stone windows, arabesque and
Sanskrit carvings on the walls; delicate pillars and mightly columns,

scalloped horseshoe arches, towers, and turrets; the Court of Lions, with its lacy arches and its fountains; the exquisite Mosque; and everywhere Arabic sayings such as "Welcome," "Peace," "There is no God but God." The Generalife, that was the summer palace of the caliphs, and the city's cathedral, where Ferdinand and Isabella are buried, are among Granada's other sights, but all pale beside the "Red Castle," the Alhambra. One can understand, at least partially, how the Moorish king, Boabdil, and his fifty soldiers must have felt when they turned back and saw this sight for the last time. Washington Irving described it as well as anyone in his *Tales of the Alhambra:* "The Moorish cavaliers gazed with a silent agony of tenderness and grief upon that delicious abode, the scene of their loves and pleasures. . . . Presently a peal of artillery, faintly heard, told that the city was taken possession of, and the throne of the Moslem kings was lost forever."

The mountaintop from which Boabdil looked back to the crenelated walls and towers of his beloved palace-fortress is called "The Last Sigh of the Moor," and to the Arabs everywhere, Spain still represents a paradise lost.

FOR THE TRAVELER'S NOTEBOOK

Official Information

Before you go: Spanish National Tourist Office, 485 Madison Ave., New York, N.Y.; Spanish State Office, 23 West Jackson Blvd., Chicago 4, Ill.; Spanish National Tourist Office, 453 Post St., San Francisco 2, Cal.

Madrid: SAS Office, 88 Av. José Antonio; Government Tourist Office, 2 Duque Medinaceli; U.S. Embassy, 75 Calle Serrano.

Barcelona: SAS Office, 277 Mallorca; Government Tourist Office, 658 Av. José Antonio; U.S. Consulate, 18 Calle Junqueras.

Seville: Government Tourist Office, 13 Quepo de Llano; U.S. Consulate, Paseo de Licias.

Money Matters

Currency: The main unit of currency is the peseta (Ptas), divided into 100 centimos. There are 60 pesetas to $1, U.S.

Tipping: Although a 15 per cent service charge is added to your bill, tip the chambermaid about Ptas 10 per day in first class hotels, 5 to 10 in second class; the porter Ptas 20 to 50. In restaurants a service charge is added to the bill but you may give the waiters Ptas 10 to 30. Theater ushers get about Ptas 1 to 2 as do taxi drivers. Tip a valet Ptas 5 per call and room waiters Ptas 5 to 10 per day. The baggage porter gets Ptas 5 per suitcase. Hatcheck girls get about Ptas 2; barbers Ptas 5, hairdressers Ptas 10.

Climate, Clothing, and Essentials

In general Spain's climate is similar to that of southern California and the Southwest. Winters are moderate, and summers hot and dry. In Madrid the average summer temperature is 75 degrees F., while the nearby Sierra Guadarrama bring the winter temperature down to an average of 46 degrees. Spring is variable but pleasant, and autumn the most uniformly agreeable season. A topcoat is needed for spring and fall evenings and a heavier coat for winter. Barcelona, being on the seacoast, has a slightly more temperate climate with winters a few degrees cooler, while in Seville it is generally five to ten degrees warmer in each season.

Dress in Spanish cities is conservative and the usual city attire is correct. Slacks and shorts are absolutely taboo except at seaside resorts, and men always wear jackets.

Hotels

The Spanish National Tourist Offices can send you a complete list of hotels with a description of prices and facilities for hotels throughout Spain. Madrid, Barcelona, and Seville have good hotels in all classes. De luxe, first, and second class hotels are best for visitors, and although hotels in a lower class may be good it would be best either to see the rooms beforehand or take them only on the advice of a travel agency or friend. There are excellent and inexpensive *paradores* (first class government operated inns) throughout the country and villas are available for tourist rental. Hotels are graded into de luxe (*lujo*), first class A and B, and pensions. Hotel prices are more or less alike in Madrid, Barcelona, and Seville, and all are authorized to raise rates during their peak fiesta seasons.

De luxe rates range from Ptas 300 to 480, single; 510 to 860, double. First class A rates range from Ptas 200 to 360, single; 260 to 420, double. First class B rates range from Ptas 180 to 240, single; 260 to 480, double. Second class hotel rates are from Ptas 120 to 180, single; 180 to 260, double.

MADRID

DE LUXE: The *Castellana Hilton, 55 Paseo Castellana,* in the most de luxe category, is a big, bustling modern hotel, with all of the facilities you would expect. The *Ritz Hotel, 5 Plaza Lealtad,* is the high society, upper crust hotel and by far the city's most elegant. The *Wellington, 8 Velazquez,* is quietly located in a residential section near Retiro Park and is formal and conservative with a good dining room. The *Palace, 7 Plaza de las Cortes,* is one of the largest hotels in Europe; it is modern and its bar is one of the favorite meeting places in the city. The *Fenix, Plaza de Colón,* with modern furnishings, good service, and a terrace restaurant, is in a fashionable residential area. The *Emperador, 53 Av. José Antonio,* and the *Plaza, Edificio España,* are modern, efficient, have their own swimming pools, and wonderfully convenient locations for shopping. The *Hotel Suecia, 19 Calle Los Madrazo,* located in the "House of Sweden," and the *Carlton* are also comfortable, quiet, and very good hotels in the de luxe category, but with slightly lower prices than the others in the group.

FIRST CLASS: Good hotels in the first class A group include the *Principe Pio, 16 Paseo Onesimo Redondo;* the quiet *Florida, 2 Plaza Callao;* the new *Zurbano, 75–79 Zurbano.* In the first class B group, you will find the *Hotel Tirol;* the *Ducal, 3 Hortaleza; Hotel Europa, 4 Calle del Carmen; Los Angeles, Costanilla de Los Angeles;* the *Bristol, Av. José Antonio;* and the excellent *Emperatrix, 4 López de Hoyos,* all more than adequate.

BARCELONA

DE LUXE: *Ritz, 658 Av. José Antonio,* is large, traditional, and many of its spacious rooms have recently been redecorated. *Avenida Palace, 605 Av. José Antonio,* is popular with Americans for its modern facilities, its good service, and handy location. *La Rotonda, 51 Paseo San Gervasio,* on the road leading to Mount Tibidabo, has balconies on many of its rooms and its restaurant is popular. *The Colón, 4 Plaza Catedral,* is in the old part of the city, facing the cathedral and has recently been refurbished. *Manila, Ramblas,* a new hotel on the city's main street, has a rooftop restaurant with a view over the city, good sized rooms, all with baths, and most comfortable. *Arycasa, 13 Ausias March,* is new, air-conditioned, and all it should be to qualify for its de luxe rating.

FIRST CLASS: Excellent hotels in this category, all run on the European plan, include the new *Condado, 201 Aribau,* and the equally new *Christina, 458 Av. Generalísimo Franco;* the *Majestic, 70 Paseo de García;* the *Oriente, 20 Rambla de Centro;* the *Emperatrix, 10 Travesera de Dalt,* and the *Astoria, 203 Calle Paris.* All have restaurants, are comfortable, and offer all facilities to make your stay pleasant. Among the best hotels in first class B are the *Esplendido, 8 Pelays;* the *Internacional,* the *Taber,* the *Gales, 120 Generale Mitre,* and the *Hotel Vienna, 22 Calle del Carmen.*

SEVILLE

DE LUXE: *Alfonso XIII, 2 San Fernando,* set in a converted palace, is as elegant as you'd expect a castle to be. *Cristina, Jardines Cristina,* faces beautiful gardens, has a fine restaurant with romantic Andalusian décor and good French food. *Madrid, 2 Mendez Nunez,* in what was once a ducal palace, is richly tiled and a veritable museum of Andalusian art.

FIRST CLASS A: *Cólon, 1 José Canalejas,* is the largest hotel in the city and is comfortable and centrally located. The *Inglatera, 11 Plaza Nueva,* has excellent accommodations and a good location. Most of its rooms have baths and its rates are at the lower end of the price category.

FIRST CLASS B: The *Niza, 5 Reyes Católicos,* and the *Rábida, 24 Castelar,* can both be well recommended in this group.

Food and Restaurants

Spanish food is excellent and you should try some of the specialties while you're there. The seafood is wonderful: lobsters (*langosta*) or prawns (*langostinos*), squid (*calamari*) fried in crisp nuggets, and salt cod (*bacalāo*) which is delectable whether served *à la vizcaína* (in tomato sauce), or in a garlic-herb green sauce (*salsa verde*). Roast pork (*cochinillo asado*) is second only to the Oriental version, and those two well-known favorites, *paella à la Valenciana* (saffron rice with chicken, seafood, sausage, peas and pimentos) and *arroz con pollo* (chicken with saffron rice) are to be had everywhere. *Gazpacho,* the cold Andalusian soup with a tomato base and minced peppers, onions, etc., is a cooling and refreshing pickup, and the garlic soup (*sopada ajo*) served with a poached egg is especially welcome in winter. *Zarzuela* is a Catalan fish stew in the style of bouillabaisse. *Jamón serrano* is a delicious sun-cured ham similar to the Italian *prosciutto* and makes a wonderful appetizer; *olla podrida* is the national stew containing virtually everything, and *butifarra mongetes* is a fine Catalonian sausage-and-bean-casserole. *Sherry* is the favored apéritif here—the pale dry *fino,* the robust *Amontillado,* and the sweeter *dulce* or *oloroso. Manzanilla* is similar to a sherry, and is an excellent apéritif. With meals you can choose from a wide variety of Spanish wines; those of the Rioja and the Valladolid districts are famous. You might try *Viña Pomal* or *Marqués del Roscal* among the red wines, or *Cepa Rhin* or *Monopol* among the white. *Sangría* is a wine punch in which fruit, sugar, and soda are mixed together. If you like wine with your dessert, try the *Málaga* or sweet sherry. Spanish beer is good and so is the brandy.

MADRID

Horcher's is one of the finest continental restaurants in the world, elegant and classic; the prices, for Spain, are high, though not by New

York or Paris standards. The *Jockey Club* is smartly international, and prices are about the highest in the city—a little-black-dress or cocktail-skirt dining place. The *Commodore,* the *Palace,* and the *Ritz* have the leading hotel dining rooms. One of the most interesting and typical places in the city is *Botín,* a late dinner spot in a seventeenth century house where suckling pig is crackling and delectable and prices are surprisingly modest. *La Barraca* is noted for its *paella; Frontón Recoletos* allows you to watch the *jai alai* game on the pelota court opposite as you try the native specialties. *El Mesón de San Javier* is an interesting Castilian inn a little way out of the city; *El Púlpito* is quaint and offers excellent Spanish food in the heart of town, and *Las Cuevas de Luis Candelas* is touristy but colorful—just off the Plaza Mayor. *Hogar Gallego* is noted for seafood dishes, *Corral de la Morería* and *Torre Bermeja* offer Andalusian food and flamenco dancing. *El Bodegón* is a favorite with Spaniards and is full of atmosphere, and *Gure Toki* is a fascinating Basque restaurant. The *California* and *Frigo* chains offer the café type of light lunch; the *Siete Picos* is famous for its modest prices and its fish stew. Cafés and tearooms border all of the main boulevards.

BARCELONA

The *Ritz Hotel,* the elegant and famous *Parellada,* and the *Finisterre,* with its summer sidewalk café, are top class international-style restaurants, serving continental as well as some Spanish food. *Las Siete Puertas,* down near the waterfront, is especially colorful for Sunday lunch, when Barcelona families come in force. Other good typically Catalan places are *Caracoles,* touristy but they serve good mussels; *Carballeira,* also on the waterfront and noted for its shrimp and seafood; *Casa Solé,* and *El Cantábrico. Oro del Rhin* and *Soley* are other good first class restaurants. *El Cortijo* and *La Masia* are pleasant in summer as is the de luxe *El Ast* with its excellent grills. *Amaya* and *Guria* feature Basque cooking, while *Kansas* and *Caneletas* are two places for the American type of light lunch.

SEVILLE

The dining room of the *Alfonso XIII* is by far the most elegant and expensive restaurant in the city. Among the best restaurants are *La Parilla, Hostería del Prado,* and *Los Corales. La Raza* is simple and good, and the *Colón* is currently popular with tourists and has a snack bar upstairs for light lunches. *Casa Luís* is simple, inexpensive, and typically "local," and the *Venta de Antequera* is a wonderful old inn a little way out of Seville that would be perfect for a long, leisurely, and peaceful lunch—unless you're there at the peak of the tourist season.

Entertainment, Night Life, and Special Events

MADRID

The Español and the *Maria Guerrero* are the two leading theaters of Madrid. Foreign opera and ballet troupes often visit Madrid, and the National Orchestra, the Philharmonic Orchestra, and the Symphony Orchestra give concerts in Madrid during the winter season. In spring and autumn, concerts are often held in the Monumental Cinema and Palacio de la Musica.

Some of the more popular night clubs are the *Rendezvous Room* at the *Castellana Hilton* and the suburban *Villa Rosa* (during the summer) while the *Pasapoga* in town is good the rest of the year. For really exciting authentic flamenco dancing don't miss the *Zambra*, near the Ritz Hotel. The *Rex* has good orchestras, charming décor, and is very popular. *Morocco* is noted for its Spanish floor show, *Florida* in Retiro Park offers summer dancing with your dinner, and *Pavillon* in the same park is lovely too. There is dancing in many of the restaurants mentioned above.

BARCELONA

The season of the Opera House is from November to February. During March the house is used for concerts, and April and May usually see foreign ballet companies giving performances here. Ancient Greek tragedies are presented on the open-air stage in the Montjuich Park during the summer season. Floor shows in the usual sense of the word are scarce, perhaps with the exception of *El Cortijo,* a nice open-air restaurant. However, there are plenty of opportunities to see Spanish dances performed at *La Macarena* or at the music hall *El Molino.* Among the numerous night clubs the de luxe *Bolero* and the *Emporium* are extremely good. For dancing try the *Atelier,* the *Bikini,* or the plush *Embassy Club.* If crowds interest you, the *Marfil* is *the* bar in town.

SEVILLE

Café sitting, walking, and dancing in the hotel dining rooms are the main evening diversions. There is gypsy dancing at *El Guajiro, El Patio Andaluz,* and in the *Bodega Parilla* of the *Cristina Hotel.*

As you might expect, here in fiesta land, there is something doing almost every minute in some part of the country. You can get a complete calendar of such events from the Spanish Tourist Offices and those listed here are the major events in and around the cities we are concerned with.

The most colorful holiday is Holy Week (*Semana Santa*), when there are numerous religious processions through the streets of the cities; these processions are most elaborate in Seville and throughout Andalusia. After Easter, the great *Feria* (Spring Carnival) is held in Seville and the city is packed with visitors from all parts of the world. On *July 7* Pamplona begins its *encierro,* the running of the bulls through the streets. The *National Fiesta,* all over the country, celebrates the opening of the bullfight season in March and April, and Madrid holds the feast of its patron saint, St. Isidro, on *May 15.* In mid-June small but typical *kermesses* (fiestas) take place in different parts of the city. Barcelona is especially gay during the fiesta of its patron, Our Lady of Ransom, held at the same time as the Mediterranean Song Festival, *September 25.*

Bullfighting will probably be a "must," especially on your first visit to Spain, and fights are held every Sunday and on most Thursdays in all major cities. The season runs from spring through early fall. Seats in the shade (*sombre*) cost more than those in the sun (*sol*). Jai alai (*frontón*) is a popular ball game played against a wall with huge scoop-shaped rackets, and there are matches in Madrid and Barcelona almost every afternoon and evening.

Shopping

There are many wonderful things to buy at comparatively low prices in Spain. Handsome woolen rugs and bedspreads; carved wooden furniture; gold and silver damascene jewelry from Toledo; embroidered cotton, linen, and lingerie; custom-made clothing; costume dolls; and leather goods are only a few of the possibilities. Excellent sherry and brandies, fans and such souvenirs as wine bottles (*porrono*) and castanets (*castanuelas*) are some others. Lace mantillas, colorful pottery, wrought-ironware and glassware all add to the delightful dilemma. There are still some bargain antiques to be had, though prices have quadrupled in the last ten years. For complete information, see the SAS booklet, "Shopping Your Way Through Southern Europe."

MADRID

In Madrid, the main shopping streets radiate from the Puerta del Sol; the Avenida José Antonio also has some excellent shops. Some of the centers of shopping interest include *El Rastro,* the Madrid flea market, where you can find antiques and "beautiful junk"; *Festival,* otherwise known as the Permanent Spanish Exhibition, with handicrafts and contemporary art at fair prices; and the *Mercado de Artesania,* with crafts from the various Spanish provinces. *Galerías Preciados* is the leading department store. For antiques and old jewelry try *Galerías Piquer, Linares,* and *Toison. Mariquita Perez* has a collection of world-famous dolls. For glass and ceramics go to *Aldonza* and *Antigua Casa Talavera.*

You will find lovely rugs, tapestries, and home fabrics at *Barasa* and *Real Fabrica de Tapices*. *Hierros Madrid* has handsome wrought-iron rails, screens, trivets, and fireplace equipment. *El Tiron* and *Jardin de Modas* have exquisite laces, blouses, and lingerie. *Coppel* and *Sanz* are noted for jewelry, watches, and clocks; *Loewe, Los Cocodrilos, Los Pequeños Suizos,* and *Varade Calle Victoria,* for leather goods. Fine men's wear can be found at *Mendiondo,* and *Sanchez Rubio,* and *Zorrila* has splendid suit fabrics. *Menkes* specializes in folk costumes and there are several high-fashion *couturiers.*

BARCELONA

There are elegant shops in the Avenida Generalisimo Franco, Paseo de Gracia, and Rambla de Cataluña; others in Plaza de Cataluña, Calle de Pelayo, Plaza de Universidad, along the Ramblas, and in Calle de Fernando. The leading department stores are *El Aguila, El Siglo, Sepu,* and *Casa Jorba. Chiquito, Grandes Almacenes,* and *Novedades Marti* are good for gifts and the local branches of *Loewe, Magda,* and *José Maria Roch* for leather goods. *Brunel* specializes in lingeries; *El Suizo* in table linens and fine embroidery. For shoes try *Creus, Durany,* or *Segarra*. For fabrics, *Almacenes Rodriguez* is inexpensive, *Royera* is exclusive, and *Almacenes Barcelona* has a wide range of woolens and suitings. *Bastida, El Dique Flotante, Pertegaz, Rodriguez Cervera,* and *Santa Eulalia* have smart boutiques and custom-made clothing for women.

SEVILLE

Most of the interesting shops are around the Calle de las Sierpes, and the leading department store is *Almacenes El Siglo. Antonio Martin Alborch* has exquisite handicrafts, including rugs and basketry and ceramic. *Santa Ana* has a good selection of pottery and wrought iron. *Peribe* is noted for leather goods; *Peyre S.A.* for linens, blouses, and shirts; and *José Rubio* has gifts of all kinds. The *Mercado Official de Artesania* has a wide range of craft objects and gifts, and *EISA* is a local branch of *Balenciaga.*

Background Reading

This is Spain, by Ignacio Olaqüé (Published by Cohen & West, London). A wonderful little book on all aspects of Spanish life, with an excellent bibliography.
Face of Spain, and *South from Granada,* by Gerald Brenan
The Spanish Temper, by V. S. Pritchett
Quest for Quixote, by R. Croft-Cooke
Spain: The Root and the Flower, by John Crow

Rose for Winter, by Laurie Lee

Homage to Catalonia, by George Orwell

Platero and I, by Juan Ramón Jimenez

Life and Death in a Spanish Town, by Elliot Paul

The Cypresses Believe in God, by José María Gironella

The Hive, by Camilo José Cela

The Broken Root, by Arturo Barea

The Three-Cornered Hat, by Pedro Antonio de Alarçon

The plays and poems of Federico García Lorca also will give you great insight into the life and temperament of the Spanish people.

Switzerland

ZÜRICH

One for all, all for one

ALTHOUGH Switzerland's capital is Berne, a flower-embroidered medieval town of clock towers and bear pits, Zürich is its largest and most important city, commercially and industrially. In any other country of the world—Scandinavia excepted—that designation would automatically imply a place of smog and smoke, grime and grayness, and the depressing pollution of gaseous waste fumes and mill-town slums. But since it is a Swiss city, Zürich, for all its industrialization, is as clear and sparkling as its Alpine lake, as cleanly picturesque as a world-of-tomorrow model village. Its factories operate electrically and are housed in attractive low buildings rimmed with gardens; and workers live in the kind of pretty suburban homes or modern apartments one would expect to find in some pie-in-the-sky utopia— idyllic conditions that are commonplace throughout the 16,000 square miles of Switzerland. They exist because of the country's great wealth and the realization that if the limited number of Swiss workers are to be kept happy and at home, they must share in the profits they help to create, a typical application of the enlightened democratic Swiss viewpoint expressed by their national motto, "One for all, all for one."

The prosperity that makes such a paradise possible is due to several

319

factors, the most important of which is Switzerland's war-free existence for the last 110 years. Although the Swiss back their peaceful hands-off policy with a well-trained citizens' militia (350,000 men can be mobilized in a day; 700,000 in three), and keep their natural mountain barricades fortified against attack, they have been left at peace only because it was convenient for the other nations of Europe to have a neutral zone in wartime. Thus they do not have to support a full-time army; they have not had to rebuild after the devastation of war; and their industries have progressed uninterrupted. No nation ever did more with what it had than Switzerland. Even the mountains, the Alps and Juras, which together take up three-quarters of the total land area, were turned into assets, not only for the hydroelectric power they supply, but as the basis for Switzerland's leading and most profitable industry, tourism.

With typical shrewdness, the Swiss realized the value of their natural and man-made wonders: the snow-capped mountains and crystal lakes; the cuckoo-clock chalets spilling over with window-box gardens; the slopes covered with edelweiss; the Gothic skylines of their antique cities; their art treasures and their good, rich food; and the contrasting regional charms of their French, German, and Italian-bordered cantons. And with typical Swiss diligence, they surrounded these attractions with everything the tourist needed to be comfortable. They built the plushiest sporting and health resorts, created the hotel- and restaurant schools that supply them (and the rest of the world) with meticulously trained staffs, set up well-informed tourist offices everywhere, advertised their charms, and in general rolled out the red carpet as no other country had ever done before—a land where every tourist is a V.I.P and every inn a traveler's dream come true.

This is apparent even in Zürich, a city as important culturally as it is commercially. It has harbored more than its share of creative exiles. It was here that Thomas Mann spent his last years and is buried; here that James Joyce wrote much of *Ulysses,* and where he too did and is buried; here that Richard Wagner worked for sixteen of his most creative years. Lenin and Trotsky plotted the Russian Revolution in the café later frequented by Joyce, the very same place, it is said, where the World War I spy, Mata Hari, once did a strip tease. Albert Einstein studied at the city's Federal Institute of Technology before going to Berne as an examiner in the patent office, where he worked out his theory of relativity in his odd moments; and Zwingli proclaimed the Protestant Reformation in Zürich's Grossmünster cathedral on New Year's Day in 1519. The most famous native son is Carl Jung, whose principles of analytical psychology are studied by students from all parts of the world in the Zürich institute that bears his name.

To sample the city's antique charms, one should start at the Lindenhof, the grassy hilltop with remains of the *castellum* built by Caesar's legions in the first century B.C. By the time the Romans came to Zürich, it was more than three thousand years old, and had been inhabited by Bronze Age lake dwellers and later by Celtic Helvetii tribes, who lived there five centuries before Christ. From the top of the Lindenhof you can look over the squares and ancient rooftops of the Altstadt, where old guild houses painted in faded pastels glow like jade and rose quartz and line the quiet old streets behind the Limmatquai. The city's slimly tapered slate-gray Gothic steeples, its churches and patrician houses, twine around the Limmat. This is a slim blue strip of river, full of colorful sailboats and swans, which opens into the Zürichsee, a sapphire lake ringed by grassy slopes leading upward to the snowy peaks above.

It is along the quais of the Limmat that you can see the twin Romanesque towers of the Grossmünster, a treasury of mellow frescoes and glittering stained glass, the cathedral of Charlemagne who built much of Zürich. Across the street is the Wasserkirche, built in fifteenth century on the spot where the town's patron saints Felix, Regula, and Exuperantius were executed. Opposite stands the stark, needle-slim tower of the Fraumünster, founded in 853 A.D. by Ludwig the German. The cloister of this Gothic-Romanesque church contains modern frescoes depicting events in Zürich's long history. With its magnificent tile stoves, carved doorways, and richly paneled rooms, the Rathaus is a masterpiece of the seventeenth century Italian Renaissance style, and the nearby St. Peter's Church, with its medieval clock tower, is the place from which Lavater, the brilliant divine who was a friend of Goethe, used to preach. Die Schipfe is a group of historic houses set on an old landing quay; the Swiss National Museum, in a Gothic building on the river bank, is full of relics and weapons gathered from all over the country, while the Kunsthaus is an art gallery full of fine European paintings and sculptures. There are a number of wooded parks, the prettiest of which is the Zürichhorn, on an arm of land reaching into the lake. A little way out of town are: the zoo and its miniature railway; the golf courses and resorts of the Dolder Mountain; and a whole ring of observatories on peaks like the Zürichberg, the Rigiblick, and the Sonnenberg, all of which can be reached by cable cars.

The modern life of Zürich mingles with its past. Its tree-lined Fifth Avenue-like shopping street is the Bahnhofstrasse, while the Niederdorfstrasse is straight out of the Middle Ages but has a bright twentieth century night life. In the Weinplatz you can see the house in which Goethe, Hugo, Dumas, Mozart, and Brahms all had lodgings at various times. If you feel like seeing more museums, there is the Rietberg, once the home of Wagner, with a collection of aboriginal artifacts from Africa and Asia, and other museums devoted to matters of the graphic, folk, applied, and ethnic arts.

Beyond this Germanic city of 450,000 lie all of the Alpine magnificence and many of the medieval antiquities for which Switzerland is valued. The old Gothic towns of Schaffhausen and Stein-am-Rhein are about an hour away. One of the most beautiful of the alpine roads, the Sustenpass, is easily reached from the city, as are the Bernese Oberland, leading to Interlaken and Grindelwald, and the Furka Pass to the Rhone Glacier and the Aar Gorge. And Zürich is just a short railroad trip away from Einseideln, the town of the Lourdes-like shrine of the Black Madonna and the birthplace of Paracelsus, the self-styled "monarch of physicians." One can then go on to the medieval walled town of Zug, halfway between Zürich and Lucerene.

LUCERNE

"Time and again it has seemed to me that
I must drop everything and flee to Switzerland . . ."

MARK Twain's longing is probably shared by every one of the half-million Americans who each year, flee to this alpine never-never land, and no place in the entire country gives them more cause for such nostalgia than Lucerne. For this sparkling city of sixty-eight thousand people is really the American dream of Switzerland come true.

Seen from the vantage points of its surrounding lookout peaks, the Dietschiberg, the Sonnenberg, and the Gütsch, it looks like a toy-town village in a Christmas shop window, a miniature play world of rustic covered bridges and tree-lined squares, white houses with red roofs and pink geraniums at every window, and church steeples as Gothic as witches' hats, all neatly laid out in the typical Swiss setting around a lake with a backdrop of towering Alps. Behind the city stands its trademark, the Musegg Türme, a strip of crenelated stone wall with nine sentinel towers—all that remains of the fortifications that encircled the town in medieval times.

Lucerne is no less enchanting at closer range. Set 1,434 feet above sea level in the very center of Switzerland, its sheltered position, its lake and woodlands combine to give it a sunny, clear, and windless climate, as much a delight to the sports enthusiast as it is to the walking-tour sightseer. In winter Lucerne is the gateway to a whole snowy string of ski slopes, less chic and therefore less crowded than the mink-lined-parka resorts such as those of the Bernese Oberland, St. Moritz in the Grisons, or Zermatt, in the Matterhorn region of the Valais. In summer Lucerne's lakeside Lido offers a full range of water sports, tennis courts and golf greens, and at the plush Kursaal-Casino you can swim or sail, ride or dance, try your luck in the game rooms or relax in open-air cafés, take an excursion to such ascents as the Bürgenstock, the Rigi, the towering Pilatus, or the Stanser-horn, among others, attend a concert, a play, or have a folklore evening.

Music lovers will want to join the thousands who flock to Lucerne for its August Music Festival, but if they do, they'd better have made reservations eight or nine months ahead to be on the safe side. Art and museum buffs will have a field day looking at the paintings in the Art Gallery of the Congress Hall, the displays in the Historical Museum, the antique vehicles in the Swiss Institute of Transports, and the handicrafts and artifacts in the very precisely named Museum of Swiss Folk Costumes and Life in the Swiss Homeland. The home of Richard Wagner, on the Tribschen Peninsula, contains many souvenirs of the composer who lived there from 1866 to 1877, and on the Löwenplatz you can see a diorama of Alpine history and military events.

Anyone who likes sightseeing on the antique side will find more than enough to keep him happy here, especially along the banks of the river Reuss, banded by its series of bridges. Of these, the most famous are the Kapellbrücke and the Spreuerbrücke— the Chapel and Mill bridges. Both are timbered and shingle-roofed, both are as fascinating inside as out, and one of the leading tourist pastimes is crossing back and forth over them. The Kapellbrücke, built in 1313, is the older and larger of the two and its rafters are covered with over a hundred sixteenth century paintings depicting the history of the entire Lucerne canton. It cuts a diagonal swathe across the Reuss to the old Chapel of St. Peter, and its octagonal stone water tower, the Wasserturm, once a prison torture chamber, is now a guild meeting hall. The Spreuerbrücke, with its red tower, dates from 1407, and its angled arches contain scenes from the medieval Dance of Death, the *Totentanz*, painted in the seventeenth century. Behind the north quay of the river is the Town Hall, with its Swiss barn roof and arched windows, facing the Kornmarkt. It is on this side of the river, too, that one can wander around such medieval squares as the Weinmarkt and the Muhlenplatz, with their statues and fountains, palatial homes, and guild halls.

Crossing to the south side of the river, one comes to the Hirschen-graben, a triangle of streets enclosing the starkly Gothic Franciscan church built between the thirteenth and fifteenth centuries, and the richly baroque Church of St. Francis Xavier, built between 1667 and 1678.

Certainly one of Lucerne's most impressive sights is the Hofkirche, the cathedral with slender twin towers dating from the sixteenth century, one of the best Renaissance buildings in all of Switzerland. Close to the cathedral is the famous Lion of Lucerne, a stone sculpture by the Dane, Thorvaldsen, carved into a natural grotto to com-memorate the bravery of Swiss soldiers who fought in defense of Marie Antoinette at the Tuileries during the French Revolution. And to show how far back Lucerne's history really goes, walk the short distance from the Lion to the Glacier Garden, with scores of fossils from the Ice Age.

The Lake of Lucerne is called, officially and significantly, the Vierwaldstättersee, the "Sea of the Four Forest States," indicating its role as the birthplace of Switzerland. Around its shores are clustered the original cantons that banded together in 1291 in mutual defense against the Hapsburgs. The three cantons that first joined to make up their "Everlasting League" were Uri, Unterwalden, and Schwyz, and the last of these gave its name to the entire country, which by 1848 consisted of the present twenty-two federated cantons. Each still has its prescribed rights and duties, just as the original three had, and though women may vote in local elections and referendums, they may not vote on the national level.

Lucerne was the fourth canton to join the league, and the other Germanic states where the language is still the dialect known as *Schweizerdeutsch,* became a part of the federation in the sixteenth century. The ring of states bordering France and Italy were designated "associated districts" and "southern bailiwicks," and served as neutral buffer zones around the central Swiss league. Now completely a part of the confederation, the population in these areas still speak their original French or Italian as first languages, though German is required in the schools. The result is, of course, that almost everyone speaks at least two languages fluently, and generally three, and there is still a sprinkling of that uniquely Swiss-Latin tongue, Romansch, spoken by the people who live in the Rhaetian district in the southeastern corner of the country. All languages are official and even the Federal Assembly proceedings are carried on in four simultaneously translated tongues, though *Schweizerdeutsch* is the most pervasive *lingua franca* in the country.

Diverse though Swiss population is, with its Mediterranean Latins in the Italianate Ticino, the gay and urbane French population in the Valais, and the solid, Tyrolean German-Austrian types in the north and east, the real miracle of Switzerland is the homogeneity these various strains have achieved. And though there are relative differences from area to area, they are all overwhelmingly Swiss, almost as though they had consciously set about pooling their talents and discarding their most marked character traits.

The Swiss take the concept of joint and concerted effort so seriously that there are very few national heroes in their history, and even their government is headed by an executive board of seven men, rather than by a single president or premier. But one hero who is very much a part of Switzerland's past is William Tell, the brave archer, half legend, half historical, whose skill with the bow and arrow enabled him to shoot the apple off his son's head and, more importantly, to kill the Austrian bailiff and help break the Hapsburg hold on his country. The settings of his epic exploits lie very close to Lucerne, just across the Vierwaldstättersee, in the fairytale town of Altdorf, the capital of the Uri canton. Every other summer the heroic legend is re-enacted in the William Tell Theater, and in nearby Bürglen, his legendary birthplace, one can see the statue erected to him in the town square and visit the chapel with paintings of his most famous adventures. All of this is a brief hour's run by railroad, or a pleasant three-hour trip on a boat that tacks between the dozens of resort landings around the lake. And from Lucerne one can also visit the other two original cantons: Unterwalden and Schwyz, or travel to any part of the country via the mountain passes that lead out from this central hub.

GENEVA

"Lake Leman woos me with its crystal face. . . ."

CHANCES are Geneva, the capital of its canton and the third largest city in Switzerland, would prove just as seductive to Byron today as it did when he wrote *Childe Harold's Pilgrimage*. For this city of light and water is a gay and sophisticated international metropolis, a place of elegant French buildings and brightly busy sidewalk cafés, fountains, and statues that are floodlit at night, wide promenades and lakeside gardens, flag-flying bridges, and a cosmopolitan array of restaurants, night clubs, and theaters. Its streets are lined with ir- resistible shops that display the wares for which Switzerland is famous. Geneva offers a calendar full of international exhibitions of everything from motorcars to musical performers, horses to watches. Its annual fete is an antique-costumed, flower-decked carnival complete with fireworks and open-air folk dancing.

In addition to its man-made attractions, Geneva boasts a magnificent setting, at the point where the silver-blue crescent of Lake Leman gives way to the vineyard-covered Jura slopes of the Rhone Valley, all in the shadow of the regal, snow-mantled Mont Blanc, the loftiest peak in the Alps. Practically straddling the border between France and Switzerland, Geneva is a French-speaking city of 200,000, with a history that goes back over two thousand years to 58 B.C. and Julius Caesar, who made it the site of an armed camp from which to control Gaul.

The Huguenot, John Calvin, made Geneva the center of his Reformation when he was exiled from his native France in 1536, and it was an episcopal see under the Holy Roman Empire. The International Red Cross was founded in the city in 1820 by the Swiss, Jean Henri Dunant, who selected his native flag in a reverse color scheme as the banner of the new organization. The handsome white buildings of the Palais de Nations in the Ariana Park, built in 1929 as a home for the League of Nations, now houses the European officies of the United Nations. Geneva is also headquarters for the International Labor Office and the World Health Organization, and the scene of innumerable peace conferences. The resultant comings and goings of visitors from every corner of the world adds to the undercurrent of excitement that runs through the city.

Although primarily modern in aspect, Geneva shows its age in its Old Town, one of the most delightful sections of the city. Narrow cobblestoned streets lined with low houses and small shops wind up to the center of this section, the Bourg de Four, with its old inn signs and gabled houses, its chimneypots and shady elms, where lacy acacia trees frame antique shop windows. Art galleries and small cafés add to the Bohemian charm. One of the oldest and most interesting streets leading off the square is the Grand-Rue. Here Jean-Jacques Rousseau was born at No. 40 on June 28, 1712. On the Rue Calvin you can see the house of the French Huguenot reformer at No. 13, and just four doors away the home of Madame de Staël.

The Rue Calvin leads to the Romanesque Cathedral of St. Peter, originally a Catholic church, but Protestant since the Reformation. It was here that John Calvin preached from 1536 to 1564. The interior is as starkly Gothic and devoid of ornamentation as the Reformation itself, though its tower carillon is as splendid as any when it rings out. Across from the cathedral is the Calvin College, a school begun by the reformer and nearby the Hôtel de Ville is the Renaissance style city hall where the Red Cross began. All through the area are statues dedicated to Geneva's local heroes and history. On the Promenade des Bastions there is the Reformation Monument, commemorating the four hundredth anniversary of Calvin's birth and on a three-hundred-foot wall opposite are carved statues of Calvin, Farel, Bèze, and Knox, flanked by bas-relief figures of all the leaders who figured in Protestant movements throughout Europe. The buildings of the Geneva University, also founded by Calvin, stand in a park across the way, and the promenade leads to the elegant Place Neuve with its Grand Theater, a miniature version of the Paris Opéra, and the Musée Rath, where art exhibits are held.

The parliament of the Geneva council meets in the fifteenth century Tour Baudet, once the headquarters of the episcopate. The thirteenth century Gothic tower that stands on the picturesque *île* is the place where Philip Berthelier was beheaded in 1519 for defending the freedom of his fatherland. From here one can stroll around the pretty pocket-size island with its colorful street markets lining the Quai des Moulins.

Geneva's antique sights are limited but nonetheless interesting, and its modern life revolves around the Place de la Fusteries and the Rue du Rhône, not far from the world's highest fountain, and the city's pride, the Jet d'Eau, a soaring stream of rainbow-tinged water that rushes five hundred feet into the air.

Close to the famed Mont Blanc ski resorts of Chamonix and the mountain railway pass through the glacial Mer de Glace, Geneva is within easy excursion distance of the upper Savoy Alps and the cable railway that leads to the lookout station of Salève, 13,450 feet in the clouds. It is also the embarkation point for one of the most delightful lake tours in the country, an idylilc boat trip on the Swiss side of Lake Leman, from Geneva to Lausanne. On the way you stop at the romantic Coppet Castle, the home of the financier, Jacques Necker, whose daughter, Madame de Staël, is buried here. You also pass Nyon, the city founded by Julius Caesar as a rest camp for his soldiers. This is the site of a sixteenth century hilltop castle and a twelfth century Romanesque church. Morges is a quiet sailing harbor and market town with a Gothic castle, a colorful grape harvest festival, and many mementos of Paderewski, who had a large estate in the nearby village of Tolochenaz. This trip through the Vaud canton ends at Lausanne, a city of ex-kings, the dethroned royalty of Europe who have taken up residence here. This pleasant resort with its fine old museum and highly respected university is the fastest growing city in Switzerland and is as beloved by visitors today as it was by Voltaire in the eighteenth century.

Should you choose to continue around the lake, you can see the market wine center of Vevey where Rousseau's heroine, Julie, shed many bitter tears, and Chardonne with a miniature castle and cypress woods. You can end your trip at the famous flowery resort of Montreux with its lakeside Chillon Castle, the prison that inspired Byron's poem, or, should you prefer, you can continue to the south side of the lake and into France.

FOR THE TRAVELER'S NOTEBOOK

Official Information

Before you go: Swiss National Tourist Office, 10 West 44th St., New York, N.Y.; 661 Market St., San Francisco, Cal.

In Zürich: SAS Office, 13 Bahnhofstrasse; Official Tourist Office, 15 Bahnhofplatz; U.S. Consulate General, 35 Talackerstrasse.

In Lucerne: Official Tourist Office, 4 Schweizerhofquai.

In Geneva: SAS Office, 30 Quai General Guisan; Official Tourist Office, 3 Place des Bergues; U.S. Consulate, Hotel du Rhône, 1 Rue du Temple.

Money Matters

Currency: The Swiss franc is the unit of currency, divided into 100 centimes. The franc is equal to about 23 cents, U.S.; there are 4.30 francs to $1.

Tipping: The service charge in hotels is usually 15 per cent for less than three days, 12 per cent for a longer visit. Most restaurants add 10–15 per cent to the check. Taxi drivers, barbers, and hairdressers usually are tipped 10 per cent of the bill or a bit more. Baggage porters get 1 franc for the first bag, 50 centimes for each additional piece. Hotel porters, cloakroom attendants, and bootblacks expect a small tip; ushers in cinemas or theaters are not tipped.

Climate, Clothing, and Essentials

Most of Switzerland's climate is similar to that of the northern United States. Summer temperatures average 65 degrees F., rarely go above 80; winter temperatures average about 33 degrees and there is lots of snow. Spring and autumn are pleasant and require a woolen suit or light topcoat, preferably one that doubles as a raincoat. Normal city attire is correct at all times.

Hotels

It's easy to see why Switzerland is called "a nation of hotel keepers"; no place can boast higher standards of service, cleanliness, and comfort. Reservations are always a good idea. The "Guide to Swiss Hotels," published by the Swiss National Tourist Office, will guide you to hotels in every part of the country. There is little difference in rates in the major cities, though Lucerne seems slightly lower. De luxe hotels charge 30 to 50 francs, single with bath; 55 to 95, double. First class rates range from 20 to 38 francs, single; 36 to 80, double. Inexpensive rooms can be had from 12 to 20 francs, single; 20 to 60, double.

ZÜRICH

DE LUXE: *Dolder Grand Hotel, 15 Kurhausstrasse,* on Dolder Hill, a few minutes from the city center (limousine service provided), is beautifully located, has tennis courts, pool, and a miniature golf course, *Baur au Lac, 1 Talstrasse,* is handsome and fashionable, set on a lake with terrace dining and dinner dancing. *Eden au Lac, 45 Utoquai,* is small, quiet and luxurious, with balconies overlooking the lake and a good restaurant.

FIRST CLASS: *Central, 1 Stampfenbachstrasse,* is close to the station and National Museum. Many rooms have balconies overlooking the river. *Savoy-Baur en Ville, Poststrasse at Paradeplatz,* has large, comfortable rooms and a convenient central location. *The Carlton-Elite, 41 Bahnhofstrasse,* is near the station and recently renovated. *The Bellerive au Lac, 47 Utoquai,* has a sun deck facing the lake. Most rooms have baths and many have balconies. The modern, charming *Storchen, 2 Weinplatz,* on the Limmat River is comfortable and expertly maintained.

SECOND CLASS and MODERATE: The *City,* the *Rothus, 17 Marktgasse,* and the *Biber,* in the old part of the city, are pleasant and comfortable at very modest rates. The *Glockenhof, 31 Sihlstrasse,* and the *Schweizerhof, 7 Bahnhofplatz,* have good service, terrace dining, some private baths, and convenience for shopping. *Hotel Limmathaus, 118 Limmatstrasse,* the most modern of the budget hotels, and the *Limmathof, 142 Limmatquai*, extremely well located, are both comfortable and pleasant.

LUCERNE

DE LUXE: *Grand Hotel National, 4 Haldenstrasse*, is the traditional luxury hotel in the city, the place for visiting dignitaries and celebrities. Balconies face the lakefront and the décor is attractively Victorian. The *Schweizerhof, 3 Schweizerhofquai*, is old and charming, and its antique electric automobile, Aunt Matilda, meets guests at the station. The *Palace, 10 Haldenstrasse*, is on the lakefront, modern and comfortable.

FIRST CLASS: The *Astoria, 29 Pilatusstrasse*, is attractively remodeled and its roof garden affords a lovely view. The *Luzernehof* is modern, with rates moderately first class. The *Carlton-Hotel Tivoli, 57 Haldenstrasse*, is a summer hotel with golf course and funicular, a good choice if you are traveling *en famille*. The *Balances et Bellevue, 7 Metzgerrainle*, on the river bank, is moderately priced and has a good restaurant featuring local specialties. The *Montana, 22 Adligenswilerstrasse*, is a hilltop hotel with lake view and an attractive paneled dining room. *Zum Wilden Mann, 30 Bahnhofstrasse*, is set in the center of the old town, convenient, charming, and an excellent buy.

INEXPENSIVE: *Raben am See* and *Hotel Bernerhof* are two comfortable, modest, and convenient hotels.

GENEVA

DE LUXE: *The Geneva Intercontinental*, opened in 1963, is the ultimate in international-style hotels, 16 stories high, with a view of Mont Blanc, Lake Leman, and everything else you can think of. *Hôtel des Bergues, 33 Quai des Bergues*, is quiet, elegant, and efficient, with old world charm and a lakeside setting. *Hôtel Richemond, Jardin Brunswick*, is friendly, informal, handsomely decorated, with a lake view and modern facilities. *Hôtel du Rhône, Quai Turettini*, has an ultramodern international décor, with a good dining room. The *President*, a huge new lakeside hotel with every pushbutton convenience boasts a miniature shopping center and commercial efficiency. The *De la Paix, 9–11 Quai du Mont-Blanc*, and the *Beau Rivage, 13 Quai du Mont-Blanc*, are two other good luxury hotels near the shopping area and with all facilities.

FIRST CLASS: The *d'Angleterre, 13 Quai du Mont-Blanc*, and the *Du Russie* are close to the shops and the city center, and offer excellent accommodations.

INEXPENSIVE: *The Cornavin, Place Cornavin*, the *Hotel des Familles, 14 Rue de Lausanne*, and the *Rex, 44 Avenue Wendt*, are very good in this price range. On the east side of the lake, the *Victoria* and *La Résidence* are comfortable and pleasant.

Food and Restaurants

Though a number of specialties are exclusively Swiss, all restaurant menus are full of French, Italian, and German dishes, depending on which border you are closest to. The most outstanding products are the superb fresh-water fish, especially trout and perch, cheeses (Gruyère and Emmenthaler, creamy Vacherin, and hard, flavorful Bagnes and Conches), chocolate, a whole array of sausages and preserves, and *bündnerfleisch,* an air-cured meat appetizer. Cheese fondue served in an earthenware dish is perhaps the most famous specialty. *Raclette,* a length of hard cheese melted and scraped onto your plate is another. Still others: *fondue bourguignonne* (bits of beef on skewers which you cook at the table); *leberspiessli,* slices of sage-seasoned liver roasted on a spit; *ratsherrentopf,* a mixed grill; *kügeli-pastete,* a Lucerne special of minced meat and mushrooms baked in pastry; and all the mouth-watering, butter-rich pastries.

Besides *Kirsch,* there are many other kinds of liqueurs, including the popular *Pflümli,* distilled from prunes. Swiss wines, little known abroad, are not bad. For white, try *Johannisberger* or *Dezaley* and for red, the *Dôle.* Swiss beer is good and cheap. For nonalcoholic drinks try *Traubensaft* (unfermented grape juice) and *Süssmost* (apple juice).

ZÜRICH

All the leading hotels have dining rooms and restaurants featuring continental food and excellent service. The *Grill Room* of the *Baur au Lac* is one of Europe's finest. *Töndury's Widder,* a fine restaurant for three centuries, has a beautiful dining room, a pleasant bar with piano music, and superb food. The *Veltliner Keller,* in the Old Town, features authentic Engadine décor and food specialties; the carved wood paneling is one of the most beautiful things in the city. *Franziskaner* is elegant and has a fine continental cuisine. If you like historic surroundings, try some of the restaurants in the old guildhouses, such as the *Rüden* or *Zimmerleuten. Columna zur Treu* is in a house six hundred years old. *Kronenhalle,* hung with original Matisses, Picassos, and Braques, is a favorite with writers and painters. The food is good and moderately priced. *Roten Gatter* is famous for chicken grilled and basted with wine; *Fluhgasse,* a country inn on the edge of the city, for fried chicken and risotto. The *Hugeunin-Zuristube* is a traditional family-style restaurant with excellent French food.

The *Chässtube* will give you anything you want that's made with cheese; *Hong Kong* offers Chinese fare; and *Sprüngli's* is a café serving heavenly pastries and good light lunches and snacks. *Mövenpick,* one of the wildly colorful modern coffeeshop-restaurants, has a branch here. The *Odeon* and the *Select* are two Paris-type cafés. The *Bahnhof Buffet,* second class dining room in the station, offers a good three-course meal for less than a dollar. *Restaurant Weisser Wind* does the same in a quaint Swiss setting. The *Felschlösschen* is a colorful, inexpensive beer garden and outdoor restaurant.

Aklin, with some of Switzerland's most superb but moderately priced cuisine, is in the town of Zug, half an hour from Zurich or Lucerne. It is set in a delightful old inn built in 1700.

LUCERNE

Zum Wilden Mann, opened in 1517, is the city's top restaurant, and *Harry's Restaurant Dubeli,* in an eighteenth century building, was a favorite with Wagner and still is with anyone who knows fine food. *Schwanen,* with a lovely terrace and breathtaking view, is noted for its *haute cuisine* and is understandably expensive. *Lapin* in the De la Paix hotel is famous for grilled sausage-by-the-yard, while the *Old Swiss House* is a quiet, moderately priced favorite of English speaking visitors. *Stadt-und-Rathskeller* is a 300-year-old beer hall full of yodelers, regional costumes, Swiss food, and beer. *Gerberstube* (the *Old Lucerne House*), in a four-teenth century building, is located in the Old Town and offers Swiss décor the gourmet fare; the *Kunsthaus* serves anything from *wurst* to a com-plete meal, inexpensively, on its terrace.

GENEVA

Le Gentilhomme of the Hôtel Richemond is undoubtedly the best and most elegant restaurant in Geneva, while the *Amphitryon* of the Des Bergues and the *Au Neptune* of the Hôtel du Rhône are excellent and elegant too. *La Perle du Lac,* a little way out of town by car or motor launch, in a lakeside park, is heavenly for lunch or dinner on a summer day. *Café du Midi* makes a superb *raclette,* and *Au Chandelier* is known for its *fondue bourguignonne. Rabelais* is a handsome, intimate restaurant featuring very good grills (especially shashlik) at moderate prices. *Au Plat d'Argent* has a pleasant atmosphere in a typical Geneva setting and a long tradition of fine food. *Le Mazot* is picturesque and offers excellent steak, and *l'Or du Rhône* specializes in chicken or beef grilled over an open hearth.

La Mère Royaume is a wonderful old inn and a standard Geneva favorite, and *Le Béarn* is one of the city's leading restaurants famous for its *tournedos* and grilled sausage. *Au Bec Fin* is another fine eating place in the same top class. *Don Quijote* is a wildly theatrical travel-poster-Spanish production with *paella* and entertainment to match. *Mövenpick* automated restaurants reach their peak here.

Entertainment, Night Life, and Special Events

Throughout Switzerland the major Christian holidays are observed, and shops and offices are closed. You can ski on slopes near all three cities, and the number of winter resorts is staggering. Write the Swiss National Tourist Office in New York for a descriptive list, also for the list of festive observances throughout the year. There are many music festivals from June through August and into September.

MEETING THE SWISS: Local tourist offices can arrange for you to meet or stay with a Swiss family; contact members of your profession; tour factories or schools; or discuss almost any activity in Switzerland with an expert.

ZÜRICH

The "Zürich Weekly Bulletin," a small brochure issued by the tourist office, gives up-to-date information on special events. The *Schauspielhaus* (Playhouse) is the leading German-language stage in Switzerland, offering classical modern dramas and comedies. The Kongresshaus is the main concert hall. There is music and dancing at many of the restaurants and hotels. The *Terrasse,* the *Embassy,* the *Bourse* and the *Odeon* offer dancing and floor shows that are only moderately interesting. *Kindli* is a gay restaurant with yodeling done community-sing fashion, and the *Mascotte* has the best dance music.

On a Monday late in April, *Sechseläuten,* an end-of-winter carnival, is celebrated. Old Man Winter is burned in effigy and there is a great pageant of children in historical costumes. *August 1,* national independence day, is celebrated with bonfires, flags, and festivities. *Knabenschiessen,* a shooting contest in which six thousand boys take part, is held in September. In June the music festival offers gala musical and theatrical performances (opera and ballet at the *Stadttheater*) and art exhibitions.

LUCERNE

Two merry beer gardens are the *Floragarteb* and the *Gütsch,* reached by funicular. *Harry's Bar,* the *Kursaal,* the *Palace,* and the *Adler* offer dancing and/or a floor show. Pre-Lenten carnival in February is a time of colorful processions, and the Lucerne International Music Festival is held from mid-August to mid-September.

GENEVA

The concert season runs from September to April with performances in

Victoria Hall. La Comédie is the scene of drama, opera, and ballet, and in summer opera is also performed at the *Grand Casino.* Geneva has its own gambling casino, and about 12 miles away, across the French border, there is the pleasant *Casino de Divonne.* In summer it is pleasant to dine and dance on the Kursaal terrace of the casino or at *Le Gentilhomme* of the Richemond. You have a large choice of cabarets and clubs, and the night life continues until dawn. *Chez Maxim's,* the *Cabaret Ba-Ta-Clan,* the chic *Moulin Rouge,* and *La Cave à Bob,* somewhat Parisian in style, all have floor shows and dancing. Strip tease is the specialty of *Piccadilly,* and a part of most floor shows.

The *International Automobile Salon* is held in March. In June, *Rose Week* brings parades, open-air concerts, ballets, and gala balls. In mid-August, fireworks, flower parades, balls, and open-air dancing celebrate the *Fêtes de Genève.* The *Geneva International Competition for Musical Performances* lasts from mid-September through October.

Shopping

Jewelry and watches are among the best buys. Many watch manufacturers have their own shops in the major cities, but all varieties are available at reliable jewelry stores. Thorens music boxes and phonographs, Alpa cameras, Hermes typewriters, Elna sewing machines, precision equipment, delicate embroideries, lovely handkerchiefs, bed and table linens are of the best quality; and prices are somewhat lower than in the United States. *Kirschwasser,* clocks, leather goods, and children's wear are also good buys. Switzerland is famous for its chocolate, including bon-bons filled with liqueurs. And for the lovers of art there are no more beautiful art books in the world.

ZÜRICH

You can stroll along the Bahnhofstrasse and on the Limmatquai past some of the world's most luxurious window displays. For a typically Swiss souvenir, visit *Schweizer Heimatwerk* (Swiss Folk Handcrafts). *Bachman* and *Monsted Polyfoto* are only two of the very reliable camera shops. There are enticing candy shops along the Bahnhofstrasse and Bahnhofplatz, and you will find jewelry and watches here too. *Jelmoli, Globus,* and *Oscar Weber* are the leading department stores.

LUCERNE

The best shops in the city are to be found along Pilatusstrasse, Haldenstrasse, Kapellgasse, and Weggisgasse. The leading department stores are *Nordmann's,* with a wide selection of gift items, and *Grieder et Cie.,* with good fabrics and men's clothing. *Innerschweizer Heimatwerk* has lovely handcrafts and gifts.

GENEVA

There are several good department stores: *Grand Passage, Bonne Génie, Samaritaine, Epis d'Or, Comptoir Tissus,* and *Kohler et Cie. Chalet Suisse* and *A l'Ours de Berne* have a wide array of souvenirs, gifts, and handcrafts. The best chocolate can be bought at *Mercure, Villars,* or *Chocolat du Rhône.*

Background Reading

Switzerland, A Democratic Way of Life, by André Siegfried
Switzerland, by Martin Hürlimann (photographs and text)
Swiss Enchantment, by Monk Gibbon
A Short History of Switzerland, by Bonjour, Offler, and Potter

Turkey

ISTANBUL

> "If one had but a single glance to give the world, one should gaze at Istanbul."
>
> —LAMARTINE

THE patina of history is everywhere in Istanbul and a gossamer haze seems to veil the city in the golden light of glories long past. Istanbul is old, and it looks it. It shows its age in the winding gray cobblestoned streets, so steeply terraced that the sidewalks are built in steps, in its antique buildings that have acquired the peeling, rusted, polychromed richness of texture that artists refer to as "quality," and in the wistful, dark eyes of the Turks. You see it too, in the deserted kiosks and kitchens of the Topkapi Seraglio, or in the sunlit silence of the Dolmabahçe Palace, the last vestige of sultanic splendor in this, the City of the Sultans.

Istanbul was Constantinople and Byzantium; Asia Minor's European touchstone and the seat of the Ottoman Empire and its Sublime Porte; the city of Suleiman the Magnificent and his dazzling Circassian odalisque, Roxelana. It evokes images of turbaned sultans and their harem wives in gauzy, blousy pajamas, lolling on cushioned divans in rooms all a-shimmer with turquoise tile; of tulip gardens and sherbet and delicate gold-leafed pastilles; of plotting janissaries, impassive black eunuchs, intriguing grand viziers, and daring seraglio abductions; of hubble-bubble water pipes, Turkish delight, and the

337

steamy sensual world of the marbled baths, the *hamams;* of brightly painted high-prowed caïques gliding along the Bosphorus from the Sea of Marmara and the Golden Horn to the Sweet Waters of Asia and the ports of the Black Sea; a hashish dream of a city with an Ali Baba skyline of golden minarets and domes, hanging like bracelet charms, suspended in the blue bubble of water, air, and sky that blend here as they do nowhere else on earth.

This was the exotic, sybaritic Oriental world that captivated Lady Mary Wortley Montagu and Lamartine, and inspired verses by Byron, novels by Loti, and paintings of darkly fair odalisques by Ingres. And as late as the Gay Nineties, no fashionable home in America was complete without its Turkish Cozy Corner. This alcove was draped, swagged, and tasseled with lengths and loopings of Oriental paisleys, brocades, and satin-stripes, with fringed ottomans and carpet-covered divans piled high with embroidered pillows. Pinpoints of light strained through the pierced brass lampshades, and the setting was not complete without at least one pearl-inlaid wooden table and a glass nargileh or two.

With its two million inhabitants, Istanbul is the largest city in the world to be divided between two continents—its head in Europe, its feet across the Bosphorus in Asia. East and West have always played a cultural and philosophical tug-of-war with it, and with the rest of Turkey as well. The resulting contradictions and incongruities can be seen everywhere. The Turks are Moslems but not Semites, and the Turkish they speak is more closely related to Finnish and Hungarian than it is to Arabic. Their flag is marked with the star and crescent of Islam, but they belong to NATO, not to the Arab League, and the fact of Israel has never been a thorn in their side. They are no longer Eastern but not yet Western, and though they have been wearing European clothes for almost three generations, one cannot help thinking that their powerfully dark, thickset beauty deserves the more dramatic costumes they abandoned. And though five times a day, muezzins call the faithful to face Mecca in prayer, men no longer wear the fez, nor do women veil their faces in observance of purdah, both religious symbols having been banned by Atatürk during his "Westernization" program in the 1920's. Polygamy was outlawed too, as were the activities of the Whirling Dervishes, though members of this Moslem sect are permitted to twirl themselves into trances once a year in December, at a festival outside of Konya.

Set midway between Russia and Egypt, the Turks drink as much scalding, smoky black tea served from samovars as they do the thickly sweet coffee that is poured from brass beakers.

They have a Mediterranean warmth, along with flashes of the Oriental ferocity that made the word "Turk" a synonym for "wildness" and "strength" when their armies were the scourge of Europe. Yet they have a generosity of spirit that will cause a flower vendor to hand you a huge bouquet as a gift simply because you took his picture, or a restaurant owner to refuse you a check because you liked his food. They have never had that particular talent for commercial matters which distinguishes the Levantines. Even in the days of Suleiman's Pax Turca, the banking and business affairs of the country were in the hands of conquered Greeks and the Jews who fled the Spanish Inquisition, and the country's trade and shipping were managed by the Venetians and Genoese.

There is more of the West than the East in the section of Istanbul known as Pera or Beyoglu, with its concentration of hotels and airline offices, one-price shops and continental restaurants, the night clubs and night lights around the main square, Taksim. But cross the bustling, traffic-filled Galata Bridge that spans the Golden Horn, and you enter the seductive and alluring Old Stamboul, with its mosques and minarets, its museums and markets, and its effervescent Oriental street life.

Here you see water vendors with gaily decorated gazebo-shaped tanks slung over their backs and shoeshine boys whose huge boxes glitter with brass domes and nailheads and painted landscapes, more like religious icons or hand organs than containers for waxes and polishes. There are casual street cafés and a tumult of bookstalls around the university. In the Balik Bazaar or the fish market, you will see giant sturgeons wearing bright blue ceramic beads to ward off the evil eye, and smaller fish with their gills turned back like blood-red rosettes so that shoppers can judge their freshness. In the flower market, peasant women wrapped in cloaks and head shawls of black-brown wool arrange their bulbs and plants in artful patterns, and in the *souks* of the coppersmiths you hear the constant hammertop as polished sheets of copper are turned into trays and bowls, pitchers and plaques. Walk through the spice market, with its pyramids of dried beans and rice, garlands of spicy sausages and slabs of pepper-cured meat, *pasturma,* all side by side with plastic hair curlers, fluoridated toothpaste, and sleazy rayon underwear, and then you are in an outdoor market place full of brightly painted metal trunks.

But of all the city's markets, none is more intriguing than the Grand Bazaar, virtually a covered city of *souks* and shops, streets and squares, cafés and yogurt kiosks. In the section devoted to antiques (or reasonable facsimiles thereof) you can buy old Victorian jewelry set with rose diamonds or superb copies, huge polished brass *tandoor* stoves that can heat an entire room, ornate little boxes of silvery-brown zinc and copper in which women carried soap to the *hamams,* and the painted leather puppets of Karagösz which one sees throughout the Moslem world from Samarkand to the Timor Sea. In one section you may buy intricately patterned red, blue, and yellow Turkish carpets, in another Turkish towels. One street is decked out with Persian miniatures and Greek icons (or excellent copies of either), while dozens of shops everywhere display creamy-white meerschaum pipes and necklaces, brocade harem slippers with toes turned up like the prows of Venetian gondolas, and silver brooches set with turquoises, the stones that derive their name from this country where they are considered a symbol of good fortune.

Not far from the Bazaar is the enticing candy shop of Haci Bekir, its windows piled high with trays of Turkish delight jeweled with pistachios and bits of citron, and giant travertine-like slabs of *halvah,* that seductive Turkish confection that is at its best on home ground. And across from here lies what may well be the most fascinating and unusual experience in all Istanbul—the Hamam, a public steam bath open to women all day and to men after five in the evening. Here you walk down a few steps and enter a stony, steamy, sulphur-scented dressing room where towels and cloths are hung out to dry. Once undressed, you are led into a huge room, thick with steam, and gradually you are aware of that fact that it is filled with about one hundred naked women stretched out on an enormous marble platform, all being scrubbed and soaped by naked attendants who look like lady wrestlers, and as the marble beneath you gets slippery with suds, you slide around bumping into the other bathers. Just off this central room are small alcoves in which one can steam some more, have a shampoo, or be covered from head to foot with what looks like mud but is really a depilatory, and accounts for the sulphur smell that hangs in the thick steamy air—all of this for as long as you like and for the equivalent of thirty-five cents in American money.

One can piece together almost all of Turkey's past by visiting the antique relics that are here in Stamboul, the original section of the city, built on seven hills. For fifteen centuries this was the hub of two of the world's greatest empires: the Christian Byzantine and the Moslem Ottoman. In its sixteenth century heyday under Suleiman, it stretched from the Persian Gulf to the gates of Vienna, from Warsaw to Cairo, and, with its fleets under the command of Barbarossa, it controlled the Mediterranean. The empire survived in this form until the end of World War I. Nothing remains here of the first Byzantium, the small settlement name after the Megarian general, Byzas, who ruled it in the seventh century B.C., but when Constantine christened it Constantinople and proclaimed it the seat of his Holy Roman Empire on May 11, 330 A.D., he and the Romans who followed him built some of the sights that can still be seen today. There is the column of nine cylindrical blocks of porphyry which Constantine brought from Rome so that, perhaps, he would feel more at home in his new capital, and the weird Yerebatan Sarayi, the Sunken Palace, that was an underground water cistern built by Justinian 1,400 years ago. Take a rowboat through this shadowy, damp cavern with its 336 magnificent columns still intact, and you'll feel as though you are in a flooded and grandiose subway, or an eerie unwordly setting for an Orson Welles thriller. There's evidence of the old Roman hands, too, in the crumbling remains of the old city walls, in the shadow of which gypsies live in ramshackle tin-and-rag huts; in the fragments of the Aqueduct of Valens; and in the Hippodrome of the Emperors, the scene of chariot races and bloody man-against-animal circuses for which the Romans were famous. There is the old Mosaic Museum, its floor tiles seemingly pale and faded until the guard obligingly wets them down with a sponge to revive the brilliant depth of color in the fruits, flowers, and hunting scenes, and the glittering Byzantine gold mosaics in the exquisitely restored Kaariye Camii, with its soulful Virgin Mary in the nave and elongated figures of the prophets lining the fluted domes.

Most spectacularly, of course, there is St. Sophia, the first great eastern Christian church, which later became a Moslem mosque and was declared a museum by Atatürk in 1935. This is actually the third church to be built on this site, and undoubtedly the greatest of them all, built by the architects of the Emperor Justinian in the sixth century, after earlier churches built by Constantine and Theodosius were destroyed. A radical departure in architecture which was to inspire all of the Eastern Orthodox churches from Venice to Kiev, this church also served as the model for Moslem mosques. Although the church is impressive from the outside for its size and mass, its interior is its most astounding feature. From the inside, the building with its enormous circular dome, 107 feet in diameter and rimmed with a ring of smaller domes, seems to bubble skyward and float away in unlimited space, above the heavy carved capitals of its magnificent marble columns, four of which came from Baalbek's Sun Temple in Lebanon. Although its breathtakingly beautiful mosaics were hidden with paint and plaster in the nineteenth century when the Hagia Sophia was a mosque, their covering is now being chipped and peeled away in a somewhat fragmentary, painstakingly slow way, to reveal again the sad, elliptical-eyed saints, the heads of queens and emperors, prophets and angels in all of their glittering, golden brilliance.

Its strategic location made Constantinople a prize worth fighting for and the strength of the Byzantine emperors was exhausted after Justinian, though real defeat did not come until the thirteenth century and the Fourth Crusade, under Dandolo, the Venetian doge of whom Byron wrote in *Childe Harold's Pilgrimage,* "Oh for one hour of blind old Dandolo/The octogenarian chief, Byzantium's conquering foe!" And a conquering foe he was, whose troops sacked and pillaged and burned the city of Constantine, which then lapsed into more than two centuries of oblivion, until the fifteenth century and the victory of the European Ottoman Turks of Bayazit and Osman over the Asian Seljuks, after the death of their leader, Tamerlane.

One of the first things Sultan Mohammed II did in 1453 to defend his newly won Constantinople was to build the castle fortress, Rumeli Hisari. This stands on the European side of the Bosphorus near what is now the resort suburb of Tarabya, one of the Turks' favorite spots to sit at twilight, sipping glasses of water, which they savor as the French do wine. Mohammed built the castle as a companion to the fortress of his father, just opposite in Asian Turkey, and the two crenelated towers stand like tiny sentinels watching over the ships that sail the narrow, winding turn from the Sea of Marmara to the Black Sea and back again. One of the earliest mosques built by the new sultan was the Bayazit, named in honor of the Osmanli leader who unsuccessfully fought Tamerlane. It is an enormous pile of hilly domes and curves, built between 1501 and 1505, the first mosque in the Turkish styles.

The sixteenth century mosque, the Suleymaniye, built by the most famous of sultans, Suleiman, is the largest in the city, and is a masterpiece of design executed by Sinan, the great Turkish architect of the time. It is set in a lovely cypress grove that rolls down to the water's edge.

The mosque that comes as the most dazzling surprise, after hearing so much about the wonders of the three already mentioned, is the Sultan Ahmed, built in the early seventeenth century, and more popularly known as the Blue Mosque. Its exterior is distinguished by six slender minarets, and it is the only mosque in the world with that number. Its greatest beauty is its interior, a world of blue tiles, covering the walls in arabesques from floor to ceiling and giving the vast room an almost iridescent underwater shimmer that seems to reflect the blue of sky and sea outside.

There are museums in Old Stamboul too, one devoted to Turkish and Islamic art with collections of Seljuk miniatures, manuscripts, gold Korans, and carpets, while another, the Fatih, displays mementos of Sultan Mohammed, and the Municipal Museum has cases full of souvenirs of Istanbul's past. There is the Oriental Museum, with relics of the Hittites and Assyrians, the Archeological Museum with, among other treasures, the sarcophagus of Alexander the Great. But beyond a doubt the most romantic museum and the most intriguing sight in all of Istanbul is the Topkapi Palace, the one and only Seraglio of the sultans from the fifteenth to the nineteenth century. As you walk through the gray stone courtyards and drab, neglected passageways, look over the tulip garden to the Bosphorus, and wander around the empty, abandoned Divan and the prettily proportioned, glassed-in Baghdad Kiosk, it is hard to imagine that this was the pivotal point for one of the largest empires in the world. It was an opulent and luxurious life that has never been equaled, an adolescent dream of sex and sensuality come true, with harems full of beautiful women sold or kidnapped as gifts for its rulers—a man's world run by women and slaves.

Walk through the Carriage Museum, the Porcelain Museum, and the rooms full of crudely hacked jewels that seem more barbarically splendid than the polished and refined Western European counterparts. And by all means see the huge funnel-chimneyed Eunuchs'

Kitchens—ten double kitchens, with cauldron-like copper vessels that were re-silvered every day, where the *hatchi-batchi,* or head chef, supervised 300 cooks and confectioners. They prepared a daily ration of 200 sheep, 100 lambs, 100 goats, 14 calves (for the eunuchs who preferred veal), 30 pairs of geese, and 100 pairs each of guinea hens, pigeons, and chickens. Each year the chefs turned 30,000 bushels of rice into pilaff, and spent $20,000 for snow from Mount Olympus, which was carried down in camel caravans and stored in pits to be turned into sherbet. (The royal favorites were those flavored with lemon, water lilies, or violets.) All this to feed a household of 800, in the time of Suleiman, to 2,000 in the reign of Mohammed IV.

One might think that everything in Istanbul pales beside the allure of the Topkapi Museum, but that is not quite true. The Eyup Mosque, reached by boat from Galata Point, has its pretty little courtyard where pigeons are fed by the faithful, and salesmen display their sacred Korans, prayer beads, perfumes, and framed holy verses. This is one of the city's most delightful sights, and from the Pierre Loti café beyond the mosque one has an unparalleled view of the Golden Horn, with the terraced buildings that seem to be rolled out flat against the sky like a huge strip of wallpaper.

Back across the Galata Bridge with its fishermen's wharves and ferries is the the Naval Museum, with souvenirs of all the Turkish fleets of history including that of Barbarossa, who would have his men draw their galleons across land if a vital waterway passage was blocked to them. Not far away is the Dolmabahçe Palace, the nineteenth century, very European seraglio built by the Sultan Abdülmecid in 1853. This is a place of polished parquet floors and crystal chandeliers, Italian marble and French brocades, but still with its pink alabaster steam baths and pierced marble screens through which the haremwives would watch the state banquets and dances in the huge ballroom below. It was in this palace that Kemal Atatürk, the father of the new Turkey, died in 1938. And from Galata Bridge you may take a boat to the white-sanded beach resorts of Princes Islands or Kadikoy, or visit Usküdar, the Scutari where Florence Nightingale had her hospital, and where there is now a cypress-shaded cemetery dedicated to the Crimean War casualties.

There is more to Turkey than Istanbul, of course. There is the new capital of Atatürk, Ankara, a city bright, white, modern, but some two thousand years old, a Hittite town, invaded by all the armies that ever came to Turkey, and the place about which Caesar issued his famed report, "I came, I saw, I conquered." Relics of its entire past exist here, from the antiquities in the Hittite Museum to the ruins of the citadel of the Galatians, the second century Temple of Augustus, the Column of Julian, and remains of old Roman baths. There is the sixteenth century Yeni Cami, a mosque designed by Sinan, and Aladdin's Mosque, for this is the city of the "magic lamp." Ankara's more modern sights include the museum, mausoleum and house of Atatürk, and a number of government buildings. A few miles from the city are the most ancient ruins, recent excavations of Hattusas, the Hittite capital, and Gordium, where Alexander cut the fabled knot.

Also in the crusty, hilly plains of Anatolia are such famous places as Kayseri, built on the ancient site of Caesarea, and the secret shrines of the Valley of Gorëme, where Christians hid in exile in weird chimney-shaped conical rock dwellings and where they first called themselves "Christians," and there is Konya, the ancient Iconium, with its relics of the Seljuk Turks and the reminders of the famous religious order that started here, the Mevlevi Whirling Dervishes.

Close to Istanbul, but still in Anatolia, is Bursa, the green-wooded mountain spa whose mineral waters treated the Empress Theodora and whose Green Mosque, covered bazaars, and elaborate old steam baths are among the country's loveliest sights. From here one can travel the route of Homer's *Iliad* to Canakkale, on the Dardanelles, twenty miles from ancient Troy, and its Roman theater and Trojan ruins, or go a little further to Izmir, the pretty seaside garden better known as Smyrna, from which the world's softest, richest figs, are exported.

There is Ephesus, with its dozens of Roman ruins and its church built on the site where the Virgin Mary lived out her life, and Adana, where Hadrian's arched bridge and Haroun-al-Rashid's castle still stand. Visit such Black Sea resorts as Sinop, the birthplace of Diogenes, and Trabzon, the Trebizond of which Rose Macaulay wrote. Turkey's Mediterranean shores boast a wealth of Greco-Roman ruins and the picturesque resort city, Antalya, from which it is a short drive to the villages in which St. Paul first preached and where the Bishop of Myra, better known as St. Nicholas, was born. Or you may travel west across European Turkey to Edirne on the Bulgarian border, a city founded by Hadrian and noted for the magnificent Selim Mosque, another masterpiece of Sinan, or fly east over the Asian Seljuk Turkey to Mount Ararat and join the search for fragments of Noah's Ark.

FOR THE TRAVELER'S NOTEBOOK

Official Information

Before you go: Turkish Information Office, 500 Fifth Ave., New York, N.Y.

In Istanbul: SAS Office, Cumhuriyet Caddesi, Altinbakkal, Beyoğlu; Turkish Tourist Office, 120/3 Istiklal Caddesi & Hilton Hotel Arcade, Beyoglu; U.S. Consulate, Mesrutiyet Caddesi.

Money Matters

Currency: The monetary unit is the Turkish lira (£T), divided into 100 kurus. £T 9 equals $1, U.S.

Tipping: The continental system prevails. In hotels and restaurants 15 per cent is added to your bill as service. It is usual to tip waiters another 10 per cent. Chambermaids may be tipped £T 1 or 2 a day. The hotel doorman is usually tipped 50 or 100 kurus for getting a taxi. Bellboys should get £T 2.50 to 5. It is customary to tip guides and drivers of hired cars about £T 10, depending on length of the service, while taxi drivers get 5 to 15 per cent of metered fare.

Climate, Clothing and Essentials

Istanbul enjoys an ideal climate in spring, summer, and autumn, with long periods of warm, dry weather, cool evenings, and only occasional rain. In July and August the average temperature is 72 degrees F. Coldest and rainiest are February and March, with an average temperature of 40 degrees, so dress accordingly. A raincoat will be useful at all times of year. If you are going to Ankara, note that summer there is warmer and winter colder. Normal city attire is correct in both places.

It is best to take all of the drugs, toiletries, and film you expect to need as these are not readily available here.

Hotels

Though Istanbul's top hotels are on a par with European counterparts, second and third class hotels are definitely not up to our standards, so don't economize here unless you absolutely have to. A complete list of Turkish hotels with government ratings, charges, and facilities is available

from the Turkish Information Office. In the de luxe class rates run from
£T 65 to 140, doubles £T 120 to 160. First class rates range from £T
40 to 50, single, from £T 60 to 80, double. Moderate-priced hotels listed
charge £T 20 to 30, single, £T 30 to 50, double. Most single rooms in
this category have no private bath, but doubles generally do.

DE LUXE: The *Istanbul Hilton,* just off Cumhuriyet Caddesi is beautifully designed, just a few steps from the main thoroughfare, new, lush,
and with a swimming pool; room service is slower than it should be. The
Divan, Cumhuriyet Caddesi, is also near Taksim Square, has a good dining room, and is smaller and more European than the Hilton. The *Cinar,*
Yesilkoy, is near the airport, on a hill with a view over the Sea of Marmara, with private beach and resort facilities.

FIRST CLASS: Also in the area of Taksim Square are the *Park Oteli,*
Ayazpasa, and the *Pera Palace, Mesrutiyet Caddesi.* All rooms in these
hotels have baths.

MODERATE: An economical but adequate hotel is the *Ipek Palace* in
the heart of the old city.

Food and Restaurants

The leading hotels have dining rooms offering a full range of continental
cuisine. Turkish food is superb and unusual. Try pilaff, rice cooked with
currants, pine nuts, and aromatic spices, usually served with chicken or
lamb; *kilic,* chunks of swordfish grilled on skewers; *midye dolmasi,* mussels stuffed with pilaff; all sorts of stuffed vegetable *dolmas;* and a rich
egg-lemon soup. *Donner kebab,* a particular specialty of lamb barbecued
on a huge vertical spit, can be had in restaurants and *kebabçis,* eating
places featuring only this dish, all over the city. The panoply of appetizers
called *mézé* here includes a variety of sausages and salads, many with eggplant, olives, *feta* cheese, fried mussels, and a very special one, chicken
Circassian—cold breast of chicken with a pink walnut sauce. Some food
shops cook "chicken only" in dozens of ways, with a dessert, *Tavuk-
Gogsu,* prepared with milk and sugar. Turks love little cups of syrupy
sweet coffee, and the tea, from samovars, is excellent.

Raki (arrack) is a national drink, a white anise-flavored liqueur served
with ice and water. Turkish beer and wines are good and the local versions
of the usual alcoholic beverages are passable. Turkish sweets are on the
flaky honey-nut variety, such as *baklava,* and the *halvah* and Turkish
delight at *Haci Bekir's* shop are the best in the world.

Few restaurants are as elegant as comparable establishments in other
European countries, and prices for very good food are moderate. *Abdullah's* serves superb food and the *kebab* with yogurt is heavenly. The upstairs dining room has a pleasantly quiet dinnertime atmosphere. *Liman*

Lokantasi is the most elegant restaurant in town, an expensive lunch-only place in the customs house overlooking the harbor and serving excellent continental and Turkish food. *Pandeli's* is an enchanting, small, tiled restaurant over the spice market; the mixed grills, wedding soup, and sweets are superb. Luncheon only, and inexpensive. *Ekrem Yegen* runs a cooking school as well as the restaurant; his Circassian chicken and *water boereck*—a concoction of noodles with sauce of *feta* cheese, eggs, and dill—are fantastically good. *Konya Lezzet* is a bustling luncheon place with excellent *donner kebab*. About twenty minutes out of the city one can dine in the very elegant, expensive, and continental *Bogazici* at the water's edge in Yenikoy, or lunch at *Fidan* in Terabja, a little café-restaurant near the water, very native, inexpensive, and with the best *mézé* in the city. For European food, light snacks, and American breakfasts, your best bet is the large hotels. Hungarian fare can be had at the *Czardas* and Italian food at *Degustation*.

Entertainment, Night Life, and Special Events

Be sure to get a copy of "This Week in Istanbul" at your hotel. Excellent theaters offer dramas ranging from Shakespeare to Sherwood, in Turkish. A highlight of the music season (October to May) is the annual visit of the State Opera Company of Ankara in the spring. The Philharmonic Orchestra gives concerts several times a week. See the Karagöz shadow puppets if you can.

For dinner, dancing, and floor shows, *Kervansaray*, the *Club 12*, *Cordon Bleu*, *Taksim Casoino*, the *Hilton*, the *Regat, Wagon Bleu, Moulin Rouge, Klob-X*, and *Cat 1* rank among the best. Outside the city, places like *Çinar, Bogazici, Lido*, and *Babek Casino* are lovely in summer. Night clubs are usually open late, often from about 10:30 to dawn. Should you like to see clubs with real local atmosphere, go to *Tepebasi* or *Casablanca* casinos.

Children's Day is celebrated April 23 with music and street dancing. *Youth and Sports Day* on May 19 is a time of athletic displays. In June and August, fairs, folk dances, and the Karagöz shadow puppet shows celebrate the spring and flower festivals. On *Navy Day,* July 1, see regattas in all the major ports of Turkey. *Republic Day,* October 29, and *Victory Day,* August 30, are celebrated with military parades. Around mid-December (check the date ahead) there is a week-long *Festival of Mevlevi* at Konya, home of the Whirling Dervishes. The *National Folk Dance Festival* is held in June and July in an open-air theater.

Shopping

The main shopping district is the Beyoğlu area, especially Istiklal Caddesi. There are attractive, expensive shops in the lobby of the Hilton. But anyone who truly loves to shop will enjoy most the Grand Bazaar (see p. 340).

Background Reading

Constantinople, by Pierre Loti
Byzantium and Istanbul, by Robert Liddell
Turkey, by Lord Kinross
Suleiman the Magnificent, and *Constantinople, Birth of an Empire,* by Harold Lamb
The Towers of Trebizond, by Rose Macaulay
Riding to the Tigris, by Freya Stark
Anyone interested in the harems of the Ottoman sultans should read either *The Harem,* by N. M. Penzer, or *Beyond the Sublime Porte,* by Barnett Miller.

Eastern Europe

and

the USSR

SPECIAL TRAVEL NOTES FOR EASTERN EUROPE AND THE USSR

Since travel arrangements for Czechoslovakia, Hungary, Poland, and the USSR cannot be made directly, you will have to rely on your travel agent when planning a visit to these countries. All arrangements must be prepaid on a varying scale.

The charges for de luxe accommodations in the Soviet Union are $35 per day, single, $50, double, from May to September. Off-season rates prevailing for the rest of the year are $30, single, $42.50, double. These prices include hotel rooms, meal coupons, sightseeing tours, and interpreter guides. You pay extra for transportation between cities, nighttime entertainments, for any meals you eat at non-Intourist restaurants and, naturally, for anything you buy. Less expensive arrangements are available for group tours. Hotels are assigned to you by Intourist on arrival, and you may not specify which you prefer.

Prices for the eastern European countries average about $13 a day for de luxe accommodations; $9 for first class; $7 for second class. Rates are slightly lower per person when rooms are shared. The per diem rate includes hotel and three meals only. Sightseeing is arranged for separately at each hotel's service bureau. One receives local currency on arrival for the prepaid dollars and the money can be used anywhere. You may book second class accommodations, eat at first class restaurants and buy more currency when you need it. Packaged tour rates are considerably lower than the above, and include sightseeing buses and transfers from terminals to hotels.

Since facilities in these countries are limited at best, it is suggested that you book the best accommodations you can possibly afford, especially when traveling outside of the major cities.

Czechoslovakia

PRAGUE

"Good King Wenceslas looked out . . ."

GOETHE was not alone in his admiration for Prague (Praha) when he dubbed it "the most beautiful jewel in the stone crown of the world." To Rodin, this city on five hills, with its magnificence of stone architecture, was "the Rome of the North," and the German historian Ranke, visiting the city in 1827, wrote, "But Prague is glorious! I have never seen such a city." This "Golden City of a Hundred Spires" is as beautiful as it ever was, with its towers and belfries silhouetted against the deep green forest hills, and its wide blue band of the Vltava River, Smetana's Moldau, spanned by eleven bridges, the oldest of which, the Charles, dates from 1357. Built during the reign of the Czechoslovakian Holy Roman emperor, Charles IV, and designed by his outstanding stonemason, Peter Parler of Gmünd, this is said to be the first stone bridge ever constructed, a Gothic landmark of sentinel towers and wide pointed arches, with a balustrade of eighteenth century statuary marching across both sides.

Prague is an old and mellow city, somber and reserved, dressed in a velvety palette of gray and gold, a city that has aged as gracefully as a beautiful woman. There is nothing trivial, nothing frivolous about it, and the adjective "gay," generally used to describe the capitals of *Mittel-Europa,* is not quite right here. Rather, Prague is substantial, solid, prosperous, secure, settled. Its men are burly and square, its women buxom and low-slung, their clothing sturdy and dark, the heels of their shoes low and wide. They are the epitome of bourgeois practicality, and nothing is more typical of them than their no-nonsense diet of pork and sauerkraut, roast goose and dumplings, with the final satisfaction coming by way of a foaming half-pint tankard of their golden Pilsner beer. With their capital set in the mathematical center of Europe, and with the conflicting interests of Germany, Poland, Russia, and Austro-Hungary impinging on their country's borders and playing a tug of war with them for eight centuries, the Czechs have an innate sense of compromise, a healthy respect for the political art of the possible, the trick of survival through the middle way.

Reluctant to discuss politics, but anxious to talk to Western visitors, slow to invite you home but quick to inquire after your comfort and well-being with an air of true concern, their native instinct for hospitality has been tempered by the facts of their political life. As one might expect in the city of Dvorak and Smetana, and the place in which Mozart lived for a while and wrote *Don Giovanni,* music is their great cultural love, and the performances in their concert halls are second to none. They have retained the ability to laugh at themselves and make jokes at the expense of their own Dutch uncle practicality, much in the manner of their fictional hero, the bumbling, bungling Good Soldier Schweik, the creation of Jaroslav Hašek, and their classic, antic puppets, Špejbl and Hurvínek. Their passion for good living and culture is obvious, not only in the abundance of theaters and bookshops, music halls and opera houses, but in the many cafeterias and cafés studded around the city, in which one can see solid housewives and shop workers relaxing over cups of steaming mocha coffee and plates piled high with meltingly rich cream and chocolate pastries. In such antique establishments as the brewhouse-restaurant U Fleků, which opened its doors seven years after Columbus discovered America, apple-cheeked Bohemian waitresses labor under their trays of beer schooners, to be served along with fat peppery sausages, wedges of tangy sheep's-milk cheese from the Tatra Mountains, and crusty sour-rye rolls.

Prague owes its quality to its architecture: an almost half-and-half combination of austere medieval Romanesque Gothic, dating from 900 to 1500 A.D., and the romantically expansive, Italianate baroque Renaissance that flourished here under Hapsburg rule from the sixteenth to the nineteenth centuries. Both styles vie with each other in the old town, crammed side by side along cobble-stoned streets of arcaded buildings and medieval courtyards, tunnels that cut under old stone houses hung with carved wooden tradesmen's signs, and Gothic back alleys between flamboyant buildings with baroque belfries and rococo cupolas. The old square of this quarter, the Staromestké námĕsti, is ringed with relics of Czech history. The Town Hall with its tower clock—the five-hundred-year-old Oroloj—that comes alive with the figures of the twelve apostles each time it strikes the hour, is a fourteenth century building that has been added to for five centuries. It was a seat of the Hussite councils, followers of the fifteenth century Bohemian religious reformer, Jan Huss, who was judged a heretic and burned alive in 1415, leaving behind him a separate Protestant church sect which still exists.

In this square too is a monumental statue to Huss, as well as the handsome Gothic Tyne Church which was the main church of the Hussites. Nearby is the little house with its delicate baroque wrought-iron railings, called the "White Horse," in which Smetana ran a music school; and the majestic curved façade of the eighteenth century baroque Church of St. Nicholas. This whole section is a Chinese puzzle of Medieval squares edged with baroque buildings, with here and there a glimpse of the river and the stone tower of the Charles Bridge. There is the little court of Ungelt, where in the tenth century merchants cleared their East-West imports through the custom-houses, a reminder of Prague's role as the leading crossroads point for merchants trading between the Orient and Central Europe. Here too is the Powder Tower, the fifteenth century defensive lookout that guarded the entrance to the old town which was used in the seventeenth century as a powder magazine—hence its name. From here one can follow the line of the old ramparts that surrounded the original Prague city center, marked off now only by the line of crumbling towers.

Close by lies the Old Ghetto, the Jewish quarter which dates from the ninth century and which in the seventh century was the leading Hebrew nucleus of all Europe. Also called the Josefov, it is an almost forgotten, quietly deserted area with a little arts and crafts museum, remnants of buildings that survived the Great Fire of 1754, and a cemetery of twelve thousand Jewish graves that are sinking into their grassy mounds. The oldest gravestone here belongs to the great Hebrew poet, Abigdor Karo, who wrote a famous *selicha,* a lament following a fourteenth century pogrom, while the most visited tomb belongs to Rabbi Jehuda Low, the originator of the Golem legend, a darkly weird folk tale, worthy of a later Czech Jew—the brooding mystic Kafka. There are the museum synagogues of Klaus and Pinkas, the former including the State Jewish Museum, a fascinating collection of relics of European jewelry that has risen from 1,000 items before 1938 and Hitler, to almost 100,000 items, a complete economic and cultural history of the Jews of Prague, who now number some 18,000 in contrast to the 100,000 there were before World War II.

From the very oldest of Prague's squares you can easily walk to the center of its modern life, the Václavské námesti, named in honor of the Czech fourteenth century king and patron saint, Wenceslas, St. Václav. This is the broad avenue of state-owned shops and cafeterias, movie houses and night lights, the National Museum, and one of the country's most famous pieces of Czech statuary, the equestrian figure of St. Wenceslas.

Each of the city's quarters has its share of architectural treasures. Across the Charles Bridge is Mala Strana, a garden suburb lined with a net work of twisting medieval alleys and Gothic cloisters, baroque castles and glittering red-tiled roofs, and in the gardens of the Wallenstein Palace, famous for its riding school and picture galleries, summer concerts are held and ballets are performed.

From the nearby Petrin Hill, the highest point in the city, one can walk to the city's leading sight and its trademark, the Hradčany Castle, a hilltop complex of buildings that includes some of the best samples of both the Gothic and baroque style to be found in the country. It is from here that Empress Maria Theresa ruled her Hapsburg empire, here that the country's leading Gothic building, the Church of St. Vitus, was built by Charles IV to replace a Romanesque basilica. Along the "Golden Street" behind the church you can see the little houses carved into the defensive walls to be used by the alchemists hired by Bohemian kings to make gold.

The Czechs have a museum for everything, one for each of its famed musicians, another, the Strahov, for literature, still another devoted to Lenin; and they are as proud of them as they are of the modern setting growing up on Letná Hill, a monument to the first

Five-Year Plan, and a glistening city of white state-owned apartment houses and public buildings. With its population of one million, this city is one of the most prosperous in eastern Europe, its shops well filled as a result of the country's incredibly high rate of industrialization.

The 49,381 square miles of Czechoslovakia are covered with forests of birch and ash, chestnuts and oaks, a richly green landscape that sparkles with lakes and rivers. The Vltava and Elbe flow through the third of the country called Bohemia and on to Germany; the Danube divides Slovakia and its capital of Bratislava from Hungary. The highest of its mountain ranges are the Tatras, and the most famous, the Giant Mountains of the Sudetenland handed over to Hitler as a result of the Munich pact.

Everywhere on this landscape, smokestacks soar into the air; some from factories making shoes, others turning out rainbow-colored Bohemian crystal; some canning Prague ham for export, others fabricating steel, processing sugar, or milling lumber. Around Plzen, breweries are busy producing Pilsner, and the V. I. Lenin plant makes machinery in the works formerly called Skoda. Oil is taken from the area of Slovakia and Moravia, pitchblende for uranium from the Ore Mountains on the Saxon border. In the picturesque villages of Bohemia, Moravia, and Slovakia, peasant girls in embroidered skirts and market squares rimmed with stepped-gable houses remind one of the settings for *The Bartered Bride*. But all this romantic atmosphere is backed by a solid, four-square practical industrialization, for the Czechoslovak Socialist Republic of almost fourteen million people is one of the most productive nations in the Communist bloc.

This country of factories and mills is also a pleasure land of spas, the most famous of which are Karlovy Vary, or Carlsbad, and Maríanske Lázně, Marienbad, both vast forest resorts of luxurious hotels and therapeutic waters, recalling the regal days of Franz Josef and Napoleon and elegant artists such as Goethe and Strauss, Wagner and Chopin, all of whom sought cures for one thing or another here.

For more serious touring, at Plzen there is the Karl Stjen Castle, once the hiding place of crown jewels; the Zbraslav Castle contains the medieval tombs of the Premysl rulers; or make a sad memorial pilgrimage north to Lidice, the Czech village wiped out by the Nazis, and now rebuilt. Its mass-grave cemetery is blanketed with roses, and it is now a living city dedicated to freedom.

Official Information

Before you go: Czechoslovak Embassy, 2349 Massachusetts Ave., Washington, D.C. Since you cannot make reservations directly, and all arrangements must be prepaid on a varying scale, you will have to rely on your travel agent when you plan a visit to any part of Czechoslovakia.

In Prague: SAS Office, 61 Stepanska, Prague II; Tourist Information, Cedok, 18 Na Prikope, Prague III; U.S. Embassy, 15 Mala Strana, Trziste.

Money Matters

Currency: The monetary unit is the Koruna (Kcs) divided into 100 Halers. There are about Kcs 7.20 to $1, U.S. Tourist rate is Kcs. 14.40 to $1, U.S.

Tipping: Although officially no tipping exists, it is customary to tip the waiters and servants approximately 10 per cent. A small tip to chambermaids and hotel porters, is much appreciated. Taxi drivers are tipped 10 per cent of the fare.

Climate, Clothing, and Essentials

Summers are hot and dry, while winters provide perfect conditions for the sports enthusiast, with temperatures the year round matching those of the middle Atlantic states. Spring, summer, and early autumn are the best times of year for a visit and the blossoms in April and May are an especially lovely sight. Normal city attire is correct at all times, with colors on the subdued side. One black dress for dinner, or a dark business suit, will do for most evening events.

Hotels

Prague has several fine hotels of international standard. Official price control insures uniform charges and that certain standards of service are maintained. Hotels are divided into de luxe, first and second class, and your accommodations depend upon the per diem rate you have prepaid. It is recommended that you stick to de luxe and first class categories, but your travel agent can supply reliable information on less expensive quarters. Although all hotels are operated by Cedok, the government tourist bureau, you can specify a choice when making your travel arrangements.

DE LUXE: *Alcron, 40 Stepanska ulice.* The city's best and most luxurious hotel, with a fine restaurant, music for dancing, and a winter garden. *Esplanade, 19 Washingtonova ulice.* Centrally located and overlooking a park, the restaurant here is noted for the wide choice offered on its menu. *Jalta, 45 Václavské náměsti.* The newest hotel in the city, this place is luxurious in the modern style and very conveniently located. *International Dejvice, 37 Jugoslávskych Partyzanu.* This modern, suburban hotel is about forty-five minutes from the city center and offers all the latest facilities.

Food and Restaurants

Czech food is good, if a little on the heavy side, and some of the native specialties you will want to try include a wide variety of sausages, an endless array of dumplings (*knedliky*), roast pork and roast goose with sauerkraut or pickled red cabbage, and Prague ham. Pickles and stewed fruits seem to be served with everything. The bread is excellent and you should try some of the Czech carp, which may be baked or served in aspic with a sauce of beer, almonds, and raisins. *Bramboracka* is the national soup made with mushrooms and potatoes; and the pastries and dessert confections are endless and superb. Fruit dumplings are certainly a native specialty and are especially good when made with damson plums. Food from the area of Bratislava has the Hungarian tinge, with lots of poppy • seeds, paprika, and sour cream. Beer from the Czech town of Pilsen (Plzěn), an incendiary white plum brandy called *Slivovice*, and wines from Moravia and Bohemia should be sampled.

In summer one can enjoy Czech or international cuisine at delightful garden restaurants such as *Barrandov; Mánes* on the riverbank; *Savarin,* with good French food and a nice bar; and from the *Zlatá Studna,* with its authentic native food, there is a wonderful view over the whole city. Other restaurants offering Czech, Bohemian, and Moravian dishes are *Valdštejnská hospoda* with its fine wine cellar, *U Kalicha,* or *U Fleku,* a brewery dating back to the Middle Ages and famous for its smoked black beer, and *U Sv. Tomáše,* a tavern that has a floor show as well. Other wine cellar restaurants worth a visit are *U Markýze* and *U Mececáše,* both serving good French food. *Monika,* a first class wine restaurant, is recommended for dinner, and the *Automat,* the country's largest restaurant, is a huge and fantastic cafeteria with standup counters for eating.

All of the hotels have excellent dining rooms serving continental dishes as well as Czech specialties. The *Palace* is one of the best, and the *Alcron* is another, its chef having taken the first prize for his efforts at the Brussels World's Fair. The *Opera Grill* has an intimate, elegant atmosphere as well as good food, and you may enjoy Hungarian food at *Budapest,* Russian fare at *Moskva,* Bulgarian dishes at *Sofia,* Balkan food at the *Balkan Grill,* and fine French food at the *Olympia.* Most of the international restaurants and hotel dining rooms have dancing.

Entertainment, Night Life, and Special Events

Opera, ballets, and drama performances are given at the National Theater, the Smetana Theater, and the Tylovo Theater. The puppet theaters offer the visitor a special treat, for their performances are a national art which has developed through the centuries. Two of the most popular are the Central Puppet Theater and the famous Spejbl and Hurvínek Puppet Theater.

Concerts are given at *Dům Umělcu* and Smetana Hall, especially during the *Spring Music Festival* which is held from late May to early June, an international event with conductors, soloists, and guests from almost every country in the world. Variety shows are presented at the *Alhambra* and the *Pražské Varieté* (Prague Variety Theater) and others. There is a large amusement park at the Fair Grounds.

For late evening entertainment and refreshments the *Alhambra* is recommended; also the *Barbara,* popular for its numerous wine drink specialties, the *Embassy Bar* at the Ambassador Hotel, the *Est Bar* of the Esplanade Hotel, and the *Jalta Club.*

Shopping

The best shops, such as *UVA, Moser-Bohemia, Dům Módy,* and *Tuzex,* are situated on Václavské nám (Wenceslas Square), Příkope, and Národní třida. Most are open all day, including Saturday and Sunday. The *Tuzex* stores in Palackého are authorized to accept foreign currency.

Bohemian crystal is one of the country's best buys and can be had in modern and traditional designs, tableware, and art glass. Christmas ornaments are especially fanciful here too, and Moravian and Slovakian textiles, laces, embroideries, national costumes, wickerwork and folk dolls are extremely interesting. Hunting rifles are good buys too, and the art books are of high quality.

Background Reading

R.U.R., by Karel Čapek
Czechoslovakia, by Harriet Grace Wanklyn

Hungary

BUDAPEST

Paprikash, gulyás, and gypsy violins

THERE is a fable often quoted these days throughout eastern Europe, concerning two dogs—one Czech, the other Polish—who met at the border between their countries. Each wondered why the other was crossing over. The Czech dog explained that he was going to Poland to bark; the Polish dog was going to Czechoslovakia to eat. Chances are, if asked, both dogs would say they wanted to go to Hungary to play. For Budapest has always been the Paris of central Europe, a city with a cultural life as rich as strudel, as heady as Tokay, with a gay and sparkling night life, dozens of theaters and concert halls, scores of romantic garden restaurants and candlelit cave-cabarets, a city where lovers stroll along the Danube quays; a place of brilliantly exuberant *czardas* dancers, and gypsy violinists so proficient at their soulful art that it is said you never have to tip them unless they make you cry.

The best thing about Budapest by far is its population, some 1.8 million Hungarians, every one a potential impresario. They are among the most amazing and inexplicable people anywhere, at once romantic and intelligent, inventive and funny, high-spirited, clever, and artistic, coldly practical in matters of finance and organization, and past masters of the stylistic *beau geste*. Their revolutions (they have had at least fifteen in the past eight hundred years) have often been planned in pastry shops, and their biting humor coupled with their Machiavellian shrewdness has made them respected adversaries whether they are producing movies in Hollywood, master-minding financial empires, or running restaurants in New York, kissing hands at high society parties anywhere, or battling tanks with sticks and stones in Budapest. "A Hungarian," the only half-joking definition goes, "is someone who can go into a revolving door behind you and come out ahead of you."

They can be as sentimental as Liszt or Lehár, as intricately intellectual as Bartok, as soundly scientific as Teller or the Nobel Prize-winner, Szent György, as gay and amusing as Molnar, as artistically original as Moholy-Nagy, as toughly clear-headed as Arthur Koestler. Even their martyred poet-heroes, Sandor Potöfi and Attila József, rooted their romantic rhymes in the solid soil of peasant patriotism, the first inspiring the great revolution of 1848. Along with the music, food, and the theater, the great pastime here is talking—arguing, conjecturing, postulating; this is a nation of gregarious gossips and one has the feeling that every Hungarian knows what every other Hungarian is up to, any place in the world.

They are quite possibly the best looking people anywhere, descendants of Magyar tribes who crossed the Urals to settle the country formerly occupied by their first cousins, the Huns. The Asian stock has mixed through the centuries with the Slavic and Teutonic strains around them to produce tall, powerfully built people with wide, flaring cheekbones and tiger eyes, with hair that can be as coal black as Bela Lugosi's, as blonde as Leslie Howard's. Hungarian women are the best dressed in eastern Europe, and wear the slimmest shoes with the highest heels, and even the men retain some of the dash one might expect in the country of the hussars.

The Hungarians are as athletic as they are musical and Budapest is full of swimming pools and thermal spas, gymnasiums and parks; as many people go to the stadium for an afternoon of football as go to the open-air theater on Margaret Island for an evening of Shakespeare, a playwright the Hungarians claim to translate better than any other people on earth.

Hungary is really two countries, just as its capital is two cities, each cut in half by the coppery-green crescent of the Danube, flowing south on its way from Vienna to Belgrade. On the right is the ancient hilly Buda, an area of medieval cobblestoned streets and Gothic arches, watchtowers and wine cellars, standing at the edge of Hungarian Transdanubia, a region of green-wooded mountains, and sparkling lakes. The newer Pest is as flat and sprawling as the great Hungarian plain, the Alföld, that backs it up, a dry level stretch of wheat and cornfields and a Van Gogh landscape of sunflowers from which Hungarians extract their favorite cooking oil. Pest is primarily nineteenth century in character, rebuilt after flood waters washed out the older town, and its wide streets full of smart shops and hotels, restaurants and airline offices, ring out in an orderly pattern from the oldest section, the Belváros, or inner city.

Between the two, lies the pretty garden-park, Margaret Island, a place of luxury resort hotels and tree-shaded cafés, hot thermal pools in which fish flicker like bits of gold leaf. A fair share of Budapest's young lovers gather here to stroll hand in hand and watch the paddle boats and pleasure launches. This lovely little island was the setting for a summer palace of a Roman emperor, and a thirteenth century convent built by King Bela IV for his daughter, Margaret, who became a nun—hence the island's name. It served as a pasture for the horses of the Turks and the site of a Hapsburg palace in the nineteenth century, a flowery, rose-strewn spa adrift mid the sophistication of the capital.

To get an over-all view of the city one should climb to the top of the Gellert Hill in Buda. From here you can see the quays of Buda and Pest and the eight bridges that stitch them together, the handsomest being the suspension bridge, the Széchenyi Lánchid, built after the flood in 1838 by the English engineers, William and Adam Clark. Looking across to Pest, you can see the huge façade of the Parliament building, etched with columns, arches, turrets, and spires, and a parade of 253 statues across its 291-yard front—a neo-Gothic work of the nineteenth century with a breathtaking white-and-gold grand stairway, under a skylight of ceiling murals, depicting legends of the Huns and their leader, Attila.

On Gellert Hill itself are the remains of a Hapsburg citadel and a brick-cave wine-cellar restaurant—a place of wrought-iron tradesmens' signs and strolling *cigány* violinists. To the north is the city's crowning touch, Castle Hill, with its stonework museum and Fisherman's Bastion, a complex of Romanesque towers, crenellations, niches with carved stone statues, and a gazebo where lovers scratch their initials. Here too is the Matthias Church, built in the thirteenth century and restored in the fifteenth, and used as a mosque by the Turks in the seventeenth. It is beautifully decorated with murals by such great Hungarian painters as Zichy and Szekely, and includes royal crypts and a marble sculpture of the Madonna and the Christ Child done by Lucas Cranach. It was from this church that Pope Calixtus III ordered all of the bells of the Christian world to be rung at exactly the same time, a clamorous commemoration of the defeat of the Turks at the hands of the Hungarian warrior, Janos Hunyádi.

The other hill worth climbing in this city is the Rózsadomb, the Hill of Roses, where narrow old streets are lined with low stone houses embroidered with window-box gardens. Much of Hungary's history centers around this older section and relics of the Copper Age have been excavated, as well as evidence of a Celtic trading center that flourished as far back as 100 B.C. The Romans made it the leading city in their province of Pannonia and called it Aquincum (now the name of the museum in this area devoted to relics of the Roman settlers), and they remained here from the first century A.D. until the arrival of the Huns four hundred years later. Attila made this his headquarters and used it as a base from which he raided western Europe, naming the city Buda after his brother.

In 896, the Huns were replaced by the Magyars central Asian warriors who shaved their heads and ate their meat raw, and who under their leader, Arpád, joined the Bulgars and Avars as the scourges of Europe, all inheriting the title "Hongroise," a fearsome epithet which has given way to our word, "ogre." Before long the Magyars settled down and became a nation of farmers; under their Arpád dynasty leader, Stephen, who was the first king and is now their patron saint, they adopted Christianity, and ultimately led three crusades against the Turks. The Hungarians had the first human rights bill on the Continent; their Golden Bull was issued just seven years after England's Magna Carta and assured them of their "right to resist"—a right they have unfortunately been forced to exercise two or three times in each century, not always with happy results.

Hungary has known two golden ages, the first in the latter half of the fifteenth century under King Mátyás (Matthias), when they founded universities and developed an artistic Renaissance, and the second time when the 150-year rule of the Turks was broken in the seventeenth century, an era that lasted through the combined Hapsburg Austro-Hungarian empire until the end of World War I when the country became free and separate. What was not destroyed by the Mongols of Batu Khan in the thirteenth century or the Turks of Suleiman in the sixteenth, was razed as a result of World War II. Later ruins and pockmarked walls resulting from the October revolt of 1956 are almost all erased.

It is in Pest that one can see the modern life of the capital, as well as many souvenirs of the past, for here are gathered such museums as the National, with its ethnic and crafts exhibits, its Roman and medieval treasures, including the throne curtain of King Mátyás and some of the most beautiful gold jewelry and altarpieces in Europe, along with the gilded illuminated pages of the Corvina manuscripts. The Fine Arts Museum has an outstanding collection of Dutch, Spanish, French, and Flemish masters from the time of Rembrandt to Renoir, while the Gallery of Art puts on exhibitions of contemporary works. There is an ethnographic museum and another devoted to applied arts; one to agricultural progress and another to the production of wine. In Pest, too, is St. Stephen's Basilica, its enormous dome towering over the whole section like a looming mountaintop, while a little way out of the center stands the forbidding Gothic watchtower of the Vajda-Hunyad Castle, a true copy of the hideaway fortress of János Hunyádi, the conqueror of the Turks, and the son of King Mátyás. This original castle still stands in the mountains of southern Transylvania, the area of legendary werewolves and Dracula monsters.

For the rest, the city is dotted with pretty squares, here and there a domed Turkish bath, a monument the Turks left behind them just as the Romans did, a pastry shop, the Ruszwurm, four hundred years old and another, the Pilvax, in which the 1848 revolution was planned. There are restful spas and fragments of towers, monuments to heroes and intriguing ancient alleyways, a year-round circus, and Vidam Park, the local version of Copenhagen's Tivoli and New York's Coney Island rolled into one.

Looping around the curve of the Danube for a day, one can see the lovely old town of Szentendre, a completely intact maze of Renaissance streets and rococo houses, a Bohemian artists' colony and a delightful place for walkers. A little north of this is Visegrad, its citadel commanding a magnificent view over the Danube. This is the court city of Hungary's Gothic kings and the ruins of King Mátyás' great palace are being excavated—remnants that came to light only in 1943 when bombings uncovered them. The most important town on this little swing is Esztergom, whose cathedral is the leading church in Hungary, with an altarpiece that is the largest in the world. Here, too, is the Christian Museum, with a collection of paintings by Italian masters of the Middle Ages, delicate Gobelin tapestries, exquisite porcelain pieces, and outstanding examples of the goldsmiths' craft. This city was the birthplace of Hungary's first king, St. Stephen, and the eastern edge of Charlemagne's empire. After World War II ruins of the twelfth century royal palace of King Bela III were discovered and diggings have revealed a storehouse of fine statuary and brilliant murals.

If you go to Hungary's "inland sea," Lake Balaton, you will find vacationing Hungarians sunning on the sandy beaches around its Tihany peninsula, swimming in its fifty-mile length, watching its regattas, and rowing in its rowboats. Ruined castle fortresses dot the volcanic hills that rim its northern shores; there are luxurious spas and therma lakes, famed for their curative powers since Roman times.

FOR THE TRAVELER'S NOTEBOOK

Official Information

Before you go: Hungarian Embassy, 2437 15th St., N.W., Washington, D.C. Since you cannot make reservations directly and all arrangements must be prepaid on a varying scale, you must rely on your travel agent when you plan a visit to Hungary. The same kind of travel arrangements are necessary for Budapest as those described on p. 352, though prices are a dollar or two higher in each category.

In Budapest: SAS Office, 1–3 Váci-utca; Tourist Information Office, IBUSZ, 5 V. Vörösmarty-tér; U.S. Embassy, 12 V. Szabadsag-tér.

Money Matters

Currency: The monetary unit is the forint (FOR), divided into 100 fillér. There are about FOR 23.07 to $1, U.S., at the tourist rate.

Tipping: Though officially no tipping exists, it is customary to tip waiters, servants, and taxi drivers approximately 10 per cent. A small tip to chambermaids and hotel porters is highly appreciated.

Climate, Clothing, and Essentials

Summer is hot and dry and lasts from mid-June to mid-September. Spring is pleasant and autumn is long and beautiful. January and February are the coldest months and offer fine skiing in the hills. The people of Budapest do not dress very formally; for evening men wear a dark suit and women a black dress. In summer only light clothing and a raincoat are needed. Spring and fall require a light overcoat, while in winter woolen clothes and a warm topcoat are necessary.

Hotels

Budapest boasts many excellent hotels, some of which, though old, have been modernized.

DE LUXE: The two leading ones are the *Grand Hotel Margitsziget,* on Margaret Island in the Danube, and the *Hotel Gellert, 4 Kelenhegyí-ut.* Both have excellent rooms with private baths, water piped in from medicinal springs, lovely terraces, and lounges. At the *Gellert* there is an indoor pool as well as an open-air pool with artificial waves. The new *Grand Hotel Royal, Leninkör-ut 49,* modern and centrally located, is also good.

FIRST CLASS: Best are the *Duna, 4 Apaczai Csere Janos-ut;* the *Astoria, 19 Kossuth Lajos-ut;* the *Palace, 43 Rakoci-ut;* and the *Beke, 97 Lenin-Körut,* with its popular afternoon café. In the Buda Mountains, within easy reach of the city, you may enjoy the hotel *Vörös Csillag* at the Szechenyi-Hegy.

Food and Restaurants

Hungarian food is excellent and enormously varied, though to most minds it summons up images of only paprika and sour cream. There are a number of famous stews like *gulyas pörkölt* and *tokany,* and a fish soup, *halaszle,* that rivals bouillabaisse. Meats and poultry are superb, as are the sturgeon, pike, and carp. Fried chicken, roast goose, suckling pig, and Transylvanian *flekken* (barbecued pork on a wooden spit) are especially good, as are sauerkraut and stuffed cabbage dishes and a delectable variety of noodle specialties. *Fatanyeros* is a mixed grill served on a plank, and the Herz salamis are justly world famous. Pastries and confections are heavenly, with dessert crepes such as *csusztatott palascinta* and *vargabeles* (a sort of custard pie), a number of tarts and *tortes* and doughnuts, and *rétes* (strudel) filled with apples, cherries, nuts, poppy seeds, cheese, or even cabbage.

Most Hungarian wines are white of the famous Tokay type, though there are some fine reds too. Some Tokay is so refined that it is used as an apéritif. More often one drinks Balaton wines with meals. A popular one is the white *Keknyelü*. For a claret ask for wines of Eger, Skekszárd, or Villány, and do try the strong apricot brandy called *Barack*.

Most restaurants and hotel dining rooms serve continental food as well as Hungarian dishes. Among the best for native food are *Red Star; Gundel*, near the zoo, an elegant and excellent dining place; *Karpatia; Fortuna; Hungaria*, a huge sort of combination coffeehouse and restaurant; and *Matyas Pince*, a smart little cellar spot with exquisite Hungarian dishes. *Rozsadomb* offers folk music and good food and is very fashionable. The *Harmashatárhegy* on the hill of the same name has typical Hungarian décor, food, and folk music, and offers a breathtaking view. *Kis Royal* and *Apostolok* are good, too. There are scores of coffeehouses and patisseries; three interesting ones are *Vörösmarty*, formerly known as *Gerbeaud*, and world-famous for its pastries; *Pilvax*, noted as the meeting place for the nineteenth century revolutionaries, though its pastry is good too; and *Ruszwurm*, more than four hundred years old.

Entertainment, Night Life, and Special Events

Hungarians love music and theater. Budapest has two opera houses, ten theaters, and two operetta stages. Summer opens up many opportunities for outdoor entertainment. Several open-air stages give performances, numerous variety theaters and cabarets provide light entertainment, and there are frequent garden concerts. An experience you will long remember is the open-air opera on Margaret Island. Reserve a seat for everything as early as possible through IBUSZ. One of the highlights is a trip on the Danube. Let IBUSZ arrange for the ticket.

There is dancing at hotels and gypsy violin music at almost all restaurants. The *Budapest* is the most elegant night club, with floor shows and full dinner menu.

A number of medicinal and open-air baths make Budapest a "city of cures." Three of the best known are *Gellert Medicinal Baths, Lukacs,* and *Imre*.

Shopping

Hungarian folk crafts are astonishingly beautiful and come as a surprise since we rarely see them outside their native land. Exquisite embroideries, laces, needlepoint, homespun textiles, rugs, national costumes, dolls and carved wood toys, and vivid peasant rugs are among the things worth buying. A good sampling of all the crafts can be found in shops along Vaci, Kossuth, and Petöfi streets and at Vörösmarty Square. Beautifully hand-decorated Easter eggs are world famous, and Herend and Zsolnay porcelain is on sale in the *Herend* shop and on Kigyo Street. Phonograph records are of high quality and inexpensive; you might be interested in the authentic gypsy music.

Background Reading

Hungary, published by Corvina
The Hungarian Revolution, by George Mikes
Hungarian Short Stories, published by Corvina
You Are All Alone, by Kovago
Flashes in the Night, by William Patrick Juliasz
History of Hungary, by Denis Sinor
The Devil and the Deep, by Sacha Carnegie

Poland

WARSAW

Behind the flexible iron curtain

OF all the countries in eastern Europe, Poland is the largest, the poorest, the freest, and the most vibrant, a land of some thirty million rebellious, indomitable, determined, and contentious people, occupied many times within the thousand years of its history, but never conquered or subdued. Its capital, Warsaw, is one of the most up-and-doing cities to be found anywhere—seething with activity, bristling with opinion, diligently rebuilding itself after the devastation of World War II. The whole city seems braced with scaffolding, construction crews are everywhere, the busiest people are the city planners, and the number one topic of conversation is architecture. No building goes up without suffering its share of criticism, none is more unanimously disliked than Stalin's gift, the Wrigley-like skyscraper that is the Palace of Culture and Science, unless it is the new American Embassy, a concrete and glass cube which, the Poles feel, is out of keeping with the traditional elegance of the embassies around Ujazdowski Park.

Two-thirds of the people living in Warsaw are newcomers to the city; half of the 1,100,000 population is under twenty-five; one out

370

of every four lives in a house less than ten years old. When the bitingly cold Polish winter gives way to summer, the sandy banks of the Vistula River blossom with bikini-clad girls, their hair piled high in towering blonde beehives. Nightclub floor shows include defiant sprinklings of political satire, beatnik-type student cabarets like the Hybrydy rock to the rhythm of the Twist, and bookstores offer the widest reading selection within the Communist bloc. Although Marxist rule brought with it a complete separation of church and state, most of the Poles are practicing Roman Catholics; religion is taught in the schools, holy days such as the feast of Corpus Christi are celebrated with elaborate street pageants, and the churches are always packed. It is estimated that 95 per cent of the population attends services, a number that might be considerably lower were churchgoing not an act of open defiance against the officially atheistic state; no one loves to protest as much as a Pole.

The Communist framework stretches in economic matters here too, ever since the Poznan uprising of 1956. When Wladyslaw Gomulka was restored to leadership, he dissolved most of the collective farms and permitted farmers to buy land, though a portion of their produce is consigned to the state, to be sold in price-fixed self-service markets such as Warsaw's Supersam. The rest (and usually the best) of what they grow is sold in open markets, such as those in the Swietokrzyska section, a teeming bazaar of second-hand clothing, luxury foods, American and European imports, and anything else that is hard to get through state-controlled channels. Private housing is encouraged, and though Russian is a required language in the schools, one hears young people conversing more frequently in English, one of the most popular electives in the academic curriculum. Socialist realism went the way of collective farms, and most Polish painters revel in the freedom of abstract expressionism and other "decadent," capitalist art movements; there is hardly a "happy proletariat" painting in sight.

Most amazing of all, however, is the superhuman accomplishment that is present-day Warsaw; nowhere else within the 121,000 square miles that make up this country can you get a better idea of the strength and persistence of the Polish people. This was the most bombed-out city of World War II. Hitler's orders concerning it were simple, direct, and systematically executed. "Warsaw," he said, "must cease to exist. Level it." At the war's end, 85 per cent of the city lay in a heap of rubble. Of its 900 historic buildings, only about 60 remained. Nearly 800,000 people were dead in Warsaw; 6 million in all of Poland, half of them Jews. Hitler could no more tolerate the hard-to-handle Poles than he could the "racially inferior" Jews. Of the dead, 4 million were slaughtered at Auschwitz, the Nazi extermination camp outside the medieval city of Cracow; the rest were marched off to Germany as slave labor—and in many cases "marched" was exactly the word.

The Poles who were alive after the war literally picked themselves up, dusted themselves off, and set about rebuilding their capital; architects, artists, skilled and unskilled laborers volunteered to repair the buildings, starting with the most historic sections, though they had neither food nor homes. In less than ten years they restored seven hundred years of Polish architectural history, brick by brick, like so many pieces in a jigsaw puzzle. When they ran out of bricks, they made new ones to match the old; when they forgot the details of a frieze or fresco, or failed to remember which building went where, they consulted the eighteenth century paintings of Canaletto, the Italian artist whose scenes of Warsaw were miraculously intact within the city.

Today the Old Town, with its Gothic and baroque buildings, its gables, iron work, and antique streets, its fifteenth century Cathedral of St. John, and the fourteenth century walls and towers of the Barbakan fortress, are living monuments to their determination. The most impressive resurrection took place in the Market Square of the Old Town, the Rynek Starego Miasta—with its rim of burghers' houses, its three-hundred-year-old wine cellar, the Krokydyl, and the restaurant Pod Bazyliszkiem where, it was said, there lived a dragon who could kill people with either a breath or a glance. Here, too, is the Institute of History, housed in the fourteenth century mansion of the Mazovian princes, an old merchant's house which is now the House of Culture, and a museum dedicated to the Polish poet, Adam Mickiewicz. He, along with Henryk Sienkiewicz, the Nobel Prize author of *Quo Vadis;* Copernicus, who, in the sixteenth century, decided that the earth revolved around the sun; Maria Sklodowska Curie, who with her husband Pierre discovered radium in Paris; and the composer-pianists Chopin and Paderewski, who was also the first president of the new Poland created in 1919, make up, in part, the roster of Poles well known to the outside world.

Thaddeus Kosciusko is especially acknowledged in America, since he fought heroically in Washington's revolutionary army, only to lead an unsuccessful uprising in his own country a few years later.

Those in search of modern Warsaw will find it along the café-shop-and-office-building avenues around the Nowy Swiat and Marszalkowska Street, in the new residential sections, and in such postwar additions as the thirty-seven-storey Palace of Culture and Science, with its tower lookout over the city and its surrounding countryside. New too, is the Tenth Anniversary Stadium, the inevitable, massive arena one always finds in Communist-bloc countries. But its older, more romantic sites are undoubtedly the greatest attractions: Holy Cross Church, where Chopin's heart is entombed; the Gothic Church of the Virgin Mary, founded in 1409 and the oldest in the city; the magnificent mansions, squares, and castles that line the beautiful Krakowskie Przedmiéscie Street; the gracious old buildings of the university; the classical nineteenth century Belvedere Palace and the older Wilanov Palace, now part of the Polish National Museum; and the newly restored Staszic Palace with Thorvaldsen's Copernicus statue standing guard outside. Perhaps the most beautiful of Warsaw's parks is the Lazienki, with its botanical gardens, its elegant Royal Summer Palace, and its eighteenth century theater that has just been rebuilt, while the saddest is the ghostly, grassy field that was the city's Ghetto, where a monument honors the Jews who fought the Germans against ferocious odds in 1943.

Fighting against ferocious odds has been a Polish trait almost since the country began. Settled in the tenth century A.D. by the Slavic Polans tribes, it became a nation in 966 under its first king, Mieszki I. He quickly converted to Christianity, out of enlightened self-interest, for a country of non-Christians was considered fair game for the Crusader kings of western Europe; it was better to join them, face eastward, and march against heathen lands. Poland was a great medieval power from the fourteenth to the seventeenth century, when her armies under King John III defeated the Turks at the gates of Vienna, thus saving European Christianity. By way of thanks, Europe has been carving up Poland ever since. With its northern boundaries on the Baltic, its southern frontiers in the Carpathians, Poland's fate has been sealed mostly by her eastern and western borders—the first touching the Soviet Ukraine, the second edging on Germany. Throughout their history, the Poles have been tugged at and occupied by both of those countries; even Hitler and Stalin came to terms just long enough to divide Poland between them.

Life is still hard for the average Polish worker; he must often have two jobs to meet the rising cost of living and even if he has enough money his chances of finding adequate housing are slim; living quarters are cramped and crowded, buses and trolleys are jammed, there is enough rationing of vital supplies and materials to be frustrating, and the easiest outlet comes by way of a glass of herb-flavored vodka or an evening at the theater or concert hall.

Essentially a country of lowlands, much of the Polish landscape is breathtakingly beautiful and dramatic, most especially the eastern Bialowieza Forest, where in the truly primeval National Park savage wolf packs prowl and one can still see bison, lynx, wild ponies, and stupendous oak trees, some six hundred years old. There are the deep-green forest slopes around Zakopane in the Tatra Mountains to the south, the gray-blue seascapes near such cities as Gdansky (formerly the free city of Danzig and the gateway to the Polish Corridor), and the salt-water resorts that center around Sopot and Gdynia. There are wooded sections known for their crystal-clear lakes—the Pomorze, the Masurian, and Kashubian, the last in the heart of the most picturesque folklore country where ancient dances are still performed and people live in carved and staved wood houses seven centuries old.

Close to Warsaw, one can visit such towns as Zelazowa Wola, where Chopin was born, and stroll through the garden of his museum-country house, or drive to Czersk with its somber Gothic castle. Traveling farther afield, there is the ancient city of Lublin, near the Russian border. Here the Old Town is a Renaissance maze of streets and arcades, churches and courtyards, and the Cracow Gate is a Gothic watchtower that has stood guard over this city since Poland's golden age.

Poznan, a city best known for its annual International Trade Fair, is even more interesting to historians and architectural buffs for its baroque town hall and palaces, its cathedral with subterranean vaults, its fine picture gallery and impressive market place. Its opera house is one of the best in Poland and outside of the city at Rogalin stands the Kurnik Castle, with a dazzling art treasury and a collection of jewel-like illuminated manuscripts.

But to anyone caught up in the romance of the past, no city in Poland is more fascinating than Cracow, the country's ancient capital and the only large city not destroyed during the war. Here is medieval Poland in all of its power and grandeur, a museum of architecture dating back to the tenth century, with one of the most beautiful squares in all Europe and with the Wawel Castle, the "Polish Acropolis," on a hill overlooking the city. Built between the tenth and sixteenth centuries, it includes within its walls a pre-Romanesque rotunda, one of Poland's oldest relics. Its square is a set-piece of arches and burghers' houses, guild halls and statuary, pigeons and people; the museums of the city include the National, with works by Rembrandt and da Vinci, and the Ethnological, with a wealth of Polish genre art; its churches glitter with brilliant stained-glass windows and its skyline is fringed with towers and spires, steeples and belfries.

FOR THE TRAVELER'S NOTEBOOK

Official Information

Before you go: Polish Embassy, Consular Division, 2224 Wyoming Ave., Washington, D.C. Since you cannot make reservations directly, and all arrangements must be prepaid on a varying scale, you will have to rely on your travel agent when you plan a visit to any part of Poland. (See note on page 352.)

In Warsaw: SAS Office, 19 Nowy Swiat St.; Tourist Information Office, Orbis, 16 Bracka St.; U.S. Embassy, 33/A1 Ujazdowskie.

Money Matters

Currency: The monetary unit is the zloty (Zlo), divided into 100 groszy. There are about Zlo 24 to $1, U.S.

Tipping: Tipping is officially frowned upon, but waiters and cab drivers usually expect 10 per cent and a few zloty is correct for baggage porters.

Climate, Clothing, and Essentials

Polish winters are bitingly cold and the best time for a visit is from mid-spring to mid-fall. Summer is dry and fairly hot with temperatures averaging 65 degrees F. from May through August. Normal city attire is correct at all times, and a dark dress or business suit is all that would be required for evening wear. Take all the camera film you'll need for your stay.

Hotels

Although standards are improving, do not expect to find de luxe hotels similar to those in the United States or western Europe. The *Grand Hotel, 28 Krucza St.,* is the largest in the city, completely modern, well located, and with all facilities including a helicopter landing. The *Bristol, 42/44 Krakowskie Przedmiéscie,* also in the center of the city, is smaller and a bit more charming and its restaurant is good. Other hotels worth considering are the *Europejeski, 13 Krakowskie Przedmiéscie,* opened in 1960 and the city's newest addition, and the *MDM Hotel, 1 Pl. Konstytucji,* the *Polinia, 45 Aleje Jerozolimskie* and the *Warszawa Hotel, 9 Pl. Warecki.*

You may specify the hotel of your choice when making reservations, but do so well in advance as accommodations are seriously limited.

Food and Restaurants

The Polish cuisine has some delightful surprises, especially in its delectable *zakouski,* cold appetizers served with iced vodka at the start of most meals. *Baraszcz* is a wonderful cabbage-beet borscht, served hot or cold with sour cream, and *chlodnik* is a kind of cold salad-soup that is refreshing and filling. *Bigos,* a hunter's stew, is practically the national dish, made with pork, beef, cabbage, and dried mushrooms (these last are by the way, the best in the world and flavor many Polish specialties) and *pieczen huzarska* is a version of sauerbraten. *Pierozhki* are pastry turnovers filled with meat or *kasha* (buckwheat groats), and many of the same fish dishes one finds in Hungary and Czechoslovakia are served here. *Colbassi* is the famous thick round garlic salami, and *babkas,* made especially at holiday times, are a great Polish yeast coffee cake. Rich desserts and *tortes* are done to perfection and the best cheeses are those of the dry cottage or farmer type. Sour milk is popular with meals and is delightful especially in hot weather, and *kwas,* a mildly fermented drink, is to the Poles what Cokes are to us. Vodka is the preferred before-dinner drink and the Polish beer is light and delicious. Tea (*herbata*) is the most common hot beverage, and is strong and good.

Continental food is served in many restaurants and in all of the hotels. which, by the way, have excellent restaurants.

The best restaurants for Polish and continental food are *Krokodyl,* the *Rarytas, Pod Kandelabrami,* the *Kameralna,* and the *Kongresowa.* Most of these have music, some dancing as well, while others double as night clubs.

Entertainment, Night Life, and Special Events

The Opera Warszawska, also staging ballets, is excellent, as are the concerts of the Warsaw Symphony Orchestra at the Filharmonia Naradowa

(National Concert Hall). Special events such as regional or foreign ballets and concerts are sometimes staged in the Sala Kongresowa in the Palace of Culture and Science. There is some fascinating folk dancing by the Mazowsze and Slask troupes. Tickets for these events as well as for sports events, etc. are normally obtainable for visitors through Orbis.

Late nightclub-type restaurants include *Kongresowa, Pod Kandelabrami,* and *Krokodyl,* and the hotel restaurants are open late with music and dancing. A few small cabarets such as *Buffo* and *Gong* might be interesting to see to.

The *Chopin Memorial Piano-Playing Contest* is held in Warsaw from late February to early March and is an international competition, and the *Folklore Festival* in Cracow takes place in early June. The *Poznan International Trade Fair* is held in June.

Shopping

Typical buys for tourists are ceramics, dolls in national costumes, embroidered tablecloths, carved wooden goods from the Cracow region, fine handmade silverware and crystal, and Zubrouka vodka. There are two shops near the Air Terminal where these souvenirs are obtainable, but you will find them also in the Old Town and in Nowy Swiat Street.

Background Reading

The Peasants, by Wladyslaw Reymont
Selected Poems of Adam Mickiewicz
Canaletto, the Painter of Warsaw, by M. Wallis
A Case History of Hope, by Flora Lewis
The Trumpeter of Cracow, by Eric Philbrook Kelly, is classified for teenage readers, but a wonderful view of medieval Poland.

Union of Soviet Socialist Republics

MOSCOW

The holy, Asiatic city; Russia
as it was and will be

Moscow has stood as the symbol of enigma to the Western world almost since the city was founded eight hundred years ago. Whether held by Suzdal princes, Tartar khans, Muscovy dukes, Romanov czars, or Communist premiers, it has represented an unknown quantity, the capital of a land cut off from the world geographically, linguistically, temperamentally, and, always, politically. Attacked time and again by the Golden Horde from the East, and the Scandinavians and Teutonic Knights from the West, the Russian rulers drew an "iron curtain" across their frontiers four centuries before Winston Churchill coined that phrase. Although the epithet was lacking, the concept had been implicit in the police states of every czar from Ivan the Terrible to Nicholas II.

Even when the official capital became St. Petersburg (later called Petrograd and now Leningrad) Moscow remained the spiritual heart of what Gogol called, "All the Russias . . . that land which has extended smoothly, glidingly, over half the earth."

Casanova, who traveled in the eighteenth century Russia of Catherine the Great, advised, "Those who have not seen Moscow have not seen Russia, for the people of St. Petersburg are not really Russians at all." A century later, Dumas *père* visited the city and wrote, "Now we are in the heart of old Russia, not the pale counterpart we had known in St. Petersburg . . . Small wonder that my heart beat high with excitement." And in 1917, John Reed, the American Communist newspaperman who reported on the Russian revolution in his book, *Ten Days That Shook the World,* explained the special thrill he felt when the Bolsheviks took Moscow, though the capital, St. Petersburg, had fallen days earlier:

Petrograd after all, in spite of being for a century the seat of government, is still an artificial city. Moscow is the real Russia, Russia as it was and will be; in Moscow we would get the true feeling of the Russian people about the revolution. Life is more intense there.

Now the capital of the entire country that is correctly called the Union of Soviet Socialist Republics (or simply the Soviet Union), Moscow is still the capital of Russia, the largest and most influential of the fifteen republics in that country. Of the 225 million people within the Soviet Union, more than half are Russians; but everyone in this vast land regards Moscow as a spiritual mecca and a place of pilgrimage, as well as a seat of government. To the people of the outside world who gain their impressions of the Soviet Union through emanations from its capital, the over-all aspect is still essentially "Russian," essentially enigmatic. No wonder then that anyone, no matter how far and wide he might have traveled in today's jet age, feels a special tingle of excitement, a mixture of apprehension and expectation, when his destination is Moscow, Pushkin's golden-headed city with the "forty times forty cupolas."

Looking down over Moscow from the Lenin Hills in front of the university, one might recall the words Tolstoy ascribed to Napoleon in *War and Peace,* when the French emperor gazed at his prize from this same vantage point, known then as the Poklonny Hill. "This Asiatic city with its innumerable churches, Moscow the holy . . . A strange, beautiful and grand city . . . She lies at my feet, though, her golden domes and crosses flashing and twinkling in the sun." How much more impressed Napoleon might be today, were he to see his city at night from one of the bridges that spans the Moscow

River. The huge complex of the Kremlin rises behind its walls as floodlights and beacons play across the cluster of golden-domed churches and five red stars atop the tallest towers glow and twirl in the darkness.

For centuries travelers have been going to Moscow expecting to find a world that is strange and different. Moscow has never disappointed them. No city on earth looks more like itself, no other capital so completely defies all look-alike comparisons. It is a world on another scale, a city viewed through a wide-angle camera lens. Great avenues some fourteen lanes wide bend and sweep toward horizons as broad as those of the Russian steppes. Buildings seem enormous, more because of their width and mass than because of their height. It takes weeks before a stranger adjusts to the perspectives and proportions, and until he does he feels dwarfed just as a Lilliputian might if he decided to turn the tables and visit Gulliver at home. After a stay in Moscow, Western capitals seem like toy towns, with narrow streets and miniature buildings. Only the somber, massive grandeur of Russian music would be a fitting backdrop for this setting. Hotel lobbies, airport reception rooms, dining rooms, and subway stations have the proportions (and often the décor) of grand ballrooms. Great arches and columns, elaborate crystal chandeliers, and murals of the boundless Russian landscapes accent the enormous scale of the interior architecture. And the suites of such prerevolutionary hotels as the National are furnished with tall, glass-fronted corner cupboards filled with elaborate porcelain vases and figurines, beds piled high with three or four pillows, bathtubs so deep one can hardly see over the edge while bathing, oversized peach silk lampshades, and writing tables that make one feel like a commissar, if not a Wall Street magnate.

To most tourists who see Moscow in summer the city's color scheme is drab and depressing. The maroon brickwork, the dark gray cobblestones, even the Italianate yellow-gold on some of the buildings, are all too close in value. But in winter the city becomes a place of sharp, frosty beauty. Magically, an underlining of white snow seems to do for the Moscow color scheme what a dab of sour cream does for a plate of thick red Russian cabbage borscht.

As soon as he drops his luggage in his room and works his way through the obstacle course of red tape at the hotel service bureau, almost every visitor to Moscow heads straight for Red Square, the

Krasnaya Ploshohad, that is the heart of the Soviet Union. It is a good instinct. Nowhere else will you get the full impact of this city all at once; no other spot offers a more accurate sampling of its tone and temper, its scale and style, and, most of all, its drama. Red Square is an enormous rectangle of cobblestones, so large it hardly seems a square at all, but more like some stupendous no man's land. At one of its short sides stands the State Historical Museum, a huge red-brick building with a white roof that always appears to be covered with snow. With its towers and dormers, this mass of nineteenth century architecture is best described as neo-Gothic, pseudo-Victorian, fake Old Russian. Far away, almost below the horizon at the opposite end of the square, looms the world's wildest building St. Basil's Cathedral, a jumble of nine convoluted mismatched domes, swirled, striped, and plaid, tossed in the air like fluted turbans. With its scalloped niches and floral frescoes, its gold crosses glinting in the sunlight, and walls that are prismatic patterns of red, white, and blue, one almost expects the whole building to tinkle out the tune of "Meadowlands," or an aria from *Prince Igor.* Built by order of Ivan IV (and Terrible) to celebrate a victory over the Tartars, and honoring St. Vasily, this church-turned-museum looks like a pasteboard carnival funhouse.

One long side of Red Square is edged by the endless length of the GUM department store, and the opposite side is framed by the red-brick Kremlin walls, with their tower gates and swallowtail crenelations. Blue spruce trees stand in front of this wall while the green domes and gold cupolas and crosses of the Kremlin cathedrals peer over it, joined incongruously, by the new, very-Bauhaus, Hall of Congresses. In the middle of the Kremlin side of the square is the great block of red and black marble that is Lenin's Tomb, topped by a reviewing stand from which high Soviet officials and honored guests watch the events held in the square. Of these, the two most spectacular take place on May Day and Revolution Day, November 7. On both occasions the square is filled with hundreds of thousands of people: Moscow citizens carrying banners and flowers, Young Pioneers in blue shorts and white shirts, factory workers in bright blue coveralls and white hats, all carrying beet-red flags that match the drapings on the buildings around the square. Gigantic photographs of Lenin and Khrushchev cover the whole façade of GUM's, fireworks shoot into the sky half the night, and all day long the square is roofed with echelons of fighter jets flying in trim formations overhead.

Almost every decisive act in Russian and Soviet history has been played out in this square, since Prince Yuri Dolgoruky founded Moscow in 1156 and built his *kreml,* or fortress, on the site of the present Kremlin. It was from this point that the Tartars besieged that fortress, burning the original wooden walls that guarded it. The square was the scene of bloody executions and tortures in the time of the Muscovy dukes, the tax collectors for the absentee Tartar khans. Here Ivan the Terrible fried victims on his oversized griddle; and here from the fifteenth to the nineteenth centuries were the bazaars and turquoise merchants of the Kitai-Gorod or Chinese city. Here the people murdered the aristocratic boyars who robbed them, and from here the Bolsheviks stormed the Kremlin in 1917 and poured into the hallowed grounds through the Spassky Gate. No one who has read John Reed's account of the masses who marched in victory to this square to bury their revolutionary dead will ever quite be able to forget the image. Five hundred of these proletariat heroes are buried in the grounds outside the wall with later Soviet leaders and heroes, as is John Reed himself, who died of pneumonia while visiting Moscow in the thirties.

Perhaps the only place in the Soviet Union more crammed with history than Red Square is the Kremlin itself, that great triangular enclosure of sixty-five acres surrounded by its high walls and towers. Within these walls are the most historic and dramatic relics of Russia's past. Enter this ancient compound through the Spassky Gate, for the most impressive effect. Stand in Cathedral Square where Boris Godunov was crowned and see the three fairytale gold-domed cathedrals, their walls shimmering with magnificent illuminated icons, some paneled with hand-wrought silver, others glittering with jewels. The oldest and most beautiful is the Uspensky, or Assumption Cathedral, built in 1479. This was the coronation church of all the czars. Here Ivan the Terrible sat on his carved walnut throne to repent his sins, which were considerable. The Annunciation Cathedral, built ten years later, is the smallest of the three Kremlin churches, but has the best icons and most exquisite detailing, and the Archangel Cathedral, built in the early sixteenth century, was the pantheon of all the czars until Peter the Great forsook Moscow for St. Petersburg. There are wonderful murals here, too, of Ivan Kalita

(Money Bags), the first Muscovy duke to turn against the Tartars, of Ivan III (and Great), who wanted to make Moscow a third Rome after Constantinople had fallen, and of all the czars who followed him.

Also in the square are the enormous gilt bell tower built for Ivan the Great, the gigantic Czar Kolokol, the black iron Czar Bell that cracked before it was ever rung, and the Czar's Cannon, from which the remains of the "false Dimitri" were fired toward his native Poland when the people found out that he had betrayed them.

The new Hall of Congresses and the Grand Kremlin Palace, where the Supreme Soviet deputies meet, are other sights worth seeing within the Kremlin. But, beyond doubt, the most dazzling place is the Armory Museum, where room after room, case after case, is packed with ermine-trimmed crowns, brocaded coronation robes, and sable-trimmed cloaks, royal carriages, ruby- and emerald-encrusted Bibles, magnificent weapons and armor, and the exquisite jeweled and enameled Easter eggs, miniature watches, and *bibelots* made by Faberge.

And anyone who asks can have a special permit to see the royal apartments of the czars, low-ceilinged, squat rooms covered with floral arabesque frescoes and furnished with big tiled stoves and enormous pieces of wood-and-velvet furniture. Their ballrooms and banquet halls, their private chapels and audience chambers make this section of the Kremlin the most incredible of all, especially if you think of all the intrigues and assassinations that took place in these rooms.

In addition to its physical appearance and its treasures, Moscow is overpowering because of its crowds. From dawn to midnight, seven days a week, the streets teem with people. Shops, restaurants, parks, squares, theaters, swimming pools, museums, and stadiums are jammed, a truly amazing sight when you realize that these people work six days a week, ten hours a day. You wonder where they come from, these silent, patient people who trudge along so tirelessly with their shopping bags full of fruits and vegetables, who sit so quietly in the immaculate subway cars, who wait so endlessly on lines that are everywhere. They wait on lines at food shops and at wrapping counters in department stores, at museums, bus stops, and airports. Dozens of people line up at eight in the morning in front of a store that has announced a shipment of new rugs or sweaters, and hundreds line up to pay homage to their revolutionary saint,

Lenin, who lies embalmed in a glass sarcophagus in his tomb on Red Square.

The question most frequently asked of anyone returning from the Soviet Union is, "What are the people really like?" To Americans who have come to regard the Russians as their opposite numbers, that answer too will be a surprise. Simply stated, they are among the warmest, friendliest, nicest people in the world. And though there is no doubt that they believe what they have been told about capitalistic war-monger imperialists, the average Russian has an unmistakable affection for Americans. And among the younger generation, American jazz, American fashions, and American literature are the rage. The getup of the young *stilyagi* seems to be inspired by a combination of American beatniks and what were once known as sharpies, and any woman traveling with an American bathing suit will have no trouble selling it on the black market if she is foolish enough to run the risk.

Those who speak English wait for a chance to use it. They will ask an American how much money he makes, what about the Negroes and how about Cuba, how many rooms does he live in, does he have a car, and, with a mixture of pride, timidity, and hopefulness, how does he like Moscow. When your guide feels she knows you well enough, she might ask why you want war, and if you are a woman all Russians ask if you work, if you have children, and do you have pictures of them. If you produce such pictures, you are taken to their hearts at once. Their faces light up and they show you, in turn, pictures of their own families, and begin comparing notes on age, likes and dislikes, names, and details about schooling. My own guide, having discovered that we each had a son two years old, gave me a present to take home, "From my son to your son in the hope that they will be friends and not enemies." The gift was a small red plastic star lapel pin with a photograph of Lenin, age three, in the center. And this same guide who brought me bags of apples and oranges each morning when we started on our tours, and who told me I looked "just like our own women," the supreme compliment to the foreign traveler in any land, took me to the Tretyakov Gallery, past the wonderful canvases of the Russian masters, and straight to a hideous painting of skeletons and skulls piled on a desolate, smoking battlefield. "We show this to everyone who wants war," she said, stepping back to see if her words had hit their mark.

With their standard of living rising steadily, though slowly, the traditional image of the Russian peasant in stout shoes, black coat, and babushka is becoming less typical. Slim high heels, the latest hairdos, Paris-inspired knit dresses, and better tailoring are to be seen everywhere in Moscow. Anyone who saw the city five years ago and returns today will be astounded by the change. Young couples dancing in the Sovietskaya Hotel on Saturday night, audiences at the Bolshoi Theater or in the modern auditorium of the new glass-and-concrete Hall of Congresses, are all better dressed, though there are still a number of women to be seen wearing drab skirts with blouses and sweaters.

Makeup, jewelry, girdles, perfumes—all of the trimmings that a generation ago were considered symbols of bourgeois decadence are now accepted. There are daily fashion shows at GUM's, Russian women are dieting and growing slimmer, men wear ties, shave regularly, and wear matching trousers and jackets. And the prefab apartment houses that are piling up with lightning speed on the city outskirts are being furnished with decorative accessories unheard of here twenty years ago. And though the Russians are proud of their achievements in outer space, they are just as proud of having enough living space, of not having to share kitchens with four or five families, of their small summer homes in the country, and even cars, if they can afford them. Prices for all of these things are four or five times higher than in the United States and such luxuries are not yet common to the majority of Russians, but they become more so every day.

Though one sees shops crammed with clothing and furnishings, de luxe food stores called *gastronomes* packed with tins of fresh black Caspian caviar, slabs of smoked sturgeon, champagne from Georgia, and other such delicacies, it must be remembered that such abundance is found only in the largest cities—Moscow, Leningrad, Kiev, Riga. And for the most part the stores nearest the hotels and tourist centers have the choicest stocks.

Before you decide that all of the Soviet citizens have turned chic, visit one of Moscow's most fascinating sights, one I returned to no less than five times in a two-week stay—the Central Market. All of the people selling food here are in effect entrepreneurs, farmers who work the large collectives but who are allowed to plant a small plot of land for family use. What they do not need for their own table they sell on the open market at prices much higher than those in the government-controlled stores. Quality is better, too, and these out-door markets are always jammed. Here are Russians as we might expect them to be, strong, stalwart, peasant-farmer types with hand-some, mellow faces that would have inspired Rembrandt. Powerful men with smiling eyes sport bushy mustaches and wear three or four sweaters under their black cotton overalls. Friendly plump women with white aprons over their black overcoats and babushkas on their heads look like the *matroshka,* the painted wooden dolls-within-dolls that are a favorite Russian toy, or the padded, wide-skirted tea-cozy dolls that are popular souvenirs.

At one stall you might see a few dozen large, earth-colored, fra-grant mushrooms, laid out on clean newspapers as carefully as jewels. Another stand sells dill cucumbers, pickled green tomatoes and red peppers, and sauerkraut from brown earthenware crocks. Others dis-play great orangey-red carrots, dark-green clumps of parsley, an endless variety of white, black, and red radishes and all sorts of root vegetables, cabbages the size of basketballs, and speckled red apples so crisp and winey they'll remind you of the first frosty autumn days in the country. In one section of the Central Market live fish are sold from tanks of icy water, while in another wooden crates are set up to display huge bunches of flowers and potted plants. Meats are sold in a covered pavilion, as are dairy products, and shoppers invariably stop to enjoy a glass of yogurt. Here you find the world's best coarse black bread and dried mushrooms, strung up in thick gray garlands. Nowhere are tourists made to feel more welcome and, with few exceptions, the people working here love to have their pictures taken, especially if you think enough of their produce to photograph that too.

"Seeing the people" is really the most fascinating and rewarding thing of all in the Soviet Union. No one should miss a visit to one of their delightful day nurseries where the children of working mothers are cared for, and no one should fail to spend an evening in Gorky Park with its Ferris wheel and carnival rides and its dance hall where, often, girls dance with girls and boys with boys. Join the Russians at their stupendous puppet shows and at their spectacular circus, where dancing bears are a star attraction just as they have been in

Russia for the past three centuries, and at their vigorous, inspired ballets, an art form in which they are the world's masters. You will find these people place a tremendous importance on education and literacy. The classic and most scathing insult is to be pronounced *nye kulturny*—without culture—an epithet used for everything from bad table manners to a failure to appreciate a poem by Pushkin. It is amazing to see how few intimate settings are available to young people here. Park benches are placed under brilliant overhead street lanterns, giant chandeliers brighten dance floors, and few restaurants have tables for two; strange couples share tables at the whim of the manager.

The more facets one discovers in the Russian personality the harder these people are to understand, much less explain. Like their landscapes, they are given to extremes and excesses. They rarely smile unless there is a good and specific reason and consider the *Amerikanskys* silly because they smile so much. One Russian woman told me she thought it made them look simple and childish. But the Russians love to laugh, and do so often, not only in their theaters but always at parties, especially after a glass of vodka or two. As for tears, "a good Russian cry" is said to be like no other.

No people in the world seem more aware of man's tragedy, and nowhere else do you find such patience and endurance, such an innate sense of irony. One has only to read through the Russian writers to know how true this has always been. The tender plays of Chekhov; the "proletariat poet" Pushkin, whose folk tales inspired many of the great Russian operas and who cried, "I crave more life, more dreams, more agony!"; the anguish of Dostoevsky's tragic heroes; the novelist-playwright Peshkov, whose pseudonym, Gorky, means bitter; Gogol, whose "subject was life," whether in a comedy like *The Inspector-General* or in a tragedy like *Dead Souls;* Aksakov, who said he had "a feeling of pity for all human suffering"; and the Byronic poet, Lermontov, who was killed fighting the Avars in the Caucasus; Leskov, Tolstoy, Turgenev, even today's renegade poet, Yevgeny Yevtushenko—all have dealt with the essential beauty and tragedy of man, all have described "life" tenderly in its minutest details.

Keys to the Russian personality lie in the minor-key, monumental quality of their music, whether it is chorale singing, the more serious works of Borodin, Glinka, Moussorgsky, Shostakovich, and Stravinsky, or the works of Rimsky-Korsakov, the sentimental Tchaikovsky, or the amusing Prokofiev; in the wildly complicated design of buildings such as St. Basil's Cathedral, and in their national history. Read only a little of Russia's past and you will find that this has always been a land of orthodoxy and authoritarianism, of censorship and controls. In the seventeenth century, painters were told how saints should be depicted in the icons. They had to "conform to their accepted images" and the "modern realist" group of painters cropping up at that time were reprimanded for portraying "our Saviour Emmanuel with a puffy face, red lips, curly hair, thick hands and arms, swollen fingers, fat thighs, and the whole of him paunchy and fat like a German . . . nothing lacking but a sword at his hip!" Anyone who sees the modern, socialist realist "happy proletariat" paintings done in the Soviet Union today will realize that the more things change the more they remain the same. The visiting prelate of the Greek church in Aleppo was stunned by the exacting, elaborate ritual in the seventeenth century Moscow churches. "All Russians will undoubtedly become saints," he said, "they outdo even the desert hermits in piety." No wonder Communist party leaders saw fit to clothe Marxist doctrines in numerous religious trappings.

And throughout Russian history, its rulers were prey to *coups,* purges, and plots. Almost every czar crowned mounted the throne over the murdered corpse of his predecessor. Catherine the Great killed her husband; her son Paul was killed by his son Alexander I; and this is just the merest sampling of such events. Rasputin and the Romanovs; Boris Godunov and the "false Dimitri"; Ivan the Terrible who killed his son in a fit of rage; and the civilized Peter the Great, who was educated in Europe and modeled his court after France, but had the head of an unfaithful mistress cut off, pickled, and packed in a glass jar which he kept in his bedchamber. Intrigue and excess might well be the motto on the Russian flag, whether its coat of arms is the imperial eagle or the hammer and sickle.

Perhaps the Russian passion for extremes is in proportion to the size of their country. This is the largest country in the world, the largest single land mass, and comprises one-sixth of the earth's surface. Its nine million square miles spread across two continents and through eleven time zones. Its borders reach from Germany to China, from the Baltic Sea to the Bering Straits, from Finland to India. It includes frozen Arctic wastes in Siberia and tropical gardens in the Crimea, and the temperatures within its borders range from 70 degrees below zero to 115 above. It includes almost a complete assortment of the world's flora and fauna, from polar bears and snow owls to camels and flamingos, from birch and pine forests to grape vineyards and palm groves. Soviet citizens speak almost seventy different languages and more than two hundred dialects and are descendants of more than a hundred nationalities. There are fiercely handsome Georgians in the rocky villages of the Caucasus Mountains and in their historic capital, Tiflis, not far from Gori, where Stalin was born, almost the only town in the Soviet Union where one now hears his name or sees his picture. Circassians near the Turkish border are known for their dark-eyed beauty and their skill with daggers; the Slavic Ukrainians wear brightly embroidered blouses and farm the rich black soil of their wheat fields. Vacationers go to the warm lake resorts of Sochi and Sukhumi, Yalta and Odessa. Moslem rug weavers in Bukhara produce carpets just as their ancestors did; and in the Baltic republics one sees traces of the ancient Swedish rulers in the blue eyes and blonde hair, the colorful folk costumes. Baku in Azerbaijan has enough oil derricks to remind you of Texas; Yerevan is the Armenian capital in the shadow of Mount Ararat; Samarkand and Tashkent are full of blue-tiled mosques and memories of Genghis Khan and Tamerlane.

But whether they are Asian Uzbeks wearing embroidered skull caps or the white-coated, fur-hatted Cossacks of the Don River region who perform in horse shows such as those held in Pyatigorsk; descendants of the invading Mongols who now live in Irkutsk; or Georgians who toast you with a silver-banded cattle horn filled with their local white wine; Turkoman shepherds in white woolly astrakhan helmets; or Caucasian herdsmen in square-shouldered capes and wide white mantles—all are Soviet citizens; all yearn to make at least one pilgrimage to Moscow.

If you cannot get to all of the fascinating and remote corners of this gigantic land, you can see most of its people, costumes and all, in the capital. For at the Agricultural Exhibition (also called the Exhibition of Economic Achievements), are the separate pavilions of the fifteen republics, each with its native products and native architecture.

Besides the museums and cathedrals within the Kremlin walls and the staggering collection of paintings in the Tretyakov Gallery, Moscow has a beautiful array of impressionist works in the Pushkin Gallery. Any student of the Russian Revolution will have a field day here, for at least a dozen museums are devoted to its high spots and memorabilia.

Certainly one should visit the Moscow university, especially if classes are in session, the Church of Ivan the Great, built for Peter I in 1713, the three enormous stadiums, and GUM's with its glass arcades, potted palms, and fountains. Even a traveler on the most limited time schedule should take a side trip to the fourteenth century city, Zagorsk, with its ancient walls, its Troitse-Sergieva Monastery, and its eleven antique churches. Visit Tolstoy's home; take a boat trip along the Moscow River, or a drive to Gorky, where you can visit the country house where Lenin spent the last years of his life.

Almost every visitor to the Soviet Union will want to see the other great cities that were once capitals—Novgorod, Kiev, Leningrad. Of these, the last is the most interesting. Although Leningrad can be reached easily and swiftly by the Soviet passenger jets, a train trip would be much more of an experience and the overnight ride to this city is one of the pleasantest to take. These are the most spacious trains anywhere, with giant samovars steaming away in every car so that you can draw water for tea any time you like. Russian men travel in their pajamas for comfort and male and female passengers share the same sleeping compartments whether they are strangers or not.

Leningrad, the beloved St. Petersburg of Peter the Great, is a European-looking city on the Gulf of Finland, a place of long "white nights" in summer. To Peter, who had traveled extensively in the capitals of Europe, this was to be his "window on the West" and his deep-sea port. He had the whole city built to order by French and Italian architects, and the checkerboard layout of the wide avenues, the parks and squares, the quays and canals, make the city look something like Helsinki, Copenhagen, Amsterdam, and even, now and then, Paris. Now officially dubbed a "Hero City" for its part in the last war, when the Germans besieged the city for nine hundred days and almost two million people starved to death, Leningrad is rich in treasures of art and history. Standing in the courtyard of the great blue-and-white Winter Palace, modeled after Versailles, it is not hard to imagine what the scene was like when the imperial troops opened fire on the masses who gathered there on Bloody

Sunday, or when the Bolsheviks stormed the palace during the October Revolution. Within this palace are the apartments of the czars, now a museum, and the wonderful paintings of the Hermitage. Here are works of all the great Flemish, Italian, Dutch, German, Spanish, and English schools, with more Rembrandts than any museum outside Holland. The paintings of Picasso, Renoir, Matisse are here in staggering numbers, along with what must be the most delicate, silken blue-and-green pear orchard Van Gogh ever painted.

One afternoon drive out to the Peterhof, the summer palace of Peter the Great, where hundreds of fountains are terraced down from the palace, along a narrow strip of a canal, and out to the Gulf of Finland. There are numerous trick fountains, too, in the beautiful gardens here—realistic trees made of iron, which spray water when certain rocks in the ground around them are stepped on. In addition to the palace, with all of its expected chandeliers and marble halls, its gilt and mirrors, see the little wooden *ibza,* the informal cottage which Peter used to get away from it all.

Leningrad's Kazan Cathedral is another unique sight—a museum dedicated to the crimes of the Church against the masses. One floor depicts the evils of all religions, another is devoted entirely to the Catholic Church. Paintings "prove" that priests turned hungry children from their door and a "model room" of an Inquisition torture chamber is complete with thumbscrews, iron masks, and dried blood on the stone floor. Try to see this on a Saturday or Sunday, when mothers take children here on outings and everyone walks around eating apples and ice cream as they look at the fake copies of newspapers and other such "evidence."

Leningrad's main street is the Nevsky Prospekt, a wide thoroughfare where people stroll late into the night, stopping at ice cream parlors and looking in shop windows. This is, traditionally, a liberal and intellectual center. If you ask your guide in Moscow why Dostoevsky is no longer mentioned along with other great Russian writers, she will tell you "he is not a writer for our times." Your guide in Leningrad will probably answer, as mine did, "The state may not approve of him, but I think he was our greatest writer."

Not far from Leningrad, and also on the Neva River, is Novgorod, one of the earliest capitals of the Varangian Swedes who settled the lands originally held by Slavic tribes. This was the city of Alexander Nevsky, who drove both the Swedes and the Teutonic Knights of

Germany and Poland out of Russia in the thirteenth century, and who was allowed to take the name of the river Neva as a mark of honor.

Kiev, "the mother of Russian cities," was the first capital of the Swedish rulers in the ninth century, and the first to adopt Christianity in the tenth under Prince Vladimir. Kiev, in contrast to Moscow and Leningrad, is gay and brightly colored. It rises from the banks of the broad Dnieper River, with its power plants, bridges, and white sand beaches where blonde Ukrainians swim and sun bathe. All Kiev seems like one brilliantly arranged garden. Busts of Lenin and Khrushchev are reproduced in formal flower beds, palms and horse chestnut trees line the main street, Kreshchatik, and the fairytale domes of the city's famed churches rise like golden bells against the clear blue sky. Of these, the eleventh century Sofia Cathedral is the most beautiful, with its icons, mosaics, frescoes, and the tomb of Yaroslav, one of the earliest Kiev princes, who ordered this church built. The Pechersk Monastery, one of the holiest places in the Soviet Union, is here, too. Some of its churches were destroyed during the war but others remain, as do its catacombs and many of its art treasures. Kiev's other sights of interest include the old market quarter, the Podol, half-a-dozen museums, statues of its sainted Vladimir, and the Golden Gate of Prince Yaroslav, which was built to defend the city against the Golden Horde from the East.

FOR THE TRAVELER'S NOTEBOOK

Official Information

Anyone visiting the Soviet Union must pay for his stay in advance through his own travel agent, who books all accommodations with the official government tourist bureau, Intourist. For details see note on p. 352.

Before you go: Intourist, 355 Lexington Ave., New York, N.Y.

In Moscow: SAS Office, Hotel National, 14 Prospekt Karl Marx, Room 206; U.S. Embassy, 19/21 Tchaikovsky St.; Tourist Service Bureau in every hotel; main office, 16 Prospekt Karl Marx.

Money Matters

Currency: The monetary unit is the ruble, divided into 100 kopeks. There are 90 kopeks to $1, U.S.

Tipping: Theoretically, tipping is not practiced in Russia and tips may be refused. However, 5 per cent is a good rule of thumb in restaurants and taxis.

Climate, Clothing, and Essentials

The average temperature in Moscow during the month of July is 67 degrees F., and in January 35 degrees. Naturally, the climate varies throughout the year, but it is for the most part similar to that of other northern European regions. Take along sturdy, informal, practical clothing. In summer, light clothing will generally do, but include a warm suit and a raincoat. Fur coats, boots, and woolen clothes are necessary in winter, as there is a great deal of snow.

Hotels

All hotels in the Soviet Union are operated by Intourist, and visitors are assigned to them on arrival. Although you can request a specific hotel through your travel agent, you may not get what you ask for. Changes in accommodations can rarely be made. There is little point, therefore, in going into great detail on the differences between Moscow hotels, but in general here are a few highlights:

Those traveling on de luxe Intourist plan will have rooms with private baths. The *National Hotel, 14 Prospekt Karl Marx,* is the best hotel in the city. It is located just across from the Kremlin, and it is comfortable, full of atmosphere, and has a pleasant staff. *Hotel Metropol, 1 Prospekt Karl Marx,* is equally well situated, but is big, rambling, and gloomy. The *Ukraina,* on *Dorogmilovskaya Quai,* the *Sovietskaya, 32 Leningradskoye Prospekt,* and the *Leningradskaya, 21/40 Kalanchovskaya Street,* are all skyscraper hotels looking vaguely like Chicago's Wrigley Building. They are enormous, far-flung, and palatial by Russian standards, but absolutely without charm. Other hotels used for Intourist accommodations are the *New Warsaw, Budapest,* the *Pekin,* the *Bucharest,* the *Grand,* the *Moskva,* and the *Berlin.*

Food and Restaurants

The food in Russian restaurants is generally poor, but there are some interesting things to try if you have great patience. Service is incredibly slow, so start early and eat lightly if you are bound for the theater. Tables are large and usually they are shared by two or more parties. Your food coupons entitle you to eat in any Intourist restaurant or hotel dining room. The *National Hotel* offers good food and the fastest, friendliest service (this is all comparative, of course). Among the better appetizers are mushrooms in sour cream, hot crab canapé, and a kind of *pâté* called "cheese of game." Borscht and *solyanka* (a soup of sturgeon, cabbage, tomatoes, lemons, olives, and capers), are almost meals in themselves. Good entrées include grilled fresh sturgeon, shashlik, chicken Kiev, *pojarsky* cutlets, beef Stroganoff, and *lula kabobs,* ground lamb patties broiled on skewers. Caviar, black bread, and smoky hot tea are wonderful everywhere, and on street corners numerous stands sell ice cream and a mildly fermented, extremely refreshing drink, *kvass.* All Intourist restaurants have the same menu, plus some specialties of their own. You will find good Czechoslovakian food at the elegant *Praga;* Hungarian food at the *Budapest,* one of the better eating places in the city; Polish dishes at the *Warsaw;* passable Chinese food at the *Pekin;* and good shashlik at *Zolotoi Kolos* (The Golden Sheaf) at the Agricultural Exhibition.

By far the best restaurant is *Aragvi.* It features Georgian specialties with wonderful appetizers (try the chicken with walnut sauce), a superb bread, and grilled chicken on the bricks. *Ararat* offers Armenian fare and is the only place that has anything like atmosphere. *Ararat, Aragvi,* and *Zolotoi Kolos* are not run by Intourist and you must pay cash for the meals you eat there.

Vodka is the before-dinner drink here, always served with some *zakouski* appetizers. The beer isn't bad and Russian wines from Georgia are surprisingly good—try some. Coffee is appalling—better forget it and drink tea.

Entertainment, Night Life, and Special Events

An evening spent at the Bolshoi Theater is simply a "must" for every visitor to Moscow. This is the home of classical nineteenth century ballet and genuine classical Russian opera. The Moscow Symphony Orchestra is the best in the Soviet Union and ranks among the finest in Europe. If the Red Army Chorus, the Moiseyev Dancing Troupe, or the Berjoska Troupe, appear while you are in town, be sure to see them. They perform in Tchaikovsky Hall and in the Palace of Congress, where some of the principal symphony concerts are also held. Other concerts are given in the Bolshoi Hall, and in the smaller Maly Theater. There are many theaters in Moscow, among which is the famous Moscow Art Theater, where the Stanislavsky tradition is meticulously preserved. At the Roman Gypsy Theater, gypsy drama and music are presented in intimate surroundings; the performance is in vivid pantomime and easily understandable. The Moscow Circus is a sight worth seeing if it's on when you're in the city, and you'll enjoy the *Kukolny* or Central Puppet Theater, where remarkably good shows are staged. The Gorky Park open-air theater offers a variety of programs, and in the Ermitage Park there are several theaters performing both indoors and in the open air. Outdoor cafés, a restaurant, and a chess pavilion add to the pleasures of these parks. Ask your hotel service bureau for tickets to theaters, concert halls, ballet, cinemas, and sporting events.

For a big night out in Moscow, go to the *Sovietskaya,* the city's most popular spot for dinner-dancing with Russians and visitors alike. Do not expect atmosphere here, and women need wear nothing more formal than a darkly colored daytime dress.

The two most interesting annual events from a tourist point of view are *May Day* (May 1 and 2) and the anniversary of the Communist Revolution (*November 7 and 8*). These are times of parades and gymnastic exhibitions and displays by the Soviet armed forces.

Shopping

Most of your souvenir shopping will be done at GUM, the endlessly long, glass-arcaded government department store complete with fountains and palms, and TSUM, the Central Department Store. You'll find some amusing toys at *Children's World (Detsky Mir),* and attractive gifts at the *podarkis* (gift shops) such as *Staleshnekavb* and *Petravka, 8.* Good buys include multicolored lacquer work in big canisters and small bowls, ladles and trays, tea cozies, enameled thimbles, cups and tea-glass holders, carved ivory, *paalag* art (a kind of polished, intricate, and expensive lacquer work), and records, though you'll need your guide to translate here while you make selections.

Background Reading

Main Street USSR, and *Travel Guide to Russia,* by Irving R. Levine
The Dukes of Muscovy, by Harold Lamb
Dragon in the Kremlin, and *Eastern Exposure,* by Marvin Kalb
Adventures in Czarist Russia, by Alexandre Dumas
The Sabres of Paradise, by Lesley Blanch
Russian Duet, by Willie Snow Etheridge
The Thaw, by Ilya Ehrenburg
The Silent Don, by Mikhail Sholokhov
Life and Thought in Old Russia, edited and translated by Marthe Blinoff
The works of Chekhov, Tolstoy, Dostoevski, Turgenev, Gogol, Gorky, and Pushkin all provide excellent glimpses into the tone of life in Russia's past.

THE MIDDLE EAST

Iran (Persia)

TEHERAN

The modern capital of an ancient land

ASK someone what comes to mind when he thinks of Iran, and the answer will undoubtedly have to do with oil and caviar, the beautiful ex-queen, Soraya, and her shah of shahs, Mohammed Reza Pahlavi, who finally had his heir by his second wife, Farah Diba. If this were all, a trip to the land would hardly be worthwhile, but it is far from all, for Iran is the country that once was Persia. As such it recalls far more romantic and exotic images. This was the world of *Thousand Nights and a Night,* the wondrous tales of Hajji Baba of Isfahan and the *Rubáiyát* of Omar Khayyám. Its very name brings to mind a sumptuous dream of ruby-handled scimitars and the Peacock Throne, turquoises and silver, apricots and pomegranates, blue mosques and the lush carpets of Kermanshah, the nightingales, roses, and poets of Shiraz, and exquisite gardens as intricately landscaped and embroidered with flowers as those shown in the polished, collage-like Persian miniatures.

There are associations that date back even farther than those above, to the culture of the Assyrians, the Hittites, and the Sumerians, and to such great kings as Cyrus the Great, who formed the Persian empire by uniting the Medes with the Aryans, the Indo-

Germanic people who settled between the Indus and Tigris rivers in what roughly is now Iran. It was Cyrus, too, who in 538 B.C. conquered Babylonia and restored Jerusalem to the Jews. His son, Darius I, invaded Greece only to be defeated on the plains of Marathon; Xerxes I, the son of Darius, crossed the Hellespont (the Bosphorus) and beat the Spartans at Thermopylae, but later lost the battle of Salamis.

This country was held by the Macedonians under Alexander, by the Seleucidae and the Parthians, the Sassanians and the Arabs, and its greatest cities were destroyed by the Mongol invasions of Genghis Khan and Tamerlane. It was the art and architecture of Persia that inspired the Mogul rulers; the cupola domes and wide pointed arches, the arcaded courtyards and splashing fountains, the perspective of the paintings and the luxurious dress of the rulers were considered the "Mogul" style from Tiflis and Tashkent to the Taj Mahal.

This was the second time Persia had served as the artistic wellspring of a vast empire for, two thousand years before, the arts of Sumer and Assyria filtered through the biblical world, and the Athenians, who considered these people barbarians in spite of their huge palaces and powerful sculptures, were to learn much from them about governmental organization, for which the Persians had an unusual flair. Though they worshiped a number of pagan deities such as Mithras, the god of light, and Ormazd, the god of benevolence, at least six hundred years before Christ Zoroaster introduced the idea of a monotheistic religion with a just and omnipotent god, Ahura-Mazda. The Parsee religion he founded still exists in Persia and other sections of the East; and some of the fire temples of Zoroastrianism are still in the city of Yazdi.

In the sixteenth century the country was at the height of its sophistication, a crossroads point on the trade routes of East and West, well versed in the cultures of Islam, Venice, and China. It was perhaps at its most beautiful when it was most decadent, in the seventeenth century, when its paintings were peopled by sad-eyed, fainthearted, brocade-draped dandies, who looked at each other with a puerile tenderness and wan beauty.

At the foot of the rocky, snow-capped Elburz Mountains and in the shadow of the cone-shaped, volcanic Mount Demavend, lies Teheran, the country's capital only since 1788, so that on the surface it seems barely a part of Persia's past. But Teheran is a direct result of that past, a city that was settled when the inhabitants of the nearby former capital, Rey, fled before the Mongol invasions in 1220, and it grew in importance and by the eighteenth century was Iran's chief city. Its location was ideal for its new function, for it was close to the Caspian shore, where a major part of the country's population has always clustered, and it was far enough inland to be easily defended against the Russians, with whom the Persians had a series of wars over the disputed areas of Georgia and Armenia. The present boundaries of Iran were, in fact, the result of a territorial agreement between Russia and Great Britain in 1907, when both had spheres of influence in the area. In addition, Teheran draws a plentiful supply of water from the nearby mountain springs—no small consideration in a country that has one-quarter of its 628,060 square miles taken up by salt deserts.

This capital is a modern city of two million people, with a complex of government buildings from which the present shah works to bring about land reforms, irrigation projects, and new programs of health and education for his 20,678,000 subjects. Iran's current income is based on the oil fields of the Persian Gulf, potentially the richest in the world; the supply of sturgeon and caviar, the Caspian Sea; her golden melons, glistening emeralds, and Oriental carpets.

All of the city's antique sights are relegated to its mosques and museums: the Gulistan Palace, where one may see the richly jeweled Peacock Throne from which Shah Jahan ruled the Mogul world in his Red Fort palace of Old Delhi, and here too are the vast imperial library and rooms full of royal regalia; the ethnological museum, with its old costumes and samples of traditional Persian folk crafts; the Iran Bastan Museum, with archeological relics dating back to 4,000 B.C.; the Bank Melli Iran, with its collection of glittering crown jewels and bowls full of loose emeralds, pearls, rubies, and diamonds; and the Fine Arts Museum, with modern Iranian paintings and pottery, textiles, rugs, and woodwork.

The Persians have always had an eye for beauty and a high level of taste that they have maintained up to the present, and nowhere is this more obvious than in Teheran's Bazaar. The workmanship in metal displayed in the halls of the coppersmiths, silversmiths and goldsmiths is sheer perfection, and the array of richly colored hand-loomed carpets is equally dazzling. But there is beauty even in the more ordinary objects here—in the collars of turquoise ceramic beads worn by domestic animals to ward off the evil eye; in the brightly embroidered saddlebags; and in the cone-shaped pyramids of rice, beans, and sugar.

Of the city's mosques, the most impressive and regal is the Sepalsalar, the scene of official mourning and funeral ceremonies, though the older Masjed-i-Shah, with its golden dome, graceful minarets, and intricate, glittering mosaics, is perhaps more exquisitely detailed and spiritually rewarding.

In addition to providing Iran with its wealth of sturgeon and caviar, the Caspian Sea, some 175 miles from the capital, serves as a playground for Teheran's more affluent inhabitants. It is ringed with luxurious resorts set in mountainside gardens and evergreen forests, and a traveler might well spend a few days here before or after covering the more ancient sights of the country.

Among those sights, none is more impressive than Persepolis, truly one of the Middle East's most spectacular ruins. Here, and in the neighboring Pasargade, the ancient royal capital, are the palace of Darius I, and an earlier palace of Cyrus; the Hall of a Hundred Columns, which was completed by Xerxes; the richly carved staircase of the Apadana; a forest of carved columns and massive gates; and a veritable zoo of powerful stone sculptures—winged lions and flying bulls and the sharp-beaked Achaemenian eagle, the forerunner perhaps of the emblems of later European empires. In Pasargade one may see the remains of "Solomon's Prison," the tomb of Cyrus, and the exquisitely designed Palace of Audience. Four miles from here, in what is now called Naghsh-e-Rustam, is the necropolis of the ancient Persian kings. Here stand Zoroaster's Shrine and the tombs of Darius the Great and Xerxes. To reach them one must climb a ladder to the rocky cliff which shelters the royal burial place.

Shiraz, about 425 miles south of Teheran, is the starting point for a visit to the ruins of Persepolis, and is in itself worth visiting. The city, with its lush rose gardens reflected in crystal-clear pools, its beautiful mosques and tree-shaded parks, and its nightingales, is the pride of Iran. It is rich in memories of the great Persian poets: Hafiz, whose erotic and mystical verses beguiled Tamerlane and whose alabaster tomb nestles on the banks of the river Ruknabad amid groves of orange trees and cypresses, and Sadi, whose life-size statue stands in the midst of the city he loved.

But whatever one sees in Iran, no one should miss Isfahan, the greatest of the remaining treasures from the empires of the shahs. Now a city of more than half-a-million people and the country's leading textile center, this is the city of the blue mosques of Persia— those glittering turquoise domes that rise like bubbles against the red backdrop of the Zagros Mountains surrounding them. Set with a zigzag pattern of glazed tiles and gold striping and accented by the slashing white ribbons of Arabic script, these mosques, with their slender minarets of fawn-colored brick, are just as close to perfection as the equally intricate designs of the paintings and carpets for which the Persians are famous.

Isfahan, the city the Iranians say is "half the world," was the capital of the great Shah Abbas, who reigned from 1587 to 1629 and who was responsible for some of the city's most beautiful buildings as well as for its arrangement. The center of the town still stands as it was in his time—the Maidan, a rectangle 550 yards long, the scene of polo matches in Shah Abbas' day and now a handsome park. Around this are some of the city's most famous mosques, most notably the Masjed-i-Shah, or Great Shah Mosque, a turquoise jewel unsurpassed by any other in the city, its tiles set in a shining, fragmented geometric pattern, and its courtyard a wash of blues, as the huge dome is reflected in the pool below. Shah Abbas' personal mosque, the smaller Lutfallah, is halfway down the Maidan, an exquisitely proportioned miniature of domes and soaring spires. Opposite this is the Ali Qapu, or Sublime Porte, with a graceful pavilion balcony over its great archway, from which Shah Abbas would watch polo matches or receive foreign dignitaries.

More rugged in style and even more powerful if less decorative, is the Masjid-i-Jami, built in the eleventh century with a Gothic severity about its huge stone columns and arches, its subterranean arcades and two brick domes. Its simple and austere architectural style has the wonderful sense of space-beyond-space that Islamic buildings always seem to suggest.

Isfahan has a fascinating bazaar, the Menar-i-Joombam, or Shaking Minaret, the lovely blue and sun-yellow arabesque-inlaid tilework of the Madrasah Chehar Bagh, once a religious school, and the amazing bridges built by Shah Abbas to span the city's narrow trickle of a river. Built in three-tiered arcades of neatly pointed arches, these handsome and elegant porticos were used as a place of cool repose, pavilions to which the city's residents could come in summer to enjoy the sound of rippling water. The shah had a special channel designed to collect every drop of dry-season water so that the effect could be created, and the greatest of these bridges, the Khajoo, is still used as a place for wedding celebrations, as it was three hundred years ago.

FOR THE TRAVELER'S NOTEBOOK

Official Information

Before you go: Iranian Embassy, Press & Information Dept., Washington, D.C.

In Teheran: SAS Office, 73 Ave. Ferdowci; Tourist-Iran, 341-40 Ave. Shah Reza; U.S. Embassy, Ave. Takhte Jamshid & Roosevelt Ave.

Money Matters

Currency: The monetary unit in Iran is the rial. $1, U.S. equals about Rials 75.

Tipping: Tip as you would in most European cities: 10 to 15 per cent over and above the service charge which will be added to the bill. In hotels and restaurants, porters expect a tip of 20 to 30 rials. No tips to taxi drivers, ushers in cinemas or theaters.

Climate, Clothing and Essentials

The climate of Iran is similar to that of the European continent. The winters are mild and sunny, with temperatures rarely falling below 40 degrees F. Summer is hot and dry with day temperatures around 95 degrees and a very low humidity.

In Teheran dress as you would in any American or European city. You need woolen clothes, including a warm overcoat, during the winter months, and lightweight clothes during the summer. Bring all the film you'll need during your stay.

Hotels

A number of good hotels are available at prices roughly comparable to those in Western capitals. Besides the hotels there are many excellent boarding houses offering less expensive accommodations. Reserve hotel room well in advance.

DE LUXE: *The Royal Teheran,* a new, modern Hilton hotel, has been open only a year. The atmosphere is best described as "international." Ranking at the top are two de luxe hotels, the *Darband* and the *Park.* Hotel Darband is situated nine miles north of Teheran at an altitude of

5,525 feet. It is particularly nice in summer, when you will enjoy its tennis courts and swimming pool. During the winter you might prefer the *Park Hotel, Avenue Hafez,* located downtown. These hotels charge about Rials 650 to 1,200 for a single room with private bath, and Rials 1,200 to 1,600 for a double room with bath. Other deluxe hotels worth considering are the *Sina,* the *Semiramis, Teheran Palace,* and the new *Commodore.*

FIRST CLASS: Among first class hotels are the *Naderi, Ave. Naderi,* and the *Jam, Ave. Takhte Jamshid,* both newly opened. Expect to pay Rials 500 to 700 for a single room and Rials 1,000 for a double room. The *Tourist Iran, Ave. Pahlavi,* is also very good. Here you may have a single room from Rials 450 and a double room would cost from 600 to 800.

PENSIONS: If you are going to stay in Teheran a week or so, perhaps you would prefer a good pension. Rates include room and breakfast. Among the best pensions are the *Villa Delfi, Ave. Paris;* the *Pension Paprika (same address)* and the *German Hotel-Pension, Koutcheh Arbab Jamshid.* Pension prices vary from Rials 300 to 800 per day.

Food and Restaurants

This is the place to eat your fill of Caspian Sea caviar—it's superb, and a great bargain. The Iranian national staple is rice, and food here includes all of the specialties described for Lebanon and Turkey. For a meal in genuine Iranian surroundings try the restaurants *Fard* or *Shamshiri* near the Bazaar. The most popular Iranian dish here is *chelow kebab,* grilled meat and rice. Persian melons, white peaches, and other fruits are heavenly. Restaurants will generally offer you any kind of international drinks (vodka is best with the caviar), but imported liquor is expensive because of high customs duties. Among the local table wines we recommend the red Chahin No. 6, and the white Riesling No. 5, which are always good.

Most hotels serve international food in their dining rooms but besides these, Teheran has other excellent restaurants, among which the *Coq d'Or* (try *kebabs* of fresh sturgeon), *Leon's Grill Room,* and *La Résidence* are good and have lovely gardens for dinner. *L'Auberge* serves good Russian food, especially the cutlets Kiev. During the summer most restaurants serve evening meals outdoors. Restaurant prices are moderate by our standards.

Entertainment, Night Life, and Special Events

The *Darband* and *Park* hotels have dancing and floor shows. The *Colbeh* in the *Darband* resembles international night clubs anywhere. Other night clubs include the new *Miami* (with floor show) and the *Beluguette* (music, dancing, and good food). A new attraction is the native Iranian night club and restaurant *Shoukoufeh*. The floor show includes Arabian belly-dancers, acrobats, and magicians. The atmosphere here is really different and exciting.

Shopping

First on the list are, of course, Persian carpets. You will find carpets of many qualities and types in the Bazaar and in the large stores. Silver objects are fine souvenirs, as are bronze and brass. Ladies will be impressed by the *geeveh* (shoes), and the linens and tablecloths with handmade designs, which are reasonably priced. Old Persian miniatures are real treasures but hard to export, and there is beautiful inlaid woodwork. The main shopping districts include the Avenues Ferdowci, Naderi, Lalezar, and Istanbul. For genuine Iranian art we can confidently recommend the *Christmas Shop,* on Avenue Ferdowci, and the *Teheran Art Gallery,* Avenue Naderi. It's better not to buy in the Bazaar unless you know the ropes or have a local resident with you.

Background Reading

Blind White Fish in Persia, by Anthony Smith
The Valley of the Assassins and Other Persian Travels, by Freya Stark
Iran, Past and Present, by Donald N. Wilbur
Arabesque and Honeycomb, by Sacheverell Sitwell
Hajji Baba of Isfahan, translated by James Morier
The Art of the Middle East, by Leonard Wooley
Persian Art, published by Skira

Israel

TEL AVIV

The Hill of Spring

FIFTY years ago, Tel Aviv was a straggling community just beginning
to crop up along a strip of sand dunes near the mouth of the Yarkon
River, a suburban stepchild of the great and ancient city of Jaffa.
Today the offspring has far outgrown the parent and, with a population of almost four hundred thousand has become the largest and
most vital city in Israel. It is a sprawling, bright Mediterranean
metropolis, with broad avenues and busy traffic circles, a skyline of
sugar-cube apartment houses and balconied hotels, and a wide white
beach lined with palm trees and edged with dozens of sidewalk cafés.
It is, in every way, a modern commercial city, a thriving seaport and
a tourist center, and it bristles with a cultural life that includes symphony orchestras and opera companies, repertory theaters and dance
groups, chamber music ensembles and art museums. Its street vendors
sell ice cream and hot dogs, buttered corn-on-the-cob and salted
chick peas, and its hundreds of shops display everything from French
perfumes and Persian rugs to a native array of Yemenite handcrafts,
such as silver filigree jewelry and jade-green bronze work, richly
embroidered cottons and rough-textured pottery.

Sitting at its cafés sipping ices or lemon tea, you are surrounded by a babel of languages that will probably include Hebrew and English, Italian and Russian, Rumanian and Polish, French and Arabic, Turkish and Hungarian, impeccable German or Yiddish, the German dialect of central European Jews. At the newsstands you may choose between two dozen daily papers printed in twelve different languages.

Like all of Israel, Tel Aviv is a melting pot, its population made up of immigrants from eighty different countries—Jews who flocked to their biblical home during the "ingathering" that followed the Nazi disaster in Europe, a return they believe to be a fulfillment of the prophecy of Ezekiel: "Thus saith the Lord God: I will gather you from the people and assemble you out of the countries where ye have been scattered, and I will give you the land of Israel." Since the Arab-Israeli armistice in 1949, that population has increased by 70,000 refugees each year and has nearly tripled to its present 2,365,000—a growth no less astounding for its variety than for its rate. Those who came to Israel had for the most part only one thing in common: they had been born to Jewish parents (or, more specifically, to Jewish mothers, since that is the qualifying requirement, on the theory that you can never be sure who a child's father is, but you are always certain of its mother). Within that rather broad spectrum were gathered believers and nonbelievers; intellectuals from Central Europe and cave dwellers from the Sahara Desert; sari-draped Indians and warrior tribes from the shores of the Red Sea; blonde-haired, blue-eyed "Aryans" from the West and olive-skinned, dark-eyed Arabic-looking Jews from the casbahs of North Africa; the Yemeni tribes of artisans from Saudi Arabia, who had never heard of airplanes until they flew in them, and scientists from Germany and Russia, such as the country's first president, Dr. Chaim Weizmann.

"Israel," says one of the government tourist brochures, "is the land of milk and honey and the electric current is 220 volts, 50 cycles." That sentence is perhaps as good a summation of the country and its paradoxes as any other. As a nation it is less than twenty years old yet its history dates back to 1300 B.C., when Joshua settled the first of the biblical Hebrews in what is now the divided city of Jerusalem, and the present Israeli capital. It is a land where the Bible is the best guide, whether you are a tourist in search of such ancient sights as the Nazareth of Christ's boyhood, or the Dead Sea setting of Sodom, or an engineer looking for the copper-rich mines of King Solomon, now being worked again after a lapse of three thousand years. This is the Promised Land, founded on the laws of Moses but organized and flourishing on the basis of the latest scientific and technological advances. Its official language, the ancient Hebrew, is spoken better by Israel's children, the native-born *sabras,* than by their immigrant parents and grandparents who are more at home with the "modern" European tongues. And this five-thousand-year-old language has been revised to cope with problems and concepts the prophets never dreamed of—with income tax returns and nuclear physics, engineering and meteorology, existentialism and advertising, television and Telstar.

Here, where a modern plough turning the soil of a new cooperative farm *kibbutz* may uncover the mosaic floor of an antique synagogue or the street of a Roman village, the water spouts that irrigate the Negev are symbolically set in the seven-branched shape of the traditional candelabra, the Menorah.

Considering the odds against Israel's survival at its outset—its present-day achievements are as awe-inspiring as any biblical miracle. The vast Negev Desert, which covers almost two-thirds of the country's 7,993 square miles and spearheads south to the Gulf of Aqaba between the heavily patroled borders of Egyptian Sinai and Hashemite Jordan, now receives most of the new immigrants and is being mined for its phosphates and copper, drilled for its oil and tapped for its natural gas, and a 100-mile pipeline leading from the river Jordan will irrigate 100,000 acres of new farmlands. The sea that has been called "Dead" because of a salt ratio that makes life impossible in its waters is now alive with potash and bromine works.

It is hard to decide whether Israel's past or present is the more interesting, and visitors to the country are torn between marveling at its modern activity and climbing its antique ruins; fortunately, it is almost always possible to do both simultaneously. Present-day Israel can be seen operating at its peak in Tel Aviv, but just outside is the quiet old port town of Jaffa, the biblical Joppa, from which Jonah sailed to his adventure with the whale and where St. Peter lived with Simon the Tanner. Drive from old Jaffa to modern Jerusalem and you pass the spot on which David is said to have slain Goliath with his slingshot. The Israeli capital is the modern half of Jerusalem; the more ancient and fabled portion lies across the armistice frontier in Jordan. Here one can visit such symbols of Israeli progress as the Hebrew University or the Knesset, the country's parliament building, wander through the exhibition halls of the Israeli Pavilion, tour the sparkling new Hadassah Medical Center, or pay respects at the tomb of Theodor Herzl, the founder of the Zionist movement. But if you prefer, you can travel back in time by visiting Mount Zion, the site of King David's tomb, and the room that is reputed to be the scene of the Last Supper. There are scores of ancient relics in the archeological museum, and in this city too is Ein Kerem, the birthplace of John the Baptist.

Beersheba, now the capital of the Negev, and an important Bedouin market center, was the city of Abraham and the seven wells from which he drew water for his flocks, and it was a capital too of the Judean kings and Roman legates.

The Sea of Galilee provides Israel with much of its fresh-water fish even as it did in the days when Christ preached along its shores. Tiberias, the city built by Herod and used as a place of refuge when the Jews were driven from Jerusalem by the Romans in 70 A.D., is now a smart week-end resort. You may swim or boat on the lake, or visit the tomb of Maimonides, the twelfth century philosopher, or try the waters of the sulphur springs which drew the Romans there two thousand years ago. Also along the Galilee shores is the remnants of the third century synagogue of Capernaum, the town where Christ did much of his early healing; and a little way further is Bethsaida or Tabgha, said to be the place at which Christ fed the five thousand with five loaves of bread. From here you can climb the sloping hill that is the Mount of Beatitudes, with its Franciscan church and a palm-fringed view of the lyre-shaped Sea of Galilee.

It was in the town of Cana, which is near Christ's early home in Nazareth, that he turned the water into wine. In this vicinity also is Mount Tabor, the traditional scene of the Transfiguration, with its Greek Orthodox church noted for its fine mosaics.

If you plan to spend a seaside week end in Israel's southernmost city, Eilat, on your way you pass the smelting furnaces of King Solomon's mines; and if you are interested in seeing the evaporating pans of the potash works on the Dead Sea, you can also gaze at the salt column which is supposedly the remains of Lot's wife, for this lowest point on earth, some 1,290 feet below sea level, was the site of the doomed city Sodom.

You may spend a delightful half day in the pretty seaside town of Caesarea and view the remains of Roman tombs and an aqueduct, Crusader castles and cathedrals, in this, the harbor town of Herod where St. Peter preached to the Gentiles. Or you can spend half a week in the lovely old city of Haifa, Israel's only deep-water port.

Here a scenic road winds up from the bustling harbor sections to the top of Mount Carmel, with its impressive gold-domed, white Bahai church, the caves where Elijah preached, and a view over the beautiful old port city. It is especially rich in art museums, with its Marc Chagall house and its collections of modern and ancient paintings and sculptures, its many galleries and the Ein Hod artists' colony. A group of Crusader castles is strung along the coast beyond Haifa in the Frankish towns of Acre and Athlit, and from here you may drive along the ancient caravan routes of the Valley of Jezreel past Megiddo, the ancient battleground of Armageddon, where ruins five thousand years old are being excavated.

All around the country the *kibbutzim*, the communal farms, and the *moshav*, which are villages of small private farms, stand side by side with Arab towns, a welfare state where capitalism, syndicalism, and collectivism coexist. This is one of the world's newest nations with one of the world's lowest illiteracy rates, where more American books are read per capita in a year than in any other country outside of the United States. Whether you visit this country for its antiquities or its modern advancements, its folk dancing or its religious shrines, you will be forced to wonder at the stamina and drive of its cosmopolitan people.

FOR THE TRAVELER'S NOTEBOOK

Official Information

Before you go: Israeli National Tourist Office: 574 Fifth Ave., New York, N.Y.; 5 South Wabash, Chicago, Ill.; 9350 Wilshire Blvd., Los Angeles, Cal.

In Tel Aviv: SAS Office, 22 Rothschild Blvd.; Israel Government Tourist Corp., 7 Mendele St.; U.S. Embassy, 38 Hakashet St.

Money Matters

Currency: The monetary unit is the Israeli pound (I£). I£ 3 equals $1, U.S.

Tipping: A 10 per cent service charge is added to all hotel and restaurant bills. Luggage porters are tipped half a pound, while barbers in large hotels only are tipped 10 to 15 per cent of the bill. Taxi drivers are not tipped.

Climate, Clothing and Essentials

Israel has a sunny Mediterranean climate with a hot, somewhat humid summer from the middle of June to October, when the temperature averages 86 degrees F. January and February are inclined to be rainy and the best months for a visit are mid-September to November, and March through June. Temperatures in winter (December, January, and February) average 53 degrees. Except in orthodox areas, dress is casual, with shorts and slacks popular by day. Bring enough film for your stay.

Hotels

Accommodations are good but limited, so be sure you have confirmed reservations well in advance. Hotels are graded A, B, C, and accommodations are available for bed and breakfast, half board, or full board. Single rooms with baths in class A hotels range from I£ 25, with breakfast, on up to 48, American plan. Doubles start at I£ 45 and go up to I£ 75. Class B hotels charge from I£ 12 to 21.50 for a single room with bath and breakfast, and from I£ 25 to 35 for a double room with full meals for two.

CLASS A: *The Dan Hotel, 99 Hayarkon St.,* is one of the city's best. Located on the Mediterranean, it has a roof garden, travel bureaus, and all hotel facilities. *The Sheraton Tel-Aviv, Hayarkon St.,* is the newest hotel in the city. It offers air conditioning, efficient service, and is conveniently located. *Ramat Aviv, Nathanya Rd.* Set just a few miles out of the city, this hotel has a lovely swimming pool, tennis courts, and bridle paths. Three lovely resort hotels, located a few miles from Tel Aviv at Herzlia-on-the-Sea, are the *Accadia Grand,* which has a children's playground as well as all of the usual hotel conveniences; the *Sharon,* with gardens, tennis courts, and dinner dancing; and the *Tadmor,* which is smaller and more personal than the other two and offers most of the same facilities.

CLASS B: Good class B hotels include the *Yarden, 130 Ben Yehuda St.; Savoy, 5 Geula St.; Armon, Hayarkon St.;* and the *Park, 76 Hayarkon St.* Class B hotels have some rooms that are air conditioned and have private baths with showers, and all have restaurants and full hotel facilities.

For a complete list of hotels throughout Israel, write to one of the Israeli National Tourist Offices listed above and ask for the pamphlet "Israel Tourist Hotels."

Food and Restaurants

Because Israel is made up of people who emigrated from all parts of the world, there is a wide variety of national cuisines one can sample, particularly those of Central Europe. Native dishes parallel those of the other Middle Eastern countries and so do the local products, especially the fruits (dates, figs, and Jaffa oranges). *Peeta,* the native unleavened bread, is delicious, and you should also try *humus,* a combination of pureed chick peas and sesame oil, and *taheena,* a sesame seed puree. *Felafel* is the favorite Israeli snack and is made of ground chick peas, onions, garlic, and chili peppers, fried into croquettes and sold on all street corners. Lamb is the main meat, served as shashlik, or ground into patties, or broiled on skewers (*kebab*), or used to stuff vegetables (*machshi*) such as green peppers. The fish is excellent, the *leben,* or yogurt, delicious and refreshing. You will also find all of the dishes generally classified as "Jewish" here, including *gefülte* (stuffed) fish, the egg bread, *challah,* and *cholent,* a lima-bean-and-meat casserole. Pork is forbidden to the Israelis and the beef leaves a lot to be desired. Native wines and beers are good and both tea and coffee are equally popular beverages.

Middle Eastern food is served at *Tel Yam, Tzli Esh,* and *Orley,* three very popular Tel Aviv dining places. *Zuckerman* features vegetarian specialties, and the *Rishon Cellar* is the most popular restaurant for European food. *Lucky's Bar* is noted for its Italian food, and *Jeanett's* specializes in fish dishes. There are also a number of delightful sidewalk cafés throughout Tel Aviv.

Entertainment, Night Life, and Special Events

The Tel Aviv Opera House has frequent performances, though the operas are performed in Hebrew. The Israeli Philharmonic performs at the handsome new Frederick Mann Auditorium, and there are weekly chamber music concerts in the city's museum. Ballet and folk-dancing and singing exhibitions are constantly going on somewhere and you should check your hotel desk for any that take place during your stay. There are theaters with amateur groups giving performances in English, plus professional troupes doing Hebrew and Yiddish dramas. The Habima Theater is one of the best in this last category.

There are a number of night clubs with floor shows, dancing, and food. Among these are the *Theater Club,* the *Omar Khayyam,* and the *Adria.* The bars and clubs in the leading hotels are popular as well.

Among the most colorful celebrations in March or April are the *Adloyda* parades in all of the main cities. There is a music festival at Passover at Ein Gev on the Sea of Galilee; and folk dances are held at *kibbutz* Dalia every third August—due next in 1966. Since most of the holidays are figured by the Hebrew lunar calendar, these dates are only approximate and should be checked from year to year. *Israeli Independence Day* on or about April 20 is a time of parades, pageants, and street dancing.

Shopping

One of the best buys in Israel is the delicate filigree jewelry made by the Yemenites and Persians, handsome copper- and enamelware, ceramics, costume dolls, and cloisonné. There are beautiful brocades, embroideries, and furs. Custom-made clothes are very reasonable since they are sold free of local taxes to tourists, who receive the finished garments at the ship or plane as they leave the country. Diamonds are also good buys here.

There are shops and bazaars all over Tel Aviv and in the lobbies of some of the better hotels. Allenby Road is one of the best shopping districts and it is here that you will find the excellent folk crafts shops, the *Wizo Center*, the *Rivoli*, and the *Maskit* and *Menora*. Other shopping centers include Dizengoff St., Ben Yehuda Rd., Frishman St., and Mograbi Sq.

Background Reading

The Splendour of Israel, by Robert Payne
Thieves in the Night, by Arthur Koestler
The Whole Loaf, by Sholom Kahn
The Bible, and *Baker's Bible Atlas*
Everyone's Guide to Israel, by Joan Comay
A Concise History of Israel, by M. A. Beek

Jordan

JERUSALEM

Bride of kings and mother of prophets

OLD Jerusalem, the Jordanian city, is divided from its modern half, the capital of Israel, which lies across an armed border just beyond the defensive wall built by Suleiman the Magnificent. Three of the world's greatest religious sects—the Jewish, the Christian, and the Moslem—claim this half-city as their shrine. More than one-third of the earth's population has spiritual roots in a city that was nineteen centuries old when Christ was born; a town the Egyptians knew as *Urusalimu,* and which was first recorded in the Bible as Salem, in the time of Melchizedek, "Priest of the Most High God." It was the city of Abraham, David, and Solomon, Nebuchadnezzar and Herod the Great, the scene of Christ's condemnation, crucifixion and resurrection, and the place from which the prophet Mohammed ascended to Allah's heaven. And between the ring of biblical hills and valleys that rim the city are crammed the holy places of all three religions, superimposed, one over the other, so that it becomes virtually impossible to sort them out as to sect, or to place them in time, or to know which is historical fact or fancy.

A perfect case in point is the Dome of the Rock, *El-Harem esh-Sharif,* the Noble Sanctuary. A magnificently domed and minareted mosque built in the seventh century A.D. by the Ommiad caliphs to mark the site of the prophet's apotheosis, the shrine stands on Mount Moriah of Genesis, the traditional spot where Abraham prepared to sacrifice his son, Isaac, the setting for King David's altar and Solomon's first temple which was destroyed by Nebuchadnezzar in 586 B.C. After the Roman conquest Hadrian built a shrine to Jupiter on this site. Since it was a pagan temple, the Christian Empress Helena ordered it razed when she came to Jerusalem in the fourth century.

Helena was canonized for her successful search for the True Cross, which she found in Jerusalem, thereby establishing the location of Calvary and her son, the Emperor Constantine, built a church to mark the discovery. Called the Church of the Holy Sepulcher and containing the Sepulcher itself, the last five Stations of the Cross are located within its walls. Each Friday the Franciscan fathers retrace the steps of Christ on His way to Calvary (some of the paths of the Via Dolorosa are still paved with the Roman stones on which He walked) and pass under ancient arches, the most famous of which is Hadrian's *ecce homo,* the place where Christ appeared in His purple robe, wearing the crown of thorns, and where Pontius Pilate, after having declared he "found no fault in him" said, "Behold the Man." Pilgrims come from all over the world to follow the way of the cross and at Eastertime thousands take part in the procession on Good Friday.

The fourteenth century citadel of the Egyptian sultans was the site of David's Tower and Herod's Palace, and the excavations at the Russian Orthodox church of Alexandros Nephki revealed remains of a Roman triumphal arch, an ancient entrance to Constantine's basilica of the Holy Sepulcher, and parts of a wall that enclosed the temple of Venus built by Hadrian.

A few of the shrines belong exclusively to one religion: Christianity claims the Crusader-built Church of St. Anne, commemorating the birthplace of the Virgin Mary, while Jews revere their traditional scene of mourning, the Wailing Wall, parts of which date back to Herod's reign. The Mosque of Omar marks the place where the caliph prayed on his entry into Jerusalem, and the Islamic Museum, with its glittering array of heraldic armory, contains some of the richest Moslem treasures in the world. The Palestine Archeological Museum, with many findings of recent excavations, houses the Dead Sea Scrolls, discovered in 1947 near the Jordanian village of Khirbet

Qumran by shepherds who were looking for a stray goat. Experts are now at work deciphering the scrolls.

Beyond the city's walls lie more relics of Jerusalem's biblical past. Eleven miles away is the town of Bethlehem, where one can see Rachel's tomb and Solomon's Pools, the ancient source of Jerusalem's water supply. Within the city, the Church of the Nativity has been a place of pilgrimage since the fourth century. Essentially the work of the Emperor Justinian in the sixth century A.D., parts of Constantine's fourth century mosaic floors can still be seen. A little beyond the city, on the Shepherds' Field, a commemorative watch is held each year on Christmas Eve.

The lovely olive-shaded Grotto of Gethsemane, where Christ received the Judas kiss and prayed on the night of His betrayal, is connected by a narrow passage to the Church of the Assumption and the tomb of the Virgin, built by Melisande, the consort of the twelfth century Crusader king of Jerusalem. The Garden Tomb, said to be the place of Christ's interment, and the first century necropolis of the kings of Adiabene are both nearby.

In spite of its religious associations, Jerusalem is anything but spiritual or detached. It is a lively, effervescent city of 800,000, a noisy hubbub of winding *souk* bazaars filled with trays and vessels of hammered brass and copper, olivewood boxes, old coins, and, inevitably, carpets. Camels and donkeys brush against Volkswagens and Cadillacs, derricks and lorries, and in the city most women wear Western dress, while on the outskirts many wear traditional long white gowns, bright with embroidery, as they draw water from wells in huge terra-cotta jars as their ancestors did in biblical days. Sticks of sugar cane lean against market stalls, waiting to be cut into sweet chewy snacks for children, bearded monks in woolly brown robes proceed from shrine to shrine, and everywhere there is thinly nasal Arab crooning drifting out of open shops from radios inside. Five times a day muezzins atop the city's minarets sing their haunting cry, "God is great, God is great. There is no god but God, and Mohammed is His Prophet."

Like Damascus, Jerusalem has been heavily inhabited all through its long and winding history and it has never been possible to excavate enough of it to completely reveal its past. Jordan, the land in which it lies, became a British mandate in 1917 after four hundred years of rule by the Ottoman Turks. Following World War II and the Arab-Israeli armistice, its 37,500-square-mile territory was set up to include the areas known as Trans-Jordan and Central Arab Palestine. It is a constitutional monarchy—officially the Hashemite Kingdom of Jordan—and the ruling king, Hussein, is the grandson of the first monarch in the Hashemite royal family, Abdullah, who reigned under the mandate. It is primarily an agricultural country with rich mineral deposits of potash and phosphates, and it exports olivewood, handcrafts, mother-of-pearl, dried fruits, olives and their oil, hides, and wool. Vast irrigation projects are under way to increase the land's productivity. It faces all of the problems of the other Middle Eastern countries—poverty, poor health, lack of education, and Palestinian refugees, but under its modern and progressive king, great improvements are being made in all of these areas.

Of its almost two million people, over 85 per cent are Arabic Moslems, but Jordan also includes sprinklings of Circassians, Copts, Persian Bahais, Syriacs, Turcomans, Kurds, Armenians, White Russians and 220 Samaritans who live in Nablus, the ancient Shechem, and are direct descendants of the biblical tribe. The mixture makes for such a diversity of secular and ecclesiastical dress that the country is virtually a living costume museum.

Jerusalem and the area immediately surrounding it does not contain the sum total of the country's antique sights. There is Hebron, with its Al-Haram Al-Ibhrahimi Mosque that encloses the Grotto of Makpelah and the graves of Abraham (as sacred to the Moslems as he is to the Jews and often called "the first Moslem"), Sarah, Rebecca, Leah, and Jacob. In the present-day town of Hebron you can wander around the narrow streets lined with gleaming houses that have picturesque cupolas, and watch the masters going about such ancient crafts as glass blowing and silversmithing. The walled city of Jericho, with Elisha's fountain and the Mount of Temptation where Christ fasted for forty days, is also the scene of excavations of the biblical walls and towers that tumbled before Joshua.

Even Jordan's modern capital, Amman, a city of 200,000, has its roots in Assyrian and Babylonian times and boasts several excellent hotels and a Roman theater that seated 6,000, King Hussein's modern palace and an archeological museum, a temple to Hercules and a Nymphaeum.

But none of Jordan's sights are more rewarding than Petra, a city settled by the Nabatæans in the fifth century B.C. and which grew to its golden age between 100 B.C. and 100 A.D. It was literally carved out of the pink marble rock of the desert mountains, a city tucked away in a valley on the main trade routes over which traveled the spice caravans of Arabia and Syria. The Nabatæans amassed a fortune in tolls in return for safe passage through these parts. It is a sight most breathtaking when the fiery light of the setting sun strikes the pastel marbled rock so that it shimmers like watered silk—recalling the description of Petra by the British poet John Burgon, "A rose-red city, half as old as time."

FOR THE TRAVELER'S NOTEBOOK

Official Information

Before you go: Jordan Tourism Information Service, 5 East 57th St., New York, N.Y.

In Jerusalem: SAS Office, Jerusalem Cinema Bldg., Port Said St.; Information Office, Tourism Authority, Salah Ed Din St.; U.S. Consulate, Nablus Rd.

Money Matters

Currency: The local currency unit is the Jordanian dinar (JD), divided into 1,000 fils. One JD equals $2.80, U.S.

Tipping: The basic rate is 10 per cent, generally added as service to hotel and restaurant bills. Apart from this, tipping is largely left to the generosity of the visitor. Taxi drivers, barbers, and hairdressers do not expect tips but naturally accept a small gratuity gratefully.

Climate, Clothing, and Essentials

Jerusalem is almost 2,500 feet above sea level and the climate is pleasantly bracing. The average summer temperature is about 75 degrees F., and even if the day is above average in warmth, the evening usually provides balmy coolness. Visitors in summer should have a light raincoat and a cardigan or casual jacket for outdoor evening wear. Winter succeeds fall about November and lasts into March. The average temperature then is 50 degrees, and warm clothing is essential.

Bring all the film you need.

Hotels

Jerusalem is immensely popular with both tourists and pilgrims, and you need confirmed reservations, particularly during the Christmas or Easter period. Accommodations range widely in price and style. If you like a picturesque setting, you will prefer one of the old Arab monasteries or mansions modernized to meet European standards of comfort. In addition there are a number of recently built first class and second class hotels operated on international lines.

Rates are usually reasonable. A single room with bath can be had for between JD 0.800 to 2.500 a night. A double with bath will cost anything between JD 1.500 and 4.400, plus service.

It is customary for guests to take all their meals in the hotel, and generally prices are quoted on this basis. Naturally it is possible to make special arrangements to lunch or dine elsewhere, with a deduction from the hotel bill. But be sure you understand what the quoted price covers when you register.

A sparkling new *Jerusalem Intercontinental Hotel* is due to open during spring 1964, with every modern, de luxe facility imaginable, including air conditioning, shops, restaurants, and a swimming pool. In the top category are the *Ambassador, Nablus Rd.*, on the Mount of Scopus north of the Old City, and the *National, Port Said St.*, close to the center of town. Slightly less expensive are the *New Orient House, P.O. Box 148*, with a large garden in which guests enjoy meals and refreshments; *Shepherd's Hotel, Mt. Scopus;* and the *Knights Palace Hotel, P.O. Box 316*, in the Old City near the Latin Patriarchate. A *YMCA* near the Damascus Gate accommodates women as well as men at a moderate price.

Food and Restaurants

Food is good and prices low in Jordan, and you may eat occidental or local fare. On the menus of many of the larger hotels you will find an extensive selection of European and American dishes, besides a diversity of Arab specialties similar to those in Lebanon and Syria.

Among the favorite eating spots for Arab dishes are the *Assalam Restaurant*, the *Jerusalem Oriental*, and the *Ommiad*. For a fine choice of both Western and Arab foods, dine at the *National Hotel*. For those who want European cuisine in a distinctly different atmosphere, we recommend the *Benedictine Convent* on the Mount of Olives or *Dom Polski* in the bazaar not far from the Damascus Gate. In both cases reserve a table in advance.

Entertainment, Night Life, and Special Events

With the exception of the *Ambassador Hotel*, night spots in the international sense are practically nonexistent in Jerusalem. Nevertheless you can dance most evenings at the larger hotels, often to first class European bands during the summer. One favorite rendezvous is the *New Orient*

House, with its lovely garden. Fashionable too are the *Grand Hotel* and the *Carlton* in the town of Ramallah. The casino at the *Dead Sea Hotel* is also easily reached. But few nighttime attractions can match the panoply of life that swirls before you as you sit at a café table in the Old City.

Most popular among the religious festivals are *Christmas* in Bethlehem, with the beauty of the carol singing in the Shepherds' Field at half-light and midnight mass in the Church of the Nativity. *Easter* in Jerusalem is equally impressive. All through Holy Week services, processions, and pageants commemorate and re-enact Christ's last days on earth. *May 25,* Independence Day, is celebrated with a most spectacular show of daring sportsmanship and magnificent discipline by the army, air force, cavalry, and camel corps. Moslem holidays are the same as those celebrated in other Arab countries.

Shopping

Many treasures are to be found in the bazaars and stores of Jerusalem. This is a coin collector's paradise, with emphasis on coins of Greek and Roman origin and from the Crusade period. The Crusade era has left behind too the beautiful traditional designs omnipresent in the wraps and jackets you will see. King Solomon's Street and David Street constitute the main shopping center, but almost everywhere are big bustling bazaars and small back-street *souks* with particularly beautiful cross-stitch embroideries at near-bargain prices. Dolls dressed in the traditional costumes of the Holy Land make charming souvenirs for both children and adults. There are also earrings, cuff links, bracelets, and brooches, all delicately worked in silver filigree or mother-of-pearl.

Background Reading

From an Antique Land, by Julian Huxley
The Bible, and Baker's *Bible Atlas*
Caravan, Story of the Middle East, by Carleton S. Coon
The Art of the Middle East, by Leonard Woolley

Lebanon

BEIRUT

In the land of milk and honey

ARCHEOLOGICAL gossip runs high in the Levant, and one is quickly
dazzled by a kaleidoscopic zigzag of names and places, cults and
cultures, myths and miracles, idols and altars, history and hearsay,
reaching back some five thousand years, almost before time had
memory. Lebanon is, as Philip Hitti puts it, "heir to all the ages"—
a country of 4,300 square miles, half the size of the state of New
Jersey, with some 1,600,000 people, one of the smallest sovereign
republics in the world but containing, probably, more history per
square foot than any other place on earth.

This is the land which was Phoenicia and knew, in turn, the civilizations of the Canaanites and the Aramaeans, the Hebrews and
Egyptians, the Persians and Assyrians, the Greeks, Romans, and
Byzantines, the Crusaders, Mamelukes, Turks, and French, among
others. It is the country that founded Carthage, invented the alphabetic system of writing, and first learned to navigate by the polar
star. The Phoenician seamen sailed around the tip of Africa a thousand years before the Portuguese, and crossed the Pillars of Hercules
to discover the Atlantic Ocean.

The country has played host to gods and goddesses, pagans and prophets, saints and saviors, wise men and warriors, conquerors and crusaders. It has been home to the followers of Baal and Jupiter, Adonis and Aphrodite, Astarte and Atargatis, Isis and Osiris, Abraham, David, and Solomon, St. George, St. Paul, and St. Peter, Christ, Moses, and Mohammed. It has felt the power of Rameses and Cleopatra, Herod and Agrippa, Pompey and Augustus Caesar, Nebuchadnezzar and Napoleon, Saladin and the Sultan Selim, Haroun-al-Rashid and Tamerlane, Darius the Persian and Alexander the Great, Baldwin of Lorraine and Richard the Lion-Hearted, Suleiman the Magnificent and Al Jazzar the Butcher—to name just a few at random.

Lebanon was the garden spot of the biblical world, a fertile, golden strip of land, rich in olives and lemons, figs and dates. Its terraced vineyards produced a wine which David said "maketh glad the heart of man"; and the *Song of Solomon* describes "a fountain of gardens, a well of living waters, and streams from Lebanon." Here also were great forests, "the trees of the Lord—the Cedars of Lebanon," and even today one can see in Becharre a few descendants of those ancient trees which were used for the coffins of the First Dynasty Egyptian Pharaohs and for the temple in Jerusalem. Solomon ordered them from Hiram of Tyre, saying, "Now therefore command thou that they hew me cedar trees out of Lebanon . . . for thou knowest that there is not among us any that can skill to hew timber like unto the Sidonians," and Hiram arranged to "convey them by sea in floats" to Palestine.

Sidon and Tyre today are drowsy little fishing villages with silvery nets drying on the salt sands, close to the remnants of crumbling Crusader castles. On the sea wall are great mounds, some as high as 150 feet, of mollusc shells, from which the ancients made their famous murex dye, Tyrian purple; the very name Phoenicia meant "land of purple." It was said to be the fastest, richest purple dye known to man; it dyed the sails of Cleopatra's barge and the robes of Helen of Troy, and colored the draperies hung in the delivery rooms of Byzantine noblewomen whose children received the title, *Porphyrogenite* ("born in the purple").

The Lebanese capital, Beirut, the Roman colony of Beryte, has been a center of law and learning since the fourth century A.D. and still is today, with its American University one of the finest schools in the Middle East. Cut off by mountains from the Bedouin deserts of its Arab neighbors, Lebanon faced westward to the Mediterranean and was consequently a place of trade and commerce, a land of seafarers and colonizers, with little time to develop a culture of their own but borrowing instead from those with which they came in contact.

Today Lebanon is the Switzerland of the Middle East, dedicated to commerce and banking with a complete free exchange. Beirut, its capital, is a free port. And though at first glance one might think this capital, with its pastel houses terraced above the Mediterranean, is a relaxed seaside resort, an Amalfi out of season, be assured that behind this balmy, casual façade, the city is teeming with the business at hand. This is the world of the asking price and the quick bargain, sealed with cold cash and hot coffee—exactly what one might expect from the descendants of Phoenician traders and Arab merchants.

Its pace is not the only thing deceptive about Beirut's appearance, for certainly the city does not show its age; the only antiquities are confined to the fantastically beautiful museum. Its buildings are modern, its diversions cosmopolitan. French is heard as much as Arabic, and the city has more than its share of superb international restaurants, cafés and espresso bars, a casino that outdoes Monte Carlo's for sheer lavishness, and so many ultrasmart night clubs and boîtes that it's impossible to keep track of them. The excellent hotels have pools and marinas, and in January one may bathe from a seaside cabana, or travel for an hour and ski on snow-covered slopes close to the biblical cedars.

But above all, in this world of highly touted tourist attractions, Lebanon comes as a complete surprise, one that generally leaves travelers with a sense of indignation, a sort of why-didn't-I-know-about-this-before feeling. For while any child of ten is familiar with such travel-poster sights as the Forum and the Colosseum, the Acropolis and the Pyramids of Giza, the Taj Mahal and the leaning Tower of Pisa, only the archeologist or historian is prepared for the grandeur of Baalbek, the grace of Byblos, or that gorgeous flower of the Damascus style, the palace of Beit-ed-Din.

Of these three, the most spectacular by far is Baalbek, a Roman acropolis set in the Bekaa plain between the Lebanon and Anti-Lebanon mountain ranges. The Phoenicians had a shrine dedicated to their god, Baal, on this site; with the conquest of Alexander the

Great, it took on the Greek name, Heliopolis; then, under the Romans, a compound of temples was built honoring Jupiter, Venus, and Mercury. Constantine made his mark on Baalbek by destroying the pagan temples and building the church of St. Barbara. This existed until 634 A.D., when it was destroyed to make way for a mosque, the one in which Saladin was educated as a boy. The Crusaders added their touch by building fortifications on top of the ancient walls in the thirteenth century, and it was further altered, and irreparably so, by two earthquakes, one in 1640, the other in 1751. At present Baalbek plays host to a summer festival of international folk music and theater groups. Here the Lebanese perform their national folk dance, the *dabbke,* accompanied by a primitive flute, a tambourine, an Oriental violin, and the castanet-like *snouj,* small brass tips worn on the thumb and index fingers and beaten together rhythmically.

To reach Baalbek, you drive northeast on the Beirut-Damascus Highway, once the caravan route of Abraham and David, up over the Lebanon Range through green gardens, lazy hillside villages, and the lovely resort towns of Chtaura and Zahle. Almost all along the way you can look back and see Beirut, set like a rose-gold scallop shell at the edge of the cerulean sea, a sea that meets the sky in a blue-white haze of horizon. As you top the mountains, snow-capped the year round, clouds hang low and fog the windshield; then suddenly you are descending the deforested, cinnamon-colored slopes of great camel-back hills that roll down to the fertile plain. And then, through a feathering of silvery poplars, comes the sudden, breathtaking sight of Baalbek, set high and wide in what seems to be the middle of nowhere, an absolutely stunning tribute to the Romans who built so tremendous a city, so far from home. The Acropolis is overpowering not only for its architecture but also for its height, raised as it is upon a gigantic substructure, the building of which is a source of astonishment to engineers today. It is built of tremendous granite stones and each of the three that form the famous trilithon measures 62 by 14 by 11 feet and weighs close to 1,000 tons.

The most obvious wonder of Baalbek is the Temple of Jupiter with its columns which rise 65 feet from base to capital, the tallest columns ever built by man. The six that remain today are topped by an entablature 16 feet high—architrave, frieze and cornice—cutting across the sky in a golden band of richly carved garlands and bulls' heads, modillions and dentils, Greek frets and acanthus leaves, and lions' heads with mouths open wide to serve as gutters for roof drainage. The temple originally measured 96 by 55 yards and was flanked on four sides by 54 columns, fragments of which can be seen all over the grounds, now a garden of architectural bits and pieces, a playground for lizards, and a joy to photographers.

Only slightly less awesome and more perfectly preserved is the nearby Temple of Bacchus, though historians believe this to be an error in name. It is, in any case, avowed to be the best example of Roman Corinthian architecture existing in the world. Weathered gold by sun and time, this temple is a jewel box of fluted columns, with a colossal sculptured doorway and entablatures, capitals and cornices rich with bouquets of poppies and sheaves of wheat, grapevines and trailing ivy, and again the heads of bulls and lions, evidence of the Oriental influence on Roman art and artisans.

About two or three hundred yards from the main compound is the circular Temple of Venus, a masterpiece of grace and delicacy, a later work than the other two temples and infinitely more refined, with pilasters instead of columns and intricately carved garlands hung from the capitals.

If Baalbek is the most impressive of the Lebanese sights, Byblos is certainly the most enchanting, a stage set of ruins and fragments, a miniature garden of the past, just at the edge of the sea. To reach it you drive north along a coastal crescent of land, starting in Beirut at the spot where St. George is said to have slain the dragon, past the Dog River, Nahr el Kelb. Its rocks bear the inscription of every invader who came to Lebanon, beginning with Rameses II, almost as though history had chosen to inscribe itself in one small spot, in much the way the Ten Commandments are sometimes minutely engraved on the head of a pin. Just a few miles off this road are the Caves of Jeita, a subterranean grotto, with great rock stalactites and stalagmites forming a fantastic backdrop like some gigantic papier-mâché creation in a Coney Island tunnel of horrors.

From here the road curves along the glass-blue Bay of Juni, where St. Peter set sail for Rome, past the glamorous cliff-top gambling casino, and on to the Nahr Ibrahim, the river that was the birthplace of the Adonis-Astarte legend. Finally, you come to Byblos, the Gebal of the Old Testament, and the oldest continuously inhabited town in the world. (Damascus claims the distinction of being the oldest inhabited city.)

As early as the fourth millennium B.C., Byblos was a center of religion and commerce, and its inhabitants, the Giblites, were the forerunners of the earliest Phoenicians. It was Byblos that gave the Bible its name, since the papyrus on which the first scriptures were written came from here.

Exhibited in the Beirut Museum are the earliest examples of the alphabetic system of writing, inscribed on the sarcophagus of King Ahiram, dating from about the twelfth century B.C., one of the many such treasures which were excavated from this site. Hundreds of other relics—pottery and jewelry, Egyptian alabaster vases and Mycenean pots and ivories, carvings and papyrus fragments—are collected in this museum, souvenirs of the centuries which reach back to the earliest settlements in the chalcolithic period, more than three thousand years before Christ.

The present-day Byblos is a quiet Arab village and the ruins are set behind a drowsy little square, where one can sit at a café and have syrupy-sweet Turkish coffee poured from small brass beakers into thimble-sized cups. Just across the square is a small mosque and from the needlepoint minaret comes the piercing, plaintive cry of the muezzin calling the faithful to prayer.

The collection of ruins at Byblos are really a jumble of history: Phoenician walls and Crusader ramparts, Roman colonnades and fragments of Egyptian and Greek columns, the pagan obelisk Temple of Rechef and the twelfth century Church of St. John the Baptist. One enters the site through an old Crusader keep, a square-towered building with small arched windows, built of great blocks of limestone now weathered to a gold-and-silver-leaf patina. Between the Frankish castle and the sea stand the remnants of the Phoenician ramparts as well as the nine subterranean tombs of the Phoenician necropolis, interesting in themselves though all of the treasures found there are now in the Beirut Museum.

Nearby is the delicate Roman colonnade, its odds and ends of columns and capitals framing the clear blue of sea and sky; twisting olive trees with silver-green leaves and driftwood trunks lean over the crumbling ruins. From here it is just a few steps to the enchanting little Roman theater, partially rebuilt with its best seats preserved, a gracefully proportioned semicircle with the Mediterranean for a backdrop. These are ruins amongst which one would like to stroll or picnic and imagine what it all was like when the first Egyptian galleys sailed into the hospitable little harbor some five thousand years ago.

Though neither as old as Byblos, nor as overwhelming as Baalbek, the palace of Beit-ed-Din is, nevertheless, a Lebanese treasure not to be missed. Built between 1790 and 1840, it was the château of Emir Beshir II, one of Lebanon's most powerful rulers, though he was nominally under Turkish authority. His château was an Arabian Nights palace, embellished with polished marble and glittering mosaics, fountains and courtyards, painted wood ceilings with polygonal coffering, and wide arches. It is set high on a promontory across a ravine from terraced vineyards, amid cypress gardens and umbrella pines which frame the setting in lush greenery. There are several lovely rooms within the palace itself, the most impressive of which is the Tribunal Hall, with its stained-glass windows and intarsia floor. There is also the richly paneled Lamartine Room, so called because it is believed that the French poet lived here for a while. Perhaps, however, the most exotic rooms of all are the Moorish baths, with their pools and fountains, intricate inlay, and pink-marbled splendor. Light bubbles into these rooms through bottle ends stuck in the domed ceilings, and from the outside these domes, rising above the building, resemble giant clove-studded hams about to be served.

And there is more: the beautiful bedroom of the emir, with its painted loggia overlooking the gardens and ravine, the open arcades rimming the building, the costume museum, and everywhere the magical wash of light and space, always a feature of Islamic architecture. In all, Beit-ed-Din is an outstanding example of the Damascus style at its most developed and refined stage. As such, it is an important link between Lebanon's present and its antique past, a past so full of splendor and achievements that one can understand how great a blessing Isaiah meant to bestow upon his people when he promised, "The glory of Lebanon shall come unto thee."

FOR THE TRAVELER'S NOTEBOOK

Official Information

Before you go: Lebanese Consulate General, 9 East 76th Street, New work, N.Y.

In Beirut: SAS Office, Riad El-Solh St., Abboud A/RAZZAK Bldg.; Tourism Office, Rome St.; U.S. Embassy, Rue de Paris.

Money Matters

Currency: The unit of Lebanese currency is the pound (L£), divided into 100 piasters. L£ 3.08 equals $1, U.S.

Tipping: In most hotels and restaurants a service charge of 10 or 12 per cent is added. If not, you are expected to tip 12 to 15 per cent. Porters get 50 piasters per load. Taxi drivers are not tipped, and hairdressers in the large hotels get 5 to 10 per cent of the bill.

Climate and Clothing

Few places in the world have a pleasanter climate than Lebanon. The best time to visit is spring (April to mid-June) and fall (mid-September through November). Winter (50 to 55 degrees F.) brings intermittent rain, and in summer (85 to 95 degrees) a great number of people leave the capital for mountain resorts. Raincoats are advisable from October to the end of March. You will want your bathing suit from May to September. In general, dress as you would in any American or European city.

Hotels

Beirut has a number of handsome and comfortable hotels with service and facilities comparable to European standards. Prices in de luxe hotels range from L£ 27 for a single room, from L£ 35 for a double. First class rates start at L£ 14 for a single and at L£ 22 for a double.

DE LUXE: Undoubtedly the most spectacular hotel is the Intercontinental's *Phoenicia, Rue Minet el-Hosn,* where terraced rooms hang over the Mediterranean and which has a rooftop cocktail lounge and swimming, boating, night club, and restaurant facilities. It is absolutely the end, Hollywood style, with prices to match. More on the quiet-elegant side, the *St. Georges, Rue Minet el-Hosn,* is traditionally *the* hotel of the city, beautifully run, on the beach front with pools and a marina, and with at least half the rooms having terraces overlooking the sea.

FIRST CLASS: A whole group of modern, efficient hotels are near the two larger ones. Some have pools, all have smart cocktail lounges and complete facilities. Among these are the *Excelsior, Rue Minet el-Hosn;* the *Commodore, Rue Hamra;* the *Riviera, Corniche du Phare;* the *Carlton, Rue Chouran;* and the *Capitole,* near the main city square, Place Riad el-Sohl. The *Bristol, Rue Mme. Curie,* is in a nearby residential section and extremely gracious.

MODERATE: Modern and comfortable, with pools and beach front locations are the *Palm Beach, Rue Minet el-Hosn;* the *City, Rue Rustum*

Pacha; the *Fédéral, Rue Chouran; Lord's, Rue Chouran; Biarritz, Rue Chouran; Plaza, Rue Hamra;* and the *Normandy, Ave. de Français.* In the most moderately priced budget category, the *Eden Rock, Rue Jénah,* the *Mayflower, Rue Sidani,* and the *Triumph, Rue Lyon,* are good choices.

Food and Restaurants

Since Beirut is a sort of international clearinghouse for the Middle East and has for centuries attracted people from all over the world, the city has an inordinately large number of superb restaurants offering a wide assortment of national cuisines. One finds the usual continental fare at any of the large hotels: wonderful French food at *Lucullus* and the *Bristol;* interesting Rumanian food at the *Bucharest;* a number of Italian restaurants along the Rue de Phénicie, especially *Quo Vadis;* the *Chinese Restaurant* serving guess what; and a whole string of espresso cafés where you can have light lunches and snacks in the vicinity of Rue de Phénicie and the Place des Canons.

But be sure to sample the food of Lebanon for it's surely the best and most delicate version of Arab food. The *mezzeh* appetizers here include the national dish, *kibbeh,* ground lamb and cracked wheat served raw or baked; *tabbouleh,* a salad of parsley and mint leaves; *hommos,* sesame paste, garlic, and lemon; and *baba gannouj,* a smoky eggplant purée. All Lebanese restaurants serve *mezzeh,* which you eat with the native drink *arrack,* a licorice-flavored liqueur served with ice and water. One establishment, *T. Mirza,* specializes in these appetizers alone—we counted forty-two dishes, each prepared differently. Other local specialties include grilled lamb on a vertical spit, here called *chourma;* broiled chicken with garlic sauce (*farrouj mishwi*); *kofta,* ground meat broiled on skewers; rice pilaff; and *machshi,* which are stuffed vegetables similar to Turkish and Greek *dolmas.* Fruits are exquisite, and a whole rainbow of cool sherbets is made from them. Seafood is excellent too.

The best restaurants for Arabic food are *Ajammi,* where the *chourma* and preserved dates with cloves are exceptionally good, *Al-Mataam, La Gondole, La Grotte aux Pigeons, Ghalayini,* and *Nasr,* overlooking the famous rocks and the sea. *Mansour, Arabi,* and *Lahoud* are also excellent. Anyone driving to the ruins at Baalbek should arrange to lunch or dine at *Akl* in the mountain resort of Chtaura.

Entertainment, Night Life, and Special Events

Beirut jumps after dark and has more than its share of noisy, smart little bars and cocktail lounges, among them the *Eve, Kit-Kat, Lido, Macumba, Les Caves du Roy, Eden Rock, La Casbah,* along with the club at the *Phoenicia Hotel.* Most have music and dancing and a few have cabaret floor shows. The *Beryte,* a stunning little lounge off the Rue de Phénicie, is rather like a snug private club. The area around the Place des Canons and the waterfront is packed with wilder places, off limits to any but the most courageous. The *Casino du Liban,* an hour's drive from Beirut, is one of the smartest gambling casinos anywhere and attracts a chic international crowd.

There are no legitimate theaters in Beirut but you may sometimes hear a concert at the Lebanese Academy of Music. For the tourist the event of the year is the *Baalbek International Festival* in July and August, when foreign dancers, musicians, and theatrical groups, and Lebanese folk singers and dancers perform nightly in the ruins of Baalbek.

Shopping

In the shops and stores of Beirut you will find a mixture of Western and Oriental goods. Most of the shops have fixed prices. If you insist on bargaining for fun go to one of the bazaars instead. Browse for miscellany at the Souk Sursock bazaars. The most attractive articles are Damascus brocades, embroideries, and laces at *Asfar & Sarkis* (St. Georges Hotel), *Papa George,* and *Tarazi;* hammered Persian silver, brass trays, and ivories at *Daouds, Bachour & Barakati,* and *Achkar;* gold filigree jewelry, silver, and jewels at *Najib Tabbah* and *Albert Assi;* rugs at *Khoren Tahan, Kalbian, Jawad,* and *Shukri Haddad.* Other places worth a visit are the *Linen Center, John Sarkis, Ras Beirut,* and *UNRWA* at the UNESCO Building, as well as the *YWCA Craft Shop* of the vocational school in Rue Ain Mreissé. *Patriarche Howayek* and other shops specializing in Oriental articles are found on Avenue des Français, and in the big hotels.

Background Reading

From an Antique Land, by Julian Huxley
Lebanon in History, by Philip Hitti
Lebanon, Land of Cedars, by Marie Karam Khayat and Margaret Clark Keatinge
The Bible, and Baker's *Bible Atlas*

Syria

DAMASCUS

A desert port

IT is said that when Mohammed saw Damascus from the desert hills surrounding it, he decided not to enter the city, for he thought it wrong for a man to taste the joys of paradise while still on earth. And when Lamartine looked down over the city from almost the same vantage point, he wrote that his eyes fell on "the most magnificent and surprising landscape that ever stunned the human mind —a labyrinth of flower gardens, orchards, palaces and streams, in which the vision was bewildered and could but quit one enchantment to be spellbound by another."

This Syrian capital of 500,000 inhabitants is still the most beautiful city in the Middle East, whether you see it first from the air, or approach it by car from the Beirut-Damascus Highway. It is a lushly green garden set amid the yellow haze of desert sands, with a skyline of somber green cypresses and feathery poplars, slim golden minarets and sugar-white domes—an Arabian Nights mirage, rising against the parched, tobacco-brown slopes of the Anti-Lebanon Range. And within the city, tucked away behind the plain walls of the Arab villas, fountains splash against tiled courtyards as families sip sherbet under the shade of the orange and lemon trees, the sycamores and date palms.

432

Damascus is an oasis, and its history hinges on that fact. It lies in a fertile plain at the foot of Mount Qasyun, and the seven streams of the Barada River which water the city have earned it its historical reputation as the oldest continually inhabited city in the world. It has always been a large city, never abandoned nor allowed to deteriorate to village status. Damascus served as a cool and shady respite to desert travelers a thousand years before Abraham; its khans accommodated caravans from India and China carrying treasures of silks and spices, porcelain and jewels westward, and traders up from Africa with their black ivory cargoes of slaves. Since the tenth century, pilgrims have rested here before setting out on the last leg of their journey to Mecca. Even today the city is a vital midway refueling point for airplanes, trucks, and jeeps, traveling between East and West.

But Damascus is more than a garden, more than a caravansary. It is a bustling, noisy center of trade and commerce, and nowhere is this more apparent than in the *souks*—the narrow alley bazaars that wind between the city streets. Of these, the most colorful and exciting is the Souk Hamidieh, the Long Market—a coolly shaded, quarter-of-a-mile arcade of stalls and shops, crammed between the remnants of Roman arches and Corinthian columns. Everywhere there is the din of voices, French, Arabic, English, Greek, selling, haggling, arguing, and sometimes flinging a subtly involved Semitic curse after a customer who has decided to go elsewhere to make his purchase.

Here the eye is dazzled by a kaleidoscopic display of damascene bracelets and trinkets, tooled leather and Damascus linens, embroideries and gold and silver brocades; richly patterned prayer rugs in tones of sapphire and ruby; and basketry with the hot, primitive colors one associates with Mexican handcrafts. Shop fronts, covered with gaudy prints of Moslem heroes, are stacked with trays, boxes, frames, and furniture of lacquered wood, gleaming with mother-of-pearl inlays; turquoise jewelry and frosted silver filigree; hammered copper and brass; and mounds of oranges and lemons from which are made sherbets and long, thirst-quenching drinks. Anyone with a sweet tooth will certainly be led astray by the mosaic of candied fruits: almond-stuffed dates, scented with cloves; sugared Damascus plums; thin rolls of pressed apricots to chew on; boxes of glazed pineapple and cherries, as intricately arranged as jewels; pyramids of jellied candies and slabs of marbled *halvah,* all seductively flavored with pistachios, almonds, citron, and golden honey.

To add to the breathtaking array there are the people and their costumes: Bedouins in from the desert, wearing dark woolen cloaks and white headshawls; women bundled in yards of cotton, their heads and faces covered with blue or black scarves in observance of purdah; portly Arab bankers in dark blue suits and red velour fezzes; and everywhere the quick, dark boys in pajama-striped *kaftans* who dash about delivering trays with brass beakers of sweet Turkish coffee to a shop or office where an honored guest (or good customer) must be welcomed in the traditional Arab manner.

The wonders of Syria's past are no less dazzling than those of its present, and most of them are amassed in the National Museum, a veritable bazaar of antiquity, and one of the most handsomely arranged exhibitions in the world. Its most impressive feature is the third century Dura-Europo Synagogue, transported here from its original site on the banks of the Euphrates. Its magnificent frescoes were preserved accidentally, when shortly after its completion in 245 A.D. the city had to defend itself against the Sassanians, and the temple was filled with sand and packed with earth to make an embankment fortification for the city walls; it was then forgotten until it was discovered by a team of Yale archeologists. The paintings depict biblical scenes and are done in a subtle scheme of Pompeiian reds, burnished golds, and velvety-greens; the painting of the prophets is a most unusual feature in a synagogue, since only for a brief period in Jewish history did rabbis ignore the scriptural interdiction against producing graven images.

This museum also houses a reconstructed desert château, originally built in Palmyra in 727 A.D. for the last Ommiad caliph, Hisham, with an impressive gateway and tower. On the first floor of the museum, showcases are filled with Roman bronzes, Assyrian gold jewelry as thin as autumn leaves, ancient glass and earthenware, and the most haunting and unforgettable sculpture from Marii—long patriarchal heads with huge burning eyes and a wild elemental quality about them, very much like the mystical figures painted by El Greco.

Another of the city's fascinating sights is the Ommiad Mosque, on the spot where a great temple stood four thousand years ago, dedicated to the Aramaean god, Hadad. The Romans transformed it into a temple to Jupiter and later into the Basilica of St. John the

Baptist, whose head was supposed to have rested on this site. In the eighth century it became a Moslem mosque, thus recording many of the civilizations that have influenced Syria and Damascus. The mosaics in this temple are its outstanding feature—sparkling gold-leafed Byzantine landscapes and townscapes, with a flat primitive perspective reminiscent of Persian miniatures.

The two smaller mosques of Damascus are graceful and historic: the Mosque of Sultan Suleiman the Magnificent, built in 1554, with a pair of needlepoint minarets and an enormous cupola dome, and the Mosque of the Sultan Selim, noted both for its sensitively proportioned interior and for its handsome exterior architecture.

For a romantic glimpse into Syria's more recent past, one must visit the El Azem Palace, built in the eighteenth century for the emir Essaad Pasha El Azem. It is one of the most beautiful examples of the Damascus style, with polychromed wood ceilings and wall panels, marble mosaicked floors and arches, and a coolly green courtyard with trickling fountains and fragrant lemon trees. And should you forget that Damascus was the scene of St. Paul's conversion, you will be reminded of that fact on the Street Called Straight, a narrow lane that passes under a fragment of a Roman arch—the very same street St. Paul walked on when he visited the house of St. Ananias, another of the city's sights and the place where Paul miraculously recovered his eyesight. Finally there is St. Paul's window, from which he was lowered in a basket by his fellow Christians to escape the Roman soldiers.

Modern Damascus is a place of building and street repairs, automobiles and a new university, and aside from Cairo, it is the most Arabic city in the world, noted for a fierce nationalism and xenophobia. None of the conquerors who have come to Syria ever managed to graft themselves onto the city—not the Assyrians, who followed the Aramaeans in 732 B.C., nor the Persians, who took it from them, nor the Romans, who came to power in 64 B.C. Under Arab rule since 635 A.D., it never gave way to the Crusaders; it is still a stronghold of Moslem resistance, and violently anti-French after its years under the mandate following World War I and the decline of Ottoman rule. It became a republic in 1932, independent in 1945, and since 1957 has been playing a game of in-again-out-again with Egypt, and Nasser's dream of a United Arab Republic. Writing of Syria in 1954, Julian Huxley observed, "Syria is visibly in the throes of transition—but transition to what?" The answer to that question is not any clearer today than it was ten years ago. In Damascus secrecy is the rule, and it is said that if one wants to know what is happening there he must go to Beirut to find out.

Damascus is, of course, not the country's only place of historic interest. Its second largest city, Aleppo, is one of the East's oldest, and its Crusader citadel with its three magnificent gateways—the Weeping Lion, the Serpents, and the Laughing Lions—is one of the most impressive of the Frankish keeps, with huge towers rising from the table-topped peak outside the city. Other outstanding Crusader castles in the country which can be reached with Latakia as a base, are the Sahyun, with its ninety-foot-high fortifying walls; the Marqab castle, overpowering and ominous, with walls of black basalt; and the most famous, perhaps, the Krak des Chevaliers, the very epitome of what we imagine a Crusader castle to be, with vaulted halls and moats, double walls and drawbridges, underground cisterns, wine caverns, and a beautiful thirteenth century chapel where Geoffrey de Joinville is buried.

But for sheer romance, no city in the country can vie with Palmyra, the lengendary capital of Queen Zenobia, who dressed as a man and hunted game, learned Greek and Egyptian as well as Syriac, and who, astride her famous Arab steed, led her armies into battle. Here are ancient tombs of Palmyran aristocracy, truncated ruins of the Temple of Bel with its graceful porticos and peristyles, golden fragments framing the turquoise sky and fawn-colored desert, where Arab shepherds wrapped in woollen cloaks tend their flocks—a sight that lured and held such famous Victorian travelers as Sir Richard Burton and his irrepressible Isabel. When Lady Hester Stanhope rode up to the city in full Bedouin regalia in 1813, to be greeted by Arab musicians and girls dancing gracefully between the temple columns, she was so enchanted that she pitched camp amid the desert ruins and stayed a week.

FOR THE TRAVELER'S NOTEBOOK

Official Information

Before you go: Arab Information Center, 120 East 56th St., New York, N.Y.; 37 South Wabash Ave., Chicago, Ill.; Dupont Circle Bldg., 1346

Connecticut Ave., Washington, D.C.; Ferry Bldg. (World Trade Center), San Francisco, Cal.

In Damascus: SAS Office, 14 Shoukri Kouatly Blvd.; Syrian Government Tourist Office, Al-Joumrieh St.; U.S. Embassy, Shami Bldg.

Money Matters

Currency: The monetary unit is the Syrian pound (S£), divided into 100 piasters. About S£ 3.50 equals $1, U.S.

Tipping: Hotels and restaurants usually add 10 per cent service charge; if not, tip 10 per cent. Taxi drivers and cinema ushers do not expect tips. Hairdressers are pleased to be tipped 10 per cent, though it is not obligatory. Porters should be tipped as you would do in any other city.

Clothing, Climate, and Essentials

The ideal time for a visit is in spring or autumn. July and August are the hottest months, with temperatures sometimes over 100 degrees F., though as a rule between 86 an 95. However, the mornings are cooler and even in the peak of summer, nights are cool and fresh. During this period white cotton dresses are recommended. During winter the temperature usually fluctuates between 40 and 60 degrees. December to March is generally rainy. For a winter visit heavy clothing is needed and it is best to have a raincoat or umbrella handy.

Some European drugs and toiletries are available but it is safe to take them and camera film along.

Hotels

There are several good hotels in Damascus, all subject to government control to insure high standards of comfort and fair prices. Advance reservations are recommended. Prices in de luxe hotels start at S£ 26.00 for a single room with bath, and S£ 35.00 for the same with full board. First class hotels charge S£ 20 for a single with bath, S£ 30 with all meals. Second class hotel rates for single rooms with bath start at S£ 17.50, S£ 20.00 with full board.

In the de luxe category the *New Ommayad* and the *Semiramis* are both excellent and conveniently located. First class hotels include the *Cattan*, the *Kassioun*, and the *Orient*. The *Semire*, the *Rami*, and the *Karnak* are second class hotels that are reliable and comfortable.

Food and Restaurants

The native food consists of all the Arabic specialties, including the appetizer course, *mezze*. All the food served in Lebanon is featured here as well. Damascus sausage is famous throughout the Middle East. If fresh apricots are in season, try them. Syrupy Turkish coffee is the main beverage and is served as a gesture of courtesy in shops, offices, or wherever a visitor calls. It is courteous to accept it, whether or not you want it. Arrack is the popular alcoholic drink. The leading hotels serve European and native food, while the *Morocco* is a very attractive new restaurant, Arab in décor but less authentic in cuisine, which features native specialties tempered to foreign tastes. Other good restaurants are the *Silver Tower, Socrat, Oasis, Agha,* and the *Airport Restaurant* (the Mezze). For superb Arabic food, very authentically prepared and served, visit *Ghazal & Sirdah,* where the check for a complete meal will come to about $1 or $1.50.

Entertainment, Night Life, and Special Events

The *Mezze Restaurant* at the airport has dinner dancing summer and winter, and the *Orient Seville* and the *Ashbilia* in summer only. The latter sometimes offers a floor show, as do the cabarets *Shehrezade* and *Florida.* Other night clubs include *Syrianna, Al-Caza, Caravan,* and *Semiramis.* These have floor shows with Oriental music and dances.

International trade fairs are held here frequently; the largest takes place in September.

Shopping

Shopping among the bazaar *souks* is one of the most exciting things to do in Damascus. The main shopping center is the Souk Hamidieh around the citadel, along the Street Called Straight and Madhat Bacha Street, and around the Sanjakdar Mosque. Prices are low here for beautiful hammered copper, basketry, brocades, embroidered table linens, leatherwork, and glass and wood boxes intricately set with mother-of-pearl. The *Sagha,* or goldsmiths' shops, have attractive costume jewelry. This is the place that calls for all of your mastery in the art of bargaining, and it is not always to your advantage to rely on the help of an official or private guide when shopping.

Background Reading

From an Antique Land, by Julian Huxley
The Bible, and Baker's *Bible Atlas*
Journey through the East, by Alphonse de Lamartine
History of Syria, by Philip Hitti
Caravan, Story of the Middle East, by Carleton S. Coon
The Art of the Middle East, by Leonard Woolley

ASIA

HONG KONG

The fragrant harbor

HONG KONG is a marvelous mess; one of the world's siren cities that everyone seems to love at first sight, though that "first sight" is often glimpsed from an airplane thousands of feet up in the air. Even from that height one is aware of the intense beauty of the place, of the green island hills, heavy with age, rimmed by white skyscrapers curving around the bright blue harbor of the China Sea; a view still more breathtaking at night, when necklaces of lights glitter from the harbor craft and dockside buildings, giving the city all the dazzle of a jewelry shop window.

But beauty is only part of the story, for there is about this city a kind of free-wheeling excitement that is electric and which defies analysis—a total charm equal to much more than the sum of its parts. Everything here can be found in some other city of the world; Hong Kong's magic lies in the mixture.

Walk the labyrinth of ladder streets that climb behind the city's modern office buildings and you'll find terraced stalls selling miles of cotton fabrics, pungent spices, ducks as crisp as parchment drying in the air, cameras, elastic bands, hairpins and diamonds, transistor radios and the bowl-shaped Chinese pots called *woks,* nylon stockings and straw coolie hats, jade, ginger, and Coca Cola, and everywhere ambitious shopkeepers invite strollers to "come have a look-see."

Drugstores display baskets of gnarled roots and musty herbs, bleached bones to be powdered into cures, and great glass jars full of coiled snakes in wine; one would not be at all surprised to see a jar labeled "Eye of Newt." Signs advertise letter writers, fortune tellers, bone setters and doctors specializing in leech treatments, spoon treatments, love potions, gold needle treatments, and the Treatment of the Pinch. Streets are lined with smoky black tenements, warrens in which the Chinese live and cook in constant terror of the greatest danger of all on the island, fire. Across the fronts of the buildings hang endless lines of tattered laundry strung out to dry on long bamboo poles.

The life of the city is lived on these streets and you can see women cleaning bean sprouts or having their hair done, families eating or selling their wares, mothers carrying babies strapped to their backs and men balancing huge burdens from the ends of bamboo poles that hang across their shoulders like gigantic scales, and on these pavements children play or stretch out for midday naps.

The faces in these streets represent more countries than belong to the United Nations. Tall, powerful Punjabi Sikhs, bearded and turbaned, sit armed with rifles guarding banks and jewelry shops; wiry coolies pull rickshaws; stern-faced Red Chinese go about their business of banking and espionage. There are visiting commissars and members of defunct White Russian royalty; Indian women swaddled in sheer cotton saris; emaciated refugees from the Chinese mainland; togaed Africans and Moslems in nightgowns. Crew-cut Americans investigate import-export possibilities, and sport-shirted Californians just off a cruise ship pursue bargain tailors, bargain jade, and bargain women, all agog at the lithe-boned Chinese girls in their slit-skirted *cheongsams;* and everywhere are the British colonials, only slightly less Maughamish than we may remember them.

And with it all goes the noise—the drilling, hawking, arguing, the cacophony of languages and dialects that would put Babel's famous tower to shame. English is the official language; add to that a dozen Chinese dialects, throw in every European, Oriental, African, and Middle Eastern tongue you ever heard of, and you'll know why it sounds as though no two people in Hong Kong speak the same language.

Watch the left-handed traffic whirl by and you'll see rickety rickshaws clacking beside lumbering double-decker buses straight from Piccadilly; green tramcars clanging beside Mercedes-Benzes and

Cadillacs; Chevrolets and Volkswagens pulling up next to bicycle-propelled pedicabs. In the bustling harbor bat-winged junks anchor beside flat-topped aircraft carriers and gleaming white cruise ships; bright blue sampans scuttle along between the swift Star Ferry, the electric *wallah-wallah* excursion boats, elaborate yachts, and Greek merchant ships.

The buildings of the city include modern steel-and-glass towers, palm-covered Victorian colonial buildings, terraced luxury apartments set up in the cool green hills, and tropical villas overlooking the harbor. There are also the musty tenements and wattle huts of the refugees and hill squatters. The most incredible dwelling places of all are the sampans of the *hakka,* the water people who live in the typhoon shelters and are born, marry, have children, earn a living, and die on their sampans, jammed one against the other in a city with a unique water life, with brothel boats and music boats, cook boats and fishing boats.

Hong Kong became a British crown colony in 1841, when it was ceded to Britain as a partial indemnity for the Chinese loss of the Opium War. It was then a barren island, home only to fishermen, a few farmers, and a hideaway for pirates who raided the China Seas. Captain Charles Eliot, who accepted the prize, was regarded as something of a laughing stock and the British foreign secretary of the time, Lord Palmerston, remarked, "It seems obvious that Hong Kong will not be a mart of trade," thereby uttering what well may be the most incorrect of famous predictions. Albert, the prince consort, was much amused at the prize his Victoria had won, and refined English ladies who could control their tempers no longer permitted themselves the euphemistic curse, "Go to Hong Kong." But if the island the Chinese called "the Fragrant Harbor" was a joke, it wasn't funny for long, for the city prospered as a cache for opium which the British sent up the Pearl River to Canton in exchange for tea and silk and in lieu of colder cash. The island attracted adventurers of every sort, nefarious and otherwise (it still does), and it soon hummed with trade in merchandise, trade in currency, and that trade in information which has long been a Hong Kong specialty, espionage.

The colony has always profited from the tribulations of the mainland, and hard-working Chinese flocked into Hong Kong, fleeing from repeated famines and recurrent wars. As a result of the Japanese invasion of Manchuria in the early 1930's, 1 million Chinese were added to the 230,000 who already lived there. During World War II Hong Kong was held by the Japanese, who left it a shambles. British bankers and investors boldly saved the island economy by making good on all of the fiat currency the Japanese had issued. The victory of the Red Chinese brought in industrious, cheap labor from south China and shrewd businessmen from Shanghai, who combined to turn this into a manufacturing city, and a boom town. Before the war 90 per cent of the city's exports were re-exported goods; now 75 per cent of the exports are produced on this island, where anything in the world can be made faster and cheaper than anywhere else. Existing solely by the grace of Red China, which needs Hong Kong as a source of currency and information, the colony has the freest form of laissez-faire capitalism in existence today, with emphasis on quick profits and liquid assets, easily movable should the mainland Chinese decide to call a halt to the colony's assorted enterprises, if not to the colony itself.

Hong Kong, with its total area of 398 square miles, includes the island of Hong Kong with the capital city of Victoria and the sampan settlement of Aberdeen. Two-thirds of Hong Kong's 3 million people live in these 32 square miles. The rest of the territory consists of the Peninsula of Nine Dragons, others known as Kowloon, five minutes from Hong Kong island by the ferry that runs on a continuous schedule. The area known as the New Territories (on a lease from China until 1997) stretches behind Kowloon for twenty miles to the Red Chinese barbed-wire border, and the frontier station of the Kowloon-Canton Railway. There are also innumerable small islands belonging to Hong Kong, and just a few hours away by luxury excursion boat lies the much romanticized Portuguese colony of Macao, perhaps the world's most overrated capital of vice, but one that still attracts tourists who by night try their luck at roulette and by day peer across the border to see what's doing in Communist China.

To tourists who are sore of foot and weary of brain from having "done" the "must-see" museums and "can't-be-missed" temples of the rest of the Orient, Hong Kong is a gorgeous respite—excellent hotels, exquisite food, familiarly Western or exotically Eastern, bargains galore, and, best of all, no important "sights" as such, to bedevil visitors and leave them conscience-stricken.

If necessary you can do all your sightseeing in two days. From Victoria Peak (reached by cable car) you can look down eighteen hundred feet over the city and harbor. You can walk through the crazy splendor of Tiger Balm Gardens for an hour or so, tour Kowloon and the New Territories, then circle Hong Kong Island in a boat, visiting Aberdeen and the sampan settlements. There is the incredible market at Taipo, where all livestock is sold on the hoof, and chow dogs are considered a special delicacy. Here are fish that look like silvery slivers of mica and others, called parrot fish, that seem to have a ceramic glaze of blue and orange. There are strange, beautiful vegetables and live suckling pigs strung up in cylindrical baskets and, if you take your camera, be quick in using it for the scene changes rapidly here. Wander through the shops in the Thieves' Market, buy dress cottons in Cotton Alley, have your shoes repaired on the Street of Cobblers, and lunch on the Street of the Hundred-Year-Old Eggs. (The eggs are only thirty days old and have been chemically aged until they are black and sulphurous inside; they are served hard-boiled, though aficionados claim the only proper way is to drink them raw.) This is all part of a routine day in this city of many worlds—a place of mah-jongg palaces and cricket matches, home to missionaries and mandarins, where you may see Chinese opera or way-off Broadway drama, a capital of banking and commerce, the world of the British club in which no Asians are allowed, and the world of Suzie Wong.

FOR THE TRAVELER'S NOTEBOOK

Official Information

Before you go: The Hong Kong Tourist Association: 501 Madison Ave., New York 22, N.Y.; 10 North La Salle St., Chicago 2, Ill.; 291 Geary St., San Francisco, Cal.; or write directly to the head office of the Association, 1 East Wing, Peninsula Hotel, Kowloon, Hong Kong.

In Hong Kong: SAS Office (also the office of Thai Airways International Ltd.), 18B Gloucester Bldg., Hong Kong, and Lobby, Peninsula Hotel, Kowloon; Hong Kong Tourist Association, 1 East Wing, Peninsula Hotel, Kowloon, or the Information Center on Star Ferry Pier, Hong Kong; U.S. Consulate, 26 Garden Rd., Hong Kong.

Money Matters

Currency: The monetary unit here is the Hong Kong dollar (HK$), divided into 100 cents. $1, U.S. is equal to about HK$ 5.70. Hong Kong is a free money market and a good place to buy any currencies you may need for the rest of your trip.

Tipping: The usual rate of tipping is 10 per cent at your hotel, 10 per cent to waiters, cab drivers and hairdressers. Ushers are not tipped.

Climate, Clothing and Essentials

Spring (March, April, and May) is warm during the day and cool at night with occasional rain. The average temperature is 71 degrees F. Summer (June, July, and August) is warm and humid with frequent showers. The average temperature is 83 degrees, requiring light, washable summer clothing and a raincoat or umbrella. Autumn (late September through mid-December) has warm days and cool evenings and very little rain. The average temperature is then 76 degrees and you will need sweaters and jackets towards November. Winter (January and February) is on the chilly side, with an average temperature of 63 degrees, and you need topcoats and winter woolens. In general, you will need the type of clothing worn in any large city, with some resort wear if you plan to spend time at any of the resort hotels such as the Repulse Bay.

Hotels

It is always necessary to have confirmed reservations well in advance here. Accommodations vary from luxury suites and rooms with private bath, telephones, radio, and TV, to economy hotels for the traveler on a limited budget. In general, floor service in the better hotels is excellent, though somehow one feels remarkably detached from the front desk. A few hotels are on the Hong Kong Island side; most are on Kowloon, which is not as inconvenient as it may sound since it's just a five-minute ferry ride to the Victoria side, the boats leave and arrive continuously, and both sections have an equal share of tourist attractions, sights, shops, and restaurants.

De luxe hotel charges range from HK$ 70 for a single room with bath, from HK$ 100, double. First class hotel charges start at about HK$ 32 for a single room, HK$ 40 for a double, while moderate, tourist-class hotels charge from HK$ 25, single, HK$ 32, double.

HONG KONG ISLAND (VICTORIA)

DE LUXE: The two newest and most modern de luxe hotels are run by large American hotel chains; both are in the heart of Victoria's business and harbor sections, both feature a type of décor that might be called "Oriental-International," and a group of Easternized restaurants, coffee shops, and bars. Rooms have a harbor view and there are swimming pools at both. The *Hong Kong Hilton* and, Intercontinental's *Mandarin* are fully air conditioned and their décor is rich in Chinese accents, so you will know where you are.

MODERATE: *Sunning House* on *Hysan Avenue* on Causeway Bay is a reasonably priced, modern, air-conditioned hotel, about ten minutes from the center of Victoria.

KOWLOON

DE LUXE: The *Peninsula, Salisbury Rd.* Set at the point where the Star Ferry docks, this is of course the fabled hotel of Hong Kong. Services are excellent, rooms are commodious and brightly attractive. *Peninsula Court (Peninsula Hotel Annex), Nathan Rd.* This newly modern annex offers compact apartment-hotel facilities of the most efficient type and boasts the most highly touted (and most expensive) tourist restaurant in town, the Marco Polo.

FIRST CLASS: *Miramar Hotel, 134 Nathan Rd.* This excellent hotel is in the heart of Kowloon's activity and has an arcade full of reputable and attractive shops.

MODERATE: *Carlton Hotel, Taipo Rd.* A comfortable and pleasant hotel, a few minutes from the center of Kowloon, with a lovely harbor view, and brightly clean, small, air-conditioned rooms and good food. Hotel buses take you to the center of Kowloon regularly, and prices are moderate. The *Ambassador, Nathan and Middle Rd.* A new, modern hotel complete with night club, coffee shop, a veritable city full of shops, and conveniently located. The *Imperial, 32–34 Nathan Rd.*, is another new, modern skyscraper hotel with a reputation for good service, a view from many rooms, a roof-garden restaurant, and a Japanese restaurant. Well located. The *Park, 61/5 Chatham Rd.*, is among the newest hotels in the city. It is huge and complete with air conditioning, cocktail lounge et al. The *August Moon, 25 Kimberly Rd.* This small efficient hotel, just a few minutes from the center of activity, is one of the best buys in the tourist class. The *Austin Hotel, 140–142 Austin Rd.*, the *Grand Hotel, Carnarvon Rd.*, the *Golden Gate, 136/8 Austin Rd.*, and the *International, 33 Cameron Rd.*, are other reliable hotels in the moderate, tourist-class category.

RESORT HOTELS: *Repulse Bay Hotel.* Overlooking the bay, this elegant resort hotel smacks nostalgically of late Victorian colonial days, complete with potted palms, sprawling veranda, huge dining room, and dance floor. Excellent service and fairly expensive.

Food and Restaurants

Anyone interested in food will have a field day in Hong Kong, for along with a number of excellent restaurants serving a wide variety of European dishes, there are dozens upon dozens of outstanding Chinese restaurants featuring the different cuisines of the provinces: Canton, Peking, Shanghai, Szechuan, and Swatow. Familiar and superbly prepared Cantonese specialties such as lobster, chicken, fried or steamed, with a lemon sauce, and roast suckling pig are excellent at *The Star, Tai Tung, Kam Ling,* the *Golden City* and the *Hotel Luk Kwok,* on Hong Kong Island, while a stew of bears' paws, eggs scrambled with crabmeat and sharks' fins, and Beggars' Chicken, baked in a coating of clay and banana leaves, are the Hangchow dishes featured at the absolutely sensational, inexpensive (by our standards) *Tien Hong Lau* on Kowloon. Shanghai food includes a number of sweet and salty dishes, an interesting appetizer of boiled peanuts, fried seaweed, and bamboo shoots, chicken in a peppery sauce, and honey-toffee apples for dessert. In autumn, fresh-water crabs are not to be missed. All these are obtainable at the *Kowloon Restaurant* on Nathan Road. For Szechuan food (sour-peppery soup, pepper prawns, and spicy duckling) there is the *Capitol Winter Garden* on Kowloon, and here too the *Princess Garden* specializes in the crispest version possible of Peking Duck. One of the best and most interesting ways to spend an evening is to have dinner at *Tai Pak,* one of the floating restaurants in the sampan settlement of Aberdeen, where fish is caught and cooked to order and a dinner might consist of fried crab claws, exquisite lobster Cantonese and a special native fish, *garoupa,* half steamed with ginger, the other half crisply fried. *Pai Lai Hsuin,* on Hong Kong, serves the Mongolian hot pot, for which each diner cooks his own mutton and vegetables in a potful of boiling stock set in the middle of the table and then blends his own sauce-dip from a choice of about ten or twelve ingredients.

No one should miss the typical Chinese tea-lunch, *Yum-cha,* served at the *Café de Chine* and *Sky Room,* on Hong Kong, the *Highball* on Nathan Road, or, most interestingly, the *Luk-Yu Tea House* on Hong Kong, a hangout for Chinese opera stars. In all of these places waitresses circulate like cigarette girls in a night club, each carrying a different variety of meat- or fish-filled dumplings (*dem-sem*), an assortment of soups, *chow fan* (fried rice) steamed in packets of lotus leaves, and over eighty such assorted delicacies. You examine each tray and decide which of the varieties you care to sample. Your bill is tallied by the number of saucers stacked up on your table.

There is excellent European food at *Jimmy's Kitchen* (the onion soup and pepper steak are quite special). Also good are the *Parisian Grill, Gaddi's* in the *Peninsula Hotel* and, next door, the *Marco Polo,* a splashy restaurant with both Chinese and European foods and prices as extravagant as the décor. *Maxim's* is a cool and comfortable place for a light snack or a cool drink all day long, and adds a floor show, dinner, and dancing in the evening. If you are seized with a sudden longing for steppes, samovars, and *smetane* go to the Russian *Tkachenko* on Kowloon for *zakouskis,* vodka and shashlik. All of the larger hotels have European dining rooms and the veranda of the *Repulse Bay Hotel* is pleasant for Sunday lunch or dinner and a late brandy. *Dairy Farms Restaurants,* of which there are several, are perfect for quick, light lunches.

Hotel breakfasts are the large, British variety and tea is the native drink, sometimes perfumed with flower blossoms as an elegant end to a meal. Sticky rice sweets and a version of frozen custard known as "soft ice" are the confections sold everywhere.

Entertainment, Night Life, and Special Events

Hong Kong is a whirl of color and activity at night with floor shows and excellent Philippine dance bands at most of the chic dinner places, such as the *Marco Polo, Maxim's,* the *Champagne Room* in *Sunning House,* and in the very popular *Miramar Hotel* on Kowloon. The *Paramount,* the *Majestic* and the *Highball* are more strictly dance-and-music places, some with Chinese hostesses in slit-skirted *cheongsams.* Those who remember that this is "the world of Suzie Wong" will be aware of some of the other aspects of Hong Kong's night life.

There is very little theater life outside of amateur shows put on by local dramatic groups. Concerts are occasionally given by touring orchestras and soloists, but every Hong Kong visitor should try to see a performance of the Chinese (Peking) opera, one of the most fascinating arts in the world, a vivid combination of music, ballet, and singing. Above all, the colorful costumes, exotic makeup, and tricky acrobatic stunts will appeal to the Western visitor. Ask your reception desk to book a seat. One of the most fascinating sights is the open-air opera given at night in the Lai Chi Kok Amusement Park, where the audience is every bit as interesting as the performance.

Most of the Chinese festivals and ceremonies are based on traditions and historical events thousands of years old. The three main Chinese feast days of the year are the *Chinese New Year* (late January or early February), a four-day celebration that brings the city virtually to a standstill; the *Dragon Boat Festival* in June, when the colorful boat races can be watched from hired launches; and the *Mid-Autumn Festival* in September, when bakeries sell enormous "moon cakes" to honor the harvest moon. Since the Chinese calendar is based on lunar months, no festival will fall on the same Western calendar date in two succeeding years.

Shopping

Hong Kong is a free port and shopping is as heady and dazzling an experience as they tell you it is. Tailors will come to your hotel and arrange for suits, dresses, and coats to be made quickly and expertly—though it is best to allow for forty-eight hours and two fittings. Swiss watches, German and Japanese cameras, Japanese pearls, English leather, china, crystals, cashmeres, and cutlery, French perfumes, and Oriental fabrics are available here and are often cheaper in Hong Kong than in the countries of origin. A great deal of Oriental merchandise is manufactured in the colony. At least one thousand factories and workshops in Hong Kong turn out silk and cotton goods, leather goods, camphorwood chests, teak, blackwood, and rattan furniture, silks, and embroidered linen. (If you are interested in visiting a local factory, call the Hong Kong Tourist Association.) In addition, there are exquisite pieces of jewelry and jade, and a wide range of Oriental antiques at better shops in the major hotel arcades, along Nathan Road, and most exciting of all, in the area known as the Thieves' Market.

This is as good a place as any to remind you that American citizens are not allowed to import to the United States merchandise (old or new) originating in China or North Korea. Certain shops and factories can provide a special "certificate of origin" issued by the Hong Kong government for purchases made covering locally manufactured goods. These certificates are accepted by the United States Customs for entry of the articles listed thereon.

When shopping in Hong Kong you are expected to bargain everywhere, except in the department stores. It may take a lot of time, but shopping is part of the entertainment in Hong Kong. Beware of brand-name imitations, and *never, never* engage a guide who solicits you in the street for a shopping trip.

There are so many shops clustered around Nathan Road on Kowloon, in the arcades of the large hotels, and in the streets around the European business section on Hong Kong, that it is difficult to single out all of the good ones, but here are a few to start you off.

There are beautiful fabrics at the *British Textile Company,* and *Kawamali's,* and a full range of Japanese silks at *Kanebo,* where prices are almost as low as in Japan. You will find the boutique-type of fashion and decorative accessories at *Charlotte Horstmann's, Eileen Kershaw's,* and the *Star of Siam.* For beautifully embroidered linens, handkerchiefs, and lingerie try *Swatow Weng Lee* and the high-fashion silk lounge-wear of *Dynasty* is on sale in the Peninsula Hotel. The best known of the men's tailors are *Jimmy Chen, George Chen, James S. Lee, Tailor Chueng,* while *William Yu* and *M. K. Loo* tailor for women as well. *Morocain Chang* and *Betty Clemo* do beautiful clothing for women, as do the boutiques already mentioned above. Reliable shops for jade, pearls, jewelry, and watches include *Sennett Frères, Falconers,* and the *Hong Kong Jade Center.* For cameras, visit *A. Sek, Wood's,* or *Cinex,* and for film or special developing services, *Kodak,* in Shell House on Hong Kong. Beautifully carved furniture can be found at *Cathay Arts, Hong Kong Old Mary, The Majestic Co.,* and *George Zee;* exquisite rugs in the Peninsula Hotel arcade. In addition to small shops, several large department stores offer a good sampling of all merchandise along with ready-made British clothing and china. For a complete list of reliable shops in Hong Kong check the guide, "Around and About Hong Kong," published by the Hong Kong Tourist Association, which indicates shops issuing the "certificate of origin."

Background Reading

A History of Hong Kong, by George B. Endicott
Hong Kong Holiday, by Emily Hahn
Hong Kong, by Gene Gleason
Hong Kong, by Martin Hurlimann (photographs and some text)

India

CALCUTTA

The pride of India and the Black Hole

CALCUTTA was a British invention—a quiet fishing hamlet in the seventeenth century, destined a hundred years later to become the center of one of the world's largest empires, and now surely one of the world's most fascinating and intriguing places. This was the city of Clive, the true founder of British India, a man who changed trading settlements into territorial dominions in the name of his beloved "John Company," the East India Company, an arm of empire concerned with affairs more governmental than mercantile. Calcutta, even then a fine seaport and now the largest in the East, was valued for its harbor on the Hooghly River, a forty-mile passageway to the Bay of Bengal and the oceans of the world, an invaluable port for receiving and transshipping the treasures of all the Indies: calico from Calicut, silk, jute, and indigo; emeralds and rubies; tea and rice; cloves, pepper, cardamon, ginger, and the dozens of spices so necessary to European palates.

This was the headquarters of that colonial empire, the pukka-sahib world of the British Raj, where topi-topped Englishmen went out in the noonday sun while their children were cared for by native ayahs and their wives played whist at luxurious "for Europeans only" clubs,

452

or competed with each other via the curry tiffin. This luncheon, an endless parade of Indian dishes, was evaluated by the number of "boys" needed to serve it, so that a woman offering a "nine-boy curry" far out-statused the previous hostess who presented only a "seven-boy curry" the day before.

Calcutta is the largest city in India, with a population close to four million. It is also the capital of West Bengal; the world's largest producer of jute; a leading industrial and commercial center, with paper mills, iron foundries, steel plants, tanneries, printing presses; and has the largest cantilevered bridge in the world. It numbers among its attractions the green park and playing fields of the Maidan; the fashionable hotels, restaurants, and shops along Chowringhee; lush botanical gardens and a banyan tree so large that several hundred people can sit beneath its shade; the Taj-like Victoria Memorial; and the huge Indian Museum. There are many imposing government buildings around Dalhausie Square; and the mosaic jewel that is the Jain temple is reflected in its own lagoon like a shimmering stained-glass window. But one can know all Calcutta's past and be aware of its present claims to fame and still be totally unprepared for the stunning impact of the city itself.

For Calcutta is awash with humanity, a sprawling, teeming mass of people—crowds that reach nightmare proportions around the Kalighat Temple, a Hindu holy place older than Calcutta itself, and which, in fact, gave the city its name. This is a Hieronymus Bosch world come to life, with cripples and beggars and fanatics working themselves into frenzies around the "fertility tree," or grabbing at the clothing and cameras of foreigners foolish enough to venture there without protection of guide; and over all the hysterical bleating of shriveled goats, sensing their fate and trying to escape the temple's sacrificial altar. And these crowds can be pitiful too, especiallly along the burning ghats of the Hooghly, where each morning gaunt corpses with marigolds in their hair are stretched on rope cots to wait their turn on the funeral pyres, with a moaning mourner or two nearby and scatterings of maimed children begging for alms, displaying their infirmities to touch the hearts of potential donors. Any night along the thoroughfares thousands of the poor wind their clothing around them and lie down to sleep, their only beds the city streets; and in front of the smart hotels beggars whine their plea in a toneless chant, "Have no father, have no mother, Give *baksheesh*," at the same time, perhaps, exhibiting the stump of an arm to make the plea more eloquent. And along these streets sit professional ear cleaners, sidewalk chiropodists, fortunetellers, and vendors selling the salted chick peas which the Indians relish for snacks as we do popcorn.

But with all the poverty there is beauty, dignity, and fascination, not only in the city's main sights, but in the crowds as well, mostly around the busy market areas. Here pyramids of spices—hot orange turmeric, fiery paprika, earth-toned cinnamon—are piled in front of open shops, and in the stalls of New Market with their polished brass water jugs and food pails, the exquisite brocaded silks from the holy city of Benares, or carved and inlaid ivory boxes and figurines. But most beautiful of all are the women—paragons of grace and elegance in their flowing saris, the parts in the hair stained bright with henna to indicate they are married.

In a book of the early 1900's called *Administrative Problems of British India,* the author, John Chailley, describes Calcutta as

. . . the pride of India, the city of wide open spaces, where you find cattle grazing in the heart of town. A city of work and pleasure, a colossal business center which is at one and the same time an immense emporium and a gigantic workshop. A worthy capital of empire this; magnificent for its growth and life; products of the slow conquest of a marshy and melancholy land; intolerable during the summer but delicious in the cold weather; feared and almost despised by those who know her not, but seductive and retentive to those who visit her.

The wide open spaces are there even now and the sacred cattle still graze in the heart of town. And though Calcutta is no longer a "capital of empire," perhaps she is destined always to be a city at once "feared and despised, seductive and retentive."

NEW DELHI

The phoenix city

LIKE the mythological phoenix, the bird that rises reborn from its own funeral ashes, Delhi has risen time and again from the ruins of former cities. Each new ruler builds his own capital, sweeping away remnants of the former regime or letting them fall into neglect and decay, leaving only the most fragmentary record of its past. Believed to be three thousand years old, this city on the Yamuna River was important before Rome, before Alexander, and since the tenth century has been the capital of Hindu kings and Rajput chiefs, Persian shahs and Mogul emperors; it was the scene of Gandhi's triumphs and assassination and is now the home of his political and spiritual heir, Panditji, Jawarharlal Nehru.

Today there are two Delhis: Old and New—five miles and three hundred years apart, with a population total of two million. New Delhi is more a state of mind than a city; a far-flung collection of grandiose government buildings that are in effect monuments to the Indian Civil Service. Designed by Sir Edward Luytens in 1911 and completed in 1931, Delhi was "planned" along the symmetrical lines of Europe's eighteenth century cities. It is a place of broad tree-lined boulevards and neatly clipped gardens, spacious parks, sparkling pools and fountains, and wide man-made vistas. It is a constant frustration to anyone who likes to see a city on foot, for distances between areas are so great as to discourage even the most intrepid walker. This is true even within the city's hub, a circular maze of streets that ring out concentrically from the Secretariat and Government House to the rim of Connaught Circus—a whirlpool of activity with eager civil servants and earnest foreign diplomats, bedazzled tourists and cautious traders, all dashing about on their diverse missions, a place long on activity but short on native color.

But Old Delhi is another matter entirely. For this is the India of Kipling and the stalwart British garrisons, with a skyline of mosques and minarets and the teeming street life of the bazaars clustered around Old Delhi's most famous buildings: the picturesque Mogul citadel, the Red Fort, a rosy sandstone compound of crenelated walls and cupola domes, a combination palace and fortress which includes the Pearl Mosque, where once stood the fabled Peacock Throne. The walls of the Audience Hall bear the Persian inscription:

IF THERE BE PARADISE ON EARTH,
IT IS THIS—IT IS THIS—IT IS THIS!

Nearby stands the largest Mosque in India, the Jama Masjid, both buildings constructed in the middle seventeenth century in the reign of Shah Jahan, the man also responsible for the Taj Mahal.

In the shadows of these buildings, amid the jumble of market activity, streets are alive with mystics and beggars, soothsayers and merchants. As you walk along shopping for bargains in spices or silks, brass or ivory, or antique temple carvings (real and fake), you are accosted by a string of turbaned or pajama-clad entrepreneurs who may invite you to witness a fakir rope trick or applaud a dancing bear. Others open hive-shaped baskets to reveal wide-headed cobras, offering to charm them with music before your very eyes, to promote a fight between a cobra and a mongoose, or allow you to watch a cobra devour a live rat. Perhaps a bearded mystic will promise, in honeyed tones, to guess your mother's name for $5, U.S. When he fails he meekly suggests that perhaps he is losing his powers, as he shyly, slyly pockets the five.

It is in Old Delhi, too, that you may shop for lengths of gold and silver cloth along the Chandni Chowk, or step into the cool courtyards and see the handsome carved doors and fantastic chandeliers in the old houses tucked away behind the Street of Silver; or view the remains of the ancient wall which ran around Shahjahanabad, the city of Shah Jahan. Here, jackals prowl the streets at night and flower sellers approach you with snowy garlands of sweet jasmine; here, street vendors sit wrapping betel-nut snacks—the after-dinner fresheners so beloved by Asians from Saigon to Bombay.

Scattered through both Delhis are the relics of the past, among them the Qutb Minar, supposedly the most perfect tower ever built, a fluted, mauve-pink shaft constructed by Delhi's first conqueror, Mohammed Gori, in the early thirteenth century. Nearby stands one of the true wonders of the world, built by a Hindu king, the Iron Pillar of almost pure iron, still unrusted though exposed to sun and rain for fifteen hundred years; and the two tombs that represent the first and last examples of Mogul architecture in India, the tomb of Emperor Humayin, dating from 1565, and the 1753 tomb of Safdar Jang.

Among the modern buildings is the phantasmagorical rainbow of inlaid stone that is the Hindu temple, Lakshmi Narayana, and the most important place of pilgrimage is the Rajghat, Gandhi's memorial and cremation site, a simple stone platform blanketed with fresh flowers and enclosed in a small park. The United States Embassy is well worth a stop, with its graceful pierced-stone façade and interior pool; and, of course, there is the morass of government buildings, most of which are open to the public at one time or another: the Parliament House and the President's Residence, the National Museum and the Secretariat Buildings.

It is from these buildings that Delhi governs one-seventh of the earth's population, 430 million people, jammed into an area roughly half the size of the United States, to make this the second largest country in the world. Only 20 per cent of these people are literate, their life expectancy is thirty-five, and they speak fourteen languages and some 250 dialects. In these vital statistics one can glimpse the problems the government is attempting to solve through a series of five-years plans. The agenda includes birth control, improved health standards, education, and the development of industry and of India's untapped resources. All this is combined with a program of land reform which was given a tremendous boost by the Bhoodan program of Acharya Vinoba Bhave in 1951. So far, it has resulted in land grants to the poor from over half a million donors. Then, of course, there is

India's special problem, its apparently immutable Hindu caste system, a rather hopeless division of classes based on birth. The highest caste is headed by the Brahmans and the Untouchables form the lowest and largest strata; between these two are a number of castes and subcastes.

The four racial types which comprise the Indian population—Indo-Aryans and Mongolians in the north, short, dark Dravidians in the south, and the isolated primitive peoples dotted throughout the hillside villages—are descendants of a five-thousand-year-old civilization. Some of its many contributions to world culture and knowledge have been the mathematical concepts of zero, the decimal system, and the value of infinity, and two of the world's leading religions, Hinduism, which covers a multitude of sects, and Buddhism, based on the teaching of a native prince, Lord Buddha, who reached Enlightenment under the bo tree of Buddh Gaya. These teachings traveled along with the art and culture of India, spreading throughout Southeast Asia, China, and Korea to the easternmost shores of the Japanese islands.

Along with the Hindu religions are its offshoots: Jainism, a sect of over a million-and-a-half followers, strict vegetarians who will not even eat eggs and who wear gauze masks over their mouths and noses to avoid killing any bacteria that might enter the body. The Sikh group of six million people are mostly from the province of Punjab. These tall, turbaned, bearded men are famous for their loyalty and fighting prowess and they are employed throughout the Orient wherever unusually stalwart guards are needed. Added to these are the Moslem followers of Mohammed, the Christians, the Jews, and the Parsees, fire worshipers of Zoroaster. Driven from Persia in the eighth century, most of the Parsees settled in India around Bombay. They built the Tower of Silence where corpses are taken to be picked clean by vultures.

Delhi's historical role as India's capital is due primarily to its geographical location. It is at midpoint on the subcontinent, halfway between the Mogul gardens of Kashmir where one may live on a houseboat tended by a private corps of servants, and the incredible sculpture of the Hindu temples that abound in the southern provinces around Madras; halfway between India's gateway, Bombay, with European cafés, espresso bars, and wide malls rimmed by Victorian Gothic buildings, and the teeming swarm of humanity that is Calcutta. And for the tourist, Delhi is just a day's excursion from the fabled beauties of Agra's Taj Mahal and the ghost city of the Mogul Akbar

—Fathepur Sikri; half a day from the rose-hued city of Jaipur, one of the cleanest, most orderly, and most beautiful cities in India, famed for its jewels and Rajasthan paintings, and the silken saris of its women. Here you may ride an elephant up to the golden splendors of the Amber Palace or marvel at the Maharajah's Wind Palace, with its organ-pipe façade of delicately pierced pink sandstone.

FOR THE TRAVELER'S NOTEBOOK

Official Information

Before you go: Government of India Tourist Office: 19 East 49th St., New York 17, N.Y.; 685 Market St., San Francisco, Cal.

In Calcutta: SAS Office, 18 Park St.; Government of India Tourist Office, 13 Old Court House St.; U.S. Consulate, 5/1 Harrington St.

In New Delhi: SAS Office, Claridge's Hotel; Government of India Tourist Office, 88 Janpath; U.S. Embassy, Bahawalpur House, Sikandra Road.

Money Matters

Currency: The monetary unit in India is the rupee (Rs.) which is divided into 100 naya paisa. There are about 4.75 rupees to $1, U.S.

Tipping: Hotels add a service charge of 12½ per cent to their bills. In restaurants the maximum tip is 10 per cent; porters get Rs. 0.25 per suitcase (minimum Rs. .50); hairdressers expect at least Rs. .50 or 10–25 per cent, depending on the total bill. Taxi drivers and cinema ushers are not tipped.

Climate, Clothing and Essentials

In Calcutta the winter months are from mid-October through March, when the weather is cool and pleasant with an average temperature range of 55 to 80 degrees F. Light clothing will be comfortable in all but the northern areas. Summer is hotter and from April to mid-October temperatures range from 75 to 97 degrees and of course you will want the thinnest tropical clothing. In New Delhi the temperature ranges are more extreme, with summer (April to July) temperatures often going as high as 110 degrees, and the air is extremely dry. In winter the thermometer often drops as low as 45 degrees and you will need woolen clothing and at least an in-between coat. The months of the monsoon rains are July to September and in all parts of India you will need a raincoat and umbrella during that time.

Unless you plan to attend special functions, extremely formal wear is unnecessary in New Delhi or Calcutta and normal city attire is correct at all times.

Though tap water is said to be safe, it is even safer to be sure that any water you drink is bottled or boiled, and in any outlying areas tap water is to be avoided. Some European drugs and toiletries are available in Calcutta and New Delhi, but if there is anything very special you need it is better to take a full supply with you. American film is available but extremely expensive.

Hotels

Though hotels in India's major cities are up to international standards in the de luxe and first class categories, it is not a good idea to stay at any lower class hotels unless you know someone who has been there and the recommendation is firsthand. Prices in all categories are a little higher than they would be for European counterparts but facilities are modern, service fairly good, and most hotels are fully or partially (often erratically) air conditioned. All of the major hotels have dining rooms with adequate food and several have cabarets.

Rates in the best hotels for a single room with bath are about Rs. 30/ without air conditioning, Rs. 50/ with. Double rates are respectively about Rs. 60/ and Rs. 100/, while the good medium class hotels offer slightly lower rates. A fixed price of about Rs. 20/ per day will be added for three meals. A complete list of government-approved hotels throughout India (with facilities and prices) can be obtained from the Indian Tourist Offices listed earlier.

CALCUTTA

DE LUXE: The best hotels in Calcutta are: the *Oberoi Grand Hotel, 15 Chowringhee Rd.,* with a large dining room, the Princes Night Club, and located in the midst of the main shopping section; the *Great Eastern Hotel, 1 Old Court House St.,* with a Chinese restaurant, Maxim's Night Club, and a convenient location.

MODERATE: *Spence's Hotel, 4 Wellesley Place,* is a good hotel in the medium price range with a restaurant and cabaret, air-conditioned rooms, and private baths.

NEW DELHI

There are many more hotels in New Delhi and Old Delhi than in Calcutta and a wider range of prices and accommodations. Generally rates are a little higher here too with single rooms starting at about Rs. 50/, double at about Rs. 100/.

DE LUXE: *Ashoka, Diplomatic Enclave,* is practically a city itself, a huge sprawling hotel "compound" complete with shops, cabana-pool, and all hotel facilities. *Oberoi Imperial, Janpath,* within walking distance of the best shops, has all of the usual comforts.

MODERATE: *Claridge's, 12 Aurangzeb Rd.* This is a jewel of a place, and anyone who prefers personalized service in a small, continental hotel will enjoy this. The dining room is attractive and the food excellent. Swimming pool and all facilities. *Hotel Janpath, Janpath.* A comfortable commercial hotel, close to the main shopping section, with full facilities and moderate to high rates.

OLD DELHI

Oberoi Maiden's and *Oberoi Swiss,* both on Atipore Road in Old Delhi, are inexpensive by Indian standards and comfortable, if a little on the fallen grandeur side. Both have nice grounds, swimming pools, and are excellent for parents traveling with children. The Swiss is the less expensive of the two.

Food and Restaurants

Continental food is available in all of the major cities, hotels, and restaurants in India, and standards vary from place to place. In general, preparation is adequate and occasionally good, with the exception of beef dishes, which are not to be recommended any place in India since it is doubtful that beef will be the meat you get—water buffalo will be more likely since cattle are sacred here. Fish is excellent, so is lamb, and the chicken is edible.

Indian food is interesting, very good, spicy, quite varied, and certainly to be tried. Curries are famous, of course, and there are several types, dry and sauced, some with a base of tamarind juice, others with coconut milk or tomatoes. All kinds of fish, shrimp, meats (Korma curry is a special favorite), and vegetables go into curries, and one can order several different kinds, to be eaten with spiced rice pilaff or *biryani,* the rice cooked with meat and vegetables in the latter. Tandoori cooking (spicy meat or chicken cooked in a circular stone oven) is superb, perhaps the best food in India, and is served with a wonderful bread (*nan*)—a sort of pizza dough baked on the hot stones of the oven. *Seekh Kabab* is another broiled skewered favorite. Indian pickles (*achar*) and fruit chutney are extremely delicate and delectable and the assorted breads—crisp *pappadums,* soft wheat *chapattis,* and golden balloons known as *poori,* are all excellent. Eggplant (*brinjals*) and lentils (*dal*) are the most commonly used vegetables, served fried or curried, and there is a wide range of tropical fruits, especially the custard apple, which are strange to us and worth sampling. Much Indian food is served with hot chilies, green or red, so be careful when trying them. Soups are good, especially the famous mulligatawny which varies from region to region. Desserts include a honey-sweet halvah, rose-water custard (*firni*), often dressed up with flecks of silver leaf, and sugared anise seeds, served in place of our after-dinner mints by the better native restaurants. Since the more religious Hindus are vegetarians, each city has several interesting restaurants featuring an incredible variety of meatless, eggless creations.

Tea is the major drink and is often served with jasmine blossoms at the end of an elegant dinner. Spiced chilled promegranate juice is one of the more exotic and delightful thirst quenchers. You can have coffee but it is not generally very good.

Imported liquor is available but rather expensive. India produces all sorts of alcoholic beverages and the gin and beer are almost as good as the better brands produced abroad. Indian liquor laws vary in each state—in some there are dry days, in others you must go into a special permit room to drink. Some allow you to drink in your room but not at a bar, and some do not permit any liquor of any kind, ever—so check on the local laws when your itinerary is planned.

CALCUTTA

There are reliable international restaurants at each of the three hotels already mentioned and you can also get a few Indian dishes there, though they are usually well tempered to Western palates. Other good restaurants in the city include *Firpo's* featuring continental food and dancing upstairs, less expensive luncheons downstairs; the *Mocambo,* which has music, dancing, and European food; the *Trinca;* and the *Skyroom.* For good Chinese food, try the restaurant at the *Great Eastern,* the *Nanking, Chung Wah,* or *Waldorf.* Calcutta clubs have excellent food, and visitors are welcome when introduced by a member.

NEW DELHI

All of the hotels have restaurants, of course, and the best of these is the one at *Claridge's.* The two most interesting restaurants in the city, featuring excellent Indian food, are in Old Delhi: *Motimahal,* a huge sprawling place with indoor and outdoor dining, features the best *tandoori* cooking in India, while *Khyber* has more variations in the same type of cooking plus a number of other excellent dishes, especially the tandoori chicken in tomato-butter sauce. *Gaylord's,* a sort of restaurant, tearoom, late night dancing spot, is somewhat *fin de siècle* in décor and serves fairly good continental and Indian food, desserts and coffee, or drinks and snacks. *Volga, Standard, Alp's, Kwality,* and *Wenger's* for confections and candies are all interesting and worth trying.

The *Vegetarian,* attached to the *Tea House* is an orthodox Hindu and Jain restaurant serving only vegetarian dishes in the traditional way and is a must for anyone really interested in native fare. The mango juice cocktail here is very good as are most of the other beans, vegetables, and grains with spiced sauces and condiments.

Entertainment and Night Life

The large hotels in Calcutta and New Delhi all have floor shows and dancing every evening and you will find the same attractions at the restaurants already mentioned.

Exhibitions of Indian dance, drama, and music are put on in the major cities regularly, and it is best to check at your hotel desk as to the performances scheduled during the time of your visit. Of these the native dances of the various provinces are most interesting to see and you should not miss any that take place while you are there.

Big game hunting is one of India's most popular sports and the tiger hunt, the Shikar, is one of the most famous of safaris, while other game includes bear, buffalo, elephants, panthers, rhinoceros, and deer. For more information on big game hunting, consult your travel agent or write to the Publication Department, Old Secretariat, Delhi.

SPECIAL EVENTS: There are a number of national and, especially, religious holidays in India, and while it is difficult to give exact information, the following may prove useful: *National holidays:* January 26 is *Republic Day,* the commemoration of the republic's foundation with celebrations, military parades, and mass meetings, principally in New Delhi. August 15 is *Independence Day.* October 2 is *Gandhi Jayanti:* On this day the people of India celebrate the birthday of Mahatma Gandhi, father of the nation. *Religious holidays: Holi* is a gay and noisy festival celebrating spring. During this festival it is customary for both adults and children to greet each other with a shower of colored powder from the sacks they carry or to spray friends and relatives with colored water. This is the Indian equivalent of our Halloween "trick or treat" when children chalk each other's clothing or swat victims with flour-filled sacks. The festival takes place around the end of March. *Sri Ramanavani* is another Hindu festival; it commemorates the birthday of Sri Rama in mid-April. *Id-ul-Fitr* is a Moslem festival to celebrate the end of Ramzan, the month of fasting. It is held in mid-May. *Id-uz-Zuha* is another Moslem holiday on which the Mohammedans commemorate the sacrifice of Abraham. It is accompanied by animal sacrifices and mass prayers and takes place in mid-July. *Muhurram* is a Moslem holiday in memory of the martyrdom of Immam Hussain in mid-August. *Dussehra* and *Durga Puja* is the greatest Hindu festival of the year, celebrating the triumph of good over evil as exemplified in Rama's victory over the demon, Ravana. This is held sometime in October. *Diwali,* the Festival of Lights, marks the victorious return of King Rama to his capital. This holiday, twenty-one days after Durga Puja, is the beginning of the fiscal year for business.

In addition to these holidays, another picturesque event is the *Car Festival* at Puri (about twelve hours' journey from Calcutta), the most famous religious procession in all India. The center of the procession is the huge wooden chariot, forty-five feet high, which is drawn by pilgrims and carries the image of Lord Jagannath, the Hindu deity. The Car Festival is held during June or July.

Shopping

Anyone on an extended tour of the Far East should set aside a good portion of his shopping budget for India, for few countries offer such a staggering array of exquisite handwork, whether it be sheer silks and glistening brocades in piece goods or in sari lengths, thinnest wool stoles or papier-mâché from Kashmir, handsome brass and ivory-inlaid wooden pieces, fanciful toys, and what is probably the most beautiful jewelry in the world—precious stones inlaid and enameled in necklaces, bracelets, and brooches. There are wonderful things made of leather, and magnificent old carvings and paintings. When it comes to jewels and fine arts, you had best know what you are buying or go with someone who does, or shop only at the government emporia where you are sure of getting what you pay for.

There is also a vast array of colorful lacquered furniture from the Sankeda works in the government shops, and delicately inlaid silver *bidri* work. Evening bags embroidered in glistening golden threads, thousands of beautiful scarves, gold-trimmed slippers, toe rings and ankle bracelets, and cool-looking summer rugs are just a few of the other things worth considering.

CALCUTTA

In Calcutta you will find an especially good selection of gold-brocaded Benares stoles, as well as all of the other things already mentioned. The best shopping area here is the district around Chowringhee Road and Park Street, between the Grand Hotel and the SAS Office. You will also want to visit the fantastic conglomeration that is *New Market,* and the *Bengal Home Industries Association, West Bengal Government Emporium, Handloom House,* and the *Women's Friendly Society,* with especially lovely children's and infants' clothing.

NEW DELHI

Every major Indian city has its shopping sections, but if you are going to New Delhi, I would strongly suggest you do most of your shopping at the *Central Cottage Industries Emporium* on Janpath. This shop is a government cooperative which sells the best of what is made in all of the Indian provinces. The merchandise is exquisite and so are the displays, and the choice is the largest in the country. New Delhi has a number of other shops worth seeing. There are also official emporia of other provinces, particularly the *Kashmir Government Shop,* the *U.P. Government Handicrafts Shop,* and the *Emporium of Rajasthan.* You will also find rows of shops around the arc of Connaught Place, along Janpath and Chandni Chowk, and a number of fine shops in the major hotels.

Background Reading

This is India, Remember the House, and *Home to India,* by Santha Rama Rau

The Lotus and the Robot, by Arthur Koestler

Walking the Indian Streets, by Ved Mehta

Krishna Fluting, and *Flight of White Crows,* by John Berry

The Last Days of the British Raj, by Leonard Oswald Mosley

Nectar in a Sieve, by Kamala Taylor

Binodini, by Rabindranath Tagore

Kim, by Rudyard Kipling

Ambassador's Report, by Chester Bowles

The Tiger House Party, by Emily Hahn

Indonesia

DJAKARTA

Where gentlemen do Not *prefer blondes*

CONSIDERING the breathtaking beauty of the Indonesian archipelago, the country's capital comes as something of a disappointment. For Djakarta, the Batavia of Dutch colonial days, is a hot and humid city of two million, devoid of charm and comfort (though not of interest), and rampant with all of the problems besetting this struggling but promising young nation: the ravages of the most wanton colonial exploitation, poverty, overpopulation (ninety million people make this the sixth largest country in the world), poor health, illiteracy (only 5 per cent of the population could read and write when the Dutch left), and a vast treasury of undeveloped resources. There is a kind of worn-out and leftover look about the place, and the apathy of the people is no small problem to the ambitious leader of this "guided democracy," President Sukarno, whose diligent sloganeering is designed to instill much needed pride and ambition in his people.

First occupied in the sixteenth century by the Portuguese, who named it Batavia, the city passed to Holland, then briefly, to the British in the early nineteenth century, and back again to the Dutch rulers. They made it the pride of the East Indies, a miniature Holland, complete with sparkling white houses roofed in red tiles and tulips that grew around man-made canals, while the natives were confined to *kampongs*—settlements of palm-and-bamboo huts, many of which still remain today.

Almost all Djakarta has to show for the four hundred years of foreign rule are a few crumbling houses; Heinekens beer; a network of muddy, torpid canals, the largest of which bisects the city, serves as a community laundromat, dishwasher, and bath, and is definitely off-limits to candid camera fans out for native color; and a ferocious

466

xenophobia which, for a while, was directed against all Europeans, especially those who were blond and fair.

The first task the Indonesians set for themselves after gaining independence in 1949 was to remove all traces of everything foreign, and Dutch names were changed to their equivalents in the native tongue, Bahasa Indonesian, a Malayan derivative. The famed Hotel Des Indes, long a setting for colonials of the Maugham type in solar topis and *stengah*-shifters, became the Hotel Duta Indonesia (the same initials could remain on linens, tableware, and floor mats); the East Indies became Indonesia; Batavia is now Djakarta; such fabled islands as the star-shaped Celebes, with its sleekly rigged prahus that sail the waters of the archipelago, became Sulawesi; Borneo, the steaming, rubber-rich island where Conrad's fat and florid Dutch planters went to ruin over native women and Holland gin, is now called Kalimantan; Java is Djawa; and the recently liberated Netherlands New Guinea will soon appear on maps as Irian Barat.

Thanks to an intense and enlightened governmental program in the interests of tourism, the situation now is considerably eased, and the snarl of red tape one had to unravel before entering the country has been simplified to a mere knot. With the newly completed Hotel Indonesia the traveler's life is far more comfortable than it might have been three years ago, but not even this added convenience would make a trip worthwhile were it for Djakarta alone. The city has a few sights of interest, such as the museum, with its Hindu-Brahmin sculptures and one of the world's best ethnological collections (the country's history dates back half a million years to the fossils of the Java man), its colorfully effervescent Glodok Chinatown, its bustling market places such as Pasar Baru and Pasar Ikan, and the enormous stadium built by the Soviet Union for the 1962 Asian Games. But still the only real reason for going to Djakarta is to see Indonesia, for the capital is the gateway to a land of fabled beauty and exotic wealth.

Indonesia, the world's largest archipelago, stretches three thousand miles across the equator from Asia to Australia, an emerald necklace of nine thousand islands reaching from the Malayan peninsula to the tip of Timor, between the Indian Ocean and the Pacific. It is a land of lush tropical forests and watery green rice paddies, volcanic peaks and white coral beaches, a floating garden of almond-scented frangipani and sprays of wild orchids, giant banyan trees, reedy bamboos, and feathery coconut palms, with such improbable fauna as the twin-horned rhinoceros and the dwarf deer, birds of paradise and lizards nine feet long, free-flying parrots as gaudy as New York taxicabs, and chirping monkeys that hop about everywhere busily picking fruit from the wide-leafed banana trees.

If beauty were Indonesia's only claim to fame, her history might have been happier. But it is her more material wealth of rubber and tin, petroleum and palm oil, sugar and rice, coffee and tea, mother-of-pearl and cinchona bark from which quinine is made, and her aromatic treasures of sandalwood and spices that have made this country a prize since Marco Polo first returned to Europe with stories about the Moluccas. These are the same Spice Islands for which Columbus was searching when he discovered America instead. And before the Europeans discovered it, the country was valued by Indians, Chinese, and Arabs who swept through the islands in turn, bringing with them their religions (Hinduism survives now only on Bali, while the rest of the country is Moslem) and adding their own racial strains to the original Malayan-Polynesian stock. The mixture has resulted in extremely attractive, small, sturdy, tawny people, with exquisitely round features and well-set bodies typified, in fact, by Sukarno him-self, in appearance an archetype Indonesian.

Of the three thousand inhabited islands, the most important is the cultural and agricultural center, Java. It is here that one finds not only the capital, Djakarta, but the overpowering eight-hundred-year-old Hindu-Buddhist *stupas* of Borobudur, near Jogjakarta, which itself is worth a visit for its folk dancers, silversmiths, and batik print cottons. Also on Java is the cool, crisply clean mountain retreat of Bandung; colorful Surabaya, the ancient city of the Madjapahit empire, now an important seaport with zoological gardens that house the world's most extensive collection of tropical birds and animals; and Surakarta or Solo, where one may still see exhibitions of traditional Javanese court dancing and the shadow puppet plays, *wayangs.*

The northern end of the island is tipped by the promontory known as the Java Head, a hideout for whales and whalers since the days of Moby Dick; just below, the Sunda Straits cut off the country's largest (and the world's fifth largest) island, volcanic Sumatra, with its rich oil fields and crater lake, Toba, a beautiful resort that can be reached by car from the city of Medan.

But of all the islands, none is more famous than Bali, every man's dream of a tropical paradise come true. And though rumor has it that Bali is not what it used to be, and one meets there bored and restless teenagers who want to be discovered by Hollywood, it still seems as relatively idyllic as it must have to the first Dutch traders who arrived there in 1597 and returned home to report on this new Eden. It is everything paradise should be—a balmy, palmy island with a water-color landscape of cerulean blue and iridescent green, where dusky, bare-breasted women, their neat hips wrapped in bright sarongs, walk barefooted and rhythmically along dirt roads, carrying on their heads great intricate towers of fruit which they present as temple offerings for the festivals held constantly all over the island.

Balinesian Hinduism, a unique animistic religion, is the focal point of life. Days here are made up of one religous ceremony after another and guided tours take tourists to see them all. One morning it may be a tooth-filing ceremony where several teenagers, smeared with sandal-wood paste and draped in parrot silks, lie on a wooden table to have their front teeth filed with rasps so their souls may enter heaven when they die; or perhaps in the afternoon there is a wedding, or a rite in honor of a teenage girl who has just reached puberty. If one is lucky he may view a cremation—a week-long ritual during which live chickens are impaled on iron hooks as offerings to the gods, and the body to be cremated is carried by hundreds of people in a funeral pyre fifty feet high; it is a ceremony so expensive that a family cannot always afford it when a relative dies, so the body is buried, often for years, and exhumed when enough money has been saved for the cremation.

All over the island one hears the plink-plonk atonal music of *gamelan* orchestras, native instruments that look like primitive xylo-phones, which accompany the dozens of dances the young, lithe Bali-nesians perform. Some dances honor such natural events as the full moon or the rice harvests, while others enact episodes from the Hindu *Ramayana*. Of these, the weekly *Ketjak,* or monkey dance, is a classic. It depicts the legend of the abducted Queen Sita who is rescued by monkey-soldiers and returned to her husband, King Rama. The dance, most effective when seen by moonlight, is an electrifying display of human forms, with 150 dancers snaking their arms into the air, moaning and sobbing, and often going into trances. In the shadowy half-light one is almost convinced that they have indeed turned into monkeys. The *legong,* performed by very young girls under the starry southern sky, is a more graceful and whimsical dance, well worth seeing.

Driving along the road you pass hundreds of picturesque *kampongs* —open, platformed huts with sugar-palm matting, towering temples with thatched pagoda roofs, women seated under shade palms plaiting straw mats for temple decorations, men carving flowing wooden figures from blond or ruby woods, brilliant belligerent roosters in rattan cages preening themselves as they wait to do battle at the cockfights staged on the island, and small boarlike pigs that are an island delicacy when spiced with chili and roasted in the oven-pits dug into the earth; and everywhere one catches the heady scent of burning joss sticks, and the sharp, sweet perfume of the clove-flavored cigarettes the Indonesians love.

Den Pesar, the main town on Bali, is the setting for open-stall shops and colorful markets. In the local museum one can see displays of Bali's indigenous, antique arts: masks, ceremonial headdresses, batiks, jewelry, water colors, wood sculptures, and painted leather puppets. Modern paintings of extremely high quality are exhibited in the handsome museum outside of the artists' village Ubud, about an hour's drive from Den Pesar.

Presided over by one of the last local princes, Tjokorda Gde-Agung, the pride of the village is the Puri Hotel, the last word in luxury, native style. One-bedroom cottages with palm-thatched roofs center around a luxuriant tropical garden courtyard—the community center of this hotel compound. Here the prince's wives and children work, play, or try to talk to guests, who have probably donned native dress. This courtyard is the scene of *gamelan* concerts and Balinesian dance exhibitions, performed almost every evening.

Wrapped in sarongs and, likely as not, wearing flowers in their hair, guests are served exotic local foods—roast pigs, vegetables flavored with peanut butter and chilis, satés, fruit juices, lemon squash, and beer—in the dining room or in the open dining pavilion, family style. After two or three sleepless nights you should get used to the wooden table-beds padded with palm-matting, the lack of electricity should seem more charming than primitive, and you might get to love dipper baths so much you eschew tubs and hot water forever. Ubud's charms, like those of the hotel, are simple and authentic. There are weekly markets to visit, artists to call upon, dances and festivals galore. Of the celebrities who have sampled Tjokorda Agung's unique hospitality, none has been more eloquently enthusiastic than Santha Rama Rau. Before you dash off a letter to Ubud and make your reservation, read the account of her visit in her book, *View to the Southeast.*

FOR THE TRAVELER'S NOTEBOOK

Official Information

Before you go: Indonesian Embassy, 2020 Massachusetts Ave., N.W., Washington, D.C.; Indonesian Consulate, Information Section, 5 East 68th St., New York, N.Y.

In Djakarta: SAS Office, 5 Djalan Modjopahit, and 193 Tromol Pos; Nitour, the Government Tourist Office, 2 Djalan Modjopahit; U.S. Embassy, 5 Medan Merdeka Selatan.

Money Matters

Currency: The monetary unit in Indonesia is the rupiah, and the current rate of exchange is about Rp. 45 to $1, U.S., but it is often subject to change. While it is possible to get a much better rate on the open market, there are strict prohibitions on the import (and export) of Indonesian currency.

Tipping: As in most Eastern countries, tipping is at the visitor's discretion. As a rule 10 per cent is added to the hotel bill for service; a small tip may be given for extra services. In restaurants 10 per cent is correct. Porters receive a few rupiahs per bag; sightseeing guides from Rp. 10 to 45, depending on the length and quality of their service.

Climate, Clothing, and Essentials

Though the average year round temperature is 82 degrees F., this does not tell all about the climate of Indonesia. Due to the extremely high humidity and often higher temperatures, it can more accurately be described as scalding. The dry season is from April to November, and June and July are the best of those months for a visit. But even then there can be days when the temperature hits 95 to 100. The east monsoon, bringing with it a constant downpour, comes between May and September; the west monsoon, during which there are intermittent showers, falls from October to April.

Clothing should be the lightest possible, with tissue silks and cottons predominating. All but the airiest of synthetics are to be avoided, and drip-dry clothes are a good idea if you are sure the fabrics are sufficiently porous. If you are planning to go to Bali, take summer resort clothes of the informal type.

All water must be boiled to be potable. If you are not sure that it has been, do not drink it. Ice cubes should be avoided too for complete safety. Iced tea, Heinekens beer, and a bottled soft drink are available.

It is practically impossible to find familiar drugs, toiletries, soap, and film, so stock up in advance.

Mosquito repellent is essential here and an English product, Flypel, is highly recommended for its non-greasy, non-smelly effectiveness. It can be found in any city in the East.

Hotels

With the new, luxury International Hotel Indonesia now opened and operating, Djakarta's facilities are somewhat improved but there remains a serious shortage of accommodations and at best those that do exist range from mediocre to poor. The only way to obtain confirmed reservations is through an agency representing the government tourist organization, Nitour. Single rooms and rates are available only at the Hotel Indonesia; elsewhere you must take and pay for double accommodations. There is hot water only upon request, when it is brought to you in pails, shower heads are placed over drains in the middle of your bathroom floor, and there are few luxury appointments such as toilet seats (though there are toilets). Mosquito netting or screening encloses most beds and large ceiling fans are the only cooling device. All hotels, except for the Hotel Indonesia, are American plan. Though hotels are graded, there seems to be little difference, in point of fact, in price or quality. Hotel rooms always seem to come within the neighborhood of $10 to $15 per day.

DJAKARTA

Hotel Indonesia, the newest Intercontinental hotel, was opened for the 1962 Asian Games and rates a de luxe classification in this city. It brings such innovations as room phones, private baths, a swimming pool, air conditioning, and all facilities. *Duta Indonesia, Djalan Gadjah Mada.* Formerly the famous Hotel Des Indes, not much remains but the initials, and of the 160 rooms it is *said* that a few are air conditioned. Most have private baths. *Dharma Nirmala, Seagar St.* One of the best European restaurants, the Ambassador, is located in this hotel, but not much else can be said for it. One-fifth of its rooms have air conditioners that work one-fifth of the time, some have baths, the rest have wash basins.

BALI

The *Bali Hotel* in Den Pasar is a large, rambling place in the center of Bali's main town. Accommodations are fairly comfortable and the food is adequate. This same hotel operates the *Sanur Beach House,* twenty minutes out of town at the edge of the Indian Ocean. The bathrooms have only dipper baths and the food, again, is just adequate. Next door, the *Segara Hotel* has rooms which are small, separated cottages on the beach. Facilities are absolutely minimal, though livable. Beautiful view and excellent swimming at both the Sanur and Segara, and both are inexpensive— about $5 single, $6 or $7 double, with meals.

Food and Restaurants

Djakarta, and in fact any part of Indonesia, is a good place to take off a few of the extra pounds you may have picked up on a Far Eastern tour. Dieting should be easy, for though there are several interesting food specialties it is almost impossible to sample them in their best form in restaurants or hotels. However, if you are lucky enough to be invited to someone's home or if you do venture forth into the one or two acceptable restaurants, here are a few of the native dishes worth sampling. Rice is the dietary staple and is the basis of the Dutch-invented Indonesian specialty, *rijstafel* (rice table), a dish of rice served with a wide variety of native specialties: spicy curries, dry and sauced; salted duck's eggs; *satés* (barbecued meat on tiny skewers with chili-peanut dip), *gado-gado,* a spiced vegetable mixture; and an array of *sambals,* pickled vegetables, and fruits of various kinds. *Nasi goreng,* the local version of Chinese fried rice, is good and can be ordered instead of plain rice with *rijstafel* or eaten as a main course by itself, and *soto* is a very good almond-flavored consommé. *Kopjor* ice is a refreshing cold drink or sauce for fruit, made of iced coconut meat and milk. Tea is the native drink, *Heinekens* beer is made on local franchise, and bottled lemon squash is generally available. Restaurant service and appointments are minimal in Djakarta and even more so on Bali, where the menu is even more limited unless you can get your hotel to do a barbecued suckling pig to order for a group of people.

Hotels have restaurants featuring European dishes with one or two Indonesian choices for each meal, generally at luncheon. Though you pay for meals with room, if you stay more than a day and a half you'll want to try at least one or two of the other possibilities: The *Ambassador* in the Hotel Dharma Nirmala features fairly good European food and steaks, and is air conditioned. *Chez Mario* is somewhat Bohemian looking and has surprisingly good Italian food, notably the *pastas. Wisma Nusantara.* Just across from the Duta Indonesia, this ʼry. spacious restaurant has dancing at night and at lunch and dinner serves the best available *rijstafel* in town. It is a good idea to order it a few hours in advance.

Entertainment, Night Life, and Special Events

There is little night life in Djakarta, though most of the hotels offer dinner dancing and the *Club Nirwana* at the Hotel Indonesia includes floor shows of the supper-club type. Performances of regional Indonesian dances and music are often given at hotels. It is sometimes possible to see native puppet shows and operas but the schedule is irregular and it is best to check at your hotel.

Bali abounds in native dance performances and local *gamelan* music and the famous *Ketjak,* monkey dance, is performed every Saturday night. At Jogjakarta there are monthly dance performances at the Prambana temple. On August 17 great celebrations are held in Independence Square in front of the Presidential Palace.

Life on Bali is one special event after another, so check on festivals, ceremonial dances, and such activities when you arrive on the island.

Shopping

Shopping in Djakarta and in all Indonesia is limited to a few interesting souvenirs here and there. The best of the articles sold come from Bali: water colors, wood carvings, brightly painted fish, hand-printed batik cottons, figures made out of Chinese coins, and headdresses for ceremonial dances. All are available in Djakarta but are better buys in Bali if you are going there. Buddha statuettes and silver jewelry set with stones are available too, but they are very expensive.

DJAKARTA

The main shopping areas are in the arcades of the Hotel Indonesia and the Duta Indonesia although prices are a bit high here. There are other shops along Djalan Modjopahit and in the native market, Pasar Baru and Nusantara.

BALI

Visit *Pandy's Art Gallery* in Sanur for paintings and wood carvings; *Klungkung* for curios and wood carvings. The town of *Den Pasar* is a center for various Balinese handicrafts, with an especially good collection at the *Foundation of Balinese Arts Museum Shop.*

Background Reading

View to the Southeast, by Santha Rama Rau
The Malay Archipelago, by Alfred Russell Wallace
Island of Bali, by Miguel Covarrubias
Malaya, Indonesia, Borneo and the Philippines, by Charles Robeguain
Indonesian Adventure, by Karl Eskelund
Story of Indonesia, by Louis Fischer
Revolt in Paradise, by K'tut Tantri
Flowering Lotus, by Harold Foster
Bliss in Bali, by Jacques Chegaray

Japan

TOKYO

Who put the sake in the Coca-Cola?

IF ever there was a city with its eye on the future, a city frenetically intent on making up for lost time, Tokyo is it. The whirl of activity is far more hectic and confusing than anything one can find in any other major metropolis, New York and London included. No one walks when he can run, no automobile takes a corner on four wheels if it can possibly be done on two, and the flash of neon at nightfall is more dazzling than anything this side of the aurora borealis. Many people will tell you that Tokyo is a waste of time; that it is just like any other large city and that to see the "real" Japan you'd best be off for the ancient capital, Kyoto. And it is true, of course, that Kyoto depicts Japan in all of its travel-poster splendor, while in Tokyo the Japanese sandman has been replaced by tranquilizers, there are more espresso bars than teahouses, and the geisha is fighting a losing battle to the stripper—in short, Madame Butterfly has flown. But it is also true that Tokyo is what Japan wants to be, and, like any capital, presents a distillation of the nation's dreams and aspirations. To evaluate Japan solely on the basis of Kyoto would be only slightly less misleading than to judge the United States in terms of colonial Williamsburg, or Egypt in the light of Luxor.

Furthermore, let me assure you, Tokyo is not like Paris, nor London, nor Rome, nor any city other than itself. It is a classic example of East breaking its neck to meet West, but always on its own terms; for whenever one country adopts the customs of another, it gives them a veneering (or in this case, a lacquering) of its own culture, producing something new and unique. This results in a series of wild incongruities and contradictions, making Tokyo one of the most astounding cities in the world, a city easier to describe than to explain.

Everywhere you see slick little Japanese automobiles, Toyopets and Datsuns, with white lace curtains stretched across the rear-view windows, blonde Caucasian mannequins modeling kimonos in shop windows, office girls in white blouses and plaid skirts carrying umbrellas of oiled paper and bamboo, young men in slacks wearing platformed *geta* sandals, and kimono-clad maidens mincing along with tiny transistor radios pressed to their ears. Pedestrian traffic backs up while two Japanese businessmen in gray flannel suits exchange alternate bows of greeting and respect. Beauty salons do a land-office business bleaching jet-black hair to henna, and plastic surgeons advertise in daily papers offering to "Westernize" the almond-slanted, underturned eyelids of Japanese girls. Department stores open each morning to the strains of Mozart and Handel as the entire staff lines up at the door, bowing greetings to customers. In these stores you may buy kimonos or blue jeans, obi sashes or Merry Widow waist cinchers, *hibachis* or pressure cookers, and, in the huge food departments, sharks' fins or slabs of dried bonito, *bento* box lunches or frozen TV dinners, gummy bean curd or seaweed crackers, éclairs or *kugelhopfs,* jello or cornflakes.

Willow-lined shopping thoroughfares like the Ginza are cut by backwater canals and alleys, where open-front shops sell everything from aphrodisiacs to Zen Buddhist tracts. Shoeshine women, as formless as laundry sacks, squat in front of modern office buildings and everywhere you hear the rhythmic click-clack of steel pellets coming from the crowded pachinko parlors, where, day and night, the Japanese give themselves up to the hypnotic allure of this vertical pinball game.

At night, Tokyo takes on a weird magic with waterfalls of neon splashing against the dark sky—red, yellow, blue, orange, purple, and green, flashing up and down, round and round, back and fourth—a crazy carnival of lights symbolizing the city's frenzied night life.

Tokyo seems to have no coherent silhouette or form. The over-all effect is one of seething movement; the swarming, scurrying young people moving as quickly as figures in a stepped-up movie film and the automobiles and kamikaze taxicabs going at breakneck speed make for a traffic pattern reminiscent of the Coney Island attraction, Dodge 'em. Add to this that none of the streets runs a straight course; all swerve, curve, and change directions every three or four blocks, and—the final touch to the nightmare confusion—few of the streets have names. Addresses are divined by an intricate process involving the ward (*ku*), the precinct (*cho*), the block area (*chome*), and finally, the number, distributed at random, therefore not consecutive, and rarely posted on the outside of the building. (During the American occupation, from 1945–1950, streets and avenues were designated by letters and numbers, never taken seriously and now rarely used.)

In makeup, this sprawling, flat, humid, and hazy city, is an intricate puzzle of sections (*machis*), eight townships, three counties, and seven islands of Izu, and contains scores of parks and a dozen Piccadillies. Tokyo is situated on Honshu, which, with Hokkaido, Shikuko, and Kyushu, is one of the four main islands of the Japanese archipelago. Inhabited since the Stone Age, it was established as a city in the twelfth century and named Edo, meaning estuary, since it straddles a delta of three rivers which empty into Tokyo Bay. It became the seat of the powerful Tokugawa shogunate in the early part of the seventeenth century and finally succeded Kyoto as the nation's capital in 1868, the first year of the Meiji Restoration, when the city's name was changed to Tokyo (Eastern capital). Since that time, it has been the center of Japan's Westernization and industrial development, and the most sensitive barometer of Japanese thought and opinion. Whatever happens in Jàpan happens first in Tokyo.

Today, Tokyo is among the three largest cities in the world, with its 10,020,000 people comprising about one-tenth of the nation's total population. The government is a constitutional democracy, with Emperor Hirohito serving as the symbol of state. He descends from a line that claims to be the world's oldest existing royal family, said to have been established in 660 B.C. The nation's constitution, written in 1946, was the first in the world to include a section outlawing war. The long, narrow chain of Japanese islands stretch for thirteen hundred miles off the Asian mainland, with a landscape reminiscent of a Hokusai print; almost every view includes a snow-capped mountain volcano such as the most famous Mount Fuji, reflected in a calm lagoon, framed by gnarled pine trees, and edged by the turbulent sea. It is a lushly green and fertile land with every inch of soil farmed to capacity, a country fabled for its seasonal charms: the frosted cherry blossoms of springtime, the flaming beauty of maples and chrysanthemums in autumn, the frozen lakes and snow-mantled mountains that delight the winter sports enthusiast, the wide Pacific beaches, hot springs, and cool hillside retreats of summer, all peaceful attractions in striking contrast to the violent tricks nature plays on this Land of the Rising Sun, by way of typhoons, earthquakes, and volcanic eruptions.

When early settlers from the Chinese mainland came to the Japanese archipelago during the Stone Age, it was already inhabited by the indigenous primitive people, whose descendants, the Caucasian-looking, bearded Ainus, can still be seen on the northernmost island, Hokkaido. The country has always been remote because of its island location and language differences (the Japanese language bears no relation to the Chinese, and its picture word construction makes it necessary to memorize three or four thousand ideograms in order to be able to read a newspaper or nontechnical book, six or seven thousand to read serious literature).

Japan's natural isolation has been interrupted by waves of "borrowing" from the successive cultures with which it has come into contact. Always "quick studies," the Japanese have learned to borrow wholesale, whether it be an idea for a camera or cigarette lighter, architecture or philosophy. The first great outside influence on Japan came in the sixth century when priests from China and North Korea brought with them the art, science, and philosophy of the T'ang Dynasty, the architecture still evident in the temples of Nara, and, most important of all, Buddhism, which flourished side by side with the indigenous cult of ancestor worship, Shintoism, as it does even now. All over Japan one sees Shinto shrines and *torii* gates, Buddhist temples, and Christian churches, representing the three main religions in the country today.

The second wave of borrowing lasted for four hundred years, from 1200 to 1600, and the style this time was far more flamboyant, as can be seen in the lacquered splendor of Nikko's temples. European missionaries and traders found their way to the islands in the sixteenth century, a brief period which came to an end with the rise of the

Tokugawa shoguns, who closed the country completely for the next two hundred years.

Japan's isolation ended forever with the arrival of Commodore Perry, who sailed into Tokyo Bay in 1853 and began to negotiate trade pacts committing Japan to a policy of world trade, a program which led to her Westernization and industrialization under the Emperor Meiji, and which finally led her into World War II in search of markets for her mass-produced exports.

With the first military defeat at the hands of the Americans, the Japanese religious belief in the divine right of the emperor and their own invincibility crumbled, and they reached out again to adopt a new culture, this time that of their conquerors. Unfortunately, when the Japanese let go of their rigidly patterned way of life, chaos resulted, with the kind of wild force one expects when the tightly wound mainspring of a watch snaps and flies out in all directions. Prescribed patterns and rules, governing things such as tea ceremonies, offered no guide to behavior in a subway rush, and traditional concepts of art and beauty, unchanged for generations, were no help at all to the Japanese when they began to adopt Western dress and furnishings.

It is true that even in Tokyo one can glimpse gracious living, Japanese-style, but you must know your way around, know which wall to peer over, which corner to turn, to find the shimmering green gardens and quiet streams, the world of chrysanthemums and silken kimonos. Even the most commercial of the city bus tours take sightseers to an abbreviated tea ceremony in an enchanting teahouse set in a rocky garden so elegantly peaceful it is hard to believe you are close to the city's roar of activity. Even in Tokyo you can see men and women carrying packages tied in the lovely silk-scarf wrappings, *furoshiki,* buying the intricately packed *bento* box lunches; and even here you may stay at a *ryokan,* the traditional inn, with sliding *shoji* panels, *tatami*-matted floors, and careful flower arrangements in the *tokonuma* (niche). Here you remove shoes as you enter and are given a light robe (*yukata*), and you sleep on floor mattresses (*futon*). You may have a traditional, sweet-scented, scalding bath in a wooden tub (you wash before getting in to soak) and you may have all of your meals cooked to order and served in your room by a kimono-clad waitress. You eat here (as in most Japanese restaurants), seated on floor cushions, and though the Japanese do this leaning back on their haunches it's a trick few Westerners can manage for more than five minutes at a time.

If you like, you can, while in Tokyo, study the intricacies of *haiku,* the seventeenth century poetic form which gives the writer just seventeen syllables with which to make his point, or attend the fifteenth century drama, the *noh* play, a highly formalized scenic opera in which masked players move imperceptibly against a musical background of atonal chanting and where every movement of fan or finger means something to initiates. If understatement is the art of *noh,* overstatement is the specialty of the brilliantly colorful seventeenth century *kabuki,* and in the amusing *banraku* puppet shows, which you should see if you have the chance, though these are more a feature of Osaka than Tokyo.

One can attend classes in *ikebana,* the Japanese art of flower arranging, or learn to grow *bonsai,* the miniature potted trees which are pruned and wired to look like the gnarled trees of the Japanese landscape. You can arrange a private party at an inn where you are served and entertained by doll-like geisha, their faces powdered porcelain white and hair piled and lacquered into gleaming coiffures. These girls serve your food, smile at you, sing to you, make amusing conversation, and teach you such entrancing games as scissors, paper, rock, as you dine on the delicately arranged dishes the kitchen has dreamed up. Contrary to popular misconception, geisha do not necessarily perform any functions other than those described, though further arrangements are always within the realm of possibility, depending on you, your geisha, and your wife, if she happens to be along, as wives often are at such parties.

At the Korkuen Hall there are regular judo matches where men and women display the technique of using an opponent's strength against himself, or you may watch *sumo,* the two-thousand-year-old national sport, a wrestling match which commences only after salt has been sprinkled on the ground to purify it, prayers have been said, and the wrestlers' long hair has been done up in tiny topknots —a fantastic sight on men who often weigh three hundred pounds or more.

There is much in the way of Western-style entertainment too, including baseball games, which the Japanese play with unmatched ceremony and courtesy, Broadway musicals, and European movies.

American style night clubs feature Japanese crooners rocking and rolling or oozing Neapolitan love songs in memorized Italian of which the singer understands not a word. Or you can visit one of Tokyo's most fascinating nighttime attractions, the fish and vegetable markets, which are in full swing from about 2 to 5 A.M. The fish market is particularly colorful with great tuna, bonito, and sharks lined up on the platforms while fishermen nap between them, resting until the real business of the market gets under way.

By day Tokyo is, of course, jammed with interesting things to see, though only a few of these are bona fide "sights" in the usual tourist sense, and two or three days should be more than enough to cover those comfortably. The city's most outstanding sight is unquestionably the Imperial Palace, set over ruggedly massive stone walls, framed by Japanese pines and surrounded by a moat complete with gliding white swans, delicate foot bridges, and an old feudal gate. The palace is open to the public on New Year's Day, January 2, and on the emperor's official birthday, April 29. Though built as late as 1920, the Meiji Shrine, with its wood *torii* gate made of seventeen-hundred-year-old cypress wood, is another sight worth seeing. Ancient music and *bugaku* dances are performed in front of the main building on special shrine festival days.

I suppose something must be said about the Tokyo Tower—1,092 feet high, more Eiffel than the Eiffel, and said to be the highest independent steel tower in the world. It has the usual restaurants, panoramic viewing platforms, science museum, and souvenir counters, and, oddly enough, though a bore to most foreign visitors, it seems a constant source of wonder and delight to the natives. Located in Shiba Park, the tower is in real life a television and radio broadcasting antenna.

After the "sights" are off one's conscience, there is more time to wander around, sans guide, and sample the other city delights, notably the museums. Ueno Park, Tokyo's largest and most beautiful, covers 210 acres and contains the National Museum of Modern Art, the National Science Museum, the Toshogu Shrine, with its stone and bronze lanterns, and the Metropolitan Fine Arts Gallery, the most important museum in the city, with its examples of old and modern masters. The National Museum of Modern Art is also essential for anyone interested in the current art movement in Japan.

About three-quarters of an hour from the center of town, the Folk-craft Museum houses a beautifully displayed collection of old handi-crafts, stoneware, and lacquer pieces, furniture, primitive clothing, and artifacts. Those with more esoteric interests would perhaps be interested in the Theater Art Museum, with its collection of costumes, masks, and musical instruments used in the *noh* and *kabuki* dramas, the Paper Museum, displaying all of the objects the Japanese so skillfully create from paper (and the tools used in creating them), and the Gotoh Museum, displaying Buddhist relics—statues, mir-rors, *sutras,* paintings, ceramics, and books. There are more Japanese fine arts at the Bridgestone Gallery, and if you hunger for a look at such famous European art works as those by Matisse, Picasso, or Rodin, stop in at the National Museum of Western Art.

Once out of the museums, Tokyo's greatest sights are in the var-ious sections of the city, each with its own personality and specialties. The Ginza is, of course, the main shopping street, with a conglomera-tion of shops, gaudy and in good taste, selling most of the things tourists want to buy. Kanda is the student section of the city and here one can find rows of bookstores and open stalls selling new or secondhand volumes in any language you can think of, old scrolls and colorful prints. Shibuya is a shopping and amusement center, alive with stores, cinemas, restaurants, and a huge department store named Toyoko. Shinjuku offers the same attractions on a lower, more economical, and more colorful level, plus what surely must be an overabundance of bathhouses. Asakusa is still another nightclub, restaurant, shopping, and amusement park center, and is perhaps the wildest and most native area of all with a maze of enticing bar-gain shops, bars, and burlesque palaces. It is here that you can see the enormous stage revues at the Kokusai theater and visit the temple to the goddess Kannon, a place with a gaudy splendor that seems particularly well suited to the dazzling night life of Asakusa.

From a tourist point of view, Tokyo is a jumping-off place for all of Japan's many wonders. One may visit the seaport of Yokohama and industrial Osaka, or the more antique delights, such as the Great Buddha at Kamakura or the colorful splendor of Nikko's temples. It is in Tokyo that you can arrange to spend a few restful days at the Atami seashore, or relax at the hot springs resort at Hakone National Park, where you can view Mount Fuji and stay at one of the world's most famous and beautiful hotels, the Fujiya, at Miyano-shita, itself a place hat should be considered one of the country's leading sights.

KYOTO

The city of purple hills

Anyone who has been to Japan can tell you that the Japanese take an inordinate amount of pride in their railroads, and the trains are paragons of comfort and cleanliness, and, most of all, prompt-ness. So when your train schedule tells you that Kyoto is six hours and fifty-two minutes away from Tokyo, you can expect to arrive in exactly that amount of time, for no line is more an object of pride than the one running between those two cities, especially if you're lucky enough to ride the train called *Tsubame* or Swan. In that short amount of time, you can expect to be transported between two worlds, from the uproar that is Tokyo to the travel-poster charm that is Kyoto. It might be noted here that both cities are comprised of the same syllables—To-kyo and Kyo-to, both meaning capital city, since that was Kyoto's role for the ten centuries from 794 to 1868, before the honor passed to Tokyo.

It has often been said (and correctly, at least in part) that Kyoto is to Japan what Florence is to Italy: the seat of art, culture, and handicrafts, both modern and antique; a repository of the country's golden age in art and architecture; and the traditional home of creative ferment even down to the present. Physically the cities are somewhat similar too, both ringed by a haze of hills, both surrounded by an easily accessible wooded countryside, and both large and thriving (Kyoto is the country's third largest city with a population of over 1.2 million). Except for the small modern section around the railroad station and the city's department stores, Kyoto is quiet and serene, with small native craft shops, bookstores, and old print shops, open stalls displaying odds and ends of porcelain tableware, and enticing little galleries featuring the most elegant and expensive Oriental *objets d'art*. These are pleasant streets for random strolling, and even getting lost is not as dismaying an experience here as it might be in the bustle of Tokyo. This is the place to shop for lacquer, or track down bits of beautiful junk, or to see the work of Japan's fine modern painters and ceramists. Here you might find an authentic print by Hiroshige or Hokusai or buy a startlingly handsome modern painting by the internationally famous Ohno whose works are displayed at the Yamada Gallery on Shinmonzen Street.

And Kyoto's sights are those one dreams of when planning a trip to Japan: the gorgeous temples, castles, and shrines (over two thousand in all) of the great imperial era and the incomparable gardens, especially the green velvet world that is the Moss Garden of Kokedera, the abstract arrangement of raked white sand and fifteen rocks that make up the "garden" of the Ryoan-ji Temple, and the ethereal landscapes and interiors of the Katsura Detached Palace. Though these are among Japan's most memorable sights you will find they are not scheduled on tours, and the special passes (which are easy to obtain) must be applied for through your hotel desk or guide.

Nijo Castle, built in 1603, is one of the architectural treasures of the city, with its exquisite paintings and decorations and its so-called "nightingale floors," especially constructed so that the boards "sing" when stepped on as a protection for the shogun against assassins. The Heian Shrine with its beautiful garden and red-lacquer elegance, the Chion-in Temple, one of the largest in Japan, with a most imposing gate, and the much photographed Silver Pavilion (*Ginkakuji*) and the Gold Pavilion (*Kinkakuji*), the Old Imperial Palace, one of

Kyoto's great landmarks, and the Kiyomizu Temple, perched up on a cliff commanding a view of the entire city from its wooden veranda, are all musts for any visitor interested in developing an insight into Japan's past.

The Kyoto National Museum has a rich collection of objects— artistic, historic, and religious—which once belonged to Buddhist temples, Shinto shrines, and private citizens, and the Nishijin Textile Museum displays the outstanding silk weaving and dye work produced in this city. Since Kyoto is the original home of the geisha, it is no surprise to find the loveliest girls in Japan in its Gion district and at night one sees these doll-like beauties mincing along to their evening appointments. If you're lucky you might even catch a glimpse of the exquisite little geisha trainees, the *maiko,* with their embroidered obi sashes and garlands of silken flowers hanging in their hair. It is in this district in April and May that one may see the springtime *Miyako Odori,* the Cherry Dances, performed by both geishas and *maikos.* And in July the city's most colorful festival, the *Gion Matsuri,* is held at the Yasaka Shrine each year.

And finally, no trip to Japan's past would seem complete without at least a day's excursion from Kyoto to the even more ancient capital, Nara, with its green-wooded deer park, its *Daibutsu*—the largest Buddha image in the world, made of bronze cast in 749. The bright red shrine, Kasuga, also at Nara, has three thousand hanging lanterns; and the Horyuji Temple, built in 607, is believed to be the oldest wooden building in the world. These are just samples of the many splendors to be seen in this beguiling and antique land.

FOR THE TRAVELER'S NOTEBOOK

Official Information

Before you go: Japan National Tourist Association, 45 Rockefeller Plaza, New York 20, N.Y.; 333 North Michigan Ave., Chicago 1, Ill.; 651 Market St., San Franciso 5, Calif.; 1420 Commerce St., Dallas, Tex.; 109 Kaiulani Ave., Honolulu 15, Hawaii.

In Tokyo: SAS Office, 2 Sangyo Kaikan, 1-chome ohtemachi Chiyodaku; Japan Travel Bureau, Tourist Information Office: the main offices are at Tokyo International Airport, the Marunouchi Building, Hotel Imperial, Hotel New Japan, and the Kokusai Kanko Building; U.S. Embassy and Consulate, 1 Enokizakamachi, Akasaka.

In Kyoto: Kyoto City Information Office, in front of Kyoto Station. Japan Travel Bureau, in Kyoto Station Hotel. American Cultural Center, Sanjo Karasuma-nishiiru.

Money Matters

Currency: The yen is the main monetary unit of Japan; there are about 360 yen to $1, U.S.

Tipping: Hotels in Tokyo usually include a 10 per cent service charge on your bill; it is unnecessary to tip anyone except bar attendants and hall porters. In inns and restaurants 10 to 20 per cent of the bill is adequate; do not tip a taxi driver unless he has gone to a great deal of trouble for you. Doormen are tipped under the same circumstances.

Climate, Clothing, and Essentials

You will find the climate in Japan not very different from that of the central United States or central and southern Europe, although it is generally more humid. Spring (March to May) is gay and flowery. June brings a rainy spell and fine weather returns early in July when summer gets under way. September is the typhoon month and somewhat rainy, but October is one of the pleasantest months to visit Japan. Autumn is delightful, with the weather just cool enough to enjoy. Winter can be chilly and damp (especially December and January) but with appropriate clothing you won't be uncomfortable. Except for the height of summer, you will be glad you brought a light sweater or jacket and a raincoat. Normal city attire is generally correct.

Hotels (Western Style)

TOKYO

Modern Japanese hotels reflect the best traditions of their European counterparts and it is one of the few places in the Orient where it is not necessary to stay at the most expensive hotels. Good service, and comfortable and clean accommodations can be found at almost every price level and all hotels have the usual range of facilities: air conditioning, bars and restaurants, laundry and dry cleaning services, newsstands, tourist bureaus, shops, and the like. Though hotels are not officially graded, in general, rates run as follows: De luxe charge from 2,100 to 3,200 yen single, 3,400 to 6,000 yen double; first class are 1,800 to 2,800 yen single; 3,000 to 5,000 yen double; Moderate from 1,200 to 2,300 yen single, 1,800 to 3,300 yen double.

DE LUXE: *Tokyo Hilton, Akasaka.* Opened in 1963, this is a Hilton production, Japanese style. See Hilton hotels listed for any other city and read "Tokyo." *Imperial Hotel, Uchisaiwaiche, 1-chome, Chiyoda-ku.*

Famous old modern hotel, done by Frank Lloyd Wright in the twenties—a maze of lobbies and levels and a sight worth seeing, though the modern wing is less so. Centrally located, comfortable, and charming. *Hotel New Japan, 29 2-chome, Nagatacho, Chiyoda-ku.* Designed by one of Japan's foremost architects, Isamu Kenmochi, this hotel has Western rooms, Japanese *ryokan* rooms, or a combination of both. *Hotel Okura, 3 Aoicho, Akasaka, Minato-ku.* This modern building is in the center of things with a swimming pool, a Japanese spa, a Turkish bath, classes in tea ceremony, flower arranging, and painting . . . in short, everything. *Palace Hotel,* (the ex-*Hotel Teito*), *10 1-chome, Marunouchi, Chiyoda-ku.* This has been rebuilt and is just across the moat from the royal palace, a few steps away from the main shopping and business section.

FIRST CLASS: *Nikkatsu Hotel, 1 1-chome, Yurakucho, Chiyoda-ku.* Located in the downtown area with a view of the royal palace from some of its rooms, this is a comfortable and efficient commercial hotel in the first class category. *Hotel Kokusai Kanko, 1 1-chome, Marunouchi, Chiyoda-ku.* Part of an office building which bears the same name as the hotel, this is located in the heart of Tokyo's business and shopping district. Convenient and efficient. The *Marounouchi Hotel, 1 1-chome, Marunouchi, Chiyoda-ku.* This is another well-located, comfortable, commercial hotel in the first class price range.

MODERATE: Among the economical but reasonably comfortable hotels are: the *Shiba Park Hotel, 3 6-gochi, Shiba Park, Minato-ku,* ten minutes by taxi from the Tokyo station; the *Fairmont Hotel, 4 Sambancho, Chiyoda-ku;* and the *Dai-Ichi Hotel, 32 1-chome, Shiba Shimbashi, Minato-ku.*

For a list of Japanese Western-style hotels, complete with all details, prices, and picture, ask the Japan National Tourist Association for a copy of the latest Japan Hotel Guide.

KYOTO

DE LUXE: *Miyako Hotel, Sanjo Keage.* Fifteen minutes away from the heart of Kyoto, this luxury hotel has Western or inn-type rooms and is absolutely enormous. Comfortable, but prices are a bit overdone.

MODERATE: The *Kyoto Hotel, 537 Ichinofunairicho, Minami-iru, Kawaramachi-Nijo, Nakagyo-ku.* Though less idyllically situated than the Miyako, this hotel is comfortable, has good service, and is a better buy for those who can skip the glamour. *International Kyoto Hotel, 284 Aburakoji 2-jo, Sagaru, Nakagyo-ku,* is Kyoto's newest, most modern hotel, built and opened in 1961. Comfortable and beautifully located near the Nijo Castle. *Kyoto Station Hotel, 849 Higashishiokojicho, Shimogyo-ku.* Very moderately priced and efficient, this place has one of the handiest locations in the city and is a real buy. The *Mount Hiel Hotel Ipponsugi,*

Hieizan, Sakyo-ku, is set up on a mountain, not too convenient for sight-seeing but a lovely resort for a summer weekend.

Japanese inns (Ryokan) exist in every city of Japan, Tokyo included, and vary from the completely authentic and traditional to those adapted to Western tastes. Anyone visiting Japan should spend at least one night in one of these gracious and enchanting inns. However, if you plan to go to Kyoto, or any of the other outlying cities, it is preferable to wait and visit an inn there. The pace of life in the capital is not quite in keeping with the relaxed *ryokan* routine, and you will find it more convenient to have familiar facilities and appointments in the hectic capital. But if Tokyo is your only stop, by all means try an inn there, or, at the very least, stay in one of the Japanese rooms as described in the hotel listing above. Prices in inns range from 1,000 yen for rock-bottom accommodations to 4,500 yen for the peak of luxury, and average prices are about 2,500 yen per night with two meals and all the hot baths you can stand.

Fukudaya is one of Tokyo's oldest, most revered, and most de luxe inns and if you want a room here you had better negotiate for it well in advance through your travel agent or you might be disappointed. Other good inns in Tokyo include the *Seiken Hiran* and the *Sekitei,* a little less expensive and a few minutes out of the city center. Kyoto's most famous and loveliest inn, the *Tawaraya,* is the one written about by Elizabeth Vining in her book, *Return to Japan.* In the same moderately high price category is the *Hiiragiya,* similar in appointments and accommodations.

You can get complete information on these inns and their facilities from the Japan National Tourist Association. They will also suggest other inns along the way when you have worked out your itinerary.

Food and Restaurants

There seems to be no middle-of-the-road attitude toward Japanese food; people seem either to think it the most exquisite cuisine in the world, or to flatly detest it. In any case, almost everyone agrees that it is always intricately arranged and beautifully served. The platters of cold appetizers with flowerets of lotus root, bits of fish, raw or cooked, often with scales left on for texture, a delicate abalone in its pretty shell, and morsels of chicken or duck meat, are the sort of things you will find as a starter to accompany your first sips of the warm rice wine, *sake* which is served in thimble-size porcelain cups. Clear soup (*sui-mono*) or the thicker *miso;* salads of pickled vegetables (*tsukemono*); *sukiyaki* cooked in stock, or better yet in butter, when it's called butter-*yaki; tempura,* the lightly fried shrimp, fish, vegetables; buckwheat noodles (*udon*); *chawan-mushi,* a custard flecked with bits of meat, fish, and vegetables; and a wide variety of noodle, meat, and soup stock (*nabe*) dishes are all worth trying. One of the best things to eat in Japan is *yakitori,* nuggets of chicken, duck, quail's eggs, and vegetables, barbecued on small wooden skewers and served with a spicy dip.

Rice is, of course, the dietary staple. Japanese products worth sampling include the excellent seafood and perfect beef, the best being that of Matsuzaka with Kobe beef a close runner up; a fruit called *nashi,* a cold crisp cross between a green apple and a pear; and giant strawberries, each the size of a tomato, tended by hand and grown over heated bricks. Japanese beer is considered as good as any, and whisky and other spirits are available as well as wines and soft drinks. Green tea is the most popular beverage among Japanese. Black tea and coffee are also becoming popular.

Restaurants in Japan generally serve one kind of food only—*tempura* or *yakitori, sukiyaki* or *sushi,* bits of raw fish and vinegar-rice wrapped in seaweed, in addition to a soup, a salad, tea, and desserts. There are some restaurants, generally traditional inns, that serve multicourse dinners, though you do not order from a menu but eat what you are served.

There are various ways of eating in Japan. Some things such as *tempura* and *yakitori* are served at counters, while traditional meals are eaten in private dining rooms with *tatami*-matted floors where the food is served on low tables and the diners are seated on cushions. Chopsticks are standard utensils and while forks and knives are sometimes available, this is not true in the best and most authentic places.

TOKYO

For excellent *sukiyaki* and butter-*yaki* try *Okahan* where the famous Matsuzaka beef is served, or *Yugiri,* which is almost as good. *Yakitori* is superb at *Isehiro* and *Torisin.* *Do Hana* and *Hanacho* have excellent *tempura,* while at *Sasanoyuki* you can have anything you want as long as it is bean curd. Eel cooked in a number of ways is the specialty at *Chikuyo.* *Yumano Chaya,* set in a pretty garden, features excellent broiled eel, *kaba yaki.* *Akahane* is one of the city's best restaurants, specializing in game caught by falconers and fish caught by cormorants, superbly prepared; dinner here costs from $6 to $10 per person. To sample *sushi* try *Ozasa* or *Sushi Sen.*

Misono and *San Kyu* specialize in delectable meats and vegetables grilled at your table. For the most elegant, traditional, lengthy Japanese meals it is best to have a small group of diners (Japanese consider five the ideal number). Have your hotel clerk or guide call and make your reservations, as such inns will rarely serve Westerners who just chance by. *Fukudaya, Shiobara, Ichinao,* and *Shinkaraku* are four lovely inns, all expensive ($10 to $15 per person), exclusive, and excellent. *Chinzanso* is a restaurant situated in a beautiful garden, serving Mongolian grilled meat—moderately expensive and definitely on the touristy side.

Western food can be had in wide variety in Tokyo: Hungarian food at *Irene's*, German dishes at *Lohmeyer's* and *Ketel*, the best French pepper steak I have ever had was at *France Ya*, and pizzas at *Nicola's* until four in the morning. The *Imperial Hotel* serves Scandinavian smorgasbord in the *Viking*, continental seafood in *Prunier's* as well as *tempura* and *sukiyaki* in its Japanese restaurants, and the new *Hilton* offers an even wider range. *Sun Ya* and the spectacular new *Liu Yuan* serve good Chinese fare.

KYOTO

Junidanya is undoubtedly one of the handsomest restaurants anywhere, an old inn full of beautiful modern Japanese paintings and sculpture, antique bric-a-brac, and furniture. The Mongolian hot pot, called here *Mizutaki*, is the main feature—slivers of meat, vegetables, noodles which you cook yourself in a copper pot full of boiling stock set in the middle of the table. *Hyotei* is one of Japan's most traditional inns, expensive and absolutely authentic. *Shinmiura* serves a chicken dish similar to the Mongolian hot pot, and *Kawarmachi Ya* features chicken which you broil on a grill in the table. There is excellent *tempura* at *Yotaro*.

There are only a few restaurants serving Western food in Kyoto, though you may also get such fare in hotel dining rooms. *Suehiro, Prunier's,* and *Alaska* run branches here similar to their Tokyo establishments; there is French food at *Manyoken*. *Grill Mantei* and *Grill Java* serve steaks and a general assortment of Western dishes.

Entertainment, Night Life, and Special Events

Frantic is exactly the word for Tokyo's night life and anyone who likes night clubs might well consider settling here. There are clubs more Copa than the Copa where the strip teasers are a cross between the Radio City Rockettes and the performers at the Paris *Folies*—all extremely expensive, if not outright clip joints. Some places have hostesses who are hospitable in varying degrees. Tokyo's main sections for night life are the Ginza and Shinjuku, with clubs, bars, and lots of little red lights everywhere. At Shibuya and Akasaka you will find exclusive, expensive clubs and a concentration of geisha (these parties can be arranged for you in advance by your hotel and, contrary to popular belief, women do attend with their husbands) and Asakusa is a lower class, native nighttime area. In all of these districts you will see tiny alley-streets mosaicked with pocket-sized bars, each just large enough to hold eight or ten patrons.

The *Queen Bee*, the *Crown*, the *Hanabasha*, and the *Mimatsu* are a few of the brassiest clubs in Tokyo and the *Mikado* may well be the brassiest in the world. The *Rat Mort* is a de luxe bar with expensive hostesses; *Lady Fair* is a basement bar popular with American tourists; the *Playbill* is intimate and has good piano music, while *Papagayo* offers strippers of above-average talents. The *Albion* is an extremely interesting place done up in harlequin plaid Day-glo colors, where Japanese and GI's drink beer to the tune of a blaring jukebox and semiclad hostesses do the serving—the Japanese idea of an American night club and somewhat of a revelation. Espresso houses are dotted all over the city.

If you're looking for typically Japanese entertainment there are two principal types—the classical *kabuki* drama and the *noh* plays. The *kabuki* drama is performed daily at the Kabukiza Theater, and the *noh* drama periodically. There are several *noh* stages—the Hoshokai or the Kanze Kaikan just to name two.

If you are in Tokyo at the right time, you may be lucky enough to see a Japanese puppet play. The Bunraku-za Theater in Osaka presents these fascinating performances all year round, but they visit Tokyo on occasions and are well worth seeing. In the beginning of April leading theaters present Cherry Dances, a distinctive Japanese spectacle. In the magazine, Welcome to Metropolitan Tokyo, which is available in all hotels, you will find a list of current entertainment.

KYOTO

One of the most obvious things to do in Kyoto at night is to go to the bars; there are so many of them, one behind the other in an endless maze through the Gion district. There are night clubs too, similar to those in Tokyo, and the *Bel Ami* and *Osome* are two of the better known. Kyoto is also famous for its geisha district, and you can arrange parties where you will be entertained by these girls as you dine, but this must be done for you by a Japanese. There are three *noh* theaters in Kyoto and one for *kabuki,* in addition to the Yaska Kaikan, where the program shifts to include all of the Japanese theater and dancing arts.

Visitors will be intrigued by Japanese wrestling. Whereas judo or jujitsu is the art of self-defense, *sumo* is the traditional spectator sport noted for its huge muscular protagonists, who in the main are professional wrestlers.

No one loves a good festival more than the Japanese, and their calendar is crammed with dozens and dozens of holidays the year round, nationally and locally. It would be best to check on those occurring at the time of your visit.

In early January there is a display of acrobatic skill on the part of the Tokyo Fire department; in mid-March the *Kannon Festival* at the Asakusa Temple when the "celestial" children (the best behaved) parade in exquisite costumes; May 3 to 5 brings dances, archery contests, and *noh* plays for the *Festival of the Meiji Shrine*, and for several days in mid-May the *Kanda Festival* is one of the biggest and most elaborate parades through the Kanda area. Superb fireworks are displayed on the third Saturday in July for the *Sumida Festival*, and during the August 15 *Festival of Lights*, paper lanterns float down the Sumida River in early evening to honor the dead. On November 15 parents and colorfully dressed children meet at major shrines throughout the country for the Seven-Five-Three Festival. In Kyoto, January 1 brings a promenade of women in their finest kimonos; on January 15 geisha are carried on palanquins to the Ebisu Shrine; there are special *Cherry Dances* performed by geisha from mid-April to May, and the *Hollyhock Festival,* one of the largest in Japan, takes place on May 15. In early June a *noh* play is performed outdoors in front of the Heian Shrine at night by the light of torches. The greatest Kyoto festival, the *Gion Matsuri,* is celebrated from July 16 to July 24 with parades and floats and incredible costumes, a festival handed down from 876 as a protection for the people against plague.

In addition to the festivals there are, of course, the seasonal wonders of this lovely country—cherry blossoms in early April, primarily in Tokyo; chrysanthemum displays in October.

Shopping

The problem in Japan is not so much what to buy but rather what not to buy. The country is full of beautiful things, all at prices much lower than in the States. Among the better-known bargain purchases to consider are cameras and electronic equipment; pearls; fine lacquerware; handsome cookware and tableware; antiques; silks; kimonos; prints; lovely objects made of paper; costumed dolls; fishing equipment; and such folk objects as traditional swords, amusing kites, and *noh* masks.

Shipping costs from Japan are high so buy the better-quality merchandise and avoid the novelty store items.

TOKYO

This is Japan's best city for shopping. Merchandise of the entire country is represented in the capital and with few exceptions includes the best designs. The Ginza and Nohombashi are the main shopping streets of the city, lined with modern department stores and specialty shops. One of the best places to find a representative assortment of almost everything in town is *Takashimaya,* the huge department store in the Ginza section. If your time is short, you can rest assured that here you will find a more than adequate sampling of the best Japan has to offer at fair prices; do not overlook the basement antique department where you will find some really gorgeous treasures at moderate prices. Other department stores you should visit are: *Daimaru,* where the Dior department makes high-fashion copies at bargain prices; *Mitsukoshi,* with its special art exhibits; and *Maruzen,* with its wonderful book department and craft center.

For old books and antique prints, visit the shops in the student section, Kanda, where you will find especially good assortments at *Iseda* and *Izara.* A collection of the best merchandise from all of Japan's prefectures is displayed in the *Kokusai Kanko Building,* and Mikimoto pearls are hard to miss in department stores, hotel shops, and in the *Mikimoto shop* on the Ginza. Go to *Haibara* for all kinds of beautiful paperware; to the *Kochukyo Company, Mayuyama* and *Heisando, Yanagawa,* and *Asahi Art* for art treasures. The last two are situated on the famous Antique Row, a wonderful place for browsers, as you might imagine. Cameras are to be had everywhere; fishing equipment at *Tsuraya;* hi-fi supplies and transistor radio at department stores and at the Sony showroom. The *Japan Sword Company* has swords old and new as well as cutlery; *Ichy's* features *noh* masks; *Ciro's* and *Pacific House* specialize in furniture; and *Takumi* offers assorted folk crafts. For silks try *Kanebo* and *The Silk Gallery.* The best lacquer ware in Japan is at the shop of *Yamada Heiando.*

KYOTO

Though Kyoto also has its share of good department stores such as the local branches of *Takashimaya, Daimaru,* and *Marabutsu,* shopping here is more pleasant and interesting in the many small artisan and craft shops that abound, especially in the area on Shin-monzen and Furumonzen streets, and downtown beyond Kawaramachi and Shijo streets is the *Shinikyogo-ku* shopping arcade, with a jigsaw puzzle of variety shops. Though Kyoto is most noted for its antique splendors, it is also the center of Japan's modern art movement; and handsome prints and spectacular painting by some of the country's most important young artists are exhibited and sold at *Tetsuo Yamada's* gallery on Shin-monzen Street. Also on this street you will find old prints at the *Red Lantern Shop,* fabrics and happi-coats at *Y. Murai,* and a number of shops selling traditional Japanese dinnerware, art pottery, and the like. In another part of town are *Ori-dono* and the *Tatsumura Silk Mansion* collections; *Yamanaka,* a show place in itself, features *objets d'art,* Oriental style, as does *Yokoyama. Koshida Satsumaya,* on Furmonzen Street, specializes in porcelain and china; and lacquerware can be bought at the *H. Nishimura* factory. Flea markets are held in Kyoto each month, at Toji Temple on the twenty-first, and at Kitano Shrine on the twenty-fifth of the month.

Background Reading

To understand modern Japan:

Meeting with Japan, by Fosco Maraini, a superb book with an excellent bibliography covering books on all phases of Japanese life.

The Lotus and the Robot, by Arthur Koestler

Some Prefer Nettles, and *The Makioka Sisters*, by Jun'ichirô Tanazaki

We Japanese, published by the Fujiya Hotel and available at bookstores.

Things Japanese, by Basil Hall Chamberlain

Bridge of the Brocade Sash, by Sacheverall Sitwell

Japan, Past and Present, by E. O. Reischauer

Windows for the Crown Prince, and *Return to Japan*, by Elizabeth Vining

Welcome Honourable Visitors, by Jean Raspail

For some romantic background:

The Tale of Genji, by Lady Murasaki

Japanese Miscellany, by Lafcadio Hearn

Japanese Inn, by Oliver Statler

The Honourable Picnic, by T. Raucat

The best guide book to Japan is: *Japan, the Official Guide*, published by the Japan Travel Bureau and available at bookstores here as well as in Japan.

Pakistan

KARACHI

A new city in an ancient land

In July 1961, Bashir Ahmed, a Pakistani camel driver, met the then vice-president of the United States, Lyndon B. Johnson, in Karachi and accepted an invitation to visit his Texas cattle ranch. If one had to select a single incident typifying the spirit and atmosphere of life in Karachi, this unlikely encounter might well be it. For all worlds meet in this city today; it is a crossroads both of time and place, a meeting point for East and West, past and future. Karachi's airport is Asia's largest, the first and last stop in the Far East for every major airline going to every part of the world, and its Arabian Sea harbor is one of the finest on the Indian subcontinent, a port for Arab dhows up from Mozambique and Zanzibar, American cruise ships, oil tankers en route to the Persian Gulf, pleasure sailboats, and the merchant fleets of more than a dozen countries.

In appearance, this rambling, dusty city (its name derives from the ancient word *Kalachi,* "Land of Sand Dunes") looks like one big construction camp, with digging, derricks, and dredges around every corner and along every thoroughfare, encouraging (though often uncomfortable) evidence of the city's constant growth.

The streets are crowded with colorfully ornamented camels and donkey carts, limousines and taxis and horse-drawn carriages called gharries. Snake charmers, fortunetellers, bazaar hawkers, Moslem women observing purdah, their faces veiled in heavy black *burkas,* and Pakistani men in the native costume of full slim trousers (*shalwars*) worn under the long tunic coats (*sherwanis*), sporting the caps of independence which are a traditional tribute to their greatest national hero, *Quaid-i-Azam* (Great Leader) Mohammed Ali Jinnah, all mingle with sailors, construction workers, and foreign diplomats, engineers searching for oil and European businessmen here to buy and sell or help Pakistan develop its own industries based on native products: jute and cotton, tea and wool, fish and tobacco, leather and sugar.

Though Karachi was no more than a quiet fishing village two hundred years ago, today it is Pakistan's largest city, with a population of three million. It was the capital of the country from its birth in 1947 until 1959, when the capital was moved to the cooler climate of Rawalpindi. Formerly part of the British Indian empire, after India had gained her independence the Pakistanis, under Mohammed Ali Jinnah, fought for their own state. This resulted in the partitioning off of the predominantly Moslem areas. There are really two Pakistans now: East Pakistan, which borders on Tibet, Nepal, Burma, and the Bay of Bengal, is separated by a thousand miles of India from West Pakistan, bordered by Russia and Afghanistan, the Himalayas and the Hindu Kush, and edged by the vast plains of the Punjab and the Arabian Sea coastline to the south.

With Moslem refugees from India pouring into their own homeland, Pakistan is now the largest of the countries following the crescent and star of Islam, though it still affords complete religious freedom to the 15 per cent of its population made up of Hindus, Christians, Buddhists, and Parsees, the fire worshipers of Zoroaster. The country is now a constitutional republic and a member of the British Commonwealth. Pakistan's president, Mohammed Ayub Khan, has established a program of "grass roots" democracy which is dedicated to alleviating the country's most basic needs in the areas of education, health, and economic growth, and the establishment of industry. The main languages spoken by the 93 million people are Urdu in West Pakistan, Bengali in the East, and English, which is widely used in courts of law, official, and commercial circles, and as the medium of instruction for higher education.

Though Pakistan is new as a nation, the land itself is among the most ancient in the world and the historic sights all testify to this antique past. The valley of the Indus River, which flows through Karachi, was the cradle of one of the oldest civilizations in the world, dating back three thousand years before Christ; and the ruins of the city Mohenjo-Daro (Mound of the Dead) show a well-planned town with kiln-baked brick houses, wide streets, and a highly developed underground drainage system. Many relics removed from this fairly intact ruin can be seen in Karachi's National Museum, along with other collections gathered from the similarly ancient cities of Horappa and Taxila.

Successive waves of invaders destroyed these great civilizations and from 1500 B.C. the country was dominated in turn by Turks, Afghans, Turkomans, and the hordes from Central Asia, led by such conquerors as Babur the Tiger, who swooped down from Samarkand along the Khyber Pass through Peshawar to become the first Mogul ruler of all India. Peshawar is still a fascinating city to see, with museums and antiquities illustrating its past as one giant caravansary for merchants and travelers from Kabul; and at Lahore one can enjoy the breathtakingly beautiful Mogul gardens of the Shalimar.

The most intriguing aspect of Karachi is, of course, the mixture of people and the blend of past and present, though the city has a few "sights" of real interest to visitors. Among them are the Frère Hall, one of the city's oldest buildings, the National Museum, Clifton Beach, where camels promenade along the water's edge, and the nearby seaside resorts of Manora and Manghopir. But perhaps the most fascinating sights are just a few minutes away from the smart European shopping section along Elphinston Street, where one enters an exotic world of Orientalia in the great bazaars. Here you can buy almost anything at almost any price, in a place of shouting and haggling, colorful cloth and glistening gems, Bokhara carpets and tinkling gold necklaces, camel saddles and polished boxes inlaid with ivory.

FOR THE TRAVELER'S NOTEBOOK

Official Information

Before you go: The Consular Division, Embassy of Pakistan, 2315 Massachusetts Ave., N.W., Washington, D.C.; or the Consulate General of Pakistan, 12 East 65th St., New York 21, N.Y.; 2606 Pacific Ave., N.W., Washington, D.C.

In Karachi: SAS Office, Hotel Metropole Bldg., Club Rd.; Karachi Government Tourist Bureau, Club Rd.; U.S. Embassy, Victoria Rd.

Money Matters

Currency: The monetary unit is the Pakistan rupee (Rs.), divided into 100 paisas. There are a little less than 5 rupees to $1, U.S.

Tipping: Not obligatory. Hotel bills normally include a service charge of 10 per cent. It is customary to give a rupee or two to porters and room servants prior to departure. Waiters, taxi drivers, and hairdressers receive 10 per cent.

Climate, Clothing, and Essentials

Due to its geographical situation, Karachi has only two seasons, summer and winter. Summer begins in March and lasts until the end of November. May, June, and October are the most uncomfortable months. It is usually hot and dry with average temperatures from 85 to 95 degrees F. The remaining months of the year comprise the winter season when temperatures are somewhat cooler (60 to 75 degrees) and more comfortable. During the summer, gentlemen are advised to bring linen or Palm Beach suits. Ladies may wear coolest cottons, linens, and silks and only the sheerest of synthetics. Light woolen clothing is appropriate for winter wear. *Tap water is not safe for drinking purposes unless boiled,* so stick to bottled water, soft drinks, or beer, which is readily available at hotels and restaurants. Take all drugs and sundries and film you might need, for the supply here is not too dependable.

Hotels

Hotel accommodations are limited in Karachi and air-conditioned rooms (for which there is usually an extra charge of Rs. 10) must always be reserved well in advance. Rates at luxury hotels range from Rs. 48 for a single with private bath, Rs. 65 double. Since there are few restaurants in Karachi, most visitors prefer to take most of their meals at their hotels. A new and de luxe American-operated hotel is due to open here some time in 1964. Called the *Intercontinental-Karachi,* it will be fully air conditioned, attractively modern, and offer much needed up-to-date hotel facilities.

The best of the existing three first class hotels is the *Metropole, Club Rd.,* which is convenient to shops and offers comfortable rooms and good service. A little way out of the center is the *Palace, Kutchery Rd.,* which has a good cabaret and reportedly good food in its Le Gourmet Room. The *Beach Luxury Hotel* (no beach and not much luxury) is fairly comfortable and attractive—about fifteen minutes from the center of town by cab. Good medium-priced hotels include the *Columbus, Clifton Rd.,* the *Excelsior, Kutchery Rd.,* and a little out of town near the airport, the three excellent hotels: *BOAC's Speedbird House; KLM's Midway House;* and the *Hostellerie de France.*

Food and Restaurants

Pakistani food is a cross between Middle Eastern and Indian cuisines, and in general is hot and spicy. The most popular national dish is *biryani,* rice cooked with spiced meat or chicken and sometimes potatoes. It tastes like curried rice or the pilau of India, though the latter is not made with meat. *Zarda* is a milder rice dish, made without meat or vegetables, but flavored with saffron; and *tandoori*-spiced grilled chicken is as popular here as it is in India.

There is a wide range of curries, especially the mussel version; skewered kebabs and meatballs (*kofta*), and quorma, chopped meat cooked in spices and served with a strong gravy. *Murgh-i-mussalam* is a delectable stuffed and fried chicken, and the Pakistani breads, *chappati* and the flaky thin *paratha,* are both delicious. Honey sweet *halvah* and *firni,* a cool dessert of rice cooked in milk and flavored with rose water, are the main desserts. The favorite drink is sherbet, fruit syrup served with ice water or soda, and tea is served at all hours everywhere.

In addition to the hotel restaurants already mentioned, the *Shezan* is recommended for European food while *Farooq* is excellent for Pakistani specialties, including the *tandoori* chicken done in small pieces and known as Chicken *tikka.* Good Chinese food can be had at the *ABC* or *Canton.*

Entertainment, Night Life, and Special Events

Night life in the Western sense is not extensive in Karachi, but there are a few good cinemas, and occasionally an amateur society will put on a play or a variety show. The three leading hotels offer dancing and sometimes a floor show or a cabaret. The *Gourmet* of the *Palace Hotel* and the club in the *Excelsior* are generally the best in this respect.

March 23 (Pakistan Day) and *August 14* (Independence Day) are celebrated with fireworks and parades. In March, the Moslem holiday, *Id-ul-Fitr,* when mass prayers are held outdoors, marks the end of a nine-month fast, and *Id-ul-Azha* in June has similar rites to mark the sacrifices of Abraham. Also in June in *Muharram,* a ten-day commemoration in honor of the martyrdom of Mohammed's family, a time of huge parades, especially on the last day of the observance.

Shopping

There is a choice of lovely handicrafts, including Persian and Kashmir carpets, furs, silver and brass, carved wooden boxes, painted furniture, embroidery, brocades, and camel-skin lampshades, just to mention a few.

The main shopping streets are Elphinstone Street and Victoria Road. At the entrance to Elphinstone Street you will find the *Kashmir Art Emporium*, where you can buy woolen shawls and other handicraft articles from Kashmir. For local handicraft products, visit the *Small Industries Corporation Shop* on the corner of Victoria Road and Preedy Street, or the *All Pakistan Women's Association Shop* in the Ilaco House Building on Victoria Road. For smaller gifts most visitors go to the *Bohri Bazaar* off Elphinstone Street. Goods are cheaper here than in the larger shops.

Background Reading

The Land and People of Pakistan, by H. Feldman
The Pakistani Way of Life, by I. H. Qureshi
The Waterless Moon, by Elizabeth Balneaves

The Philippines

MANILA

Latin America in the Orient

To anyone who has traveled through the Caribbean, the Philippines will seem startlingly familiar, a misplaced bit of fiesta land set adrift in the Pacific, and comparisons between the two will become inevitable. For there is much about Manila to remind one of Havana, much that seems more Latin-American than Oriental. Both cities are seagirt, both curve in blazing white crescents around their bright blue harbors, and in both cities one finds old Spanish missions and ruined churches, coconut palms, and cool villas with tiled courtyards framed in flaming hibiscus, luxury hotels with cabana pools in heartbreaking contrast to the ramshackle native tenements, broad boulevards and slickly modern office buildings, and the same kind of honky-tonk downtown areas that teem with a wildly lurid nighttime cabaret life.

The natives of both cities share an innate sense of rhythm and are superb dancers, and in Manila as in Havana, music pours out of every open door, and from behind every palm-fronted bar; the Philippine dance bands are headline attractions in the smartest night clubs throughout the Far East. There is the same sense of casual tropical ease (though perhaps less so in the quicker paced Philippines than in

501

the Caribbean) and men in both countries dress out of deference to
the climate in cool, loosely cut jacket-shirts—the Cuban *guayabera*
and in the Philippines the *barong,* similarly cut but more elegantly
embroidered.

History, and to some extent geography, explains all in this case, for
both the Philippines and Cuba are island nations set just below the
Tropic of Cancer. Both have advanced Indian races who came under
the iron thumb of the Catholic conquistadors, and both took on a
heavy overlay of American culture after liberation resulting from the
Spanish-American War. The Philippines were settled originally by
Malays who came in outriggers from Indonesia, followed by subsequent waves of Chinese; the islands had a highly developed civilization
and conducted a prosperous trade with China, Japan, and India two
centuries before they were "discovered" by Magellan, who landed on
the island of Cebu in 1521. Fifty years later the first colonizing wave
of conquistadors arrived under Miguel Lopez de Lagaspi, who founded
Manila, and with cross and sword secured the islands for Spain and
named them after his sovereign, Philip II. He also "named" the people
(again as in Cuba) *Moros,* the "wild and treacherous ones."

Four hundred years of Spanish rule naturally left their mark and
today there is much of colonial Spain in the food, architecture, and
music of these islands, to say nothing of the religion. Eighty-three per
cent of the 7.5 million population are Roman Catholics, making this
the only Christian nation in Asia. Spanish as well as English is still
widely spoken although the native tongue is Tagalog. Spanish rule
ended in 1898, following a native revolt abetted by the United States,
when Commodore Dewey defeated the Spanish fleet in Manila Bay.
The United States acquired possession of the Philippines and immediately got off on the wrong foot when President McKinley announced
that we had a sacred obligation to "civilize and Christianize" these
people who had of course been Christianized several centuries
before.

The Filipinos never forgot America's promise of independence, but
it took years of peaceful negotiation by Sergio Osmena, Sr., the last
president of the Commonwealth, before they achieved their goal on
July 4, 1946.

World War II brought the Philippines to the forefront as a battlefield, and the islands were lost, inch by bloody inch, to the Japanese
after such now historic battles as Luzon and Leyte, Bataan, Corregi-

dor, and Mindanao. To the Filipinos, who were cruelly treated by their Japanese conquerors, the greatest American hero will always be General Douglas MacArthur, the man who said he would return, and did. The wartime destruction of Manila was second only to that of Warsaw, and when the Japanese were driven from the city after three years of occupation, the place was a shambles with most of its antique treasures completely destroyed.

Today the only remaining relics of Manila's past are the fragmentary ruins of Intramuros, the original, walled city-within-a-city created by Legaspi on the ruins of an old Mohammedan settlement. Though much of this has been destroyed too, the sixteenth century church of St. Augustine is miraculously intact with its beautiful wooden carvings still works of art.

The city itself is of course jammed with colorful sights, and everywhere there is the overwhelming contrast as skyscrapers overlook native nipa huts, bull carts plod along beside trucks, and jeep-buses called "jeepneys" roll beside *calesas,* the little horse-drawn carriages that clatter around everywhere. Department stores are close beside *sari-saris,* the tiny native shops which, as the name indicates, sell "all sorts of things." You can take a glorious ride along the airy boulevard named after Admiral Dewey, shop in the luxurious shops of the Ermita district, or taste the assorted vices and virtues of Binondo, the city's Chinatown. Here pocket-size restaurants which serve delectable Chinese dishes are crammed against each other, while other shops sell jade or Oriental drugs. In the Quiapo section of the city you can see the riotously colorful public markets and listen to the musical hawking of the vendors, or visit Quiapo Church, with its shrine of the Black Nazarene.

The 7,100 islands that make up the Philippine archipelago are roughly equal in size to the state of Arizona, and of these only 462 cover an area of more than one square mile and only 300 are inhabited. Manila is on Luzon, the largest of these islands.

If Manila is one of the most Americanized, futuramically modern cities in the world, the rest of the country is about as unspoiled as can be. By driving just a short way from the capital in almost any direction one can view such varied sights as the Ifuago rice terraces of Banaue, the eighth wonder of the world, carved from the mountainsides by Malays with their bare hands three thousand years ago, and not far from there relax in the idyllic lake resort of Baguio, the summer capital of the Philippines, five thousand feet up in the cool mountain air.

Thirty-five miles south of Manila is Tagaytay, the beautiful Taal Vista lake resort twenty-two hundred feet above sea level, with thatched-roof houses built on stilts and groves of coconuts and mangoes. By traveling two hours from Manila you can shoot the rapids of the Pagsanjan Falls. If you have time for longer trips you can visit Cebu, the source of the country's best musicians and the island of Magellan, with a wealth of hot sulphur springs, or see Zamboanga on Mindanao, famed for its coconut palms, giant roses, orchids, Moslem temples, its water gypsies, and Moro vintas—dashing outriggers with sails as wildly cut as sharks' fins.

The most excitingly exotic sights in the Philippines are unquestionably in these outlying areas. Almost as soon as you leave the large cities you'll find yourself in a world of lush tropical scenery, of iridescent rice paddies where farmers are aided by water buffaloes; and in the noisy market places of the little village barrios. Everywhere you will hear the cries of vendors selling *balut,* hard-boiled ducks' eggs complete with embryos, still the favorite snack of the Filipinos in spite of the inroads made by pizzas, hot dogs, and hamburgers.

FOR THE TRAVELER'S NOTEBOOK

Official Information

Before you go: Philippine Travel Information Office: 535 Fifth Ave., New York 17, N.Y.; 212 Stockton St., San Francisco 8, Calif.

In Manila: SAS Information Office, Bay View Hotel, Dewey Blvd., corner Isaac Peral; Philippine Travel Center, Shurdut Bldg., Intramuros; U.S. Consulate, Dewey Blvd.

Money Matters

Currency: The monetary unit of the Philippines is the peso (P). One peso is divided into 100 centavos. P. 2 is equal to about $1, U.S.

Tipping: The general rule is 10 per cent, applicable to hotels, restaurants, taxis, hairdressers, and shoeshiners. Tip the porter P. 0.20 for each suitcase he handles for you. No tipping at theaters, cinemas, etc.

Climate, Clothing, and Essentials

There are two principal seasons in Manila: the dry season from November to June, and the rainy season from June through October.

The climate is tropical, but due to the constant sea breezes the heat seems less oppressive than in other tropical areas. The days are generally pleasant —nights are cool. Temperature averages about 80 degrees F. Late November to early March is the best season of the year, the weather then being cool and dry. The warmest months are April and May.

For your comfort in the Philippines, tropical clothing is essential. If you go out in the evening a necktie and a coat are usually required. Men generally dress informally during the day. Avoid nylon and, as far as possible, any clothes requiring dry cleaning.

Hotels

Hotels in Manila are very good, modern, and with air conditioning, private baths, standard facilities, and in many cases with swimming pools. All of the first class hotels are on or near Dewey Boulevard with a view across Manila Bay. Prices for the city's top four hotels have been mutually set and are about the same. Charges for a single air-conditioned room with bath start at P. 22, doubles at P. 28, with slightly higher charges at the Manila Hotel, the city's most expensive. Moderately priced hotels charge P. 15 for a single air-conditioned room and from P. 22 for a double, and inexpensive but comfortable rooms are available starting at P. 8.50 single, P. 15.50 double, with air conditioning. For a complete list of government-graded hotels, get the "Hotel Guide Book" from the Philippine Travel Information Office.

DE LUXE: *Manila Hotel, Katigbak Dr.* This is Manila's most famous luxury hotel, practically a complete town in itself, offering almost any convenience imaginable.

FIRST CLASS: *Hotel Filipinas, Dewey Blvd.*, offers air-conditioned rooms and private baths in both the older building and modern wing, and also has a private swimming pool. *Bay View Hotel, Dewey Blvd.*, is completely modern in décor and offers every comfort. *Shellborne Hotel, Dewey Blvd.* This excellent first class hotel boasts an underground cocktail lounge in addition to all of the expected facilities. *Hotel Mabuhay, A. Mabini St.* This first class hotel has the only indoor-outdoor pool in the Philippines.

MODERATE: The *Luneta Hotel, San Luis,* is just off Dewey Boulevard on Luneta Park and has comfortable rooms with or without air conditioning at moderate rates. *Swiss Inn, Dewey Blvd., corner Isaac Peral,* has all air-conditioned rooms at modest prices and excellent Swiss management. Two very economical but comfortable and reliable hotels with air-conditioned rooms, well located in the downtown area, are the *Hotel Great Eastern, 72 Echague St.,* and the *Congress Family Hotel, 1427 M. H. del Pilar,* in the heart of the Ermita shopping and residential district.

Outside of Manila at Tagaytay Ridge, the *Taal Vista Lodge* can be recommended, with a clear view of the lake and the Taal volcano, while in Baguio, the summer capital, the *Pines Hotel* is one of the best in the country. Prices are a little lower than in comparable hotels in Manila.

Food and Restaurants

The leading hotels and restaurants in Manila serve American and continental cuisine as well as local specialties, Chinese and other Oriental dishes. The staple food in the Philippines is rice, which is prepared in many different ways. Favorite dishes are *lechon* (roast pig), *adobo* (a stew of chicken, pork, beef, and lots of garlic), and *sinigang* (stewed fish or meat with vegetables). Tropical fruits such as pomelos, pineapple, mangoes, and bananas are superb here and fish such as the *lapu-lapu* and the baked *bango* are good.

Tuba is a native drink made from fermented palm juice. Philippine *San Miguel* beer is excellent, and at bars and cocktail lounges you eat *sitcharon* pork cracklings, served here instead of nuts or pretzels.

In addition to the hotels already mentioned, there are numerous other excellent places to lunch or dine. The *New Europe* has a cosmopolitan atmosphere and is recognized for its good service and delicious steaks. For really good Spanish food, there is the *Alba* or the *Casa Marcos,* where the food is served under a canopy of stars. Some really hot food? *Café Indonesia* is the place. Its menu comprises many popular Indonesian dishes, curries and *satés*—heavily spiced. The *Golden Lotus* specializes in Chinese food. A "combo" plays Latin airs during dinner. Philippine dishes are the specialty of the *Bulakena*. Here you can choose from various regional dishes, and you may have "curb service" if desired. The *Aristocrat* offers native food twenty-four hours a day. Another fine Filipino restaurant is the *Bamboo Room* in the *Hotel Manila*. Your meal is served by girls in Filipino costumes and the décor is genuinely Filipino throughout. If you like Italian food, try the *Cocina Italian.* Anyone longing for the cool air and the cozy chalets of the Alps should visit the *Swiss Inn*. European food is their specialty, and there is a fine wine list. At lunch time a cosmopolitan crowd gathers at the *Botica Boie Fountain* where, by the way, there is fountain service. There are a number of espresso cafés and American-style soda fountains serving snacks (*meriandas*), all clearly described along with the city's many restaurants in the booklet "Manila and Environs" available from the Philippine Travel Information Office.

Entertainment, Night Life, and Special Events

Manila's night life is colorful and gay. You may start with dinner-dancing and move on to any of the numerous night clubs offering floor shows and dancing throughout the night.

Under the heading *Food and Restaurants* we have already mentioned some very attractive places for dinner. To these may be added the *Sky-room* of the *Jai-Alai* and the *Champagne Room* of the *Manila Hotel,* which are both distinguished restaurants in a strictly "coat and tie" setting with excellent food and service. At *Nina's Papagayo,* Mexican atmosphere dominates—the food is hot and the "combo" of guitarists will play Mexican and Spanish rhythms. The *Metro Garden & Grill* is informal and cozy. The *Met* is perhaps a little on the "wild" side, a place to "let your hair down." *Bayside* is where one would turn for fine food, dancing (with hostesses), and good entertainment. At *Jimmy's* the Chinese food is famous. At the *Manhattan* there is dancing on Saturday nights only, and the mamba is very much in vogue there. On Saturday nights the *Winter Garden* of the *Manila Hotel* attracts many customers with its excellent band. In this hotel the *Jungle Bar* is another popular place, always featuring an outstanding singer or similar attraction. The *Santa Anna Cabaret* is said to be the largest in the world and the booklet "Manila and Environs" mentioned above will guide you to the hundreds of other night spots in this city.

You may watch a fast game of *jai-alai,* a game of Basque origin, every night except Sunday at the *Jai-Alai Fronton* in Manila. Cockfights can be seen on weekends. At the *Rizal Court* the native game *sipa,* or "foot tennis," is played on Sunday afternoons.

Fiestas seem to be a Philippine specialty and there often is a major holiday every week or so somewhere on the islands. In January the *Feast of the Three Kings* is celebrated with parades in every village and in Manila's Quiapo district there is a mammoth procession honoring the Black Nazarene. During Holy Week in March or April, penitents march through the streets of all the cities and, in May, the *Flores de Mayo* is a month-long festival of flowers. *Santacruzan* in May also is the biggest day of celebration with elaborate pageants everywhere marking the finding of the True Cross by the Empress Helena in the fourth century.

Shopping

Manila offers the visitors many goods, including souvenirs from other Eastern countries: India, Indonesia, and Japan. Imported goods are usually more expensive than in other cities in the Far East, so concentrate on Philippine products, of which there is a wide choice: delicate Piña cloth and *jusi* (pronounced: housee) for shawls, jackets and dresses; furniture and accessories of bamboo and mahogany, excellent Igorot wood carvings, and many fiber products (hats and bags). It will certainly not take the smoker long to find out that Philippine cigars rank high among the best in the world.

There are excellent shops in all of the leading hotels and along Isaac Peral, A. Mabini Street, and M. H. del Pilar. Two of the leading department stores in town are *Heacock's* and *Aguilnaldo's,* while *Tesoro's,* the *Oriental Handicraft Shop, Philippine Homecrafts,* and the *Philippine Education Company* have good samples of the country's varied handicrafts. But for those who love shopping for its own sake, few locales will be as exciting as the local public markets in the Plaza Santa Cruz, between Escolta and Rizal avenues.

Background Reading

Malaya, Indonesia, Borneo and the Philippines, by Charles Robeguain
The Land and People of the Philippines, by Josephine Vaughan
The Lost Eden, by José Rizal
Little Brown Brother, by Leon Wolff

SINGAPORE

The lion city, everything we desire

SINGAPORE, the island and city-state, dangles like a white diamond bauble from that outflung arm of Asia, the Malayan Peninsula, a rich and romantic seaport, busily exchanging the treasures of the East for those of the West. It is the world capital of the here and now, a city that never dwells on its past and has never been sure of its future, an exotic port of call to cruise ships and corsairs, star-crossed lovers and empire builders, writers and runaways, merchants, missionaries and marauders, princes and prostitutes. And though there is a slightly has-been quality about the city, to those with even the slightest imagination it still stands for all the fables of the Oriental tropics—the colonial outpost where Somerset Maugham first conjured up visions of Sadie Thompson, where British *tuans* sipped *stengahs* and slings at the gleaming length of the Raffles Bar, a place that is still an international hodgepodge, where a Negro native of Portuguese Timor, working in a Scandinavian airline office, asks all American tourists if they know Thelonious Monk.

Singapore is crowded and youthful, and of the 1.7 million people crammed into its 224 square miles, more than 60 per cent are under twenty-one. With its blazing equatorial climate, its tropical palms and modern office buildings, it looks very much like a Caribbean

509

Chicago with an all-pervading Chinatown, a jigsaw puzzle of contrasts, and if the pieces do not always seem to fit, they at least can
be confined within one box. Contrary to popular belief, Singapore
is no melting pot, no blend of cultures; it is, rather, a catalogue of
the world's racial, national, and religious entities who speak their
own language, live, dress, eat, and worship according to their own
traditions.

Here, on any given day, a Hindu fakir may lie on a bed of nails
or walk barefoot across live coals in the area around the temples
of Chettiar or Sri Mariamman; Chinese may pray to Buddha in the
ancient temple on Telok Ayer Street or worship the monkey god at
street-corner shrines, while Moslems bow down toward Mecca as the
muezzin calls from the Sultan Mosque. Protestants may hear a ser-
mon at the snowy-spired St. Andrew's, Catholics attend mass, and
Jews pray in the manner of Moses.

While Europeans relax in the luxurious clubs that line the grassy
seaside meadow, the Padang, or dance in noisy, smoky night clubs
to the latest American tunes played by Filipino bands, hundreds of
destitute old Chinese await death in houses along Sago Street provided for the purpose. Thousands of people join the carnival gaiety
in the Chinese amusement parks, Happy World, Great World, New
World. Lunch to some means a curry tiffin in a suburban villa, to
others a steaming, fragrant bowl of Chinese chicken-rice on Middle
Road, or a slab of the Arabic meat pie, *murtabaka;* and while some
tourists attend a full dress barbecue at a smart hotel, others sit at
sawbuck tables in candlelit back alleys eating satays, bits of meat
broiled on slim bamboo skewers over a tin drum of fiery charcoal.

Raffles Place and Collyer Quay, with their handsome white skyscrapers and sprawling Victorian emporiums, are split by the stalls
of Change Alley, a sort of open-air dime store alive with bargaining
and buying. Around all of this lie the narrow, darkly aromatic streets
where the twanging atonal music of the Cantonese opera clatters out
of open-front shops, set in lopsided buildings done up in watery
pastels all brilliant with the huge red and black Chinese calligraphy.

You may shop for fabulous jewels and rare silks in the luxury
hotel shops or walk through the musty, cracked warrens of Arab
Street, where Moslems take time out from haggling over their baskets
or carpets to sip thickly sweet Turkish coffee from thimble-size cups.

And as you stroll the length of Orchard Road with its antique shops and fashion boutiques, its espresso cafés and ice cream parlors, you may stop in at the slickly modern supermarkets—the Singapore Cold Storage Company or Fitzpatrick's—or walk past them to the more tantalizing, damply cool, Oriental market with its array of Chinese vegetables, gnarled winter melons, dried mushrooms, knobs of fresh pungent ginger, and Peking ducks as crisp as cracklings.

And everywhere, always, the conglomerate of costumes, the cacophony of tongues, for though Malay is the official language, English, Tamil, and half-a-dozen Chinese dialects are equally widespread and the Malayan radio broadcasts programs in all of these.

Singapore is one man's dream of a city come true, with a Horatio Alger success story almost unequaled in history. Though it was a thriving Malayan port called *Tumasik* (Sea Town) in the thirteenth and fourteenth centuries, it was destroyed by the Javanese. Renamed in Sanskrit *Singha Pura* (Lion City), it was promptly forgotten by the world for the next four hundred years. Sir Thomas Stamford Raffles, an experienced colonial administrator and student of all things Malayan, had dreamed of acquiring the port in the name of the British East India Company and the Crown, both of which he represented as lieutenant governor in Benkoelen. On February 16, 1819, he sailed into the sleepy harbor with its fifty native huts and received temporary rights to the settlement.

From the first the port was a success, both as a shipping center for British interests in the East and as a fortification against other Europeans who were entrenched in the same area—especially the Dutch who were just across the straits in the Indies.

Five years later Raffles purchased perpetual rights to the entire island from the sultan of Johore. The city he called "this child of my own" grew beyond his wildest dreams, and when he finally acquired full possession in 1824 he felt that it had become "everything we desire."

Perhaps one of the city's earliest signs of progress came only four months after Raffles arrived, when five thousand Chinese poured into the city, to be followed by another five thousand three months later. This pleased Raffles greatly and in a letter he wrote on June 11, 1819, he said, "From the number of Chinese already settled, and the peculiar attraction of the place for that industrious race, it may be presumed that they will always form the largest part of the community." His prediction was correct and today more than 80 per cent of Singapore's population is the same "industrious race" whose members figure actively in all affairs of commerce, industry, and the professions.

Malayan Moslems make up another 13 per cent of the population and are primarily engaged in fishing, sailing, police work and civil services, chauffeuring and gardening. Their "high huts" in the *kampongs* outside of the city are one of the more picturesque sights in the palmy countryside.

Indians and Pakistanis (some 8 per cent of the island's population) are shrewd merchants operating textile shops and department stores, while Eurasians have a part out of all proportion to their number in the arts and banking, the medical and legal professions. Filipinos play music, Arabs and Jews trade, the Ceylonese deal in public service and precious stones, Sikhs are watchmen, Chettiars are bankers.

In spite of Raffle's fantastic contribution to the Crown, he was eventually discredited in the same uniquely British manner that dealt so harshly with two of its other empire builders, Sir Richard Burton and Clive of India, and died at forty-five in debt and dishonor in his own country, far from his beloved city. Singapore went on to justify his faith in it, and after being swept away from Britain by the Japanese in World War II (the island was fortified from the sea but attacked by land) and then regained, it achieved statehood in 1959, and in 1962 voted for limited union with the Federation of Malaysia and to remain part of the Commonwealth.

In addition to Singapore itself, Raffles' most obvious contributions to the island are the museum which bears his name, with its fascinating collections of indigenous East Indian art and its natural history displays, most especially the botanical life of the area, and the Institute, the oldest school in the city, founded by Raffles himself. And just behind the Cavanagh Bridge stands the statue of the city's founder, facing the spot on the Singapore River where he made his landing less than one hundred and fifty years ago.

Whether you wander around the grotesquely painted sculpture of Haw Paw Villa, the incredible garden built with the profits of the health elixir, Tiger Balm, walk along the esplanade, or drive through the park-like suburban areas, you will marvel at the gorgeous array of flowers and trees: canna lilies and orchids, honeysuckle and hibiscus, oleander and jacaranda, spiky rain trees and orange flame trees, and the travelers' palms that stand in front of the Raffles Hotel, their fronds fanned out like stately peacock tails.

Even today it fits Marco Polo's fourteenth century description: "The city is a fine and noble one, and there is great trade carried on there. All kinds of spicery are to be found there, and all other necessaries of life."

Anyone who has had enough of Singapore's infinite variety (if that were possible) can drive north across the causeway to the sultanate of Johore Baru and onward through Conrad country—the enchanted world that is the Malayan Peninsula, a world awash in the blue-green haze of refracted light, a jungle paradise with brilliant birds and playful monkeys, swaying palms, giant fig trees, glistening rice paddies, and crystal beaches edging the cerulean sea. Everywhere you meet the gracious, easygoing Malays, who have about them a sort of Oriental *dolce far niente,* and the women, with their oval faces, dark limpid eyes, and glistening black hair are as gorgeous as peacocks in brilliant, satiny sarongs, diaphanous blouses, golden slippers, and bracelet bangles. There is a remarkably detached feeling about all of the peninsula, like a cruise ship far out at sea, an almost inexplicable peace considering how vital a role Malaya has played in the world's history, how sought after it has been for its strategic position and its wealth of rubber and tin.

Here and there the insistent jungle has been cut back to make room for cities such as quaint Malacca, with its vestiges of fifteenth, sixteenth and seventeenth century Chinese, Portuguese, and Dutch rulers, a city famous for its cane and valued as a port. Further along the Indian Ocean coast is the Malaysian capital of Kuala Lumpur (by air just one and a half hours from Singapore), one of the East's most charming cities, an almost forgotten example of the dreamy life of the colonial Orient. Among its best known sights are its musical-comedy Moorish railway station, a piece of amusement-park architecture, all pink and white and turreted, and an equally whimsical domed clock tower in the city center. This comfortable capital of 315,000 (K.L. to its inhabitants) has a miniature jungle in the heart of the city, the Weld Hill Forest Reserve, and in the Kampong Bharu, the all-Malay district, you can see breezy little native houses and the colorful bustle that is the Sunday market. And at the handi-crafts center you can buy the serpentine daggers, krisses, for which the Malays are famous as well as some of the most intricate basket-work in the world, paper-thin hammered silver, and *kain songket,* Malayan brocade with shadowy patterns woven in gold or silver threads.

Ipoh, a picturesque town with pretty villas perched over the sea, with ornate shrines and cave temples, lies halfway between Kuala Lumpur and Penang, officially called Prince of Wales Island and the first British settlement in Malaya. Here lush greenery forms a backdrop rising from the water's edge and the crowded harbor of George Town, the island's port, is jammed with Chinese junks, the *prahus* of the local traders, fanciful *bugis* vessels, modern ocean liners, steam launches, and oil tankers. The orderly, spotless streets are lined with palm trees and decked out with giant ferns, and in the peaceful city center one can visit the beautiful gardens enclosed behind the Moslem mosque built in 1800, or meditate in the courtyard of the Buddhist temple. On a nearby hillside sit the seven-storied pagoda of Kek Lok Si and the Chinese Monastery of Supreme Bliss, and if you ride the funicular to the top of Penang Peak you can enjoy an idyllic view of the enchanting little island that has earned itself the name "the Pearl of the Orient."

FOR THE TRAVELER'S NOTEBOOK

Official Information

Before you go: Singapore Tourist Section, Ministry of Culture, Coleman St., P.O. Box 484, Singapore.

In Singapore: SAS and Thai International Offices, John Little's Building; Singapore Tourist Section, Ministry of Culture, Coleman St.; U.S. Consulate, Shaw House, 9 Orchard Rd.

Money Matters

Currency: The monetary unit is the Malayan dollar (M$) most commonly called the Straits Dollar, divided into 100 cents and equal to about U.S. 33 cents.

Tipping: Tipping is not yet rampant in Singapore and a 10 per cent gratuity for good service in a hotel or restaurant is optional and adequate. Luggage porters get about M$ .50 and taxi drivers are not tipped at all.

Climate, Clothing, and Essentials

Singapore weather could best be described as "hot" and "hotter" but the most comfortable months for traveling would be from May to October as the nights are generally cooler and the humidity is a little lower—but never low enough. Tropical clothing, light in weight and color, is best for men and women. The European restaurants and hotel clubs are dressy in a summer resort way and a light stole is suggested for air-conditioned places. Laundry can be done quickly and inexpensively.

Hotels

Singapore's hotels are by and large up to the very best European standards of comfort, service, and cleanliness. Rates are on a par with most major cities and a single, air-conditioned room with bath in a de luxe hotel will start at about M$30, a double at M$35. First class hotels charge from M$25 for a single room with bath, from M$36 for a double. Air-conditioned rooms in more modestly priced hotels are from M$18 single, and from M$27 double. Reservations are essential from December through March and a good idea at other times though not absolutely necessary. For a complete list of hotels with prices, see the hotel guide available from the Singapore Tourist Section.

DE LUXE: The new *Singapura Intercontinental* is the epitome of modern design and push-button efficiency; in the heart of the Orchard Road shopping area. *Raffles Hotel, Beach Rd.,* is a Singapore landmark. With its palmed courtyards, cool, wide corridors, and louvered doors, it is typical of British colonial architecture. All facilities, but since the place is huge, the service is somewhat impersonal. *Goodward Park Hotel, Scotts Rd.,* a gracious old place in the residential district. Swimming pools and Sunday barbecue.

FIRST CLASS: *Princess Garni, Orchard Rd.,* offers superb service under Swiss management and is a favorite with Europeans, especially Scandinavians. Air conditioned, good food. Other first class hotels include the *New Cathay, Cathay Bldg.,* which also has its own movie theater and Chinese restaurant and the *New Adelphi,* located in the heart of the city's downtown area, Coleman St. The *Sea View Hotel, Meyer Rd., Katong,* is an absolutely gorgeous resort hotel about twenty minutes from town at the water's edge. A little further out and more private, the *Ocean Park Hotel, Siglap,* has a number of good suites and cottage-like rooms with fine food and a popular outdoor barbecue.

Hotel de l'Europe, 6 Oxley Rise, also called the *Cockpit.* This is real joy to those who like smaller hotels and relaxed personal service. Conveniently located but quiet. Thus is a favorite with European travelers and newspapermen. Moderately priced, but first class in all other respects.

Food and Restaurants

Singapore is one of the few cities of the world where you can find a staggering array of foreign cuisines, all expertly prepared by natives of the country.

Among the best restaurants offering European food are those in the hotels already mentioned, especially the one at the *Hotel de l'Europe* (the *Cockpit*), the Elizabethan Grill at Raffles Hotel, and the *Adelphi Grill*. *Prince's* is superb for European haute cuisine and the *Chicken Inn* at the *Sea View Hotel* specializes in chicken in a number of ways—especially fried or curried and served in a coconut shell; on Sunday there is a special feature of a curry tiffin lunch. The *Tangle Inn* is an English tavern once removed and the *Pavilion* has good European food in a simple setting. There are wonderful Chinese resturants all over the city. For a simple, native lunch, try chicken-rice at any of the little shops specializing in it along Middle Road and for more formal luncheon and dinner dishes try *Peking,* the *Cathay,* and the *Szechuan Restaurant* serving the hot and spicy food of that province.

The *Islamic Restaurant* seems to specialize in what might best be described as Indian Moslem food. It's a huge brightly lit place with upstairs and downstairs dining rooms and an enormous menu with a dozen curries, vegetable fritters (*sambosas*) and a Moslem-Singapore answer to pizza—*Murtabaka*—a flakey pie of a sort of strudel dough filled with chopped meat, onions, and spices, and pan-grilled.

The *Rendez-vous* across from the Capitol Cinema looks like an ordinary luncheonette but serves a truly great Malayan version of the Indonesian *rijstafel,* called here *nasi padang.* All of the foods served are displayed at a window counter and you choose six or eight to go along with your rice. The food is absolutely superb and extremely inexpensive, with a full luncheon as described coming to not much more than $1, U.S.

In addition to restaurants, Singapore has what is locally known as the *Satay Club*—open-air stalls that operate each evening along Beach Road, Albert Street, and in the People's Park. You decide on a stall, sit down at a sawbuck table and are served a variety of *satays*—skewered meats grilled over charcoal and served with a chili-peanut sauce. Your check is determined by the number of skewers that collect at your place, and the food is really sensational and unbelievably cheap.

For light lunches and American-type snacks, there is the *Milk Bar* on Raffles Place, and, along Orchard Road, the *Cozy Corner Café,* the ice cream parlor, *Mont d'Or,* and the *Stella D'Oro* espresso café.

Entertainment, Night Life, and Special Events

Most of the hotels and many of the more elegant restaurants, such as *Prince's* and the *Capitol,* have dancing. Two night clubs with good dance bands are the *Rosé d'Oro* and the *Arundel Room* of the *Goodward Park Hotel.* The city's outstanding nighttime attractions are the three Chinese "worlds"—Great World, Happy World, and New World, huge amusement parks with dance halls and hostesses, good Chinese food, colorful bazaars, Chinese opera, Malayan *joget* dances, and a whole raft of other such carnival attractions.

Since the inhabitants of Singapore are drawn from so many races, its festivals include those of all the major religions, and observances are held for Hindu, Buddhist, Moslem, Christian, Jewish, Taoist, Sikh, and Parsee holy days. Most of the important festivals are national holidays for everyone.

One of the most colorful events, *Thaipusam,* takes place in January, when Hindus run through the streets to their temple, Chettiar, with steel spikes stuck into their flesh and at night hold a procession for the jeweled god, Lord Subramania. In February, New Year's is celebrated by the Chinese population with fireworks and dragon dances, while in March, Moslems observe the end of the Ramadan fast. Floats and parades mark the birthday of Lord Buddha in April and pilgrims returning from the annual journey to Mecca are honored at *Hari Raya Haji* in May at the city's Sultan Mosque. *National Day* in early June is a time of carnivals and parades, and the birthday of Mohammed in August is celebrated with a Koran reading contest for the youth of Islam. The Hindu *Divali,* festival of lights, comes in November.

Shopping

Like Hong Kong, Singapore is an international free port and many of the same things are good buys in both cities. You cannot bargain in department stores, in the hotel arcades, or in the well-established shops along Orchard Road, but you can in most of the other smaller shops in native quarters. You'll find elegant shops in the Raffles Arcade and along Orchard Road, colorful native shops along Arab Street and around Raffles Place and Collyer Quay.

The most fascinating place to shop is *Change Alley,* a narrow slit of a street running from Raffles Place to Collyer Quay, with open stalls selling everything from buttons to Buddhas, and where bargaining is expected.

At *Robinson's* department store you get a good sampling of everything plus some choice British cashmeres and china. Along Orchard Road you'll want to visit *Orient Crafts, Helen Ling,* and *Moon Gate* for exquisite collections of arts and handicrafts, jade and curios. Further up the Road is *Antoinette's,* a chic boutique of clothing and accessories made from Thai and Indian silks, Javanese batiks, and European cottons. There are very fine jewelry shops in the Raffles Arcade; here too you will fine good men's tailors and the extremely beautiful home and fashion accessory shop of *Doris Geddes,* with fine imports from all over Asia and Europe.

The *Malayan Arts and Crafts Society* has a small kiosk-shop with beautiful basketry, puppets, leatherwork, and silver pieces, and the *Malayan Javanese Shop* on Orchard Road has more of the same in wider variety.

Anyone interested in baskets should see the fantastic collection at *S. Abdul Wahab* on Arab Street, who are, by their own definition, "Dealers of all kinds of Fancy Mats from Java, Batavia, China and Japan, Wholesale and Retail."

Background Reading

Raffles of Singapore, by Emily Hahn
Eastern Windows, by Francis Ommanney
Singapore, by Han Suyin, in the collection, *Ten Years of Holiday*
Books on Malaya worth reading include the following:
The Malayan Archipelago, by Alfred Russell Wallace
Malaya, Indonesia, Borneo and the Philippines, by Charles Robeguain
". . . and the Rain My Drink," by Han Suyin
Jungle Green, by Arthur Campbell

Thailand

BANGKOK

City of angels, the Venice of Asia

THE Thai call their capital *Krungthep* (*The city of angels*); we call it Bangkok, but by any name it is far and away the most beguiling city in Asia, and, to the Western eye, the most foreign. For while we have become more or less familiar with the arts and architecture, food and customs, manners and dress, of China, India, and Japan, the wonders of Thailand (the land we know best as Siam) remain relatively unknown—a never-never land of Orientalia, astoundingly exotic, in the very strictest sense of the word—with white elephants and Chiengmai roses, cats with eyes as blue as star sapphires, and star sapphires as big as cats' eyes.

Bangkok is a sparkling, kaleidoscopic whirl of color and pattern, glistening with bell-tinkling temples, intricately mosaicked with fragments of glass and crockery, set like fantastic jewels along the banks of the Chao Phya River. Tiled roofs are glazed lacquer-red and green, glittering statues of leering demons and *garudas* guard the treasure of the *wats;* and *cheddi* or *stupa* shrines, lustrously gold-leafed, rise like gigantic overturned chalices from the flat countryside. The sprawling, noisy, bustling city of two million is laced with watery *klongs,* the canals of this Asian Venice. They are always jammed with

519

paddle boats and sampans, floating markets and swimming children, housewives doing laundry and young men brushing their teeth—all side by side in front of their simple teak houses, set up on stilts over the muddy waters. In the old town, narrow, dusty streets teem with Chinese street cooks, Indian jewelers, open-air shops and fruit stands, thieves' markets, and the modernized rickshaws, the motor-samlors, and traffic jams that make Fifth Avenue at noon look like a throughway.

Enchanting as the city itself may be, Bangkok's greatest treasures are its people: the gracious, graceful Thai, delicately proportioned, intelligent, and as cheerful as smiling Buddhas—a fact that has earned Thailand the epithet, Land of the Smile. Everywhere people greet each other with the traditional gesture of courtesy and respect, the *wai,* placing hands together in front of the chest, face, or slightly bowed forehead. Though many Thai in Bangkok wear Western dress, one may still see some men in colorful pantaloons and women in their *panungs* —wrap-around skirts of brightly printed cotton with a blouse or folded scarf on top.

The Thai are superb craftsmen with a strong predilection for intricate, precise patterning, a very special talent that becomes obvious as one looks at mosaic walls, doors inlaid with pearl, fruits and vegetables in market stalls, elaborately set jewelry, or the rough-textured silks, with subtle undertones of colors—hot pinks and oranges, parrot blues and greens, woven in complicated shadow plaids and blending stripes. Their architecture is perhaps the most obviously fantastic of their arts, with curlicued gables flaring skyward like golden tongues of flame, a form repeated exactly on the jeweled fingertips worn by the traditional dancers. Stone rubbings and old paintings, almost primitive in quality, reflect this passion for intricate detailing; they reveal, too, a strong sense of whimsy, with mischievously grinning demons flying through the air and gardens full of wildly imaginative flora and fauna.

The people are largely Thai, with a great number of Chinese and lesser numbers of Indians, Malayans, Burmese, Cambodians, and Europeans. Now that Bangkok is the headquarters of SEATO (Southeast Asia Treaty Organization) and the regional headquarters of the United Nations, it is rapidly assuming the mixed racial aspects of any international metropolis. All of the Oriental and European languages are represented here, though the official tongue is Thai—a Malayan-Khmer-Sanskrit-Chinese dialect.

Ninety per cent of the population is of the Buddhist faith, a religion brought to the country from Ceylon in the fifteenth century. The Thai take their religion seriously and it is a fixed central point in their lives. Almost all men serve three months as monks, shaving their heads, dressing in robes of hot-spice colors, turmeric and saffron, receiving food offerings from devout Buddhists from sunrise to noon each day, after which they may eat nothing. Perhaps it is this gentle religion, along with the natural wealth of the country that accounts for the easygoing, placid, smiling people. Though neither indigent nor industrious, they could best be described as "casual" about their work, doing only what is necessary to produce the things they need to live. Until recently, pressure was an unknown ill in Bangkok, and it has been suggested that a fitting national motto might well be, "If at first you don't succeed, it hardly matters."

As a capital, Bangkok is less than two hundred years old, though Thai history dates back to the sixth century, when the first settlers crossed into the country from south central China, to be followed by an even larger wave, fleeing from Kublai Khan's armies, in the thirteenth century. For about four hundred years, theirs was a history of squabbles between the Burmese and Khmer kings of Cambodia, a fact causing such devastation in the ancient capital of Ayudhya that the capital was moved to Bangkok, then a sleepy Chinese trading post, by the first great Thai king, Chao Phya Chakri, Rama I.

To us, the most famous Thai king was Mongkut, Rama IV, of *The King and I* fame, who brought Thailand to its modern phase, introduced social, educational, and governmental reforms, and opened the country to the West. He did, in fact, write to President Lincoln, offering him a herd of elephants with which to wage the Civil War. He and his successors, King Chulalongkorn and King Vajiravudh, developed a policy of expedient diplomacy best described as bending to the prevailing winds, thus escaping colonization when most of southeast Asia was coming under the European thumb. Though Westerners called the land Siam, to the Thai it has always been *Mung Thai* (Land of the Free). Perhaps the most enduring of Thailand's Western contacts has been with Denmark, through the trade link of the East Asiatic Company, and it's a relationship that has been long and happy, based as it is on mutual benefits, understanding, respect, and absolute tolerance.

Thailand is now a constitutional monarchy, and the present king,

Boston-born Bhumibol Adulyade, is an ardent sports-car fan, composes music, and plays the saxophone so well that he sat in on jazz sessions with Benny Goodman in Bangkok and New York. Sirikit, his beautiful queen, is, among other things, a world fashion leader, and active in a wide range of artistic, social, and philanthropic affairs in the country. All this is a far cry from the remote lives led by Thai royalty back in 1881, when King Chulalongkorn's queen drowned in the castle moat because no commoner was permitted to touch her, even to save her life.

Though Bangkok has enough modern conveniences to keep almost any traveler happy, it is not without its discomforts, among them the dusty heat and wilting humidity (or sheets of monsoon rain), irrepressible mosquitoes, and maddening traffic jams. There are more than enough compensations, however, in the way of breathtakingly beautiful sights, most especially the amazing temples in the city.

Thai temple terminology is a pretty bewildering subject and before long your head will be swimming with words like *wat* (a compound of temples), *bot* (the main building), *stupa* or *phra cheddi* (the bell-like monuments containing the bones of the dead), *nagas, garudas, kinnara, singhs* (the various serpents, lions, and mythological figures adorning and guarding the temples), and *chofa* (gable moldings).

There are over three hundred *wats* in Bangkok, over twenty thousand in Thailand, but none is more beautiful than Wat Phra Keo (the Temple of the Emerald Buddha). Built in 1785, this royal chapel enshrines a Buddha statue, carved out of one solid piece of translucent jasper, on a golden throne. Elaborate robes of gold and precious stones drape the figure and are changed according to the seasons. This temple is especially noted for its murals illustrating episodes from the Hindu epic, the *Ramayana,* and, most delightfully, for the bells that tinkle in the temple eaves. All around this temple are dozens of *phra prangs, cheddi*-shrines, and statues that make up the grounds of the Grand Palace.

Wat Phra Jetubon, or Wat Po (the Temple of the Sacred Fig Tree, or Temple of the Reclining Buddha), is famous for its 160-foot statue of the reclining Buddha, representing the moment when the master entered Nirvana. One of Thailand's largest temples, the grounds here include a bodhi tree, sprung from a branch of a tree under which Buddha is said to have sat.

Built by King Chulalongkorn, Wat Benchamabopitr (the Marble

Temple) combines modern and traditional Thai architecture and is a gleaming combination of Italian marble, Chinese glazed tiles, and gold-stained windows, while Wat Arun (the Temple of Dawn), is one of the most impressive in Bangkok, with its "Porcelain Pagoda" standing on a terrace at the edge of the river.

Two other *wats* of more than passing interest are Wat Rajabopit, where all of the buildings are covered with Chinese tiles, and Wat Saket (the Golden Mount), enshrining a bone fragment of the Lord Buddha.

The most outstanding array of Thai treasures is housed in the National Museum: royal barges, carriages, and costumes, ancient Thai coins, weapons and fabrics, sculptures and paintings, along with architectural relics from pre-Christian eras, musical instruments, and cremation chariots. A smaller but no less fascinating collection of native art can be seen in the beautiful home built of four old Thai houses belonging to Jim Thompson. A former officer in the O.S.S., he returned to Bangkok after the war to re-establish its ancient silk industry.

No trip to Bangkok would be complete without an early morning boat visit to the floating markets. Here you see life in Bangkok as it is lived on the water—postmen delivering mail by boat, food vendors of every kind in sampans and paddle boats, floating shops, rice barges from up country, water taxis, and buses.

In addition to its more serious treasures, Bangkok boasts a wide range of native diversions. Between March and May one may see fights between "male" and "female" kites, the male having a barb with which he tries to spear the female out of the sky; and *takraw,* a native ball game. Above all, the amazing Siamese boxing matches are certainly not to be missed. Starting with a formal prayer, the bouts go on to include punching, elbowing, kicking, and jabbing.

One of Bangkok's most colorful and inspiring attractions is the classical Thai drama and dance. Based on the religious epic, the Hindu *Ramayana,* it has dialogue, choral singing, and graceful Oriental ballet, performed to the accompaniment of traditional Thai music. The masked actors (all male in the *khon,* all female in the lovely *lakhorn*) depend upon movements and gestures to tell their story and are dressed in elaborate, gold-encrusted costumes with domed headdresses, so that they look very much like the glittering *stupas* in the temple compounds.

Anyone out for real trouble can probably find it in one of the bars in the Klong Toy section, where inevitably sits a *mama-san,* serving drinks, watching her girls, and taking cash. These spots are, understandably, hangouts for visiting sailors and GI's, but are probably not a very good idea for any but the most experienced male who really knows his way around.

There are several interesting short trips one can take from Bangkok, each for a day or two. Ayudhya, the ancient Thai capital, is about fifty miles away, with magnificent ruins of old palaces and temples. On the way you pass rural villages and rice paddies being ploughed by water buffalo. Chiengmai, the second largest city in the country, considered the northern capital, is three hours from Bangkok by air and less than twenty-four hours by train. In addition to its old temples, the city is famous for roses and beautiful women, silver and metal work, cotton and umbrellas. Set one thousand feet above sea level, it offers a cool and breezy respite from the sweltering heat of Bangkok, and it is here that you can visit Thailand's famous teak forests and see the elephants at work. And Siemreap, the famed site of Angkor Wat and the hundreds of other Khmer temples of Cambodia, is within excursion distance of Bangkok too, just one and a half hours away by air.

FOR THE TRAVELER'S NOTEBOOK

Official Information

Before you go: Though the government of Thailand has no travel office in the United States, information on rules of entry can be obtained from the Royal Thai Embassy, 2940 Tracey Place, Washington, D.C., your local SAS office, which also represents Thai Airways International, or directly from the Tourist Organization of Thailand, Rajadamnern Ave., Bangkok, Thailand.

In Bangkok: SAS and Thai Airways International, 55 Oriental Ave. and 1101 New Rd.; U.S. Embassy, Wireless Rd.; Tourist Organization of Thailand, Rajadamnern Ave.

Money Matters

Currency: The monetary unit is the baht, also called a tical (Tcs.), which is divided into one hundred satang. Tcs. 20.80 is equal to about $1, U.S.

Tipping: Hotels often (but not always) add a 10 per cent service charge to the bill. Restaurants: tip 10 per cent unless a service charge is already added. Taxi drivers expect a couple of ticals, and the same goes for baggage boys at hotels.

Climate, Clothing and Essentials

Bangkok's climate can best be described as boiling, though the comparatively cool and dry months are November to February when temperatures range from 62 to 84 degrees F. May to September range from 76 to 95 degrees and there are monsoon rains. Tropical clothing is worn throughout the year, and standard attire for businessmen is light slacks, white shirt, and a tie but no jacket. Bangkok is not a dressy city, though a summer cocktail skirt or dress may be needed for night-clubbing, and it's a good idea to have a lightweight stole or sweater to throw across your shoulders in air-conditioned places. In the rainy seasons an umbrella is essential; raincoats are usually too warm.

All drinking water should be bottled or boiled, even for brushing teeth, and you'll have to give up ice cubes too if you're going to be on the safe side.

Mosquito repellents are essential here if you want to maintain your sanity. The one I've found to be superb is an English product, Flypel, sold in all Bangkok drugstores. It's non-greasy and works like magic.

Hotels

There are about eighteen hotels in Bangkok which can be recommended to foreign visitors. They are neat and comfortable, several have swimming pools, and almost all have air conditioning in the de luxe and first class categories. Unless you're extremely adventurous or traveling on the most limited budget, stay away from the "moderate" and "inexpensive" hotels, as these often have no private baths and offer, occasionally, electric fans, inadequate in the extreme heat. Prices for a double room with bath at the de luxe hotels average about $17 a day, $14 in the first class hotels, about $10 in the moderate hotels, and $7 in the least expensive places if you choose to forego all cooling devices.

DE LUXE: *Rama Hotel.* Currently the pride of Thailand, this is the newest, most modern hotel in the country, completed and opened in 1961. It is centrally located, air conditioned, and has about every facility one could imagine. *Erawan Hotel, Ploen Chit and Rajdamri Rd.* Set a little way out of the bustling city center, this hotel has long been one of the most famous hotels in the Far East. It blends traditional Thai architecture with modern design and has complete hotel facilities.

FIRST CLASS: *Oriental Hotel, Oriental Ave.* Definitely for travelers on the romantic side, this is Bangkok's only hotel at the river's edge and is the place where Somerset Maugham wrote *The Moon and Sixpence*. For real atmosphere, try the older, erratically air-conditioned rooms, while the tower wing is air conditioned and done up in a sprightly motel-type décor. Swimming pool and wonderfully convenient location. *Princess Hotel, New Rd. and Oriental Ave.* A little less expensive than the Oriental, and almost as well located, this modern hotel also has a pool and air conditioning. *Plaza Hotel, Patpong Rd.* Modern and conveniently located, this is popular with European businessmen and has a restaurant featuring Thai specialties. *Grand Hotel, Rama 1 Rd.* Relatively new and modern, this completely air-conditioned hotel, just a few minutes from the center of town, has a Japanese restaurant and a roof garden.

MODERATE: *Trocadero Hotel* and the *Metropole*, both on *Suriwongse Road*, located in the heart of the European business section, are bustling, partly air conditioned and moderately priced.

Food and Restaurants

Of all the cuisines one samples in Asia, Thailand's is the least familiar, therefore the most exotic. Though derived somewhat from Chinese cooking (meat, fish, and vegetables, finely sliced and stir-fried) and Indian (Thai curries are famous and incendiary), it has its own refinements and intricacies, its own complement of herbs and seasonings. Several of these herbs are found in almost every Thai dish and give the food its truly "foreign" flavor: *pri-kee-noo,* the blazing red or green chilies that the Thai chop up and throw into everything; lemon grass with a lemon-oil flavor not unlike citronella; *makrut,* a bay-like leaf; *pak-chee* (Chinese parsley); and a fermented fish sauce (*nam prik*) that's a second cousin to the ancient Roman *garum* and about the foulest smelling substance imaginable, though its flavor when cooked is mild and inoffensive.

Native products of outstanding quality which you should not miss in Bangkok are the giant prawns, served fried, barbecued, or in salads (*yams*); and *plakapong,* a large, white-fleshed fish, sweet and meaty to the taste, served fried, or steamed with sweat-sour ginger sauce.

Soups are a big feature of a traditional Thai meal and generally come along with the rest of the food. For the most part they are clear broths with slivers of various meats, vegetables, and noodles in them. When it comes to curries, beware—generally a meal consists of several, made of chicken, lamb, pork, shrimp, designated as Mussulman or red and green curries, but to us they simply meant hot, hotter, and hottest. Rice in Thailand is about the best in the world and is served steamed, as an antidote to the curries, or as *kao pat,* fried rice. Of all the Thai dishes, the most beautiful and typical is *mekrob:* golden, crisply fried noodles, that look like clouds of spun glass and taste heavenly. Wonderful barbecued chicken stuffed with grated coconut (*gai yang*) is a specialty too, as are *satés*, broiled meat on skewers in a peanut-chili sauce. *Salim,* a dessert of sweet noodles and iced coconut milk, is cooling and refreshing, and the most delicate Thai dessert is *sangkaya,* a coconut custard baked in the coconut husk and chilled.

Fruits are lush and exotic and in season one may sample mangoes, papaya, green oranges, and such (to us) unknown but delicious fruits as the lichee-like *rambutan; rang sard,* which tastes like a lemony grape; and *durian,* somewhat like a cross between pineapple and overripe camembert, which smells so unbelievably horrible it's difficult to believe that one can become addicted to its flavor, though they say that's exactly what happens.

Tea is the Thai beverage, generally green and mild, and *mekong,* a native rice whisky, is somewhat like rough bourbon—sample some. Good beer is available, both the local *Singha* brand and imported Danish brews, along with American cola drinks and lemon squashes.

Thai service is most attractive, the various courses served on tiny, footed compote dishes, decorated in typical jewel-like patterns. Thai use only a fork and spoon for eating and in the most traditional places, such as the excellent native restaurants, *Debaros* or *Salinee,* you can be served in the classic manner, sitting (or more exactly, lying) on the floor, leaning on a large wedge-shaped pillow in front of low lacquer tables. Other restaurants offering Thai food most authentically include *Sorn Daeng* on Rajadamnern Avenue and the *Red Arrow* (*Isra*) out near the British Embassy. Though this last looks like a crowded luncheonette, the food is very good.

Thai food, tempered to the Western palate, is served at the *Thai Room* of the *Plaza Hotel,* the *Palms Restaurant* near the Erawan, the *Thiparos,* and in the *Rama Hotel.*

Chinese food is absolutely superb at *Hoi Thien Lao* on Sau Pah Road and almost as good at the *Golden Dragon.*

There is some very good European food served in Bangkok too, most especially in the charming, provincial *Normandy Grill* atop the tower of the *Oriental Hotel.* Other good continental dining places include: the *Swiss Chalet* of the *Erawan,* the new *Rama, La Cave,* and *Nick's Hungarian Inn* on Sathorn Road. For light lunches (you can't imagine how welcome a chicken sandwich and some iced tea can be) try *Dairy Farms* on Suriwongse Road, the *Tea Room* at the *Erawan,* the *Club Keynote* on Patpong Road, the *American coffee shop* in the *Rama,* or the *Little Home Bakery.*

Entertainment, Night Life, and Special Events

Drama and dance performances can be seen from November through

May at the Silpakorn Theater, though special dance exhibitions seem to be put on at least once a week for tourists throughout the year. Rehearsals can be seen at the Academy of Fine Arts. All can be arranged for at tourist bureaus in the hotel lobbies.

There are several European-type night clubs in the larger hotels, offering dancing and second-rate entertainment. The chic *Tropicana* in the glamorous *Rama Hotel,* the intimate, pleasant *Bamboo Bar* of the *Oriental,* and the very dark, sophisticated *Ambassador Club* at the *Erawan* are in this category. Other clubs offering excellent Philippine dance bands and generally "hostesses" are the *Lido,* the *Sani Château,* the *Starlight,* and the *Club Keynote.* And for real trouble there's always the Klong Toy district.

Thai boxing is a must in Bangkok and can be seen Tuesdays, Thursdays, and Sundays at the Rajadamnern Stadium, Tuesdays and Saturdays at Lumpini. Kite-fighting during March and April is not to be missed, and most local clubs accept foreign visitors for this event.

The beautiful *Wisakha Buja Festival* takes place about the beginning of May in commemoration of the three significant events in the life of the Buddha: his birth, his Enlightenment, and his passing into Nirvana. Everyone comes to the temples to listen to the reading of the holy scriptures and at night most of the temples are illuminated.

The end of Lent (*Ork Parnsa*) in October is the time of the festival of *Sart.* This custom harks back to an ancient Indian feast, and is in the main a family ceremony, followed by canoe racing on the rivers and canals.

A ceremony is performed in memory of King Chulalongkorn in the plaza in front of the Throne Hall on *October 2.* Several other feasts take place at the end of October, and if you happen to be in Thailand at that time, you will come across many processions in the streets and roads and —perhaps the most beautiful—on the rivers and canals. Most spectacular, however, are the royal processions during the *Tod Kathin Festivals.* Another great attraction is the annual boat race and the pilgrimage to the idyllic Phra Cheddi Klang Nam, a beautiful temple on an island in the Menam River. The popular *Phu Khao Thong Fair* at the Golden Mount can also be seen in late October or early November.

Shopping

Bangkok offers shoppers a storehouse of fascinating, beautiful objects which for the most part, are almost completely unavailable in other cities of the world. Bargaining is the way of business life in Bangkok, excepting those better-known, well-established tourist shops selling silk and Thai cutlery. Thai shops are extremely reliable about sending merchandise.

Jewelry of delicate gold filigree, precisely set with tiny gem-stones, is a Thai specialty. Graceful pagoda earrings and high-dome "princess" rings, brooches and the like are extremely good buys here, but if you do not know anything about gems, go with someone who does, or you're certain to get imitations. Nielloware, the Thai black enamel on silver, shimmers in carved designs on bracelets, pins, cigarette boxes, cufflinks, tie clasps, and the like. The best shops for jewelry are *Alex's, H. Sena, Zerner's,* the shops in the de luxe and first class hotels, and *Ainslie's* for black star sapphires and unusual antique pieces.

Thai silks—fabrics, shirts, ties, cummerbunds, scarves, evening bags, and belts—are available in the widest color range we've ever seen. The rough-textured silks come in brilliantly contrasting plaids, muted checks, subtle metallic-toned solids and stripes. The best assortment is unquestionably at *Jim Thompson's Thai Silk Company* on Suriwongse Road. Other shops selling Thai silks are *Star of Siam* in the Erawan and Oriental hotels, and the *Bangkok Silk Company* on Patpong Road.

Cutlery and tableware made of charcoal black buffalo horn and shiny bronze, decorated with traditional Thai motifs has been a national art here for generations and the handsome flatware adds a striking note to modern or traditional table settings. You can see the bronzeware being made, and buy it, at *S. Samran's* on Petchburi Road. This same firm has a shop on New Road near Oriental Avenue. On New Road also you'll find the shop of the *Siam Bronze Factory* offering similar ware, and shops in the leading tourist hotels have more limited but representative selections.

Antiques, paintings, decorative accessories—otherwise known as *objets d'art,* or beautiful junk. This you bargain for everywhere, but especially in the enticing shops located in Nakorn Kasem, the Thieves' Market. One of the most outstanding shops here for fine Buddha heads, porcelain, old lacquerware inlaid with mother-of-pearl, etc., is *Peng Seng*'s shop—but don't seem over-anxious about anything you like or the price will rise accordingly. *La Boutique* on Dejo Road has an outstanding selection of decorative objects, old and new. The *Monogram Shop* in the Erawan Hotel has a great deal of this merchandise along with some jewelry as well, as does the antique-packed *Thai Antiquarium* behind the Erawan Hotel, though here and in shops at the Rama Hotel, you can be sure prices are aimed at tourists.

Special shopping note: If your time is extremely limited, you can get, in one place, an over-all sampling of Thai products. The *Tourist Organization of Thailand,* a government agency, is completely reliable and operates a large, attractive shop in its building on Sri Ayudhya Road.

Background Reading

View to the Southeast, by Santha Rama Rau
Siamese Harem Life, by Anna Leonowens

Anna and the King of Siam, by Margaret Landon
The Treasured One, by Ruth Adams Knight and Princess Rudivoravan
Land of the Lotus Eaters, by Norman Bartlett
Anyone planning to visit the Khmer temples of Cambodia should read *The Royal Road* by André Malraux, and *The Road to Angkor,* by Christopher Pym.

AFRICA

Egypt (U. A. R.)

CAIRO

A new city, one thousand years old

WHETHER Cairo looks more Oriental than European depends on the direction from which you are traveling, and your previous stop. Should you arrive after a stay in some European city, such as, let us say, Vienna, you will immediately feel yourself entering the world of the East. You will be aware of a skyline of domed mosques and slender, soaring minarets, and of men wearing red fezzes or white cotton skullcaps, and robelike kaftans or striped cotton pajamas, all twirling long-handled fly whisks or fingering the amber "worry beads" seen throughout the Moslem-touched world, from Athens to Djakarta. You will be conscious of the seductive honeyed whine of Arabic music in a world of bazaars, belly dancers, and beggars who plead for *baksheesh,* the Arabic word for "tip" that will follow you all the way to Calcutta. You will notice the Oriental smile, the intricate, formal courtesies, and the ancient superstitions that lead a shopkeeper to tell you you have "green feet" because you brought him luck on the previous day. And you are certain to feel yourself right in the middle of an Arabian Nights tale if you go to one of the native restaurants. Here you sit cross-legged on carpeted divans and dip

533

into little bowls of sesame-seed appetizers with pieces of flat Arab bread, as the waiters bring the mass of glass, brass, and tasseled tubing called the nargileh to portly Egyptians around you who prefer this soul-soothing after-dinner smoke to the acrid Turkish cigarettes.

But if you come to Cairo after a stay in any of the tangled, humid cities of the Far East, you will suddenly feel as though you have, at last, arrived in a European outpost. Then your eye is more likely to be captured by the luxury hotels with their carpeted lobbies, where music of Handel or Mozart is piped over the loudspeaker system; here glass walls and private balconies overlook the Nile quays, as the river floats by under its bridges like a miniature Seine—an impression which becomes even stronger in the violet evening when the causeway lights begin to blink on. Walk along wide, orderly, boulevards such as Soliman Pacha Street and you'll be aware of the smart boutiques, the continental restaurants, the Opera House and the chic, dark women whose clothes could have been inspired only by the *couturiers* of Paris or Rome. And though rice is still the dietary staple here, as it is throughout Asia, you will note that the taste for tea has switched to an unquenchable thirst for the hot, sweet Turkish coffee, served to you in almost every home, shop, or office you enter. Most astounding of all, after weeks in the steamy, jungle-shaded cities of Asia, is the Egyptian light—the first, hot, white wash of the Mediterranean sun that seems to be filtered through starched organdy and makes you feel as though your eyes have suddenly been unveiled. All through your visit you will see the two faces of Cairo—the city pinpointed where the Mediterranean world gives way to Asian waters—like a photograph that has been double-exposed, its two images always visible at once.

When El Kahira, the original section of Cairo, was founded in 969 A.D., Egypt was over four thousand years old and its most illustrious days were already ancient history. Behind it were the predynastic periods ruled by shadowy gods and half-gods; the lotus symbol of the Upper Kingdom of the Nile had long ago merged with the papyrus of the Lower Kingdom; and the great pyramids, built between the Third and Sixth Dynasties by Zoser, Cheops, Chephren, and Mycerinus, were well on their way to becoming "ruins" and were visited by the conquering Moslem Fatimids who journeyed on camels from their newly won capital, Cairo, to the antique sights at Giza and Sakkara.

Over twenty centuries ago, Thutmose I had his burial place cut into the rocks of Thebes to create the first of the royal tombs which were to honeycomb the fabled necropolis, the Valley of the Kings. During his reign, Rameses II added to the temples at Karnak and Luxor, erected a mortuary temple at Thebes, and constructed a rock-cut temple at Abu Simbel, which is soon to be flooded by waters released from the Aswan Dam.

Over thirteen hundred years before Christ, King Akhnaton and his queen, Nefertiti, made the first attempts at a monotheist religion; King Tutankhamen lay buried and forgotten midst his treasures; and Hatshepsut, the queen who always had herself depicted as a bearded man, shared the dim and distant past with such pagan gods as Ra, Isis, and Osiris.

Moses had received the Ten Commandments on Mount Sinai and he and his people had completed their exodus across the divided waters of the Red Sea; the great Persian rulers such as Darius and Artaxerxes had come and gone.

The "modern" Egyptians of a thousand years ago had long since forgotten how to read hieroglyphics, which were not decipherable until 1799 when Napoleon's armies found the Rosetta Stone, the key to these ancient writings, near Alexandria. The 365-day calendar had been in use for centuries; Egyptian astronomers under the Ptolemies had speculated on the probability of the earth's revolving around the sun; ancient architects and builders, sculptors and metal smiths had produced some of the most beautiful work the world has ever seen; and the science of medicine had progressed farther than it would again until well past the medieval age in Europe.

Egypt's Greco-Roman period began with the arrival of Alexander the Great in 332 B.C., when he built the city he named for himself, Alexandria. After his death it became the center of the brilliant kingdom of the Ptolemies, who held sway until 30 B.C. when the last of the line, the queen, Cleopatra, chose death rather than life without her beloved Mark Antony (or life with the hated Octavian). The Romans ruled Egypt until the Arab conquest in 313 A.D. By that time Christianity had been firmly established and the first Eastern Christian sect, the Copts, were in power. They attained even greater importance in the late fourth and early fifth centuries, when they initiated the idea of the monastery and built the interesting group of monastic retreats at Wadi Natrun, the remains of which can be seen today on the road between Cairo and Alexandria.

All this was part of the past in 969 A.D.; all this and more. Egypt had been a Moslem country for three hundred years, following the defeat of the Byzantines in 641 A.D. at the hands of the caliph, Omar, the second successor to the prophet Mohammed, and it had since been ruled by the caliphate dynasties of the Ommiads and the Abbassides.

But more was still to come, and Cairo belonged to Egypt's future rather than to its past. It was from this "new" city that Saladin ruled, as did the Mameluke soldier-slaves of the Ayyubid and Circassian sultans from 1250 to 1517, at which time the Turks of Suleiman took over. They remained in power until 1798, when Napoleon and the French army captured Cairo and held it until their fleet was destroyed by Nelson in the Bay of Aboukir, outside of Alexandria. In 1820 Mohammed Ali conquered the Sudan and became the first pasha of Egypt. In 1882 Queen Victoria of England installed an army of occupation to protect her rights on the Suez Canal, rights that had been obtained by Prime Minister Disraeli to preserve his nation's short-cut to her Indian empire. Egypt became a sovereign state in 1922, a republic in 1952, and "nationalized" the canal in 1956, one of the first acts of her new president, Gamil Abdel Nasser, who was elected in that year by a majority of 99.9 per cent of the total vote.

Cairo, with its population of 3,500,000, is the largest city in Africa, and though it is young by Egyptian standards it contains remnants of the country's entire history. The most staggering collection of antiquities is in the National Museum, with relics covering 3500 years of Egypt's past. Here are such striking, stylized, two-dimensional sculptures as the glittering black diorite figure of King Chephren; showcase after showcase full of the earliest miniature ivory figures, impeccably carved in three-dimensional perfection; and hundreds of figures in painted limestone or done in the exaggerated, distorted proportions of the latest of the ancient kingdoms. The museum is crammed with mummy cases and treasures exhumed from royal tombs: tiny figures depicting the arts and industries of villages that prospered thousands of years ago; exquisite jewelry of beaten gold, some set with enormous gems and chunks of quartz; mounds of household objects and fragments of faded fabrics; thousands of scarabs; and rooms full of the ordinary appointments of daily life. But the most fabled and fantastic of all the museum's treasures is the collection found in the tomb of King Tutankhamen, unearthed in 1922. His gold-and-enamel mummy case, his golden bed and state chariot, the dog-legged game table he used, and the gold and ivory throne from which he ruled, were all hermetically sealed with him in his tomb, and so were perfectly preserved. Here, too, are the gold fingertips which were slipped over the hands of the royal corpse, alabaster vases carved to sheer translucence, and the shriveled brown petals of funeral roses over thirty-three hundred years old. One could spend months, if not years, studying the exhibits in this museum and probably everyone who has ever been there has wished for three things: more time, better lighting, and a more orderly arrangement of the displays.

Though the National Museum may be Cairo's most fascinating and important sight, it is certainly not its most famous, for half an hour's drive from the city lie what are among the best known travel-poster landmarks in the world: the Great Pyramids of Giza and the Sphinx. No matter how many pictures one may see of these monumental tombs, he will not be prepared for the reality of them, for their overpowering, towering mass is something you cannot feel unless you stand beneath their looming shadows, climb over them, walk around them and through the winding labyrinth of their interiors. The oldest and largest of these is the Pyramid of Cheops, built in the twenty-seventh century B.C. to a height of 479 feet, though now, after having been stripped of its white limestone facing, it stands at 450 feet.

Close to the three pyramids is the Sphinx, most incredible of all to see, crouched there with a catlike smile, seeming strangely uncomfortable and out of place in the middle of the desert with the swirl of tourists and guides, the camels decked out in colored tassels and tinkling bells, and the dragoman guides selling photographs and so-called "authentic" scarabs from Egypt's antique days.

The first pyramids ever built in Egypt stand about an hour away from Cairo at Sakkara. These are great heaps of huge stones, piled up with stepped sides to flat, square tops, built by the Pharaoh Zoser. Royal tombs nearby reveal a wealth of brilliantly painted wall sculpture-frescoes and a temple with slimly fluted columns that predate the Grecian columns by two thousand years. Twenty minutes from

here, at Memphis, one can see the delicately carved, massive mum-
mification slabs used to embalm sacred bulls which were thus honored
out of respect for one of the most ancient of the pagan deities, the
bull-god Apis. Close by is a small and perfect alabaster Sphinx, and
there is a colossal figure of Rameses II, now enclosed in a wooden
shack and edged with ladders so one can climb up and examine the
huge head at convenient range.

Not all of Cairo's sights date back to antiquity: many are relics
of its Moslem lineage. Among these is the overpowering Citadel of
Saladin, that sits atop the slopes of Mount El Mokattam, providing
a panoramic view across Cairo's four hundred minarets and over the
Nile to the tops of the Giza pyramids. There are three mosques
within the fortress walls, the most beautiful of which is that of
Mohammed Ali, built of white alabaster; one may also visit the
museum of the El Gawhara Palace at this site. The Sultan Hassan
Mosque, with its 267-foot minaret and its magnificent courtyard, is
the city's grandest, but the most important by far is El Azhar, with
its university founded in 969 A.D. and still the most important center
of religious education in the Moslem world.

There are the other museums too: the relatively new Abdin Palace,
with elaborate souvenirs of Farouk's reign, and the Islamic Museum,
with its arabesque-patterned textiles and red, white, and blue ap-
pliquéd tent quilts, pottery and silver, swords and pistols of damascene, exquisite tilework and glass, ivory-inlaid wood, and pierced
brass mosque lanterns. There is the Coptic Museum, a small, perfect
jewel of a house once belonging to a rich Christian merchant and
now containing silver and painted wood icons, glass and ceramics,
and richly colored, intricately patterned textile fragments. Just next
door is the El Moallaka, the hanging church, a Coptic place of worship dating back to the sixth century, built over the walls of an old
Roman fortress. Not far from here, and also in the quarter known
as Old Cairo, is the Ben Ezra Synagogue, built in the twelfth century
by the subject of Browning's famous poem on the same spot where a
Jewish temple stood in the time of Nebuchadnezzar.

After a round of the museums and the mosques, you will be ready
for El Muski, the largest of the Oriental bazaars. It is really made
up of a dozen bazaars and narrow *souk* streets, such as the Khan-
el-Khalily, with its magnificent brocades, carpets, and silks, the Souk-
el-Mahasin, where shops display water pipes and trays, coffee beakers

and plates made by local coppersmiths, and the Souk-el-Sgaha, where you can find bargains in gold and silver jewelry, and wide-collared necklaces dripping with turquoise and coral, modeled after pieces worn by Pharaonic queens. Some *souks* specialize in fezzes, either plain or draped as tarbooshes, others sell perfume oils, such as attar of roses and haunting sandalwood; some offer kohl, the mascara of Cleopatra's time, while others have hundreds of scarabs or charms modeled after the hieroglyphic "key of life" symbol. It is a noisy, exotic world of bargaining and coffee drinking, as enticing with its jam-packed array of modern treasures as the National Museum is with its antiquities.

Cairo is also the perfect point of departure for Egypt's other wonders. A few hours away is the very cosmopolitan Mediterranean city of Alexandria, with its relics of the Greeks, Cleopatra, and the Ptolemies, as well as its wide *corniche* crescent, its cabana beaches, its sidewalk cafés and altogether European aspect. Here stood the world's first lighthouse, the Pharos, one of the Seven Wonders of the ancient world. In its prime under the Ptolemies, Alexandria boasted a library of four hundred thousand books and it was the city in which Euclid, Apollonius, Ptolemy, and Callimachus, among many others, made their contributions to science, poetry, and philosophy.

Of all the sights in Egypt, none are more impressive or incredible than those of the Upper Nile. There is Abu Simbel, with its enormous temple of Rameses II, rising like some fantastically carved rock-mountain island in the middle of the gray-green waters of the Nile. With inundation of the monuments fairly imminent (unless the world can come up with the millions of dollars needed to save them), tourists are flocking here in excursion launches from Wadi Halfa or Cairo and viewing them first by daylight and later by the light of the moon.

Another of the fascinating stops in Nubia is Aswan, with its huge, gushing dam and its ancient granite quarries, from which the twelve great obelisks were cut and floated down the Nile to such points as Luxor, Memphis, and as far north as Baalbek in Lebanon. One of these obelisks stands in the Parisian Place de la Concorde, a trophy of war brought home by Napoleon; still another, Cleopatra's Needle, is now in New York's Central Park. The largest of these obelisks, 137 feet tall, still lies in the quarry, attached to its granite bed. A boat trip on a swallowtail-sailed felucca is another pleasant pastime in Aswan, a peaceful silent excursion past Nubian villages with their fringe of palm trees, their huts built of the same fawn-colored clay that lies along the river banks, and their elegantly tall, slender people —dark and regal descendants of the Sudanese who wandered up the river and settled here centuries ago. Stop for a while at Kitchener's Island, a botanical garden of tropical flowers and trees, at Elephantine Island with its temple ruins, and glide past the huge, silent tomb of the late Aga Khan and the dozens of ant-hill burial places of ancient Egyptians, as yet unexcavated.

Luxor has about it the same quiet, windless, baking heat, the same thick blue sky with an occasional brushing of white clouds, as does the rest of the Upper Nile Valley, and it is this rainless, almost glassed-in airlessness that has preserved the relics of the tombs. This is a world that seems strangely dreamlike and far away from the activity of Cairo or the sophistication of Alexandria. Spend a day wandering through the fabulous wealth of ruins at Karnak, sixty-two acres of columns and arches, a vast compound of temples entered between a double row of ram sphinxes, the heads of which seem to nod, so lifelike are the sculptures. Here amid a forest of painted and hieroglyphic-carved pillars, and papyrus-ridged capitals, flat against the sky, is the temple that was known as the "Wonder of Thebes." The Hypostyle Hall of Rameses I and Seti I is some 338 feet across— Notre Dame could fit into it with room to spare—and the columns which rim it are richly patterned with deep relief carvings set in superb design patterns.

Within walking distance of the amazingly fine tourist hotels is the Temple of Luxor, described by guides as "a minor sight," a piece of information that will astound even the most jaded lover of ruins. Smaller it may be, but the collection of lotus- and papyrus-fluted columns and royal statuary, the exquisitely proportioned temple of Amenophis III, the more grandiose courtyard of Rameses II, and the little back garden of architectural fragments, make this perhaps a more charming and humanly believable sight than the staggering array that is Karnak.

Across the Nile from modern-day Luxor are the ruins of imperial Thebes and the Valley of the Kings. Buried under cone-shaped mountains of sand that look surprisingly like the pyramids are the tombs of the Pharaohs, some still sealed in airless splendor, others opened or in the process of being excavated. Tutankhamen's tomb, empty since its relics were removed to Cairo, still retains the deep, brilliant, blue-green color of its walls and the sharply clear red-and-white figure painting of the frieze. All of the tombs, like those of Rameses II and III, are rich with fresco paintings depicting scenes from the life of the king and prognosticating his fate in the afterworld.

There are temples here too, most spectacularly the huge, hot orange buildings of Queen Hatshepsut, set against towering rock cliff backdrop in the Dehr-el-Bahri Valley. With a long processional ramp, wide, horizontal lines, and colonnades of squared-off columns, it looks more like a grandiose modern post office than the temple of a royal queen, erected only shortly after the Stonehenge monoliths. The Rameseum, the mortuary temple of Rameses II, is most interesting for its wall carvings; its huge façade is completely covered in mosaics depicting the battles that figured in the king's career, and at the entrance to the temple lie the fragments of his sixty-foot statue with a forefinger that measures three and a half feet.

The two figures that are the gigantic Colossi of Memnon sit alone and deserted amid an expanse of sand, or surrounded by a miniature lake when the Nile overflows. The Temple of Seti nearby is worth a visit, and the excavation of this tomb is nearing completion. The whole valley is filled with hundreds of tombs of the nobles, each with its secrets and its treasures, a wealth of ancient records that makes one feel that perhaps the Egyptian rulers' obsession with the afterlife is what really made them immortal, though maybe not in the way they expected.

FOR THE TRAVELER'S NOTEBOOK

Official Information

Before you go: United Arab Republic Tourist Information Office, 630 Fifth Ave., New York, N.Y.; 257 East Delaware Place, Chicago, Ill.; 3001 Pacific Ave., San Francisco, Cal.

In Cairo: SAS Office, 2 Sh. Champollion; State Tourist Administration Office, 5 Adly St.; U.S. Embassy 5 Sh. El Walda, Garden City.

Money Matters

Currency: The principal unit of Egyptian currency is the pound (EG£), equal to 100 piasters (P.T.) or 1,000 millimes. One pound is equal to $2.30 U.S.

Tipping: Hotels and restaurants add a 10 per cent service charge to the bill and porters at hotels are usually tipped P.T. 5 for handling luggage. At the airports and railroad stations, porters get a fee of P.T. 2.50 for the first suitcase and P.T. 1.50 for each additional piece of luggage. Tipping taxi drivers, cinema and theater ushers, hairdressers, and wardrobe attendants is not required.

Climate and Clothing

Summer (June to August) can be fairly hot, often in the upper 90's, but the humidity is low and there are pleasantly cool breezes every evening. Winter (December to April) is delightfully cool, with a temperature average of about 70 degrees F. There are few rainy days and an average of eight hours of sunshine a day. Spring and autumn (March to May and September to November) are excellent for travel. Light clothing is needed, especially in summer.

Hotels

Cairo has good de luxe, first and tourist class hotels. Since there are limited rooms it is best to have reservations. De luxe hotels charge from P.T. 300 to 500 for a single room with bath, P.T. 400 to 600 for a double; first class hotels charge about P.T. 150 or 200 for a single with bath, and from P.T. 200 to 400 for a double. Tourist class rates range from P.T. 100 to 130, single, P.T. 130 to 180, double. Some Cairo hotels lower prices 15 to 25 per cent during off-season, from May 1 to October 31. For a complete list of government-rated hotels throughout Egypt, see the booklet "Tourist Information," available from the UAR Tourist Offices.

DE LUXE: The *Nile Hilton, Sh. Maspero, Corniche Ave.,* is undoubtedly Cairo's most beautiful hotel, with a view of the Nile. Room service leaves a lot to be desired, but the rest of the hotel is elegant and convenient, with all facilities. It is about a two-minute walk from the fabulous National Museum. *Shepheard's, Sh. Elhamy, Garden City,* is Cairo's legendary hotel. Though the original burned down, the modern version is a favorite with those who prefer old-world comfort and color. The staff is costumed in "operetta Egyptian" with turbans, flowing kaftans, and white pantaloons. *Semiramis, Sh. Elhamy, Garden City,* is next door to Shepheard's and also on the Nile bank, a little less expensive than the other two. For something different, try the *Mena House Hotel* at Giza, just across from the pyramids.

FIRST CLASS: First class hotels in Cairo are comfortable and good, with varying standards of cleanliness and service, and few elaborate lobby trimmings. One of the best is the *Elborg,* in Gezireh, well located and a favorite among traveling Europeans, while *Atlas, Sh. El Gomhurya,* the *Cleopatra Palace, Tahrir Square,* and the *Continental, Opera Square,* are good alternate choices, as all are newly built.

SECOND CLASS: Many visitors are happy in the more modest hotels, some of which are excellent. The *Carlton, 21 26th July St.,* the *Ambassador, 31 Ramsis,* and the *Windsor, 3 Sh. El Elfi,* are all comfortable and economical.

Since most visitors will want to see the antiquities of the Upper Nile, it might be helpful to know that the *Cataracts* and *Grand* hotels are the best in Aswan; the *Winter Palace* is the best in Luxor, with the *Luxor* a close and less expensive second; while those who visit the enchanting city of Alexandria will be happy at *Cecil's, 26th July Ave.,* the *Metropole, 52 Saad Zaghloul Ave.,* and the *Windsor Palace, 17 Rue Shohadaa.*

Food and Restaurants

The quality of food is excellent, and you may enjoy good European cooking in the well-run dining rooms of the leading hotels and in a number of restaurants like the *St. James, Kursaal, Groppi's, Ermitage,* and the *Crillon,* where you can also get some native dishes.

Egyptian food is extremely interesting and certainly should be tried. It falls into the category of Middle Eastern cookery. Some delectable specialties are *kebabs,* lamb grilled on skewers; *dolma,* a variety of lamb-and-rice-stuffed vegetables or grape leaves; *moussaka,* eggplant stuffed with lamb; *fattah,* a creamy baked combination of rice, Arab bread, chopped chicken, and yogurt; a dozen delicious bean dishes; and that staggeringly varied Middle Eastern antipasto, *mézé.* The giant prawns are excellent and there is a good local caviar, *batarikh.* Desserts are the honeyed, nutted varieties of flaky pastry and the superb tropical fruits. Coffee is usually the syrupy very strong Turkish brew. Favorite alcoholic beverages are the local *Stella* beer, Egyptian wines and the licorice-flavored arrack.

The three most interesting restaurants in Cairo serve superb Egyptian food and should all be visited. *Khomais* is the most elegant; it serves the local specialties in an authentic atmosphere where you dine on carpet-covered divans from huge round brass trays. *Mahmud el-Sammak,* one of the oldest restaurants, is a large marbled place serving sensational fish and seafood dishes to statesmen and laborers, travelers and journalists. The most native of the three and good for an inexpensive light lunch is *Eldomyati,* a small tiled spot serving only bean dishes, pickles, yogurt, and such fare. There are also several foreign restaurants in Cairo, including *Sofar* for Lebanese food, and the *München* for German cooking.

Entertainment, Night Life, and Special Events

The leading hotels have dancing and floor shows; the smartest of these are the *Belvedere Room* of the *Nile Hilton,* the roof garden of the *Semi-*

ramis, Sinbad's Cave at the *Gezirah Palace,* and the *Geisha* at the *Atlas Hotel.* There are also good night clubs with European and native entertainment. Best known are the *Auberge des Pyramides,* and the *Caravan Tent, Hilton Hotel.* Most interesting of all is *Sahara City,* a huge club in an Arab tent in the shadow of the pyramids, about thirty minutes from town. Here you are served Arab fashion on low divans. The entertainment consists of native belly dancers and folk dancing from the provinces, the Sudan, etc.

The principal Moslem religious event of the year is the month of *Ramadan,* when Moslems do not eat from early morning until sunset. In the evenings the minarets are illuminated, the mosques crowded, and the cafés are open all night. An important Coptic feast is *Sham el Nessim,* celebrated on Orthodox Easter Monday, when all Egyptians, regardless of religion, race, or class, go to the parks or the country to enjoy the spring air.

Shopping

You will find fine shops in Cairo, especially in the arcade of the Nile Hilton. The most fascinating shopping area is the bazaar, *El Muski,* where prices are considerably lower than at the hotels, particularly after you've bargained them down to one-half or one-third the asking price. Good buys include leather goods such as hassocks, slippers, and camel saddles, perfume essences, ivory inlay work, copper and brass, silver and gold costume jewelry often set with coral and turquoise, silk brocade, and the most beautiful cotton fabrics in the world. Men may have shirts made to order here at half the price they would be at home. You will also find attractive stores along July 23 Avenue and Soliman Pacha. *Khan Khalil* and *Sabry Bazaar* are two shops with a good assortment of everything and reliable packing and shipping home—but bargain like mad, no matter how adamant the salesman may seem at first.

Background Reading

From an Antique Land, by Julian Huxley
The Bible, and Baker's *Bible Atlas*
The Blue Nile, by Alan Moorehead
The Splendor That Was Egypt, by Margaret Murray
Alexandria, by E. M. Forster
The Egyptian, by Mika Waltari
Nasser's New Egypt, by K. Wheelock
Caravan, A Story of the Middle East, by Carleton S. Coon
The Lost Pharaohs, by Leonard Cottrell
The Art of the Middle East, by Leonard Woolley

Kenya

NAIROBI

The place of cool waters,
within a lion's roar

FEW cities have grown up as quickly as Nairobi. Established just sixty-four years ago as a depot on the "lunatic line" (the railway the British built to link Uganda with Kenya's Indian Ocean port, Mombasa), it is now the leading commercial and cultural center of East Africa, and, with its population of 200,000, one of the largest cities between Johannesburg and Cairo. It is the capital of Kenya, an ex-British colony of seven million that has just gained its independence.

With its office buildings of steel, glass, and gleaming white concrete, its neatly laid out, palm-lined avenues, trim parks, and garden villas, the whole city looks like one big modern shopping center, a misplaced island of suburbia, adrift in the natural wonders of the Dark Continent. Known in the past for its Kikuyu fighters and Kamba witch doctors, Nairobi is the the gateway to safari land. (This travel classic originated here and *safari* is the Swahili word for "trip.") It is now also the headquarters for Hollywood film companies shooting on location in the bush, and a center for traveling salesmen of every nation in the world, who ply their trade in nylons and pneumatic drills, automobiles and automatic washers, television sets and chewing gum, up and down the east coast of Africa. And at the sidewalk café of the New Stanley Hotel, East African waiters in wine-colored fezzes and white robes tied with wide yellow sashes serve lemon squash and espresso coffee to a world-wide assortment of people: European businessmen in suits of English or Italian cut; turbaned Sikhs and sari-clad Indian women; "white hunters" in leaf-green bush jackets and broad-brimmed hats turned back Aussie fashion; and English office girls in Liberty cottons.

Behind. the Municipal Market, with its kaleidoscopic array of tropical fruits and vegetables, is the curio section. Here Kikuyu gardeners sell flowers that cascade from their overflowing baskets, Kamba wood carvers offer primitive, polished wood sculptures, and Kisii vendors display their translucent soapstone vases, while everywhere you hear the bright friendly greetings, *"Jambo," "Ahsante,"* and *"Kwaheri"*—Swahili for "Hello," "Thank you," and "Good-bye." All of this, is, as the New Stanley's slogan puts it, "within a lion's roar," referring to the fact that only seven minutes from the hotel lies the game reserve of the Royal Nairobi National Park. Here hippos, crocodiles, monkeys, hartebeests, wildebeests, zebras, jackals, lions, crested cranes, and great hornbills live under natural bush conditions in a vast cageless zoo, without keepers, where animals fend for themselves and only the fittest survive. As you drive along in your car (the rule is that you must not get out) you can see secretary birds in search of supper and giraffes nibbling the feathery leaves of the tall mimosa trees. And at dusk, you can watch the animals go down to their watering holes, as hyenas and lions set out for the evening kill.

It is its location that gives Nairobi its glamor and accounts for its growth. For though it is only 100 miles from the equator it is set 5,500 feet above sea level on the flat, sisal-spiked Athi Plain, where gazelles skim across the horizon as gracefully as ballerinas, and the climate is so healthful and pleasant that the Masai named the site Nairobi—"The Place of Cool Waters." On one side of the town lies the blue haze of the N'Gong Hills, so beloved by the Danish writer, Isak Dinesen, the Baroness Blixen, who ran a coffee plantation in these Highlands for seventeen years. From these hills that rise out of the Great Rift Valley one can see Africa's tallest mountain, Kilimanjaro. Its flat, snow-capped peak thrusts 20,000 feet into the air, overlooking the tent camp of Amboseli and the clay-hut villages of the Masai. These are the handsome natives who plaster their elaborate hairdos with ocher-colored mud and live on the blood and milk of the cattle they raise, a diet Isak Dinesen believed was responsible for the smooth silkiness of their skins.

Nairobi with its mixed population of African natives, European settlers, Arabs and Asians, has the distinction of being the first town in the British colonial empire to be designated a city by royal charter on May 30, 1950.

The Arabs came to this land in the seventh century, converted the natives to the Moslem religion, and developed the Swahili language. The Asian population consists mostly of Indians who came originally to work on the Uganda railway and now engage in trade.

Apart from healing the tribal schisms within the country, Kenya's most desperate problem is education, and 6 per cent of the national budget is expended in that direction, to prepare its population for the responsibilities of independence. Nairobi, is, therefore, proudest of its schools, most especially the Royal College, qualified to grant degrees in engineering, commerce, and the arts. This modern school, and governmental buildings like the City Hall, the law courts, and Parliament House are all open to visitors and most interesting to see, as is the Coryndon Memorial Museum, with its relics of prehistoric and tribal lore, and a huge collection of East African flora and fauna.

But Nairobi, as fascinating as it may be, is not Kenya's greatest attraction, for there are dozens of more exciting places to visit within the 225,000 square miles that make up this country. The wildlife is beyond doubt the most amazing thing to see, on reserves such as those at Amboseli, Tsavo Park with its elephant herds and prides of lions. Murchison Falls National Park near the Nile in Uganda, or Queen Elizabeth National Park, at the foot of the Mountains of the Moon, also in Uganda. Visitors may sit up all night watching animals at their watering places, if they stay at the tree-lodge, Treetop. Elizabeth of England and Prince Philip were vacationing here when they learned of the death of George VI, and the girl who went up to the lodge a princess came down a queen.

There are beautiful flame trees and river falls at Thika; Olorgesailie Park is a prehistoric excavation on the floor of the Great Rift Valley which cuts a wide swathe from the Dead Sea through Ethiopia and

Kenya to the Indian Ocean; Lake Nakuru has a wealth of commercial soda and salts, and thousands of pink flamingos. You can travel to Tanganyika to see the lions and other wildlife on the Serengeti Plains or visit the enormous crater, Ngorongoro, nine miles in diameter, with walls that rise 2,500 feet above the crater floor. You can take a steamer from the Kenyan port of Kisumu across Lake Victoria, or sail down the coast to the clove-scented city of Zanzibar; go deep-sea fishing or skin diving in the peaceful waters of the coral reefs, or swim and sun bathe on the beaches of old Arabic towns such as Gedi or Malindi.

But to the imaginative and romantic mind, no place will be more alluring than the ancient city of Mombasa, East Africa's most important port and the Kenyan capital until Nairobi assumed the role in 1905. Here, the Old Town is a seductive maze of narrow alley streets with carved, Arab-style doorways, spice shops, coffee vendors, and carpet dealers. Five times a day the muezzins call the faithful to pray from the slim minarets of the city's sugar-white mosques. The sixteenth century Fort Jesus, built by the Portuguese, looms over the port and is now a museum of East African memorabilia. In the harbor below are the dhows of Araby with their high prows, lateen sails, and brilliantly painted hulls. For centuries these ships have sailed before the *Kaskasi,* the northeast trade wind, that brings them so swiftly from the Persian Gulf and the Red Sea each January and shifts southeast to blow them home again in April. In the true spirit of Arabic hospitality, the *nahodas* or captains of these ships serve guests dates and nuts and thick, sweet Turkish coffee as they pass around the nargileh to smokers in the group. And the crews of these long boats, half naked in their Arabian Nights costumes, look every bit as dashing as they must have in the days of Sinbad.

FOR THE TRAVELER'S NOTEBOOK

Official Information

Before you go: East Africa Tourist Travel Association, 750 Third Ave., New York, N.Y.; Information Officer, EATTA, P.O. Box 2013, Nairobi, Kenya, East Africa.

In Nairobi: SAS Office, Ottoman Bank Bldg., Delamere Ave. and Hardinge St.; Visitors' Information Office, Hardinge St. near bus station; U.S. Consulate General, Cotts House, Eliot St.

Money Matters

Currency: The monetary unit is the shilling (s.), divided into 100 cents. One shilling equals about 14 cents, U.S.

Tipping: Some hotels charge for service, and it is customary to add a tip for personal service rendered. Guests leave a shilling for the room boy for an overnight stay, five shillings for a week. For waiters a tip of 10 per cent is considered reasonable. During a safari you are expected to tip generously.

Climate, Clothing and Essentials

Since Nairobi is near the equator there is no real distinction between summer and winter. Long rains occur from March to May and short rains from the end of October to mid-December. The warmest period is January and February, with hot, dry winds. The coolest period is July and August. The temperature, however, is never unbearable—rarely above 80 degrees F. at midday and usually about 50 in the early morning. The ideal wardrobe is cotton, linen, or light tweed suits or dresses to which one can add warm jackets or wraps. Anyone planning a safari will be given details on clothing by the agent handling the tour, although you can be completely equipped on arrival.

Sunglasses are essential. Drinking water should be boiled, bottled, or treated with purification tablets.

Hotels

Good hotels are available in and around Nairobi but advance reservations are necessary. Daily all-inclusive rates vary from 35 to 65 s. a person, and only a few hotels quote bed-and-breakfast rates.

The most famous and conveniently located hotel is the *New Stanley, Hardinge St.,* which has an ultramodern wing, a bar, and a sidewalk café. Rates range from 60 s. single to 120 double, with bar. The *Norfolk, Government Rd. (P.O. Box 64),* is a little way out, has rooms and cottages, a swimming pool, and a cabaret. Rates are similar to the New Stanley. Two good tourist-class hotels are the *Hotel Ambassadeur, Government Road,* and the *New Avenue, Delamare Ave. and Sadler St.* Both offer comfortable accommodations and good service for from 45 s., single to 95 double, with bath.

Food and Restaurants

There are a number of restaurants serving European or Far Eastern food. For international menus try the *Stanley Grill,* the *Lobster Pot,* the *Topaz Grill* (in the *New Avenue Hotel*), and the *Rendezvous. Lavarini's* features Italian dishes, the *Pagoda,* Chinese, and *Chez Joseph,* French. *La Taverna* is a very good grill.

Entertainment and Night Life

A relatively young city, Nairobi has not yet an abundance of varied entertainment. For the most part, entertaining is done at home or in clubs. Some of the clubs welcome overseas visitors; ask about temporary membership at the Visitors' Information Bureau. The Donovan Maule Theater Club is famous and good; temporary membership can be arranged in Nairobi. The Kenya National Theater offers high-quality amateur and professional shows. There are several night clubs, the most popular of which is the *Equator Club.*

Special Note on Safaris

This is the center of big game, and whether you "shoot" with gun or camera, you probably will want to go on safari to see the endless variety of animals which is Kenya's greatest wonder. Safaris can be arranged in Nairobi, but it is advisable to book in advance through your local travel agent as you engage a hotel. A number of safari operators organize regular tours to suit all budgets, no matter how small. You may expect to live most comfortably on safari, and you can rent guns instead of carrying your own. For full particulars write the East Africa Tourist Travel Association (addresses under *Official Information*). Camera fans will find a telephoto lens most useful, and it is a good idea to have one roll of film developed here to test exposures in the bright sun.

Shopping

The best shops are conveniently located in the center of town. The Kamba wood carvers make very attractive polished figurines, and Kisii sellers will offer you beautiful soapstone vases, native drums, and animal skins. All the necessities of everyday life are available also. For typical native articles visit the *African Curio Shop, Mackay's, Rowland Ward,* the *Zanzibar Curio Shop, Madame Louise,* and *City Furrier.*

Background Reading

Out of Africa, and *Shadows on the Grass,* by Isak Dinesen
The Nylon Safari, by Rehna Cloete
The Green Hills of Africa, by Ernest Hemingway
Safari, by Martin Johnson
The Flame Trees of Thika, by Elspeth Huxley
The Snows of Kilimanjaro, by Ernest Hemingway

AUSTRALIA

Australia

SYDNEY

Down under, as far as you can go

AUSTRALIA'S first city is a harbor town, and the sea is everywhere, with Pacific inlets cutting patchwork patterns of parks and skyscrapers, stitched together by a network of causeways and bridges. It's a place of briny sea breezes and dancing blue-green reflections of light on water, a place of quays and bays, coves and headlands, and a harbor coastline that snakes through the city for almost two hundred miles. Twenty minutes from the steel-and-glass office buildings of Martin Place and the smart cafés and shops of King's Cross are more than two dozen golden sand beaches like Manly, Dee Why, Curl Curl, Narrabeen, Bondi, and Coogee. During the week the city's harbor bustles with tugs and lighters, freighters and passenger liners, but on weekends it reflects only the spanking white sails of pleasure boats that glide peacefully under the Sydney landmark, the silvery arc that is the Harbour Bridge.

Though the people who live here are ambitious and industrious and apply themselves to the affairs of commerce the week long, their hearts are really in the great outdoors, and on weekends the city seems deserted as its inhabitants take off for the yacht basins and beaches, race tracks and golf courses, cricket fields and football grounds that rim Sydney's eastern edge.

All of this is not to imply that the city is without its cultural side, and it is *almost* as proud of its symphony orchestra and university, its Conservatorium of Music and public library, its theater and ballet companies, the Australian Museum, the New South Wales Art Gallery, and the Applied Arts Museum as it is of its playing fields and parks.

While this is Australia's oldest city, it is primarily a modern one, and it keeps its history confined to the area around the huge park, the Domain, and the Sydney Cove, the site of the first English settlement in Australia. Here, narrow terraced streets lead up from the quay and one can see the gracious old mansions with luxurious lawns and private swimming pools, in elegant contrast to the brilliantly painted, boxlike houses of the earliest pioneers at nearby Wolloomoolo.

Sydney with its 2.5 million people is the largest city in Australia, and the fourth largest in the British Commonwealth, preceded only by London, Calcutta, and Bombay. It is the capital of New South Wales, but not of Australia. Canberra, in the same state, was created for that express purpose in 1913 and it is from here that the 11 million people living in the six federated states are governed: Queensland, New South Wales, Victoria, South Australia, Western Australia, the island-state of Tasmania, and the Northern Territory.

Though Australia is farther away from the United States than any other place on earth, it would be hard to find a country in which Americans would feel more at home. For the Australians seem almost like super-archetype Americans: gay, robust, boisterous, beef-eating, guileless, and good-humored, bubbling with optimism and good will, with an athletic sun-bronzed *brio* that smacks of Texas and the pioneering West. Indeed, this continent is one of wide open spaces and Australia's Wild West was opened up in much the same manner as our own. Cattlemen and sheepmen pushed hard across the Blue Mountain barrier behind Sydney to the grazing lands beyond and squatted there to stake their claims, start their ranches, and farm a soil so fertile it was said that if you merely tickled it with a hoe, it would laugh with a harvest. And anyone who fought alongside the Anzacs in World War II can tell you of their fierce bravery and fighting prowess. The discovery of gold in Australia, a few years after our California rush, tripled the population within thirty years and gave the country a boom-town glow that still remains.

The very size and shape of the continent matches the contours of the United States turned upside down, and the seasons, being the reverse of ours, add to that effect. Australians have an innate sense of democracy even more deeply rooted and widespread than our own, attributable to the common beginnings shared by the earliest settlers, convicts all, declared freedmen if they settled this wilderness and developed it for the Crown. And so the land was peopled by murderers, thieves, debtors, and prostitutes. Seven hundred of them came with the First Fleet under Captain Arthur Phillip in 1788, just twenty years after the land was charted for Britain by Captain James Cook, who had been assigned the task of finding what was then called *terra australis incognita,* the unknown southern land. The Dutch, under Captain Tasman, had visited the land a hundred years before, but after exploring the area now called Tasmania, Tasman decided that the continent, with its naked aborigines, would be of little value to the Dutch East India Company, in whose service he sailed, and so the land he named "New Holland" became a British colony.

Because of its geographical detachment Australia has become a repository for a number of species of wildlife long since extinct in other areas of the world. The famous marsupials, the leaping kangaroos which carry their young in their pouches, and those cuddly teddy bears, the koalas, which are only half-an-inch long at birth, and even earlier species like the duck-billed platypus and the ant-eater abound here.

The whole country is virtually an aviary of bizarre bird life, with such varieties as the kookaburra with its wild, demented laughter; the flightless cassowary; black swans; emus, second only to their ostrich cousins in size; mutton birds; one of the world's most beautiful warblers, the lyrebird; and the enchanting miniature fairy penguins whose twilight march down to the beaches of Phillip Island off Melbourne, is a favorite sight with Australians as well as major attraction for tourists.

Among its unique flora Australia boasts the two-hundred-foot-high king karri tree and almost seven hundred types of giant eucalyptus, gold blossoming wattle trees, bottle trees with trunks like Chianti casks, and the bizarre blackboy tree with its brush-on-brush silhouette.

And in this never-never country are the most primitive of the Abos, the aborigines who still exist in varying stages of evolution and are basically nomadic, having been pushed farther and farther inland by the encroachment of the Aussie whites. Some of the Abos live on reserves, and are free to pursue their tribal rituals and ceremonial customs. They are accorded full citizenship and a government organization functions in their behalf, the goal being complete education and assimilation into the white community.

MELBOURNE

The grande dame *of Australian cities*

MELBOURNE is the most European and gracious of the Australian cities. It is the mellow, charming, and dignified capital of Victoria and the financial center of the country. It is hard to believe that only 125 years have passed since the first pioneer settlers from Tasmania decided that this land on the Yarra River was the place they wanted for their home. Its climate is cooler than Sydney's, its pace more leisurely. The green-gold parks and tree-shaded bridle paths, the squares, statues, and handsome public buildings built with nineteenth century gold-rush profits, the fine European restaurants and the sidewalk cafés along Collins Street, and the great gray cathedrals lend it a distinctly continental cast.

It is here that the world-famous horse race is run for the Melbourne Cup, and each year in March the Moomba festival rivals a Philadelphia mummers' parade for color and gaiety. Within the city are a number of museums and galleries with works of the great European masters, the open-air Myer Music Bowl, and gardens, both botanical and zoological, while beyond the city are mountain ski resorts, the animal sanctuary of Healesville, and the koala colony on Phillip Island. There are spas and lakes and beach resorts and, loveliest of all, the woodlands of the Dandenoungs, just twenty miles east of the city. Here the lyrebird sings amid forests and fern gullies, the Abos make their famed boomerangs. Rhododendrons, azaleas, and violets grow wild along the bush walks and throughout the picturesque villages.

This boundless land with the golden climate is one of great beauty and contrast, as well as riches, and anyone who goes this far ought to see it all.

Tasmania, with its capital, Hobart, just an hour and a half away from Melbourne, is reminiscent of the Cotswold countryside, with apple orchards and flowered landscapes, fern forests and trout-filled lakes, misty plateaus and rugged rock hills, and everywhere are the Merino sheep, descendants of the earliest flocks which were this country's first wealth.

Adelaide, the capital of the grazing-land state of South Australia, is a city of gardens, and the flower beds provide veritable carpets of brilliantly colored blossoms, while Alice Springs, the tourist center of the outback desert land of the Northern Territory, is a frontier oasis with a rough excitement about it.

Perth, in Western Australia, is sunny and exuberant with a year round climate that reminds one of Indian summer. It is a leisurely town with a resort pace, as it sprawls lazily about the broad blue waters of the Swan River. In the southwestern part of this state you can see almost six thousand varieties of flowers that grow nowhere else on earth—among them the red and green kangaroo paws, as gay as Christmas, burning pink Geralton wax plants, royal purple Qualup bells, and fiery red bottlebrush.

Darwin reaches up toward Timor and the equatorial tropics, and here is the conglomerate of races that hints of Asia. Here you may hunt buffalo or crocodile, prospect for gold, or watch the adventurous pearl divers of Arafura at work.

For those who love the sea, from above or below, there are the resort islands of the Great Barrier Reef, along the Queensland coast, where one can swim or skin dive, fish or water ski, dive for pearls, pick wild orchids, or view the tropical fish and coral life from the secure comfort of a glass-bottomed boat.

And the Queensland capital, Brisbane, built up over seventy lavender-blue hills, midst a countryside of subtropical foliage, is worth a day or two of any traveler's time.

The rest of Queensland is range country, the place where the unofficial anthem "Waltzing Matilda" was written, the land of the Coolabah tree, the wandering swagman, and the riverbed pools, *billibongs*.

FOR THE TRAVELER'S NOTEBOOK

Official Information

Before you go: Australian National Travel Association: 636 Fifth Ave., New York, N.Y.; 153 Kearney St., San Francisco, Cal.

In Sydney: SAS Office, 13 Bridge St.; New South Wales Government Tourist Bureau, Challis House, 8 Martin Place; U.S. Consulate, 7 Wynyard St.

In Melbourne: SAS Office, 51 William St.; Victorian Government Tourist Bureau, 272 Collins St.; American Consulate, 7 Commercial Rd., South Yarra.

Money Matters

Currency: The monetary unit is the Australian pound (£) which is divided into 20 shillings, and further divided into 12 pennies per shilling. One pound is equal to a little more than $2, U.S.

Tipping: Tipping is optional following the general procedures of Europe and the U.S. In hotels it is customary to leave each of the staff a few shillings if your stay is longer than a day. Tip baggage porters a shilling or two, wine and food waiters in hotels 10 per cent of the bill.

Climate, Clothing, and Essentials

The seasons in Australia are the reverse of ours. Summer starts in December with an average temperature of 64 to 78 degrees F.; autumn starts in March; winter in June (47 to 62 degrees); spring in September. Climates vary greatly within the continent, but there are no great extremes. November through May is the ideal time to visit Australia.

Bring your lighter clothes and lots of casual attire for summer. Men will need a jacket and tie in most places for meals. Winter in southern Australia is cool, but there's still plenty of sun. Bring medium-weight woolens and a raincoat or topcoat.

Hotels

The Australian National Travel Association publishes a guide to government-rated hotels and motels throughout the country. All facilities and prices are included in this listing. Rates quoted by hotels here generally cover room and breakfasts. Reservations are necessary the year round.

De luxe hotels charge from about $11, for a single room with bath, and from $21, double; first class hotel rates start at $11, single with bath, and at $18, double. There are a number of good moderate-priced hotels in the city too, where less expensive accommodations may be had from $4, single or double without private bath, $5 to $6 with bath.

SYDNEY

DE LUXE: *Chevron-Hilton Sydney, Macleay St., Pott's Point.* The newest hotel in the city, this place is the height of luxury, has a harbor view, and is close to the city center. *Australia, 41 Castlereagh St.* This first class hotel is all air-conditioned, set in the center of the city with complete facilities. The *Menzies Hotel, Carrington St.*, is in the heart of the city, overlooks a park, and has the attractive Jungle Bar.

FIRST CLASS: *Carlton-Rex, 56 Castlereagh St.* Close to the theater and shopping district, this hotel offers just about anything you can think of to keep a traveler comfortable. *Rex, 58 Macleay St.*, is modern and located just two miles from the city center in King's Cross. It has complete facilities and offers rooms with or without bath.

MODERATE: *The Hampton Court, 9 Bayswater Rd., King's Cross; The Metropole, 8 Bent St.* and the *Wentworth, 13 Lang St.*, are three good moderate-priced hotels, all with complete facilities and convenient locations, while the *Belvedere, 81 Bayswater Rd., King's Cross,* and the even less expensive *Canberra-Oriental Temperance Hotel* are comfortable, the first with lovely gardens and good Swiss food, the second with a roof-garden view of the harbor.

Outside of Sydney, at Bondi Beach, the *Astra, 34 Campbell Parade,* and the *Bondi, Curlewis St. and Campbell Parade,* are moderately priced; both overlook the surf, and are close to golf and tennis courts as well as swimming and boating facilities.

MELBOURNE

DE LUXE: Intercontinental's *Southern Cross, 131 Exhibition St.*, is the newest hotel and modern to the last inch, with all conveniences. *Chevron-Hilton, 519 St. Kilda Rd.*, is another top hotel, with a beer garden and barbecue patio, a cabaret and all comforts, and is a ten-minute drive from the city center.

FIRST CLASS: The *Australia, 266 Collins St., Hosies, 1 Elizabeth St.,* the *Menzies, 509 Bourke St.*, the *Savoy Plaza, 122 Spencer St.*, and the *Windsor, Spring St.*, are all comfortable and more than adequate.

MODERATE: The *New Oriental, 41 Collins St.*, and the *Federal, 547 Collins St.*, and *Victoria Temperance Hotel, 215 Little Collins St.*, are good buys for those on limited budgets.

Food and Restaurants

Because it is such a large and fertile country, Australia has a great variety of superb products, prepared, by and large, in the simplest ways possible. Cooking and dining habits follow the English pattern for the most part, though there are many continental and Oriental restaurants in the major cities as well. Tea is the main beverage and Australian beer and lamb rank with the world's best. Steaks are great favorites and the seafood is superb, especially the lobster tails, the huge oysters, and the shrimp. Fruits are incredibly oversized and delectable, with such varieties as pineapples, oranges, grapefruits, loganberry, pawpaw, and a whole cornucopia of others. Australian beer is powerful, and wines are good and consumed in great quantities with and between meals.

SYDNEY

The *Chelsea,* an attractive sort of English inn, is an excellent and expensive restaurant in King's Cross, and just a few minutes from here are *Prunier's* and *Prunier After Nine,* both excellent. The *Caprice* and the *Rhinecastle Bistro* offer fine food and wine and pleasant surroundings, while *Prince's* has well-prepared food and is a night club as well, very popular with the city's smart set. *Romano's* also features good continental food while the *Sukiyaki Room,* the *Copenhagen,* and the *Nanking* serve Japanese, Scandinavian, and Chinese food in that order. *Cahill's,* a chain of cafés with seven branches in Sydney, are perfect for light lunches and snacks, and, of course, every major hotel has formal dining rooms with a wide variety of cuisines as well as informal coffee shops.

MELBOURNE

Caper's and *Molina's* are two of the best restaurants in Melbourne for continental food, while Italian food is excellent at *Florentino's* and French-Italian fare is good at *Mario's.* Some other foreign restaurants in the city and surrounding suburbs are *Chung Wahm,* the *Ceylon,* and *Tientsin.* The *Oxford Hotel* is also good for European food; and among the more moderately priced restaurants in the city *Droussous,* the *Bistro,* and the *Balzac* are most pleasant. All of the hotels have dining rooms, of course, and have dance music as well at night.

Entertainment, Night Life, and Special Events

Both Sydney and Melbourne abound in movie theaters showing European and American films and since theater-going is a popular pastime, there are several in each city featuring foreign and local dramatic groups. In Sydney, the Empire, the Elizabeth, and the Royal stage dramas as well as musicals, operas, and ballets; in Melbourne, Her Majesty's Theater, the Comedy, the Princess, and the Tivoli do the same. Sydney is famous for its symphony orchestra and the Town Hall is the scene of its concerts. This same orchestra visits Melbourne regularly, as do musical groups from all over the world, and in summer outdoor concerts are held at the Myer Music Bowl, just outside the city.

Many of the restaurants and hotel dining rooms also have floor shows and dance music and the local papers or the hotel porters will be able to guide you to those. In addition, *Chequers, Andres, Princes,* and *Latin Quarter* are smart Sydney clubs. In Melbourne, the *Embers, Tarantella,* and *Troika* are all worth a visit if you like night clubs.

In October the streets of Sydney are aglow with the crimson blossoms of the *Waratah Spring Festival.* Melbourne's classic horse race in November for the *Melbourne Cup* is one of the greatest in the world and all Victoria claims it as a public holiday. You can see a cross section of Australia's rural wealth at the Sydney *Royal Easter Show* in April, with competitions, sporting events, sheep dog trials, and the daily grand parade of champion animals. *December 26* is the start of the 640-mile ocean-going yacht race from Sydney to Hobart. The *Moomba Festival,* Melbourne's colorful carnival in March, features pageants, concerts, fairs, art shows, regattas, fireworks, parades, and dancing in the streets. *Moomba* is an aborigine word meaning "Let's have fun."

Shopping

Woolen blankets and textiles, sheepskin rugs, and articles made of alligator and crocodile are among the best buys in Australia. The opals here are world-famous and you will also find some interesting handcrafts produced by the various tribes throughout the country.

In Sydney, *Farmer's, Grace Brothers,* and *David Jones* are among the best department stores, and the *House of Proud's* specializes in fine opals. There are a number of curio shops around the *Martin Place Arcade,* and for authentic aboriginal carvings visit the *Church Missionary Society Bookshop.* Everything made of koala can be found at the *Koala Bear Shop* and *Fortune's Koala Center.*

In Melbourne, the *Myer Emporium* is the largest department store, while *George's, Buckley & Nunn,* and *Foy's* are definitely among the others worth visiting. Curio shops are all around the arcade of Collins and Elizabeth Streets and one of the most interesting of these is the *Arts and Crafts Society of Victoria.*

Background Reading

Cobbers, by Thomas Wood
The Australian Legend, by Russel Ward
The Australian Way of Life, by George Caeger
The Generation of Men, by Judith Wright
Rum Jungle, by Alan Moorehead
Stranger in Gallah, by Michael Barrett
Australian Stories of Today, edited by Charles Osborne

LATIN AMERICA

Argentina

BUENOS AIRES

The Good Winds

WHETHER the Argentine capital reminds you of New York, Paris, Naples, or a Spanish colonial holdover depends on the part of the city you're in. Viewing the skyscraper skyline and the bustling street crowds, walking along the Times Square maze of neon that lights up the Avenida de Corrientes after dark, it's easy to imagine you're in New York. But sip an apéritif at an awninged café, or shop in one of the smart boutiques along the Avenida Santa Fé or the Calle Florida, and you'll wonder if you're not in Paris, especially if you indulge in the favorite Argentinian male pastime: watching some of the world's most fashionably dressed women passing by.

Then for contrast, spend an afternoon wandering around the old Bohemian section, the Boca, near the city's wharves. Here, houses are painted in a wild array of carnival colors, and rich tenor voices singing nostalgically of Sorrento drift out of the little *trattorie* that are everywhere, for this is home to the Italian fishermen and their families (there are over two million Italian-born residents in the city), and you'll feel as though you've stepped into the middle of a stage set for a Neapolitan operetta.

And though "B.A.," as the residents call their city, has been com-

565

pletely redesigned to meet its enormous population growth and is now primarily modern in aspect, it still retains a few graceful vestiges of its colonial past. If you walk around the Plaza de Mayo, with its pink Casa Rosada or Government House, the cathedral which contains the mausoleum of San Martín, and most especially the historic Cabildo, the restored mission-style Town Hall, in front of which Argentinians gave voice to their first attempts at independence in 1810, or visit the San Telmo section where some of the oldest and handsomest Spanish buildings still stand, you will get an idea of what the city was like in the days of the conquistadors.

Inevitably, and happily, you know you are in Buenos Aires, and it is a city to be valued for itself, not merely for its resemblance to other places or other times. The city with its surrounding districts includes almost one-third of the country's population, some 6,500,000 people, to make this the world's seventh city, the largest in South America, and the largest Spanish-speaking city in the world. Argentina's population is primarily Catholic. Its citizens are of Italian and Spanish stock with some middle European elements woven in. In the towns of the Andean foothills there are mixed-breed mestizos, descendants of the Indians and early settlers, but the country's population is primarily of the white race. The *porteños* (literally, people of the port) claim for Buenos Aires the distinctions of being the largest beef-eating city in the world, with the largest opera house, the flamboyantly baroque Teatro Colón with seats for almost four thousand people, and the world's widest avenue, the tree-lined Avenida 9 de Julio, with the towering obelisk built in 1936 to commemorate the city's four hundredth birthday.

Buenos Aires was officially founded by Pedro de Mendoza in 1536, ten years after Sebastian Cabot had established a fort at Sancti Spiritu on the Paraná River and twenty years after Solis had sailed along the coast of Uruguay and traveled up the fresh-water "sea" he found, only to be massacred by Indians.

The city was originally named Puerto de Nuestra Señora del Buenos Aires (Port of Our Lady of the Good Winds) for the patron saint of the sailors. They believed it was she who provided the gentle breezes that blew the Spanish galleons into the waters they called the Rio della Plata.

Hostile Indians forced the abandonment of the city shortly after its founding, but it was resettled in 1580 by Don Juan de Garay with

10 Spaniards and 50 Criollos, who brought with them 1,000 horses and 50 head of cattle. These became the nucleus of the vast herds that now graze on the southern pampas. But there were older and more prosperous cities in Argentina even as early as this, because Spain had colonized the land, not only from the east by water but from the west through Chile and Peru.

Among the country's most fascinating sights are Santiago del Estero; Argentina's most ancient city, Tucumán; Salta (still a treasury of colonial architecture); La Rioja; Jujuy, with its hot springs known to the Incas, and its lovely old Spanish buildings; and Mendoza, the center of the wine country and the place from which San Martín set out across the Andes to liberate Chile.

In addition to being a late arrival, Buenos Aires also suffered from the Spanish trade policies, which dictated that all goods sent into or out of the city must filter through Lima, via the hazardous Andean passes, thus inhibiting the export of the city's hides and tallow and making its European imports impossibly expensive, so that smuggling became the number one occupation. And so for 270 years Buenos Aires languished as an almost forgotten military outpost in an empire that focused on Lima; but by the early eighteenth century discontent was rampant in the city and the Crown could no longer ignore it. Between 1720 and 1780 trade laws were gradually liberalized until ships called directly at the port of Buenos Aires. About the same time, the Spaniards decided to build up the city in opposition to its traditional enemy Portugal, now well established across the estuary in Colonia, Brazil. In 1776 a new viceroyalty was created, made up of what is now Uruguay, Paraguay, Bolivia, and Argentina, freeing this area from Peru.

After repelling the British, who attacked Buenos Aires in 1806 and 1807 in retaliation for the Spanish surrender to Napoleon, the *porteños* began to feel their strength and become impatient to be entirely free of Spanish rule. In 1810 they deposed the viceroy who ruled for King Ferdinand VII, then the captive of the French, and six years later declared their independence, led by their greatest national hero, José de San Martín.

Since that time, Argentina's politics have been anything but tranquil. There has been a long stretch of military governments in opposition to the representatives of the *caudillos,* the owners of the huge ranch estancias, backed by the gauchos who work for them. The overthrow of the Perón government in 1955 was merely another chapter in the long story of revolutions, dictatorships, and military coups. Argentina's constitution dates from 1853 and its first four presidents, Mitre, Sarmiento, Avellanda, and Roca, were responsible for its amazing growth and prosperity.

With all of its style and sophistication, Buenos Aires still has about it the air of a frontier boom town and is reminiscent of such Texas phenomena as Houston and Dallas, cities where the ranch owners come to enjoy life, ride around in their slick black limousines, and spend money at the local branches of the most exclusive jewelers and de luxe art galleries in the world. And when they are tired of buying what's for sale in Buenos Aires, they fly to the other great shopping cities: Paris, London, and New York, and begin all over again. Meanwhile, back at the *estancia,* the gauchos tend the herd. Somewhat like our own cowboys, with much the same daring and bravado about them, the Argentinian cowherd is noted for his songs, dances, and riding prowess. He dresses far more dramatically—in poncho and black hat, his swashbuckling wide pants bloused into low boots.

This cosmopolitan city has a full roster of night clubs and smoky and enticing *boîtes,* elegant French restaurants and European operas; but the big event of the year is the livestock show held each August in Palermo Park. Buenos Aires includes among its spectator sports auto racing and polo, soccer and horse races, but its heart really belongs to *pato,* a murderous game played on horseback, originated by the gauchos and combining the more deadly features of polo and basketball. It was only recently made legal.

Further attractions for sightseers include the colonial church of the Jesuits, San Ignacio, in the picturesque San Telmo district, the Church of La Merced, with its archives dating back to 1610, and the Convent of Santo Domingo, where the British holed up before their surrender. There is a museum for every taste too: most notably the National Museum, with its old masters and early New World paintings; the Historical Museum; and the Boca Museum, to name only three out of a possible nine. Shopping and café sitting are among the city's pleasantest activities but you might bestir yourself long enough to take an hour's journey to Tigre-delta where you can row, fish, and go yachting, or visit La Plata, with its university. The Gothic cathedral of Lujan and its Town Hall museum are worth a day of anyone's time, and a week at the fashionable seaside resort of Mar del Plata, 250 miles from Buenos Aires would rejuvenate even the most footsore traveler.

There are exciting natural wonders, too, within the country's 1,072,745 square miles. You can visit the Iguazú Falls on the Argentina-Brazil border, ski on the Andean slopes, explore the lovely lake country of Bariloche in the south, or travel still further south in Patagonia to Tierra del Fuego and see the great fjords, as icy blue as those in Norway, tipped off the glaciers of Antarctica in Ushuaia, the southernmost town in the world.

FOR THE TRAVELER'S NOTEBOOK

Official Information

Before you go: Argentine Embassy, 1600 New Hampshire Ave., N.W., Washington, D.C.; Argentina Consulate Generals: 12 West 56th St., New York, N.Y.; 105 West Adams St., Chicago, Ill.; 870 Market St., Flood Bldg., San Francisco, Cal.

In Buenos Aires: SAS Office, 728 Av. Pte. Roque Saenz Peña; Tourist Information Office, 578 Rivadavia; American Embassy, 567 Av. Pte Roque Saenz Peña.

Money Matters

Currency: The monetary unit is the peso ($), which is divided into 100 centavos. The rate of exchange fluctuates and at the time of this writing was 135 pesos to $1, U.S.

Tipping: A service charge of 10 to 24 per cent is added to hotel and restaurant bills; it is customary to leave an additional 10 per cent. Chambermaids get a few pesos per day when you leave. Taxi drivers get 10 per cent of the metered fare and a little more on short hauls. Station porters, theater ushers, and hotel doormen get about 10 pesos.

Climate, Clothing, and Essentials

Buenos Aires is south of the equator, and the seasons are the reverse of those in the United States or Europe. Spring (September–December) is a wonderful time for a visit, as is autumn (April–June). The average temperatures are in the low sixties at these seasons. Summer starts in December and ends in March; the average temperature then is in the mid-seventies with occasional heavy but short rains. June to the end of August is winter (average temperature about 50 degrees F.)—no snow, no frost, but it may at times be quite chilly. Dress comfortably, but remember that the *porteños* (residents of Buenos Aires) are conservative.

Bring enough camera film for your stay.

Hotels

De luxe hotel rates start at about 900 pesos, single, 1,200, double. Moderate first class hotels charge 600 to 850 pesos, single, 900 to 1,300, double.

DE LUXE: The *Plaza, Av. Florida and Charcas,* is a leading hotel, well located, with a good restaurant and high standards of service. The *Alvear Palace, 1891 Av. Alvear,* is large and elegant and has a new wing and a restaurant noted for its French food.

FIRST CLASS: The *Continental, 725 Av. Pte Roque Saenz Peña,* close to the business district; the *Lancaster, 405 Córdoba,* just a few minutes from the shopping center; the *Claridge, 539 Tucumán;* the *California, 1038 Talcahuano;* and the *City Hotel, 160 Bolívar,* are all good. There are many less expensive hotels which your travel agent can book for you.

Food and Restaurants

The favorite dish in all of Argentina is steak. *Bife a caballo* (steak on horseback) is served with two fried eggs and potatoes, and *asado* is a thick cut of barbecued beef. The meat pie which you will see eaten with fingers instead of forks is called *empañada.* Other popular dishes are the *puchero,* a combination of meat and vegetables cooked in Spanish style, and Spanish *paella,* rice cooked with chicken and various seafoods. *Carbonada* is a stew with peaches, and *dulce de leche* is a favorite caramelized milk dessert. Continental food is widely available. Try one of the local wines with your dinner, such as San Felipe, Sautern, Trapiche, and Norton (white), or Fond de Cave and Bianchi Cabernett (red). There are many varieties of beer, most of them good. Maté, a native tea, is available everywhere and you should try it.

Buenos Aires has a host of restaurants, the smaller ones rather "French *bistro*" in atmosphere. Generally, restaurants are open from noon to 3 P.M. and from 8 P.M. to 1 A.M., but some stay open all night. Ten is the height of the dinner hour, and dining spots are likely to be deserted earlier in the evening.

In addition to the dining rooms of the leading hotels you will find excellent continental and Argentinian food at rustic, picturesque *La Cabaña. La Estancia,* a huge ranch outside the city, has an outdoor barbecue, and the *Shorthorn Grill* also features barbecued specialties in the heart of town, while *La Tranquera* on the city outskirts has a fantastic mixed grill served with crisp, pickled vegetables. *La Emiliana* is popular and somewhat old-world, with high ceilings, marble pillars, and Italian-Argentine food and incredibly good grilled chicken. *La Rueda Criolla* has a fantastic revolving broiler and gaucho décor, while *Loprete* is a huge place also featuring the native cuisine. *Au Bec Fin* is a fine French restaurant frequented by diplomats and local V.I.P.'s, and *El Pescadito* is a wonderful spot specializing in fish and seafood at moderate prices. The *London Grill* offers excellent shrimp and curry dishes, and *El Caballito Blanco* is reminiscent of Vienna or Budapest, with its gypsy violinists. Tearoom-cafés offer light snacks and lunches. Among the most pleasant of these *confiterías* are the *Dover Coll, Queen Bess,* and *MacGregor.* The *Augustus* has some of the best pastries in Argentina.

Entertainment, Night Life, and Special Events

The Teatro Colón (opera house)—the pride of all Argentina—is said to be the largest in the world. The season is from May to October, with French and Italian works most frequently performed at the beginning of the season and German works toward the end. Throughout the year world-famous companies give performances at one or another of the many fine theaters in the city, and each year the French and Italian theaters give performances in their own languages. (Check at your hotel for what is playing where.) In summer there are many outdoor performances of opera, symphony, and ballet.

For night life, the typical places are the *Achalay Huasi* or *Mi Refugio* or *La Querenica,* with folk music and dancing. Gambling is strictly prohibited in the city, but authorized casinos are located at the summer resorts of Mar del Plata, Mendoza, Termas del Rio Hondo, Necochea, and Miramar.

You should see at least one game of *pato,* a sort of Argentine polobasketball combination, played since the Spaniards first arrived—a game so wild that it was for a time prohibited.

Shopping

The best shops are on or near the Calle Florida, which is closed to traffic from 11 A.M. to 11 P.M. to make life simple for pedestrians. The Avenida Santa Fé is another fine street for shoppers, and the beautiful window displays offer a remarkable choice of goods.

Leather work is excellent, especially those articles made of alligator, and women will delight in the exquisite hand-embroidered blouses and the large selection of antelope jackets and coats. Typical souvenirs are gaucho costumes, dolls, and silver ornaments, ponchos, rugs, vicuña and guanaco furs, matés and *bombillas* (silver tubes used for drinking maté). All these are good buys, as are recordings of native gaucho camp music.

The local branch of the English *Harrod's* and the nearby *Gath* and *Chavez* are the best department stores in the city.

Background Reading

These books provide excellent background on all the countries of South America:

The Conquistadores, by Jean Descola

The Rise of the Spanish American Empire, and *The Fall of the Spanish American Empire,* by Salvador de Madariga

This New World: The Civilization of Latin America, by William L. Schurz

Green Continent, edited by German Arciniegas

The following books apply primarily to Argentina:

River Plate Republics, by Betty De Sherbinin

Argentina, by George Pendle

Argentine Upheaval, by Arthur P. Whitaker

The Drunken Forest, by Gerald Durrell

Brazil

RIO DE JANEIRO

Where they put coffee in the coffee

Looking down from the peak of Rio's travel-poster landmark, Sugar Loaf Mountain, one sees what must be the world's most beautiful harbor: a wide turquoise lagoon almost completely landlocked, dotted with jade-green islands edged in pearl-white sands, and backed up by the 365 mountaintops that cast lavender shadows over the clear waters of Guanabara Bay. Across the bay from Sugar Loaf, the Corcovado Mountain, with its sun-washed statue of Christ the Redeemer, rises some two thousand feet into the glass-blue sky, and between the thickly forested Tijuca Mountains and the South Atlantic Harbor is the thin strip of city that is Rio, a gleaming white modern metropolis, lushly decked out with tropical parks and jeweled with intricately patterned mosaic sidewalks. And at dusk the view from Corcovado is as glittery as a Tiffany window, as the "diamond necklace" of lights along the city's coastline winks on in the blue twilight hour.

To the more than three million Cariocas (the residents of Rio), this is the *Cidade Maravilhosa* (the Marvelous City); to almost everyone everywhere, it is, more than any other great Latin-American city, synonymous with an irrepressible gaiety that is a far cry from its *fado*-singing Portuguese ancestry. Its very name is as evocative as the clack of castanets, bringing to mind an image of fiesta holidays,

573

Carmen Miranda rhythms and a samba beat, of sunny days and snowy beaches such as the famed Copacabana, and of the pre-Lenten carnival that is a three-day paroxysm of joy and abandon, making even the Fasching of Germany and the New Orleans Mardi gras look like children's birthday parties by comparison.

For the "fat" days preceding the six-week penance, the city throbs to the Latin beat of tom-toms, tambourines, and long, keglike *cuica* drums, as every Carioca in Rio dances on the gaudily decorated streets. Everyone is in costume, whether it be an elaborately designed satin ball gown, a sequin-studded bikini, or a paper costume that gradually tears away to reveal a bathing suit underneath. There are fancy-dress balls and a parade of elaborate floats and dancing all through the maze of confetti-covered streets; some of the more exuberant ranchos and masqueraders wind up in the local jail, the *xadrez,* and almost everyone winds up with an Ash Wednesday hangover from too much wine and *cachaça,* the local white rum distilled from sugar cane.

Rio is the leading city of South America's largest, and the world's fourth largest, country. Brazil encompasses almost half of the continent and more than half of the people on it, and includes the world's longest river, the Amazon. In the tropic jungles of Mato Grosso, the Iguazú Falls are 53 feet higher than our own Niagara. The country's boundaries stretch from just north of the equator through the Tropic of Capricorn, and within its 3,286,000 square miles are such diverse climates as the steaming rain forests (*hyleia*) of the Amazon basin, rich in Brazil-nut and rubber trees; the half-forest, half-desert savanna of the northeast uplands; and the mountains and plateaus of the central and southern areas. It is in these last that one find the enormous *fazendas,* the plantations that grow more than half of the world's exportable coffee, where bushes of red berries reach from horizon to horizon. Cotton, fruits, and livestock flourish here too, and more than 60 per cent of the country's 65 million people live in this cool, dry, and healthful climate.

This population is made up of many strains, for assimilation and amalgamation have been a way of life in Brazil since the first Portugese settlers under Governor Thomas de Souza established themselves in Bahia in 1549, almost fifty years after the land was discovered by Pedro Alvares Cabral. Today's mixed race, the *caboclos,* is made up of the aboriginal Indian stock, the new Iberian settlers, and later,

Negroes. The Portuguese gave Brazil its language, its basic racial type, and its Catholicism. Other European strains that figure strongly in the national makeup are the Spaniards, Italians, and Germans; and, since the war, the largest Japanese colony in the world has grown up in Brazil. With so much of its vast area uncultivated and undeveloped, and so much of its population concentrated within the cities, immigration is still being encouraged and is flourishing.

Brazil had to wait for Napoleon's conquest of Portugal to become a national kingdom. It was here that the regent Dom João sought refuge in 1808 and proclaimed the land "the United Kingdom of Portugal, Brazil, and Algaraves." He reigned there as the head of a somewhat corrupt government until he was recalled to Portugal in 1820. Two years later from Lisbon, he granted Brazil its sovereignty and acknowledged his son, Dom Pedro I, as its emperor.

Dom Pedro II, who succeeded his father, became the nation's first great ruler, developing its agricultural and educational programs, encouraging immigration, and establishing an efficient system of communication within the country. He also abolished slavery completely in 1888 after a number of liberalizing reforms, but this act earned him the contempt of the powerful plantation owners and he was forced to abdicate and flee in 1889. Since that time, Brazil has been a republic and its most famous president was perhaps Getulio Vargas, who committed suicide in 1954 after his re-election.

Rio de Janeiro, or the River of January, as it was named by the Portuguese sailors who first sighted in it January, 1502, was formally founded in 1566, but with Bahia as the nation's capital until 1763, its importance was minor. Rio became the capital in that year and remained so until 1960, when the futuramic, planned city of Brasília, in the middle of the frontier province of Goiás, assumed the role. This new city, the product of Brazil's two leading architects, Oscar Niemeyer and Lucio Costa, is a breathtakingly beautiful arrangement of lakes and fountains and handsomely sculptured buildings, and it is among the country's leading attractions for visitors. So are Brazil's other chief cities: São Paulo, the industrial center that is a miniature Chicago, with an active cultural life and a bustling cosmopolitan aspect; Belo Horizonte, Brazil's first planned city, in the middle of its beautiful Minas Gerais province; Recife in the state of Pernambuco, the dreamy, picturesque "Venice of Brazil" with a blue-green harbor and coral reefs, where one can see the leather-garbed native cowboys, the *vaqueiros,* and the vestiges of the French, English, and Dutch invaders who besieged the city at various times in its history; Santos, the island port just thirty-eight miles from São Paulo, with its fascinating coffee exchange; and, most of all, Salvador, the capital of Bahia, with its Macumba rituals and colorful African folklore life.

Petrópolis, the exclusive resort of the smart set of São Paulo and Rio, has one of the world's most magnificent hotels, the Quintandinha, decorated by Dorothy Draper, and offering every vacation lure imaginable. And within the city itself one should see the blazing crown jewels and the treasures of the palace of Dom Pedro II, who founded the city and named it after himself. Terezopólos is another popular summer resort a little farther away from Rio, and Paquetá, a brief ferry ride away, is a small island with an English colony and a lovely view of the Rio skyline from the wide white beaches that border the bay.

Rio sights are many and varied and if you can tear yourself away from the beauties of its beaches—the wide Copacabana, the little Urca, or the more exclusive tree-shaded Ipanema and Leblon, to name only a few—there are other wonders the city has to offer. Walking through its streets or riding its picturesque open-air trolleys, or its *lotação* (jitneys), one is struck by the contrasts within the city. There are the wide tree-lined boulevards such as the Avenida Rio Branco, where you find the National Library, the Palace of Justice, and the National Art School, with its impressive exhibitions of modern paintings; the winding mazes of the *favelas,* the shantytown slums which are being rapidly improved; the colorful alleys of the old town, with open front stalls and craft-work shops. You can travel to the peaks of Sugar Loaf or Corcovado, view the city and lunch at one of the excellent barbecue restaurants in the vicinity, or shop in elegant boutiques along the Rua Gonçalves Dias and walk to the end of the street to see the colorful flower market in progress.

You can visit one of the city's historic churches, such as the Lady of Gloria, built in 1671, the Convent of Santo Antonio, with its two chapels founded in 1619, or Our Lady of Candelaria, considered to be the most beautiful church in the city, or spend time in the Museum of Modern Art, the National Museum, or the Historical Museum. And at night you can choose between the city's glittering after-dark attractions or hear a concert in one of its great auditoriums, where soloists and conductors from overseas appear frequently and where the music of Brazil's great composers, Villa-Lobos and Guarnieri, gets special attention. And when you feel like relaxing, you can enjoy the city's magnificent parks—most especially the Botanical Garden, with its thousands of tropical specimens gathered from all over the world, or spend a day in the Tijuca forest with its cool, green, garden passes and cascading falls.

FOR THE TRAVELER'S NOTEBOOK

Official Information

Before you go: Brazilian Government Tourist Bureau, 551 Fifth Ave., New York, N.Y.; Brazilian Embassy, 3007 Whitehaven St., N.W., Washington, D.C.

In Rio: SAS Office, 277 Av. Rio Branco Leja 1 BD; Official Tourist Information, Departamento de Turismo da Prefeitura, 104 Rua Mexico; Government Tourist Bureau, 171 Av. Marechal Camara; U.S. Embassy, 147 Av. Presidente Wilson.

Money Matters

Currency: The monetary unit is the cruzeiro (Cr), which is divided into 100 centavos. The rate of exchange fluctuates wildly; at the time of writing 600–640 cruzeiros equaled $1, U.S.

Tipping: Hotels normally include a service charge of 10 per cent, but it is usual to tip another 10 per cent. Waiters get 10 to 15 per cent of the check and baggage porters get Cr 10 per bag and never less than Cr 20. Taxi drivers expect a tip of 10 to 15 per cent of metered fare.

Climate, Clothing, and Essentials

Rio has a tropical climate with seasons the reverse of the United States. In summer, December–March, temperatures range from 86 to 100 F., and often higher. The rest of the year Rio enjoys moderate temperatures equivalent to summer temperatures in northern Europe, rarely below 50 degrees. Through most of the year very light clothing is appropriate, but in winter a light woolen suit or dress will be useful. It is better to drink bottled water.

Hotels

Single rooms with bath in de luxe hotels range from Cr 1,400 to 2,200, doubles from Cr 2,000 to 3,000; first class, 900 to 1,800 for single room with bath, double rooms from 1,100 to 2,000. The most popular places to stay are the Copacabana seaside hotels, all of which are handsome, elegant, beautifully appointed, and with breathtaking views over the bay. As you might expect, they are all fairly expensive, though there are a few exceptions. Mention should be made, however, of the Ipanema district, where the *Hotel Ipanema, 3678 Av. Epitacio Pessoa,* near the Lagoa Rodrigo de Freitas, is recommended. The Flamengo district is even closer to the city center and has excellent hotels too, such as the fine, old-world, de luxe *Glória, 632 Rua Russel,* and the first class *Novo Mundo, 20 Praia do Flamengo.* If you prefer to stay in the center of the city, you will find comfortable accommodations at the efficient first class commercial hotels there, including the *Serrador, 14 Praça Getulio Vargas;* the *Guanabara Palace Hotel, 392 Av. Presidente Vargas,* and the *Ambassador, 25 Rua Senador Dantas.*

ON COPACABANA BEACH

DE LUXE: The *Excelsior Copacabana, 1800 Av. Atlantica,* is one of the newest and most elegant hotels on the beach, with its own night club and private beach and a pleasant dining room. Request a room facing the beach. The *Copacabana Palace, 1702 Av. Atlantica,* is one of the best hotels anywhere and has a private swimming pool, a night club, and everything you need for a comfortable stay. The *Miramar, 3668 Av. Atlantica,* near the end of the beach, is pleasant and a little less expensive than the *Excelsior.*

FIRST CLASS: The *Olinda, 2230 Av. Atlantica, Ouro Verde, 1456 Av. Atlantica,* and *California, 1470 Av. Atlantica,* are other hotels along the beach worth considering.

Food and Restaurants

Rio is very cosmopolitan and you can have the usual international dishes at all of the large hotels and better restaurants. It is more interesting, however, to try the superb native Creole dishes, like *feijoda,* a stew of black beans, rice, meat, and herbs; fish *vatapa,* a spicy fish and shrimp stew; *empadinhas da camarao,* a pastry turnover filled with minced shrimp, olives, and hearts of palm; and *camaroes à la Grecque,* shrimp grilled on skewers. Worth trying too is the mellow pumpkin soup, *sopa de abodara Amarella,* and the native hash, *picadinho.* You will also like *churrasco,* a tender piece of grilled *filet* served with *mandioca,* a flour made of cassava roots. The coffee is wonderful, generally served strong and sweet. Maté, a native tea, is a popular beverage that you should try.

One of the best soft drinks is made from the guarana berry. You will find local beer and wines excellent, and the native rum *cachaça,* sometimes called *agua ardente,* is an excellent cocktail mixer and the basis of such drinks as *batida, rabo de galo,* and *leite de camelo.* Imported drinks are available but expensive.

One of the most interesting restaurants in which to sample the cuisine of north Brazil is the *Cabeca Chata,* with its straw-matted walls, strolling musicians in leather hats, and waiters in jeans. Located on top of the Sears Roebuck Building, the *Camponeza Churrascaria* features grilled meats cooked over the charcoal broiler, and you will also find this specialty prepared beautifully at the *Parque Recreio* and the *Churrascaria Gaucha.* Bahian Creole specialties are excellent at *A Bahianinha,* and served on a patio overlooking the ocean. There is fine seafood done native style at the *Cabaca Grande* and *Rio Minho.* The *Dinabar,* which you enter through a patio of tropical plants, is a little out of the center of the city in Barra da Tijuca, and has a summer roof restaurant overlooking the water. Prices are reasonable, service is good. *Os Esquilos,* also in the Tijuca forest, has one of the prettiest locations near Rio, and *Cinelandia,* atop a local skyscraper, offers music and a lovely view of Guanabara Bay. *Bife de Oura* in the *Palace Hotel* is elegant, and a glass wall overlooks the sea. Other good restaurants featuring native food as well as continental dishes are *Mesbla, Colombo,* and *Abi.* *Al Pappagallo* and *Cantina Sorrento* offer Italian food. *Le Bec Fin* and *Au Bon Gourmet* are best for French (and some Brazilian) specialties. *Dana* has Russian food, *The Smiling Buddha* has Chinese food. There are a number of tearooms for light snacks and lunches in the downtown area, along the Copacabana, and in the Flamengo district.

Entertainment, Night Life, and Special Events

Rio is a gay city with pleasant entertainment during the day and in the evening. Gambling casinos are no longer in existence, and the enormous floor shows of former days have disappeared, so night life as a whole is less hectic than it used to be. There is tea dancing at the *Meia Noite* (Midnight Room) of the *Copacabana Palace Hotel,* at *Night and Day* in the *Hotel Serrador,* and at *Beguin* (*Hotel Gloria*). These also have dancing and floor shows in the evening. You can also go to the following restaurants and night clubs: *Sacha's, Bem, Fred's, Drink, Club 36, Ciro's, Jirau, Fafá Lemos,* and *Au Bon Gourmet.* If you are fond of music, go to the Municipal Theater where concerts with famous soloists and conductors from overseas are given by the National Symphony Orchestra between June and September. Excellent concerts may also be heard at the National School of Music.

On *September 7* a colorful dress parade marks the day in 1822 when Dom Pedro I declared Brazil independent of Portugal. *November 15* is Republic Day, which celebrates the proclamation of Brazil as a republic in 1889. The entire month of June seems to be a perpetual holiday with festivities almost every day. The carnival that takes place on the last three days before Lent is one of the gayest in the world, and everyone stops work to take part.

Shopping

Among the best buys in Brazil are aquamarines, amethysts, topazes, tourmalines, and other precious and semiprecious unset stones, leather goods—especially alligator—Portuguese silver, some antiques, handmade blouses, wood carvings, and French perfume. Most of the shops are in the city center and along the streets bordering Copacabana Beach. Among the best are *Casa Sloper* and *Magazine Mesbla,* the most popular department stores; *Casa Hugo, Charles, Tony Bill, Museo Indio,* and the *Portuguese Travel Agency* for tourist souvenirs; the *Casa Anglo-Americana* for antiques and silver; *Imperial Modas* for handmade blouses; and *H. Stern* and *Zitrin* for precious stones.

Background Reading

The Masters and the Slaves, and *The Mansions and the Shanties,* by Gilberto Freyre. Two magnificent and essential books for learning about Brazil's past and present and its future prospects.
Gabriella, Clove and Cinnamon, by Jorge Amado
Brazil, the Infinite Country, by William L. Schurz
Child of the Dark, by Carolina María de Jesus
New World in the Tropics, by Gilberto Freyre
Epitaph of a Small Winner, by Joaquim María Machado de Assis
Time and the Wind, by Erico Verissimo

Peru

LIMA

"The beautiful City of the Kings"

WILLIAM H. Prescott, in his classical nineteenth century account of the Incan civilization and its conquest, said, "Amidst the woe and destruction which Pizarro and his followers brought on the devoted land of the Incas, Lima, the beautiful City of the Kings, survives as the most glorious work of his creation, the fairest gem on the shores of the Pacific." And though the city's population of 1,215,000 is more than ten times what it was when Prescott wrote, and earthquakes and soaring skyscrapers have altered its antique appearance somewhat, Lima still has more old-world elegance and formality than any other city on the South American continent.

Here, amid the snow-capped peaks of the Andes, which reach some of their loftiest heights in Peru, llamas as graceful as ballerinas pick their way along the slopes of the Sierras, tended by poncho-clad Indians. Incan descendants, who still hammer their silver and gold jewelry, weave their brilliant primitive textiles and speak Quechua, their ancient language, just as they did in the days before the conquistadors. Gardens and mountain paths flame with the hot pinks and oranges of geraniums and roses, the fiery purples of bougainvillaea and violets; and in the mountains eagles and condors swoop down over the lairs of mountain lions, vicuñas, and sloths. And fifty miles from the ancient Incan City of the Sun, Cuzco, with its winding cobblestoned streets and open markets, its old churches rich with silver and carved wood ornamentation, and its cool Moorish patios, lies the lost city of Machu Picchu.

This is the Angkor of South America, a buried city forgotten for untold centuries, perched on the Andean slopes overlooking the wild gorge of the Urubamba River, a city not discovered by the Spaniards

581

but unearthed in 1911 by Hiram Bingham and his archeological expedition from Yale. Remnants of stairways, temples, and palaces built of massive stones fitted together without mortar are evidence of the Incas' ability as masons; and it is still a source of wonder that they were able to get such huge stones to this mountain site without knowledge of the wheel. They did, however, have a highly developed planned economy, and a decimal system of counting based on knots tied in a length of string. They also established a common language amongst the various tribes of their lands, and ruled over all of Bolivia, northern Argentina, and most of Chile and Ecuador. Their arts were among the most sophisticated of all the pre-Columbian Indians.

Peru is now a country of ten million people, mostly Spanish Catholics and mixed-breed mestizos, and within its 500,000 square miles there are three climatic sections: the coastal deserts that edge the Pacific; the central Andean "backbone" of the country, which contains most of the nation's mineral wealth; and the rain forests and tropical greenery in the area of the Montaña River, with its rich banks that yield rubber, jute, rice, fruit, and coffee, and grass for the grazing of cattle. Lima, the capital, is set on a fertile plain midway between the Andean foothills and the Pacific, with its port city of Callao some twenty minutes away.

When the Spaniards first came to Peru in 1532 they made Cuzco their capital, but the piercing cold was anathema to men raised in the sunny Iberian climate and so Pizarro sent scouts in search of a warmer setting for their city. When they found Lima on January 6, 1535, Pizarro called it the City of the Kings, in honor of the day of the Epiphany, and on January 18, he named it the capital of the Spanish colonial empire. On the same day he set the cornerstones of the cathedral and the Palace of the Viceroys. He planned the city in a pattern of 117 geometrical blocks, naming a captain to oversee each sector. Lima was also the seat of the New World Inquisition, and parts of the main hall of the courts where "heretics" were tried are still intact.

This city on the Rimac River (the city's name is a Spanish mispronunciation of the place the Incas called Rimão) was the seat of the entire Spanish American empire, and it was a crossroads point for all the treasures of the continent, which were shipped on to Panamanian and West Indian ports, and finally to Spain. Peru gained independence from Spain in 1821 through the efforts of the great

South American liberators, San Martín and Bolívar. Today, Peru is a constitutional republic with a president elected by popular vote.

Though Peru's attractions are primarily its pre-Columbian relics, Lima's charm lies in its colonial grace. In the old section of the city "below the bridge," one walks around tree-lined plazas and broad avenues laid out in the regular block pattern that was a signature of the Spaniards in every New World city they colonized. Rose-pink mission churches and carved wooden shutters and balconies still persist around the city that used to pave its streets with silver to welcome new viceroys. Pride is perhaps the most obvious characteristic of Lima's people; pride and the fabled beauty of its women. Their charms were famous even in Charles Darwin's day, when they wore the provocative *saya y manto,* a form-fitting pleated dress and a black silk head shawl that covered all of the face except one eye, a revealing and enticing costume that caused Darwin to tell of the "nicely rounded mermaids" he met, whom he considered "worth more attention than Lima's churches and buildings."

Lima's women are still worth the attention of almost any man, but so are its churches and buildings. The Government Palace on the original site of Pizarro's fortress, the Archbishop's Palace, and the cathedral where Pizarro's remains lie in a glass casket, are all centered on the city's main square, the Plaza de Armas. Near this plaza are four of the handsomest churches in Peru: La Merced, where the first mass in Peru was said; the Church of Santo Domingo, built in 1549 and containing the remains of the New World's first saint, Rose of Lima; San Francisco, noted for its paintings and carved ceilings; and San Pedro, with its impressive altar completed in 1638.

One of the most interesting architectural sights is the Torre-Tagle Palace, built in 1735 in the style of Seville with a lovely courtyard and lacy iron work. On the Plaza de la Inquisición one can see the fantastic carved mahogany ceiling that remains intact from the original Court of the Inquisition, and is now part of a building used for military councils. Lima's eighteenth century bull ring was the first in the Americas and is still in use, and the Quinta de Presa, the summer palace of the Viceroy Amat, which is said to have been built for his mistress, La Perrichole, who inspired Thornton Wilder's *Bridge of San Luis Rey,* is a favorite sight of the city.

There are a number of beautiful parks in Lima, none more so than the Parque de la Reserva, designed to represent Peru's three climatic sections. And no one should miss a day's drive through some of the elegant outlying suburbs such as San Isidro, the seaside Miraflores, the chic resort Chorillos, and Barranco, with its swimming pool and zoological gardens.

The Indian market at Huancayo, a few miles from Lima, is a "must" on a Sunday morning when the native dances and fiestas are in progress, and Pachacamac, twelve miles out of the capital, has the fascinating ruins of the Incan Temple of Fertility, built of sun-baked bricks in 1350—all a far cry from the fashionable, present-day world exemplified in the smart shops, hotels, and restaurants that border on Lima's Plaza San Martín, the center of the city's and the country's modern life.

FOR THE TRAVELER'S NOTEBOOK

Official Information

Before you go: Peruvian Embassy, 1320 16th St., N.W., Washington, D.C.; Consulate General of Peru, 10 Rockefeller Plaza, New York, N.Y.

In Lima: Guest Airway, 370 Camana; U.S. Embassy, Edificio Sud America, 117 Plaza San Martín.

Money Matters

Currency: The monetary unit is the sol (plural soles), divided into 100 centavos. There are about 20 to 25 soles to $1, U.S.

Tipping: A 16½ per cent service charge is added to hotel bills and an additional 10 per cent is generally left. In restaurants leave 10 to 15 per cent unless a service charge has been included. Taxi drivers are not tipped.

Climate, Clothing, and Essentials

Lima's climate is mild, with average temperatures from 65 to 75 degrees F. It is pleasant at almost any time of the year, though December through April is the most perfect period of all, while from May to November the days are misty and cool. Normal city summer attire is correct, and slacks and shorts are frowned on for women.

Hotels

There are several good hotels, as well as many pensions and boarding houses in Lima. Reservations are necessary from December through April. De luxe hotels charge from 200 soles for a single room with bath, from 300 for a double. A number of moderately priced hotels charge from 125, single, and 200, double. Pensions range in price from 375 to 625 soles per person per week.

DE LUXE: The leading hotel and the meeting place for local society is the *Gran Hotel Bolívar, Plaza San Martín,* with a good restaurant, night club, and central location. Slightly less expensive, the *Hotel Crillon, 589 Av. Nicolas Pierola,* has comfortable air-conditioned rooms that are well maintained. You will also find here a grill, a Scandinavian smorgasbord, and a Turkish bath.

MODERATE AND INEXPENSIVE: The *Hotel Savoy, 224 Cailloma,* is one of the newest and largest in the city, and the *Gran Hotel Maury, 201 Ucayali,* though recently remodeled, is still gracious and slightly old world. Smaller but adequate is the *Alcazar, 564 Camana.* The *Lima Country Club, Av. Golf, San Isidro,* is one of the country's best, located about five miles from the city. It has excellent facilities for tennis, swimming, and golf and is close to the airport and the race track. Three pensions in Lima worth considering are the *Morris,* the *Brandon,* and *Suiza;* and the *Astoria Noetzli, San Isidro,* is comfortable and inexpensive.

Food and Restaurants

Peru has about the most original and interesting cuisine of South America. Among its specialties you should certainly try *seviche,* bits of raw fish marinated in lime juice with onions and peppers; *arroz con pato,* duckling cooked with rice, tomatoes, peas, and brandy; *picante de camarones,* shrimp in a pink sauce with garlic flavor; *anticuchos,* bits of beef heart on skewers; and *chupe de camarones,* a sort of soup-stew of seafood and vegetables. Chili pepper (*ají*) is used in many dishes. Fish roe, sea bass (*corvina*), avocados, and other fruits are delicious. There are dozens of varieties of corn. *Chicha morada,* made from a purple corn, is a pleasant, cooling soft drink. *Pisco,* the local white brandy made from grapes, is mixed in a number of refreshing drinks, notably the Pisco Sour. Local wines are good.

Hotels *Maury, Crillon,* and *Bolívar* have elegant continental dining rooms. The fashionable *Restaurant "91,"* atop a tall office building, offers a superb view and one of the largest and best T-bone steaks you will find anywhere. There's a good French menu at the dressy and expensive *Pavillon,* and *La Toscana* is fine and colorfully decorated. *Rosita Rios,* set in the highlands of Lima, serves excellent, authentic Peruvian food; reservations are essential. You can eat in an outdoor patio most of the year, and there is no menu. *Las Trece Monedas* offers native food adjusted to foreign palates in a beautiful old colonial house. You may sample more local specialties at *Karamanduka,* with lovely Peruvian décor and folk music. *El Cortijo* features Argentine grilled meats, barbecued in the dining room. One of the newest restaurants, *Canela Fina,* offers fine native food with music to match. A little way out of the city, *Granja Azul,* in a rustic country setting, is famous for its chicken, aromatically barbecued over *algarrobo* wood. You can get light snacks at one of the restaurants in the *Crem Rica* chain.

Entertainment, Night Life, and Special Events

Lima's nightclub circuit is limited to the *Bolívar* and *Continental* hotels, a few cabarets in the Plaza San Martín area (most notably the *Embassy*), and a fascinating native club, the *Fiesta,* a few minutes from the city, with good food and lots of local color. The National Symphony Orchestra plays summer concerts in the outdoor auditorium of the Campo de Marte, indoors in winter at the Teatro Municipal, while Spanish and Italian operas are frequently performed there as well. Interesting native dance exhibitions are held weekly. Bullfights are held in the Lima ring from October through March. Cockfights are frequent, though the schedule is not formal.

A colorful carnival is held for the two days preceding Lent. The folk festival at Amancaes near Lima is worth seeing if you happen to be there *June 24.* There is also an Inca festival at Cuzco in honor of the ancient sun god on the same day. The international fair in October is a samples fair. On *August 30,* Peruvians honor their patron saint, St. Rose of Lima.

Shopping

The main shopping area is off Plaza San Martín on Jirón Union. Sterling silver (marked *esterlina*) is one of the best buys; you can see it being made at the *Camusso* factory, where it can also be bought. Leather work, blankets, Indian pottery, costume dolls, gold jewelry, alpaca slippers, and rugs are also attractive, and you should take home at least one bottle of Pisco. If you can find any remnants of old Incan textiles, buy them and frame them as wall decorations; for these try the *Tourist Shop* and *Casa Mas.* The native central market along Jirón Ucayali is a colorful spot where bargaining is the main diversion.

Background Reading

The Bridge of San Luis Rey, by Thornton Wilder
Fire over the Andes, by Carleton Beals
Four Seasons of Manuela, by Victor W. Von Hagen
The Lost City of the Incas, by Hiram Bingham
The Conquest of Peru, by William H. Prescott

Mexico

MEXICO CITY

A piñata *full of surprises*

MEXICO City has come as a surprise to almost every foreign visitor since Cortés, who arrived in 1519 at what was then Tenochtitlán, the capital of Montezumas' Aztec empire. Certainly he could not have expected to find a city of a million inhabitants here when such great European cities as the London of Henry VIII had a population of less than a hundred thousand. How could he have known that people who had neither learned to use beasts of burden nor stumbled on the secret of the wheel could build a city of vast palaces and temples, plan zoological and botanical gardens, and amass a glittering wealth of silver and gold? How could he have dreamed, when he landed at the humid little gulf port he named Vera Cruz and began his march of conquest inland, that he would come to a city he would consider "the most beautiful on earth"—one he would "regret" having to destroy two years later?

Even today no one seems to expect quite the right thing from this city, for no matter what our travel-poster fantasies may include, they are bound to topple before the facts of the place. The first shock comes from the very air itself—the thin, rarefied result of the altitude, a soaring 7,434 feet, ringed by the extinct volcanic cones and rock-

587

peaks of the Sierra Nevada range. Here you find yourself suddenly, inexplicably, out of breath, your cigarette burns twice as long as it usually does, and one drink does the heady work of three back home. And then, as you walk around, you'll feel as though the whole city has a decided pitch and tilt, for, in addition to being perched up on such lofty heights, earthquakes and shifting lava beds have jostled things around a bit, so that a street inclines steeply when you least expect it to, and when you are not puffing your way uphill, you are braking your downhill speed.

When you finally manage to adjust your pace and literally catch your breath, you'll find the city has more surprises in store for you. This is true whether you expect to find it a place of sleepy, serape-wrapped Indians dozing under the shade of their sombreros, or a populace of garlic-chewing, renegade revolutionaries such as Zapata or Pancho Villa; a mecca for the black-limousine, international night-life set, or a place of pilgrimage for barefoot country peons who wander in to worship at the holy shrines; a home for expatriate artists or expatriate opportunists; a bargain paradise for remittance men or a stronghold of the colonial *hidalgo;* the city better typified by the darkly dignified beauty of Dolores del Rio or the maverick, clownish charm of Cantinflas. Whether you think you'll find a metropolis made up of steel and glass skyscrapers, or a living museum of Spanish co-lonial architecture where *churrigueresque* cathedrals stand as ornately baroque as giant sand castles; if you think the affluent live either in glass-enclosed, split-level splendor, or in sixteenth century haciendas gleaming with Mudejar tilework—whichever of these things you ex-pect, you are certain to be surprised. For in Mexico City the error lies in "either-or"; to be correct you must expect everything, all at once.

This sun-washed capital of fiesta land, with its five million popula-tion, is the world's tenth largest city and the oldest in North America. It is a place where you may shop in Parisian-style boutiques or dime stores, plastic-lined *supermercados* or overripe native markets burst-ing with tropical fruits and vegetables, brilliant with Indian basketry and rough-woven peasant cottons in Tamayo color schemes of rasp-berry and orange, purple and crimson, parrot green and turquoise.

You will hear traffic noises by day, but the rooster's crow at dawn, the pneumatic rat-tat-tat of the street drill and the soft slap-slap of the *tortilla*-maker, and always, at any time of day, anywhere in the city, the whisk of a thousand brooms, for the Mexicans are as obsessed with sweeping as are the Moscovites. Here in the city of perpetual spring you are caught in sudden flashes of rain, and you may stroll along Maximilian's wide, tree-lined Paseo de la Reforma, designed after the grand boulevards of Paris, or pick your way along narrow winding "streets" of the Tinsmiths, the Coffin-Makers or the Mexican Thinkers. At night you can listen to jazz, see a Latin Quarter-style floor show, or be serenaded by the colorful wandering musicians, the *mariachis*. This is a city brilliant with flowers and twittering with birds, where that never-do-today-what-you-can-put-off-till-tomorrow philosophy summed up in the word *mañana* flourishes beside the cult of *machismo,* that natural, flashy propensity of the Mexican male to prove his masculinity by being quick to take insult, even quicker to take revenge, resulting in a city that has one of the world's highest murder rates. And though it has more than its share of streetwalkers and strippers, it also is home to society debutantes who are never seen in public without their duenna chaperones—the last vestige of the Moorish preoccupation with female chastity that came to Mexico by way of Spain.

It is that particular Iberian-Arabic combination, grafted on to the culture and psyche of the Indian that gives the Mexicans their national character. Their unique blend of fierce peasant stoicism with a Spanish flair for personal liberty and free-wheeling individuality ultimately served to break the grip of the conquistadors. Both the Indians and the Moorish-Spaniards had a sense of style and dash, and a dark, deep passion that expressed itself in a taste for bloody religious rituals— human sacrifices or the agonies of saints, *machismo* or the bull ring.

Of the thirty-five million people in Mexico, about 70 per cent are mestizos—a mixture of Indian and Spanish blood in varying proportions. In the days of the conquest one's social prestige depended on his having more Spanish blood than Indian, but since the Revolution and the national pride instilled by such heroes as Juárez, the pure-blooded Zapotec who led his country to reform in the mid-nineteenth century, the mestizo is prejudiced in favor of his Indian ancestry. The Catholicism practiced here strongly reflects the pagan-Christian blend of background. The very Catholic All Saints' Day is followed by the very pagan Day of the Dead, when elaborate food offerings, sugar angels, and candy-frosted skulls are placed in churches and on graves to feed the departed loved ones. Many who worship at the shrine of the Guadalupe Virgin refer to her as Tonantzin, the corn goddess of Indian lore, and back-country peasants have been known to remove the saint's image from their church and destroy it when rain fails to come in time to save their crops.

Still a poor country but now well on its way to prosperity, Mexico's history has always been one of strong men—starting with the legendary Quetzalcóatl, the plumed serpent who was half-god, half-man to the Indians, a sort of Paul Bunyan and Jupiter rolled into one. Whether he was pure fact or pure fancy, a stray Viking or an Oriental wanderer, he is said to have given the Indians the gift of corn, which has always been the food staple and is still the country's main crop, taught them the arts of spinning and weaving and how to build and make tools, and preached a message of peace through brotherhood. After Quetzalcóatl, the people worshiped their tribal rulers, and certainly no monarchs ever held them in a stronger grip, demanding sacrificial lives to appease their gods and claiming the results of their labor, just as the Spanish viceroys exacted their own sacrifices from these same people for almost three hundred years. In a way, the Indians were betrayed by their "plumed serpent," for they believed he would come again; and as luck would have it, Cortés appeared, flashing cold Toledo steel and firing cannons, on exactly the day prophesied for the return of the ancient god, and by the time Montezuma finished welcoming the Spaniards Mexico was lost for three hundred years.

Its independence was regained finally in 1815 through the efforts of such Spanish friars and soldiers as Father Hidalgo and Captain Allende. Subsequent rulers, such as the General Santa Anna, were not very much better to their people than the Spaniards had been. It was only with the reforms instigated by Benito Juárez that the common man of the country became an object of consideration. The rule of Juárez was interrupted briefly by the arrival of the Archduke Maximilian, the Hapsburg nobleman backed by Napoleon III and supported by French troops, who took the city as "emperor" with his "empress," Carlotta. Maximilian was a man both benign and naïve, and his reign was a fantasy of *noblesses oblige* and the white man's burden. He wrote books of court etiquette, taught a few privileged Indians to dance the Varsoviana at his grand ball, and had the Paseo de la Reforma built on the style of the Champs Elysées. He was ultimately deposed by Juárez, deserted by France, and shot in 1867.

To fully appreciate the diversity of the country's capital and, at the same time, piece together fragments of its history, one has only to make the rounds of the leading sights—the museums and markets, the parks and plazas, the castles and churches. The best starting point is the Plaza Mayor, or what was to the Aztecs Zócalo. Here they had their greatest temple and the palace of Montezuma, and here today stands the massive cathedral, finished in 1813 after almost three hundred years of building. It is a wonder of Spanish Renaissance architecture and decoration, inside as well as out, and the little chapel next door, the Sagrario Metropolitano, has a *churrigueresque* façade that is one of the finest in the country. On the other side of the Zócalo is the National Palace, built over the foundation of Montezuma's palace and rebuilt in 1692. It is a rosy baroque building of *tezontle,* a red volcanic stone reminiscent of terra-cotta pottery, and its Liberty Bell is rung by the president each year on September 15. The museum of this palace contains the mural by Diego Rivera that unfolds all of Mexican history back to pre-conquest days. In the archeology wing is the Aztec perpetual calendar, that huge circular slab of carved stone, weighing 25 tons and measuring 12 feet in diameter, which is the standard ornamental motif on all tourist souvenirs, and also a dazzling array of Mayan and Aztec sculptures.

One of the city's richest art collections is in the Palacio del Belles Artes, the Palace of Fine Arts, with works by Orozco and Rivera, including the latter's famed Rockefeller Center mural which was removed because of its Communist taint, the stark Indian primitives of Tamayo, and the stirring social realist murals of Siqueiros, an artistic hero and a political prisoner, jailed for his radical predilections. There are beautiful old paintings here too—colonial art in the vein of north European paintings, polished and exacting, and giving an interesting view of the *hidalgos* and their families.

This same combination of modern and colonial art is exhibited in Chapultepec Castle, set up on a hill in a pretty park with a view over the whole city. You may wander through rooms full of French trinkets imported by Maximilian and Carlotta when they lived here, or study the gilt and jeweled appointments used by the Spanish viceroys who occupied the palace before them. Here too are the modern murals, again by Orozco but most spectacularly by Siqueiros, whose figures seem to march right off the wall in a clamor of rage and indignation. A full-time guard is on duty here to keep right-wing extremists from destroying the painting as a protest against the politics of its painter.

No one should miss a Sunday afternoon visit to the park of this palace, when proud parents air their starched, polished, and combed children and the whole city seems to be out in its holiday best.

Wander through any of the city's quiet flowery parks in the early morning, when the shoeshine boys are setting up their painted boxes, almost as elaborate as those in Istanbul; or battle the noisy exuberance of such vast markets as the Merced, or the Sunday Rastro-like flea market, Langunilla. There are dozens of seventeenth and eighteenth century churches to be seen, more wonderful frescoes in such buildings as the Palace of Justice and the National Preparatory School, and the National Library collection of 250,000 books includes the first ever published in Mexico. You can get an accurate sampling of Mexican architecture, old and new, along such avenues as Alameda and the Reforma, with its flower-decked *glorietas,* perhaps the dressiest traffic circles in the world. One Sunday morning you may float amongst the flower barges of Xochimilco, or watch a *charreada,* the exacting and colorful Mexican rodeo in which the prime rule is that no animal may be hurt, and in the afternoon see a bullfight in the world's largest bull ring, where the fight is always to the death.

Take an afternoon drive to University City, a fantastic collection of modern, futuramic buildings decorated with brilliant mosaics that look like Aztec primitives. On your way drive through the de luxe, superb Jardines del Pedregal, with new glass villas built on ancient lava beds, with indoor-outdoor swimming pools and outdoor-indoor gardens of rubber trees and bougainvillaea, hibiscus and cactus, yucca plants and wild orchids.

On another day you can drive south to the Tenayuca, the sun pyramids of the Toltecs, and later see for contrast the shrine of Our Lady of Guadalupe, who appeared in 1531 to become the New World's first saint. There is the picturesque suburb of Coyoacán from which Cortés launched his attack on Tenochtitlán, and you can still visit the Municipal Hall, the house in which he stayed, built 250 years before the arrival of the Spaniards.

Once out of the shadows of Mexico City's legendary guardian peaks, Popocatepetl (the warrior) and Iztaccihuatl (the princess who chose to die rather than live without him), there is still much to be seen. Certainly everyone must know of the cities that make up the touristic beeline from the capital to the Pacific coast. The line starts with the garden town of Cuernevaca, a low-altitude resort retreat for the fashionable people of Mexico City, a place of country markets, swimming pools and inns with tiled courtyards and fountains. Cortés lived here, in what is now the capital of Moreila state, and the palace he built for his second wife still stands on the town's pretty plaza. The next stop is Taxco, the silver town, a winding cobblestoned village in the hills, with a perfect *churrigueresque* cathedral, and roofs of red tile in the manner of Toledo's houses.

The final stop is Acapulco, a thoroughly international seaside, cabana-bikini-hotel-swimming-pool resort. Night clubs are cut in the sides of cliffs, one can play golf or skin dive, marvel at the tropical fish and deep-sea gardens, or escape to the next-door resorts, Zihuatanejo or Puerto Marques, for a more peaceful and idyllic beachcomber's life.

Somewhat less frequented by tourists but far more interesting are such Mexican towns as Puebla, a green and gracious jewel of Spanish colonial architecture; the colorful tiles and pottery produced here are still done in the traditions handed down by the Spaniards. Tepoztlán is an Aztec village, almost completely intact, where Indians still speak their tribal tongue. Monterrey, Mexico's third largest city, primarily industrial, offers a breathtaking view of the Horsetail Falls, a pyramid of water that cascades down the mountainside, and a chance to see the huge grottos of the Garcia caves, with their underground "skyline" of stalagmites and stalactites. Guadalajara, the second largest city in the country, is also one of the most colorful, with its baroque cathedral and its great plazas, its gardens and parks. It is set in the midst of crystal-clear lake country and from it you can visit the Bohemian little artists' village Ajijic, or Tequila, where the famed liquor is made. It is in Guadalajara that such typically Mexican customs as the hat dance—the *jarabe tapatio*—originated, as did the *charro* costume (a cross between the outfit of the toreador and the gaucho), and the *mariachis,* the strolling musicians most commonly identified with Mexico City. One of the most picturesque sights in this state is Lake Pátzcuaro, where the huge elliptical nets of the Tarascan Indian fishermen are balanced across their rowboats and shimmer in the sunlight like the silken wings of dragonflies.

The colonial town of Oaxaca is a must for the bona fide traveler really interested in fathoming Mexico's past. With its lacing of iron grillwork and its baroque cathedral of Santo Domingo with gilt and polychromed cherubs and angels, its expert silversmiths and potters, it is a vignette of old Mexico. It is close to Indian ruins such as Mitla, once a Zapotec religious center, and Monte Alban, with its vestiges of sun temples.

Travel just thirty-eight miles west of the capital to sample the colorful delights of Toluca's Friday market, or fly as far south as possible in the country, to the peninsula of Yucatán, once the realm of the great Mayan tribes. Mérida, the capital, is a clean and sparkling city fanned by some twenty thousand windmills, and from here you can visit the most astounding of the Mayan ruins, the giant sun pyramids built at the height of this Indian culture in the eleventh and twelfth centuries. Remnants of temples and palaces can be seen in Uxmal, once a chief center of Mayan rule, and in Chichén Itzá, where a huge temple compound is in a fairly good state of preservation, complete with ball courts and limestone carvings, a sacred well sixty feet across into which beautiful virgins were thrown to placate the god Chac-Mol, and an enormous flat-topped, stepped pyramid standing like a Babylonian ziggurat, silhouetted against the *yic-yac* forest and the sky.

FOR THE TRAVELER'S NOTEBOOK

Official Information

Before you go: Mexican Government Tourist Bureau, 630 Fifth Ave., New York, N.Y.; Mexican Embassy, 2829 60th St., N.W., Washington, D.C.

In Mexico City: General Agent for SAS, Guest Aerovias Mexico, S.A., 51 Paseo de la Reforma; Tourist Information Office, 35 Paseo de la Reforma; Mexican Tourist Bureau, 89 Ave. Juárez; U.S. Embassy, 45 Paseo de la Reforma.

Money Matters

Currency: The monetary unit is the peso, divided into 100 centavos. 12.50 pesos equal $1, U.S.

Tipping: The United States pattern is followed, with 10 to 15 per cent the correct amount in hotels in restaurants. Taxi drivers are not tipped, and porters have a fixed charge.

Climate, Clothing, and Essentials

The climate in Mexico City is always pleasant, with an average temperature of 62 degrees F. The rainy season starts toward the end of May and lasts until the middle of September. This is not a steady tropical rain but generally afternoon showers. Since the city is high in altitude, the rarefied atmosphere requires you to take it easy to avoid fatigue. People usually dress in a conservative and elegant fashion. Slacks are taboo for ladies, and shorts are worn only at summer resorts. Wear the same type of clothes you would wear anywhere in spring. Winter nights may be chilly; take a light topcoat or sweater.

Hotels

There is a wide variety of accommodations at all price ranges, but it is suggested that visitors stay at de luxe or first class spots unless you know of others by close personal recommendation. All the de luxe hotels offer private baths and air conditioning and their rates range from 120 to 200 pesos, single, 150 to 250, double. First class rates start at about 90 pesos, single, 110, double, while less expensive but still first class hotels charge from 50 to 65 pesos, single, 65 to 75, double.

DE LUXE: Newest is the *María Isabel, 325 Paseo de la Reforma,* modern and posh, with all the expected facilities. The lovely old *Tecali, 736 Mariano Escobedo,* is the *grande dame* of the city's hotels and offers suites only, at the top prices in town. The *Continental-Hilton, 166 Paseo de la Reforma,* is convenient, commercially busy, and decorated with Mexican-Indian motifs. *El Presidente, 135 Hamburgo,* is older but still modern, with all the usual hotel conveniences. The *Alffer, 18 Revillagigedo,* the *Bamer, 52 Juárez,* and the *Del Paseo, 208 Paseo de la Reforma,* are also plush, smaller than those above, and well appointed.

FIRST CLASS: The *Reforma, Paseo de la Reforma at Paris,* is an old-guard tourist hotel that is well located and comfortable. *Del Prado, 70 Juárez,* is another old hub of tourist activity and still bustling, well set in the heart of things. The *Monte Cassino, 56 Génova,* is tops in service and quite comfortable, and the *Premier* and *Cristóbal Colón, 27 Colón,* are pleasant and moderately priced. The *Majestic, 73 Madero, Prince, 12 Luis Moya, Genève, 130 Londres,* and *Romfel, 123 Articulo and Revillagigedo,* are all good in the lower first class price category.

Food and Restaurants

Mexican food is varied and delicious and is perhaps the most original cuisine of Latin America. Be cautious about such things as raw unpeeled fruits and vegetables in markets and out-of-the-way places, but you can safely eat anything on the menus of restaurants mentioned here.

The real staple of the Mexican diet is the *tortilla,* a thin, baked pancake with a cornmeal base, made in many sizes and served in many ways. Folded and filled with cheese or meat they are *enchiladas.* Rolled and filled with meat, cheese, or vegetables, they are *tacos.* Toasted, they are *tostados. Tamales* are corn-flour rolls, steam cooked and stuffed with chicken or pork. *Empanadas* are little meat-filled pastry pockets. *Mole,* an aromatic sauce made (incredibly) with a chocolate base, and spiced with chili, sesame, and garlic, tastes much better than it sounds. It is served with large slices of turkey or chicken.

Beans are used a great deal in Mexico and are delectable when mashed and re-fried (*frijoles refritoes*) or when cooked with rice and served with lemon and chopped onion. *Pozole,* a common, inexpensive dish, is a favorite too, made of cornmeal, pork, and various seasonings. Try eggs *rancheros,* fried eggs on a *tortilla* with a peppery tomato sauce; *guacamole,* a mashed avocado salad; and *chicharrones,* crisp pork cracklings. You'll find many familiar Spanish dishes. Mexican hot chocolate is flavored with cinnamon and whipped to a froth—really worth sampling. Typical desserts include solid loaf-type fruit jams, custards, and tropical fruits.

Mexican beer and rum rank with the world's best, and *tequila,* powerful white liquor made from cactus plant, should be tried straight or mixed into sours and collins drinks. Coffee is strong and good.

In addition to the hotel restaurants, you will find continental food elegantly (and expensively) served at *Les Ambassadeurs* and *Focolare,* two tourist strongholds, while *Jena* has a more charming, relaxed atmosphere and offers a few Mexican dishes as well. *Rivoli* is another good continental restaurant, with a wonderful Yucatan specialty, chicken *Chichén Itzá.* *Quid* is colorful, especially when there is music, and its barbecues are excellent. For charcoal-broiled food amid the flashiest setting, try *Delmonico's. Mauna Loa* is one of the best Polynesian restaurants anywhere and the décor is as *aloha* as can be. There's French food at the *Normandie* and *La Lorraine,* Italian specials at *Alfredo's* and *Angelo's,* superb Argentine barbecues at *La Tablita,* and Chinese dishes at *Tibet Hamz.*

One of the best and most authentic places for Mexican food is *La Fonda Santa Anita,* the older branch at 1089 Insurgentes. At *La Fonda el Refugio* you'll find good native food in a dressier setting. *Restorante Lorendo's* serves a beautiful seafood soup in a ceramic coconut, and try *carne asado* here. At *Circulo Sureste* the simple décor belies the unusual menu of wonderful Yucatán dishes. From the very native-looking kitchen of *Mesón del Caballo Bayo* come simple, superb dishes. *Las Cazuelas* is another popular Mexican restaurant, and the club-like atmosphere of the *Lincoln Grill* is the perfect setting for some of the best seafood, native, and international dishes. The five *Sanborn* restaurants dotted about the city are "musts" for Americans. They are large glorified coffee-shop cafeterias with American breakfasts and light lunches. If you go to Cuernevaca, don't miss the elegant, excellent *La Mañanitas.*

Entertainment, Night Life, and Special Events

Mexico City abounds in after-dark entertainment with a selection of clubs, bars, and cabarets to suit almost every taste. Among the top cabarets in the international style (floor shows, Latin-American bands, et al.) are *Los Globos,* the softly lit *Jacaranda,* the *Afro,* and *El Patio*—all dressy and expensive. The large tourist hotels offer more of the same. For something more native go to *Gitanerias,* a series of small rooms full of Mexican atmosphere, where flamenco dancing and singing is the specialty, or go to the smaller, more moderate *Rincon de Goya.*

An interesting, colorful evening pastime is a walk around the Plaza Garibaldi where the *mariachi* bands, their strolling musicians clad in native costume, provide a musical accompaniment to your stroll among the market stalls. The same music is presented in a more formal and stylized way at *Bajo el Cielo de Jalisco,* an indoor Hollywood version of the outdoor stall area. The *Rua* and the *Ro* are jazz clubs. *Tivoli* is a burlesque house, Mexican style.

There are frequent performances of native dances and music with colorful regional costumes at many places in the city, especially at the Palacio del Belles Artes. Check your hotel for such performances. During the concert season (July and August) the symphony orchestra plays at the Palacio. There are several revue theaters: Lirico, Follies, Iris, etc., usually with two evening performances. There are also some tent shows which are informal and colorful.

Bullfights are Mexico's most popular Sunday afternoon entertainment. The Plaza Mexico holds sixty thousand people and is the largest bull ring in the world. The season runs from October to March, with fights every Sunday at four. Other popular events are the *charreadas* (rodeos) presented on Sunday mornings at Rancho del Charro. *Jai alai,* the world's fastest and most exciting game, can be seen daily at the Fronton Mexico, Plaza de la República.

Mexico is fiesta land. Every day seems to bring with it some sort of carnival in some part of the country. The most colorful of the celebrations in and around Mexico City are held in December and January, pre-Christmas to Epiphany. *New Year's Day* offers fireworks and a number of fairs. *Mardi gras* before Lent is a time of rodeos, fireworks, native dances, and fiestas everywhere. Perhaps the weirdest holiday of all occurs on *November 1 and 2,* All Saints' and All Souls' days, with pageants and food offerings to departed relatives and loved ones. Holy Week is primitive, with penitents walking the streets carrying lighted tapers. *May 5 (Cinco de Mayo)* is Mexico's national holiday, with Maypoles and an arena full of dancing children in spring costumes in nearby Puebla.

Shopping

The National Museum of Arts and Crafts opposite Alameda Park sells native handicrafts such as primitive pottery, handwoven wool and cotton, silver art objects, and serapes. Though there are many good shops in the city, it should be remembered that one can often make better buys in places like Taxco (silver jewelry), Puebla (Talavera onyx), Guadalajara (pottery, woodwork, and textiles), Toluca (baskets and wood carvings), Oaxaca (ceramics and woolen shawls called *rebozos*), and Saltillo (serapes). There are some interesting finds at the *National Pawn Shop*, the Sunday market at Lagunilla, and the wonderful market at Toluca. One of the best shops for fabrics is *Tillets,* and you'll enjoy seeing the silver at *Tony Castillo.* If you are out for antiques and know what you're buying, try the Lagunilla market and the shops along Allende. *Sanborn's* has a little of almost everything, and there are high-fashion (and high-priced) sportswear shops on the Pasaje Jacaranda.

Background Reading

The Sudden View, by Sybille Bedford
A Visit to Don Ottavio, by Sybille Bedford
Children of Sanchez, by Oscar Lewis
Life in Mexico, by Madame Calderón de la Barca
Viva Mexico!, by Charles Flandreau
The Plumed Serpent, by D. H. Lawrence
The True History of the Conquest, by Bernard Díaz, a fascinating account by one of Cortés's men.

INDEX OF PLACES

Abu Simbel, 535, 539
Acapulco, 593
Adelaide, 557
Aleppo, 436
Alexandria, 535–536, 539, 540, 543
Alps, 190, 322, 323, 327, 328
Amman, 418
Amsterdam, 218–220, 222–225
Ankara, 344–345
Antwerp, 130
Aranjuez, 297
Arnhem, 221
Aswan, 539, 540, 543
Athens, 202–208, 210–214, 222–225
Avila, 297

Baalbek, 424–426, 431, 539
Baden-Baden, 182
Baguio, 503–504, 506
Bali, 468–471, 472, 473, 474
Bangkok, 518–528
Barcelona, 298–303, 310, 311, 312, 314, 315, 317
Basque country, 289, 290
Beersheba, 410
Beirut, 422–424, 429–431
Beit-ed-Din, 428
Belfast, 96
Bergen, 27–29, 30–35
Berlin, 168–173, 190, 192, 195–196, 197–198, 200

Bethlehem, 417
Black Sea, 345
Bombay, 458
Brasilia, 575
Bratislava, 359
Bremen, 179
Brisbane, 557
Bruges, 130
Brussels, 126–129, 132–135
Budapest, 361–365, 366–369
Buenos Aires, 565–568, 569–572
Burgos, 290
Byblos, 426–428

Cairo, 533–534, 536, 541, 542, 543–544
Calcutta, 452–454, 459, 460, 462
Cannes, 152, 165, 167
Capri, 263
Carlsbad, 357
Cebu, 504
Chichén Itzá, 594
Constantinople, 337, 341–342
Copacabana Beach, 576, 577, 579, 580
Copenhagen, 3–13, 14
Córdoba, 309
Costa Brava, 303
Cracow, 375
Cuernavaca, 592–594, 596
Cuzco, 581, 582, 586

Damascus, 432–436, 437–438
Danube River, 357, 365–366, 367, 368
Darwin, 557
Delft, 221
Delhi, New and Old, 455–465
Djakarta, 466–468, 471, 472, 473, 474
Dublin, 89–95, 97–99

Eastern Europe travel notes, 352
Edinburgh, 76–81, 83–84, 86, 87
Elsinore, 7, 12
Escorial, El, 291, 296–297
Estoril, 283, 285, 287

Fatima, 284
Florence, 236–241, 264, 265, 267, 272, 275, 276, 277–278, 279
Fontainebleau, 149
Frankfurt am Main, 179–182, 191, 193, 196, 199, 200–201

Gdansky, 374
Geneva, 326–329, 331–332, 333–334, 335, 336
Ghent, 129–130
Giza, 534
Glasgow, 83, 85, 86, 87–88
Gothenburg, 41–43, 45, 47, 48, 49
Granada, 290, 309–310
Guadalajara, 593, 598

Haarlem, 221
Hague, The, 220, 225
Haifa, 411
Hamburg, 174–178, 191, 192–193, 196, 198–199, 200
Helsinki, 15–22
Herculaneum, 263
Hobart, 556–557
Hong Kong, 441–444, 445–447, 448–451

Isfahan, 402–404
Istanbul, 337–344, 346–349

Jaffa, 409
Jaipur, 459

Jerusalem, 409
  Old, 415–418, 419–421
Jutland, 8, 13

Karachi, 495–497, 498–500
Karnak, 535, 540
Kiev, 385, 392
Kowloon, 447, 448, 450
Kremlin, 382–383
Kuala Lumpur, 513
Kyoto, 483–485, 486, 487, 488, 490, 491–492, 493

Lahore, 497
Lapland, 17, 22, 41, 48
Leghorn, 241
Leiden, 220
Leningrad, 378, 385, 390–391
Lidice, 357–358
Lido, the, 250
Lima, 581–586
Lisbon, 280–282, 285, 286–287
London, 53–75
Lübeck, 178
Lublin, 374
Lucerne, 322–326, 329, 331, 334, 335–336
Lucca, 241
Luxor, 539, 540, 543

Madras, 458
Madrid, 289, 291–295, 310, 311–312, 313–314, 315, 316–317
Majorca, 303
Manila, 501, 504–505, 506–508
Mar del Plata, 569, 571
Melbourne, 556, 558, 559, 560–561
Mérida, 594
Mexico City, 587–593, 594–598
Milan, 251–256, 264, 266–267, 271, 275, 276, 277, 279
Mombasa, 548
Monaco, 155
Monte Carlo, 165, 167
Montecatini, 241
Monterrey, 593

Moscow, 378–390, 392–395
Munich, 183–190, 191, 193–194, 196–197, 199–200, 201

Nairobi, 545–547, 548–550
Naples, 257–262, 264, 269, 273, 276, 278–279
Negev Desert, 409–410
New Delhi, 455–458, 459, 460, 462, 464–465
Nice, 150–151, 153–155, 159–161, 163–164
Nikko, 482
Novgorod, 391–392

Oaxaca, 593, 598
Old Delhi, 455, 456–457, 461–462
Osaka, 482, 491
Oslo, 24–27, 29–35

Paris, 136–150, 155, 156–159, 161–163, 164–167
Persepolis, 402
Perth, 557
Peshawar, 497
Petra, 418–419
Pilsen, 357, 359
Pisa, 241
Pompeii, 263–264
Prague, 353–356, 358–360
Puebla, 593, 597, 598

Recife, 575–576
Red Square, 381–382, 384
Riga, 385
Rio de Janeiro, 573–575, 576–580
Riviera, 150–155, 165, 167
Rome, 227–236, 264, 265–266, 270–271, 276, 277, 279
Rotterdam, 220

St. Peter's, 231–232, 255
Sakkara, 534
Salzburg, 113–116, 117, 119–120, 121–122, 123, 124
São Paolo, 575, 576

Segovia, 297
Seine River, 137
Serengeti Plains, 548
Seville, 304–309, 310, 311, 313, 314, 315–316, 317
Shiraz, 402
Siemreap, 523
Siena, 241
Singapore, 508–513, 514–517
Sintra, 283–284
Slovakia, 357
Stockholm, 36–41, 43–45, 46–47, 48–49, 50
Sydney, 553–555, 558–560, 561

Tagaytay, 504, 505
Teheran, 399–402, 404–406
Tel Aviv, 407–409, 411–414
Thebes, 535, 540
Tokyo, 475–482, 485, 486, 487, 488, 489, 490–491, 492–493
Toledo, 290, 295–296
Tuscany, 241–242

Uppsala, 40
USSR, 352, 386–389

Valencia, 290
Vatican Palace, 227, 229, 231, 233
Venice, 240, 242–250, 264, 268, 273, 275, 276, 278, 279
Versailles, 149
Vienna, 103–113, 117, 118, 119, 120–121, 122–123, 124

Warsaw, 370–374, 375–377

Yokahama, 482

Zagorsk, 390
Zamboanga, 504
Zanzibar, 548
Zuider Zee, 221–222
Zürich, 319–322, 329, 330–331, 332–333, 334, 335

TRAVEL NOTES

TRAVEL NOTES

TRAVEL NOTES

TRAVEL NOTES

TRAVEL NOTES

TRAVEL NOTES

About the Author

MIMI SHERATON is one of those very fortunate people whose work combines two of her chief interests: travel and cookery. She was born in Brooklyn and attended Midwood High School there, and later graduated from New York University. From early childhood she wanted to write and to travel. Her writing, combined with the fact that her husband, Richard Falcone, is in the import-export business, permits her to travel widely.

For this book Miss Sheraton spent two years in special travel in eastern Europe and the Middle and Far East. She had already gleaned much from earlier trips to Europe. She visited all parts of the globe, making notes on the character and color of cities, sampling fascinating food, and gathering unusual merchandise for a prominent New York shop. She speaks a smattering of French, Spanish, and Italian, and can read a menu in any language, including Lebanese, so long as the alphabet is the same as ours. She collects "beautiful junk" from shops and markets in all parts of the world, and takes many color slides on her foreign jaunts.

Miss Sheraton is the author of *The Seducer's Cookbook,* and has contributed to such magazines as *Good Housekeeping, Mademoiselle, Town and Country,* etc. She was also formerly managing editor of *House Beautiful* Bride and Home Supplement. She is now working on a series of national cookbooks, with one on German cuisine as the first. She serves as food consultant for a number of New York's most famous restaurants.

The Falcones live in Greenwich Village with their small son and find it an interesting and relaxing area. Mimi Sheraton loves New York and says she would never want to live anywhere else in the United States, though she has many favorite foreign cities too—among them London, Copenhagen, Paris, Siena, Beirut, Istanbul, Singapore, and Hong Kong.